THE FREE-STANDING COMPANY IN THE WORLD ECONOMY 1830–1996

The Free-Standing Company in the World Economy 1830–1996

Edited by

MIRA WILKINS AND HARM SCHRÖTER

OXFORD UNIVERSITY PRESS

1998

This book has been printed digitally and produced in a standard specification in order to ensure its continuing availability

OXFORD
UNIVERSITY PRESS

Great Clarendon Street, Oxford OX2 6DP

Oxford University Press is a department of the University of Oxford. It furthers the University's objective of excellence in research, scholarship, and education by publishing worldwide in

Oxford New York

Auckland Cape Town Dar es Salaam Hong Kong Karachi Kuala Lumpur Madrid Melbourne Mexico City Nairobi New Delhi Shanghai Taipei Toronto

With offices in

Argentina Austria Brazil Chile Czech Republic France Greece Guatemala Hungary Italy Japan South Korea Poland Portugal Singapore Switzerland Thailand Turkey Ukraine Vietnam

Published in the United States by Oxford University Press Inc., New York

Reprinted 2009

ISBN 978-0-19-829032-2

PREFACE

One of us, Mira Wilkins, in 1988 published an article in the *Economic History Review* entitled 'The Free-Standing Company, 1870–1914: An Important Type of British Foreign Direct Investment'. After it had attracted substantial attention, the other of us, Harm Schröter, organized a session on free-standing companies at the Eleventh International Economic History Congress, in Milan, Italy, September 1994. This book is the outcome. It is *not* the proceedings of a conference. All the essays have been rewritten; we brought in additional ones. We debated the topic and learnt from one another. We incorporated newly published materials. We do not hold uniform views, as will be very evident. The book should be helpful to students of British, Continental European, US, Canadian, Australian, Latin American, South East Asian, Indian, Middle Eastern, and African economic history. Fundamentally, this is an offering in international economic and business history, a contribution to the history of multinational enterprise. The authors are economists and historians, who live in eight different countries (the USA, Germany, England, Holland, Russia, Canada, Mexico, and Brazil); the sources tapped are in ten languages (English, German, Dutch, French, Spanish, Portuguese, Italian, Russian, Swedish, and Danish); the subject matter is global.

The concept of (and identification of) the free-standing company has been called 'exciting', 'useful', and 'pernicious'. It has encountered enthusiasm and antagonism. Most of the writers in this book thought the concept enriching; a few found it quite alien. Overall, however, it pushed all of us towards a better understanding of the institutional structures associated with capital exports. It has helped us make sense of the theory and practice of international business through time. The present book is designed to introduce economic and business historians, economists, historians, political scientists, students of multinational enterprise, sociologists—as well as interested 'others'—to the insights and controversies provoked by the free-standing company paradigm. The book does not solve historical dilemmas; it probably poses more questions than it answers; but it is the first ever on free-standing companies.

Our goal is to acquaint the reader with the current status of the discourse and why the subject is important. The book begins with my (Wilkins's) explaining, revisiting, and elaborating on the original idea. In the introductory chapter, I draw on my and others' research to re-examine the views put forth in my 1988 article. I seek to clarify my own argument, to go far beyond the 1988 presentation, and, at the same time, to set the stage for the very exciting essays that follow.

We have left in many chapters the authors' definitions of free-standing companies. While this entails a little repetition, it is necessary when contributors have focused on different facets of the concept and, at times, have used different definitions. The three essays after the introduction—those by Jean-François Hennart, Mark Casson, and T. A. B. Corley—provide theories and statistics. Hennart and Casson, both economists specializing on multinational enterprise, have engaged in a vigorous debate for many years, and their chapters capture their separate approaches. Corley adds his own distinctive insights.

The second part—with essays by Peter Hertner, Natalia Gurushina, Stanley Chapman, Rory Miller, Reinhard Liehr and Mariano E. Torres Bautista, and Tamás Szmrecsányi—considers the role of free-standing companies that invested in Italy, Russia, India and the Far East, and Latin America. Free-standing companies had investments worldwide; the detailed host country (region) treatments included are selective and seek to highlight similarities and differences. With two exceptions—Hertner's paper on the variety of nationalities investing in Italy and Szmrecsányi's case study of a French-headquartered sugar producer in Brazil—all the chapters in this group are on British-based free-standing companies.

The third section shifts the perspective and studies free-standing companies from the standpoint of capital-exporting nations. Included are Ben P. A. Gales and Keetie E. Sluyterman's survey of Dutch-headquartered free-standing companies and my (Schröter's) assessment of such enterprises with Belgian, German, and Swiss headquarters. The next three chapters—on firms organized in Britain, the USA, and Canada—are sector-specific. Geoffrey Jones writes on British overseas banks as free-standing companies, while William J. Hausman and John L. Neufeld (as co-authors) and Gregory P. Marchildon respectively ponder whether and to what extent the concept casts light on the history and behaviour of US and Canadian public utilities that invested over national borders.

As a collection, the chapters form a textured approach to free-standing companies, showing the value of the concept *and* its warts and blemishes. We have included the work of sceptics, as well as enthusiasts. Most of the contributions—in seeking to apply or to criticize the concept—introduce substantive, highly original, findings on the history of business over borders. Most chapters focus on the pre-First World War years (the 'heyday' of the free-standing companies); some cover the inter-war years; and others bring the material up to the present. All of the essays are historical. The book ends with a short 'where we are at this point of time' conclusion. In it, I (Wilkins) summarize the significance and relevance of the concept, map some unexplored paths, and suggest an agenda on how the approach might open avenues for further research.

Both of us want to thank all the authors for their chapters and invaluable aid in the preparation of this volume; we thank them for their patience as we have tried to bring these papers into a coherent whole; this has been a truly splendid experience. Above and beyond all, we want to applaud Will Hausman's outstanding help in moulding this book (he has been a 'godsend'). Our thanks also go to Professor Hausman's assistants, Jonathan Kajeckas and Steve Wilson, whose tireless efforts have accomplished wonders.

I (Wilkins) want to extend my gratitude to the following individuals and funding sources at Florida International University: my incomparable department chair Panos Liossatos, my dean Arthur Herriott (Arts and Sciences), associate dean Brian Cutler (Arts and Sciences), Eduardo Gamarra (Latin American and Caribbean Center), Dennis Gayle (International Education), and Damian Fernandez (International Studies), all of whom furnished moneys for my travel to Milan and have encouraged my efforts. I thank the John Simon Guggenheim Foundation; during my year as a Guggenheim fellow, many of my earliest ideas on this subject took form. Barry Eichengreen and Gerald Feldman invited me to California, where, at Berkeley and Stanford, I had the opportunity to present my findings to thoughtful audiences. In addition, my special appreciation goes to the many individuals (including, but unmentioned herein, contributors to this volume and those at the seminars in California) who have stimulated my thinking: (in alphabetical order) Rondo Cameron, Alfred Chandler, Roy Church, Phil Cottrell, Lance Davis, John Dunning, Patrick Fridenson, Les Hannah, Charles Jones, Stuart Jones, Frank King, Stephen Nicholas, Ranald Michie, the late Edith Penrose, John Stopford, Costas Syropoulos, Alice Teichova, Raymond Vernon, Louis Wells, Maria Willumsen, Guus Veneendaal, and many, many others. Among those writing in this volume, I want to acknowledge how particularly beholden I am to my co-editor, Harm Schröter (who organized the Milan session, inspired this book, and has been a source of splendid ideas), Rory Miller, and once again Will Hausman (who wrote fine critiques of Chapter 1), Geoff Jones, Tony Corley, Jean-François Hennart, and Mark Casson (each of whom has discussed the free-standing company concept with me for about a decade and a half; each of these four had written on free-standing companies prior to their chapters for this volume; I cannot tell them how much I cherish their wisdom). To Gerry Bierwag, Howard Rock, Brian Peterson, Karen Paul, and Marianne Burge, know how great you have been. I owe the most profound debt to my so recently deceased husband, George Simmons (how I miss his insights and our joy).

I (Schröter) want to thank first of all the organizing committee of the Milan Congress, which by accepting the proposal for a session on the free-standing company provided an attractive forum for the exchange of views. I am grateful to the discussants at this session as well as those at our research seminar on the free-standing firm at the Bundeswehr Universität Hamburg. Particularly, I want to single out Verena Schröter and Mira Wilkins, as well as my research assistant Simone Gmeiner, for their work, advice, and involvements with my chapter in this book.

Mira Wilkins
Harm Schröter

April 1997

CONTENTS

PART III. COUNTRIES THAT WERE HOMES TO FREE-STANDING COMPANIES: GENERAL AND BY SECTOR

PART IV. CONCLUSION

LIST OF FIGURES

LIST OF TABLES

ABBREVIATIONS

AEG	Allgemeine Elektrizitäts-Gesellschaft
ANZ	Australia and New Zealand Banking Group
ARCF	Anglo-Russian Cotton Factories
ASAB	Anglo-South American Bank
ASARCO	American Smelting and Refining Co.
BAT	British-American Tobacco
BP	British Petroleum
BPL	Banco del Perú y Londres
CUL	Cambridge University Library
EBASCO	Electric Bond & Share Company
Electrobank	Bank für Elektrische Unternehmungen
FDI	foreign direct investment
FSA	firm-specific asset
FSC	free-standing company
FTC	Federal Trade Commission
GL	Guildhall Library, London
HLBP	House of Lords Record Office, London, Beaverbrook Papers
HVA	Handelsvereeniging Amsterdam
INEGI	Instituto Nacional de Estadística, Geografía e Informàtica
ITT	International Telephone and Telegraph Corporation
KPM	Koninklijke Paketvaart Maatschappij
LTC	London Tin Corporation
MNE	multinational enterprise
NABP	National Archives of Canada, Ottawa, Beaverbrook Papers
NKPM	Nederlandsche Koloniale Petroleum Maatschappij
Oberbedarf	Oberschlesische Eisenbahnbedarfs Actien-Gesellschaft
PRO	Public Record Office
R&D	research and development
RGIA	Russkii Gosudarstvennyi Istoricheskii Arkhiv (Russian State Historical Archives), St Petersburg
RMC	Russian Mining Corporation
RTC	Russian Tobacco Company
SDAG	Sowjetisch-Deutsche Aktiengesellschaft
SEAR	Stock Exchange Annual Reports
SOFINA	Société Financière de Transports et d'Enterprises Industrielles

SUDAMERIS	Banque Française et Italienne pour l'Amérique du Sud
UAC	United Africa Company
UBO	ultimate beneficial owner
UCL	University College Library, London

LIST OF CONTRIBUTORS

MARK CASSON is Professor of Economics at the University of Reading, UK. His research interests include entrepreneurship and the theory of international business. Among his most recent books are *Studies in the Economics of Trust* (1995) and *Information and Organization* (1997). His initial contributions on the theory of free-standing companies were published in *Business History* (1994). Professor Casson is a fellow of the Academy of International Business.

STANLEY CHAPMAN is Professor of Business History in the History Department of Nottingham University, UK, and editor of *Textile History*. He is the author of books on industrial, commercial, and financial history, including *The Rise of Merchant Banking* (1984) and *Merchant Enterprise in Britain* (1992). His research on British investment groups' overseas activities has been very influential in the study of the history of multinational enterprise.

T. A. B. CORLEY has retired as Senior Lecturer in the Economics Department at the University of Reading, UK, and teaches there part-time. His published work on international business history includes a two-volume history of the Burmah Oil Company (1983, 1988), along with a number of articles on British outward foreign direct investment. He has also done research on the history of the UK pharmaceutical industry and on patent medicines.

BEN GALES is Lecturer in Economic History at the Faculty of Economics of the University of Groningen, the Netherlands. He has written on the history of heavy industry, insurance, and social security. He published a company history of AEGON (1986) and was co-author (with Keetie Sluyterman) of 'The Rise of Dutch Multinationals', which appeared in Geoffrey Jones and Harm Schröter's *The Rise of Multinational Enterprise* (1993).

NATALIA GURUSHINA is an economist with Bankers Trust in Moscow. She is a graduate of Moscow State University and has a D.Phil. in economic history from Oxford University, where in 1996 she completed her dissertation, entitled 'British Private Capital Exports to Late Imperial Russia'.

WILLIAM J. HAUSMAN is Professor of Economics at the College of William and Mary, Williamsburg, Va., USA. He is secretary–treasurer of the Business History Conference and editor of the conference proceedings volume, *Business and Economic History*. He and John Neufeld have co-authored numerous articles on the history of pricing, regulation, and public versus private ownership in the US electric utility industry.

JEAN-FRANÇOIS HENNART is Professor of International Business in the Department of Business Administration at the University of Illinois, Urbana, Ill., USA. He is an economist by training. His research has concentrated on the transaction-cost theory of international business institutions. He is the author of *A Theory of Multinational Enterprise* (1982) and has published numerous articles in international business and strategy journals. He has also published in *Business History*.

PETER HERTNER is Professor of Economic History at Martin-Luther-Universität Halle-Wittenberg, Germany. He was previously Professor of History at the European University Institute, Florence, Italy. He has published many articles, as well as edited collections, on the history of multinational enterprise. He co-edited (with Geoffrey Jones) *Multinationals: Theory and History* (1986).

GEOFFREY JONES is Professor of Business History in the Economics Department at the University of Reading, UK. He previously taught at Cambridge University and the London School of Economics. He has written on a myriad of aspects of the history of international business. His publications include *British Multinational Banking 1830–1990* (1993) and *The Evolution of International Business* (1996). He is preparing a book on the history of British trading companies.

REINHARD LIEHR is Professor of Latin American History in the History Department and the Latin American Institute of the Free University of Berlin. He has written on the social and economic history of Spain, Mexico, and Latin America. He edited *La deuda pública de América Latina en perspectiva histórica* (1995) and *Empresas mercantiles mexicanas en la economía antes atlántica de la fundación de los bancos*, a special volume of *Ibero-Amerikanisches Archiv* (1996).

GREGORY P. MARCHILDON is Deputy Minister to the Premier and Cabinet Secretary for the Government of Saskatchewan in Canada. He has taught economic history at the London School of Economics and Johns Hopkins University and is the author of *Profits and Politics:*

Beaverbrook and the Gilded Age of Canadian Finance (1996) as well as of numerous articles in economic and business history.

Rory Miller is Senior Lecturer in the School of Historical Studies and the Institute of Latin American Studies, University of Liverpool, UK. He holds a Ph.D. from Cambridge University. He has published widely on the modern economic and social history of Peru, particularly on the development of railways and oil. He is the author of *Britain and Latin America in the Nineteenth and Twentieth Centuries* (1993). His present research is on the evolution of British manufacturing companies in Latin America.

John L. Neufeld is Professor of Economics at the University of North Carolina at Greensboro. He has co-authored with William J. Hausman articles on the history of the US electric utility industry. He is a former member of the North Carolina Energy Policy Council.

Harm Schröter is Visiting Professor of Economic History at the University of Konstanz, Germany. He has written extensively on the history of multinational enterprise, including work on the history of cartels. His *Aufstieg der Kleinen* (1993) was on the history of multinational firms based in small countries. Together with Geoffrey Jones, he co-edited *The Rise of Multinationals in Continental Europe* (1993).

Keetie E. Sluyterman is a researcher at the Research Institute for History and Culture of the Utrecht University, in the Netherlands. She is the author of many books and articles on Dutch business history, including *Ondernemen in Sigaren* (1993) and *Driekwart Eeuw CSM, Cash Flow, Strategie en Mensen* (1995) and is writing a history of the Dutch trading company Hagemeyer. She has had an abiding interest in the history of Dutch business abroad and has published widely on this subject.

Tamás Szmrecsányi is Professor of Social History of Science and Technology at Unicamp, the State University of Campinas, in São Paulo, Brazil. He has written many articles on Brazilian economic and business history and is a specialist on the history of the Brazilian sugar industry. In the early 1990s he edited four books of essays on Brazilian economic history and one volume on business history and economic development, all published in Brazil.

Mariano E. Torres Bautista is Professor of Economic History at El Colegio de Puebla in Mexico. Professor Torres previously taught at the

University of Paris, La Sorbonne. He is the author of two books on the industrialization and entrepreneurship in nineteenth-century Mexico: *Los origenes de la industrializacion en Puebla* (1995) and *La Familia Maurer de Atlixco* (1994). He is a contributor to the *Jahrbuch für Geschichte von Staat, Wirtschaft und Gesellschaft Lateinamerikas* (1995).

MIRA WILKINS is Professor of Economics at Florida International University, Miami, Florida, USA. Her books include *The Emergence of Multinational Enterprise: American Business Abroad from the Colonial Period to 1914* (1970), *The Maturing of Multinational Enterprise: American Business Abroad from 1914 to 1970* (1974), and *The History of Foreign Investment in the United States to 1914* (1989). She has written dozens of articles on the history of multinational enterprise. Her present research is on the history of foreign investment in the USA, from 1914 to the present. Professor Wilkins is a fellow of the Academy of International Business.

Part I

Introduction: Background, Theory, and Controversies

1

The Free-Standing Company Revisited

Mira Wilkins

A 'free-standing company' is a firm set up in one country for the purpose of doing business outside that country. The term 'free-standing' was adopted to contrast this type of investment over borders with the more familiar one of today's multinational enterprise that begins with business operations *at home* and *then* moves abroad, building on its competence and needs and generally pursuing a related line of business. With the free-standing company, the individual founders established a new 'free-standing' unit in the home (headquarters) country with the immediate intention of operating outside that headquarters nation.[1] My initial research on the free-standing company concentrated on the history of British-headquartered free-standing companies; quickly, however, it became apparent that other nations also were homes for such companies.[2]

The identification of the free-standing company came from a desire to understand the institutional business structures associated with international capital movements. The importance of the notion rested on its insistence that we ask questions about the essential features of international business firms as they evolve through time, including how they are managed. In my analysis, I focus on the firm. Investors in a firm and the firm itself may be one and the same, or there may be a separation of ownership and control of a firm—as in the modern managerial corporation. To understand the history of international business, I believe the attention must be on the *firm* as the actor rather than on a more generalized approach. In some cases, holders of shares (ownership) of a firm were widows and orphans, or institutional investors on their behalf; in other cases, shareholders were active participants; frequently, there was a mix of passive and active investors. There is a separate literature on British individuals as investors, and I do not attempt to add to that literature here.[3] The originality of the concept of the free-standing company lies in its emergence from an attempt to clarify the business enterprise's characteristics (including the nature of management), behaviour, performance, and influence as the firm expands over borders through time.

Resources (especially capital, technology, and management) often do not move, domestically, or to foreign countries, in arm's-length transactions. The 'visible hand' of business managers is present; business transactions are governed by those who administer the enterprise.[4] To study business across borders, we must look at the business institutions.[5] Research on the free-standing company, a special form of multinational enterprise, helps us to discern and to explain historical patterns of global economic integration and thus to understand an important aspect of global economic history. Some have suggested that such research may contribute insights into aspects of imperialism.[6]

Historiographical Background

Before I revisit the concept of the free-standing company (FSC), some historiographical background is necessary. The identification of and the labelling of the free-standing company as a type of multinational enterprise arose out of my re-examination of British capital exports of the late nineteenth and early twentieth centuries. In that period Britain was by far the world's leading capital exporter; a substantial portion of the nation's total savings was invested abroad.[7] Britain's capital exports in those years have attracted immense attention from economic historians, as well as from contemporary commentators. There are numerous studies of these British capital flows, as well as of subsequent British capital exports. Typically, at least since the 1960s, historians classified the overseas interests of British-registered companies as 'portfolio investments'; students of the capital flows considered the capital as raised in Britain and exported.[8] Many authors assumed that the bulk of British investment abroad in the late nineteenth and early twentieth centuries was passive. Yet, some scholars in the 1920s and 1930s and some writers in the immediate post-Second World War years recognized that, while this was certainly true of British stakes abroad in government bonds and other British holdings of securities, the overseas interests of British-registered companies suggested, in today's usage, 'direct' rather than passive portfolio investments, since the enterprise itself was extending across country borders to control and to manage the operations abroad. Since the 1970s scholars have tried to assemble statistics on the history of British multinational enterprise and consider the portfolio/direct overseas investment ratios. A number, beginning with Tom Houston and John Dunning, explicitly included the British-registered companies—once designated as portfolio investors—as foreign direct investors.[9] I called such British firms free-standing companies (FSCs): they were registered in Britain, had a headquarters there, but had *no operations there in the specified (or in a vertically related) industry*; their overseas business was usually set up in a single foreign country, or a single region. They were free-standing because their international business did not grow out of an ongoing business that operated at home, with the firms seeking to 'internalize' (combine) overseas operations in their existing activities. I identified thousands of British owned and controlled FSCs, with business abroad—in and outside the Empire.

My point of departure was research (beginning in 1959) that I had done on the history of American business abroad. To the surprise of many readers, I had found numerous American companies, from the late nineteenth century onwards, that had started at home and had developed domestic market expertise, and then rapidly became multinational enterprises. American businesses such as Singer Sewing Machine, General Electric, National Cash Register, International Harvester, Aluminum Company of America, and Ford Motor Company, for instance, early in their histories established formidable international operations, which evolved out of their domestic activities.[10] My own research had uncovered the historical pattern of US businesses that began at home and then expanded abroad. At the same time, in the 1960s, students of contemporary multinational corporations, including Raymond Vernon, Charles Kindleberger, Richard Caves, and John Dunning, for example, were all taking the pattern of domestic first and then foreign for granted.[11]

Louis Wells has noted that two concepts are widely held today among researchers on multinational enterprise: '(1) to survive abroad, a firm needs some kind of advantage over local competitors, and (2) a firm must have some reason to internalize that advantage through ownership rather than contracting with another firm [or outside individual].'[12] Wells's apt summation assumes that at the point when it invests abroad the enterprise has already internalized the advantage in its *home* nation. Wells has espoused 'product-cycle theory', which is what Mark Casson (in Chapter 3 below) attacks, but it was not only product-cycle theorists who accepted the notion of a firm's need for competitive advantage.[13] In a 1995 summary of the state of the art on multinational corporations, James R. Markusen discusses at length 'ownership advantages', the knowledge-based assets, which multinationals transfer; like his predecessors, he too takes for granted the existence of these advantages within the company; he also assumes that the advantages have been derived from experiences within the firm.[14]

Research on multinational enterprise, historical and contemporary, initially focused on American companies.[15] When historians of multinational enterprise turned to study the path of British multinationals, they at first applied the 'American model' (derived from the prior research) and they realized that many British industrial enterprises conformed neatly to the 'American' pattern: J. & P. Coats, Lever, Courtaulds, and others began with operations at home, and then went overseas based on their domestic business expertise.[16] From my own research (which had shifted from the history of American business abroad to the history of foreign investment in the USA), I had become aware that many *British* overseas investments carried management and potential for control over borders. Often, however, these British firms investing abroad did not fit the traditional multinational enterprise 'model' that I had previously encountered: frequently, they did not start with domestic business operations and then expand abroad based on the core competencies they had developed at home.[17] The free-standing company—the company that inaugurated foreign business afresh—could not have *at origin* advantages within the firm, since it had no domestic operations on which to base these advantages.

What did this do to the widely accepted theoretical framework? What, if any, advantages did the newly established free-standing company have? By definition, because it had no *operations at origin at home*, to conduct business abroad the company had to engage the talents of outsiders. I identified clusters of individuals and other firms with varying expertise that surrounded an individual free-standing company.[18] Stanley Chapman's research on British-based investment groups had substantial influence on my thinking.[19] Yet, my clusters comprised more than his investment groups. I considered—and debated, particularly with Jean-François Hennart—whether skills in raising capital could be considered an advantage. Owing to the absence of operations in the UK, it seemed to me that, once more by definition *at home* and *at origin*, there was a 'lean governance structure' internal to an individual company. And as I paid special attention to the many British free-standing companies—mining, cattle-ranching, brewery companies, and so forth—in the USA in the late nineteenth and early twentieth centuries, I was impressed with how often these were short-lived activities. I related this, in many instances, to the lack of effective direction and administration at origin, or subsequently.[20] Also, I noted that a number of ventures were 'scams', set up by promoters to tap British capital markets solely to enrich the promoters. In addition, I was impressed with the work of Donald Paterson, who compared British direct investments in Canada with American multinationals there. He found major differences, with the former less successful than the latter.[21] In sum, my identification and definition of the free-standing company emerged from the juncture of four distinct research trails: (1) economic historians' research on British overseas investment, (2) business historians' and economists' work on the growth of the firm, domestically and internationally, (3) economists' studies of and theories of multinational enterprise, and (4) business historians' investigations into the history of multinational enterprise.

As others joined me in exploring the nature and growth of free-standing companies, six sets of questions arose that required further clarification: (1) *Context:* where, exactly, do free-standing companies fit in British economic history? (2) *Definition:* what, more precisely, was to be included under the rubric British 'free-standing company'? (3) *Elaboration:* how do we improve and add to our understanding of British free-standing companies? (4) *Evaluation:* were British free-standing companies associated with British economic decline? Were they 'second-rate' foreign direct investments? (5) *Extension:* were there only British-headquartered free-standing companies? How general—across source-of-capital countries—was this form of doing business abroad? And (6) *Explanation:* why were numerous free-standing companies headquartered in Britain and certain Continental European nations, and why, elsewhere, was the organizational form less evident? Why did so few enterprises survive over the decades *as free-standing companies*? What functions did free-standing companies serve within the evolving world economy? The questions, as posed under the first four headings, all relate to the history of British free-standing companies, but can, by extension, apply to free-standing companies headquartered in other nations. Item 5 specifically makes that extension. And, item 6 takes the extension into account. The matters covered under all six topics are discussed from different angles in the chapters in the present volume. It is those essays along with other critiques that stimulate and inform this introductory chapter, which explores these six broad subjects. I will save for the conclusion of this book some further thoughts on the implications and significance of the research on free-standing companies and address the topic where we go from here: what are the principal unresolved questions?

Context

What is the place of free-standing companies in British economic history? Britain in the late nineteenth and early twentieth centuries was the world's greatest capital exporter. In 1914 over 40 per cent of global foreign investment was from Britain.[22] Under British joint-stock company laws, companies were registered to do business in Britain and abroad; under the relevant joint-stock acts, between 1856 and 1914, 154,817 companies were registered in London and 9,303 in Edinburgh.[23] In addition, within Britain, family firms (often partnerships) existed that did not register; these too engaged in business at home and abroad. Thus, joint-stock companies do not account for all British domestic or overseas business. Nor, for that matter, do they cover, by any means, all long-term foreign investments, for individuals and informal groups purchased securities of companies and governments abroad; most—but not all—of those bonds and stocks were portfolio holdings.[24] Christopher Schmitz counted the Scottish-registered companies and found that 853 were, by his definition, set up to engage in overseas investment; of this number 315 were still active in 1914. The Scottish overseas investors were only a small (albeit important) part of the British total. Schmitz suggests that in the late nineteenth–early twentieth centuries 'perhaps as many as 15,000 or 20,000' companies were formed for foreign business and registered in London.[25] These numbers dwarf those cited by A. R. Hall as registered in England and Scotland and listed in the *Stock Exchange Official Intelligence in 1914* and as operating mainly or wholly overseas (1,976) that I used in my *Economic History Review* article.[26] The mortality rate of English joint-stock companies, by all reports, was somewhat higher than that of their Scottish counterparts.[27]

If we view, at their origin, companies set up under British joint-stock company laws, five types that were owned and controlled within the UK seem to have participated at the start, or subsequently would engage, in overseas investment:

1. *Domestic companies.* These were basically established to take part in business at home; then, later, they developed business operations abroad that involved making investments. Some of these companies also acquired portfolio investments outside Britain.
2. *Domestic/international companies.* These participated in business at home and began business abroad *before* they were registered, so at the time of registration they were already international (J. & P. Coats is an excellent example). Some were, at origin, international, for different historical reasons (e.g. Borax was a merger of an American and a British company; it was British-controlled and British-headquartered).
3. *Trading and shipping companies.* Many of these connected activities at home with those abroad. They started with a need at home and meshed it with some Anglo-foreign relationship(s).
4. *Investment trusts and certain other financial intermediaries.* These often made sizeable foreign portfolio investments, but had little or no direct investments abroad.
5. *Free-standing companies.* These were organized for the specific purpose of undertaking business abroad, typically in a particular country or region.

All five of these categories of joint-stock companies served as international capital flow conduits. Category 4—investment trusts—excepted, all seem to have had, or in the future would make, more overseas direct than portfolio investments, and all were associated with networks of trade, technology transfer, information dissemination, and managerial extensions abroad. Above and beyond these five categories there were *foreign-controlled* companies (part of foreign multinational enterprises or controlled by foreign individuals) registered in Britain; some of these companies became conduits for outward from Britain foreign direct investments.[28]

Joint-stock companies established under British law were required to keep stockholder lists. They had registered capital. Many remained family or closely held firms. The securities of others were traded, yet still closely held. Recently, William Lazonick has written that the critical transformation in US capital markets, which supported technological innovation, came with the rise of the market for industrial securities in the USA in the 1890s. He argues that the existence of this market meant that owner-entrepreneurs who had built up their firms from new enterprises to major ones 'could now monetize their accumulation of real assets through a transfer of ownership. The old owners could now exit from their enterprises', leaving control in the hands of career managers and easing the transfer to managerial capitalism.[29] As I read that passage, I wondered about its relevance to British-registered companies and, particularly, to British free-standing companies. There were markets in Britain for the securities of the registered companies that participated in overseas business. The British knew how to package companies to sell their securities and raise moneys that would in turn be exported. Many of the registered companies were listed and traded on stock exchanges. Yet the presence of that market in England and Scotland did not necessarily mean a transition to managerial capitalism. There is no question in my mind that all the above categories of registered companies provided conduits for capital export, that only some of the companies were actively traded on the London or Edinburgh (or Liverpool or Glasgow) stock exchanges, and, of those that were, most (at least at origin) did not have broad managerial capabilities within the firm. The fact that they could go to British capital markets (and the existence of active securities markets) did not in and of itself replace the owner-entrepreneur with managerial organizations. Indeed, what turned my initial attention to the free-standing company was that, unlike the classic multinational enterprise, the model for which was derived from empirical research on US-headquartered enterprises, the free-standing company did not first develop a business and managerial structure *at home*, which it could then at low marginal cost transfer abroad.

None the less Lazonick's point is critical. To operate over distance (as these companies did when they made foreign direct investments) required different kinds of managerial capabilities from those of local business. Because of this, the free-standing company at origin was usually associated with clusters of outsiders.[30] Since it lacked at formation competencies internal to the company, it had to obtain them from outside the firm. Britain—and especially the City (the financial district of London)—had an extraordinary 'service' sector capability on which these companies could draw.[31] It has been and will be my argument that, following on the theory of multinational enterprise—as articulated in the earlier quotation from Wells—a firm must have advantages over actual or potential local competitors in order to survive abroad. I believe we need, therefore, to study the nature of that advantage. We cannot assume away management. We need to ask how the production of goods and services over borders was managed and how the managerial structures evolved. We also have to consider how the clusters of outsiders related to that advantage. Does the starting advantage have to be 'internal' to the company? Could that advantage lie exterior to the company, in the financial, commercial, accounting, engineering, and other services accessible to those in the City? Were there available talents in other locales in the UK? Did merchants—whether in London or elsewhere in Britain—engaged in international trade provide the experience and information to serve the new enterprises (at least the ones that survived)? What were the institutional networks associated with these businesses conducted over borders?

A significant part of the context for free-standing companies in Britain is that they proliferated in the most advanced, most capital-rich nation in the world, the country with the most sophisticated stock market. They emerged in a nation that dominated international trade as well as international investment. Free-standing companies furnished the basis—or so it was thought—for residents within Britain to get a better return on capital than could be obtained at home.[32] The investors' belief was that opportunities existed in the newer parts of the world; these opportunities, opened by Britishers (under capable British direction), would bring forth greater rewards than investments in the more mature home economy.[33] Investors knew of these prospects because of Britain's experience in overseas commerce. Founders of free-standing companies, as investors and as mobilizers of capital, understood the premiss of higher returns. Free-standing companies would offer conduits for capital to flow into the freshly identified overseas investment opportunities. But did the companies have sufficient 'advantage', or were they able to obtain sufficient 'advantage', to derive the hoped-for profits? The services of the City might supply the advantage; so, too, might other knowledgeable businesses and businessmen.

Free-standing companies multiplied in number in late nineteenth and early twentieth century Britain, where there was a rising demand for new goods and services as economic growth occurred and incomes increased. They spread in the Age of High Imperialism, when the 'Sun Never Set on the British Empire'. In the mid-nineteenth century, Britain had been the industrial workshop of the world; by the late nineteenth century, with the development of new industrial technologies, the USA and Germany were challenging Britain. The overseas business of free-standing companies has to be considered in the context of both Britain's domestic economy and that country's changing role in the global economy. As noted, throughout the pre-First World War years, the UK remained the world's largest trading nation and the world's greatest international investor. One truly significant group of companies that were free-standing at origin were the British multinational banks. Significance is measured not by the count of companies, but by their impact—and these banks had vast influence. As Geoffrey Jones has shown, these banks did not emerge as extensions of existing British domestic banks; rather they were newly set up with the aim of doing business in a single country or region overseas.[34] There were other major British firms that began as free-standing ones, such as British Petroleum Company and Rio Tinto. While many of the free-standing companies were transient, a number had profound consequences.

Of the \$18 billion–\$20 billion total British overseas investment on the eve of the First World War (1914), T. A. B. Corley (in his chapter in this volume) has estimated that \$8.2 billion was direct investment and \$6.6 billion of the direct investment was by free-standing companies.[35] I am not entirely comfortable with these figures, but I believe Corley is, indeed, accurate in his conclusion that the greater part of British direct investment overseas in 1914 was initially established by free-standing companies.[36]

Definition

Many questions have arisen concerning the definition of free-standing companies: which companies qualify and which do not? What began, in my view, as something simple and straightforward is clearly not.[37] The attempts at clarification have served the vital purpose of stimulating more careful analysis of the institutional forms of conducting business over borders. In providing definitions, I do not want to pigeon-hole.

Rather, as we try to delineate the principal characteristics of business over borders, we need to ascertain where or whether the free-standing company 'model' fits the evidence. To do that I must define my terms and recognize where there are ambiguities. I will discuss seven separate definitional matters that have arisen.

There no longer seems to be much—or any—dispute over *a first definitional matter* that once created confusion and controversy, yet the point must be reiterated. An individual who migrates and sets up a business abroad has *not* established a free-standing company.[38] As I have written elsewhere, it is bizarre to call the Scottish-born Andrew Carnegie a 'British investor in the United States'. I follow this rule globally: a Britisher resident in China, who started and ran a business there, and formed a company that had no parent (or headquarters) domiciled in Britain was not to be included as a British overseas investment. The latter required residence in Britain.[39] There are no difficulties in this definition when we consider the USA as a host. On the other hand, the Hongkong and Shanghai Banking Corporation, registered in Hong Kong, but with shareholder lists in both Hong Kong and the UK, does present some definitional quandaries. For consistency, it is probably better to call it a Hong Kong registered company and exclude it.[40] To do so provides the opportunity to compare, for example, cotton textile mills registered in India and run by Britishers with those operating in India and registered in the UK; or diamond mines registered in South Africa and run by Britishers with those South African diamond mines registered in the UK. We want to enquire were there basic differences between those businesses with and without a UK-registered parent? I believe there were.[41] It makes us ask why and when a headquarters in London, or elsewhere in Britain, was established. Whenever there was British registration, there was at least a nominal British headquarters. Note that in host countries—Russia, the USA, and Italy, for example—domestic registration, e.g. incorporation, was required or was the procedure of choice for business operations. The British free-standing company doing business in Russia and, in some cases, the USA held stock in an operating subsidiary.[42] As Peter Hertner's chapter shows, 'foreign companies'—those founded abroad—had to register to do business in Italy.[43] For our purposes, the determinant point was whether there was *a parent* in the UK. To qualify as a British free-standing company, there had to be British registration—that is, at least a nominal British head office. There had to be supervision by—or the extension of—a company domiciled in, resident in, Britain. This is vital, for ours is the study of the operation of business *over borders*. This said, I share the caution of my co-contributors to this volume on the matter of equating registration and headquarters (more on this below).[44]

A *second definitional problem* involved a total misunderstanding by some readers of the crucial distinctions between the 'classic' multinational enterprises—as described above—and the free-standing companies.[45] A *third set of questions* homed in on foreign 'direct investments': are there only two kinds, the free-standing type and the classic multinational, or do a wide variety of forms exist? There were overseas direct investments made by British individuals, for instance in real estate. Individuals and groups of UK residents controlled companies set up abroad. These direct investments do not fit the free-standing company definition, nor do some of them meet the classic multinational enterprise criteria.[46] Several authors in this book make extremely valuable suggestions on different sub-types of free-standing companies.[47] The answer is that there are more than the two forms of foreign direct investments. If, however, we focus solely on joint-stock companies registered in Britain, categories (1), (2), and (3) above would seem to fit as classic multinational enterprises; category (4) did not involve much direct investment (but, to the extent that it did, it would seem to conform to the classic type). Category (5) is the free-standing company case, by definition, and we can expand it to include various subcategories. Were there any joint-stock companies that did not go under any of these five rubrics and yet engaged in overseas direct investments? British-American Tobacco Company (BAT) combined the international business of two firms that were classic multinationals, but it does not belong under heading (2) since it was not British controlled at origin. It was similar to a free-standing company in that it was set up in the UK to do business abroad, yet, because, at origin, it was American controlled and managed, it would not qualify for inclusion in category (5). Over time, the ownership and control of BAT moved to the UK. Did it then become a free-standing company? We will return to the important matters of nationality and of change through time later in our consideration of definitions.

An associated and more challenging definitional problem—*our fourth one*—looks at how we define a firm. If there is a coterie of companies, commonly managed, I have no difficulty in defining the collection as a firm, even if the companies are separately registered.[48] How does this apply to the activities abroad of 'investment groups', so well documented by Stanley Chapman.[49] Some of my colleagues have asked: is an analysis of investment groups and their overseas activities an alternative to a free-standing company type of analysis? I believe the two approaches are entirely complementary. As noted, I had read and admired Chapman's work and was influenced by it when I started to write on free-standing companies. I never perceived the free-standing-company concept as a substitute or rival one, but considered rather that free-standing companies were often part of Chapman's investment groups. Yet, free-standing companies were also associated with other business clusters. These findings led to the broader dilemma of defining the firm. Is 'the firm' the cluster of companies, or the single free-standing one? If one moves away from formal registrations to the business history of enterprises, usually—but not always—the query resolves itself.[50] Jean-François Hennart's, Natalia Gurushina's, Rory Miller's, and Geoffrey Jones's chapters herein—each from different perspectives—capture the various relationships between free-standing companies and the associated clusters.[51] Jones finds the term 'free-standing' a 'misnomer', since these companies were frequently part of wider enterprise groups. In a sense he is right, yet the phrase was adopted solely to differentiate free-standing companies from the classic multinational enterprise; and in that respect, it is not a misnomer.[52] But to return to the investment groups of Chapman. Whereas I had seen the constituent, separately registered in Britain companies within these collectivities, as 'free-standing', Chapman does not like that designation. In his chapter in the present volume, he provides a very convincing story of the growth of British business in India and the East. 'The firm' for him is the cluster, the group of companies associated with the agency house.[53] Robert Greenhill, in 'Investment Group, Free-Standing Company or Multinational? Brazilian Warrant, 1909–1952', posed many of the same issues in a different geographical setting.[54] Greenhill's case study dealt with the evolution of a trading firm. Such 'networked' businesses prompt us to ponder what, in fact, constitutes common management, which is critical to our discussion of the nature of the firm and how business was governed over borders.[55] Chapman's narrative and that of Greenhill seem closer in their descriptions to that of the classic multinational enterprise than to the free-standing company one: the merchant houses (the wider enterprise groups) develop on the basis of internally generated talents; their investments are associated with their 'advantage' in marketing; they have 'advantage' in information; they have appropriate experience and skills. Interestingly, the classic model was to a large extent formulated on the basis of American *industrial* companies; Chapman's and Greenhill's centre firms are merchants. Yet, I have never felt this paradigm need apply only to manufacturers.[56]

The role of the clusters *vis-à-vis* the free-standing company seems crucial. If, at least at origin, the company did not—by definition—have internally generated headquarters expertise then it had to obtain the talents from outside. In the renditions of Chapman, Greenhill, and

Hennart, the cluster has a pivotal firm with minority interests in a collection of satellite free-standing ones (albeit Chapman does not see the satellite units as 'free-standing'). Hennart's theoretical analysis seeks to explain two related phenomena—that of the free-standing company proper and that of the firm that takes the minority stakes. There seems, however, to be an added element in the clusters—that is, the exogenous group of interested parties in any single free-standing company. These clusters of services surround and assist the free-standing company, with no clear centre.[57] Thus, in my 1988 article I wrote of promoters, solicitors, accountants, investment trust company representatives, and so forth, as part of the clusters. Sometimes, these firms (or their principals) had equity interests in the free-standing company, and sometimes not. Gurushina—in Chapter 6—and Reinhard Liehr and Mariano E. Torres Bautista—in Chapter 9—are excellent on interlocking directorates and clusters of companies. The 'business world' in late-nineteenth- and early twentieth-century Britain was small enough for studies of who's who on boards of directors often to be a good start in tracing the networks and nuclei.

A *fifth definitional problem* sprang up apropos of nationality: if I define the British free-standing company as one registered in Britain, under British ownership and control, I must specify the meaning of '*British* ownership and control'. If a company was headquartered in Britain (as nominally it must be under British registration), what percentage of the ownership must be British to call it British owned or British controlled? Are the two identical? Does the size or proportion of ownership necessarily indicate control?[58] Share registers reveal that British-registered companies were often not wholly British owned. As pointed out in other chapters, Bolivian Francisco A. Aramayo participated in the organization of a free-standing company in London in 1906; he held control.[59] In Chapter 6, Gurushina considers the Russian Tobacco Company, set up in Britain by Russians, to invest in Russia.[60] While, formally, such companies looked like *British* free-standing ones, that might not be the case at all. How does the free-standing-company notion fit when an Aramayo (or a group of Russians) makes a 'direct investment' in a company in the UK that, in turn, becomes the vehicle for an investment in Bolivia (or Russia)? Equity investments (in Hennart's discussion) are designed to carry control, but the equity held by the Bolivian (or the Russians) rather than by many (or few) Britishers is the key here in understanding the development of the business activity.[61] If a resident of a host country sets up a company in Britain, which he owns and controls, but which is registered under British law and raises only debenture capital in Britain, is that a British free-standing company? Take the same circumstances and have the firm raise equity as well as debt capital; how much equity must be held in Britain to move the ownership 'control' to that country? Clearly, ambiguities abound.

A number of large German, French, and American investors made third-country investments (in public utilities and mining in Latin America and in the British Empire, for example) through British-registered companies.[62] American multinationals often used British subsidiaries for business abroad. At origin, the British-American Tobacco Company (set up in London) was two-thirds owned by American Tobacco; its key management was American; it was 'American owned and controlled'; as noted, I excluded it at origin as a *British* free-standing company. Likewise, when Singer Sewing Machine administered a major portion of its foreign business through London, I believe this was decentralization within a US-headquartered multinational enterprise and not *British* business abroad.[63] In sum, it is important to establish whether a British-registered entity taking part in overseas investments was ultimately 'British directed', or, in effect, German, French, or American direct investments and not a *British* free-standing company at all.

In brief, a British-registered company need not be British owned and controlled. My definition of a *British* free-standing company has required British ownership and control of the parent and the overseas operations.[64] Exactly what constitutes British ownership and control may be hard to determine.[65] We have to examine the individual firm to establish the actual 'headquarters' and thus the nationality. As a further complication, the nationality of ownership and control (and the headquarters) could change through time.

A sixth definitional question arose out of and was linked with the last. It was not only the nationality issue that posed quandaries in the determination of a headquarters. What constitutes a 'headquarters'? Corporate structures (registration) were used for many purposes: raising money, liability, tax, and national rules and regulations. 'Registration' *per se* is not adequate to determine the home office. Yet, I have used British registration merely as a convenient handle, recognizing it as imperfect and well aware that the only way to identify the true head office of an enterprise is to look at the firm's records.[66] Ownership *of the firm*, if concentrated, is linked with control. If not concentrated, control may be separate. When I discuss tiers of ownership and control of the overseas business, the firm is my focus. 'Control' of the firm may be separate from ownership. None the less, as a company extends abroad, it is possible to say that there is 'control', or at least potential for control of the foreign operations. A headquarters is the place from which 'control' or potential control emanates. Jean-François Hennart and Mark Casson in their chapters herein debate some of the highly complex issues of control. When Edith Penrose wrote of the growth of the firm, she focused on the expansion of an administrative core. Yet, administration within the firm can be decentralized. Every student of multinational enterprise knows how murky some of the control issues are.[67] Because a number of free-standing companies were 'brass plates in the City', some authors have assumed that I believed that in the case of free-standing companies control from Britain was always weak.[68] I have never, however, argued that this is the distinction between classic multinational enterprises (where control could be minimal) and free-standing companies (where control could be carefully maintained).[69] Casson suggests that with certain free-standing companies, there was no direct investment at all, that the investment abroad was a 'portfolio one'.[70] In my view, by definition, the free-standing company has a headquarters in one country and extends abroad; by definition, it makes 'direct investments'. What seems crucial is that the free-standing company, at least at origin, confronted *different* choices relating to control and governance from those of the classic multinational enterprise. That accepted, the nature of control and the structure of governance by free-standing companies become important research topics. The spectrum of headquarters control presented by Corley in his chapter herein seems an excellent starting point.[71]

Our seventh and last set of definitional questions relate to the time dimension—the evolution of the firm. There appear to be three separate queries. The first two have easy answers; the third is the most problematic. (1) Can a firm through time change its headquarters, its nationality? Yes. (2) Could existing companies over time *become* free-standing ones? Yes, again. A company in a host country could be taken over by a British free-standing company. There was often a sequence of free-standing companies, acquiring the same assets, each better capitalized or more skillfully chartered, each hopefully able to raise new moneys.[72] On the other hand, I would argue that when, for example, the British-American Tobacco Company became British controlled—that is, changed its 'headquarters'—it did not qualify as a free-standing company, since within its organization the basic managerial capabilities had by then been fully internalized. Indeed, at origin, BAT—unlike the typical free-standing company—operated abroad in a number of countries and regions. It had core competencies drawn from American Tobacco *and* from Imperial Tobacco. (3) If a company began as a free-standing one, what characteristics must it maintain to remain in that category? In the past, my answer had been that, if a surviving enterprise internalized managerial capabilities on an international scale, it no longer qualified as a free-standing company. Yet, this response was not precise; it did not address exactly what characteristics a company had to sustain to persist under the label 'free-standing'. By definition, lean governance existed at the start; the firm did not have operations in Britain, at origin, other than those related to the establishment of the head-office. But was lean governance from that small head-office fundamental to my definition of a *continuing* free-standing company? In my 1988 article 'The Free-Standing Company', I wrote: 'The limited size of the typical home office was ultimately the crucial feature that distinguished these companies from contemporary US multinationals.' What I had meant to say was that 'At the start of their overseas business, the limited size of . . . '.[73]

As my colleagues (including the authors of the chapters herein) have pursued research on free-standing companies, I have had to think more carefully about the firms that survived—some for generations. My concern at this juncture focuses on definitional dilemmas. Clearly, individual companies that began as free-standing followed different paths. What is unclear is how long in the course of an individual company's history the term 'free-standing' continues to be meaningful. What does 'lean governance' entail? When, more exactly, can we say managerial capabilities have been internalized? Just how much of a home office *and* overseas corporate administration are required before we drop the designation free-standing?[74] It seems to me that at this point in our research flexibility must substitute for rigidity, and, probably, we must accept imprecision. We need to study the emergence of a broader business (if that occurs), the shaping of administrative structures, and how and what kinds of managerial and technical expertise developed. As in the growth of any business firm, this is a process. A single foreign plant, plantation, or bank office can be administered by a few individuals within the host country or from abroad. Enterprises, however, that come to employ thousands and comprise multiplant, multioffice, multifunctional, multinational activities require administrative hierarchies and the internalization of technical know-how. The British overseas banks (so well described by Geoffrey Jones), which founded and acquired multioffice outlets, had to create managerial organizations and obtain knowledgeable personnel for survival. They had different needs from the single mine, plantation, or jute factory that persisted over time. Some free-standing companies came to be drawn into wider enterprise groups after their origin. This was true of a number of mining ventures and of some of the companies that Chapman describes.[75] As we seek to refine our considerations on what happens over time, our understanding of the realities and the nature of business over borders deepens. Contributors to this volume do not apply the free-standing concept to business through time in the same manner. This is, however, in my view, entirely acceptable, because our purpose is to use the concept as a means of comprehension, of guiding our questioning.[76]

Thus, while it is useful and necessary to try to be reasonably careful in definitions, taxonomy can get tedious and we should try to avoid over-classifying. Premature definitions should not be allowed to divert attention or create blinders. What is central to the research on free-standing companies is that thousands were established, owned, and controlled in the home country, to conduct business abroad through direct investments, generally in a particular host country or region, and that the foreign business of these companies did not evolve out of ongoing business operations *at home*. These companies, therefore, had to develop anew and to find the know-how to run such enterprises abroad if the businesses were to survive.[77] How, when, and where they did so is vital to an analysis of the international business relationships and to the understanding of global economic history.

Elaboration

Elaboration (based on newly assembled evidence) helps with some of the definitional difficulties and puts them into a broad perspective. As noted, Christopher Schmitz has recently scrutinized the 9,303 companies registered in Edinburgh (1862–1914) and identified 853 companies set up for overseas business. Of these, 87 (roughly 10 per cent) were 'investment trusts, general investment'.[78] These probably would not be free-standing companies in my definition, because most had no business operations abroad; typically, they made their foreign investments from their home-base or appointed independent agents to make foreign portfolio-type investments in capital markets outside the UK.[79] Thirty-one were 'general trading, agencies'; I have long classified most trading companies as service multinationals, in keeping with the 'classic' multinational enterprise, since they had a domestic business rationale (to export or import goods), which linked operations abroad with those at home.[80] Thus, they would be excluded from the free-standing company category. There were, however, some trading companies set up to operate solely overseas and not to conduct trade with Britain, which would qualify them as free-standing companies. Most of the rest of Schmitz's 853 would seem—at least on the surface—to fit under the rubric, free-standing companies.[81] Table 1.1 summarizes Schmitz's findings.

One of the most helpful elaborations of the free-standing company concept relates to industries. Schmitz's research confirms Mark Casson's argument that, at least for the Scottish free-standing companies,

TABLE 1.1. *Scottish-registered companies set up for overseas investments, 1862–1914*

Industry	%	%	Number	Number
Mining	44		376	
Gold		19		163
Copper		3		29
Agriculture, ranching	22		184	
Rubber plantations		5		46
Tea plantations		4		30
Livestock, ranching		2		21
Manufacturing	4		34	
Jute spinning		1		7
Transportation, communication	2		18	
Services, utilities	5		42	
General trading, agencies		4		31
Investment, real estate	17		148	
Investment trusts		10		87
Mortgage companies		3		29
Land, real estate		4		31
Miscellaneous	1		10	
General, unspecified	5		41	
TOTAL	100		853	

Source: C. J. Schmitz, 'Patterns of Scottish Portfolio Foreign Investment 1860–1914', unpublished report to ESRC (1994).

there was a disproportionate share in what Casson calls 'property-related' investments.[82] The paucity of stakes in transportation and communication may be the case with Scotland and not England. British Inland Revenue Department data show a heavy concentration of British companies abroad in railroads and transport in the late nineteenth century.[83] My earlier writings had stated that free-standing companies existed in all sectors—primary products, manufacturing, services; I still hold to that but am prepared to amend the conclusion. Casson has made a major contribution in insisting that the concept is more suitable in analysing economic behaviour in certain sectors than others.[84] Hennart also emphasizes this, arguing that the free-standing form was appropriate in capital-intensive projects where there was little collateral—that is, an inadequate basis for borrowing.[85] Many of the contributors to this volume have noted the free-standing company's viability as a form for new mining ventures, especially when there was high risk, and also because there were active groups of mining engineers and investment bankers in London which were experienced in financing mining ventures. London was the 'premier metal market at that time'.[86] Nowhere was there better information on the market for the output of new mining ventures and on the demand for copper, lead, zinc, phosphates, tin, and other minerals. So, too, the free-standing-company form also became a viable one for plantations, especially those in rubber and tea. In the past, I suggested that the classic multinational enterprise often had no advantage in backward integration over the free-standing company. For example, Ford Motor Company had no knowledge within the firm on the cultivation of rubber. It had to hire specialists. The free-standing companies with their rubber plantations in Malaya probably had an advantage over Ford with its rubber plantations in Brazil. The former were frequently set up or came to be managed by experienced agency houses; they were thus better positioned to draw on outsiders' talents.[87] Geoffrey Jones shows that the free-standing-company form was utilized for British overseas banking.[88] While there were free-standing companies in manufacturing, none was in a 'high-technology' industry that required ongoing complex technical assistance from a parent organization. The complete absence of free-standing companies in high-technology production is one of the most crucial findings of recent research.[89] Likewise, few free-standing companies sold branded, trademarked goods.[90] For high-technology products, the multinational enterprise needed control over research and development and its transmission within the firm. For branded products, there had to be careful governance to promote the good or service and to avoid debasement of the name. Each involved managerial control that seemingly needed to be internalized to be efficient. The manufactured output did not, however, have to be high technology (only new technology) or branded merchandise for the classic multinational to perform better than the free-standing company. As a case in point, there is evidence that Japanese cotton-spinning companies that made direct investments in Chinese spinning (and behaved as American-model classic multinationals) created more efficient operations than British free-standing companies in the identical Chinese industry. Existing theories of multinational enterprise would predict this; the Japanese advantage was managerial.[91]

A principal feature of many free-standing companies seems to lie in their relationship with other companies, with the loose clusters of outsiders.[92] Alice H. Amsden and Takashi Hikino have maintained that 'late-industrializing enterprises . . . pursued strategies of vertical integration and unrelated diversification simultaneously, in unsystematic and complicated ways'. They cite as an example a mid-1980s statement by the chairman of Korea's Lucky-Goldstar Group:

> My father and I started a cosmetic cream factory in the 1940s. At the time, no company could supply us with plastic caps of adequate quality for cream jars, so we had to start a plastic business. Plastic caps alone were not sufficient to run the plastic-molding plant, so we added combs, toothbrushes, and soap boxes. This plastic business also led us to manufacture electrical and electronic products and telecommunication equipment. The plastics business also took us into oil refining which needed a tanker-shipping company. The oil-refining company alone was

paying an insurance premium amounting to more than half the total revenue of the then largest insurance company in Korea. Thus, an insurance company was started. This natural step-by-step evolution through related businesses resulted in the Lucky-Goldstar group as we see it today.[93]

As I read this statement, I had a sense of *déjà vu*. Balfour, Williamson & Co.'s acquisitions, for example, seem to have been made in much the same kind of natural, step-by-step evolution.[94] A similar pattern can be seen in studies of British investments in South Africa; one investment led to information about other semi-related activities.[95] These added businesses required new capital and different expertise. Often companies were set up separately. If they called for sizeable amounts of capital, they might be registered in the UK. If not, they need not have been. The internalization that the chairman of Korea's Lucky-Goldstar Group described might not exist, although the same kind of cluster sequencing was apparent—principally, but not necessarily, in host late industrializing countries (Balfour, Williamson & Co., which carried on the step-by-step approach, did so not only in Latin America but also in the USA). The notion of 'wider-enterprise' groupings gets us back to the definitional problem of 'defining the firm'.

Geoffrey Jones notes that the British overseas banks—which were unquestionably free-standing, at least at origin—were not part of any broader enterprise collectivity. Yet, John Dunning and E. V. Morgan have included them in 'the financial nucleus' present in the City. Jones would agree. And not only were they linked in a financial network, but these banks had to recruit from outside personnel to administer their banking operations. Until they developed capabilities internal to their organizations, they were forced to turn to banks within Britain for staffing. The overseas banks would apply to their home office for the names of clerks 'able and willing to take up the challenge of banking in colonial or foreign markets'.[96] In time, the British overseas banks that survived provided their own expertise, established their own on-the-job training programmes, and generated their own distinct bank 'culture'. Yet, as Jones argues, they continued to rely on and remain part of London's agglomeration of financial institutions and markets.

A very useful elaboration of the concept of free-standing companies comes when detailed applications are made to different host countries and regions. The chapters in this volume are a wonderful beginning in country and regional treatments, but we need many more such essays for comparative purposes. What is confirmed at this point is that British free-standing companies were in business in Empire and non-Empire host countries. These companies operated in the most developed regions of the world as well as in less developed ones. There is no neat centre–periphery pattern. None the less, there may well be some systematic differences between those within Empire and non-Empire (or between parts of the Empire and non-Empire), relating to British registration.[97] And a major divergence between those in developed and less developed host areas did exist in longevity: all the research finds that the lifespan of British free-standing companies in less developed host countries was longer than in the USA, for example.

Were the 'cluster' patterns similar in each host region? Were the modes of doing business the same or unique? Even though at first free-standing companies were specific to a country or region, there seem to be common features as we survey the global characteristics of British overseas investments. The British merchant groups that Chapman has chronicled operated in a similar manner in various parts of the world.[98] So, too, the overseas banks that Geoffrey Jones has researched appear alike in genesis (if not in continuity) from one region to the next.[99] Yet there were special aspects by geography. Thus, Chapman argues that key London promoters of international companies had no experience with India and the Far East.[100] Another difference lay in staffing. British free-standing companies in less developed countries often hired British expatriates—already settled there—or sent personnel from the UK. In developed countries, nationals within the host countries were fully capable of carrying on activities, which may explain why the domestication of free-standing companies (the elimination of the British headquarters) usually came more rapidly in developed than in less developed countries.

Some businesses in the same industries and same countries, often associated with identical clusters of companies, were established as free-standing ones in Britain, while others had only local registration. Why did this dissimilarity exist? The answers are not yet entirely evident, but, *ceteris paribus*, companies registered in Britain tended to be larger (with greater capitalization) than those in the same industries—in the same cluster—formed in host countries.[101] The high cost of floating a company in Britain (for example, the costs of lining up and paying directors, fees to accountants, charges for British specialists' trips overseas for verification purposes) had to be offset by the capital acquired. Chapman (in Chapter 7) and my own research confirm this high cost. G. D. N. Worswick and D. G. Tipping indicate that, with both a head office in Britain and an operating establishment abroad, 'a fairly large minimum size is therefore pre-supposed'.[102] Hennart, who in Chapter 2 gives his own answers on the different reasons for British rather than host-country registration, points out that some locally incorporated 'Western' tin mining companies in Malaya were reincorporated in London when their capital needs grew. In the same chapter, he hypothesizes that, the more a firm was oriented towards export from a host location, the more likely it would have a foreign registration; he shows, for instance, that, in Ceylon, tea growing was undertaken by both sterling (London-registered) and rupee (locally incorporated) companies; sterling companies specialized in the highest quality tea, which was sold in London, while the generally smaller rupee companies sold most of their produce on the local market.[103] On the other hand, there were many British free-standing companies that did not participate in exporting from the host country.[104] In the case of South Africa, where sometimes there was London registration of diamond- and gold-mining companies and sometimes not, the advantages of *South African* incorporation have been summarized as follows: (1) avoidance of the inconvenience and constraints of English company law; (2) no need to hold annual meetings in London; and (3) no need to provide shareholder registers.[105]

A. R. Hall, in *The London Capital Market and Australia 1870–1914*, studied the relative use of various types of securities issued by companies operating in Australia in 1914, broken down by those companies registered in the UK and those registered in Australia; he found that the bulk of 'Australian securities' in London were issued by companies registered in the UK. 'Most of the ordinary shares of companies registered in Australia were held there, only preference and debentures being issued in London and these made up a relatively small proportion of the resources of the companies concerned.'[106] This coincides with Hennart's more recent findings. R. P. T. Davenport Hines and Geoffrey Jones, in their introduction to a volume on British business in Asia since 1860, discuss London-registered and locally registered 'British' businesses in that region, including in the latter discussion the business of expatriate locally resident Britishers and suggesting that the place of registration gave no consistent guide to sources of capital, 'although as a general rule locally registered companies seem to have drawn at least some of their capital from locally resident Europeans and occasionally Asians'.[107]

The British-registered free-standing company usually sought to tap British capital markets. Lance E. Davis and Robert J. Cull have pointed out that, in 1910, 18.2 per cent of American stock issues were traded on both the New York and London stock exchanges. Davis and Cull found that, in sectors other than railroads, American commercial and industrial firms were traded on both stock exchanges, 'however, the same firms were seldom listed on both exchanges'. They concluded that 'a substantial fraction of American securities traded in London were not even imperfect substitutes for many of the stocks and bonds traded in

New York'. Apparently, British free-standing companies, with their securities denominated in sterling, would *not* be traded in New York.[108]

As noted, there were costs as well as benefits to founders of a business in forming a free-standing company in the UK. When a free-standing company was organized, however, there was some kind of management over borders, no matter how lean the head office. If the purpose of setting up a free-standing company was purely to obtain capital in Britain and if the initiative came from abroad, perhaps the free-standing form was used differently from those cases where the initiative came from the UK. There are not enough studies on whether there were managerial or other systematic differences between companies in the same industry that were registered in a host country (employing foreign capital) and those registered in Britain. Did it matter to management structures as to where the initiative came?

The discussion of British versus local registration of companies dominated by British capital has prompted new research on the functions of a head office. In the administration of business over borders, what does a head office do? At the very minimum, if there was a registered company, the secretary of the company filed reports required by law. In Chapter 4, Corley presents a spectrum, from that of a 'brass plate' to that of a fully operational head office. This is very helpful. Some addenda might be made. First, what were the proportions in each category (which types of head offices were more common)? Secondly, what were the changes through time (were companies once and forever in a set category, or do companies through time move from one category to the next)? Thirdly, how did the nature of the headquarters relate to survival through time? Fourthly, were there systematic industry and host country/region differences in the functions of the British registered company's head office? Finally, as a fifth point, we need more details on those free-standing companies where the head office was or became 'fully operational', 'in regular correspondence', and 'concerned mainly with financial matters'. Corley provides a fine beginning to this elaboration. Geoffrey Jones shows that the head offices of successful British overseas banks played a major role in the provision of financial and recruitment services, while remaining 'lean' in 'size' (in numbers of individuals). I would classify them, however, in Corley's terms, as 'fully operational'. Natalia Gurushina's chapter reveals the complexities of activities of British head offices in dealing with the financing of Russian business.[109]

To conduct a successful business involves a certain amount of know-how; resources do not combine automatically; management matters. If, by definition, a new company is established that does not have within its midst the learning experience, as in the case at origin with free-standing companies, in order for it to continue it must obtain knowledge from outside. This brings us to one of the most significant contributions of the chapters in this volume. Many focus on what happened to free-standing companies over time. What were the patterns? We are back to the time dimension, now summarizing recent findings and adding new insights on the validity of different definitional choices. An individual free-standing company could—even before it started to function or after many years—exit (through failure, full absorption by another company, or abandonment of the British headquarters).[110] In my 1988 *Economic History Review* article, I commented on the high drop-out rate, which I attributed to scams and lean governance (inadequate management from the UK). I believed then, and still do, that many more of these companies were failures than successes.[111] Yet, there were long continuities and success stories.[112] It is thus wise (and necessary) to devote attention to what happened to those companies that began as free-standing and persisted over many years. And, if the business abroad was viable, we need to ask *why* was a foreign (British) head office retained? Assuming no 'exit', the firm's subsequent history could follow one of several paths: (1) the business could remain as a single purpose, single (or occasionally several) facility enterprise within the host country, keeping a separate identity; if so, there was usually no reason to expand the size of the home office; (2) it could be partially absorbed within a wider enterprise group, still maintaining a small head office in Britain; and (3) it could grow into a more extensive enterprise, internalizing within its business organization managerial and technical capabilities. In this third category, some companies continued for many years with lean governance from Britain that proved efficient and appropriate to the business undertaken, while at the same time developing *abroad* an impressive administrative organization. Others that began as free-standing companies created large head offices (and added operations) in Britain and became multifunctional, multiproduct, multioffice, multiplant, multifacility businesses—resembling the classic multinational enterprise. I am convinced that the principal feature of free-standing companies, at origin, was *not* their absence of business in Britain, but rather the lack of business *experience* in Britain, *internal* to the company, on which to draw.[113] How they coped with this deficiency through time tells us a great deal about the microeconomics of economic history.

Mark Casson suggests that free-standing companies were more adept at development of new activities than at maintenance.[114] This requires much more research; it is challenged by Gurushina.[115] Hennart notes that as late as 1967 UK-registered free-standing companies were producing over 75 per cent of Nigeria's tin output; presumably they had their own managerial structures.[116] Rory Miller shows how railroad companies created within their organizations professional management and survived.[117] Did the single purpose tin-producing and railroad companies remain 'free-standing' through the years? This depends on the definition of the free-standing company adopted. If one argues that they persisted as single-activity ventures within a single host country, albeit with a professional management, does that qualify them for continuing free-standing status? At least one contributor to the volume believes that to be the case.[118]

A key set of survivors was a small collection of British overseas banks, whose history Geoffrey Jones has documented. They began as free-standing companies. In response to business opportunities in certain regions they generated banking skills *and* managerial capabilities within their organizations.[119] As these overseas banks expanded, by my original (1988) definitions they were no longer free-standing businesses, for they internalized their managerial talents and did not depend on buying basic services (core competencies) from outsiders.[120] Note, however, it was not the British overseas banks that extended into the USA, Austria, or Italy that persisted, but those that were established in much less developed regions.[121] In the cases of the railroads and overseas banks, the British home office continued to be modest, but served more than a fund-raising function. In Corley's terms, it seems to me (as I have earlier noted in relation to overseas banks), both had head offices that were 'fully operational'. When we discuss 'operations', we must consider production of *services*. These head offices produced important recruiting, purchasing, as well as financial services on an ongoing basis for the overseas activities. The head office also produced other 'client' services. It had access to and the ability to transmit information. The costs of the head office appear to have been offset by the benefits.

One major company that started as free-standing demonstrates vividly the process of transformation over time. Rio Tinto (in the early and mid-1990s RTZ Corporation, briefly RTZ-CRA, and then in early 1997 back to its original name, Rio Tinto) began as a free-standing company, operating a mine in Spain; it became a giant international mining enterprise, with vast expertise internal to its business organization. In 1990 the RTZ Corporation employed 73,612 individuals worldwide, of which 15,459 were in the UK. When, in 1993, RTZ, which had 50 per cent of its operating assets in the USA and Canada, considered reducing its currency exposure by migrating to the USA, its British management rejected the idea, in part because 88 per cent of its shareholders were in the UK but also because, as Sir Derek Birkin, chairman, declared, 'We do think that being British is helpful. There's an image of fair play, of cultural skills.'[122] This company is no longer free-standing by my definition; yet, the exact point that it changed from a free-standing company to a modern multinational enterprise is difficult to determine, but it may not be necessary to make that determination with exactitude.

Another case of transformation through time is Anglo-Persian, now the British Petroleum Company (BP), which began as a free-standing company with an oil concession in Iran; by 1947 it had 14,456 employees in the UK (out of 107,269 worldwide) and was a leading oil multinational.[123] In 1990 it employed 118,050 worldwide, of which 30,693 were in the UK.[124] In this instance as well it is hard to decide exactly when capabilities became internalized. Corley's discussion of the origins of British Petroleum highlights some of the difficulties of the free-standing-company paradigm, but also the concept's value.[125] The origins of BP go back to the D'Arcy Concession of 1901. In 1903 William Knox D'Arcy formed the First Exploitation Company, a prototypical free-standing company.[126] In 1905 Burmah Oil became involved in D'Arcy's venture and a new corporate structure emerged.[127] When, in 1909, the direct predecessor to BP (Anglo-Persian) was formed, we could—following Corley—call that company a part of the multinational, Burmah Oil. The latter provided skills, but they proved to be insufficient; Anglo-Persian used a managing agency with poor results. Burmah Oil's chemists were unfamiliar with the properties of Persian oil. In time, as Corley points out, Burmah Oil could not handle the management. Anglo-Persian increasingly internalized its own managerial needs. We are back to defining a firm.[128] Clearly, for a while, Anglo-Persian was part of a larger multinational enterprise.[129] As Burmah Oil's investment became passive, Anglo-Persian emerged as 'the firm', and, as it internalized its expertise, it behaved as any multinational enterprise would do. The free-standing-company concept seems valuable in dealing with the origins of this company (and in thinking about its subsequent development). We do not want to employ the concept as a strait-jacket. Yet, having the concept as a guide, does show how, as this oil firm's business grew, its needs changed, as did its strategies and its managerial structures.[130] It overcame the limitations of a free-standing company.[131]

Schmitz's research on Scottish companies offers new data on continuity. His study indicates that 764 companies were set up in Scotland before 1914 for business abroad (I have taken his original 853 companies and subtracted 87 investment trusts and 2 other investment companies on the grounds that these would not, at origin, fit my definition of free-standing). Of these, only nineteen were still active in 1992. Schmitz kindly provided me with their names (see Table 1.2). With two exceptions, these companies had begun business within the

TABLE 1.2. *1992 survivors of Scottish-registered companies set up for business abroad, 1862–1914*

Company name	Date of registration	Primary activity at origin	Primary location at origin
1. Scottish Assam Tea	1865	Tea plantation	India
2. Tharsis Sulphur & Copper	1866	Mining	Spain
3. Samnuggar Jute Factory	1874	Jute manufacture	India
4. African Lakes Corporation	1878	General trading	British East Africa
5. Victoria Jute	1883	Jute manufacture	India
6. Titaghur Jute	1883	Jute manufacture	India
7. Doloi Tea	1884	Tea plantation	India
8. Burmah Oil	1886[a]	Oil exploration	Burma
9. Dharmai Tea	1894	Tea plantation	India
10. Consolidated Tea & Lands	1896	Tea plantation	India
11. Amalgamated Tea Estates	1896	Tea plantation	India
12. Kanan Devan Hills Produce	1897	Agriculture	India
13. Anglo-American Direct Tea Trading	1898	Tea, coffee, cocoa plantations[b]	India and Ceylon
14. Shelford Rubber Estates	1906	Rubber	Malaya
15. Third Mile (FMS) Rubber	1906[c]	Rubber	Malaya
16. Anglo-Sumatra Rubber	1907	Rubber	Dutch East Indies
17. South Georgia[d]	1909	Trading	British Empire
18. Juru Estate[e]	1910	Rubber	Malaya
19. Kajang Rubber Estate[f]	1910	Rubber	Malaya

[a] Reconstructed 1902.
[b] The company's name notwithstanding.
[c] This has been subsequently reconstituted as an investment company.
[d] Renamed Christian Salvesen in 1969.
[e] Renamed Dean Park Hotel Group in 1986.
[f] Renamed Inch Kenneth Kajang Rubber in 1933.
Source: Data from Christopher Schmitz, 28 Feb. 1994. He had 21 non-financial survivors. I dropped North British Canadian Investment (a land company) and Scottish Trust & Loan Co. of Ceylon (which invested in tea plantations) from the list, considering them investment companies.

British Empire. There are on this survivor list, as I would anticipate, no Scottish companies with business (at origin) in the USA. The roster also suggests the need to consider continuities by industry. It contains three manufacturing facilities, all in jute, and all of which were part of the Thomas Duff & Co. managing agency group. As for the persisting tea companies, nos. 10–13 were part of the James Finlay & Co. group. The earliest of the continuing tea companies, Scottish Assam Tea (no. 1), was in the Williamson, Magor & Co. group. Others of these long-lived companies were either associated with managing agency groups or were no longer free-standing.[132] Hennart argues that 'free-standing companies were created to internalize the international market for equity capital. When this market became more efficient, they lost their *raison d'être* and evolved into domestic companies. Their disappearance was the logical consequence of changed market conditions.'[133] Does this explain these survivors?

Three aspects of the history of free-standing companies over the years require attention. The first, which we have just discussed, deals with the ongoing activities of free-standing companies established before 1914. In this regard, Tamás Szmrecsányi has made the tempting suggestion that the free-standing form could perhaps be seen as transitional.[134] Following this approach, companies that lasted pursued different tracks, but in each case developed workable business organizations. This raises the definitional question of whether we want to reserve the term free-standing for only 'origins' or for firms that remain over time single-function, single-country businesses. *Or*, alternatively, do we also want to include firms—such as the British overseas banks—that did not develop in Britain 'operations similar to those done abroad'? If the home office came to produce the required services to administer the business abroad, even if the home office stayed small, should we drop the term 'free-standing'? As noted, there were several paths through time. If the firm's economic activity continued on and became domesticated in the host country, it ceased to be a continuing free-standing company; it came to be controlled and managed in the host country. One type of survivor (with a continuing British head office) was a business that maintained the single-core activity and never became part of a large multifunctional, multioffice, many-country operation. Another type of survivor was a firm transformed into the familiar category of multinational enterprise. There also seem to be 'intermediate' survivors—i.e. those with a single-core or single-country (or region) activity, but with a sizeable business; in addition, there were survivors that were for all practical purposes not independent, but closely associated with a wider enterprise group (usually a trading company) so as to have the latter constitute the multinational firm. Writing in 1931 on British overseas investments in 1929, Robert Kindersley noted that 'almost every British company operating abroad [and registered in the UK] maintains an expensive London head office or agency, which absorbs part of the company's capital'. What Kindersley seemed to be saying is that those persisting British free-standing companies established important (or at least costly) head-office activities.[135] Whereas a number of companies did continue on during the inter-war period as basically single-function, single-country enterprises (and probably should still be designated 'free-standing'), such lasting entities dwindled in the decades after the Second World War, as Britain lost her colonial Empire and as Third World countries intensified the process of industrialization, and economic nationalism triumphed. As the world economy changed, the free-standing-company form seemed increasingly inappropriate.

A second approach to the free-standing company over time looks at new British companies organized after 1914. The period prior to the First World War was the heyday of the free-standing company. Hennart observes, however, that free-standing companies were still being floated in the 1990s, yet his list includes none that is British. He found that in the 1920s, in parts of the British Empire (from Malaya to Nigeria) where capital markets were poorly developed, many free-standing companies were floated in Britain for rubber plantations and tin-mining.[136] Other data point to more British free-standing companies in existence in 1927 than in 1909—suggesting that many new companies were established in the 1920s. On the other hand, these same data—based on the 'number of assessments' by the Commissioner of Inland Revenue—show that, as a percentage of the total tally of domestic and overseas company assessments, there was a sharp decline from 1909 to 1927 in the overseas portion. Moreover, an increase in the 'number of assessments' might not necessarily mean more new companies; it could mean existing companies had taxable revenues in 1927 but not in 1909.[137] Rory Miller's research on the west coast of South America, which revealed numerous British free-standing companies before the First World War, found few new ones in that region in the 1920s. Jones's corporate biographies of British overseas banks include less than a handful set up after 1914.[138] My own research on the USA as a host to foreign investment uncovered no new British free-standing companies investing there after 1914.[139] Rory Miller points out that, in the early 1920s, the British government placed restrictions on capital exports and 'raising money [in Britain] for enterprises outside the Empire was particularly difficult'.[140] Once again, Kindersley is also helpful. He wrote that in the nineteenth century 'the British company was the favourite medium for the investment of British capital overseas. The high rate of income tax now [referring to 1929–1930] payable by British registered companies as compared with companies registered abroad, and the rapid industralisation of foreign countries has now left but little scope for the further development of this method of investment . . . '.[141] After 1929–1930, this became ever more true.

A third approach is to consider the changing industry composition of free-standing companies through time. This is virgin territory, but British Commissioner of Inland Revenue figures on 'numbers of assessments' are revealing. Table 1.3 gives the total number of assessments of British overseas companies, broken down by the largest industry categories. What is most striking is the decline in the use of the form in railroads and transport over time. Also there is the confirmation of the data in Table 1.2—i.e. the continuing relative importance of plantation companies. Remember, however, that 'numbers of assessments' reveal nothing about the size of investments, nor the importance of individual investments, only that these were providing profits subject to tax. The sharp 1932 drop in number of assessments of plantations

TABLE 1.3. *British overseas companies, number of assessments, by largest industry category*

Industry category	1890/1		1895/6		1909		1927		1932		1938	
	No.	%	No.	%	No.	%	No.	%	No.	%	No.	%
Railroads and Transport	621	33	527	28	410	13	202	6	125	5	104	4
Mines	295	16	246	13	614	19	330	9	264	10	231	9
Oil concessions		n.a.		n.a.	69	2	78	2	60	2	31	1
Land and Mortgage	281	15	238	13	194	6	273	8	255	10	120	5
Plantations		n.a.		n.a.	930	29	1,194	34	486	19	1,018	40
Public utilities	59	3	96	5	67	2	82	2	99	4	63	2
Others	624	33	746	41	919	29	1,343	38	1,264	50	976	38
TOTAL	1,880	100	1,853	100	3,203	100	3,502	100	2,553	100	2,543	100

Notes: Percentages may be off due to rounding.
n.a. = not available.
Source: G. D. N. Worswick and D. G. Tipping, *Profits in the British Economy 1909–1938* (Oxford, 1967), 93, 146.

might well be explained by the fall in commodity prices and the resulting losses experienced. The number of overseas banks was small (and because of this not included in Table 1.3), yet these were some of the most significant British free-standing companies—significant in their impacts on the trade and banking systems in the regions where they operated. These data do not provide host locations, which might help explain not only the use of the form but also the shifting industrial composition.

Evaluation

The concept of the free-standing company, when introduced, was meant to be descriptive; it was not value-laden, nor normative. I described what I found in my research. Yet the concept stirred a controversy I had not anticipated, albeit perhaps I should have. At the very time the idea was aired, British economic historians were paying attention to the roots of British economic decline and there was a new scrutiny of the history of British corporate performance, both at home and abroad. Alfred Chandler's appraisals of the weaknesses of managerial capitalism in Britain disturbed British economic historians.[142] Geoffrey Jones had written of unsuccessful British manufacturing multinationals.[143] My discussion of the small head office and 'lean governance', my contrasting of the classic multinational that transferred the advantages of its own experiences with the free-standing company that had started anew, my noting that many free-standing companies were short-lived and had a high failure rate, along with the conclusion by many observers that free-standing companies were not in advanced-technology industries, seemed grist to the mill of a literature seeking to explain British inadequacies. It surprised me how easily the 'free-standing-company' idea was incorporated into the British concerns over 'declinology'—that is, explanations of British decline. Charles Jones saw my rendition of the free-standing company as a 'kind of 2nd rate' foreign direct investment; T. A. B. Corley interpreted my discussion as one of looking at 'an inferior' form of foreign direct investment. Casson countered the argument that 'the free-standing company is just an inferior culturally-specific form of multinational enterprise'.[144] With no such intention, my evidence seemed to provide ammunition to students of the roots of British decline and to raise the blood pressure of some serious scholars, who came to the defence of British business enterprise.

The resulting debate has been fruitful. Corley defends the viability of British companies and the monitoring from their home office. He presses us to scrutinize more closely what monitoring was done. Casson sees these firms not as a less entrepreneurial type of multinational enterprise, but rather as playing an important entrepreneurial role. Geoffrey Jones demonstrates clearly that many British overseas banks, which began as free-standing companies and did not develop banking networks at home (at least until very recently), were successful for decades by every criterion—profits, provision of services, and so forth. Chapman finds that surviving free-standing companies had often been initially, or were later folded into, an experienced British mercantile firm, hardly a sign of 'failure'.[145]

The notion of second-rate foreign direct investment has different normative implications when judged in terms of: (1) the firm itself; (2) the home country; and (3) the host countries. These three vantage points for 'evaluation' are conceptually separate. In the concluding chapter of this volume, I will address these three distinct categories. (I will also deal with its success in the facilitation of global integration.) Here we need note only the juxtaposition of research on free-standing companies and that on the competitive advantages of firms and nations.

Extension

Were free-standing companies exclusively British headquartered? In my own writings and above, I have concentrated on British free-standing companies because they were the most numerous of all nationalities and because, when they proliferated and took on importance in the late nineteenth and early twentieth centuries, Britain was the world's largest capital exporter. None the less, I have long been aware that the form was far from confined to British-headquartered enterprises.[146] Students of the history of Dutch, Belgian, and French business abroad, in particular, have found that the concept enriches their research.[147] Harm Schröter has identified a small number of Swiss and German free-standing companies.[148] Gregory Marchildon, in his chapter in the present volume, is wonderful in using the idea to illuminate Canadian business abroad.[149] Miller points out that in the pre-First World War years, Cerro de Pasco, the US-owned company that mined in Peru, fits the mould;[150] certain US sugar producers in Cuba conformed to the pattern.[151] Obviously, there was no British monopoly on the free-standing company form. In addition, for some headquarters countries, leaving aside the UK, the free-standing-company concept may have validity in analysing outward direct investments in the 1920s—and perhaps even later.[152]

All the comments on context discussed above can be considered in relation to the free-standing companies headquartered in European and North American capital-exporting nations. With one exception—the paper by William Hausman and John Neufeld (which deals with the 1920s)—the chapters herein that discuss non-British free-standing companies begin their analyses with the late nineteenth and early twentieth centuries; most extend to a later period as well. This research has opened new horizons. The emerging consensus seems to be that free-standing companies were a principal type of conduit for capital exports for the Netherlands and Belgium.[153] Regrettably, we do not have in this volume a general paper on French free-standing companies, albeit the Hertner and Szmrecsányi chapters cover French companies and my own reconsideration of the data suggests that this form of starting business abroad seems to figure importantly in the French capital export story.[154] The chapters herein confirm preliminary conclusions that free-standing companies were less frequently headquartered in the USA, Germany, Switzerland, and Sweden.[155] Marchildon describes Canadian free-standing utilities in Latin America and the Caribbean.[156] Schröter suggests that countries with empires—Britain, Holland, Belgium, and France—tended to have more free-standing companies than countries with smaller, or without, empires—the USA, Germany, Switzerland, and Sweden.[157] Yet the geographical extension of free-standing companies from imperial countries was far from exclusively within Empire.[158] Moreover, companies from countries with overseas empires were *not* 'more international' than those from nations without or with relatively small empires; thus, there were large outward foreign direct investments by classic multinational enterprises from the USA, Germany, Switzerland, and Sweden in the pre-1914 years. Can it be that, in general, countries with sizeable capital surpluses in the late nineteenth and early twentieth centuries tended to be the most important homes to free-standing companies?

Virtually all the definitional matters posed above in relation to British companies have arisen as the study of free-standing companies has been stretched to include other headquarters countries. The problems of migration are important. A company formed by a German settler (immigrant) in Russia, Guatemala, Brazil, or China does not qualify under the rubric free-standing (or as part of a classic multinational enterprise), if there was no home office.[159] Likewise, a Dutch expatriate in the Dutch East Indies or a French settler in Algeria who initiated a business *with no parent company back home* is not counted as a 'foreign' investor. By definition, a free-standing company required business over borders—that is, registration/residence in a headquarters nation. 'Registration' *per se*, however, might not indicate headquarters. The Suez Canal Company, for example, was 'registered in Egypt', but its administrative head office was in Paris; its *legal domicile* was at its Paris administrative headquarters.[160]

The classic multinational enterprise—with a headquarters and economic activity in continental European countries—had a long history.[161] There were also many 'wider-enterprise' groups that bore strong resemblance to the British ones chronicled by Chapman. There were clusters. Hennart—in Chapter 2—notes, for example, the role of the Belgian Empain group and the Belgian free-standing traction companies associated with it. As Hennart indicates, the clusters of companies domiciled in Belgium pose many of the same kinds of difficulties in defining a firm as were encountered in our examination of the British groups.[162] Some Dutch trading groups, described in Ben Gales and Keetie Sluyterman's chapter, are analogous.[163] Szmrecsányi found hints of a connection between a French sugar *machinery* manufacturer and the large French free-standing sugar producer in Brazil.[164] Thus, with not only British free-standing companies, but European Continental ones as well, we have to reflect on the history of corporate networks, of loose groupings of companies. Marchildon's study of Canadian free-standing utilities is superb on Canadian clusters that helped the utilities overcome the limitations of being free-standing units.[165] Networks and alliances in business history have been studied in the context of cartels; perhaps more important were these clusters of interactions that we saw in British business history and that seem more generally in evidence.

The matter of defining the nationality of a business over borders raised questions when we studied British free-standing companies; the same is true of the non-British counterparts. The first complication lies in what constituted a 'country'. In the British case, we defined all parts of the overseas Empire as 'foreign'. Although wary, we used registration in Britain as a proxy for headquarters. The authors of the chapters herein have adopted that protocol to make our papers consistent. But

Harm Schröter—in his chapter—shows some of the bizarre consequences of following that pattern rigidly in relation to Belgium and the Belgian Congo in the post-First World War years.[166] Moreover, on the European Continent, where borders were redrawn through time, scholars have struggled with how to define 'foreign' business. Is an Austrian company's investment in what became Czechoslovakia in the inter-war years a domestic investment before 1914 and a foreign one after the war; and if we define investments in overseas empires as 'foreign', what do we do about empires that cover contiguous territory (i.e. were not overseas)?[167]

A second matter of nationality related to ownership and control of a firm registered in one country to do business abroad. Ben Gales and Keetie Sluyterman have considered Dutch free-standing companies, adopting the same criteria as I used for British ones. If residents of one country invested back home or in a third country through a Dutch-registered entity, they argued that this was not a *Dutch* free-standing company.[168] This is important. So frequently did foreign individuals and companies use Dutch intermediaries in the pre-First World War years, as well as later, that the Dutch literature had special names for this practice. Gales, writing on the period before the First World War, found that Germans often formed companies in Holland to tap Dutch capital markets for *German* business activities—so-called 'bypass investments'. In addition, he points out that it was very common for French and Belgian investors to set up companies in the Netherlands to invest in the Dutch East Indies—so-called 'transfer investments'. Gales notes that the German 'bypass investments' seemed to have been German managed, while, with the 'transfer investments', the nature of the management varied.[169] Similarly, to operate in Belgian or French colonies, non-Belgian or non-French multinationals registered in, or acquired companies registered in, the mother country.[170] After 1914 the 'nationality' problem takes on much more complexity (see below).

With Canadian-registered public utilities abroad, a third matter of nationality arose. In these cases, the management and direction might well be by Canadians from a Canadian head office, but the majority of the ownership could be American and/or British.[171] With the Canadian public utilities in Latin America and the Caribbean, the clusters on which they relied for talents in many instances extended into the USA. Obviously, we need to look carefully at the business activities and get behind the corporate edifices. Ford Motor Company, for example, for years let its Canadian affiliate own and handle all British Empire business (outside Great Britain); its Canadian affiliate was, however, a part of the Ford Motor Company's multinational business.[172]

One has to sift the evidence to decide where the headquarters of a firm is located, from where the direction of the business arises. As in the British case, this may not be apparent from the place of registration. Especially after the First World War, the location of registration (incorporation) more and more might reflect tax and other considerations. As we pass through time, there is a growing imperative to raise the 'legal veil' and study the nature of the business activity *per se*. The value of the free-standing-company concept is that it presses us to consider the business history of enterprises that operate over borders in terms of strategies and managerial structures. The interest is in the *firm*—its impact and performance—and goes beyond the capital flows.

Research on free-standing companies headquartered on the European Continent and in North America has added substantial richness and depth to what we know of international business history. The industry composition of the involvements of non-British-headquartered free-standing companies provided some surprises. One was the truly heavy participation of Dutch free-standing companies in tropical agriculture (sugar, coffee, tobacco, and rubber).[173] The share seems out of keeping with any other national record on free-standing companies.[174] On the other hand, given the heavy concentration of Dutch free-standing companies in the Netherlands East Indies, the surprise evaporates. Likewise, the use of Belgian companies for investments in tramways seems distinctive. While this has been noted before, it comes out very strongly in the international comparative context and can be understood in terms of learned capabilities within Belgium. So, too, Canadian entrepreneurs' unique way of organizing business in public utilities in Latin America seems to have no global counterpart. Marchildon provides the rationale.

In many Continental European nations, banks played a very different role *vis-à-vis* foreign direct investment than was the case with US or British business abroad. The precise relationships between banks and free-standing companies remains elusive.[175] By contrast, one of the most fruitful outcomes of the research on non-British free-standing companies has been the re-examination—on a global scale—of the nature of business over borders in public utilities. Hausman and Neufeld's excellent chapter is a major contribution. They explore outward US foreign direct investments in electric power companies in the 1920s. When, years ago, I wrote on the history of American business abroad, I had no difficulty in seeing such stakes as part of the discernible activity of US multinational enterprise. No 'flags' went up then that these investments failed to conform with the pattern I had perceived as general. Indeed, when Hausman proposed this paper for the Milan Conference session on free-standing companies, I nervously agreed. Had I been blind in my previous findings? Hausman and

Neufeld concluded (to my relief) that the free-standing-company paradigm was in general *not* appropriate; in the main, the most important of these investments arose out of the participants' experience in their home enterprises—and built on that knowledge base.[176] The use of the free-standing concept, however, encouraged Hausman and Neufeld to try to answer questions they would not otherwise have asked. In addition, I began to wonder whether there was one large American-based utility that might go under the rubric free-standing: International Telephone and Telegraph Corporation, formed in 1920.[177] The fit is awkward, and, on consideration, I believe that the application of the free-standing-company concept to this public utility does not contribute much to our understanding of its strategies or structure.

Marchildon's chapter finds the concept useful in studying pre-1914 Canadian utilities abroad.[178] Yet, over time, the concept seems to become less helpful. Indeed, when it is applied to the inter-war financing of Latin American (and other) power, light, and telephone companies through Canadian (or, I might add, American, Belgian, or Swiss) holding-company structures, perhaps we need to search for superior models. Yet, here again, as with Hausman and Neufeld's considerations of US investments abroad in this sector and Hennart's treatment of the Empain group (he believes that the free-standing-company concept is applicable at least in the pre-1914 years), research on the free-standing company has spurred a more careful scrutiny of the way business is managed and financed over borders. Reflections on management, along with finance, give us a fresh view of the clusters of companies involved, offering valuable insights into the development of public utilities on a global scale.[179]

Research on non-British free-standing companies seems to confirm their presence in certain infrastructure investments, in plantation agriculture, and in mining. Most important, it verifies their absence in economic activities involving high-technology differentiated trademarked products—in modern *industrial* activities that required management of scale and scope economies.

The geographical spread to host regions or countries of non-British free-standing companies is noteworthy. Gales and Sluyterman's findings for the pre-First World War years (as well as subsequently) on the overwhelming importance of the Netherlands East Indies and the relative unimportance of the Netherlands West Indies and Surinam are of great interest.[180] And, it was not that the Dutch were uninterested in the Western Hemisphere; the USA ranked second (a distant second to be sure) to the Netherlands East Indies as a host to Dutch free-standing companies.[181] Just as in the case of the classic multinational enterprise, so, for free-standing companies, the geographical distribution of outward foreign direct investments varied greatly by home-country nationality.[182] Also the geographical direction of free-standing companies (at origin) and later in their development may have differed (at least in proportions) from that of classic multinationals of the same nationality.[183]

Gales and Sluyterman's study of free-standing companies that operated in the Dutch East Indies shows that, of new companies starting operations there, the ones registered in Holland were far larger than those registered locally. They write, 'Registration in the mother country was preferred if links with the capital market were important.'[184] This coincides with the earlier findings on British free-standing companies within a common industry, within empire. Gales and Sluyterman's research uncovered, however, no connection (by place of registration) between companies in the host country that exported and those that did not—challenging one of Hennart's hypotheses on British free-standing firms. Another of their pertinent discoveries was that, unlike the classic Dutch multinationals where the initiative for foreign direct investments generally came from the parent company, with free-standing companies, more often than not, the initiative came from abroad. I am not, however, prepared to accept this as a general rule for differentiating classic multinationals and free-standing companies—since with the 'classic' American multinationals I know of many instances where entrepreneurs, customers, or agents abroad were responsible for the initiation of foreign investment plans and I am also aware of many instances with British free-standing companies where the initiative came from men in the UK.[185]

The studies of non-British free-standing companies (like those of their British counterpart) seem to emphasize the importance of the use of the form in the pre-First World War period and the decline in its usage as the twentieth century progressed. A possible ambiguity lies in the 1920s and whether, as the USA became a major creditor nation, the form was used more often in the USA in that decade than earlier (and, as noted above, some authors have argued that, in the 1920s, the British—in certain activities and in certain regions—continued to use the form extensively).

In the post-First World War era, as indicated earlier, as taxation became a key issue, the use of corporate structures for tax reasons became commonplace. Foreign-exchange restrictions affected corporate conduits for capital. In my view, the free-standing-company concept fades in significance as these other international considerations loom. The proxy use of 'registration' for headquarters becomes less viable and the requirements of penetrating corporate veils to identify patterns of corporate direction and management become ever more crucial.

Networks of public-utility financing of operations in the 1920s crossed national borders with extraordinary complexity. Yet in the 1920s and well beyond, in some activities, as was the case with British firms, a number of non-British free-standing companies did persist as single-core-function, single-host-country activities with limited head offices.[186] New free-standing companies were organized in the inter-war years and in the aftermath of the Second World War. Still the concept seems to me to have less neatness in fit in the post-First World War years and less explanatory power. Moreover, as we move into the 1920s and particularly into the post-Second World War era, the composition of international direct investments changed; the diffusion of modern industrial process and products could not be done through free-standing companies. What the concept does (and should do), however, is to prompt us to consider more carefully historical *networks of business from different vantage points*: legal, ownership, financial, and managerial structures and at the same time to examine intra- and inter-company trade, technology, and information-transfer structures—as they alter over time and as they are part of and have impact on the changing world economy. As most students of the history of multinational enterprise are aware, these different structures—all linked with business over borders—frequently do not coincide.[187] Clearly, as we decipher the post-First World War forms of business abroad, we need to pay more careful attention to where the true headquarters of a firm is located, since registration often is less useful as a proxy. The headquarters–business abroad relationships merit more careful scrutiny.

Explanation

It is not sufficient to describe free-standing companies. We need explanations. In Chapters 2 and 3, Jean-François Hennart and Mark Casson seek to test existing theories and develop their own. I will leave them to speak for themselves. To their contributions, I want to add, however, several thoughts of my own, focused on explaining *why* pre-1914 free-standing companies were so frequently headquartered in Britain and did not so often have headquarters in the USA;[188] why in certain Continental European nations the form was often adopted and why, elsewhere, it seemed inappropriate; why the form was employed at all; what kinds of free-standing companies survived through time; and what functions such companies served within the evolving world economy.

The explanation for why the headquarters of free-standing companies were so prevalent in Britain and not so apparent in the pre-1914 US environment seems clear. In Britain by the late nineteenth century there was abundant capital, seeking higher returns. At the same time, worldwide, British traders were experienced in handling exports (and imports). British entrepreneurs went abroad, searching for opportunities. Information was abundant. Britain was connected with the rest of the world. As this happened, individuals saw opportunities. An infrastructure developed in London to float companies to raise moneys for the ventures identified by Britishers and by individuals of other nationalities. The British could offer the services. The free-standing company was a superb institutional vehicle to take advantage of perceived opportunities—opportunities for investors, promoters, traders, and shippers of British and of other nationalities. As Hennart points out, for high-risk projects where collateral was lacking and where there was unfamiliarity, for projects that could not borrow, the British-registered free-standing company was a brilliant institutional device.[189] It seemed to provide safety to the British saver (since it was registered under British law and its head office was domiciled in Britain); it was a channel of information; it was a way of mobilizing funds that would not otherwise have been transmitted over borders. It was far from a 'second-rate' kind of foreign direct investment.

In the USA, as the geographically extended market unified by railroad lines grew in size and as population rose, domestic companies emerged in new industries to fill national needs; there was a tremendous demand for capital at home (before the First World War the USA was a debtor in world accounts), so there was no special urge by individual savers to seek financial opportunities abroad; yet, American *companies* quickly became multinational ones, naturally and logically extending their range to world markets (and when necessary seeking sources of supply) as part and parcel of their growth at home. US industry developed differently from that of Britain.[190] Since the pace of development, the industrial composition, the geographically dispersed national market, and America's resource base were unlike that of Britain, it followed that what was reflected abroad would not be identical.[191] There is no difficulty in explaining the separate paths of these two countries which were sources of foreign direct investment: the main differences were based on the extent of opportunities at home, the level and nature of the industrialization process, the characteristics of the domestic market, the amount of capital available in the source nation, and the existing financial infrastructure.

This explains why London and not New York (why Britain and not the USA) was the centre for headquarters of free-standing companies in the pre-1914 years. By extension, one can argue that because, in each Continental European nation, the course of industrialization was different, so too we would expect varying usages of the free-standing form. A comparison of Holland and Germany is instructive—and might well follow a discussion parallel to that of Britain and the USA. The Dutch had a well-developed stock market, abundant capital, a relatively small domestic market (relative to Germany), as well as a long history of international involvements. By contrast, German political unification had opened up a sizeable national market. Like US business, German enterprises' first priority was domestic, and only secondarily international. We would have predicted more free-standing companies headquartered in Holland than in Germany.

The explanations appropriate to the cases of France, Switzerland, Belgium, and Sweden are still being shaped. As noted, the current thinking is that France and Belgium were important homes for free-standing companies, while Switzerland and Sweden were not. Explanations have been offered that deal with France and Belgium as imperial powers, the nature of national legislation (including tax laws), the characteristics of capital markets in these countries, the relationships between banks and enterprises, the stages of development, the domestic industrialization processes, the changing size of domestic markets, and more generally, the business history of firms in these nations. These explanations are as yet tentative and not conclusive. Perhaps, however, most cogent, France and Belgium in the pre-1914 years had capital surpluses; Switzerland and Sweden did not; this was especially true of Sweden.[192]

The free-standing-company form of business was used when it supplied a need. In the late nineteenth and early twentieth centuries, the global economy became integrated as never before in history. Business organizations were required to serve in a world where people, goods, money, and information were crossing borders to an unprecedented extent. Free-standing companies offered many connections. They linked expatriates abroad with home sources of capital. They gave traders (and shippers) ways of taking advantage of newly identified prospects. They seemed to present a fine institutional conduit for available capital to move abroad (for individual savers and for investment-trust companies they seemed to offer a means of reducing risk in investment and gaining a higher return than available domestically—and to do so with low transaction costs). And, most important, with the spread of information, they furnished a form that could capture and employ newly available knowledge in a manner to raise the output of goods and services. They were, to repeat, not an inferior form of foreign direct investment, just different from the form that students of multinational enterprise had been studying.

The free-standing form of business seemed a good way to start up projects or to introduce new capital to existing projects abroad. There would not have been the multiplication of such companies if they were not seen as appropriate. Why, however, did so few companies survive as free-standing ones? I have earlier explained the short-lived companies in terms of scams and lean governance. I maintained that, when managerial competence was internalized, there were survivors (but the term free-standing no longer applied). Hennart has criticized my analysis as being too much based on the experience of high-risk mining firms (which he admits did make up a large proportion of British free-standing firms). Miller has argued that there were not that many scams (especially when one leaves out the mining sector), and that lean governance was a problem but was readily overcome and thus was not the principal reason for lack of survival. Miller claims that quite a number of companies that the west coast of South America hosted lasted over long periods, developing means of coping with lean governance. He suggests that the reasons for the exits lay in British involvements in declining industries (rubber, nitrates, railroads). That there were few new British free-standing companies in Latin America in the inter-war years and that some older ones did not persist was—according to Miller—based on problems in the British capital market, tax considerations, and capital-outflow restrictions.

Miller's reasons for the small number of start-ups after the First World War makes good sense to me (and they also would explain the decline of older ones). Ranald Michie reminds us that between 1914 and 1979 (1925–1931 excepted) the British had foreign-exchange controls.[193] In the 1920s the USA became the centre for cosmopolitan finance.[194] Both Geoffrey Jones and T. A. B. Corley feel there were still a sizeable number of new British free-standing companies in the 1920s. Clearly, however, by this decade, a variety of additional international business forms had developed, some of which were similar to the free-standing company seen in pre-war Britain, but many of which were quite different.[195] Most important, worldwide economic conditions altered, and, as new industries arose, the free-standing company form—once highly suitable—seemed less so.

While I am convinced by the new evidence that, at least for poorer countries, I did in my earlier writings underestimate the longevity of many of the free-standing companies and the foundations for future operations that they established, I am not prepared to abandon the importance of focusing on managerial structures and managerial arrangements for persistence. Every survivor described in the chapters herein (by Hennart, Miller, Marchildon, and Jones) seems to have introduced substantial internalization of administration and technical abilities or at least to have regularized inter-firm connections. The French company studied by Szmrecsányi worked out a way of managing the business that proved satisfactory for years (it was for a while one of the leading sugar producers in Brazil), but it is not clear that this company with its lean governance from Paris was able to make adjustments over the decades; in time its market share declined, and eventually the administration of the business from Paris came to an end.[196]

Explanations of the course of the free-standing company must rely heavily on the study of the growth of the firm. Research that considers when and why vertical and horizontal integration take place and when and why related and unrelated diversification occur is germane. Free-standing firms are no different from other enterprises. Even the starting point is not unique, for, if we turn to purely domestic companies, we recognize that at origin these too have to locate outsiders to run the operations. As the business grows, a company hires and develops its own experienced personnel. Where the free-standing company differs is its extension over borders; in this respect it encounters problems common to all multinational enterprise.

The world economy changed after 1914, which more than anything else accounts for the absence of a proliferation of new free-standing companies. Corporate structures took on a different role. Successful enterprises expanded and became more complex. Taxation became a key influence. Britain's relative decline as a world power meant it no longer had the pivotal place in the international economy of prior years. New modern industries arose where the free-standing form was not adequate (it could not cope with the business requirements). An explanation of the free-standing company and its course through time must be grounded in the history of the world economy.

None the less, in the era of their prominence, free-standing companies played a key role within the evolving world economy. They mobilized business resources; they provided 'connections' between the 'old' world and the rest of the world. The Suez Canal Company was a typical free-standing company. Free-standing companies established railroads, opened mines and plantations, developed resources to make them commercially viable, set up tramways in urban areas, and furnished telephone and power and light services. They offered long-term capital and short-term credit. They transferred more advanced ways of producing goods and services. They did not, however, move 'high technology'. In some cases, they provided the beginnings for activities with long histories within a host country, but that were no longer controlled from abroad. In other instances, they internalized management and served as the launch pad for long-lived important multinational enterprises. Free-standing companies persisted during the inter-war years and after the Second World War, but, as the world economy was transformed, new industries and new needs surfaced. There came to be available far superior business conduits for the spread of industrialization on a global scale. There are still free-standing companies today, yet they are dwarfed in the overall panorama and have been superseded—in the main—by other forms of business over borders.

NOTES

1. M. Wilkins, 'The Free-Standing Company, 1870–1914: An Important Type of British Foreign Direct Investment', *Economic History Review*, 2nd ser., 41 (May 1988), 259–82.
2. My first three publications that dealt with free-standing companies were in 1986. In 'Defining a Firm, History and Theory' (in P. Hertner and G. Jones (eds.), *Multinationals: Theory and History* (Aldershot, 1986), 80–95, esp. 84–7), while I recognized that the concept had broader implications and advocated more research, I considered only my findings on the history of British companies in the USA. That same year, in 'European Multinationals in the United States 1875–1914' (in A. Teichova, M. Lévy-Leboyer, and H. Nussbaum (eds.), *Multinational Enterprise in Historical Perspective* (Cambridge, 1986), 55–64), I commented on the existence not only of British, but of French free-standing companies. My third 1986 publication was 'The History of European Multinationals: A New Look' (in *Journal of European Economic History*, 15 (Winter 1986), 483–510, esp. 501–3), wherein I noted British, French, and Dutch headquartered free-standing companies. In 1987 (in 'Efficiency and Management: A Comment on Gregory Clark's "Why isn't the Whole World Developed?"', *Journal of Economic History*, 47 (Dec. 1987), 981–3), I used the free-standing-company concept as a handle to consider Clark's appraisal of 'British' textile firms in India, China, and elsewhere. I noted that in 1910 not a single Lancashire cotton textile mill operated as a multinational enterprise in China, India, or Brazil. I employed insights from my work on free-standing companies to evaluate 'British' management of cotton-textile enterprises. The next year, 1988, I wrote on free-standing companies in two more contributions. In one, 'European and North American Multinationals, 1870–1914: Comparisons and Contrasts', *Business History*, 30 (Jan. 1988), 8–45, esp. 14–19, I once more put free-standing companies in the overall context of business over borders. In the second, 'The Free-Standing Company, 1870–1914', published in *Economic History Review*, for the first time I devoted an entire article to the concept, specifically as it applied to British overseas investments, not merely in the USA but worldwide. That article summarized much of my earlier thinking about free-standing companies and was—until now—the only contribution that I have made solely devoted to the topic. Two added 1989 publications of mine are, however, germane. In my lengthy book, *The History of Foreign Investment in the United States to 1914* (Cambridge, Mass., 1989), I discussed the presence of British, French, and Dutch free-standing companies in the USA as part of all foreign investment in that nation. My earlier research for that book was what had in the first place turned my attention to free-standing companies. In 'The Impact of Multinational Corporations' (*South African Journal of Economic History*, 4 (Mar. 1989), 4–20, esp. 7–20), I tried to discern whether the free-standing-company concept would aid in understanding direct investments in South Africa. More recently, in 'Multinational Corporations: An Historical Account', in R. Rowthorn and R. Kozul-Wright (eds.), *Transnational Corporations and the Global Economy* (London, forthcoming), I have sought to fit the impact of free-standing companies into a more general perspective. Meanwhile, many

other authors have been writing on the subject; some of their work will be reviewed as this chapter progresses.

3. That literature is concerned with the savers and asks who in Britain invested (by region, social class, religion, and so forth).
4. The term 'visible hand' comes from A. D. Chandler, *The Visible Hand* (Cambridge, Mass., 1977); I use the phrase in exactly the sense that Chandler does; indeed, Chandler's work has been very influential in my thinking. When Oliver Williamson discusses the governance of firms, he too is talking about the visible hand. On the firm as a transmitter of technology, see, for example, M. Wilkins, 'The Role of Private Business in the International Diffusion of Technology', *Journal of Economic History*, 34 (Mar. 1974), 168–88. In discussing the growth of the firm I have been very influenced by Edith Penrose. See her *The Theory of the Growth of the Firm* (Oxford, 1959; 3rd edn., 1995).
5. Douglass North makes the distinction between institutions (the rules of the game) and organizations (the players). See his 'Economic Performance through Time', *American Economic Review*, 84 (June 1994), 359–68, and his *Institutions, Institutional Change and Economic Performance* (Cambridge, 1990). I use the word 'institution' differently, more as a synonym for organization; as I use the term, I mean a study of the channels, structures, and edifices that frame transactions. My usage involves more than (but also less than) the rules of the game.
6. Several chapters in this volume make that suggestion, either implicitly or explicitly.
7. In this chapter I use the words abroad, overseas, and foreign synonymously to indicate outside the UK. I consider a British investment in a colony to be a 'foreign' investment. A British investment abroad is by my definition one made by an individual or company resident in the UK.
8. On this use of the phrase 'portfolio investments', see H. Segal and M. Simon, 'British Foreign Capital Issues, 1865–94', *Journal of Economic History*, 21 (Dec. 1961), 567–81; M. Simon, 'The Pattern of New British Portfolio Foreign Investment, 1865–1914', which first appeared in J. H. Adler (ed.), *Capital Movements and Economic Development* (London, 1967) and was republished in A. R. Hall (ed.), *The Export of Capital from Britain 1870–1914* (London, 1968), 15–44; and M. Simon, 'The Enterprise and Industrial Composition of New British Portfolio Foreign Investment, 1865–1914', *Journal of Development Studies*, 3 (1967), 280–92. These articles set the stage for the designation of companies that raised money in Britain for capital export as 'portfolio investments'. See also L. E. Davis and R. Huttenback, *Mammon and the Pursuit of Empire: The Political Economy of British Imperialism, 1860–1912* (Cambridge, 1986), and 'Theories of Capital Exports: Lessons from the British Experience', in B. Stallings, *Banker to the Third World: US Portfolio Investment in Latin America, 1900–1986* (Berkeley, Calif., 1987). In some of the even more recent literature, this formulation continues to be maintained. See, for example, C. H. Feinstein, 'Britain's Overseas Investments in 1913', *Economic History Review*, 2nd ser., 43 (May 1990), 289. It is true that in the main the investors in these firms were 'portfolio investors', but the *firm* itself made the overseas investments, extending itself abroad; the firm was responsible for the conduct of the overseas business operations. Since the existing British literature at that time had used the words 'direct investments' to signify those investments overseas by firms that bypassed securities markets in their capital exports, Simon and others—in employing the phrase 'portfolio investments'—wanted to indicate that they were excluding these other overseas investments that were made 'directly'. As far as I can determine, the use of the words 'portfolio investments' to deal with British overseas investments evolved from the work of Simon.

George Paish and Robert M. Kindersley, the most prominent earlier students of British overseas investments, did not use the term 'portfolio investments'. See M. Wilkins (ed.), *British Overseas Investments, 1907–1948* (New York, 1977), for reprints of Paish's and Kindersley's most important papers on British overseas investment. Likewise, neither C. K. Hobson, *The Export of Capital* (London, 1914), nor H. Feis, *Europe: The World's Banker, 1870–1914* (New York, 1965; repr. of 1930 edn.) uses the words 'portfolio investments'.

9. The contemporary distinction between portfolio and direct investments lies in the matter of control. Portfolio investors are passive; direct investors are not. This distinction was not always the norm. The literature on British overseas investments and that on American investments abroad evolved with very different vocabularies and the result has been great confusion. As indicated in note 8, the British spoke of investments made directly as those that bypassed the stock market. In the American literature, covering both US long-term outward and inward investments, there has been since the 1920s the category 'direct investments' (defined by control). The US Department of Commerce came to define a direct investment as 25% or more ownership of a business abroad; in time, it lowered this threshold to 10% (first for US business abroad and then later for foreign business in the USA). In the US literature 'direct investments' carried with them the potential for control. Cleona Lewis in her *America's Stake in International Investments* (Washington, 1938) included British companies that extended into the USA as direct investments. So, too, a 1949 United Nations publication (undoubtedly because of American influence) applied the term 'direct investment'—following American usage—to British companies operating abroad (United Nations, *International Capital Movements during the Inter-War Period* (Lake Success, NY, 1949), 32–3). In the mid-1950s, R. V. Clements specifically challenged what he believed was the prevailing assumption that historically all British overseas investment had been of a passive nature. See, for example, his 'British Controlled Enterprise in the West between 1870 and 1900 and Some Agrarian Reactions', *Agricultural History*, 27 (1953), 137–41. John Dunning's student, T. C. Coram ('The Role of British Capital in the Development of the United States, 1600–1914', M.Sc. (Social Science) thesis (University of Southampton, 1967)), did not understand the difference between the US investments of British immigrants and British residents, but he did perceive that there were many British direct investments in the USA. Coram labelled some of what I would later call free-standing companies, 'syndicate' investments. There were many other historical studies of British investments in the USA—on cattle and mining companies—that discussed these stakes in terms of 'direct investments', although not using that phrase. In the early 1970s, J. M. Stopford, in 'The Origins of British-Based Multinational Manufacturing Enterprise', *Business History Review*, 48 (Autumn 1974), 303–35, was puzzled over how to classify certain British investments, those which he saw as having only a financial 'shell' in Britain; he was not, however, ready to call them direct investments. Indeed, my first thinking about 'free-standing companies' arose from my discussions with Stopford on a preliminary draft of his 1974 paper. Then came T. Houston and J. H. Dunning, *UK Industry Abroad* (London, 1976); D. G. Paterson, *British Direct Investment in Canada 1890–1914: Estimates and Determinants* (Toronto, 1976); I. Stone, 'British Direct and Portfolio Investment in Latin America before 1914', *Journal of Economic History*, 37 (1977), 690–722; D. C. M. Platt (ed.), *Business Imperialism 1840–1930: An Enquiry Based on British Experience in Latin America* (Oxford, 1977); P. Svedberg, 'The Portfolio Direct Composition of Private Foreign Investment in 1914 Revisited', *Economic Journal*, 88 (1978), 763–77; and J. H. Dunning, 'Changes in the Level and Structure of International

Production: The Last One Hundred Years', in M. Casson (ed.), *The Growth of International Business* (London, 1983), 84–139. In the interim, and even earlier, there were many studies that could be reread as works on British managed investments overseas by companies organized in Britain to do business abroad. The American vocabulary—distinguishing portfolio and direct investments in terms of control—is now becoming established in the literature on British capital exports: see, for example, M. Edelstein, 'Foreign Investment and Accumulation', in R. Floud and D. McCloskey, *The Economic History of Britain since 1700*, ii. *1860–1939* (2nd edn., Cambridge, 1994), 173–96.

10. My first book on the history of American business abroad, based on Ford Motor Company archives in Dearborn and worldwide, was M. Wilkins and F. E. Hill, *American Business Abroad: Ford on Six Continents* (Detroit, 1964). This was followed by a broader two-volume study of all American business abroad: M. Wilkins, *The Emergence of Multinational Enterprise: American Business Abroad from the Colonial Period to 1914* (Cambridge, Mass., 1970), and M. Wilkins, *The Maturing of Multinational Enterprise: American Business Abroad from 1914 to 1970* (Cambridge, Mass., 1974). Thus, during the 1960s, when everyone was discussing American multinationals' challenge in Europe, I was pursuing *the history* of US-headquartered multinational enterprises. To write that history involved an immense amount of research and reading and developing a framework of analysis. My framework emerged out of archival evidence, along with the contemporary studies of business history, especially those of Allan Nevins and Alfred Chandler; Edith Penrose's work on the growth of the firm was very helpful; and then there were the highly germane studies of contemporary international business, particularly those of Raymond Vernon, Charles Kindleberger, John Dunning, and, to a far lesser extent, Stephen Hymer. My approach to the evolution of US business abroad took shape after using business archives, reading hundreds of US business histories, numerous inter-war studies of US foreign direct investment (from those of Cleona Lewis to Frank Southard), as well as the huge cartel literature. My research was novel, since I was asking a new set of questions about my findings. My results were also novel: few scholars had realized how quickly in their historical evolution innovative American companies had moved into international business.
11. My own research differed from most of the contemporary studies in the 1960s in that I included backward integration of multinational enterprises into raw material production; I also included service-sector multinationals.
12. L. T. Wells, Jr., 'Mobile Exporters: New Foreign Investors in East Asia', in K. A. Froot (ed.), *Foreign Direct Investment* (Chicago, 1993), 182.
13. In my own research, I was influenced, but not convinced, by product-cycle theory, yet I found fundamental the notion of advantage. All the early theorists, considering multinational enterprise, accepted the notion of 'advantage'. See R. E. Caves, *Multinational Enterprise and Economic Analysis* (2nd edn., Cambridge, 1996), 1–2.
14. J. R. Markusen, 'The Boundaries of Multinational Enterprises and Theory of International Trade', *Journal of Economic Perspectives*, 9 (Spring 1995), 169–89. The point should, however, be made that contemporary scholars differ from earlier ones, and among themselves, on what constitutes 'advantage'. Sometimes these assets are called proprietary assets or firm-specific assets.
15. This was even true of the British leader in studies of multinational enterprise, John Dunning. His first book was on American business in Britain: J. H. Dunning, *American Investment in British Manufacturing Industry* (London, 1958). In Chapter 2 herein, Jean-François Hennart discusses Dunning's 'eclectic

theory' of multinational enterprise; in keeping with the pattern, it too assumes 'advantage'.

16. See, for example, G. Jones (ed.), *British Multinationals: Origins, Management and Performance* (Aldershot, 1986).
17. When, at the start of the 1970s, I turned from studying American business abroad to do research on the history of foreign investment in the USA, my plan was to turn the coin over and write on the history of foreign multinationals in the USA as I had previously written on US business abroad. (Raymond Vernon's big project at Harvard Business School had begun with US business abroad and then turned to non-US headquartered multinationals.) To understand foreign direct investment in the USA (inward investment), I read the immense general historical literature on international capital flows; I came across many direct investments that were not like those of the US multinationals that I had come to know so well. I asked, were these specific only to the host USA or more general? And, since I was reading the capital-flow literature, I decided to write on *all* foreign investment in the USA: the outcome was my earlier cited *The History of Foreign Investment in the United States to 1914*, published in 1989; a second volume is in process.
18. See my 'The Free-Standing Company'.
19. S. D. Chapman, 'British-Based Investment Groups before 1914', *Economic History Review*, 2nd ser., 38 (May 1985), 230–51.
20. Wilkins, 'European and North American Multinationals'; Wilkins, 'The Free-Standing Company'; Wilkins, *The History of Foreign Investment*. Note that many that invested in the USA were short-lived as British free-standing companies, but some became the basis for very viable and sustained American-headquartered enterprises.
21. See D. G. Paterson, 'The Failure of British Business in Canada, 1890–1914', in H. Krooss (ed.), *Proceedings of the Business History Conference* (Bloomington, Ind., 1975), and his *British Direct Investment in Canada*.
22. Depending on the source, the percentage varies, but it was clearly huge. See Wilkins, *The History of Foreign Investment*, 145, for one set of numbers. On the importance of British overseas investment, see M. Edelstein, *Overseas Investment in the Age of High Imperialism: The United Kingdom, 1850–1914* (New York, 1982).
23. C. J. Schmitz, 'Patterns of Scottish Portfolio Foreign Investment 1860–1914', unpublished report to ESRC (1994), 2 n.6; see also Davis and Huttenback, *Mammon*. Schmitz uses the term 'portfolio foreign investment' in the traditional manner (as applied to the British data).
24. Portfolio investments, as I am using the term in this chapter, are those wherein the outward foreign investor is not planning to (not able to) influence the outcome of the investment; there may be intervention, but only when something goes wrong. Investments in foreign government securities are portfolio ones; likewise, most British investments in American railroads were portfolio ones. Foreign portfolio investments can be in debt or in equity. They can be made by firms or individuals. I am discussing here long-term foreign portfolio investments, not short-term bank deposits or other short-term 'portfolio' assets (these are sometimes designated as 'portfolio investments' and sometimes not). By contrast, I use the following definition of direct investments: foreign direct investments are those where the investor has control or potential for control and/or the investment relates to the business operations (that is, it is integrated with a business *operations* strategy). Some British-resident individuals made direct investments; many of the investments of the 'investment groups' so

well described by Stanley Chapman did not go through companies registered in the UK, but were clearly direct investments.

25. Schmitz, 'Patterns', pp. i, 3 n.7. Companies could be registered in London or in Edinburgh. London-registered companies might, however, have a 'registered head office' in Liverpool. See Rory Miller, Chapter 8 herein, on 'Liverpool-registered' companies.
26. Wilkins, 'The Free-Standing Company', 262 n.12. Companies could be traded in London, in Edinburgh, on provincial exchanges, or *not* traded at all. The numbers of 'registered' companies far exceeded those listed in stock-exchange manuals.
27. T. A. B. Corley, Chapter 4 herein. Some have suggested that the reason for this lay in managerial ability. Thus, W. G. Kerr (*Scottish Capital on the American Credit Frontier* (Austin, Tex., 1976), 2), writes that 'British [Scottish and English] ranching interests by the mid-1880s spread from Montana and Wyoming range south to . . . Texas'. Most of the investment failed, mainly 'because the British investors knew nothing about ranching on the western plains. [While Kerr does not say so, some of the few successful ones were Scottish.] Such was not the case with Scottish mortgage companies organized to do business in Texas, the South, the Midwest, the Pacific Northwest, and the plains states. The directors of these companies knew their business and their investments prospered.' The ranching companies and the mortgage companies were both direct investments.
28. Note that this approach to classifying the registered companies results in an inevitable lack of synchronization between my findings and the data assembled by George Paish, Herbert Feis, Matthew Simon, Lance Davis, and others. They were trying to determine capital flows, while I have been studying business over borders. Paish's careful 1909, 1911, and 1914 articles (and discussions on his September 1909 and 1911 papers) on British overseas investments are in Wilkins (ed.), *British Overseas Investments*. They are and have been over the years a primary source for anyone doing research on British overseas investments before 1914. Paish indicated in 1909 that in his estimates of overseas investments he had not included the 'private investments of mercantile and banking houses'. In his totals he made informed allowances for these investments. As noted earlier, Paish never used the words 'portfolio investments'; he never actually used the phrase 'direct investments' either, as far as I can establish. It was Feis, *Europe: The World's Banker*, 15 n., interpreting Paish, who in 1930 would employ the term 'direct investment', as that investment, which did not leave 'traces in the form of securities issue'. What the literature on British capital exports came to call direct investment (after Feis and Simon) was what Paish referred to as 'private capital employed abroad' by banking houses, 'branch manufacturing, mercantile, and trade undertakings, &c., &c.'. (See his 1911 article, 'Great Britain's Capital Investments in Individual Colonial and Foreign Countries', *Journal of the Royal Statistical Society*, 74/2 (1911), 187, repr. in Wilkins (ed.), *British Overseas Investments*). The reason for lack of synchronization in the current research with prior studies lies in the different (and new) questions being asked. Paish, Feis, Simon, Davis, *et al.*, were all considering the amounts of British overseas capital. The student of free-standing companies seeks to understand, to repeat, the nature of and the investments made in the course of conducting British *business over borders*. They are not identical. Paish and his contemporaries were well aware that some British overseas investment was passive and some carried control, but they made no attempt to quantify this particular distinction. The same was true of Feis, *Europe: The World's Banker*, 29 (Feis writes, for example, that in 1914, 'Almost all of the mine properties financed by British capital were held under

British control and management. . . . The gold and diamond mines of South Africa and West Africa were almost entirely under British management . . . ').

29. W. Lazonick, 'Learning and the Dynamics of International Competitive Advantage', in R. Thomson (ed.), *Learning and Technological Change* (New York, 1993), 187.
30. Wilkins, 'The Free-Standing Company'.
31. This suggestion was made by an anonymous reviewer of the manuscript for this book, and it is, of course, crucial to the storyline. On the services of the City, see R. C. Michie, *The City of London: Continuity and Change, 1850–1990* (London, 1992), and J. H. Dunning and E. V. Morgan, *An Economic Study of the City of London* (London, 1971).
32. Jean-François Hennart has made this point in a number of different articles.
33. This is consistent with the traditional view (the textbook rendition) that, *ceteris paribus*, investors seek the highest return on their money. See Edelstein, *Overseas Investment*, and Sir Alec Cairncross, *Home and Foreign Investment, 1870–1913* (Cambridge, 1953), for more on British capital exports in this era.
34. G. Jones, *British Multinational Banking, 1830–1990* (Oxford, 1993), 9–10, and Jones, Chapter 13 herein.
35. On the accepted $18 billion–20 billion figure, see Wilkins, *The History of Foreign Investment*, 145, 156. These are stock figures. For Corley's estimates, see Chapter 4 herein.
36. My discomfort lies in a concern over the underlying data; it lies in the fact that foreign-direct-investment data and 'capital' of free-standing companies represent statistics collected in divergent manners. I do, however, greatly admire Corley's efforts to make these estimates.
37. Part of my before-noted reservations over Corley's numbers are associated with the definitional questions: if we do not have uniform definitions, how can we put exact numbers on the categories? In this chapter and in the following chapters in the present book many definitional issues surface. Likewise, in articles published elsewhere on free-standing companies, the phrase has been interpreted in diverse ways.
38. None of the contributors to this volume has included the companies of immigrants or expatriate (locally resident) investors under the rubric 'free-standing company'. We are unanimous in that regard.
39. This means that books such as C. F. Remer, *Foreign Investment in China* (New York, 1933), must be used with special care; he included the businesses of expatriates. Indeed, very frequently in much of the literature on British investments in Asia (and elsewhere), no differentiation is made between the Britisher resident in the host country *and* the British enterprise with a home office in the UK. There needs to be a 'home office' in the UK for there to be a business investment over borders, a foreign direct investment.
40. Geoffrey Jones includes it as a British overseas bank, basically because its behaviour pattern was completely in keeping with the other British overseas banks registered and definitely headquartered in the UK. He, however, is very clear in noting its place of residence. As indicated in note 7 above, we defined 'foreign' to include colonies. Reinhard Liehr and Mariano E. Torres Bautista, Chapter 9 herein, seek to justify the inclusion of Canadian-registered companies in Mexico as a special type of British free-standing company. Their argument is that these were, in reality, British companies. I have strong doubts, but their chapter addresses the same problem of economic activity within an empire and wherein lies the 'headquarters'.
41. This is true at least in the cases of cotton textiles and diamond mines. See the section on 'Elaboration' for more on this matter.

42. Natalia Gurushina, Chapter 6 herein, on Russia; the US generalizations are based on my own research on foreign investments in the USA. (In the USA domestic registration was not required, but for tax, liability, and other reasons it was often the procedure of choice.)
43. Peter Hertner, Chapter 5 herein.
44. There could be a British head office *without* British registration. There needs to be studies of how frequently this was the case of new firms set up to do business abroad. My research indicates that, at least in the period before 1914, this was not the norm. A firm might have a London representative, or a London office that pursued specified functions (related, for example, to finance, purchasing, and staffing), but that did not provide overall administrative direction. For some of my earlier thoughts on the firm established abroad, with no UK registration, that attracted both British capital and management, see my 'European and North American Multinationals', 16–18. Clearly, this matter has to be addressed. Thus, Rory Miller, going through *Stock Exchange Yearbooks* for the 1890s, found British-owned Chilean-registered railway companies with twice-yearly shareholders' meetings in Liverpool, obviously dominated by Liverpool merchants (Miller to Wilkins, 10 Mar. 1995). Geoffrey Jones also warns about the problems of 'registration' (Jones to Wilkins, 15 Dec. 1995). Later in this chapter I elaborate on some of the problems. By the early twentieth century, the British Inland Revenue Department had separated out three groups of 'identifiable income from abroad'. The first group consisted of portfolio investments (as we would define the term today). The second group included the profits of British companies operating abroad. The third group involved British firms doing business mainly at home but also overseas. The second category—those of businesses typically registered in the UK—appears to coincide quite closely (albeit not exactly) with our free-standing companies; on the other hand, Worswick and Tipping, in dealing with British companies (with British headquarters) operating abroad, identified a number that were 'non-corporate' (presumably without British registration under British joint-stock company laws): G. Cassel *et al.*, *Foreign Investments* (Chicago, 1928), 126, 140–1, and G. D. N. Worswick and D. G. Tipping, *Profits in the British Economy 1909–1938* (Oxford, 1967), 86, 93, 116, 118. I am indebted to T. A. B. Corley for directing me to this last reference.
45. Some early commentators, who had not read the literature on multinational enterprise, failed to comprehend the basic distinction. I can only refer them to the authors cited in notes 10, 12, 13, and 14 above, and particularly to the Wells and Markusen formulations as given in the text of the present chapter. Some chapters in the present volume contrast the free-standing company and the multinational enterprise; I believe the more appropriate contrast is between the free-standing company and the *classic* or traditionally conceived multinational enterprise. As I earlier wrote, 'I view them [free-standing companies] as a type of MNE' (Wilkins, 'Defining a Firm', 86).
46. Some family and individual investments, however, fit very well into the traditional multinational-enterprise category. Thus, the early international activities of the Coats family firm, J. & P. Coats (before it was incorporated), conform nicely with the model of the classic multinational enterprise. Likewise, the international business of Lipton and Beecham (see T. A. B. Corley, 'Britain's Overseas Investments in 1914 Revisited', *Business History*, 36 (Jan. 1994), 73–4) fit, in my mind, easily into what to me was the familiar 'American' model. On this matter, I totally agree with Corley. I would also put the trading companies that were *not* registered in Britain yet had managing partners there in the category of the classic multinational enterprise. On the other hand, as noted,

Group 2 of the British Inland Revenue Department categories (see note 44 above) contains income from operations abroad not linked with free-standing companies. See Worswick and Tipping, *Profits*, 88.

47. Gurushina, Chapter 6, Miller, Chapter 8, and Jones, Chapter 13 herein, for example. Gurushina's chapter differentiates between the functions of 'core' and intermediary free-standing companies. Miller and Jones show other different types of free-standing companies.
48. Multinational enterprises are typically a group of separate corporations commonly managed. We drop the corporate veils as we discuss the nature of the 'enterprise'.
49. S. D. Chapman, *Merchant Enterprise in Britain* (Cambridge, 1992).
50. See my 'Defining a Firm', for some of the fundamental issues. Alfred Chandler has recently written, 'As a historian who has spent a career in examining the operations and practices of business firms, I have not given much thought to precise definitions of the firm. I have had little trouble locating information on literally hundreds of individual enterprises' ('Organizational Capabilities and the Economic History of the Industrial Enterprise', *Journal of Economic Perspectives*, 6 (Summer 1992), 79–100, esp. 79). While I generally agree with Chandler, I do think there are often problems in defining the multinational firm (and firms within firms). Yet, at the same time, I do believe that the business history of enterprises often resolves these problems. Chandler never puzzled, for example, at the time Du Pont had major interests in General Motors, whether he was talking about one firm or two. The data seemed to resolve the issue. Interesting insights on these questions come from R. H. Coase, 'The Nature of the Firm', *Economica*, NS 4 (Nov. 1937), 387–9; Penrose, *The Theory of the Growth of the Firm*; and G. B. Richardson, 'The Organisation of Industry', *Economic Journal*, 82 (Sept. 1972), 883–96.
51 See their chapters herein.
52. Jones, Chapter 13 herein. See also Mark Casson, Chapter 3 herein, who agrees with Jones.
53. Chapman, Chapter 7 herein. Chapman sees truly free-standing companies as ones floated in London, but *not* associated with the agency houses. These—at least the ones with operations in India—were, he believes, 'on the margins of the system'.
54. R. G. Greenhill, 'Investment Group, Free-Standing Company or Multinational? Brazilian Warrant, 1909–1952', *Business History*, 37 (Jan. 1995), 86–111.
55. M. Casson, *The Organization of International Business* (Aldershot, 1995); see also Casson, Chapter 3, and Hennart, Chapter 2 herein. See Wilkins, 'Defining a Firm', 90, on 'firms within firms'.
56. See also Hennart, Chapter 2 herein, for his views on this. Chapman—in his discussion—sees no importance in the place of registration for the companies within the group, aside from commenting on the expense of setting up companies in the UK. In the introduction to the 1995 3rd edn. of her *The Theory of the Growth of the Firm*, p. xviii, Edith Penrose discussed the metamorphosis of the firm in the 1980s and 1990s in terms of core firms and networks. She felt that the firm as she had described it in her earlier work has in recent years become less coherent. Yet, as one studies the growth of certain groupings of overseas businesses in the late nineteenth and early twentieth centuries, one sees the same kind of rough edges in the conception of the firm. Later in this chapter, I mention the 'free-standing' companies in the USA in which Balfour, Williamson & Co. played a pivotal role. The loose cluster—with minority interest but attention to management—was a clear form of doing business.

Unlike Chapman, I do see a difference between those companies registered and not registered in Britain.

57. Neither the service provider nor the free-standing firm is the centre. The service firms assist other unrelated companies, as the need arises.
58. For more on the matter of ownership and control, nationality aside, see Casson, Chapter 3 herein, and my 'Defining a Firm'.
59. Miller, Chapter 8, and Hennart, Chapter 2 herein. To complicate matters, Aramayo was apparently *resident* in Paris.
60. Gurushina, Chapter 6 herein.
61. J.-F. Hennart, 'International Financial Capital Transfers: A Transaction Cost Framework', *Business History*, 36 (Jan. 1994), 51–70, and Hennart, Chapter 2 herein. The 'entrepreneurial activity' in these cases was Bolivian and Russian.
62. Rory Miller reports that by 1913 the Chilean Electric Tramway & Light Co. Ltd., London, was German owned. The Lagunitos Oil Co. Ltd., London, in business in Peru, was by 1913 American, owned by a group associated with Herbert Hoover. Miller, Chapter 8 herein; William J. Hausman and John L. Neufeld, Chapter 14 herein; and Wilkins, *The Emergence of Multinational Enterprise*, 185. Germans and Frenchmen used British companies as instrumentalities for South African investments (Wilkins, 'The Impact of Multinational Corporations').
63. Wilkins, *The Emergence of Multinational Enterprise*, 42–4.
64. See above. Rory Miller asks: can a free-standing company have a *shared* home? On the west coast of South America, Aporama Goldfields Co. and Corocoro United Copper Mines (both registered in London) had considerable French interests on their boards. Presumably, French businessmen could visit London 'to look after their interests'. Would this count as a 'shared' home? (Miller to Wilkins, 14 Oct. 1996). Is a 'shared' home tantamount to shared ownership and control?
65. The US Department of Commerce faced this problem in its studies of foreign direct investment in the USA. Its solution was to label the first foreign parent the foreign direct investor, and then to go beyond that and ask further questions on the UBO—ultimate beneficial owner.
66. A business could be registered abroad and owned and controlled from Britain (see note 44 above for more details). When one consults business archives, usually it is possible to determine 'headquarters' and the allocation of responsibilities within the firm. While British registration is far from a perfect proxy for 'a headquarters', when it was absent—as indicated—often the British 'headquarters functions' were hard to maintain.
67. A splendid introduction to the complexities of ownership and control can be seen in D. K. Fieldhouse, *Merchant Capital and Decolonization: The United Africa Company 1929–1987* (Oxford, 1994). Fieldhouse's book is on the United Africa Company (UAC), a subsidiary of the multinational enterprise Unilever. UAC was itself a multinational, within the larger Unilever. It was fully owned, yet potentially but only partially administratively controlled by Unilever. It was a separate administrative entity within the large multinational, Unilever. UAC in turn had a range of affiliates that it administered with different degrees of decentralization. Caves (*Multinational Enterprise*, 1) calls what constitutes control a 'judgmental issue'.
68. Corley, 'Britain's Overseas Investments in 1914 Revisited', 74. This is not the view Corley takes in the chapter included in this volume.
69. In my studies of the history of traditional multinational enterprises, I have found many instances where parent companies did not exercise strong control over subsidiaries. Amount of control unquestionably varies by company,

function, time, and many other variables. Within single multinationals, it was not strange to find subsidiaries that had autonomy for years. The contemporary literature on multinationals is filled with survey articles whose authors asked subsidiary managers, 'how much autonomy do you have?' On control by free-standing companies, see Wilkins, *The History of Foreign Investment*, 306.

70. Casson, Chapter 3 herein.
71. Corley, Chapter 4 herein.
72. Gurushina, Chapter 6 herein, is wonderful on this. See also Liehr and Torres Bautista, Chapter 9 herein, on the sequence of companies that began with United Mexican Mining Co. Ltd. My own research has found similar sequences of free-standing companies.
73. Wilkins, 'The Free-Standing Company', 264; also 279, wherein I state that the lean governance structure 'at origin' was responsible for many failures of free-standing companies.
74. Jones, Chapter 13 herein, for example, sees the British overseas banks as continuing through time as free-standing. They were, we all agree, set up as free-standing firms, yet they developed a lean but entirely adequate home office and abroad an extensive professional management. Chandler, in *The Visible Hand* and in his *Scale and Scope: The Dynamics of Industrial Capitalism* (Cambridge, Mass., 1990), considers the evolution of overall administration and the relationship between a central staff office and corporate administration. His insights are helpful in this regard.
75. Chapman, Chapter 7 herein; see also R. T. Stillson, 'The Financing of Malayan Rubber, 1905–1923', *Economic History Review*, 2nd ser., 24 (1971), 589–98. And we are back to the fourth definitional problem on what constitutes a firm.
76. Perhaps, as Miller and Jones, Chapters 8 and 13 herein, suggest, we need different typologies in dealing with free-standing firms as they evolve through time.
77. Both Corley, Chapter 4, and Miller, Chapter 8—exempting mining companies—see a higher survival rate than I do; I do not think we should exempt mining companies. The US evidence seems clear on a very high mortality rate; other evidence I have seen seems to confirm this. I am, however, convinced by all the authors in this volume that it is very important to pay much more attention to what happened to companies through time; see the section of the present chapter on 'Elaboration'.
78. Schmitz, 'Patterns', 11.
79. Many investments trusts (more the English than the Scottish ones) made domestic investments in free-standing companies, which, in turn, made the overseas investments. If an investment trust made an investment in American railroad securities, for example, usually that investment could be made in the UK and did not involve any activity by the investor in the USA. Some investment trusts invested in dollar securities within the USA and to do this they usually used an agent—banker or broker—and did not have an office, a direct investment, in the USA. See Wilkins, *The History of Foreign Investment*. See also R. Kindersley, 'British Foreign Investments in 1929', *Economic Journal*, 41 (Sept. 1931), 371, repr. in Wilkins (ed.), *British Overseas Investments*; Kindersley wrote on the problems of 'double counting' of British overseas investments, which was true before 1914 as well as later.
80. See, for example, Wilkins, *The Emergence of Multinational Enterprise*, and M. Wilkins, 'Japanese Multinationals in the United States: Continuity and Change, 1879–1990', *Business History Review*, 64 (Winter 1990), 585–629. My view of trading (and shipping) companies is consistent with that adopted by the British Inland Revenue Department, which classified such companies in Group 3

rather than Group 2. See note 44 above for the groups and Worswick and Tipping, *Profits*, 86, for the classifications.

81. Once again it is to be noted that there is an absence of full synchronization between what I call 'free-standing companies' and the overseas companies discussed by Paish, Simon, Davis, and most recently Schmitz. All the companies discussed by them were not necessarily free-standing ones by my definition. Also, I become increasingly wary of lists. The more one goes beneath the surface, the more apparent it becomes that especially over time seemingly 'free-standing companies' may often be anything but.
82. M. Casson, 'Institutional Diversity in Overseas Enterprise: Explaining the Free Standing Company', *Business History*, 36 (Oct. 1994), 96.
83. Paish's figures—14 Feb. 1914 (in Wilkins (ed.), *British Overseas Investments*)—and Corley, 'Britain's Overseas Investments in 1914 Revisited', 80, which uses them, deal with transactions rather than numbers of companies; they do indicate important British involvements in overseas tramways, telephones, and telegraph. Miller, Chapter 8 herein, notes heavy British concentration in railroads in the host countries that he considers. Schmitz's work provides paid-in capital by 1913 ('Patterns', 12); these are the figures that are used by others for 'accumulated stock'; they do not indicate sizeable Scottish stakes in this sector. Worswick and Tipping (*Profits*, 146), contains data showing the relative importance of 'railroads and transport' in the late nineteenth century. See also Table 1.3. There needs to be more research on the use of the free-standing company form in railroads.
84. Casson, 'Institutional Diversity', 96; Corley, Chapter 4 herein, also makes this point.
85. Hennart, Chapter 2 herein.
86. See Hennart, Chapter 2, Hertner, Chapter 5, Gurushina, Chapter 6, Miller, Chapter 8, and Liehr and Torres Bautista, Chapter 9 herein. It has often been noted that mining projects were speculative ones, which perhaps is another way of saying high-risk ones. The quotation in the text is from Michie, *The City*, 63. For a splendid article on the role of the City in mining projects, see C. E. Harvey and J. Press, 'The City and International Mining, 1870–1914', *Business History*, 32 (July 1990), 98–119.
87. It could be argued that Ford Motor Co.'s 'advantage' was that it had an assured market for the rubber produced. But the experienced merchant firms that were associated with the free-standing companies in the rubber business had a comparable advantage in commodity markets. Moreover, the rubber-plantation companies that were set up and managed by agency houses might not be considered free-standing at all. It should be noted that Ford was very unsuccessful in its efforts to grow rubber. Wilkins and Hill, *American Business Abroad*, ch. 8.
88. G. Jones, *British Multinational Banking*.
89. I did make this point in Wilkins, 'The Free-Standing Company', 277. For some companies that started in industries (oil, for example) where new technologies were essential, the firm found it needed to have within its own organization the asset-specific talents—that is, the companies developed managerial structures and hired their own engineers.
90. Most of the typical 'American-model' multinationals sold trademarked products. On this, see M. Wilkins, 'The Neglected Intangible Asset: The Influence of the Trade Mark on the Rise of the Modern Corporation', *Business History*, 34 (Jan. 1992), 66–95. There were some free-standing companies, which had branded goods. Pillsbury-Washburn Flour Mills Co., Ltd. in the USA in the late nineteenth century was a British-owned free-standing company, floated in

London in 1889 (Wilkins, *The History of Foreign Investment*, 320–2). Also, some of the breweries abroad that were owned by free-standing companies had beers with trade names. But read Wilkins, *The History of Foreign Investment*, on the baneful experience of Pillsbury when it was a British free-standing company.

91. Wilkins, 'Efficiency and Management', 982.
92. I emphasized this in Wilkins, 'The Free-Standing Company'.
93. From A. H. Amsden and T. Hikino, 'Borrowing Technology or Innovating', in Thomson (ed.), *Learning and Technological Change*, 256.
94. Miller, Chapter 8 herein. See also W. Hunt, *Heirs of Great Adventure: The History of Balfour, Williamson and Company Limited* (2 vols.; London, 1951, 1960).
95. Based on the research I did for Wilkins, 'The Impact of Multinational Corporations'.
96. See Jones, Chapter 13 herein, and his *British Multinational Banking*. Dunning and Morgan, *An Economic Study*, 156 (these comments are for a later period but are applicable for earlier times). The quotation is from E. Green, 'Export Bankers: The Migration of British Bank Personnel to the Pacific Region, 1850–1914', in O. Checkland, S. Nishimura, and N. Tamaki (eds.), *Pacific Banking 1859–1959* (London, 1994), 82. Green looked at personnel records of British domestic banks and showed that the latter were recruiting grounds for the overseas banks.
97. Within parts of the Empire, there were special issues on British registration that did not prevail elsewhere. Otherwise, it seems remarkable how few differences there were between Empire and non-Empire stakes.
98. Chapman, *Merchant Enterprise*.
99. G. Jones, *British Multinational Banking*.
100. Chapman, Chapter 7 herein.
101. This was true only *vis-à-vis* the *identical clusters*. Thus, Otis Steel (a British free-standing company in the USA) was far smaller than US Steel. The British free-standing breweries in the USA did not consistently have larger capitalization than the US-owned ones.
102. Chapman, Chapter 7 herein, and Wilkins, *The History of Foreign Investment*, 493–4. Worswick and Tipping, *Profits*, 88: the context of this comment lay in comparing the 'supposed' capitalization of the average overseas company with the average British domestic one.
103. Hennart, Chapter 2 herein.
104. Hennart's suggestion that sizeable exports from the host country made British registration more appropriate than local registration might apply to mines and plantations (and jute factories), but it did not apply to American cattle companies or American mortgage companies that were set up as free-standing, or for that matter to British free-standing breweries in the USA, South Africa, and Peru.
105. R. V. Kubicek, *Economic Imperialism in Theory and Practice: The Case of South African Gold Mining Finance 1886–1914* (Durham, NC, 1979), 88.
106. A. R. Hall, *The London Capital Market and Australia 1870–1914* (Canberra, 1963), 97–8.
107. R. P. T. Davenport Hines and G. Jones (eds.), *British Business in Asia since 1860* (Cambridge, 1989), 10. Rory Miller, Chapter 8 herein, suggests that merchant groups used local registration when they did not need the resources of the London stock market and 'for reasons of commercial confidentiality'.
108. L. E. Davis and R. J. Cull, *International Capital Markets and American Economic Growth, 1820–1914* (Cambridge, 1994), 66, 71. When I wrote *The History of*

Foreign Investment, it did not occur to me to compare the American stock issues traded in New York and London. Yet, the matter is extremely germane to the history of free-standing companies. Davis and Cull see the lack of synchronism as based on British capital flows being targeted at 'economic activities that lay outside the scope of the still embryonic American financial market'. See Davis and Cull, *International Capital Markets*, 71. Perhaps there were institutional explanations as well. Americans wanted to trade in dollar issues. Britishers were willing to buy dollar-denominated American railroads and large industrials such as US Steel, but were not prepared to invest in many of the less familiar 'commercial and industrial' firms. Americans were not interested in trading in sterling-denominated companies. The free-standing companies were sterling-denominated.

109. Corley, Chapter 4 herein, puts the banks' head offices in the category of 'maintaining regular correspondence'. See Gurushina, Chapter 6 herein, on the head offices of British free-standing companies in Russia.
110. Hertner, Chapter 5 herein, notes a huge British free-standing bank in Italy—of which he found no further trace: also a typical exit. If a company was replaced by another free-standing one, the first company is considered as an 'exit'. If the company continues on within the host country with no London head office, we can consider this to be the end to a British business abroad, i.e. an exit.
111. There is a problem in defining success: see the section on 'Evaluation'. The research of Reinhard Liehr and Mariano E. Torres Bautista on Mexico (see Chapter 9 herein) confirms the short-lived characteristics of many of these ventures.
112. The point is made by a number of contributors to this volume.
113. See earlier discussion on the third query under the seventh definitional problem: if a company began as a free-standing one, what characteristics must it maintain to remain in that category?
114. Casson, 'Institutional Diversity', 96, and Chapter 3 herein.
115. Gurushina, Chapter 6 herein.
116. Hennart, Chapter 2 herein. Many of these may well have been only nominally free-standing. See Jones, Chapter 13 herein, for an indication that in the 1930s at least some of these may have become part of the London Tin Corporation group. The London Tin Corporation appears to have been a multinational enterprise, with interests in Malaya, Nigeria, Thailand, and Burma (J.-J. van Helten and G. Jones, 'British Business in Malaysia and Singapore since the 1870s', in R. P. T. Davenport-Hines and G. Jones, *British Business in Asia since 1860* (Cambridge, 1989), 168–70, 184–5.
117. Miller, Chapter 8 herein.
118. Miller, Chapter 8 herein, thinks it legitimate to call these ongoing, continuing free-standing companies. He argues that they did not become classic multinationals (at least by conventional definitions), and, if they did not remain free-standing companies, we need another category of foreign direct investments (Miller to Wilkins, 14 Oct. 1996).
119. G. Jones, *British Multinational Banking*, and Jones, Chapter 13 herein.
120. Miller, Chapter 8 herein, accepts my view and does not include, for example, the Anglo-South American Bank (ASAB) as a free-standing company. By 1913 Miller notes that the ASAB operated (or at least had offices) in several countries in Latin America, in the USA, and in Europe. Miller sees the geographical expansion (along with the internalization of management) as creating 'a more or less' classic multinational in the financial service sector. Like other British overseas banks, it had, however, he agrees, started as a free-standing company

(the Bank of Tarapacá & London in 1888) and—in Miller's view—remained free-standing until 1900, when it expanded into business in Argentina (Miller to Wilkins, 14 Oct. 1996).

121. I do not think that the failure to survive in the USA was based on regulatory restrictions, which did exist, but instead was based on the absence of a need for overseas banks (US banks could suffice). On Anglo-Austrian's two incarnations as a British bank, see G. Jones, *British Multinational Banking*, 228–9. On the exit of a British overseas bank from Italy, see Hertner, Chapter 5 herein. In Canada, the longest lasting British overseas bank was the Bank of British North America, founded in London in 1836; it had first-mover advantages and had a long history. In 1918, however, its assets were taken over by the Bank of Montreal. There was by that time no need for an overseas bank in Canada. When R. Cameron and V. I. Bovykin were planning their edited volume *International Banking 1870–1914* (New York, 1991), I tried to push contributor Ian Drummond to deal with overseas banking in Canada; he argued that locally incorporated banks did the largest share of the business, and that portion increased in the period under study (p. 192). By 1913 the Bank of British North America had a mere 3.9% of the commercial banking assets in Canada (ibid.). In Australia, it is true that the British role lasted longer and was more important. Yet, Australia was far less developed than the USA or Canada. On the role of British banks in Australia, see G. Jones, *British Multinational Banking*, 57, 98. By contrast, in some less developed countries, these banks were truly important. By one estimate, in 1914, British overseas banks controlled a third of the deposits in the Brazilian banking system and over a quarter of those in Argentina and Chile (G. Jones, *British Multinational Banking*, 56). The role of the Imperial Bank of Persia was even more substantial, although comparisons should be made with great care, since there existed an active pre-modern banking business—in bazaars (see G. Jones, *Banking and Empire in Iran*, i. *The History of the British Bank of the Middle East* (Cambridge, 1986), 205, 235). Yet, after 1929, in Iran the domestic Bank Melli increasingly took market share from its foreign competitors (ibid. 236).
122. This firm became RTZ-CRA at the end of 1995 and then readopted the name Rio Tinto in 1997 (*Financial Times*, 21 Dec. 1995 and 28 Feb. 1997). On its earlier history, see C. E. Harvey, *The Rio Tinto Company: An Economic History of a Leading International Mining Concern, 1873–1954* (Penzance, Cornwall, 1981); J. M. Stopford, *Directory of Multinationals* (1992), 1168–70; and *Financial Times*, 11 Aug. 1993.
123. J. H. Bamberg, *The History of the British Petroleum Company*, ii (Cambridge, 1994), 268. On its early history, see R. W. Ferrier, *The History of the British Petroleum Company*, i. *1901–1932* (Cambridge, 1982), and T. A. B. Corley, *A History of the Burmah Oil Company 1886–1924* (London, 1983).
124. Stopford, *Directory*, 220.
125. See Corley, *A History*, and an earlier draft of his chapter published herein.
126. Ferrier, *The History*, 53.
127. Ibid. 70.
128. See Wilkins, 'Defining a Firm', 90, where I puzzled over this same case. My rendition now is slightly different from that one.
129. Corley is an expert on Burmah Oil and I have to agree with his analysis here.
130. In this regard, we could spend time tracing it from its origins and show how different its experiences were from say Standard Oil of New Jersey (now EXXON) or Shell. What the free-standing-company concept does is push us to look closer at the course of the business history of particular enterprises. It provides an analytic frame of reference.

131. The phrase is borrowed from the title of Gregory Marchildon, Chapter 15 herein.
132. Data from Geoffrey Jones and Stanley Chapman on the managing agency groups. We need more business histories. Burmah Oil, for example, was no longer free-standing; it is doubtful that Tharsis would so qualify. Survivors and paid-up capital data from Christopher Schmitz, 28 Feb. 1994.
133. Hennart, Chapter 2 herein. Hennart also points out that some existing free-standing companies survived after their *raison d'être* had disappeared.
134. The suggestion was made in discussions in Milan, in October 1994. He made this suggestion as a way of considering the differing paths of surviving companies. He did not make it in the same context as Casson, who refutes those who argue that the 'free-standing company may be just a transitory phenomenon . . . called into being by speculative bubbles on the stock exchange . . .' (Casson, Chapter 3 herein).
135. Kindersley, 'British Foreign Investments in 1929', 376, repr. in Wilkins (ed.), *British Overseas Investments.* (Kindersley was arguing that part of the capital of these companies was employed at home and should not be included as a capital export.) For more details on expenses of home offices, see Kindersley, 'British Overseas Investments, 1938', *Economic Journal* 49 (Dec. 1939), 687–8.
136. Hennart, Chapter 2 herein.
137. Worswick and Tipping, *Profits*, 137. The percentage of total number of assessments was less than 1%, dropping from 0.76% in 1909 to 0.33% in 1927. Worswick and Tipping believed the increase in foreign assessment numbers 1909–27 was 'barely significant' (p. 88).
138. Miller, Chapter 8 herein, and G. Jones, *British Multinational Banking*, 403–13. The Anglo-Austrian Bank (in its second reconstruction) was a post-First World War creation, as was its successor the Anglo-International Bank (1926) (Jones, *British Multinational Banking*, 228–31). There were others post-1914, but they were few and far between.
139. This research is as yet unpublished.
140. Miller, Chapter 8 herein.
141. Kindersley, 'British Foreign Investments in 1929', 378. Kindersley pointed out that most of the British-registered companies still operating abroad had been set up in an earlier era. Michie (*The City*, 131) has a fine summary of the role of the City in overseas investment 1913–79, which provides a good context for the decline in the use of the British free-standing company.
142. On British decline, see W. P. Kennedy, *Industrial Structure, Capital Markets and the Origins of British Economic Decline* (Cambridge, 1987); Kennedy believed overseas investment substituted for domestic investment. This was *not* a new idea but was now given new currency. In 'The Growth of the Transnational Industrial Firm in the United States and the United Kingdom: A Comparative Analysis', *Economic History Review*, 2nd ser., 33 (1980), 410, Chandler wrote: 'The British failure to participate fully in the growth of the new industries and to meet competition from the United States and the continent has often been explained as entrepreneurial failure. A better term may be managerial failure: that is the continuing existence of the family firm helped to deprive Britain of a class of trained managers and sets of technological and managerial skills that became increasingly essential, not only to technically advanced industries but also to the operation of modern urban, industrial economies.' In *Scale and Scope*, 235–7, Chandler wrote of the inadequacies of British 'personal management' and the absence of managerial hierarchies in modern industries. For criticisms, see, for example, L. Hannah, 'Delusions of Durable Dominance OR The Invisible Hand Strikes Back: A Critique of the New Orthodoxy in

Internationally Comparative Business History 1980s', manuscript (1994); see also G. Jones, 'Big Business, Management and Competitiveness in Twentieth Century Britain', in A. D. Chandler, Jr., F. Amatori, and T. Hikino (eds.), *Big Business and the Wealth of Nations* (Cambridge, 1997).

143. G. Jones (ed.), *British Multinationals.*
144. In the initial draft of C. Jones, 'Institutional Forms of British Foreign Direct Investment in South America', *Business History*, 39 (1997), 21–41; Corley, Chapter 4, and Casson, Chapter 3 herein. Ben P. A. Gales and Keetie E. Sluyterman, Chapter 11 herein, also interpreted my rendition as describing a form 'inferior' to the US multinational enterprise.
145. Chapters of Corley, Casson, Jones, and Chapman herein. The experienced mercantile firms in India, in particular, provided on-the-spot management for both sterling and rupee companies. These wider enterprise groups within India had under their jurisdiction many companies and vast numbers of employees (in 1913 Andrew Yule & Co. provided managerial services to some sixty companies with 200,000 employees, while in 1939 James Finlay & Co. had under its supervision 139,260 employees). See Chapman, *Merchant Enterprise*, 125, and C. Jones, *International Business in the Nineteenth Century* (Brighton, 1987), 195.
146. I have discussed, albeit briefly, free-standing companies from other nations in a number of places, including my *The History of Foreign Investment.*
147. On non-British free-standing companies, see Chapters 2, 3, 4, 5, 10, 11, 12, 14, and 15 herein, but especially Gales and Sluyterman, Chapter 11, and Harm Schröter, Chapter 12 herein, which are the first attempts to treat systematically Continental European free-standing companies. Tamás Szmrecsányi, Chapter 10 herein, considers the history of a French free-standing company. In addition, see B. P. A. Gales and K. E. Sluyterman, 'Outward Bound: The Rise of Dutch Multinationals', in G. Jones and H. G. Schröter (eds.), *The Rise of Multinationals in Continental Europe* (Aldershot, 1993); and H. G. Schröter, *Aufstieg der Kleinen: Multinationale Unternehmen aus fünf kleinen Staaten vor 1914* (Berlin, 1993).
148. Chapter 12 herein; see also Hertner, Chapter 8 herein.
149. Gregory P. Marchildon, Chapter 15 herein.
150. Miller, Chapter 8 herein.
151. Corley, Chapter 4 herein, using Cleona Lewis's data, wants to push the US free-standing company share of total US outward foreign direct investment to some 18% in 1914.
152. Hennart, Chapter 2, Schröter, Chapter 12, Szmrecsányi, Chapter 10, and Marchildon, Chapter 15 herein—for such suggestions.
153. Gales and Sluyterman, Chapter 11, Schröter, Chapter 12, Hertner, Chapter 5, Corley, Chapter 4, and Hennart, Chapter 2 herein.
154. Szmrecsányi, Chapter 10, and Hertner, Chapter 5 herein. Corley, Chapter 4 herein, gives an estimate of free-standing companies as 10% all French foreign direct investment. I think that has to be low. Years ago, R. Cameron (in *France and the Economic Development of Europe 1800–1914* (Princeton, 1961)), insisted that French investment abroad was far from passive; recent research confirms this. I have found that there were not only many French multinational enterprises of the classic model sort, but numerous French free-standing companies with direct investments abroad.
155. At least that is the way I interpret the data. This does not exactly correspond with Corley's conclusions, Chapter 4 herein.
156. Marchildon, Chapter 15 herein.
157. Germany did, however, have colonies before the First World War.

158. But see the striking conclusions of Gales and Sluyterman, Chapter 11 herein, on the relative importance of the Dutch East Indies, and Schröter, Chapter 12 herein, on the special role of the Belgian Congo in Belgium's investments abroad.
159. There were sizeable German immigrant and expatriate communities in many parts of the world. These were often linked with German multinational enterprise, providing employees, markets, and information. See, for example, Wilkins, *The History of Foreign Investment*, for Germans in the USA.
160. Schröter, Chapter 12, and Gales and Sluyterman, Chapter 11 herein, deal with some of the special problems of including colonies as 'foreign'. On the Suez Canal Co. (which I would call a free-standing company), see E. H. Tuma, 'Suez Canal: Another Dimension in the European Network', *Journal of European Economic History*, 24 (Winter 1995), 626.
161. See, for example, L. G. Franko, *The European Multinationals* (Stamford, Conn., 1976), and Jones and Schröter (eds.), *The Rise of Multinationals in Continental Europe*.
162. Hennart, Chapter 2 herein. On Belgian banks and free-standing companies, see also Herman Van der Wee and M. Goosens, 'Belgium', in Cameron and Bovykin (eds.), *International Banking*, 122–7.
163. Hennart, Chapter 2, and Gales and Sluyterman, Chapter 11 herein.
164. Szmrecsányi, Chapter 10 herein.
165. Marchildon, Chapter 15 herein.
166. Schröter, Chapter 12 herein.
167. My solution to reflect realities would be to call the contiguous Austro-Hungarian Empire the political unit and business outside it would be 'foreign'. After the break-up, the new nations are the political entities and some business that was once domestic becomes, by definition, 'foreign'.
168. Gales and Sluyterman, Chapter 11 herein.
169. B. Gales, 'In Foreign Parts: Free-Standing Companies in the Netherlands around the First World War', unpublished paper prepared for the Milan Conference (1994). Just as American multinationals used British intermediaries to do business in certain parts of the world, so too they used Dutch intermediaries to do business in the Netherlands East Indies—in Gales's term, transfer investments. Thus, Standard Oil Company (New Jersey) in 1912 formed N. V. Nederlandsche Koloniale Petroleum Maatschappij (NKPM) to operate its new concession in the East Indies (I. H. Anderson, Jr., *The Standard-Vacuum Oil Company and United States East Asian Policy 1933–1941* (Princeton, 1975), 205).
170. When the British Lever Brothers wanted to do business in the Belgian Congo, in 1911 it set up La Société Anonyme des Huileries du Congo Belge. In French West Africa, Lever Brothers bought what appears to have been a typical French free-standing company, Compagnie Propriétaire du Kouilou Niari (and, like many free-standing companies, it turned out not to live up to expectations) (C. Wilson, *The History of Unilever* (3 vols.; New York, 1968), i. 168, 179).
171. Marchildon, Chapter 15 herein, treats these companies as Canadian free-standing ones, while Liehr and Torres Bautista, Chapter 9 herein, consider them as 'British'.
172. None of this had anything to do with free-standing-company activities (Wilkins and Hill, *American Business Abroad*). Ford's Canadian affiliate in its early decades had an immense degree of managerial 'autonomy'. This was a case of a multinational enterprise, where administrative 'control' from headquarters was minimal, albeit the Canadian company gained from being part of a

multinational enterprise in what was transferred from the parent *vis-à-vis* product and production knowledge.

173. Gales and Sluyterman, Chapter 11 herein.
174. At least this is the tentative conclusion from the present state of research. The British had many free-standing companies in agriculture (but not the *share* that the Dutch had); none the less, the new data in Table 1.3 on Britain does show the importance of plantation companies in the inter-war period. Interestingly, although the Germans had few free-standing companies, in terms of numbers Schröter found those in agriculture were pre-eminent (Chapter 12 herein). We do not have any industry distribution figures on French-headquartered free-standing companies. Our one case study of a French business abroad is in sugar (milling and plantations) (Szmrecsányi, Chapter 10 herein).
175. Cameron and Bovykin (eds.), *International Banking*, contains numerous useful insights in this regard. In some cases banks were clearly central to the clusters surrounding free-standing companies. See, for example, J. Thobie, 'European Banks in the Middle East', in ibid.
176. Hausman and Neufeld, Chapter 14 herein.
177. See T. Abo, 'ITT's International Business Activities, 1920–1940', *Annals of the Institute of Social Science*, 24 (1982–83), 104–28.
178. Marchildon, Chapter 15 herein.
179. This new research set me thinking about multinational enterprise and the establishment of infrastructure within the world economy (Wilkins, 'Multinational Corporations').
180. Interestingly it was a Dutch multinational, the Royal Dutch Shell group, that made the largest pre-war investment in Curaçao (in the Dutch West Indies), in a refinery there, designed to process crude oil from its new Venezuelan oil properties. Royal Dutch Shell, of course, had large investments in the Dutch East Indies as well.
181. Gales and Sluyterman, Chapter 11 herein.
182. Wilkins, 'European and North American Multinationals', for differences in direction.
183. Our evidence here is weak.
184. Gales and Sluyterman, Chapter 11 herein.
185. See also Marchildon, Chapter 15 herein, where, in the case of the Canadian free-standing public utilities abroad, some (but not all) of the initiative came from Canada. F. S. Pearson—an American entrepreneur—was important in many of the Latin American investments. I found a number of third-country entrepreneurs would participate in British free-standing companies. That, however, fits the notion of Gales and Sluyterman that the initiative came from abroad.
186. Szmrecsányi, Chapter 10, discusses a French company in Brazil, a less developed country where the arrangement was entirely viable.
187. I cannot overemphasize this when dealing with the history of the classic multinational enterprise. One can look at multinational enterprises and draw charts; depending on the structure that one is trying to document, the charts look entirely different. The research on free-standing companies brings forth comparable conclusions.
188. Corley, Chapter 4 herein, suggests that they represented 80% of British outward compared with roughly 20% of US outward foreign direct investment at the eve of the First World War.
189. Hennart, 'International Financial Capital Transfers', and Hennart, Chapter 2 herein.
190. Chandler, *Scale and Scope*, makes this point. The paths to economic

development were different. On US business abroad, see Wilkins, *The Emergence of Multinational Enterprise.*

191. Wilkins, 'European and North American Multinationals'.
192. See Schröter, Chapter 12 herein, for his very useful explanations on why Belgium was particularly attractive as a headquarters locale for free-standing companies. He throws important light on these questions.
193. Michie, *The City*, 106.
194. M. Wilkins, 'Cosmopolitan Finance in the 1920s', in R. Sylla, R. Tilly, and G. Tortella (eds.), *The State, the Financial System, and Economic Modernization* (Cambridge, forthcoming).
195. M. Wilkins, 'The History of Foreign Investment in the United States from 1914', manuscript in process.
196. Szmrecsányi, Chapter 10 herein. I will admit that it did have quite a long life.

2

Transaction-Cost Theory and the Free-Standing Firm

Jean-François Hennart

Since the publication of Mira Wilkins's seminal *Economic History Review* article[1] where she described the free-standing firm as an important type of pre-1914 multinational enterprise, business historians have started to pay serious attention to this phenomenon. There is increasing evidence that this type of investment made up a substantial proportion of British foreign direct investment before 1914 and that there were a significant number of French, Belgian, and Dutch free-standing firms, and some US-based ones as well. While free-standing firms were overshadowed by the more traditional type of multinational enterprises after the First World War, they continued to be formed in both the UK and the USA, and some are still being floated in the 1990s.[2]

Free-standing firms share a number of characteristics. They were domiciled in the dominant equity markets of the time (in London, but also in Brussels, Paris, Boston, etc.) and raised equity there by selling shares directly to the public to finance investments that were located abroad. In their country of registration they had a head office, but no industrial activity, all their actual operations (plants, mines, plantations) being in foreign countries: in the least developed part of Europe (Spain, Italy, Russia), in the regions of recent settlement (Australia, Canada, the USA, Argentina), and in developing countries, both under colonial rule (India, Malaysia, the Dutch East Indies, Africa) and outside it (Russia, Persia, Siam, Latin America). While they were engaged in a wide variety of businesses, from services (hotels, utilities, docks, newspapers, banks) to manufacturing (breweries, jute mills, fish-canning, flour-milling), the majority of free-standing firms were in two sectors, ranches and plantations—natural rubber, tea, sugar cane, cinchona—and mining and petroleum. In Christopher Schmitz's list of companies registered in Edinburgh between 1862 and 1914 to do

I want to thank John McKay, Tom Roehl, Charles Harvey, and Adrian Tschoegl and especially Mira Wilkins, Geoffrey Jones, and Mark Casson for useful discussions and valuable comments on this topic. Dixie Zietlow and Georgine Kryda provided excellent research assistance.

business abroad, nearly half of the companies whose activity is known were in mining, quarrying, and oil, and nearly another quarter was in agriculture and ranching.[3] Forty per cent of the 2,544 British free-standing firms operating outside the USA and Canada listed in a 1916 US Federal Trade Commission report were in mining, and another 28 per cent were in agriculture.[4] Sixty-nine per cent of the Dutch free-standing companies identified by Ben Gales and Keetie Sluyterman as active in 1913 were in tropical agriculture and in mining and petroleum extraction.[5]

Another important aspect of these firms is that they were financed in large part by selling equity directly to the public. This mode of financing is only one among many ways in which foreign projects are financed, as we will see later.

Most free-standing firms were single project firms: they operated a single plantation, a single mine. Yet these seemingly independent free-standing firms were often linked in clusters.[6] A single promoter could spin off a number of firms. For example, the thirty-six separate companies engaged in the exploitation of Chilean nitrates in 1913 can be traced back to five groups of British capitalists.[7] Numerous Malayan rubber and Indian tea estates were promoted by British trading companies, such as Harrisons & Crosfield, and remained partly owned by them. Similarly, one finds a small number of mining engineering firms linked to many of the tin-mining companies in Malaya. For example, the partners in Osborne & Chappel, mining and consulting engineers based in Ipoh, Malaya, had by 1908 stakes in half a dozen Malayan tin-mining companies.[8] Bewick, Moreing & Co. and John Taylor & Sons, two London-based mining consultants, became part owners of a large number of mining free-standing enterprises at the turn of the century.

An explanation of free-standing firms would, therefore, seem to require a simultaneous understanding of two related phenomena: the phenomenon of the free-standing firm proper, a single project firm with no domestic operations, and that of their clustering around a firm that takes minority stakes. Both of these phenomena are hard to explain in terms of the eclectic theory of the multinational enterprise, although, as we will see, they can be explained by a suitable extension of transaction-cost theory.

How does one Explain Free-Standing Firms?

The eclectic theory, one of the best-known theories of the multinational enterprise, posits that multinational enterprises arise when firms have firm-specific advantages (for example, unique technologies), when these advantages can profitably be exploited abroad, and when the most efficient way to exploit these advantages is through foreign direct investment.[9] Free-standing firms do not fit this model very well. Having no operations at home (besides their headquarters) and no cadre of professional domestic managers, it is difficult to see how they could have long-lasting firm-specific advantages to exploit abroad. Indeed, it is this lack of domestic firm-specific advantages, manifested by their lean governance structure, that Mira Wilkins saw as the cause of their allegedly short life and high failure rate.[10]

The minority investments of trading companies and mining consulting engineers that we have described above are also difficult to explain in terms of the eclectic model. That model posits that firms take equity in other firms (internalize) because the exploitation of their firm-specific advantages through arm's length or contractual sale is subject to high market transaction costs. It makes sense then to bypass the market and, instead of selling advantages at arm's-length to a foreign firm, to transfer those advantages to a wholly owned subsidiary, which will then sell to the public products or services that incorporate these advantages. In other words, internalization is efficient because it allows the owner of firm-specific advantages to bypass inefficient markets for these advantages in favour of more perfect markets for final products incorporating these advantages.

In this context, taking partial equity (internalizing through a joint venture) suffers from major defects. Since equity control means getting paid for one's firm-specific advantages not in the form of direct payment for these advantages, but through the sale of the products incorporating these advantages, a firm that exploits these advantages through a partially owned subsidiary must either charge the joint venture for those advantages, or give up part of the profits that result from the transfer gratis of these advantages to the venture. For example, a firm transferring proprietary technology free of charge to its 50 per cent owned joint venture will receive only 50 per cent of the contribution of its knowledge to the venture, with the other partner getting a 50 per cent free ride. Licensing the knowledge to the joint venture is a solution that is by definition less than optimal: if knowledge could be sold at a price acceptable to the innovator, it would have been licensed already. The very fact that the innovator has sought to internalize the transaction suggests that the knowledge is difficult to price. Hence, at least at first blush, the eclectic model does not provide obvious reasons why some firms would ever take small, minority stakes in other firms.

In the following pages I will show that the existence of both free-standing firms and of minority equity links to their sponsors can be explained by extending the eclectic model in three directions. First, we must reconsider the link between internalization and the exploitation of advantages. The crucial point here is that, while equity links between two firms result from the internalization of markets, including markets for advantages, they do not require that one or the other firm possesses any type of advantage. Multinational firms exist to internalize markets, not to internalize advantages.[11] Secondly, the internalization model must be extended to financial capital if one is to make sense of free-standing firms, and, more generally, of the various types of institutions chosen to transfer financial capital across countries.[12] We will argue that free-standing firms are firms that internalize markets for international financial capital and that they will prosper as long as there is a pay-off to internalizing such markets, independently of whether they possess any type of firm-specific advantage or not. Lastly, the existence of minority stakes can be understood in terms of the transaction-cost theory of equity joint ventures.[13] Minority equity stakes are taken when full internalization is not necessary and would substantially increase management costs.

A Theory of Minority Equity Stakes

As a starting point, consider the reasons why firms decide to organize internally (as opposed to through an arm's-length market) the interaction between two stages of production linked by the exchange of inputs. The standard explanation is that the cost of organizing the transaction internally is lower than that of organizing it on markets.[14] Thus firms take equity into other firms when the interaction between these two firms is more efficiently organized through hierarchical than through price coordination.

The reason why interaction can, in some cases, be more efficiently organized within the firm has to do with differences in the incentive systems used in firms and in markets. Consider two firms (firms A and B), one of which generates knowledge while the other could profitably use it. When that knowledge is exchanged through the market (i.e. through licensing), the rewards to the knowledge seller are a function of the price he can charge for the knowledge. If the buyer has difficulty in cheaply assessing its value, the seller will be able to cheat (to sell the knowledge for more than it is worth). Given this expectation, the market may break down.[15]

The internalization solution consists in having the seller and the buyer of knowledge joined within a firm. Why does this improve the efficiency of the transfer? The answer is not that the firm organizes a better 'internal market', but instead that a shift to intra-firm exchange changes the incentives facing the parties to the exchange. The essence of the hierarchical mode of organization that is used in firms is that individuals (employees) are rewarded not for their output, but for obeying managerial directives. Hence the knowledge seller no longer benefits from selling overpriced know-how, but instead is rewarded for facilitating the transfer to the buyer, now another member of the firm. By breaking the link between output and rewards, firms reduce the incentives that employees have to cheat in internal trades. Note, however, that an unintended consequence is that they now have greater latitude to slack in their effort (to shirk), since they are not directly rewarded for their output, but instead for their willingness to follow managerial directives.[16]

The problem with taking partial equity (through a joint venture or a partial acquisition) is that it re-creates the perverse incentives of the market. If the knowledge buyer is now only partly owned by the seller, then the seller still has incentives to overprice the knowledge. If the buyer was 100 per cent owned by the seller, each dollar by which the knowledge transferred to the buyer is overpriced would be offset by a dollar reduction in the profits of the (wholly owned) venture. When the buyer is only partly owned (say 50 per cent), then each dollar extracted through overcharging is only offset by a 50 cents reduction in the profits of the joint venture that accrue to the seller.

Why would firms then ever take less than full equity stakes? Leaving aside the problem of government restrictions on full ownership, one can think of the following reasons:

- first, it may be possible to internalize the interaction between the two firms without owning all of the shares. If ownership of the shares is widely dispersed, control can be obtained with only a minority stake. It may also be possible to avoid fully sharing the profits of the venture with the majority (but dispersed) shareholders.
- second, the activity undertaken may require the combination of two or more inputs, each of them owned by a separate firm, and each subject to high transaction costs.[17]

Consider our previous example of firms *A* and *B*, and assume now that the buyer of knowledge (Firm *B*) possesses another type of know-how (perhaps a knowledge of local conditions) that is necessary to do business but is subject to high market transaction costs, and hence costly to transfer through licensing. Then the efficient solution is for both parties to take equity in the venture: this solution alleviates simultaneously the problem of transferring *B*'s knowledge to *A* and that of transferring *A*'s know-how to *B*.[18]

While the simultaneous failure of the markets for two or more inputs provides a necessary condition for the existence of less than full equity, this condition is not sufficient. An additional condition is that the alternatives of replication or full acquisition must be more expensive than the sharing of existing assets through a joint venture or a partial acquisition. To return to the same example: one additional solution is for *A* to replicate the knowledge held by *B*; another is for *A* and *B* to merge.

One possible reason why a joint venture or a partial acquisition might be preferred to a full acquisition might be government or institutional barriers to acquisitions/mergers. Most countries put restrictions on acquisitions of domestic firms by foreigners in 'strategic' industries.

Another reason why replication and full acquisition may be undesirable arises from shirking, the unavoidable by-product of internalization. To reduce incentives that sellers have to cheat, internalization breaks the connection between price and rewards, but this encourages shirking by employees. When firm *A* buys all the shares of firm *B*, it reduces the incentives that the erstwhile independent owners/top managers of *B* had to perform by reducing the claim that they have on the profit stream for which they are responsible. They are now employees of *A*, and the relationship between their actions and their rewards is likely to be weaker. They will thus have greater incentives to shirk.

One way to control shirking is to monitor the behaviour of employees. This is made more difficult by geographic and cultural distance. When these factors create management problems, one solution is to leave some of the equity in the foreign venture to the existing owners/top managers of *B*. The result is a joint venture or a partial acquisition.

Similarly, replication means creating in-house the capability that is possessed by the potential joint venture partner. This necessarily means increasing the size of the firm, and often the range of activities undertaken, resulting in greater management problems. By contrast, a joint venture or a partial acquisition allows access to the needed inputs without having to manage their production.

To summarize, a firm will take a minority stake in another firm when some interactions between the two firms need to be organized through hierarchy, some of the capabilities of the other firm cannot be obtained in the market in disembodied form, yet a full acquisition of the firm owning these capabilities would unduly increase management costs.

Consider the case of sellers of heavy industrial equipment. They want to generate a stable market for their output. In emerging industries, there may be a significant information asymmetry between them and their potential customers. They typically have a more sanguine view of the prospects for investment in the industry than their customers, but may be unable to communicate it credibly. An equipment manufacturer eager to develop the market for its capital goods may then be forced to integrate into the production of the goods using its equipment because of the failure of local entrepreneurs to enter the industry or to adopt the new technology.[19]

Such downstream integration is not without costs. First, it tends to tie up a considerable amount of capital. Secondly, it increases the size of the equipment seller, and extends the firm into activities with which it may not be familiar. This suggests that an ideal strategy is to foster the creation of new potential customers, but to sell most of the equity of the customer to other firms or to the public, keeping just enough equity to obtain contracts for the original equipment, for maintenance services, spare parts, and the replacement and upgrade of the equipment when the original equipment has worn out. As we will see, this process will result in the creation of free-standing firms if the capital of the customer firm is obtained in a country that is different from the country of operation and through equity directly subscribed by the public.

A good example of this process is the system of *Unternehmergeschäft* used by German manufacturers of heavy electrical equipment. Peter Hertner notes that the large German manufacturers of electrical equipment

> created their own market by founding local and regional electric power, tramway and lighting companies or by taking over and 'electrifying' existing firms in those countries (for example Spain, Italy, Russia, the Latin American states) and for those customers (particularly local and regional public authorities) which suffered from a chronic lack of capital or which were too reluctant to adopt this new technology. The newly-founded or transformed companies were then obliged by statute or by more flexible means to buy all or most of their electromechanical material from their big industrial founders.[20]

The German firms created financial holding companies, which held the shares and bonds of the newly created utility companies and sold them to the public as soon as the companies had yielded profits, keeping only a minority holding. To insure their own liquidity during the construction period, the holding companies floated shares, and, if possible, issued long-term bonds in their own name.[21] Whether this process resulted in free-standing companies or not depends on where the utility companies were domiciled. If they were domiciled in Belgium and sold their shares to the public there, while operating in other countries, then they became Belgian free-standing firms. If the companies were registered locally, they became indigenous companies with minority foreign ownership. In all cases the common link between these companies was the limited control exercised by the German makers of electrotechnical equipment through their financial holding companies.

There are many other examples of this type of investment. Hence the French equipment-maker Schneider took minority stakes in foreign enterprises to secure orders for its French plants.[22] The Belgian Empain group followed a similar strategy to sell its equipment to foreign electric tramway companies, thus creating a large number of Belgian free-standing firms.[23]

The investments of mining finance houses follow a similar pattern. Mining finance houses emerged in the 1890s in South Africa. They were created by diamond merchants who raised money in their own name in Europe to finance the development of deep-level gold mines. When the development of these mines was advanced enough to interest the investing public, their shares were sold to the public in European stock markets. The mining finance houses kept a controlling minority interest which allowed them to keep selling managerial, secretarial, technical, and administrative services to the members of the group.[24] The result was the system of 'Group Administration' which was eventually adopted throughout the South African mining industry, consisting of a large number of European-based free-standing mining firms grouped in clusters around mining finance houses.

The behaviour of trading companies is very similar to that of equipment sellers and of mining finance houses. Trading companies make money through commissions on the sale of commodities, or, when they take title to the goods, through temporal or geographic arbitrage. Their profits are thus directly linked to the volume of business which they have a contract to handle. Trading companies are always looking for new business for which they can have trading rights. In the case of new and risky business, however, a trading company may have difficulty convincing entrepreneurs to enter the field, and may be forced to put up the capital for such ventures. The idea then is to develop the enterprise to the point where it can be floated as a public company, and to sell the shares to the public or to other firms so as to recoup the initial investment and make profits from the flotation.

In most cases, it does not make sense for the trading company to take full ownership of the new firms it has helped establish. First, the commissions earned on the business of the new firms provide a much higher (and much quicker) return on invested capital than the profits that will eventually be generated by the venture. Secondly, a public flotation makes it possible to offload the risks inherent in the enterprise. Thirdly, it keeps the trading firm small and nimble. Trading firms will therefore take a share that is just large enough to guarantee that they will retain the trading rights in their offsprings.[25] As a result, traders typically own a large number of minority participations.

Whether these minority ownerships will be in free-standing firms or not will depend on the form taken by the financing of their progeny.

The history of British trading firms in the East provides a good example. British traders (such as Harrisons & Crosfield and Guthrie & Co.) played an important part in the early development of rubber-planting in Malaya, when there was still considerable uncertainty as to the future of the industry. British trading firms had a clear interest in developing the industry. Rubber plantations could offer them a profitable business as they required supplies, both capital goods for the estates and consumer goods for the imported labour force, and assistance with the selling of rubber in consuming countries. The trading companies had experience in import/export, and their good names in London helped convince the British public to subscribe the capital needed for the development of what was still a speculative business.[26] British trading companies sponsored the London flotation of a large number of rubber estates. They sold most of the shares to the public, keeping only a minority stake. This minority stake allowed them to guarantee that they would get the commission business of the estate (usually 2.5 per cent on the sales of produce and on the purchases of inputs).[27] In this process the trading companies became involved in giving commercial and technical advice to the rubber estates; they slowly evolved from trading companies to agency houses. There is some evidence that they saw their agency role as accessory to their main trading business. Because these companies were financed through the sale of shares directly to the British public, this process resulted in a large number of UK-based free-standing rubber plantations in which a small number of trading companies had minority stakes.

This pattern was not particular to British trading companies in Malaya, but also applied to British and non-British trading companies in the rest of the world. American and British trading companies, such as Grace, set up and ended up owning minority shares in manufacturing and extractive ventures in South America.[28] Dutch trading firms floated the shares of plantations set up in the Dutch East Indies and became their managing agents.[29]

In the post-Second World War years Japanese trading companies have followed similar strategies, sponsoring a number of manufacturing and service ventures overseas as a way to increase their trade opportunities. They have played a pioneering role in the overseas expansion of Japanese manufacturing firms and in the development of new industries (for example in the development of chicken production[30] and in the import of natural gas). As in the case of all other trading companies, they have tried to keep their equity investments to a minimum, helping the development of new customers through loans, or, when equity was needed, through the establishment of joint ventures rather than wholly owned subsidiaries. As of 1979 the nine major Japanese trading companies had made equity investments in 1,360 overseas projects, with the trading company share generally less than 30 per cent and as low as 1 per cent.[31] In contrast to nineteenth-century British traders, the firms they have sponsored abroad have never been home-based (that is, Japan-based) free-standing ones. Instead, they have been overseas-registered joint ventures with local (and also sometimes Japanese) partners.[32]

Belgian, French, and German sellers of electrical equipment, South African mining houses, British, Dutch, American, and Japanese trading companies all exhibit similar behaviour: in all cases expansion of the business required an increase in the number of customers, but the high level of uncertainty and the size of the investment discouraged the spontaneous emergence of new firms or the transformation of existing ones. Sellers of equipment and of managerial and trading services then took the initiative of developing potential customers by sponsoring the establishment of new firms. With the exception of the eastern 'agency' houses, they were not interested in running these new businesses. Hence they tried to limit their stake to a level just sufficient to guarantee that their offspring would give them their business. They ended up with minority stakes in a large number of firms. In the case of the agency houses, the business—the service sold—was management; the agency houses, however, benefited most from the trade that these new units in the group generated.

Yet it is clear from the previous examples that a theory of minority ownership cannot fully account for free-standing firms. The overseas joint ventures established by Japanese trading companies have not been floated on the Tokyo stock exchange as free-standing firms, but instead have been registered locally. Most of their financing has not been subscribed directly by the public, but has come from the venture's parents. Our next step must therefore be to investigate the conditions under which the offsprings of trading companies and/or equipment vendors are likely to take the form of free-standing firms.

A Transaction-Cost Theory of International Transfers of Financial Capital

Consider the London-based rubber planting free-standing firms discussed earlier. We call them free-standing firms because they were registered in London and transferred equity capital to Malaya.[33] This set-up is only one of eight alternative ways in which firms can be financed. A firm can be funded (1) through local or through foreign sources, (2) through equity and through debt, and (3) through intermediated or through non-intermediated capital transfers (Fig. 2.1).[34]

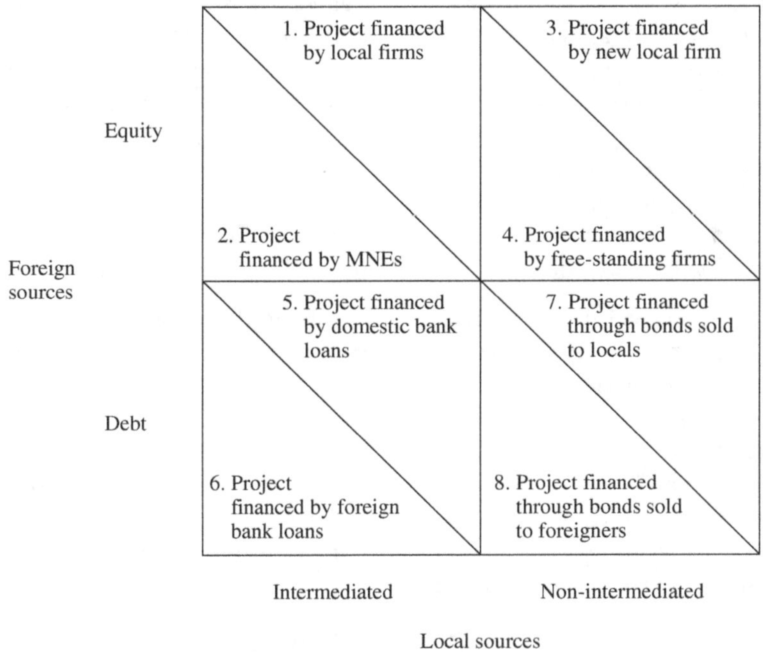

Fig. 2.1. Types of international financial capital transfers
Note: Intermediation occurs when firms or individuals raise funds in their own name and transfer them to other entities, thus allocating capital internally.

Malayan rubber plantations could have been locally registered and financed through the sale of shares to Malayan investors (as were the so-called 'dollar' companies) (cell 3), they could have been set up as wholly owned subsidiaries of locally registered companies (cell 1), or of foreign-based multinational firms (cell 2) (some American rubber-tyre makers invested in Malayan rubber plantations). The plantations could have been financed by locally registered firms through the sale of bonds to local investors (cell 7) or to foreign investors (cell 8). Lastly, the plantations could have been financed by loans extended by local banks (cell 5) or by foreign banks (cell 6). Instead, the case of free-standing firms (cell 4) corresponds to that of foreign-registered firms selling their shares on foreign stock markets.

To explain the free-standing firm one must therefore answer the following questions. Why was capital obtained in London, and not locally? Why was capital raised through equity, as opposed to debt? Why was not equity intermediated (why was it subscribed directly by the public, as opposed to taken by intermediaries, such as other firms or banks)?

The answer to the first question would seem obvious. Capital was raised in London because the mobilization of savings and their channelling to investments was more efficiently performed there than in Malaya. As noted above, not all rubber estates established in Malaya during the rubber boom were registered in London. Dollar companies were floated in Singapore. One observes the same coexistence between foreign-based and locally registered companies in other countries and industries (for example, in the Dutch East Indies, in India, in Ceylon, and in tea, sugar cane, and cinchona).

One would expect that companies would be floated in foreign stock markets rather than locally when the following conditions obtain:

- The less developed and the less liquid the domestic stock market, the greater the proportion of firms in that country registered in foreign countries.
- The larger the investment, the more likely the firm will be foreign-registered.
- Firms which are oriented towards exports are also less likely to find favour with local investors, and more likely to be registered in another country—and especially in importing countries—especially at early stages of the development of an activity.

The heavy concentration of free-standing firm operations in the least developed parts of Europe, in the regions of recent settlement, and in developing countries, and their registration in countries with liquid equity markets are consistent with the first of these expectations.

Some evidence on the second point is given by Ben Gales and Keetie Sluyterman, who compared free-standing companies registered in the Netherlands in 1912 to the population of all Dutch limited liability companies.[35] They found that free-standing firms had higher capitalization than domestic firms, since the former made up 9 per cent of all Dutch limited liability companies in 1912, but accounted for 31 per cent of all paid-up capital. Another bit of evidence comes from a comparison of companies registered in the host country with their free-standing firm counterparts. In the Dutch East Indies, free-standing companies registered in the Netherlands worked side by side with locally registered firms. Their capital, according to Gales and Sluyterman, was substantially larger than that issued by locally registered firms and Gales and Sluyterman note that 'registration in the mother country was preferred if links with the capital market were more important'. In Malaya, London-based (and Australia-based) free-standing firms coexisted with local Chinese or Western companies. The same link between access to capital and foreign registration is shown by the fact that some locally-registered Western tin-mining and smelting firms reincorporated in London as their financial needs grew. For example, Bruseh Hydraulic Tin, one of the first hydraulic mines in Malaya, was floated as a dollar company in Singapore in 1901 by the Borneo Company, and reconstructed as the Bruseh Tin and Rubber Estates in London in 1911. Similarly, the smelter built by Leh Chin Ho in Penang to smelt local tin ores and incorporated locally as the Eastern Trading Company was reincorporated in 1911 in London as a free-standing company. The Chinese directors argued that by floating the firm in London 'they could get fresh capital there more easily than they could get it locally'.[36] Sluyterman notes the same pattern of existing Dutch East Indies sugar factories and tea plantations switching their registration to the Netherlands to raise additional funds.[37]

The third hypothesis has been advanced by M. D. Morris, who, to explain the peculiar pattern of British free-standing firms in India, argues that exporters are more likely to obtain finance in the importing country than in the country of production.[38] British free-standing firms dominated the Indian jute industry by 1914, but were nearly absent from the cotton sector where Indian enterprise flourished. He argues that British firms had a comparative advantage in jute because its demand was international, while that for cotton textiles was primarily domestic. British trading companies, with their extensive involvement in international trade, were in a better position to forecast the former than the latter, and may therefore have been obliged to play a larger role in the development of jute than in that of cotton-spinning enterprises. A similar pattern can be found in Ceylon, where tea-growing was undertaken by both sterling (London-registered) and rupee (locally incorporated) companies. Sterling companies were located up-country and specialized in the highest tea quality, which was sold in London, while rupee companies, which were generally smaller than the sterling ones, sold their produce on local markets.[39]

So far we have shown that in some cases it is easier for a firm to find financing overseas than at home. We must now explain the particular form taken by the London financing of our rubber free-standing firms. Floating free-standing firms was not then (and neither is it today) the only way of funding plantations. In the 1990s most plantations in developing countries are not financed by floating free-standing firms on the stock markets of developed countries, but by having locally incorporated firms obtain loans from foreign banks or sell bonds and shares to foreigners. A third possibility is to sell the estate to a foreign-based multinational enterprise. For example, a decade after British trading companies started to float rubber estates as free-standing firms in London, the US Rubber Company, an American rubber manufacturer, established wholly owned subsidiaries to plant rubber in Malaya.[40]

Hence, to explain free-standing firms one must show why the transfer of financial capital from capital-rich to capital-poor countries took the form of equity (as opposed to loans) and why this equity was subscribed directly by the public (as opposed to held by a multinational firm). The first issue involves the choice between equity and debt. The second has to do with the optimum degree of intermediation.

Assuming that capital could be obtained more cheaply in the UK, why did the owners of rubber estates in Malaya choose to float the firm on the London or Edinburgh stock markets, rather than keep the company private and borrow from London banks? Why did the British trading companies not finance the development of these estates exclusively through debt?

One possible clue might be to look at debt and equity as alternative governance structures.[41] Seen in this light, the difference between debt and equity is that debt does not give the lender any right to the residual value of the venture—i.e. it does not remunerate the provider of funds through a share of the profits, while equity control does. Compared to equity owners, lenders have also much more limited rights to direct the behaviour of borrowers.

Remunerating savers with the profits of the venture and giving them the right to direct the implementation of the investment using their savings is a better solution than lending if the market for loanable funds is subject to high transaction costs.

There are two main reasons why lending money is subject to significant transaction costs.[42] The first one is the non-simultaneity between the two sides of the transaction: the lender makes funds available today to the borrower, to be repaid later with interest. Secondly, the chances of default are increased by a difference in incentives between lenders and borrowers: borrowers have incentives to take on risky projects, since they get to keep the entire gain over the stipulated interest costs if the venture is successful, while they may escape relatively unscathed if the project fails and they default.

Lenders can use a number of strategies to protect themselves against default. One of them is to ask the borrower to pledge collateral to be forfeited in the case of default. If borrowers have no private fortune, they will have to pledge the assets financed through the loan. The collateral value of these assets may vary a great deal across projects: transportation equipment is an excellent collateral; mines and research and development facilities are not.

A second strategy is to screen projects and applicants based on past record. As a result, new investors and new projects are likely to be turned down. A third option is to monitor the use of funds. While lenders are not allowed to interfere in the day-to-day management of a company, they can have loaned funds earmarked for specific investments.

When none of those strategies is effective in reducing default, the best solution is internalization. Internalization in this case means that savers will take equity in the projects financed by their savings, giving them the right to decide how the funds will be invested, or to direct employees to do it in their name. The pay of these employees need no longer be related to the profits of the venture, so as to reduce the incentives they have to misrepresent projects.[43] Default is also less likely because savers can now carefully monitor the behaviour of their employees. The efficiency of the internalization solution hinges, however, on the costs of monitoring the behaviour of the employees carrying out the investment.

The preceding considerations suggest circumstances where the international transfer of capital is likely to be internalized (i.e. to take the form of equity). We would expect this to be the case when (1) the activity to be financed does not provide good collateral, (2) when prospective projects are new and unproved, and (3) when potential borrowers are relatively unknown to lenders. Inversely, projects which provide good collateral and which are in more established fields of business are more likely to be undertaken by locally organized firms selling bonds to foreigners or borrowing from foreign banks.

Some of the empirical evidence on free-standing firms is consistent with our hypothesis. We have seen that free-standing firms were concentrated in mining and plantations. Mining is a very risky endeavour. Most of the money invested in mining is sunk in diggings which offer little collateral. As a result, new mining ventures cannot generally obtain debt financing, and have to be financed through equity. Initial exploration and development are generally financed by the personal funds of owners of mining claims and by those of their friends and relatives. Once minerals are found, a public stock offering is usually made on stock markets. In the 1980s and 1990s, shares of small companies developing North and South American mines are sold directly to the public on the penny stock markets of Spokane, Denver, and Vancouver,[44] as they were in London in the heyday of the free-standing firm. The reliance on equity is due to the poor quality of the collateral of mining ventures.

Plantations seem to have been the second largest field of activity of free-standing firms. The type of plantations financed through free-standing companies is consistent with our theory. Free-standing companies played a large role in the early development of rubber and cinchona in South East Asia.[45] The production of both these products in South East Asia was very speculative when introduced around the turn of the century. The investment was substantial, since it takes seven years between planting and yield for rubber and fifteen years for cinchona. It was risky because there were then no settled techniques of cultivation and the size of the market was unknown.[46] The main collateral for plantations is land. Whether plantations can or cannot borrow depends on whether their land has value for alternative uses. When previously undeveloped land is used for new, speculative export crops, as was the case with rubber in South East Asia, it probably has little collateral value, and equity financing must be sought.

Activities that provide good collateral are more likely to be financed through lending, either bank lending or bonds. Hence the foreign financing of railroads in nineteenth-century USA was different from than that of mines. While the bulk of foreign investment in US mining took the form of UK-registered free-standing companies, most of the financing needs of US railroads were obtained through US-incorporated firms selling bonds to foreigners.[47] The land owned by US railroads provided good collateral. Railroads were also the first regulated enterprises in the USA, and as early as 1909 had to follow a standard balance sheet, making it easier for lenders to monitor the borrowers.[48] The risk of default was therefore much lower than for mining.

N. Ramachandran's study of the financing of free-standing firms in the rubber and tea industry of Ceylon at the turn of the century also supports the hypothesis that equity is used to finance activities with poor collateral.[49] He found that the ordinary share was the only type of security used by rubber companies to raise initial funds, while the tea companies made greater use of debentures when they were established in the 1890s. He attributes the difference in finance to differences in riskiness for lenders. By the time tea plantations were established in Ceylon, tea cultivation was well established in India. Debentures could therefore be secured by the value of the estates. By contrast, rubber-growing was quite speculative at the time: methods of cultivation were still unsettled, and the size of the market was unknown. The land on which rubber was grown had been previously uncultivated, and thus had little collateral value.

The third distinctive aspect of free-standing firms is that most of their equity was held directly by the public, as opposed to taken by intermediaries, such as other firms or banks. Our third question was, why was not equity intermediated? We have already noted that at early stages of the development of some projects outside financing (whether through shares, bonds, or from banks or other lenders) is very difficult to obtain. The flow of capital for projects at very early stages usually comes from the profits of existing concerns (manufacturers, traders) or from the funds of project initiators and of their friends and relatives.

But when initial development is completed and outside capital can be obtained, the initiator can either decide to keep full equity in the project or to float all of it, or part of it, to the public.

When capital comes from an existing firm, this corresponds to the case of the modern multinational enterprise. Financial capital transferred through the multinational enterprise is intermediated in the sense that the funds transferred to the foreign subsidiaries have been raised by the parent for general purposes, and have not been earmarked for any particular investment. The multinational enterprise then allocates the funds thus raised between all of its new and existing projects. In that sense, multinational firms intermediate the fund-raising process. The case of zero intermediation is that of free-standing companies, created by professional promoters, who eventually placed all of the shares allotted to them with the general public. The third possibility (partial intermediation) is that of free-standing firms partially owned by trading companies, mining finance houses, and manufacturers of electrical equipment.

Since investors can choose between intermediated and non-intermediated channels for their investment, it would appear that for intermediated channels to be selected they must be more efficient than non-intermediated ones. As I am defining it, intermediation means that an intermediary (a firm in the case of equity transfer, a bank in the case of loans) screens projects and allocates the funds it receives from savers. In the case of non-intermediated transfers, there is no intermediary between savers and investors: screening is done by savers.

Hence the extent of intermediation should depend in part on the costs of obtaining information about projects. The greater the complexity of projects, the more it pays to have someone (the intermediator) specialize in screening them. We would expect more intermediation, everything else being constant, for new industries and for more complex technologies. For example, the part played by British trading companies in floating rubber-planting companies in London declined as the industry became more established; then an increasing number of firms were created by London stockbrokers as fully independent entities i.e. without any intermediation.[50]

The second factor is the minimum size of the investment. When the investment has a larger minimum size, the personal funds of the promoter are no longer sufficient to bring the project to flotation, and it becomes necessary to finance its initial development from the profits of other businesses. For example, the shift from outcrop mines to deep levels in South African gold-mining led to the establishment of the Group Administration system, in which the profits from existing mines were used to generate the significant sums necessary to bring the capital-intensive deep levels to the state where a public flotation could be attempted.[51] Similarly, as gravel-pumping was replaced by dredging, a technique thirty times more capital intensive, many of the free-standing tin-dredging firms operating in Thailand, Burma, Malaya, and Nigeria were floated by mining finance houses, such as Anglo-Oriental, that owned minority stakes in a portfolio of mines.[52] Earlier, many gravel pump mines had been floated by individual sponsors.

In conclusion, free-standing firms were characterized by low intermediation. Some of them—such as the large British-controlled railway companies on the West Coast of South America or most of the British free-standing mines in the American West—were totally independent.[53] Others were linked into networks organized around a trading company, a mining finance house, or an equipment seller. In that case there was a limited amount of intermediation, caused by the increased complexity of the business and the need to finance the early development of new projects from the profits generated by existing ones.[54]

In brief, within the category of firms that had been set up by sponsors (promoters, equipment sellers, sellers of management and of marketing services), free-standing firms had three distinguishing characteristics: they were registered in foreign countries, they raised the bulk of their finance by floating shares, and most or all of those shares were placed directly with the public. In the preceding pages we have analysed the conditions necessary for choosing this distinctive way to raise capital. Free-standing firms appeared because tapping foreign sources of finance was cost-effective, but obtaining loans from foreign banks or selling bonds to foreign investors was impossible or very costly because of the high risk of default. Most or all of the equity was sold directly to the public as opposed to intermediated via a multinational enterprise because the projects were simple enough to assess and small enough in scale, so that they could be nursed to the flotation stage by single-project promoters or syndicates.

Some Testable Implications of the Theory

The model developed in the previous section has interesting implications as to the reasons for the emergence of free-standing firms, the type of projects we would expect to see financed through them, the characteristics of countries which should be home and host to them, and lastly the conditions under which they should flourish.

First, the model suggests that free-standing firms existed primarily to internalize the market for equity capital between home and host countries. While one might see free-standing firms also contributing other factors (such as technology), the capital contribution is both necessary and sufficient for free-standing firms to emerge.

Secondly, one would expect to see free-standing firms used to fund ventures which cannot usually rely on debt because of the poor quality of their collateral: mining, new speculative export-oriented agriculture, and research-and-development intensive ventures are all examples.

Thirdly, we would expect free-standing firms to be based in the most liquid equity markets of the time. Because the internalization of equity finance through free-standing firms makes sense only if local equity markets are inadequate, we would not expect to see many free-standing firms created to operate in countries with efficient equity markets (for example, a Brussels-based free-standing firm operating in the UK should be an anomaly).

Fourthly, setting up a new venture as a free-standing firm is efficient as long as equity capital can be raised more efficiently in the foreign country (the UK, Belgium, etc.) than locally. More precisely, this arrangement is efficient as long as the savings in the procurement of equity capital overseas are greater than the additional cost of managing the operation from afar. The development of efficient equity markets in the free-standing firms' country of operation should reduce the gains from internalizing capital from foreign bases and one should witness a gradual reduction in the number of new free-standing firms created to operate in that country. Likewise, the need to internalize the procurement of capital should decrease as the industry becomes more established.

Existing free-standing firms—those created before the development of local equity markets or when the industry was still seen as speculative—may survive some time after their *raison d'être* has disappeared, but, if access to cheap equity capital was the sole reason for their existence, the costs of being managed at a distance should start to reduce the efficiency of these firms relative to their local rivals, and we would expect free-standing firms to be eventually liquidated, sold to local firms, or reincorporated as local concerns.

The empirical evidence provides some support. The first point, that the rationale of free-standing firms must be found in the desire to internalize the market for equity capital (and not necessarily that for technological know-how), is supported by evidence that shows that in some cases technical expertise was held not at headquarters, but instead in the country where the investment was made.[55] Gravel-pumping, the technology used by the early British free-standing firms mining tin in Malaya was not used in Cornwall, but was transferred to Malaya, from California gold-mining.[56] So, too, Gales and Sluyterman note that the Dutch owners of free-standing firms operating in the Dutch East Indies could not draw on their domestic experience, as 'metropolitan and colonial agriculture had almost nothing in common'.[57]

Secondly, we have seen that the activities undertaken by free-standing firms were concentrated in sectors (such as mining) which provided poor collateral and which still in the late twentieth century must rely on equity capital.

Free-standing firms were also based in countries boasting efficient and liquid equity markets (the UK, Belgium, etc.). The development of US-based free-standing firms after 1900 also supports the view that the main factor determining where free-standing firms are based is the relative efficiency of equity markets (while the main factor determining where they will operate is the country's lack of an efficient equity market). Miller notes that by the 1920s the informal controls exercised by the Bank of England made it very difficult to raise money in London for ventures located outside the Empire.[58] By 1902 a thriving equity market had developed in the USA.[59] British capital controls helped New York displace London as the world's largest stock market.

Wilkins, among others, has documented the demise after 1914 of the British free-standing firms operating in the USA and the absence of new London flotations to operate there.[60] That fate, which she attributed to the free-standing firms' lack of firm-specific advantage, makes sense when one considers that by 1914 the *raison d'être* of British free-standing firms operating in America—to procure cheap access to equity financing—had disappeared with the development of an indigenous stock market.

By contrast, many new British free-standing firms were created after 1914 to operate in parts of the Empire with poorly developed capital markets. Fifty-nine Malayan rubber-growing free-standing companies were floated between 1923 and 1929.[61] The flow of British capital invested in free-standing tin-dredging firms in Malaya peaked in 1925–7,[62] while the bulk of the capital of British-based free-standing tin-mining firms in Nigeria was also invested in the inter-war period. All these firms prospered until the late 1960s. As late as 1967 UK-registered free-standing companies were producing over 75 per cent of Nigeria's tin output. These firms lost their free-standing status the following year when the Nigerian government forced them to re-incorporate in Nigeria.[63] The fate of British free-standing firms in Malaysia was similar: they were bought by the Malaysian government in the mid-1970s. By then most of their stockholders were Malaysian. The demise of British free-standing firms in America and their survival in countries with undeveloped equity markets is consistent with the view that their *raison d'être* was to internalize the market for equity capital.

Also consistent with our theory is the flotation of American free-standing companies in the 1920s to operate mines, utilities, and plantations, mostly in Latin America. One sees US-based free-standing companies running mines in Mexico and other Latin American countries. For example, a large number of American free-standing firms were organized in the 1920s to prospect for oil in Colombia and in Venezuela.[64] Much of the Cuban sugar-cane industry was developed by US-based free-standing firms after the First World War.[65] In some cases these free-standing firms purchased the plants of UK-based free-standing firms.[66] Miller's statement that 'difficulties in raising new finance to expand facilities may have lain behind some of the decisions taken at the end of the 1920s to sell [British free-standing] assets in Latin America to US businessmen'[67] supports our point that the main *raison d'être* of free-standing firms was access to finance and that the USA had by then replaced the UK as the most efficient source of equity capital.

Some Criticisms of the Model

How does the model presented here differ from those presented by Casson and Wilkins? In the next chapter, Casson disputes the view that the transfer of funds within a firm constitutes the internalization of an international market in capital and that the free-standing firm is therefore a direct investor. For Casson, the internalization concept cannot be applied to financial capital, and hence the only direct investors are firms that internalize other markets, such as those for technological knowledge.[68]

Casson's criticism reflects what seems to be major differences in our views on the meaning of internalization and control. Casson believes that it is inappropriate to speak of internalization of capital markets:

> For a start, capital is a factor of production and not an intermediate product. According to internalization theory it is intermediate product markets that are internalized, and not factor markets. Factor markets link household with firms, and cannot normally be internalized, whereas intermediate product markets typically link one firm with another, and can be internalized quite easily.[69]

The idea that capital transfers cannot be internalized because capital is a factor of production may arise from a confusion between households as consumers and households as economic agents. When consumers invest, or when they borrow to support a business, they are acting as economic agents. Were one to follow Casson's view, one would speak of the internalization of capital flows when capital is intermediated (for example, when a bank acquires a firm to which it intends to lend) because the resulting transaction links one firm with another, but not when an entrepreneurial nephew with a good business plan persuades his rich uncle to bankroll his project and to hire him to implement it (a transaction between two households). Yet clearly the two phenomena must be explained by the same theory. Interestingly, Casson himself has discussed this last example in his book, *The Entrepreneur* (1982).[70] In that book he argues that entrepreneurs will often experience difficulties borrowing from banks and may find it easier to get financing from family members, thus internalizing the capital market.[71]

We also seem to have different views on what constitutes internalization. For Casson, internalization theory 'explains why two distinct activities in two different countries are brought under common control'. Because he subscribes to this view, he finds it difficult to deal with the free-standing company, since that company has no manufacturing activity in the home country, only a headquarters. Casson adopts the convention that 'being a headquarters is not an activity, so that a headquarters office is not an activity unless it performs some other functions as well'. This assumption leads him to the conclusion that free-standing firms in which the directors did not have specific expertise were not foreign direct investments at all, and are therefore of limited theoretical interest.[72]

My view of internalization is somewhat different. I see internalization as the extension of managerial control across national boundaries. Internalization takes place when the coordination of agents in two separate countries is effected not by prices, but by managerial directives. This does not require that there be extensive manufacturing activities in the home country. In the case of free-standing firms, we have internalization because coordination between lenders in one country and borrowers in another is being organized within the free-standing firm through employment contracts. Hence the free-standing firm is a transnational (or a multinational) firm.

Casson's view of internalization is linked to his definition of what constitutes a multinational firm. Casson defines a multinational as an enterprise that owns and controls activities in more than one country. Framed in these terms, whether the free-standing firm is a multinational or not again hinges on whether the headquarters is an activity. There is, however, a much simpler and general way to define a multinational firm, and that definition avoids the somewhat artificial question of whether the headquarters constitutes an 'activity'.

The issue that captured my interest in the multinational enterprise in the 1970s—and that of many other scholars—was why, in spite of the costs of doing business in a foreign country, firms exercised managerial control across national boundaries.[73] I defined a multinational (or transnational) firm as one that uses hierarchical links to coordinate the behaviour of agents located in more than one country, without much concern as to whether employees at home or abroad were in R&D, marketing, extractive activities, or manufacturing. Other researchers, interested by the extent to which national firms were becoming more independent of domestic economic and political conditions, defined multinational firms in terms of the extent of their foreign manufacturing activities and of the international dispersion of these activities.[74] Then the level and type of foreign activities and their international dispersion becomes relevant. The issue raised by free-standing firms is obviously of the first type: we want to know why a tea plantation in India was registered and ostensibly run from London, given the communication and control problems involved.

Casson's definition of what constitutes a multinational firm forces him to make a complex distinction between multinationality and foreign direct investment. His final conclusion is that most of the free-standing firms described in this chapter are neither multinationals nor foreign direct investors. Only when headquarters export both technology and information is the free-standing firm both a multinational firm and a foreign direct investor. He classifies many of the free-standing firms described in this book, where the headquarters had neither technological expertise nor the knowledge to direct day-to-day operations, as neither direct investors nor even quasi-multinational firms, and little more than 'shell companies for tax avoidance, or even devices for "laundering" illegal funds'.

The complex distinction between foreign direct investment and multinationality is unnecessary if one sticks to the definition that a multinational firm is an institution that organizes the interactions between agents located in at least two distinct countries through an employment contract, and foreign direct investment is the financial consequence of that relationship. Casson's analysis is, however, useful in bringing up the point that there are two separate issues concerning control in free-standing firms: (1) was control exercised by the owners? (2) were owners always resident of the country of registration?

The first issue is whether the equity stake taken by the suppliers of capital in the implementation of their foreign investment plans qualifies as the extension of hierarchical control across countries. If one joins Casson in denying it, then the free-standing firm is not, according to my own definition, a multinational firm. The second issue is whether effective control in free-standing firms always emanated from the country of registration. This is not crucial to my definition of free-standing firms as multinational firms, since this issue has to do with where control was located, and not whether it was exercised by owners.

The main reason why Casson denies the status of multinational and of foreign direct investor to all free-standing firms whose headquarters did not transfer technology or management to their foreign operations is because he denies that equity carries control. For him, 'possession of equity is not synonymous with the right to control'. The control right of shareholders is embedded in the right to vote. Casson argues that this right is more often symbolic than effective, especially in large corporations.[75] For Casson, control is located where 'competence and integrity reside'. He sees an apparent contradiction between my observation that competence was often located overseas and my statement that control was always held at headquarters.

My theory of free-standing firms is based on the assumption that the type of control held by equity owners on the use of their funds differs from that obtained by lenders. If there are no differences between the type of control exercised by owners and lenders, then the choice between lending and owning is trivial, and the rationale for free-standing firms must be found elsewhere (for example, in a transfer of knowledge from headquarters).

Casson's argument that equity does not carry control seems at odds with his earlier writings in *The Entrepreneur.* There he anticipates my argument that lenders can reduce the risk of default by becoming owners of ventures and taking entrepreneurs as their employees because equity (ownership) gives owners greater control over borrowers than that available to lenders:

> So far as the lender is concerned, full and accurate reporting of the information is crucial in minimizing the risk of loss. A lender is not automatically entitled to information of this kind. Even if he were to contract to receive such information, he would still need to check that there is no concealment, or deliberate distortion. . . . To check that the entrepreneur is not concealing information, the lender needs to be able to monitor the implementation of the activity himself. He must have unrestricted access to the premises where the activity is carried on. As new information becomes available he must have the right to consult with the entrepreneur and, if things turn out badly, the right to overrule the entrepreneur in the interests of reducing the loss and protecting the repayment of his loan. This suggests that the lender should participate in the project as one of its principals, with the entrepreneur assuming the role of delegate. . . . The simplest way for the entrepreneur to act as delegate is to become an employee.[76]

Casson's more recent position that equity does not provide control may, however, apply in the case of the modern corporation where he asserts that 'collective control by shareholders is obviously a myth'. This point seems, however, somewhat overdrawn. While it is true that in many cases the control rights of some shareholders in firms with dispersed ownership seem more potential than real, a shareholder's right to vote assures potential ultimate control, though the way this control is exercised can take many forms. First, core shareholders or groups of shareholders often exercise effective control in many corporations, and the same appears to have been true in many free-standing firms.[77] Secondly, coalitions of stockholders can be formed to oust poorly performing managers (IBM, American Express, Compaq, Digital Equipment, Kodak, Hartmarx, Tenneco, Westinghouse, Morrison-Knudsen, and W. R. Grace are recent examples).[78] Thirdly, votes can be bought by outside raiders intent on displacing existing managers. In short, while shareholders may choose not to exercise control in most circumstances, this does not mean that they do not have it.

The same distinction between potential ultimate control and day-to-day control, or between strategic and operational control, plays out in multinational corporations of the 1990s. Because competence often resides in the foreign subsidiary, the headquarters of most multinational firms do not intervene in the day-to-day operations of their foreign affiliates. Instead the head offices make strategic decisions, such as where to reinvest the cash flows generated by the enterprise, which subsidiaries to expand, and which ones to liquidate. That ultimate control is held by headquarters is widely accepted by managers of multinational firms.[79]

The separation of strategic control from operational responsibilities which characterize the modern multinational seems also to have been the norm in free-standing firms. While the head office of many free-standing companies was small, it was not always ineffective. Drawing from the histories of a number of Dutch free-standing companies, Gales and Sluyterman conclude that the board in Holland exercised strategic control because it held the purse strings.[80] The distinction between strategic and tactical control is also nicely described by Geoffrey Jones in the case of Britain's multinational banks: he notes that the London offices, despite their small size, added significant value to the operations of the bank by providing overall strategic direction, by hiring and firing managers, by instilling a company culture, and by tightly supervising and monitoring the business of the overseas branches.[81] T. A. B. Corley also provides examples of British free-standing firms where headquarters maintained strategic control through their power to hire and fire managers and to authorize expenses.[82] It is because the stockholders of free-standing firms had—or had the potential to have—strategic control over the use of their funds, including the right to fire the overseas managers responsible for the day-to-day conduct of foreign operations, that they were more willing to subscribe shares in the enterprise than to buy its bonds.

The second issue is whether control in free-standing firms was always exercised from the place where the company was registered. This does not seem always to have been the case.[83]

While Casson denies that the internalization of capital could provide a rationale for the free-standing firm, another group of authors represented by Clark C. Spence, Donald G. Paterson, and Wilkins agree that free-standing firms made foreign direct investments, but they have emphasized the short-lived character of these firms.[84] Wilkins wrote:

> Fundamental to the free-standing company was its inherently weak managerial structure at origin, causing it to depend on outside providers for service. This initial lean governance structure was responsible for the short life or failure of many of the British businesses operating overseas.[85]

These authors tend to stress the inefficiencies of free-standing firms and their high failure rates due to incompetence and fraud. This verdict is in large part based on the experience of mining firms, which, we have seen, made up the largest proportion of free-standing firms, and more particularly, of those in North America.

Lending to mining firms is a very risky proposition because of the lack of good collateral. Hence mining has always relied on equity financing. While the floating of mining stocks has often been accompanied by fraud, the efficiency of this process must be assessed in relative, not in absolute terms. The 1980s performance of international bank lending to mining firms in developing countries suggests that, in spite of considerable abuses, free-standing firms were a comparatively efficient method of funding foreign mining ventures.

When one looks at mining firms outside North America, and at free-standing companies in other industries, free-standing firms do not seem to have a particularly high failure rate. As mentioned above, were it not for political factors, British free-standing tin-mining firms would still be active today in Nigeria and Malaysia. The British overseas banks—another group of free-standing companies—were still very much in evidence in the 1960s.[86] Gales and Sluyterman show that the survival rate of Dutch free-standing companies varied with their industry and location: 77 per cent of all companies doing business in 1913 in the Dutch Indies (mostly plantations) had not disappeared twenty-four years later, versus 41 per cent for those in other countries (principally mortgage companies).[87] These rates compare favourably with some studies of the 1980s and 1990s survival rates of foreign affiliates.[88] Many British free-standing firms in the West Coast of Latin America did also survive for long periods.[89]

Since the rationale for free-standing firms was the funding of risky ventures overseas, keeping the firm no larger than that of an efficiently sized production unit may have been efficient, since it made it possible for investors to diversify their investment across a large number of firms. Keeping free-standing firms small reduced their cost of raising funds. Subcontracting basic administrative services, marketing, and local management avoided diseconomies of scale. Developing a sizeable corps of managers at headquarters would have been useless if the main role of headquarters was to give strategic direction and not detailed operational instructions.

Wilkins's second point was that British free-standing firms failed because their contribution 'was often solely financial; the British free-standing firm had no sustained advantage'.[90] This assumes that a firm needs advantages to operate abroad. Yet observation of vertically integrated multinationals shows that this is not the case. Multinational firms arise to internalize markets, not necessarily advantages. Steelmakers have invested in foreign iron-ore mines even though they have no expertise in mining (most of their captive mines are managed by specialist iron-ore-mining firms). They have developed foreign mines to internalize the market for iron ore, not to exploit abroad some type of advantages. One would expect them to sell off their mines or to operate them at arm's length if the market for iron ore became competitive.

Similarly, free-standing firms were created to internalize the international market for equity capital. When this market became more efficient, they lost their *raison d'être* and evolved into domestic companies. Their disappearance was the logical consequence of changed market conditions. When markets improve, vertical disintegration follows, and this is as true in the market for equity capital as in that for iron ore.

Conclusion

The goal of this chapter has been to develop a theory of free-standing firms, looking both at the way they were created and at the particular form they took. While some free-standing firms were clearly completely free-standing, others were linked in clusters to traders, sellers of capital equipment, and mining consulting and engineering firms. Free-standing firms have two main characteristics that challenge the usual rendition of the eclectic theory of foreign direct investment. First, in contrast to the prediction of the theory, these firms did not grow from a domestic base from which they could transfer 'ownership advantages' to their foreign operations. Secondly, many were linked to their sponsors through minority stakes. These stakes are difficult to explain in terms of the eclectic theory, for they were not taken by parents internalizing proprietary knowledge through wholly-owned subsidiaries, as is the usual pattern with today's multinational firms.

In this chapter I argue that the existence of free-standing firms and their minority equity links to sponsors can be explained by a three-pronged extension of the eclectic model. First, we need to understand that the presence of equity links between firms does not require the exploitation of advantages. Multinational firms arise to internalize international markets, not necessarily international advantages. They do not need to possess advantages to expand abroad. Their expansion can be explained by the internalization of markets. Secondly, while the focus of the international business literature has been on the internalization of markets for technological know-how, the theory can be extended to that for financial capital. Free-standing firms can be seen as institutions that reduce transaction costs in the markets for financial capital by having savers control the investment of their funds in a foreign project through an employment relationship. This is shown to be efficient when the market alternative of lending would experience high costs because the project is new and unproved, it does not provide good collateral, and its sponsors are unknown to lenders. This explanation is consistent with the main features of free-standing firms: their registration in countries having liquid equity markets, the absence of domestic activities (other than those of the head office), their lean headquarters staff sometimes lacking technical expertise, the concentration of their activities in risky projects in capital-starved countries, their high capital intensity, and their reliance on equity.

The presence of minority equity links between free-standing firms and their sponsors can be explained by the desire of sellers of goods and services to integrate vertically forward. Sellers were forced to sponsor the establishment of customer firms because such enterprises would not have appeared spontaneously otherwise. The involvement of sellers can be explained by the superior information they possessed and their inability to transfer it to local entrepreneurs because of the well-known problems encountered in the sale of information.[91]

But while suppliers had to establish equity links between themselves and their potential customers, they generally did not need to take full equity. Full integration would have involved more costs than benefits. Sometimes the suppliers did not have all the requisite skills to operate locally, especially a knowledge of local conditions. Taking more equity than the minimum required to obtain the custom of their progeny would have yielded few benefits to suppliers of heavy equipment and to traders, while substantially increasing the size of their operations and hence their management costs. Hence traders and heavy-equipment makers ended up owning minority stakes in a large number of customer companies.

Lastly, under the free-standing firm pattern each project was basically undertaken as a separate firm, as opposed to as part of a large firm, with funds raised by the large firm and then internally allocated to each project, as is the norm with today's multinational enterprises. The reason is that, given the small minimum efficient size and the relative simplicity of the technology involved, there was no need to transfer funds internally from existing to new projects. Instead independent sponsors could finance the early development of projects and bring them successfully through flotation. Some partial intermediation did take place when the scale of the project was so large that it could not be prepared for flotation by isolated sponsors. Then the development of new projects was financed by trading firms, financial holding companies, and mining finance houses from the cash flows of existing ones.

NOTES

1. M. Wilkins, 'The Free-Standing Company, 1870–1914: An Important Type of British Foreign Direct Investment', *Economic History Review*, 2nd ser., 41 (May 1988), 259–82.
2. The following are just a few examples gleaned from press articles: Affymax NV, a public company incorporated in the Netherlands whose only activity is doing research on combinatorial chemistry in Palo Alto, California; Vengold Ltd., floated on the Vancouver Stock Exchange to develop gold properties in Venezuela; Musto Explorations, a Canadian company traded on the Vancouver Stock Exchange, whose main asset is a 50% interest in a copper/gold project in Argentina; Gold Reserve Corp., an American company initially floated on the Spokane stock exchange, now on NASDAQ, whose sole asset is a gold mine in Venezuela. See *Wall Street Journal*, 27 and 31 Jan. 1995; *Financial Times*, 27 Apr. 1995; *Spokesman Review*, 28 May 1994.
3. C. J. Schmitz, 'Patterns of Scottish Portfolio Investment 1860–1914', unpublished report to ESRC (1994). See Table 1.1 herein.
4. US Federal Trade Commission, *Report on Cooperation in American Export Trade* (Washington, 1916), pt. 2, 537.
5. Ben Gales and Keetie Sluyterman, Chapter 11 herein.
6. Wilkins, 'The Free-Standing Company'.
7. J. F. Rippy, *British Investments in Latin America, 1822–1949* (Minneapolis, 1959), 59.
8. A. Wright and H. A. Cartwright, *Twentieth Century Impressions of British Malaya* (London, 1908).
9. J. H. Dunning, *International Production and Multinational Enterprise* (London, 1981).
10. Wilkins, 'The Free-Standing Company', 279.
11. The point is made implicitly in J.-F. Hennart, *A Theory of Multinational Enterprise* (Ann Arbor, Mich., 1982); and explicitly in M. Casson, 'General Theories of the Multinational Enterprise: Their Relevance to Business History', in P. Hertner and G. Jones (eds.), *Multinationals: Theory and History* (Aldershot, 1986), 42–63.

12. J.-F. Hennart, 'International Financial Capital Transfers: A Transaction Cost Framework', *Business History*, 36 (Jan. 1994), 51–70.
13. J.-F. Hennart, 'A Transaction Costs Theory of Equity Joint Ventures', *Strategic Management Journal*, 9/4 (1988), 361–74; J.-F. Hennart, 'The Transaction Costs Theory of Joint Ventures: An Empirical Study of Japanese Subsidiaries in the United States', *Management Science*, 37 (Apr. 1991), 483–97.
14. Hennart, *A Theory of Multinational Enterprise*.
15. G. Akerlof, 'The Market for "Lemons": Quality Uncertainty and the Market Mechanism', *Quarterly Journal of Economics*, 84 (1970), 488–500.
16. Shirking can be defined by the failure of employees to live by the spirit of their employment contract. Shirking takes the form of failure to work during work hours, to show initiative, to collect information, to respect company property, and/or to obey managerial directives. Note that our description of what goes on in firms simplifies in assuming that firms use pure hierarchical control modes. In fact, firms use a mix of price and hierarchical controls. See J.-F. Hennart, 'What is Internalization?', *Weltwirtschaftliches Archiv—Review of World Economics*, 122/4 (1986), 791–804; J.-F. Hennart, 'Explaining the "Swollen Middle": Why Most Transactions are a Mix of Market and Hierarchy', *Organization Science*, 4 (Nov. 1993), 529–47.
17. Hennart, 'A Transaction Costs Theory'.
18. For some empirical evidence supporting the theory, see Hennart, 'The Transaction Costs Theory of Joint Ventures'.
19. See the case of tramways in J. McKay, *Tramways and Trolleys* (Princeton, 1976) and the hypothesis of Tamás Szmrecsányi, Chapter 10 herein.
20. P. Hertner, 'The German Electrotechnical Industry on the Italian Market before the Second World War', in G. Jones and H. Schröter (eds.), *The Rise of Multinationals in Continental Europe* (Aldershot, 1993), 157.
21. Some of these financial holding companies were established in joint ventures with banks in Switzerland and in Belgium. Hence AEG established in 1895 the Bank für Elektrische Unternehmungen (Elektrobank) in Zurich with the Deutsche Bank and in cooperation with the Credit Suisse and other German, Swiss, and Italian banks, and in 1898 SOFINA in Brussels in collaboration with Belgian banks. Those two countries were ideal locations to finance operations outside Germany because they were neutral and had very liberal company law and stock-exchange regulations. The US General Electric Company seems to have adopted a similar strategy. In 1905 it set up the Electric Bond and Share Company to finance the acquisition of utilities. That subsidiary acquired or created a large number of electric traction and lighting companies. At least some of those were free-standing companies with stock sold to the public—for example, the Cuban Electric Company (incorporated in 1927 to supply electric power to Cuba). In 1923 Electric Bond and Share organized the American and Foreign Power Co. to hold its foreign properties. See M. Winkler, *Investments of United States Capital in Latin America* (Boston, 1929), 190; M. Wilkins, *The Maturing of Multinational Enterprise: American Business Abroad from 1914 to 1970* (Cambridge, Mass., 1974), 131; W. J. Hausman and J. L. Neufeld, Chapter 14 herein; Hertner, 'The German Electrotechnical Industry'; A. Broder, 'Banking and the Electrotechnical Industry in Western Europe', in R. Cameron and V. I. Bovykin (eds.), *International Banking, 1870–1914* (New York, 1991), 468–84.
22. In 1898 Schneider took an 8% participation in the Société Franco-Russe pour l'Industrie Électrique in order to obtain orders for their electrical works in France. See C. P. Beaud, 'Investments and Profits of the Multinational Schneider Group: 1894–1943', in A. Teichova, M. Lévy-Leboyer, and H. Nussbaum (eds.), *Multinational Enterprise in Historical Perspective* (Cambridge, 1986), 87.

23. J. McKay, *Pioneers for Profit* (Chicago, 1970), 100–2. Electric tramways needed a large and reliable supply of electricity, and hence were a good market for companies that were selling heavy electrical generating equipment. See, for example, D. McDowall, *The Light: Brazilian Traction, Light and Power Company Limited, 1899–1945* (Toronto, 1988).
24. R. Turrell and J.-J. van Helten, 'The Rothschilds, the Exploration Company, and Mining Finance', *Business History*, 28 (Apr. 1986), 188; M. Fraser, 'Editor's Introduction', in L. Phillips, *Some Reminiscences* (Johannesburg, new edn., 1986).
25. Having a trading firm as a minority share owner is also useful to the free-standing firm, since it helps guarantee marketing support from the trader and provides credibility *vis-à-vis* customers. For a discussion in the context of Japanese trading companies, see T. Roehl, 'A Transaction Cost Approach to International Trading Structures: The Case of the Japanese General Trading Company', *Hitotsubashi Journal of Economics*, 24 (1983), 119–35.
26. J. H. Drabble and P. J. Drake, 'More on the Financing of Malayan Rubber, 1905–23', *Economic History Review*, 2nd ser., 27 (1974), 108–20.
27. J. H. Drabble, *Rubber in Malaya 1876–1922* (Kuala Lumpur, 1973), 85.
28. R. Miller, Chapter 8 herein.
29. Gales and Sluyterman, Chapter 11 herein.
30. Mitsubishi Shoji was in the mid-1960s the largest importer of animal feeds. As an outlet for its feeds, it fostered the development of broiler farms and of processing plants. To absorb the resulting broiler meat, it entered a 50–50 joint venture with Kentucky Fried Chicken to introduce fried chicken fast-food restaurants into Japan. See Y. Tsurumi, *Multinational Management* (Boston, 1977); M. Yoshino and T. Lifson, *The Invisible Link* (Cambridge, Mass., 1986).
31. K. Hayashi and S. Robock, 'The Uncertain Future of the Japanese General Trading Companies', *Kajian Ekonomi Malaysia*, 19/2 (1982), 45–67; K. Kojima and T. Ozawa, *Japan's General Trading Companies: Merchants of Economic Development* (Paris, 1984).
32. An example is Sangkasi Thai Co., a manufacturing joint venture between Mitsui & Co. (24% owner), C. Itoh (16% owner) and local interests (60%) which manufactures galvanized iron sheets in Thailand. These sheets used to be exported from Japan by the trading companies. They set up Sangkasi Thai and similar ventures when their export business was threatened by Thai tariffs. Mitsubishi Brunei LNG project is a three-way joint venture between the Government of Brunei, Royal Dutch/Shell, and Mitsubishi Shoji. The joint venture (Brunei LNG Sendirian Berhad) is domiciled in Brunei. See T. Cappielo, 'The Changing Role of Japan's General Traders', *Journal of Japanese Trade and Industry*, No. 4 (1982), 18–30.
33. Note that they sometimes transferred other inputs besides capital. In this chapter, however, we focus on their role as conduit for financial capital.
34. In practice, pure types are rare, most firms being financed through a mix of debt and equity, through both intermediated and non-intermediated transfers, and through both foreign and domestic sources. It is, however, convenient to look at pure types to understand the trade-offs involved. Note, also, that the underwriting of bonds and stocks by banks or other intermediaries is not considered intermediation here. In this chapter, intermediation is considered to occur when individuals or businesses raise funds in their own name and transfer them to other entities, thus allocating capital internally.
35. Gales and Sluyterman, Chapter 11 herein.
36. Article on Leh Chin Ho in the centenary number of the *Pinang Gazette* cited in J. W. Cushman, 'The Khaw Group: Chinese Business in Early Twentieth Century Penang', *Journal of Southeast Asian Studies*, 17 (1986), 58–79.

37. K. Sluyterman, 'Dutch Free-Standing Companies between 1870 and 1940', unpublished paper (1994).
38. M. D. Morris, 'South Asia Entrepreneurship and the Rashomon Effect, 1840–1947', *Explorations in Economic History*, 16 (1979), 341–61.
39. K. Stahl, *The Metropolitan Organisation of British Colonial Trade* (London, 1951), 167.
40. C. Lewis, *America's Stake in International Investments* (Washington, 1938), 284.
41. O. E. Williamson, 'Corporate Finance and Corporate Governance', *Journal of Finance*, 63/3 (1988), 569–98.
42. For a more extensive discussion, see Hennart, 'International Financial Capital Transfers'.
43. On the other hand, they will be less motivated to exert effort and to collect information, and more motivated to embezzle.
44. R. Mikesell and J. Whitney, *The World Mining Industry* (Boston, 1987).
45. Hennart, 'International Financial Capital Transfers'; Gales and Sluyterman, Chapter 11 herein.
46. R. T. Stillson, 'The Financing of Malayan Rubber, 1905–1923', *Economic History Review*, 2nd ser., 24 (1971), 589–98; C. G. Allen and A. G. Donnithorne, *Western Enterprise in Indonesia and Malaya* (London, 1957).
47. M. Wilkins, *The History of Foreign Investment in the United States to 1914* (Cambridge, Mass., 1989).
48. J. Baskin, 'The Development of Corporate Financial Markets in Britain and in the United States, 1600–1914: Overcoming Asymmetric Information', *Business History Review*, 62 (Summer 1988), 228.
49. N. Ramachandran, *Foreign Plantation Investment in Ceylon, 1899–1958* (Colombo, 1963).
50. Drabble, *Rubber in Malaya*, 85.
51. P. Richardson and J.-J. van Helten, 'The Development of the South African Gold-Mining Industry, 1895–1918', *Economic History Review*, 2nd ser., 38/3 (1984), 319–40.
52. Yip Yat Hoong, *The Development of the Tin Mining Industry of Malaya* (Kuala Lumpur, 1969).
53. Miller, Chapter 8 herein; M. Wilkins, 'The Impact of Multinational Corporations', *South African Journal of Economic History*, 4 (Mar. 1989), 4–20.
54. Miller (Chapter 8 herein) observes that free-standing companies in the West Coast of South America fell into two such categories: those basically independent and those linked to traders, such as Gibbs and Balfour, Williamson & Co.
55. J.-F. Hennart, 'Free-Standing Firms and the Internalisation of Markets for Financial Capital: A Response to Casson', *Business History*, 36 (Oct. 1994), 122.
56. Ibid. Similarly, dredging was not a British technology, but was borrowed from New Zealand gold-mining.
57. Gales and Sluyterman, Chapter 11 herein.
58. Miller, Chapter 8 herein.
59. T. Navin and M. Sears, 'The Rise of a Market for Industrial Securities', *Business History Review*, 29 (1955), 105–38.
60. Wilkins, 'The Free Standing Company'.
61. Drabble and Drake, 'More on the Financing', 116.
62. Yip, *The Development of the Tin Mining Industry of Malaya*.
63. L. Schatzl, *The Nigerian Tin Industry* (Ibadan, 1971).
64. Winkler, *Investments of United States Capital in Latin America*, 118–23 and 158–75.
65. Farr and Co., *Manual of Sugar Companies* (New York, 1925).
66. This pattern can be seen in mining and petroleum, with US firms buying

British free-standing firms in Mexico and Venezuela. For example, Lago Petroleum, incorporated in Delaware in 1923 to prospect for oil in Venezuela, acquired in 1924 the British Equatorial Co. Ltd.; the Colon Oil Corp. was organized in the USA in 1928 to take over the Colon Development Company Ltd., registered in 1913 in the UK to explore for oil in Venezuela. International Telephone and Telegraph, which seems to have had the characteristics of a US-based free-standing firm, acquired in the late 1920s a series of British-based free-standing telephone utilities (the Chili Telephone Co. Ltd. and the Montevideo Telephone Co. Ltd. in 1927; the Peruvian Telephone Co. Ltd. in 1930). See Winkler, *Investments of United States Capital in Latin America*; Miller, Chapter 8 herein.

67. Miller, Chapter 8 herein.
68. Casson, Chapter 3 herein.
69. Casson, Chapter 3 herein.
70. M. Casson, *The Entrepreneur* (Oxford, 1982).
71. Casson (ibid. 199) writes: 'It is worth noting that the family is capable of internalizing not only the labour market, but the capital market too.'
72. Casson, Chapter 3 herein.
73. Hennart, *A Theory of Multinational Enterprise.*
74. See, for example, R. Vernon, *Sovereignty at Bay* (New York, 1971).
75. Casson supports his point that possession of equity is not synonymous with right to control with the example of Chinese railways, where the bondholders had the right to name the general manager. He also argues that control of firms that have failed to make interest payments has been taken over by committees of bondholders. These two examples are not persuasive because they correspond to abnormal situations. In the case of Chinese railroads, the first best solution of lenders would probably have been to hold equity in the railroads, but this was probably frustrated by the Chinese government's insistence on ownership. Hence to attract funds the Chinese government was probably obliged to offer additional control rights to bondholders. The second example corresponds to a case where lenders, having suffered the consequences of lack of control, try to obtain it ex post. See Casson, Chapter 3 herein.
76. Casson, *The Entrepreneur*, 212–13.
77. This is the case in many family-controlled public corporations. For some evidence of tight family control in some British free-standing firms, see Hennart, 'Free-Standing Firms'.
78. See, for example, H. Smith, *Rethinking America* (New York, 1995), 274–92.
79. As the British managing director of an American-owned subsidiary put it to Michael Brooke and Lee Remmers, 'the manager of a subsidiary must accept that he enjoys a subordinate status, that a subsidiary company is an organ of the parent company, and that policy is basically formulated and handed down by the parent company'. See M. Z. Brooke and H. L. Remmers, *The Strategy of Multinational Enterprise* (New York, 1970), 8.
80. Gales and Sluyterman, Chapter 11 herein.
81. Geoffrey Jones, Chapter 13 herein. The London offices also performed banking functions, such as the discounting of bills received from their foreign branches, the confirmation of letters of credit, and the purchase and sale of bullion and securities.
82. In his comment on Hennart, 'International Financial Capital Transfers', Corley argued that the evidence of effective strategic control by directors over the operations of free-standing companies shows that the directors were internalizing knowledge from headquarters, and that the need to include financial capital as an intermediate factor becomes therefore less compelling. My point is that

the free-standing firm was the vehicle to link through hierarchical processes individuals with projects (entrepreneurs) and those with funds (investors)—i.e. the savers became owners of the project. Sometimes the entrepreneurs became co-owners of the firm, sometimes they became employees of the savers, and sometimes they were themselves savers. In all cases the market for financial capital was being internalized. My views are therefore compatible with those of Corley if one realizes that the market for financial capital links individuals with projects (with privileged information on profitable use of funds) and those with financial resources. See T. A. B. Corley, 'Free-Standing Companies, their Financing, and Internalisation Theory', *Business History* 36 (Oct. 1994) and Corley, Chapter 4 herein.

83. For example, Aramayo Francke Ltd., a company floated in London to mine tin in Bolivia, was controlled by the Bolivian Aramayo family. Miller (Chapter 8 herein) provides other examples. Many free-standing companies floated in London to mine in South Africa were German and French controlled. See Wilkins, 'The Impact of Multinational Corporations', and Wilkins, Chapter 1 herein.
84. C. C. Spence, *British Investment and the American Mining Frontier* (Ithaca, NY, 1958); D. G. Paterson, *British Direct Investment in Canada 1890–1914: Estimates and Determinants* (Toronto, 1976); Wilkins, 'The Free Standing Company'.
85. Wilkins, 'The Free Standing Company', 279.
86. Jones, Chapter 13 herein.
87. Gales and Sluyterman, Chapter 11 herein.
88. For example, only 41% of the foreign subsidiaries of a sample of Norwegian firms in 1982 were still active ten years later. See G. Benito, 'Disvestment of Foreign Production Operations', paper presented at the 2nd Workshop in International Business (University of Vaasa, Finland, 1995). The survival rate of Japanese manufacturing subsidiaries in the USA between 1980 and 1989 is 89% (author's database of Japanese subsidiaries in the USA).
89. Miller, Chapter 8 herein.
90. Wilkins, 'The Free Standing Company', 276.
91. See, for example, Hennart, *A Theory of Multinational Enterprise.*

3

An Economic Theory of the Free-Standing Company

Mark Casson

The free-standing company flourished in the age of high imperialism, 1870–1914. It was a company typically based in London or some other European financial centre which owned purely overseas operations. It was a distinctive form of international business enterprise, although, as indicated below, it evolved from antecedents elsewhere.

According to the product-cycle theory of foreign direct investment, successful overseas operations hinge on the exploitation of competitive advantages developed in the home market.[1] From this perspective the free-standing company appears paradoxical because it has no domestic operations from which it can derive competitive strength. This has suggested to some writers that the free-standing company is inherently weaker than the kind of multinational enterprise described by the product-cycle theory. The free-standing company may be just a transitory phenomenon, it is suggested, called into being by speculative bubbles on the stock exchange, and doomed to failure in the long run. It has been further alleged that the nineteenth-century free-standing firm was a typical product of European capitalism, in that it lacked professional management, and so failed to exploit economies of scale and scope in the way that US multinationals subsequently did. The apparent decline of the free-standing firm after 1914 is cited in support of this view.

It is possible to challenge this interpretation on several grounds. First, product-cycle theory is not a general theory of foreign direct investment, but merely a generalization of specific post-war US experience. It takes the spread of overseas branch plants exploiting new technology and converts it into a general account of foreign investment. In fact there is no reason why, in general, a firm's competitive advantage has to derive from its domestic operations, and hence no reason why a firm's overseas operations have to resemble its domestic ones. There is,

I am grateful to Jean-François Hennart, whose paper at the International Economic History Congress, Milan, provoked this essay, and to Tony Corley, Geoff Jones, Harm Schröter, Keetie Sluyterman, and Mira Wilkins for comments on earlier drafts of this chapter.

therefore, no paradox about the free-standing company, and so no reason to allege a competitive weakness either. Secondly, although the free-standing form was far more conspicuous amongst European investors than amongst US investors, the existence of significant US free-standing investments in Mexico and South America belies the idea that the free-standing company is just an inferior culturally specific form of multinational firm. The free-standing firm appears to have been important wherever particular types of investment—notably the project-oriented investments typical of mining, agriculture, and utilities—needed to be organized. When there was a frontier to be explored, an imperialist drive to exploit it, and infrastructure to be created, the free-standing firm usually had an important role. During the age of high imperialism frontier activity was focused on Africa, Australia, and the American West. The first two were European spheres of influence, while the third frontier was, of course, internal to the USA. This is one simple reason why it is European firms rather than US firms which appear as leading free-standing foreign investors in the period 1870–1914.

The main sources of information used to establish the number of free-standing companies based in a particular country are company registrations and (less frequently) stock-exchange handbooks. These sources are not particularly informative about the nature of the company's operations, and certainly reveal little of its internal management structure. Until more archives have been located, the overall picture concerning the organization and management of these companies will remain difficult to discern. Although there are business histories which provide secondary source material on some of the larger and more successful companies, their coverage is too patchy to permit reliable generalizations. This deficiency of primary material has made it difficult to resolve theoretical controversies by a direct appeal to the evidence.

Even where the evidence is abundant, though, there is still a problem for business historians in reconciling their inductive approach, based on business records, with the deductive approach, based on theory.[2] Steps have already been taken to interpret the available evidence on free-standing companies using international business theory, notably by Mira Wilkins and Jean-François Hennart.[3] This chapter contends, however, following my own approach, that these interpretations are unduly speculative, and that the conclusions to which they point may be premature.[4] It develops an alternative schematic approach which, it is suggested, provides historians with a useful technique for future research.

The approach also helps to clear up a confusion about whether all free-standing firms are direct investors or not. According to Wilkins, they are.[5] At first sight this view seems quite reasonable, since the free-standing firm maintains an equity linkage between home and overseas countries. Equity is normally assumed to confer control, and the exercise of control over foreign operations is the defining characteristic of direct investment so far as international business theory is concerned. But then, in her infamous reference to 'brass nameplates', Wilkins goes on to argue that in many cases effective control was not exercised from the head office at all. It would appear that in these cases equity was not issued in, say, London because it was intended that control should be exercised from there, but for some other reason instead. But what might this other reason be, and what bearing does it have on whether the investment was direct or not?

The issue is clearly important because, as T. A. B. Corley has noted, the existence of an unrecorded concentration of managerial control in London, transmitted abroad through free-standing firms, would substantially alter the common perception of the declining competitiveness of the British economy after 1870.[6] If such control existed, then the statistics of British foreign direct investment should clearly be revised upwards, by reclassifying indirect portfolio investments as direct ones. But, if no such control existed, then the previous classification of these investments as indirect would seem to be correct, and there is no reason to re-evaluate the standard interpretation of declining competitiveness in post-1870 Britain.

Unfortunately the issue has been further clouded by Hennart's claim that the internalization theory of international business supports Wilkins's view.[7] He claims that direct investment occurs whether active managerial control is concentrated in London or not. Free-standing firms internalize equity markets, he asserts, and this is a sufficient condition for direct investment.

It is argued below that Hennart's interpretation of internalization theory is incorrect. It is suggested that a correct application of internalization theory would focus on the export of information or technology instead. It is shown that this approach identifies four main types of free-standing firm. Type A exports both information and technology, Type B exports information but not technology, Type C exports technology but not information, and Type D exports neither. Types A and B are direct investors but Types C and D are not. Types A and C are the most interesting from a theoretical perspective, and Type D is the least interesting of them all. Unfortunately, most of Hennart's examples relate to Type D.

The point of most immediate relevance to the historian is that Types C and D are typically embodied in wider business networks in which other kinds of firm—notably managing agencies—are involved. In these cases it is the other firms that supply the information and managerial expertise that the free-standing firm itself lacks. In this sense the term 'free-standing' is somewhat misleading, because, although the foreign operation is free-standing in the sense that it is independent of any domestic operation, it is not free-standing in the sense of being independent of other firms.[8] Indeed, the more 'free-standing' the firm is in one sense, it could be argued, the more likely it is to be embedded in the other sense. In this respect the term 'free-standing' represents a rather unfortunate choice of words.

Because Types C and D are not direct investors, they are not covered by conventional theories of the multinational firm. This suggests that conventional international business theory is too narrow a perspective from which to examine the free-standing firm. A broader perspective can, however, be developed, in which indirect investments may be analysed as well. This makes it possible to consider why individual free-standing firms are of a particular type, and why certain types may be concentrated in certain industries. This perspective is set out in the schematic analysis presented later on.

The Concept of Control

As indicated above, the defining characteristic of foreign direct investment is the exercise of control over local operations from a foreign headquarters. A free-standing firm that exercises no control from its headquarters cannot be a direct investor.

The significance of control for the foreign-direct-investment literature is illustrated in many ways. The treatment of multinational holding companies is one. Most previous empirical work has excluded holding companies from measures of foreign direct investment for the simple reason that they do not exercise significant control from headquarters. For similar reasons banks which hold a major proportion of the equity of a foreign company have not been regarded as foreign direct investors.[9] Because a bank is a corporation, it would be possible to regard firms owned by a bank as subsidiaries of the bank, but because of their 'hands-off' approach to the management of their equity investments banks are usually regarded as indirect portfolio investors instead. The emphasis on control is also reflected in the political economy of foreign direct investment, where debates usually centre on the 'branch plant syndrome'—the fear that control exercised at a distant headquarters may impinge adversely on the plant because of ignorance or simple disregard of local interests.[10]

Unfortunately, however, control is a potentially ambiguous concept because of the various stages through which the exercise of control can pass. Nominally, control is conferred by the shareholder's right to vote. Votes can in principle attach to any kind of share, but in practice they usually attach to equity. Some firms have various tiers of equity, though, with shares in a higher tier having more rights than others. Some equities may even have no votes at all.

Voting rights are to some extent residual rights, in the sense that they do not apply to matters on which the firm has already surrendered control through contractual commitment. The equity-holders cannot vote to suspend payments to bondholders in order to increase their dividends, for example. In some cases, indeed, bondholders may restrict the rights of equity-holders by giving themselves the right to manage instead. Some Chinese railway bonds, for example, conferred on bondholders the power to appoint the railway's general manager, in order to prevent the principal equity-holder—the Chinese government—from attempting to influence operational matters.[11] In other cases committees representing bondholders have taken over effective control of firms which have failed to meet their interest payments. These examples illustrate quite nicely the general point that possession of equity is not synonymous with the right to control.

Most shareholders simply vote on the election of board members, and on any capital reconstructions, mergers, etc. that may occur. In effect, they delegate day-to-day control to the chief executive, who in turn delegates to managerial subordinates, and so on. While control ultimately resides with the shareholders, therefore, *de facto* control over operations usually resides with managers on-site. Whatever instructions or guidance these managers are given, they can, in the short run at least, do exactly as they please. The really interesting question is how control is allocated within these limits. This is the key question for the organization of the free-standing firm, just as it is for any other kind of firm.

There is some confusion in the economic literature, however, about how far delegation really can occur. According to Frank Knight, control is always located where responsibility ultimately lies.[12] Financial responsibility clearly rests with the equity shareholders, since they bear the residual risks—that is, those risks that have not been shifted onto other people through the firm's contractual arrangements. (Creditors too bear risks, arising from the bankruptcy of the firm, but this complication is ignored.) Since financial responsibility rests mainly with the equity owners, Knight argues that they will collectively exercise control.

Collective control by the shareholders is obviously a myth, though. In practice shareholders normally trust the managers to take decisions on their behalf. If the shareholders cease to trust the managers, then they simply sell out, provided that there is a good secondary market for their shares. It is actually a quite different principle that governs where control is really located. Control is located where competence and integrity reside. Here competence refers to the ability to access and interpret relevant information about the firm's environment in order to make correct decisions. Integrity refers to the way that the decision-maker is trusted to keep the shareholders' interests at heart.

The question then becomes one of where the relevant competence is located. This may vary from one industry to another, and even from one stage of the firm's existence to another. If strategy is dominated by the timing, location, and design of an initial investment project, then the relevant competence may reside in one place (say the headquarters country), whereas, when strategy is dominated by efficient utilization of the completed investment, then the relevant competence may reside elsewhere (overseas, for example).

Hennart is implicitly a follower of Knight: he construes control as virtually inalienable by the equity-holder. Yet he also asserts that managerial competence was often located entirely overseas.[13] The inescapable conclusion is that in free-standing companies control resided where competence was lacking, violating the fundamental principle of efficient delegation enunciated above. The organization of free-standing firms was thus obviously very poor. Hennart's proposition therefore runs directly counter to the general stance of internalization theory—which he claims to support—that competitive pressures will select efficient organizational forms. It is interesting to observe, however, that his view accords quite closely with Alfred Chandler's view of British firms as being inefficient because they lacked professional management.[14] Hennart's analysis supports the view that enterprising individuals overseas were let down by the weakness and incompetence of the firm's headquarters in Europe. It remains an enigma, however, as to how the world's most sophisticated capital markets tolerated such apparently incompetent management structures for so long. It is little short of a miracle that any free-standing firms were successful, given the conditions suggested by Hennart's theory.

Hennart's dismissal of British managerial competence leads in nicely, though, to his alternative explanation of why free-standing firms were headquartered in London—namely, to gain access to its equity market. Hennart notes that free-standing firms procured capital in London in order to transfer it to another location where it would be used. Hennart's analysis of the advantages of London as a source of equity funds is quite standard and unobjectionable. What is objectionable is that he claims that equity raised through a company office there must be classified as direct investment, whereas in fact it could just as well be indirect investment instead. Hennart claims that the transfer of funds effected by the firm constitutes the internalization of an international market in capital and so, by appeal to internalization theory, turns the free-standing firm into a direct investor.

To an economic theorist there is something suspect about this argument. For a start, capital is a factor of production and not an intermediate product. According to internalization theory it is intermediate product markets that are internalized, and not factor markets. Factor markets link households with firms, and cannot normally be internalized, whereas intermediate product markets typically link one firm with another, and can be internalized quite easily.

Initial doubts over Hennart's approach are reinforced when it is recalled that the function of a market is coordination. Markets and hierarchies are alternatives because they are different methods of coordination. Coordination by a market involves reconciling the plans of the buyers and the sellers. Internalization brings the market within the firm, and allows management to draw up an integrated plan instead. This coordination process is quite distinct from the transfer of the intermediate product itself. The truck driver who actually takes the product from the upstream plant to the downstream plant is not a coordinator—the coordinator is the manager responsible for deciding how much product is to be transported in the first place.

In the case of the free-standing company, it is the equity market that determines how much equity capital will be subscribed to the firm. Coordination is effected by a market process that drives the equity price to its equilibrium level and thereby determines the amount of the funds that the firm can raise through a given issue of shares. The subsequent transfer of these funds overseas may be little more than a simple banking operation. Their transmission is merely a 'truck-driver' activity, in other words. All the key decisions have been taken by the participants in the external equity market. Indeed, Hennart's own reference to 'transfers' in the title of one of his papers conflicts with his contention elsewhere that it is *markets* and not mere *transfers* that are internalized by the firm.[15] The principles of internalization, as set out by Hennart himself, clearly indicate that the internal transfer of equity funds is not the same thing as the operation of an internal equity market.

Another way of expressing this criticism is to say that the free-standing company as described by Hennart functions rather like a special type of holding company. It is special in the sense that it normally holds only one investment in its portfolio. It has already been noted that holding companies are normally excluded from statistics of direct investment on the grounds that they do not exercise significant control. Yet even a normal kind of holding company can decide whether to reinvest the earnings from one project in a different project or not. In this sense a normal holding company has an internal capital market of sorts, though it is technically not an equity market. But a typical free-standing company does not even have this option because, having only one project, there is no other project to consider investing in. Its only decision is whether to distribute dividends or to reinvest profits instead. A free-standing company as described by Hennart therefore has even less of an internal market than a normal holding company would have.

Hennart does not claim that the London office of a free-standing company did absolutely nothing at all. He notes, quite correctly, that head offices fulfilled a useful function in selling equity to speculative investors through the use of prestigious addresses and the recruitment of prestigious names to the board. He recognizes that incorporation under English law enhanced the perceived security of the shareholders' claims against the company, whilst the depth of the London equity market conferred a liquidity on the shares far in excess of the real liquidity of the assets in which the funds were invested. Moreover, despite the limitations of Knight's approach, it remains true that a power of monitoring resided at head office, and reserve powers of intervention in a crisis were located there. But the literature on foreign direct investment has a well-developed code of practice, according to which such activities, even in total, do not constitute the exercise of active control. The role of London as a capital market is not sufficiently compelling to turn all of the free-standing firms located there into direct investors, as that term is commonly understood.

Multinationality and Direct Investment: Traps for the Unwary

A peculiar feature of the free-standing company is that the usual connection between foreign direct investment and the multinational enterprise breaks down. A multinational is conventionally defined as an enterprise that owns and controls activities in more than one country.[16] It tends to be assumed that a multinational enterprise necessarily engages in foreign direct investment, and that foreign direct investment is necessarily carried out by a multinational firm. The two concepts are therefore often employed in an interchangeable way. This is incorrect, however. The point at issue here concerns the second part of the proposition—namely, whether foreign direct investment is necessarily carried out by multinational firms: the first part of the proposition is considered later.

The foreign-direct-investment concept is concerned with the location of control relative to the activity being controlled. The multinationality concept, on the other hand, is concerned with whether two activities in different countries are under common control, wherever that control is located. Thus, if an activity located in Country *B*, which has no analogue in Country *A*, is actively controlled from a headquarters in Country *A*, then foreign direct investment occurs even though the firm is not a multinational enterprise.

This problem does not arise in the context of 'product-cycle' investments because control is normally exercised from the country in which production first begins. (Indeed, the traditional emphasis on product-cycle investments probably explains why the problem is so often overlooked.) The problem is a serious one in the case of the free-standing firm, however.

The problem can be overcome by classifying the headquarters as a separate activity. The firm then has activities in both *A* and *B*, both of which are controlled from *A*, and so foreign direct investment is now once again effected by a multinational firm. This approach involves an element of circularity, though, for *A*, as headquarters, now controls *A* as activity. The approach only works on the convention that each headquarters controls itself.

While a fudge of this kind may suit the empiricist, it creates theoretical difficulties. So far as internalization theory is concerned, it means that orders given by headquarters to affiliates become information flows that are internalized by the firm. Thus an internal market in information is created quite independently of any other markets that the firm may have internalized too. This then raises the question of where the coordination of this new internal market is located, and if this locus of coordination also qualifies as a separate activity as well. To justify the fudge, the condition must be imposed that all coordination of internal markets in information is effected by one of the activities that handles the information (normally the activity that sources the information, though this is not necessarily the case).

In the interests of clarity it is best to adopt the convention that being a headquarters is not an activity, so that a headquarters office is not an activity unless it performs some other function as well. The obvious candidate for an additional function is the provision of technological advice or some other intangible service. Such services have always played a crucial role in rationalizing the existence of multinational firms. Analysing an internal market in services of this kind does not raise the problems of circularity discussed above. The advantages of coordinating an export of services from the location that generates them are fairly self-evident, and can be explained in terms of conventional internalization theory.

TABLE 3.1. *Typology of free-standing firms*

Export of information	Export of technology	
	Yes	No
Yes	A multinational direct investor	B direct investor
No	C quasi-multinational	D —

Internalization theory therefore makes clear the importance of distinguishing an export of information, embodied in the exercise of control, and an export of technology embodied in a supply of intangible services. It is the interaction of information and technology flows that creates the typology of free-standing firms referred to above. This typology is formally presented in Table 3.1.

The Type A firm, that exports both information and technology, would, under the recommended conventions, qualify as both a direct investor and a multinational firm. It takes information from sources close to headquarters, synthesizes this with information received from the foreign plant, and encodes it in the form of orders sent overseas. It is a direct investor because it exercises control and a multinational firm because its headquarters qualifies as a separate activity.

In an earlier article, I discussed the Type A firm and argued that the typical firm of this type exported project management services.[17] These services related to the planning and execution of major infrastructure investments. Empirical support for this view was found in the concentration of free-standing companies in industries such as mining, railways, harbours, and oil, where infrastructure investment has a crucial role. The role of the headquarters, it was suggested, was to take an initial entrepreneurial idea—to sink a mine or to build a railway, for example—and refine it. The headquarters teamed up specialists on engineering, marketing, property law, and procurement to generate a detailed specification which enabled the project to be completed on time and within budget.

In terms of the more conventional interpretation of international business theory within a manufacturing context, a suitable analogy is between project management and research and development (R&D). While R&D produces a detailed specification for a new product or process, project management produces a detailed design for an infrastructure investment instead.

The analogy is not exact, of course, but the differences involved are, in fact, the very differences that explain the unusual features of the free-standing firm. For a start, the output of R&D has potentially global application, while the output of project management is specific to one particular site. This explains why R&D-intensive firms operate in many overseas locations, while free-standing firms normally operated in only one. Secondly, R&D is a continuous activity which feeds back information from regular operations to refine and improve the product or the process; by contrast, project management is a once-for-all activity because its output is embodied in equipment and infrastructure which is difficult to alter later on. This explains why R&D-intensive firms are long-lived firms with a continuing capacity for innovation, whereas free-standing firms were often short-lived firms whose innovative capacity dried up once their projects had been completed. Finally, R&D-intensive firms typically commence their feed back of information using their domestic operations, which are closest to the laboratory. Free-standing firms, however, could not feed back information so easily because their operations were usually tailored to the unique geography and resource endowments of the overseas location which had no exact parallel at home. The home-based skills used by the free-standing firms were the general skills possessed by the scientific community and exploited through consulting firms, rather than the specific skills found amongst employees in the domestic industry. This explains why R&D-intensive firms expand by replicating domestic operations overseas while free-standing firms did not.

The Type B firm exports information but not technology. It is a direct investor because the information exports are encoded in the form of orders, but it is not a multinational because its headquarters, being specialized entirely in coordination, does not qualify as a separate activity. The Type B firm illustrates quite nicely the kind of semantic paradox that a free-standing firm can create. A Type B firm is created when, for example, it is found easier to manage at a distance than to manage on the spot. A plantation on the West African coast may be managed from London because the local environment is too uncongenial for managers to work there for too long. Information generated by the London commodity markets may also be of greater strategic importance to the firm than information obtained in Africa itself.

To understand firms of Types C and D it is necessary to consider the first part of the proposition with which this section began—namely, that a multinational enterprise is necessarily a foreign direct investor. The issue concerns whether the exercise of control can be externalized or not. It has already been shown that control can be delegated. The managing agency system, described below, demonstrates that control can in fact be delegated to independent agents, provided that a contract with suitable performance incentives can be drawn up. Of course, the owners still retain residual rights not to renew the contract (indeed, they may also have rights to terminate the agreement if certain minimum performance norms are not met). The externalization of control raises the possibility that a company might be a multinational owner, in the sense of owning outright activities in several different countries, without exercising multinational control. It would not be a true multinational, for this by definition both owns and controls, but it could be described as a quasi-multinational instead.

The Type C firm exports technology or project management services, but without the responsibility for coordinating them. The coordination is arranged by consultants or managing agents who have an arm's-length relationship with the firm. It is not a direct investor, and is only a quasi-multinational firm. There is evidence to suggest that a number of Type C firms were actively promoted by managing agents—particularly those operating in Asia—as a device for expanding their operations without diluting the partners' control of the agencies themselves.

The Type D firm exports neither technology nor information. Its role is basically to own overseas assets which other people manage. The reputation of the independent management is crucial to this arrangement. The logic of it also hinges on the fact that there may be little that the management can do to influence the performance of the activity, apart from carrying out routine operations in a professional manner. The value of the asset—such as an opencast mine—may be subject to economic fluctuations according to the state of business confidence, and all that is required is a large and diversified group of investors who are prepared to tolerate the speculative exposure that such assets invariably create.

The Type D firm is neither a direct investor nor even a quasi-multinational firm. Unfortunately it seems to be this type of firm on which Hennart places the greatest emphasis. He may be correct in his judgement that this type of firm is statistically well represented in the population of free-standing firms, but all this really shows is that there are a large number of firms which have been classified as free-standing which are of very limited economic significance. They are of limited theoretical interest since they are merely a device for marketing equity in risky projects, and of limited historical interest since the real coordination was done elsewhere—by the people who promoted the firms in fact, and the agents who managed the operations on a regular basis. It has also been suggested that Type D firms may have been 'shell' companies for tax avoidance, or even devices for 'laundering' illegal funds. Firms of this kind have existed ever since company law afforded loopholes which could be exploited in this way; it would seem rather disappointing if the study of free-standing firms were to degenerate into a study of such operations, when there are more important issues connected with the other types of firm that warrant immediate investigation.

Hennart himself seems unaware of the distinction between direct investment and multinationality in his application of internalization theory to the free-standing firm. The distinction is important for his purposes, though, because internalization is first and foremost a theory of the multinational firm. It explains why two distinct activities in two different countries are brought under common control. In analysing the Type D company, Hennart identifies the head office as one of the firm's activities, because he considers the sale of equity to be an important function so far as his theory is concerned. In this way Hennart turns the Type D firm into a multinational. According to Hennart, this head office is set up on the initiative of individuals overseas, who deploy it to access funds that could not be obtained through local equity sales. In many cases this account of Type D firms' origins may well be accurate. But it implies that the overseas firm is actually making the direct investment in the home country rather than the other way round. Foreigners or expatriates are investing in a registered London office, for example, in order to procure additional funds. They control this office from overseas. What Hennart actually explains, in terms of his own approach, therefore, is foreign direct investment in Britain by overseas firms, to the value of the office premises that they use. He employs the concept of multinationality in such a way that he generates, not a large British direct investment overseas, as Wilkins claims, but a small overseas direct investment in the London office property market instead. Such direct investment almost certainly did occur, but is this what the free-standing firm is really supposed to be all about?

A Schematic Analysis of the Free-Standing Firm

To account for the behaviour of all the firms identified by Wilkins, a theory is required which encompasses both direct and indirect investment. Since the theory of direct investment has been discussed at length above, and the theory of indirect investment is not a controversial area, a synthesis of this kind is easy to effect. It appears, indeed, that this is exactly the kind of synthesis that Hennart is striving to achieve. He is correct to surmise that considerations of financing and control need to be integrated to provide a complete account of the free-standing firm. Hennart asks all the right questions, and, although some of his answers are unsatisfactory, he also provides constructive insights as to how the integration can be carried out.

The approach taken here is to embed the analysis of the free-standing company within a more general view of the imperial system of which it formed such an important part. The free-standing company is viewed as part of a larger international business system, in which other types of company—notably the managing agency—also played a role. Free-standing companies of the type emphasized by Hennart—which were not direct investors in the normal sense of the word—appear in this model as adjuncts to the managing agencies. They allowed the more reputable agencies to raise large sums of money on the security of relatively illiquid assets. This was an alternative to floating shares in the agencies themselves, which would have created large high-risk firms and would have led the partners in those agencies to lose their overall control (as noted above).

The concept of imperialism used in this analysis is an economic rather than a political one. It certainly embraces the classic forms of imperialism, such as the British in India, but it includes the USA in Latin America too. There is a widespread view that imperialism is a specifically European vice, but from an economic perspective the subsidization of a pro-Western government in a 'banana republic' has much the same consequence for foreign investment as overt political control by a colonial power. The analysis therefore not only addresses the role of British and Dutch investments in Asia and Africa, say, but US investments in Mexico too. The distinctive features of European investment, as compared to US investment, are explained within the model; they are not prejudged at the outset.

The analysis begins by distinguishing three different types of international flow (a fourth type is introduced later). The 'imperial template' suggests that an appropriate illustration of resource flow would be a raw material which is exported from a colonial mine to a smelter in the home country. (To apply the model properly, the term 'colony' needs to be interpreted very broadly, to include not only self-governing dominions but any country that is heavily dependent on overseas trade and capital for its development). A flow of this kind is illustrated in Fig. 3.1. The conventions used in this and the subsequent figures are explained in detail elsewhere.[18] The upstream production plant—i.e. the mine—is denoted Y_1 and the downstream production plant—i.e. the smelter—is denoted Y_2. For future reference, the ship in which the mineral ore is transported is also shown, indicated by *V*. It is a convention that production plants and physical equipment such as ships are noted by squares and that the product flows that link them are indicated by double lines.

The export of mineral ore is coordinated by a flow of information. This information flow informs the decisions which govern the quantity of material that is shipped at any one time. Information flows are indicated by single lines in the figure. Unlike the material flow, which is one way, the information flow is two way, as indicated by the arrows pointing in each direction.

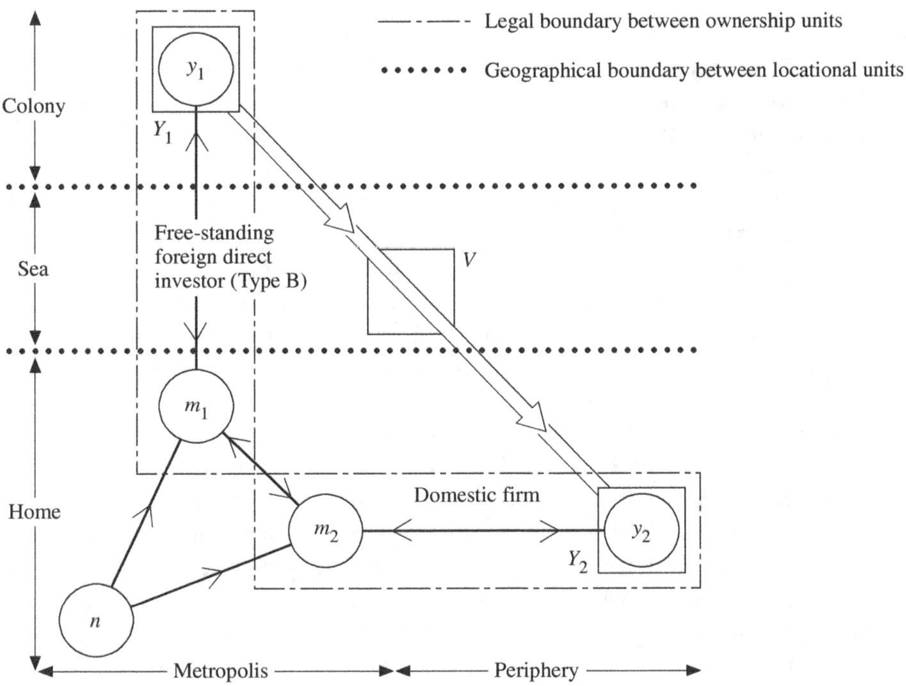

Fig 3.1. Intermediation in the coordination of a raw material export flow
Source: M. Casson, *Information and Organization* (Oxford, 1997), 231.

Information is processed by individuals; individuals are indicated by circles to distinguish them from production plants. When an individual is based at a plant—as in the case of the production managers y_1 and y_2—then they are shown as circles within the corresponding squares. The coordination of product flow is not necessarily effected by direct communication between the managers of the plants, however. When modelling information flow it is crucial to recognize that information flow is often intermediated by third parties. If the same firm owned both plants, so that the product flow was internalized within a vertically integrated multinational, then both production managers might well report to a single intermediator—namely, the senior production manager at headquarters.

The free-standing firms were not of this type, however. When a free-standing firm exported to its home country, then the product was usually sold to an independent local firm for further processing. In this case the intermediation typically involved two parties who were linked by a market transaction. This is the case illustrated in the figure. The intermediator m_1 (an import merchant at the free-standing firm's headquarters in the home country) negotiates with the intermediator

m_2 (his 'opposite number'), who purchases on behalf of the smelter firm and who is typically based at the smelter firm's headquarters. Once these two merchants have fixed the price through their negotiations, the quantity information is transmitted back to their respective production managers. The mine manager y_1 sets an appropriate level of output, and the smelter manager prepares to adjust his own output ready for when the consignment of ore arrives.

The figure also shows the location of the various plants and people. In particular it shows that both intermediators are located in the home country. Intuitively this captures the tendency for intermediation to be concentrated in the metropolitan centre in the home country, where organized markets for products are most likely to exist.

The two-way flow of information between y_1 and m_1 does not, of itself, identify m_1 as being the headquarters, since it does not indicate which direction of flow is the most important. The importance of m_1 relative to y_1 is determined by the fact that m_1 also has access to the supply of news n which y_1 lacks. The managers m_1 and m_2 are agglomerated in the metropolis not only so that they negotiate face to face (and avail themselves of organized markets), but also because they get privileged access to the news. To some extent, of course, they are themselves a source of this news because they are helping to form the prices of products which are later reported to others. But by agglomerating in a locality that has specialized information workers, such as journalists, they gain priority access to information collected more widely than their own social contacts would permit.

It is because m_1 can combine information on overseas production conditions obtained from y_1 with the general news n that he is better placed than y_1 to take decisions. The manager m_1 encodes his synthesis in instructions given to y_1, rather than the other way round, because m_1 has superior access to information. This is why authority runs from m_1 to y_1 and why m_1 is therefore the headquarters of the firm.

Because control over colonial operations is based in the metropolis, the firm is a direct investor, but because the headquarters does nothing but coordinate, it is not a true multinational firm. It therefore corresponds to the Type B firm described above. This is the type that illustrates the apparent anomaly of the free-standing firm most clearly.

Besides the flow of materials and the flow of information, the flow of equity finance is also distinguished. Equity finance is the third of the flows mentioned above. Such flows are identified in Fig. 3.2 using the notation of a spring. This rather unusual notation is used to suggest that the equity holders buffer the firm against fluctuations in its profits. They insure the firm's creditors by absorbing all shocks to the profit

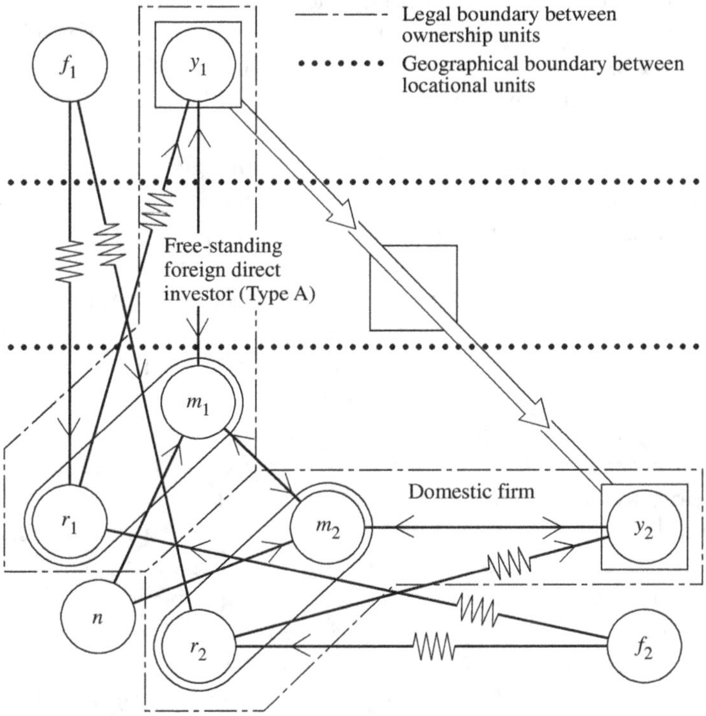

Fig. 3.2. Intermediation in financial flows
Source: Casson, *Information and Organization*, 233.

stream through changes in their dividend stream or through changes in the value of their undistributed reserves.

The ultimate source of equity finance is individual savers—particularly those of a speculative disposition—who may live either at home or overseas. They prefer to channel their funds into assets using companies incorporated in the metropolis because of the greater security and liquidity that this affords, as explained above. Funds are therefore transmitted to the metropolis for this purpose. The managers at the headquarters incorporate themselves into a legal entity with limited liability by promoting the firms r_1 and r_2. The funds collected from the sale of equity are then channelled to the plants. In the case of the smelter, they are channelled to a peripheral region of the home country where heavy industry is located—near to the coast and close to a major coalfield, for example. In the case of the mine they are simply channelled overseas.

It can be seen that each headquarters therefore intermediates not only in the coordination of the intermediate product flow but also in the flow of equity too. Such a dual role is not inevitable, but it can be seen that the two types of intermediation are related. It is Hennart's contribution to spot this relationship, even if he does not keep the two forms of intermediation sufficiently distinct in his own analysis.

By setting the model up in this way, the mine and the smelter are put into roughly symmetric positions. Both are engaged in the raw material market, and both are recipients of capital raised in the metropolis. They are both constituents of the empire too. They just happen to be in different countries within the empire. This demonstrates that the free-standing firm which owns the mine may well be an international analogue of the domestic firm that owns the smelter. The arrangements relating to the former may be deemed to have evolved directly from the arrangements that related to the latter, as explained below.

This suggests that, even though the product-cycle model does not apply in the physical sense that domestic plants are replicated overseas, it may apply in the organizational sense that patterns of intermediation, exemplified by the free-standing company, that have proved themselves in a domestic context are later used for the organization of overseas activity. Just as the bureaucratic structures of post-Second World War US investment may be traced back to the managerial revolution begun by the transcontinental US railroads, so the lean and flexible structures found in the London-based free-standing companies may be traced back to the speculative enterprises used to finance the early Industrial Revolution in Britain.[19]

Maritime Operations and the Managing Agency

No account of the imperial system would be complete without some discussion of maritime activity. Voyages of discovery played a crucial role in the foundation of the Spanish, Portuguese, French, and Dutch empires, whilst a combination of the search for a northern passage to the Orient and organized piracy created the early momentum for the British Empire. Before the Industrial Revolution the maritime sector was instrumental in developing a consumer society in Europe, based on the conspicuous consumption of imported luxuries, whilst later on—during the years of the scramble for Africa, for example—it brought the raw materials to feed the heavy industries of Europe.

Of particular relevance to the free-standing company is the way that the joint stock principle of finance developed in the maritime sector, both in the ownership of ships and in the financing of voyages. For example, one-sixty-fourth shares in ships were widely traded by the sixteenth century.[20] One way in which a shipping company can be factored into the imperial system is shown in Fig. 3.3. The vessel V is

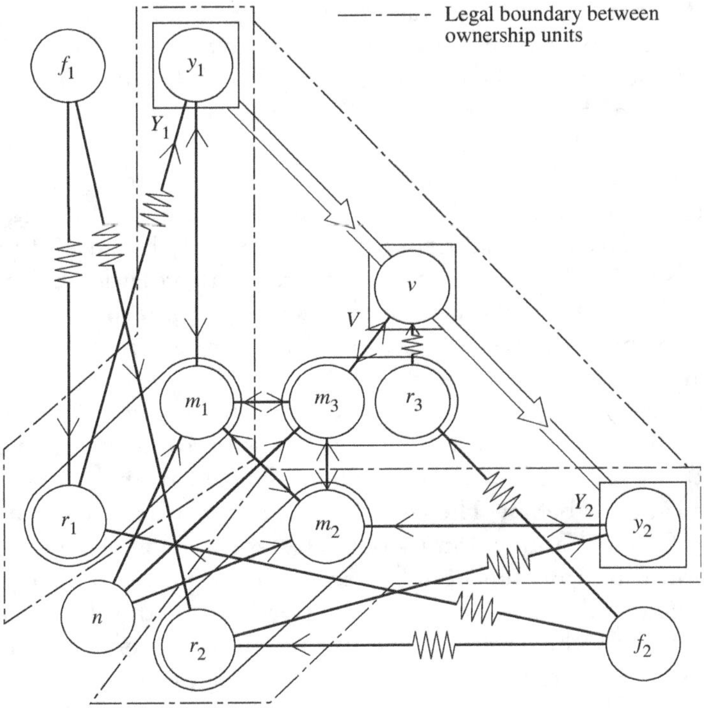

Fig. 3.3. The role of shipping firms
Source: Casson, *Information and Organization*, 235.

controlled by the master, or captain, v, who coordinates the arrangements for the voyage with the manager of the shipping company m_3. The manager is appointed by the director of the company r_3, who controls the equity funds subscribed by the shareholders f_2. As shown, only domestic shareholders own the shipping company, although there is no reason in principle why colonial investors could not be involved as well.

The shipping company r_3 occupies a line of intermediate position on the spectrum between the free-standing direct investor r_1 and the domestic company r_2. The company is domestically financed, like r_2, but its asset base is not confined to domestic territories in the sense that the ship it owns can sail to foreign ports. In so far as the ship is domestically registered, however, the company technically remains a local investor like r_2. If, however, the ship were foreign registered, in order to use cheaper labour, for example, then the company would technically become a free-standing direct investor like r_1.

In fact, the organization of maritime activity did not evolve in quite this way, though. Instead of having a few shipping companies with substantial fleets, each ship was typically organized as a separate company in order to control the financial risks involved. It neutralized the 'domino' effect which the loss of one ship could have on the finances of other ships in the owners' fleet. Ships have always been amongst the largest, most indivisible, and most risky assets in which people can invest. Merchant ships are floating containers, and economies of scale encourage them to be built as large as possible compatible with access to port facilities. Financial risks are great not only because of the risks of loss at sea, but because charter rates are highly volatile on account of the durable nature of the fleet and sensitivity of international trade to the state of business confidence, particularly where raw material shipments are concerned.

With many small shipping companies, each owning a single vessel, it became quite common for the owners of a ship to vest the management of it with an agent. The agent, for example, could arrange to charter out the ship on their behalf. The agent would be rewarded by some combination of salary and commission. The agent had to enjoy a good reputation for competence and integrity, however, because he personally carried only a very small proportion of the financial risks associated with the vessel's operations. To make efficient use of a specialized ship agent's time, it was necessary for an agent to manage several ships. This, of course, allowed agents to accumulate enormous expertise. To capitalize on this—in other words, to exploit the economies of scope afforded by their general knowledge of the shipping trade—they could take on junior partners to expand their agency, provided, of course, that they could also procure the finance to buy more ships. This provided an inducement for reputable agents to promote the building of ships (or in some cases the acquisition of second-hand ships), incorporating a new company for each additional ship, and inviting wealthy speculators to subscribe equity. Although the historical details are sometimes rather sketchy, it seems clear that the subscribers often included merchants who were interested in chartering the vessels for themselves.

The intelligence gathered by the captains of these ships would inform the managing agents of business opportunities overseas—in particular, opportunities for procuring larger return cargoes by developing mines, plantations, and so forth. Individual shipping routes tended to be highly competitive because, unless they were controlled by a charter monopoly that was effectively policed, vessels could easily be switched onto routes where existing operators were enjoying profits higher than elsewhere. Vertical integration into the procurement of export cargoes made little sense, therefore, when the arrival of ships to collect the cargoes could not be accurately predicted, where the export products were difficult to store, and where it was costly to vary the rate of production at short notice. It was far better to ship the exports on the first available ship than to try to coordinate production and sailings within the constraints of using only vessels from a particular owner's fleet.

Managing agents seeking to develop an export trade would therefore find it advantageous to promote a company that invested in a mine or plantation quite independently of the shipping companies that it might otherwise control. By analogy with the shipping company, the mining company or plantation company would be promoted on the basis that management would be effected by the agency rather than by the company itself. The shareholders would have the residual right to take the management of the company out of the agent's hands if it performed persistently badly, but it was anticipated that such action was most unlikely to occur.

The resulting situation is illustrated in Fig. 3.4. The separation between ownership and management effected by the managing agency system is shown schematically by separating the plant or vessel,

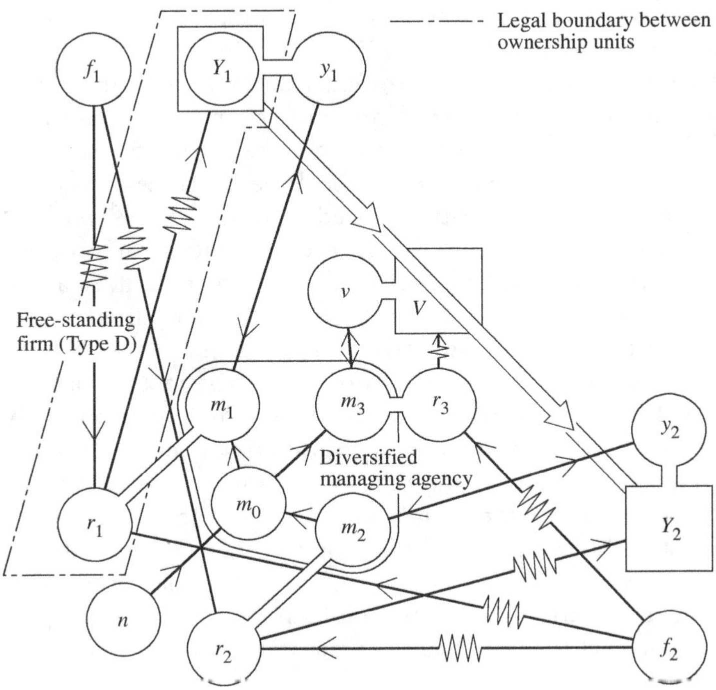

Fig. 3.4. The managing agency and the promotion of free-standing firms
Source: Casson, *Information and Organization*, 237.

denoted by a square, from the individual manager of the plant, or captain of the vessel, denoted by a circle. The managers and the captains are under the control of intermediators in the metropolis, just as before, but these intermediators now work for a managing agency whose activities are coordinated by a senior partner m_0. This senior partner is networked to the major private sources of news, and takes policy decisions based on this news which are communicated to the more junior partners who deal with the individual firms. The owners of these firms—the investors f_1 and f_2—channel their funds through the company headquarters r_1, r_2, and r_3 into the plant and equipment Y_1, Y_2, and V which provides their main collateral. As Hennart has noted, the highly speculative nature of this collateral explains why equity finance rather than bond finance is normally required. The 'downside' of these investments is so large—their entire value could be wiped out—that there is no effective way of protecting ordinary creditors such as bondholders.

The separation between the ownership of the company and the management of its headquarters is shown by separating the two circles involved. The circle r_1 represents the owners acting as a corporate body, while the circle m_1 indicates the independent agent to whom they have delegated control. The line enclosing them indicates that they are linked: the managing agency and the promotion of free-standing firms by a management contract. The shape of the line is different from that in Fig. 3.3 because the agent is no longer an employee of the firm.

The separation between ownership and control explains the lack of control which Hennart so eloquently describes in his discussion of the Type D firm. The registered office of the Type D firm is indeed merely a conduit through which the capital raised from f_1 and f_2 is transferred to the overseas plant Y_1. This is because coordination of product flow, drawing on the news n, is being effected by the merchant m_1 and not by the registered office r_1. Management has been externalized by the contract between the free-standing firm and its agent.

The free-standing firm is not a direct investor in this case because control has been placed in other hands. It is possible, though, that the managing agency may qualify as a multinational firm. This multinational dimension of managing agency operations has received little analytical attention so far. It is clear, however, that if the managing agency m_1 also holds responsibility for the management of the mine Y_1, so that the manager, y_1, is an employee of the same firm, then multinational operations are in principle involved. The agency is internalizing the market for information between m_1 and y_1, just as the Type B multinational did before.

It goes without saying, of course, that the mine and the smelter used in these examples have been chosen only for purposes of illustration.

The model applies to other industries too. It may, for example, help to explain Scottish investments in the Indian jute industry, and English investments in Brazilian agriculture. In both these cases managing agents appear to have played an important role in a major export trade. The link with managing agents is not ubiquitous, though. It is certainly the case, as Hennart has argued, that some free-standing firms in mining were quite unconnected with managing agencies based in London. It is well known, for example, that many freelance concession-holders took up temporary residence in London to attempt to float companies there—though often with little success. Similarly, not all managing agencies originated in the maritime sector: many of them were ordinary merchants or factors who diversified out of commodity trading when the innovation of the telegraph and liner shipping rendered their short-term speculations obsolete. The picture given here is for expository purposes only; it is not claimed to portray a situation that is fully representative of free-standing firms as a whole, or any given export trade in particular.

The Role of Technological Expertise

It must be recognized that even the most speculative investors are unlikely to subscribe shares in an asset such as a mine or smelter, and particularly one that is overseas, unless they are reasonably confident that the technology exists to operate it properly. In the case of underground mine workings, for example, it is important to understand the geology of the seams, to arrange the shafts to provide adequate ventilation, and to install pumping equipment of appropriate capacity. Specialized scientific knowledge must be obtained from geologists, mining engineers, and mechanical engineers to ensure compliance with these requirements. The source of this technological expertise is indicated in Figure 3.5 by the triangle in the bottom left-hand corner labeled t. The flow of technological knowledge is indicated by a single line with an asterisk along it. It is a single line rather than a double line to indicate that it is a flow of information rather than materials, whilst the asterisk is used to indicate that it is not ordinary coordinating information such as prices and quantities that is involved, but know-how instead.

The know-how is shown as being supplied to the companies themselves rather than to the managing agencies. This is because the information is vital to reassure the shareholders. The technological assessments are more in the public domain than the private one; summaries may well appear in the company prospectus, for example. In the early stages of the venture, therefore, while the company is being

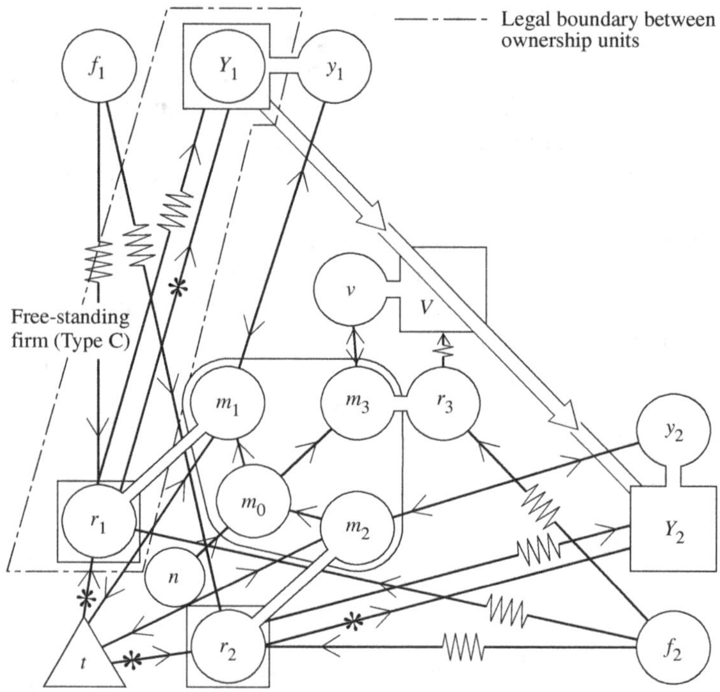

Fig. 3.5. Technology and the supply of project management services by the free-standing firm
Source: Casson, *Information and Organization*, 239.

launched, and immediately afterwards, the headquarters of the company may well have an active role to play. But once the innovations have been completed, and the funds supplied by the shareholders have been allocated to their purposes, the headquarters may assume a purely passive role.

The technology acquired by the firm is not purely for public consumption, however. It will be passed on to the overseas operation too. A synthesis of the various kinds of expertise required by a complicated project qualifies as an activity in its own right. A square has therefore been drawn around the circle that represents the company to indicate that, so far as internalization theory is concerned, a proper activity is now under way in the home country. The input, synthesis, and onward transmission of the expertise remain coordinated by the agent m_1, however.

In this case the free-standing firm is of Type C. It is a quasi-multinational because its headquarters generates exports of technology embodied in project-management services. Because all coordination is in the hands of the managing agency, however, no direct investment is involved. As indicated earlier, the export of technology may cease once the initial project is complete, in which case the firm becomes Type D, as illustrated in Fig. 3.4.

The final possibility is that the free-standing firm is actually akin to a conventional multinational, with the qualification that it just happens to lack domestic operations similar to its foreign ones. Like a conventional multinational, it exports technology from the country in which it is headquartered, and controls its own operations too. This is the case of the Type A firm shown in Fig. 3.6. Because the internal structure of the firm is slightly more complicated than in the previous cases, the firm has been abstracted from its environment to give the diagram greater clarity.

Because the Type A firm is so conventional, it fits not only with internalization theory but with John Dunning's eclectic theory too.[21] Hennart has claimed, in the light of his own analysis, that free-standing firms did not have ownership advantages of the kind described by Dunning, but Type A firms clearly do. Certainly their ability to convert technological expertise into project-management services can be construed as an ownership advantage (or, equivalently, a competitive

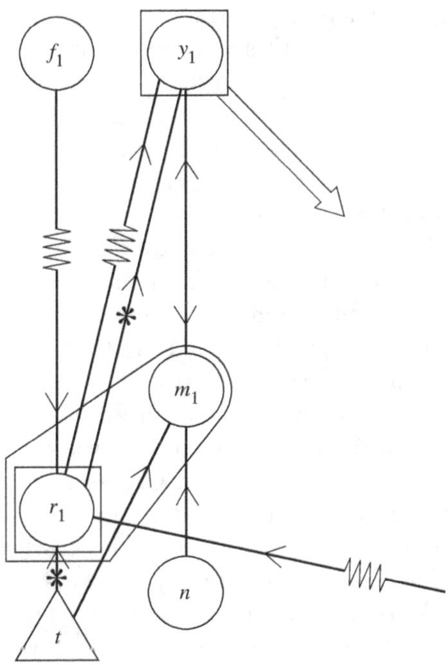

Fig. 3.6. The Type A multinational direct investor
Source: Casson, *Information and Organization*, 241.

advantage) in Dunning's terms. This underlines the fact that Hennart's analysis overstates the differences between free-standing firms and conventional ones. It is not necessary to reject Dunning's eclectic theory in order to explain the free-standing firm, but only the product-cycle theory. Dunning's theory can be criticized on other grounds, but it does not seem to be at fault in this particular case.[22] It is worth noting that much of the technological expertise available in London during the nineteenth century had been accumulated in the operations of domestic companies such as the one portrayed in the figures above. The Newcastle coal industry, the Shropshire iron industry, and the Birmingham engineering industry, for example, all incubated pragmatic expertise which gave birth to the professional consultancy firms on which the free-standing companies drew. Because many such regional industries were financed, at least in part, using London funds, these domestic firms may be seen as progenitors of the free-standing firms in respect of both technology and capital. The organizational methods incubated in the shipping industry were refined in domestic industries such as coal and iron before they were exported to the colonies in the nineteenth century by the free-standing firms.

So far as the free-standing firm is concerned, this analysis suggests three things. First, that the free-standing firm forms part of a system predicated on arm's-length contracts rather than vertical integration in international trade. It is this that explains why, in the example discussed, the mining company and the smelting company are not just different divisions of a multinational enterprise of a conventional type.

The second is that the separation of ownership and management effected by the managing agency system is designed to distribute the enormous risks involved in the process of colonial and imperial development as widely as possible. It avoids concentrating too many large and speculative assets in the hands of the same firm. Thus any difficulties encountered in one area of the managing agency's operations—a particular colony, or a particular export trade—cannot bring the whole company down and disrupt the entire process of imperial development.

Thirdly, despite the contractual separation of ownership and management, quite a lot of management activity was carried out in the colonial metropolis, even though it did not necessarily take place in the headquarters of the firms that the agents managed. A great deal of trading activity was managed in London on a day-to-day basis because of the importance of accessing commodity markets—for example, to hedge commercial risks by buying futures. Access to the financial markets was also important not merely for raising equity finance, but for the important function of raising and then arranging for the discounting of the bills of exchange by which trade was financed.

Summary and Conclusions

This chapter has claimed that the classification of all free-standing companies as foreign direct investors is unsound. The way in which researchers trawl through data on company registrations in search of free-standing firms makes it inevitable that a rather varied assortment of firms will be caught in the net. It is hardly surprising that the resulting firms turn out to be of different types. Labelling them all simply as free-standing firms tends to obscure important differences between them that merit further study. Following the pioneering work of Wilkins and Hennart, it therefore seems natural that the next step should be careful differentiation of types and a close examination of each type.

To understand these types it is important to realize that the seemingly straightforward concepts of foreign direct investment and multinational enterprise present a semantic minefield for the unwary researcher. The concept of foreign direct investment relates to the *location* of control, whereas the concept of multinational enterprise is concerned with the *breadth* of control. It is much more important to keep these issues distinct when analysing free-standing firms than it is when analysing the more familiar type of product-cycle investment.

Rather than stretch these concepts to breaking point in an effort to clarify the nature of the free-standing firm, this chapter has pursued an alternative strategy based upon a schematic technique. This technique is well equipped to analyse the internal organization of the free-standing firm, which is an issue of considerable historical interest. It also serves to embed the free-standing firm in a wider context. In this context the boundaries of the firm emerge quite naturally from the partitioning of ownership within a complex system. This partitioning generates other complementary types of firm as well. The overwhelming historical evidence for the existence of these complementary types suggests that the analysis is basically along the right lines.

The schematic technique relates material resource flows to information flows, technology flows, and financial flows. It also highlights the importance of intermediation, particularly in information flows. The comparative advantages of different locations in the intermediation of information flows explains the location of control, and hence bears specifically on the direct investment issue. It explains, for example, why the headquarters of a free-standing company is typically in the home country and not the colony, and therefore explains why the home country is a direct investor in the colony and not the other way round. The comparative advantage of different locations in the intermediation of finance explains why equity is sold from the home country and not in the colony, and hence why the registered office of the company is in the home country too.

The home country, in other words, normally has a comparative advantage in both forms of intermediation. A key reason for this is that the home country has many organized markets. These markets are supported by a large amount of face-to-face contact between merchants, and this is in turn associated with economies of agglomeration in a metropolitan area. A conventional firm based in the metropolis will intermediate both information and finance from a registered office which is also its operational headquarters. The distinctive types of investments in which free-standing companies were involved, however, often favoured the separation of these intermediating functions.

The fundamental rationale for this special type of institutional specialization can be found in the economies of scope afforded by the information available in the metropolis. The European Empires of Britain and Holland were based on global trading systems coordinated by market rather than by hierarchy. International trade was coordinated not by vertically integrated enterprises with a single locus of control, but by disintegrated enterprises linked through the metropolitan markets. The price information used for coordination purposes was basically common knowledge to those participating in the markets. By combining this information with information received from explorers and adventurers in the colonies it was easy for entrepreneurial merchants to identify profitable opportunities overseas. To avoid the diseconomies of managing a large diversified conglomerate, the most entrepreneurial merchants chose to establish each new project as a profit centre, bringing in consultants at critical stages, such as start-up, temporarily to strengthen their management team. Moreover, to facilitate the financing of their expansion, they chose not to issue equity in a conglomerate company but to adopt the principle of raising mortgages on the assets associated with each project. Because of the highly speculative nature of the investments, however, it was deemed prudent to raise the mortgage using equity rather than fixed-interest debt. Given the popular euphoria over imperial expansion in the late nineteenth century, there was little difficulty in raising funds in this way provided that endorsements from reputable non-executive directors and consultant engineers could be obtained. Indeed, many entrepreneurs, given their superior knowledge, may have been quite sceptical about the long-term value of these investments. They recognized, however, that under the terms of their management contract their short-term returns were secure, and that, even if the business failed later, the equity-holders, unlike bond-holders, were not creditors and so could not forcibly liquidate the investment.

The German Empire was less reliant on disintegrated firms and on metropolitan markets, with foreign investments being perceived much more as elements in an organized strategy for imperial self-sufficiency. The greater dependence on integrated structures may explain the relative paucity of free-standing firms in Germany.

It is quite misleading to perceive British free-standing firms, with their lean management structures, as symptomatic of the weaknesses of unprofessional family capitalism. Free-standing firms were a key component—though not, in themselves, the driving force—in a dynamic imperial system.

Within these systems control resided where competence lay, namely with the merchant entrepreneurs. If there is a question mark about the system, it lies perhaps in the question of whether competence was always linked with integrity too. The system of management contracts created potential moral hazards, and it is possible that some of the managing agents placed short-term gains ahead of long-term viability. The system was also heavily committed to the principle of vertical disintegration in trade. As production and transport technology changed, and the imperial dream lost political legitimacy, the system as a whole began to collapse. Weaknesses in the free-standing companies were not the cause of this collapse. The companies went into decline because they were specifically adapted to the needs of the system, and the system itself was no longer well adapted to altered economic circumstances in the aftermath of the First World War.

NOTES

1. R. Vernon, 'International Investment and International Trade in the Product Cycle', *Quarterly Journal of Economics*, 80 (1966), 190–207.
2. T. A. B. Corley, 'Firms and Markets: Towards a Theory of Business History', *Business and Economic History*, 22 (Fall 1993), 54–66.
3. M. Wilkins, 'The Free-Standing Company, 1870–1914: An Important Type of British Foreign Direct Investment', *Economic History Review*, 2nd ser., 41 (May 1988), 259–82; Wilkins, Chapter 1 herein; J.-F. Hennart, 'International Financial Capital Transfers: A Transaction Cost Framework', *Business History*, 36 (Jan. 1994), 51–70; Hennart, Chapter 2 herein.
4. M. Casson, 'Institutional Diversity in Overseas Enterprise: Explaining the Free-Standing Company', *Business History*, 36 (Oct. 1994), 95–108.
5. Wilkins, 'The Free-Standing Company' and Chapter 1 herein.
6. T. A. B. Corley, 'Foreign Direct Investment and British Economic Deceleration 1870–1914', in Hans Pohl (ed.), *Transnational Investment from the 19th Century to the Present, Zeitschrift für Unternehmensgeschichte*, (Occasional papers, 81; Stuttgart, 1994), 153–72.
7. Hennart, 'International Financial Capital Transfers'; J.-F. Hennart, 'Free-Standing Firms and the Internalisation of Markets for Financial Capital: A Response to Casson', *Business History*, 36 (Oct. 1994), 118–31; Hennart, Chapter 2 herein.

8. S. D. Chapman, *Merchant Enterprise in Britain* (Cambridge, 1992); G. Jones, 'Organization and Strategy of British-Based International Business before and after 1914', unpublished paper (University of Reading, 1995).
9. There are exceptions to this. See, for example, G. Jones (ed.), *Banks as Multinationals* (London, 1990).
10. Indeed, as pointed out by Mira Wilkins in Chapter 1, most of the multinational-enterprise, foreign-direct-investment literature has dealt with manufacturing companies.
11. R. W. Huenemann, *The Dragon and the Iron Horse: The Economics of Railroads in China, 1876–1937* (Cambridge, Mass., 1984), 58.
12. F. H. Knight, *Risk, Uncertainty, and Profit* (Boston, 1921).
13. Hennart, 'Free-Standing Firms'.
14. A. D. Chandler, *Scale and Scope* (Cambridge, Mass., 1990).
15. Hennart, 'International Financial Capital Transfers'.
16. P. J. Buckley and M. C. Casson, *The Future of Multinational Enterprise* (London, 1976).
17. Casson, 'Institutional Diversity'.
18. M. Casson, 'Internalisation Theory and Beyond', in P. J. Buckley (ed.), *New Horizons in International Business: Research Priorities for the 1990s* (Aldershot, 1991), 4–27; M. Casson and H. Cox, 'Modelling Interfirm Networks', University of Reading Discussion Papers in Economics, No. 278 (1994) (a revised version of which is in M. Casson, *The Organization of International Business* (Aldershot, 1995), ch. 3); M. Casson and I. Paniccia, 'Business Networks and Industrial Districts: A Comparison of Northern Italy and South Wales', University of Reading Discussion Papers in Economics, No. 301 (1995).
19. For the formal analogy, see Casson and Paniccia, 'Business Networks'.
20. W. R. Scott, *The Constitution and Finance of English, Scottish and Irish Joint-Stock Companies to 1720*, i. *The General Development of the Joint-Stock System to 1720* (Cambridge, 1912).
21. J. H. Dunning, *International Production and the Multinational Enterprise* (London, 1981).
22. M. Casson, 'General Theories of the Multinational Enterprise: Their Relevance to Business History', in P. Hertner and G. Jones (eds.), *Multinationals: Theory and History* (Aldershot, 1986), 42–63.

4

The Free-Standing Company, in Theory and Practice

T. A. B. Corley

Überhaupt ist es für den Forscher ein guter Morgensport, täglich vor dem Frühstück eine Lieblingshypothese einzustampfen—das erhält jung.

Konrad Lorenz[1]

Business history can be studied either from the historical or from the scientific viewpoint. The historical approach tends to concentrate on the unique aspects of past occurrences, with some (but limited) comparisons with similar events being made. By contrast, the scientific method involves observing and seeking to analyse regularities. It likewise requires a continuous search for new and improved techniques for processing the available empirical evidence. Most business historians broadly follow the historical approach. However, some have looked to the social sciences, and most notably to economics, in order to find techniques to analyse and to explain these regularities and hence go some way towards making business history into more of a rigorous academic discipline than it clearly is at present.[2]

Mira Wilkins's concept and descriptions of the free-standing company are urgently in need of re-examination along the scientific lines referred to above. She first unveiled the concept at an international conference in 1983, her paper being published three years later. A full-length article, partly entitled 'The Free-Standing Company, 1870–1914', followed in 1988. She has made use of this concept in various other works, most of which are noted in the present chapter.[3] Although a number of scholars have identified historical cases of free-standing companies in various countries, no comprehensive academic critique has until now appeared in the literature. In 1994 some follow-up articles were published on specialized aspects.[4] This chapter is designed to offer a survey on the subject as a whole.

As a historian who has charted the emergence and maturing of American multinational enterprises and is currently writing the history

I am grateful to colleagues with whom I have discussed problems connected with this topic.

of foreign inward investment in the USA, Wilkins sees the free-standing company in heuristic terms: she has felt it worth following up because (in her opinion) it exists. Hence her denial that she was trying to develop 'a "watertight" theory, a universal concept'; instead (in her words) 'I was seeking more modestly to delineate what I was uncovering in my research.' However, scientifically oriented business historians would argue that to study a concept from a purely historical angle, restricting examination of it to one country and/or period and making only limited comparisons outside these limits, is doing only half the job. If a concept appears to have merit, then it and its implications should be followed through, to see if it is of wider validity. She has admitted that her concept 'is meant to be suggestive', and she hopes it 'has analytic as well as heuristic value'. In the conclusion to the present volume, she decides that it does have both analytic and heuristic value.

In my examination, two basic questions are addressed. First, has she justified the concept? Does it help to illuminate aspects of business history that were hitherto not fully explored or understood, and is there no existing term that is equally valid? Secondly, do her findings from her use of the concept accord with the facts? The next section, therefore, discusses the theoretical underpinnings of the free-standing company, followed by a section on the empirical evidence. Finally, I offer some conclusions.

Free-Standing Companies in Theory

According to Mira Wilkins, a free-standing company is a multinational enterprise set up in the home country to do business outside that country. It has not grown out of (and thereby further internalized) an existing company at home. As such, its head office is much weaker than that of a domestic company going overseas. Its 'lean governance' would seem to make it free-standing, because host-country activities could be said effectively to stand on their own. Hence, a further rationale for the striking term which she has invented. As indicated in her Chapter 1, her rendition of the phrase 'free standing' is slightly different—that is, a firm set up anew.

To test her concept rigorously, free-standing companies need to be considered in general terms rather than being associated with particular countries. The country-specific aspects of these companies can then be examined from a practical viewpoint. As multinational enterprises, free-standing companies are the fruit of outward foreign direct investment, defined by her in terms laid down by the US Department of Commerce—namely, 'investment abroad made for business purposes, with the investors intending to control or having the potential to control the foreign operations'.

Incidentally, those who have had to work through earlier controversies and misunderstandings over the word 'direct' might prefer a more appropriate and less ambiguous phrase such as 'foreign entrepreneurial investment'. That would both emphasize the decision-making entrepreneurship required and avoid confusion with the older usages of *direct*, in two rather diverse senses: (i) all non-public sector investment abroad which did not pass through a stock exchange, and (ii) the method of calculation which involves totting up lists of companies rather than working back from the accumulated net holdings of overseas assets in balance-of-payments estimates.

Foreign direct investment needs to be contrasted with foreign portfolio investment, where the relationship between investor and recipient is at arm's length, the investor having no control over how the invested funds are used. While firms, including unincorporated ones which in the British social accounts are allocated to the personal sector, undertake foreign direct investment, portfolio investment can be carried out by firms and individuals alike.

There are two distinct types of multinational activity (note that these are conceptual, not legal distinctions):

1. *Branches.* Some subsidiaries or affiliates produce the same variety of goods and services (allowing for different consumer tastes abroad) as does the home-based firm. Others result from backward integration, into primary or intermediate products, or forward into activities connected with sales. Here the moneys (or claims on resources) usually come from retained profits or from the entrepreneur's pocket, or they may be raised from outside on the strength of the firm's reputation at home. In quite a separate process, tangible assets—either spares from the factory or newly bought-in items—are shipped abroad, as well as the production, marketing, technological, and other skills required to set up and maintain the physical branch assets.
2. *Overseas companies.* Here companies are established in the home country to operate wholly or mainly outside its borders. Setting them up involves a two-stage process, as with branches. First, the company's promoters seek funds from investors, who carry out portfolio investment in that country to gain interest or dividends. Secondly, the directors then use the proceeds to export tangible (plant and machinery, etc.) and intangible (know-how, managerial, and marketing skills, etc.) assets.

Analytically speaking, these two forms are quite distinct, having different characteristics, origins, and modes of operation. A logical problem arises because Wilkins portrays her free-standing companies as in many instances an 'alternative' to foreign branches of well-established home enterprises. Since again and again she compares and contrasts them as alternatives, the differences have to be made quite clear. First, however, the general question of alternatives calls for discussion.

An alternative connotes the existence of free choice between two or more courses of action. Once this free choice is seen not to have existed in the case of overseas companies, the validity of Wilkins's argument is thereby weakened. In any scientific analysis, *like* must properly be compared with *like*.

The reasons why branches and free-standing/overseas companies are not valid alternatives to each other can be explained as follows:

1. Branch activities arise from relatively mature enterprises, themselves normally survivors out of the many which had started out with high hopes but had then fallen by the wayside. The survivors' early entrepreneurial efforts helped to build up managerial expertise, suitable corporate structures, markets for their goods or services, and business connections for the satisfactory provision of inputs.
2. By contrast, overseas companies perforce had to start up their operations abroad entirely from scratch. In this respect the more accurate comparison is with fledgling domestic companies in facing uncertainty and heavy (often terminal) penalties for misjudgements, and in painfully building up goodwill with customers and suppliers alike.

An analogy can be drawn with the frog and the tadpole, or pollywog. Frogs are fully grown and robust creatures, capable of surviving in predator-free environments for between five and fifteen years. On the other hand, as parents know all too well from pond forays, tadpoles emerge in large quantities, many perishing along the way and only a relatively few making it to maturity. In the economics literature about the growth and death of firms, the theme of natural selection is a common one, portraying the many as going to the wall and the few winning through.[5]

Why, then, do branch operations and overseas companies exist side by side? Although Wilkins has denied that she believes that managerial shortcomings have caused many entrepreneurs to take the free-standing route as an alternative to opening branches, the whole tenor of her arguments conveys this impression. For example, she writes: 'The free-standing company, therefore, served as an alternative in many instances to the extension of the home-based operating enterprises abroad, though the need to manage the business overseas was still there and provided a formidable challenge, and one that the free-standing companies often failed to meet.'

In reality, home-country-specific considerations are paramount in explaining which of the two modes are used. If country *A* is geographically large, with most raw materials within its borders, and has a comparative advantage in high-technology products, then most of its multinationals will tend to be of the branch kind. If country *B* is of small dimensions, lacking resources at home and enjoying a comparative advantage in branded and fairly simple consumer goods and in services, then it is likely to have a preponderance of overseas companies. Thus the question of relative entrepreneurial efficiency takes second place to those of geographical size and resource endowment.

When a firm becomes involved directly abroad, it encounters greater risk than at home. Yet Wilkins has demonstrated that at least some overseas companies surmounted all these risks, prospered, and grew as successfully as had home-country firms which went on to open branches in host countries. She might indeed have given credit to these overseas companies for staying the course over the years when they were at their most vulnerable. To repeat, in their early years overseas companies *of necessity* lacked the maturity and business expertise enjoyed by those which have opened branches.

Was Wilkins logically justified in equating overseas companies with free-standing companies? Did the former possess such relatively small and weak head offices that operations in the host country were to all intents and purposes independent and self-generating?

1. According to the strict definition, Wilkins's reasoning is far from internally consistent, as can be illustrated by the following propositions:
   (*a*) The key element of foreign direct investment is that of exercising control over the assets abroad by the firm in the investing country.
   (*b*) If a free-standing company stands on its own, it must logically be free of home-country control. It is therefore simply a uninational firm in the host country, financed from home by portfolio investment.
   (*c*) If, on the other hand, control from home *does* exist, the overseas company's head office and operations abroad combined add up to a viable multinational enterprise. The concept of the free-standing company thus has no meaning.
2. Wilkins herself clearly does not see overseas companies in such

logically rigid terms, but envisages an intermediate category where the head office has varying degrees of strength and effectiveness. Hence sometimes in her writings the free-standing company had a 'familiar legal structure', with a board of directors often comprising 'men who had knowledge and expertise related to the line of business and [who] might even be involved full time at home in similar activities'. Here, then, it is in my view a properly constituted multinational exercising decisive control.

Elsewhere, however, she has found the head-office structure to be of far less consequence. Apart from a board of directors and a corporate secretary, there was 'little else', so that many such companies could be referred to as scarcely more than a 'brass nameplate' of 'an enterprise that could disappear as suddenly as it had emerged'. Since the board was part-time and the secretary possibly the sole full-timer, the head office was 'tiny', 'did not amount to very much', and was 'virtually non-existent'. She has indicated the lower limit of that muchness (or meagreness) by the phrase 'however minimal its function'. As tellingly, when control of certain real-life free-standing companies changed hands from home to host country, she describes the former corporate structure as 'essentially superfluous': when broken off, the shoot was found to have been already long dead. Sometimes, she adds, a free-standing company's head office 'became an albatross' generating 'only cost and no benefit to the ongoing business' in the host country.

So as to classify Wilkins's various descriptions of the strength or weakness in a free-standing company's home-country headquarters, it seems useful to build up a framework of cases. This might help us to see whether such a spectrum—see Table 4.1—would modify the perhaps over-rigorous sequence of propositions in (1) along the lines of her suggestions in (2). Thus, notwithstanding the in-between category which

TABLE 4.1. *Spectrum of free-standing companies: Declining strength of control*

Board	Secretary	Head office	Types of overseas company
Full-time Part-time	Full-time	Fully operational	Multinational
Part-time	Part-time	In regular correspondence overseas	Multinational
Part-time	Part-time	Concerned mainly with financial matters	Multinational?
Ineffective between	Annual general meetings	Solely share registration	Uninational in host country
Ineffective/sinecure	A once-a-year signature	Accommodation/ forwarding address with brass plate	Uninational in host country

she seems to visualize, in my view all but one doubtful case fall neatly into the category of either multinational or uninational companies.

Although Wilkins correctly draws a distinction between the initial portfolio investment in an overseas company and that company's subsequent foreign direct investment, in her various treatments she does not always make clear whether she is referring to financial capital or real capital being moved abroad. By definition, foreign direct investment comprises real investment—namely, the transfer to the host country of both tangible and intangible assets, as explained above. Those potentially productive assets have been well defined as a 'package of resources'.[6] Although, in the limiting case, some money could be remitted to the host country in order to acquire tangibles and intangibles on the spot, essentially movements of real resources are at issue.

However, Wilkins envisages free-standing companies as conduits of financial capital which, rather than being sent abroad in a 'disembodied' (presumably monetary) fashion, would be in the corporate form. Often these free-standing companies were established 'purely and simply' to seek a higher return in the host country, 'although the investment was *designed* as a managed business abroad'. She thus appears to be portraying at least some overseas companies as types of financial investment abroad, determined by interest-rate differentials between countries.

She further states that, in a country rich in (financial) capital, the free-standing company would be 'the means by which capital was mobilized, *managed*, exported and allocated' (italics in original); this capital 'was to be managed through known channels by reputable men'. In the home country 'usually only capital markets (and sometimes human capital markets) were tapped. The new foreign enterprise did not draw on the expertise of an operating parent with know-how about a product and process and their management.' Her reference to human capital markets is puzzling, since none (such as head-hunters) for management then existed. However, there were numerous channels in advanced countries for obtaining professional and technical services.

Thus far I have examined, from the theoretical standpoint, Wilkins's treatment of the free-standing company. Three aspects of this treatment in particular have been seen to be wanting. First, her comparison of branches and overseas companies as alternatives was a flawed one. Secondly, she did not at all adequately justify calling overseas companies by the name of free-standing companies. Thirdly, she appeared not to be clear as to whether the capital she described as being sent overseas was financial or real capital.

Free-Standing Companies in Practice

Wilkins's heuristic portrayal of the free-standing company has in the main been a two-dimensional one, since she has largely concentrated on those in one home country—namely, the UK—over the limited period 1870–1914. To give an extra dimension to this concept, we need to see how far the free-standing company was a country-specific phenomenon, or whether, and to what extent, it was to be found all over the world.

As yet, not enough information is available in order to compile global figures for 1870. Table 4.2 sets out estimates for 1914, covering all known outward direct investing nations of the world.

The left-hand column lists the total accumulated stock of foreign direct investment country by country, which I took from the latest estimates (of 1992) by John Dunning, but incorporated more recent data for the UK, Germany, and the Netherlands.[7] In the right-hand column is listed the total capital of the free-standing/overseas companies belonging to (headquartered in) the nations concerned. The latter were compiled as follows. For the UK, I had published estimates for 1913 of all UK quoted overseas companies' capital, totaling about 78 per cent of its accumulated foreign direct investment.[8] As for the rest of

TABLE 4.2. *Accumulated foreign-direct-investment stock and free-standing-company capital by country of origin, 1914 ($m.)*

Country of Origin	Total FDI Stock	Estimated Capital of FSCs
UK[a]	8,172	6,550
Germany	2,600	260
France	1,750	175
Netherlands	925	370[b]
Italy Belgium Sweden Switzerland	1,000	100
Russia	300	30
USA	2,652	489
Canada	150	15
Japan	300	30
Australia New Zealand South Africa	180	18
WORLD TOTAL	18,029	8,037 = 44.6%

[a] 1913.
[b] Amended (see text).
Source: T. A. B. Corley, 'Free-Standing Companies, their Financing, and Internalisation Theory', *Business History*, 36 (Oct. 1994), 111.

the world outside the USA, Wilkins found many French and Dutch free-standing companies but very few Swiss ones; she was less sure about how common they were in Germany. Since an informed estimate has put German ones at a little less than one-tenth of that country's aggregate foreign direct investment stock,[9] the proportion of 10 per cent is taken here as a reasonable minimum for all non-US and non-UK outward investing countries. The sole exception was for the Netherlands, where, based on Ben Gales's work, I estimated the proportion at 40 per cent.[10]

As for the USA, Wilkins has stated that there were American-headquartered free-standing companies in the Cuban sugar industry, mining in Latin America, and so on; 'the relative importance in US direct investment, 1870–1914 was, however, minuscule in comparison with their role in the United Kingdom'. In her various works, she has provided examples of sugar plantations in Cuba and Mexico, banana plantations in Jamaica, and sugar and rubber concerns in Mexico. Nickel was another resource not found in the USA, but available in Canada, where US firms—many undoubtedly overseas companies—also supplemented indigenous supplies of copper, lead, zinc, and iron as well. In Canada there were American-owned paper mills which an authoritative survey has judged to be 'scarcely typical branch plants', while half the US-owned lumber companies were equally 'not the offspring of previously existing such ventures in the US'.[11]

To allow for these supply-based activities, the relevant figures for the USA in Table 4.2 were compiled from the capital of sugar, fruit, rubber, and other agricultural product companies, to which have been added a conservative one-fifth of the American-owned mining and smelting companies in Latin America. The data were taken from Cleona Lewis's tables for 1914; in total they suggest that overseas companies made up some 18 per cent of all US outward foreign-direct-investment stock that year.

Summing up on Table 4.2, for the world as a whole in 1914 free-standing/overseas companies apparently accounted for nearly 45 per cent of the total foreign-direct-investment stock. Thus Wilkins's lengthy discussion of the British free-standing company and sketchy treatment of their counterparts elsewhere must be viewed as partial and—in the statistical sense—biased. None the less, my figures do show that the capital of British FSCs equalled about 81 per cent of the estimated FSC total.

Like all estimates of quantities which have not been obtained from census and other compulsory returns, those in Table 4.2 can be questioned, as Wilkins has questioned other estimates, for being tentative and impressionistic. Yet orders of magnitude are important in empirical research as helping to put the relevant issues in perspective. The estimates here thus provide a basis on which to carry out a more rigorous examination than has hitherto been undertaken.

For example, Wilkins makes a good deal of the low survival rates of British free-standing companies, implicitly when contrasted with the American experience. Such generally poor chances of survival come as no surprise to those who accept the tadpole analogy provided above: the branches of established companies that have become large enough to diversify outside their borders have a far greater chance of being survivors than the myriad 'tadpoles' struggling for a place in an unwelcoming and hostile world. To test her second assumption, relative corporate rates of survival in Britain and the USA need to be compared.

In her Chapter 1 in this book, Wilkins cites unpublished figures given by Christopher Schmitz, stating that, under the relevant joint-stock acts between 1856 and 1914, 154,817 companies were registered in London and 9,303 in Edinburgh. These figures agree tolerably well with those in the Board of Trade returns over this period, of 142,168 companies registered in England, 9,294 in Scotland, and 4,053 in Ireland: a total for the (then) United Kingdom of 155,515. Of these, the total number still on the register at 30 April 1914 amounted to 58,164 (40.9 per cent) in England, 4,598 (49.5 per cent) in Scotland, and 1,930 (47.6 per cent) in Ireland.[12] The mortality rate for English-registered joint-stock companies was thus slightly (but not *far*, as she has claimed) higher than for the Scottish-registered ones.

Any further stage in the discussion involves entering the realms of conjecture: according to the leading British quantitative economic historian, C. H. Feinstein, 'an opinion formed on slight or defective evidence or none'.[13] *If* Christopher Schmitz found that 9.2 per cent of all the Scottish companies in the relevant period were 'set up to engage in overseas investment' (but doubtless a smaller percentage engaged in direct investment, once, say, investment companies were taken out), and *if* the English overseas companies were of a comparable percentage, then there may have been as many as 13,000 of them. On the other hand, the number may have been as low as 10,000 or as high as 15,000; we just do not know.

As long as an atmosphere of uncertainty and conjecture hangs over these questions, the only logical course is to concentrate on the most reliable information which we do have. (Sir) George Paish's data of the 2,172 British non-railway overseas companies, and their capital and income in 1907/8, are of signal importance here. He found that on average these companies earned 7.7 per cent on their capital, compared with 4.0 per cent from government and municipal loans and stocks and 4.4 per cent from railways. The highest income was from enterprises engaged in mining diamonds and other stones (30.3 per cent) and the lowest, of 3.3 per cent, from 'financial, land and investment' companies. According to the Inland Revenue, there were also 107 railway companies controlled from Britain, earning £13.5 million. Their total capital is not known, but that income is included in the 4.4 per cent earned by all British overseas railway company stocks.[14]

Paish was editor of the respected British journal the *Statist*, and an expert on British and American railway and other statistics. His findings therefore carry weight, as do the concurrent data of Edgar Crammond, secretary of the Liverpool Stock Exchange. In his studies of British investment abroad, Crammond took the capital of an unknown number of British overseas securities in 1906 from the *Stock Exchange Official Intelligence*. The data cannot be precisely allocated to overseas companies: over and above 'government stocks' and 'railways', his categories were 'corporation stocks, banking, financial, land etc', 'mines', and 'miscellaneous'. The total capital for the last three categories amounted to £955 million and for the last two to £784 million, higher than the £737 million of the non-railway overseas companies in Paish's tally for 1907/8. Crammond usefully calculated the approximate market value of each category, in total, by continent and by country. Globally, the market value of the shares in the three categories—corporation stocks etc., mines, and miscellaneous—exceeded their nominal value by 10.8 per cent, and in the last two categories by 8.7 per cent.[15]

These calculations were by two men who both knew personally about many overseas companies and could ask questions of those who knew about others. Their findings suggest that somewhere between 2,200 and 2,500 British overseas companies were doing rather well. These broadly agree with statistical evidence from Inland Revenue sources, of assessments in 1911/12 which roughly relate to performance in 1909. There were 3,203 assessments in the 'adventures [= ventures] out of the UK' category, 2,419 being corporate and 784 non-corporate; total gross true income was just under £63 million. While these overseas companies numbered less than 1 per cent of all the (overwhelmingly domestic) UK companies assessed, they accounted for nearly 15 per cent of the total profits earned. Of these, no fewer than 773 incorporated and 157 non-corporate plantations, which could hardly have adopted US-style hierarchical structures, earned between them £6.75 million. The presenters of these figures admit that here are no more than orders of magnitude; yet they yield confirmation of quite a solid bedrock of flourishing British overseas businesses.[16]

We are still left with perhaps 10,000 overseas companies—whether more or fewer is anyone's guess—which by 1914 were no longer quoted or in existence or had escaped the compilers' nets. Of those which had disappeared, the perhaps many abortive companies are of some interest. According to Professor D. H. Macgregor, these 'represent a factor in enterprise, an aspect of "stimulus" in industry', by linking intangibles (potentially profitable entrepreneurial ideas, some ahead of their time) with the very material consideration of inadequate cash being forthcoming from subscribers.[17]

There were any number of good reasons why British overseas companies found themselves having to be dissolved. Oil prospectors set up companies and then closed them down when concessions were lost or oil shows proved uncommercial. Many, such as the Burmah Oil Company, found reconstruction with a new company under an identical name the simplest way of writing up their capital. Blights such as those in India and Ceylon around the 1870s caused many coffee-plantation companies to go under, new tea-growing ones often being established in their place. Single ships were sometimes registered as companies, which closed when the ships were scrapped. Success permitted amalgamation with rivals for technical (e.g. raw-material access) reasons or to achieve scale economies. Forward or backward integration at times became worthwhile. It is misleading to dwell at too great length on the incompetents and crooks who undoubtedly existed, in Britain as in every other country with overseas companies.

If we try to substitute reasonable approximations for a raft of single cases, then the 2,500 or so survivors may have been nearly one in five of the 13,000 or so overseas companies. Wilkins has stated (admitting the lack of precision) that 'the number of free-standing companies with continuity, flourishing as successful, profitable enterprises, represented a very small percentage of the total number established'. An authoritative handbook for writers of English prose, which contains a suggested measure of proportion, identifies a 'very small part' as 5 per cent, somewhat below the 20 per cent suggested above.[18]

Turning now from the British to the American corporate experience, it is very unfortunate that no comparable figures for US dissolutions and survivals, either in aggregate or for those operating overseas, at this period appear to exist. The system there of business incorporations being registered state by state has clearly deterred scholars from undertaking a national study of this kind. The Dun & Bradstreet data from 1857 onwards merely give annual totals of business formations and business failures; they are no substitute for the comprehensive figures available in Britain from official sources, since they do not tabulate corporate dissolutions for other reasons.[19] Works such as George H. Evans's *Business Incorporations in the United States 1800–1943* (1948), concentrating as they do on some but not all states, cannot help much.[20] Until a systematic research project, attempting to harmonize data in both countries, has been undertaken, no certain conclusions can be drawn about the extent and causes of business successes and failures in the UK and the USA. Even then, the still more intractable problem remains of identifying overseas companies and their performance.

In the light of the broader perspective on this topic furnished by Table 4.2, with the national breakdown by headquarters of free-standing companies, and of the immediately preceding discussion about corporate births and deaths in the two countries, it is now possible to pursue some of Wilkins's empirical assertions.

An integral part of her empirical approach is the distinction she drew between the 'American model'—the branches we described earlier—and the (largely) British 'model' of overseas companies. As already shown, she regarded these two categories as substitutes for each other. According to her, Britain's relatively small domestic market gave its entrepreneurs all too little scope to develop organizational skills. By contrast, the geographical vastness of the USA allowed multiregional and then multinational enterprises there to be developed by dynamic managerial teams. Thus a free-standing company—of the British type—was a 'compromise' which 'may in many cases have substituted [i.e. represented an inferior substitute] for British firms that apparently found the extension of management internationally a difficult proposition'. In short, free-standing companies served as an 'alternative in many instances to the extension of the British home-based operating enterprises abroad'.

To investigate in empirical terms this hypothesis of multinational enterprises with branches and overseas companies being substitute organizational forms, it is necessary to look at the reasons why the overseas companies were set up in the first place.

1. According to Wilkins, British overseas companies existed to tap UK financial markets, the availability of funds being Britain's important (and about its only) comparative advantage. However, because such companies were 'unable to capture the very advantages (experience, technology, goodwill) that provide the basis for effective and efficient multinational enterprise', the 'presence of a British superstructure [i.e. the headquarters at home] brought only additional cost'. Hence in the USA as host country, 'the introduction of a British legal corporate entity was usually redundant, that is, unnecessary for securing property rights and inadequate in or of itself for securing effective control'.
2. The more immediate reason for their establishment, that of home-country-specific differences in resource endowments, has little attraction for Wilkins. Yet it remains true that the USA was

> more or less self-sufficient in all but tropical products, whereas Britain was short of many primary products from raw cotton to oil and a range of non-ferrous metals. Wilkins not only dismisses UK resource-based investment as 'highly selective' but also finds the raw-materials-shortage argument unconvincing. Thus she points out that British firms invested in tea, crude rubber, nitrates, and tin to a greater extent than US corporations did before 1914, even though the Americans also needed to import these commodities. Her explanation was that Britain had the capital and sent it abroad because favourable alternative investment opportunities at home were hard to find through flaws in its domestic economy.

Here Wilkins's assertions and findings are tested against evidence in respect of Britain. The present author's estimates for 1913 indicate that over one-quarter of the capital of British quoted overseas companies, and about half by number, were resource-based, in mining, oil and tea, coffee and rubber plantations. Railway ventures came to nearly 30 per cent and banking and insurance to about 5 per cent, while 28 per cent comprised a variety of utilities and services from gas, electricity, and water to tramways, telegraphs, shipping, docks, and land. Overseas companies in manufacturing (and processing) made up less than 13 per cent of the whole. Thus, British entrepreneurs actively pursued both national resource needs and comparative advantages in a range of different industries.

As to foreign-direct-investment responses to raw-material shortages, a crucial question is whether ample supplies of resources were available from abroad *through the market* on acceptable terms. Widespread concern in Britain about resource supplies had arisen from the 1850s onwards as the country's industrial potential grew.[21] Where efficient markets existed—such as for raw cotton—foreign direct investment was not required; however, foreign direct investment by Britain had already performed a vital market-creating role. In the 1820s UK investors had begun to acquire interests in the US cotton trade in order to build up necessary supplies of raw cotton.[22]

By contrast, oil can be cited as an increasingly vital product where foreign direct investment by oil-scarce countries—most notably Britain—helped to combat the very intensive efforts by the then giant oil corporations to monopolize the market for their products on a global scale. The British government's investment in 1914 to acquire a controlling stake in the Anglo-Persian Oil Company had the explicit purpose of discouraging outside companies from charging excessive prices for fuel oil bought in by the Admiralty, since a substantial proportion of naval requirements would be coming from a secure source. In the metal-mining industries too, once the availability at home of raw materials declined after the 1870s, company promoters in Britain 'responded to deficiencies of supply and high prices by developing mines overseas'.[23]

On the empirical side, therefore, Wilkins has seriously weakened her case for the existence of free-standing companies in two respects. First, she is weak in her investigations of the free-standing company on a global scale. Secondly, she compared two quite dissimilar types of cases: the so-called American model of branches and the overseas company, which are radically different in structure and sprang from different basic circumstances. Since Table 4.2 indicates that nearly one-fifth of the USA's own outward foreign-direct-investment stock in 1914 comprised overseas companies, there was clearly no justification for portraying the two types as substitutes for each other.

The composition and structure of the overseas company's head office, discussed earlier from the theoretical viewpoint, requires empirical investigation for two reasons. First, if the head office contained no intermediate factors such as managerial and other know-how, it would find it very difficult to set up its overseas operations in the first place. Secondly, a head office with no substantive assets would be unable to maintain effective control once the productive activities abroad were in place.

A representative comment (already quoted) by Wilkins about British free-standing companies was that the need to manage these activities overseas 'provided a formidable challenge, and one that the free-standing companies often failed to meet'. To test this statement, elsewhere the structures of three major British companies operating abroad, and also of less important ones in widely differing industry groups, have been examined.[24] The former comprised the Anglo-Persian Oil Company (later British Petroleum), the Burmah Oil Company,[25] and the Rio Tinto Company.[26] All of these have been characterized by Wilkins as free-standing companies, at origin. Yet the evidence for each makes clear that the head office of every one from the outset effectively controlled its overseas operations. All three companies in time adopted management structures that resembled those found in the American 'model'. This subsequent managerial development by them and by other successful British enterprises is of scarcely greater interest than the fact that tadpoles—if lucky—grow into frogs. Had there been a more appropriate way of administering its assets abroad, no doubt each of these companies would have pursued that rather than the American route.

The four cases in the latter, more modest, group belonged to the food manufacturing, oil, utilities, and services sectors respectively. These were Liebig's Extract of Meat Company Ltd. (better known as Oxo Ltd.), the Assam Oil Company Ltd. (smaller and more remote than the large oil enterprises considered above), the Imperial Continental Gas Association Ltd., and British multinational banks.[27] Rather than conforming to Wilkins's definition of free-standing companies as ones with minimal functions at home, all their head offices maintained regular correspondence with operational managers abroad, both by mail and by international cable, monitoring local activities through setting targets and the periodical submission of reports and financial returns. They hired and fired senior staff. While the home directors were all part-time, the company secretary had a key role as the regular channel of communication with the overseas managers. He issued formal instructions and less formal advice, and accompanied directors on (often annual) visits of inspection abroad.

A recurrent theme of Wilkins is that the British free-standing company had only a slender chance of success because of its fundamental weaknesses. In her words, 'with its tiny home office', it 'had either to find or create [a management] package; otherwise it was doomed to dissolution'. To be sure, some examples have been given of the more successful UK overseas companies, later coming somewhat to resemble the American model in creating departments which ranged from marketing to research. Yet they remained overseas companies since—at least until 1914—there were no domestic oil activities on which to base their operations abroad. All of them had to begin on a small scale, gradually building up their organizations as they gained both financial strength and managerial expertise. As suggested earlier, their achievements were more impressive than those of the American-style multinationals, which ventured into far riskier business abroad well equipped with the tangible and intangible assets representing the fruits of their home operations. To sum up this empirical section, the historical evidence presented here throws further doubt on Wilkins's concept of the free-standing company.

Conclusion

The main findings of this chapter can be outlined very briefly. The concept of the free-standing company as an overseas company with minimal head-office structure or power of control cannot be justified in theory and had little, if any, validity in practice. Reality lies elsewhere. The overseas company, operating wholly or mainly abroad and thus a different species from the branch operations of multinational enterprises with productive activities in the host countries, adequately covers all aspects of the topic which Wilkins has sought to address.

Finally, any attempt to launch a new concept on the academic world is always a hazardous undertaking, especially when a satisfactory name already exists for it. As John Dunning has written, 'it is one of the more irritating characteristics of academic researchers (and the present author is no exception!) that they sometimes invent their own nomenclature for concepts which are familiar under different names to other researchers'.[28] Even so, Wilkins's path-breaking contributions to the study of past multinationals must be freely acknowledged. It is to be hoped that she will be encouraged to take a more scientific look at the overseas company's operations throughout the world, especially during the era of unprecedented global economic expansion before 1914.

NOTES

1. 'It is, above all, a useful morning routine for a scholar to shed a pet hypothesis every day before breakfast. That keeps one young' (K. Lorenz, *Das Sogenannte Böse: Zur Naturgeschichte der Aggression* (*On Aggression*) (1963), ch. 2). My thanks to Felix Corley for the translation.
2. These ideas were developed in T. A. B. Corley, 'The Ultimate Synthesis? Towards an Integration of Business History, Social Science and Managerial Theory', in M. Davids, F. De Goey, and D. De Wit (eds.), *Proceedings of the Conference on Business History, October 1994* (Rotterdam, 1995), 78–90.
3. The unreferenced quotations are all taken from the following works by M. Wilkins: 'Multinational Enterprises', in H. Daems and H. van der Wee (eds.), *The Rise of Managerial Capitalism* (Louvain, 1974), 213–35; 'Modern European Economic History and the Multinationals', *Journal of European Economic History*, 6 (Winter 1977), 575–95; 'Defining a Firm: History and Theory', in P. Hertner and G. Jones (eds.), *Multinationals: Theory and History* (Aldershot, 1986), 80–95; 'The History of European Multinationals: A New Look', *Journal of European Economic History*, 15 (Winter 1986), 483–510; 'European Multinationals in the United States 1875–1914', in A. Teichova, M. Lévy-Leboyer, and H. Nussbaum (eds.), *Multinational Enterprise in Historical Perspective* (Cambridge, 1986), 55–64; 'The Free-Standing Company, 1870–1914: An Important Type of British Foreign Direct Investment', *Economic History Review*, 2nd ser., 41 (May 1988), 259–82; 'European and North American Multinationals, 1870–1914: Comparisons and Contrasts', *Business History*, 30 (Jan. 1988), 8–45; *The History of Foreign Investment in the United States to 1914* (Cambridge, Mass., 1989); 'The Free-Standing Company Revisited', unpublished first rendition (Aug. 1994).
4. J.-F. Hennart, 'International Financial Capital Transfers: A Transaction Cost Framework', *Business History*, 36 (Jan. 1994), 51–70; M. Casson, 'Institutional Diversity in Overseas Enterprise: Explaining the Free-Standing Company', *Business History*, 36 (October 1994), 95–108; T. A. B. Corley, 'Free-Standing Companies, their Financing, and Internalisation Theory', *Business History*, 36 (Oct. 1994), 109–17; J.-F. Hennart, 'Free-Standing Firms and the Internalisation of Markets for Financial Capital: A Response to Casson', *Business History*, 36 (Oct. 1994), 118–31.
5. A. Marshall, *Principles of Economics* (9th edn., London, 1961), i. 240–2; D. H. Macgregor, *Enterprise, Purpose and Profit* (Oxford, 1934), 101.
6. N. Hood and S. Young, *The Economics of Multinational Enterprise* (London, 1979),

9, and M. Casson, 'The Theory of Foreign Direct Investment', in P. J. Buckley and M. Casson (eds.), *The Economic Theory of the Multinational Enterprise* (London, 1985), 113.
7. J. H. Dunning, *Multinational Enterprise and the Global Economy* (Wokingham, Berks., 1993), 117.
8. T. A. B. Corley, 'Britain's Overseas Investments in 1914 Revisited', *Business History*, 36 (Jan. 1994), 71–88.
9. Estimate supplied by Harm Schröter, whose wife Verena calculated the overall German foreign-direct-investment figure cited in Table 4.2. See also V. Schröter, *Die deutsche Industrie auf dem Weltmarkt 1929 bis 1932* (Frankfurt, 1984), 114–36, 384–447.
10. B. P. A. Gales, 'In Foreign Parts: Free-Standing Companies in the Netherlands around the First World War', unpublished paper presented at the International Economic History Congress, Milan (Sept. 1994), 12.
11. C. Lewis, *America's Stake in International Investments* (Washington, 1938), 583–7, 590–4; H. Marshall, F. A. Southard and K. W. Taylor, *Canadian–American Industry* (New Haven, Conn., 1936), 54, 56.
12. Twenty-seventh Annual Report of the Board of Trade, *British Parliamentary Papers* VII, 709 ff., appendix VI, 10–11.
13. C. H. Feinstein, 'Capital Formation in Great Britain', *Cambridge Economic History of Europe*, vii, pt. I (Cambridge, 1978), 28.
14. G. Paish, 'Great Britain's Capital Investments in Other Lands', *Journal of the Royal Statistical Society*, 72 (1909), 471–5.
15. E. Crammond, 'British Investments Abroad', *Quarterly Review*, 207 (1907), 249–53.
16. G. D. N. Worswick and D. G. Tipping, *Profits in the British Economy 1909–1938* (Oxford, 1967), 99–118.
17. Macgregor, *Enterprise, Purpose and Profit*, 101.
18. R. Graves and A. Hodge, *The Reader over your Shoulder: A Handbook for Writers of English Prose* (London, 1943), 72.
19. US Bureau of the Census, *Historical Statistics of the United States from Colonial Times to 1970* (Washington, 1975), series V 20–30, 'Business Formation and Business Failures 1857–1970', pp. 912–13.
20. G. H. Evans, *Business Incorporations in the United States 1800–1943* (New York, 1948). An intensive search of the computer catalogue in the Library of Congress has yielded no further books or articles of relevance to this particular issue.
21. H. J. Habakkuk, 'Free Trade and Commercial Expansion 1853–1870', in J. Holland Rose, A. P. Newton and E. A. Benians (eds.), *The Cambridge History of the British Empire*, ii (Cambridge, 1940), 773.
22. T. C. Coram, 'The Role of British Capital in the Development of the United States, 1600–1914', M.Sc. thesis (University of Southampton, 1967), 168.
23. C. E. Harvey and J. Press, 'Overseas Investment and the Professional Advance of British Metal Mining Engineers, 1851–1914', *Economic History Review*, 2nd ser., 42 (1989), 66.
24. T. A. B. Corley, 'Foreign Direct Investment and British Economic Deceleration 1870–1914', in H. Pohl (ed.), *Transnational Investment from the 19th Century to the Present, Zeitschrift für Unternehmensgeschichte* (Occasional Papers, 81; Stuttgart, 1994),162–3; Corley, 'Free Standing Companies', 115–16.
25. R.W. Ferrier, *The History of the British Petroleum Company*, i. *1901–1932* (Cambridge, 1982); T. A. B. Corley, *A History of the Burmah Oil Company 1886–1924* (London, 1983).
26. C. E. Harvey, *The Rio Tinto Company* (Penzance, 1981).

27. C. Scarborough, . . . *about* Oxo (London, 1965), 3–8; *The Story of the Assam Railways and Trading Company Ltd. 1882–1951* (London, 1951), ch. 8 (on 'oil'), and information from the Assam Oil Company archives at Swindon, by kind permission of Burmah Castrol plc.; *Imperial Continental Gas Association 1824–1974* (London, 1974), 1–28, kindly lent to me by G. Jones; Geoffrey Jones, *British Multinational Banking, 1830–1990* (Oxford, 1993).
28. J. H. Dunning, *Explaining International Production* (London, 1988), 68.

Part II

Countries and Regions that were Host to Free-Standing Companies

5

Free-Standing Companies in Italy, 1883–1912

Peter Hertner

Italy was, economically speaking, a country of the European periphery from the second half of the seventeenth well into the twentieth century, after having been at the heart of Europe's cultural and economic development during the Middle Ages and the Renaissance period.[1] During the second half of the nineteenth century, despite Italy's overall 'economic backwardness', its more advanced parts, mainly in the north-west, received considerable flows of financial and human capital as well as technology from abroad.[2] Some of these flows, but only a relatively small amount, went also into the less developed central and southern parts of the peninsula. The leading capital exporter to Italy in the 1850s and early 1860s was France, followed by Britain. Belgium and Germany took on an increasing role from the 1880s onwards. When Italy's economic growth accelerated markedly in the second half of the 1890s (after an abortive start during the preceding decade), the relative importance of foreign investment for capital accumulation and technological progress in industry and infrastructure diminished gradually, whereas foreign investment's contribution to Italian public finance lost its former weight in the course of a few years starting in 1895/6.[3]

Foreign capital invested in the joint stock companies registered in Italy between 1883 and 1911/12 amounted to almost 30 per cent of the entire nominal capital subscribed in Italian joint-stock companies in the early 1880s. A decade later, when the country went through a major economic crisis, this share moved up to between 50 and 60 per cent. With Italy's first breakthrough to self-sustaining industrialization coming at the end of the 1890s, the percentage decreased rapidly and stabilized at a rate of about 10 per cent between 1905 and 1910.[4] By this time the internal rate of capital accumulation was almost sufficient for sustaining the quite impressive rate of growth of industrial production achieved between 1897 and 1907.

Did 'free-standing companies', as defined by Mira Wilkins, play a role in this flow of investment?[5] Were they used as tools of investment to an equal extent by all the source-of-capital countries? Were they used to the same extent over the entire period considered in this chapter—i.e. from 1883 until 1912? These are the questions to which we shall try to give some provisional answers.

Focusing on Italy enables us to observe conditions in this recipient country and consider them as one of the causes for the inflow of capital. Since the flows came from different nations, a closer look at conditions abroad will then help us to draw a better picture of the reasons why the free-standing company and not another juridical type of commercial organization was chosen. Finally, a look at the economic activities in which free-standing companies were particularly in evidence (or, on the contrary, absent) will acquaint us indirectly with other characteristics of this particular type of firm.

Our analysis starts in 1883 because during the previous year a new *codice di commercio* had been introduced to the Kingdom of Italy. This new commercial law finally abolished governmental concessions by charter for joint stock companies. In the purest tradition of the Napoleonic *code de commerce* adopted in most parts of Risorgimental Italy, these concessions had been reiterated in the 1865 commercial code of the recently unified state. The commercial legislation of 1882 required only registration in court for joint-stock companies and enacted basic rules for the procedures of statutory constitution and the functioning of these companies. The individual act of registration, for which 30 per cent of nominal capital had to be paid in, had to be published in a new periodical bulletin of the Ministry of Agriculture, Industry and Commerce, the *Bollettino ufficiale delle società per azioni*. This bulletin was also supposed to publish the yearly balance sheets, as well as any decision taken by the companies' boards or shareholders' general meetings concerning capital increases or cuts or the eventual winding-up of these firms.[6] Companies founded under foreign law and with their legal seat outside Italy—many of them of the free-standing type—had, in case they wanted to do business in Italy, to register in the country according to the 1882 law. Their registration was published in the *Bollettino ufficiale*. It is from this source that the figures provided in Table 5.1 have been derived.[7] Based on these data, I made the determination as to whether a company was of the free-standing type, and grouped these companies according to industry and source-of-capital country.

Tables 5.2 and 5.3 demonstrate that foreign free-standing companies registered in Italy between 1883 and 1912 were largely of UK origin, with Belgian and French-based companies also possessing significant shares. This holds for both the total amount of nominal capital declared at the moment of foundation of these firms as well as for the number of free-standing companies registered in Italy.

TABLE 5.1. *Foreign free-standing companies founded not earlier than 1880 and registered in Italy between 1883 and 1912* (nominal capital at foundation in 1,000 lire)

Years	Mining	Gas, water, electricity	Transport	Manufacturing	Banking	Other businesses	Total
1883–8							
UK	38,250	7,500	12,625	—	—	—	58,375
Belgium	—	—	24,480	—	—	—	27,480
France	4,750	—	400	—	—	8,000	13,150
Switzerland	1,200	—	—	—	—	—	1,200
Germany	125	563	—	—	—	—	688
1889–94							
UK	2,500	525	5,000	1,500	50,000	3,750	63,275
Belgium	—	2,000	6,700	—	—	—	8,700
France	200	100	—	450	—	—	750
Switzerland	—	—	1,500	—	—	—	1,500
Germany	—	—	—	—	—	—	—
1895–1900							
UK	30,625	5,000	2,500	1,250	—	13,250	56,625
Belgium	3,000	9,000	1,000	5,000	—	—	18,000
France	805	900	1,100	2,000	—	2,000	6,805
Switzerland	—	400	—	—	—	2,750	3,150
Germany	—	—	—	—	—	—	—
1901–6							
UK	8,700	—	—	750	—	3,750	13,200
Belgium	1,000	—	5,000	—	—	—	6,000
France	4,450	150	5,000	5,400	—	3,200	15,000
Switzerland	—	—	—	—	—	—	3,200
Germany	250	—	—	—	—	—	250
1907–12							
UK	23,050	—	—	75	500	1,450	25,075
Belgium	1,500	—	13,000	6,000	—	—	20,500
France	2,450	—	18,500	100	—	—	21,050
Switzerland	—	—	—	—	—	500	500
Germany	125	—	—	—	—	—	125
	122,980	26,138	99,405	22,525	50,500	38,650	

Note: in this period, £1 = 25.3 lire, $1 = 5.2 lire.
Source: Bollettino ufficiale delle società per azioni (Roma 1883 ff.).

Table 5.1 showed that mining was the leading sector for free-standing companies registered in Italy and that in this branch the lion's share was from companies founded in the UK. This is hardly surprising to those doing research in the field of mining history and seems to be in line with basic evidence produced in the framework of the free-standing company hypothesis. The companies were mining zinc, lead, copper, sulphur, silver and gold, with zinc and sulphur probably the most important.[8] The role of the City of London in the financing of mining in all parts of the world resulted from the experience of British mining engineers, the position of the City as the hub of global finance until 1914, and the City's 'special position . . . at the centre of a global

TABLE 5.2. *Total nominal capital of foreign free-standing companies registered in Italy from 1883 until 1912* (in 1000 lire)

Country of origin	Capital
UK	212,550
Belgium	80,680
France	56,005
Switzerland	9,550
Germany	1,063

Source: See Table 5.1.

TABLE 5.3. *Number of foreign free-standing companies registered in Italy from 1883 until 1912*

Years	UK	Belgium	France	Switzerland	Germany
1883–8	8	8	5	1	2
1889–94	11	4	3	1	—
1895–1900	9	7	7	3	—
1901–6	8	4	8	2	1
1907–12	10	6	6	1	1

Source: See Table 5.1.

information network'. This has recently been emphasized by Charles Harvey and Jon Press as well as by Jean-Jacques van Helten.[9]

At first sight, more surprising (see again Table 5.1) seems to be the strong position of the transport business among the free-standing companies and, above all, the leading role that Belgian capital played in this sector, especially during the 1880s and the early 1890s. A closer look reveals, however, that most of these free-standing firms were tramway companies, and in this field Belgian capital had a dominant position among foreign investors in Italy: between 1875 and 1886, there were 2,006 kilometres of new tramway lines established in Italy; 1,357 kilometres of these were financed and controlled by Belgian investors, which contributed no less than 92 per cent of all foreign participations in that particular field. Our source for this is a German dissertation, defended in 1920, which appears to have been based on systematic research undertaken by the German army during its occupation of Belgium in the First World War.[10] According to more recent results, published in Michel Dumoulin's work on the economic relations between Belgium and Italy between 1861 and 1914, 90 per cent of all Belgian investments in Italy by 1885 were in public transport. In 1914 this share was reduced to 77.7 per cent, whereas the total amount of Belgian capital in Italy had, according to Dumoulin, almost doubled during the three intervening decades. Dumoulin's figures for 1885 give 'chauffage et éclairage' and water an added share of 5.2 per cent, which would make it the second largest branch of Belgian investments in Italy.[11] This corresponds roughly with our results calculated in Table

5.1. The category 'banking' in the same table gives an unrealistic picture due to the foundation of an *English and Italian Banking Corporation* in 1891 with a registered nominal capital of not less than 2 million pounds sterling (which equalled roughly 50 million lire).[12] This huge venture must have had a very short-lived existence or perhaps did not even get off the ground. There is no mention of it in Geoffrey Jones's comprehensive *British Multinational Banking*.[13]

This leads us directly to the results given in Table 5.4, where another method of assembling statistical data has been applied: instead of taking at face value the nominal capital declared at the moment of foundation of those companies identified as free-standing, only the capital declared afterwards *as having been subscribed* has been counted; this then was subdivided according to its national origin. The UK figures are excluded, because in the case of companies founded in the UK, the legislation of 1856 (which made limited liability 'freely available') did not link the subscription of shares to the actual raising of capital. As Philip Cottrell has explained, 'the only requirement by the Act [of 1856] was the filing of a memorandum of association with the Registrar, signed by seven shareholders, who needed merely to have taken up one of the company's shares, for which there was no prescribed minimum value, and on which no money needed to have been subscribed. English company law now became the most permissive in Europe.'[14] Thus in the UK case neither the nominal capital formally indicated at the moment of a company's foundation nor the number and the value of shares stated as having been subscribed reflect the amount of capital really invested. This is the reason behind the omission of UK figures from Table 5.4. As for the other four countries of origin, Table 5.4 conveys a rough impression of the nominal capital actually subscribed in the free-standing companies.

Table 5.5 tries to establish the proportion between the effectively subscribed nominal capital of free-standing companies and the total nominal capital of joint-stock companies held by foreigners and registered in Italy, regardless of the law—Italian or foreign—under which

TABLE 5.4. *National origin of nominal capital subscribed at foundation of free-standing companies registered in Italy from 1883 until 1912* (in 1,000 lire)

Years	Belgium	France	Switzerland	Germany
1883–8	26,493	12,750	1,137	600
1889–94	4,775	750	1,500	—
1895–1900	9,224	9,448	2,876	1,162
1901–6	5,453	12,390	2,916	297
1907–12	8,103	8,077	200	375

Note: UK figures are excluded because they are not considered to be reliable.
Source: See Table 5.1.

TABLE 5.5. *Share of nominal capital of free-standing companies (at foundation) in total nominal foreign capital of joint-stock companies registered in Italy from 1883 until 1912 (%)*

Years	UK	Belgium	France	Switzerland	Germany
1883–8	92.5	66.8	61.8	9.4	1.6
1889–94	100	39.3	12.9	7.8	—
1895–1900	63	43.3	59.8	11.6	2.8
1901–6	70.4	65.4	38.6	5.9	1.3
1907–12	22.1	32.9	24.4	1.0	2.1

Source: See Table 5.1.

these companies had been founded. We have estimated the UK figures from available data.

Our findings are interesting. They corroborate the view that, at least in the Italian case and with the exception of the last years before the outbreak of the First World War, 'the free-standing company was . . . probably the most typical mode of British direct investment abroad'.[15]

The figures in Table 5.4 showed that, apart from the UK case, Belgium played an important role as a seat for free-standing companies, and that French firms of that type were far from negligible. By contrast, neither Swiss nor German free-standing companies had any importance. Another look at Table 5.5 confirms this conclusion: until the middle of the first decade of the twentieth century, free-standing companies absorbed by far the largest part of UK investments in the Italian economy. This seems evident despite the reservations made above concerning the reliability of the UK figures. Belgian as well as French free-standing companies held an important position within the overall investment flows from these source-of-capital countries into the Italian economy. Swiss free-standing companies played a subordinate role in this context; in the case of German investment, free-standing companies were practically nonexistent.

Two sets of problems remain to be explained: (1) *the chronological development*; in other words, why did the relative importance of free-standing companies compared to the overall amount of foreign capital invested in joint-stock companies shrink so visibly at the end of the period under investigation? And, (2) *the national imbalance*; or, why were free-standing companies so normal in the UK and Belgian cases and why were they so uncommon with the Swiss and the German investors?

As to the development of the free-standing company in the course of time, one must keep in mind that the nature of investment in the Italian economy was profoundly modified beginning at the end of the 1890s. The 'breakthrough' to industrialization meant that the share of investments in manufacturing and in the trade of investment goods increased. This was to the detriment of the free-standing company with 'its inherently weak managerial structure', which very often failed to provide its offspring abroad with necessary guidance and with technical advice that only a multinationally organized structure could guarantee.[16] One must agree, when looking at the Italian example, with Wilkins's assertion 'that advanced technology could not be effectively transferred via this type of intermediary and that the lean governance structure was the constraint'. Therefore 'such companies tended to be absent from the high-technology industries of this era, notably the electrical and chemical industries'.[17] In the Italian case this can be clearly demonstrated. The best example is supplied by electrical and electrotechnical manufacturing, where practically none of the firms which ever gained any importance were organized as free-standing companies. The ongoing transfer of a steadily evolving advanced technology, the necessary permanent control and monitoring of these investments, and the comparatively huge amounts of capital required for founding and developing firms in this quickly oligopolized sector prevented the free-standing companies from offering a viable alternative to the direct investments of multinationally structured corporations.

Regarding the possible causes for the striking source-of-capital national imbalance in the use of the free-standing form, conditions in the countries of origin were crucial to these choices: an important role was played by the legal system and by the structure of the capital markets in each of these countries. The UK, with its extremely lax company laws (relative to the standard prevailing on the European Continent at least until about 1900), offers the best example. Add the attractiveness of the London capital market and its role in global information transfer, and you have most of the ingredients for a successful environment for free-standing companies.

Much less well known is the case of Belgium, generally considered to be the first industrializer on the European Continent. But there again the necessary preconditions seem to have been provided by a combination of low taxes on both stock-exchange transactions and company earnings, by very permissive company laws (at least between 1873 and 1913), and by a well-functioning capital market fed by a high rate of capital accumulation within the country as well as by a steady inflow of capital from abroad, especially from France.[18] Given these circumstances, the foundation of a company in Belgium, whether free-standing or not, must have been attractive. Many of the Belgian-based investments in Italy took place in technologically undeveloped parts of infrastructure and mining. It is, therefore, not by pure chance that Belgian investments in the tramway sector (mostly, as we have seen, organized in the legal form of Belgium-based companies, free-standing or not) stagnated after the end of the 1890s, when electrification became general and when strong links with the electrotechnical industry favoured German, Swiss, and US multinational enterprises of the 'classic' variety.[19]

The factors that acted in favour of UK and Belgian free-standing companies were absent, or less incisive, in the German and Swiss cases. In Germany (and to a lesser extent Switzerland), company laws and taxation were more stringent. What is probably more important, German and Swiss capital markets were dominated by the banks. Their outflow of foreign investment—apart from the special case of the Swiss textile industry—started later, more or less together with the so-called Second Industrial Revolution (from the 1880s to the early 1930s).[20] Conditions in the industries of this new era were then, as we have already seen, unfavourable to the adoption of the free-standing type of company.[21]

Summing up, one might say that the 'free-standing model' has so far shown a lot of vitality. Further research into particular industries and national case studies is certainly desirable. Where it has been tried, as in this chapter on the Italian example, much remains to be done. I have not used the available sources to assess the lifespan of free-standing firms. Scattered evidence seems to confirm that, for the companies focusing on the Italian market, especially in the case of the mining companies, 'a large majority never entered production'.[22] Other aspects of the 'free-standing model' have been confirmed or extended.

NOTES

1. See I. Berend and G. Ranki, *The European Periphery and Industrialization 1780–1914* (Cambridge, 1982), 73ff.; V. Zamagni, *Dalla periferia al centro: La seconda rinascita economica dell'Italia, 1861–1981* (Bologna, 1990), where the introductory chapter was titled 'Dal centro alla periferia'.
2. The reference to Alexander Gerschenkron, *Economic Backwardness in Historical Perspective* (Cambridge, Mass., 1966), is, of course, obligatory, especially since Italy serves as one of his principal case studies. For a recent discussion of Gerschenkron's contributions to the debate on Italian economic development, see G. Federico and G. Toniolo, 'Italy', in R. Sylla and G. Toniolo (eds.), *Patterns of European Industrialization: The Nineteenth Century* (New York, 1991), 197–217.
3. See P. Hertner, 'Das Auslandskapital in der italienischen Wirtschaft, 1883–1914: Probleme seiner Quantifizierung und Auswertung', in K. Borchardt, E. Schremmer, and W. Zorn (eds.), *Weltwirtschaftliche und währungspolitische Probleme seit dem Ausgang des Mittelalters* (Stuttgart, 1981), 93–121.
4. Ibid. 109 (graphs 2 and 3).
5. M. Wilkins, 'Defining a Firm: History and Theory', in P. Hertner and G. Jones (eds.), *Multinationals: Theory and History* (Aldershot, 1986), 80–95; Wilkins, 'The Free-Standing Company, 1870–1914: An Important Type of British Foreign Direct Investment', *Economic History Review*, 2nd ser., 41 (May 1988), 259–82.
6. See G. Ferri, 'La disciplina delle società nel codice de commercio del 1882', in *Cento anni dal codice di commercio: Atti del Convegno Internazionale di Studi, Taormina 4–6 Novembre 1982* (Milan, 1984), 91–125; C. Ghisalberti, *La codificazione del diritto in Italia, 1865–1942* (Rome, 1985), 60ff., 154ff.

7. Calculations of capital effectively invested are particularly problematic in the case of insurance companies and of foreign agencies of shipping companies. They have, therefore, been completely omitted from our calculations.
8. See Wilkins, 'The Free-Standing Company'; it also seems to fit with Mark Casson's argument that free-standing companies were to be found mainly in 'property-related industries'. See M. Casson, 'Institutional Diversity in Overseas Enterprise: Explaining the Free-Standing Company', *Business History*, 36 (Oct. 1994), 95–108.
9. C. E. Harvey and J. Press, 'The City and International Mining, 1870–1914', *Business History*, 32 (July 1990), 98–119; J.-J. van Helten, 'Mining, Share Manias and Speculation: British Investment in Overseas Mining, 1880–1913', in J.-J. van Helten and Y. Cassis (eds.), *Capitalism in a Mature Economy: Financial Institutions, Capital Exports and British Industry, 1870–1939* (Aldershot, 1990), 159–85.
10. H. König, 'Belgische Kapitalanlagen in Italien', unpublished dissertation (University of Kiel, 1920), 200.
11. M. Dumoulin, *Les Relations économiques italo-belges, 1861–1914* (Académie Royale de Belgique, Mémoires de la Classe des Lettres, Collections in 8°, 2nd ser., vol. 68, pt. 2, Brussels, 1990), 316.
12. Ministero di Agricoltura, Industria e Commercio (ed.), *Bollettino ufficiale delle società per azioni* 49 (1891), 64 ff.
13. See Geoffrey Jones, *British Multinational Banking, 1830–1900* (Oxford, 1993), for a context.
14. P. L. Cottrell, *Industrial Finance 1830–1914* (London, 1980), 52.
15. Wilkins, 'The Free-Standing Company', 261.
16. Ibid. Mark Casson distinguishes between the ordinary free-standing company as presented by Wilkins and which he does not consider to be a direct investor and the 'expatriate multinational', as he calls it, which, in his definition, 'actively controlled its overseas operations on a continuing basis'. See Casson, 'Institutional Diversity', 102.
17. Wilkins, 'The Free-Standing Company', 277.
18. See C. Colinet, *L'Organisation professionelle des bourses de valeurs mobilières en Belgique* (Brussels, 1913), *passim*; W. Bürklin (ed.), *Handbuch des belgischen Wirtschaftslebens*, pt. I (Göttingen, 1916), 268 ff.; B.-S. Chlepner, *Le Marché financier belge depuis cent ans* (Brussels, 1930), 73 ff.; R. Piret, *L'Évolution de la législation belge sur les sociétés anonymes* (Tournai/Paris, 1946), 37 ff.
19. See Dumoulin, *Les Relations économiques italo-belges*, 316 ff.
20. For Switzerland, see Paul Bairoch, 'La Suisse dans le contexte international aux XIXe et XXe siècles', in P. Bairoch and M. Körner (eds.), *Die Schweiz in der Weltwirtschaft (15.–20. Jh.)/La Suisse dans l'économie mondiale (15e–20e s.)* (Zurich, 1990), 103–40; H. G. Schröter, 'Etablierungs- und Verteilungsmuster der schweizerischen Auslandsproduktion von 1870 bis 1914', in Bairoch and Körner (eds.), *Die Schweiz in der Weltwirtschaft*, 391–407. For Germany, see the almost contemporary estimate and description by F. Lenz, 'Wesen und Struktur des deutschen Kapitalexports vor 1914', *Weltwirtschaftliches Archiv*, 18 (1922), 42–54.
21. A good example is offered by electricity production and distribution in Italy, where, according to Luciano Segreto's recent calculations, in 1913 the German share in joint-stock company capital amounted to 18.27% and the Swiss share to 8.28%, whereas Belgian and French capital reached percentages of only 2.05 and 1.17 respectively. See L. Segreto, 'Imprenditori e finanzieri', in G. Mori (ed.), *Storia dell'industria electrica in Italia*, i (Roma, 1992), 333. The part of German- or Swiss-based free-standing companies in this branch was negligible (see Table 5.1 in this chapter).
22. Harvey and Press, 'The City and International Mining', 115.

6

Free-Standing Companies in Tsarist Russia

Natalia Gurushina

The majority of British companies involved in conducting business in Russia at the end of the nineteenth and the beginning of the twentieth centuries followed an identical organizational pattern. The distinctive feature of this pattern was the existence of complex, multilevel structures that included intermediary companies, special companies for financing, Russian-affiliated enterprises, and Russian and British banks.

Many British companies that financed business in Russia were so-called free-standing companies. This term was first introduced by Mira Wilkins, who defined a free-standing company as an 'administratively as well as legally independent' venture the purpose of which was

> to obtain capital by bringing together profitable or potentially profitable operations overseas with British investors seeking financial opportunities superior to those at home. . . . The free-standing companies would provide an institutional framework that minimized . . . risks, managed the savings of British investors, and could attract foreign as well as British investment.[1]

Free-standing companies did not originate from a domestic manufacturing base. They were floated in the UK and had their head offices in London, but conducted business overseas. The difference between free-standing companies and investment companies was that the latter usually operated 'solely within Britain as institutional portfolio investors'.[2]

Wilkins argued that the type of capital export represented by free-standing companies was a direct investment rather than portfolio investment, since these ventures 'were designed to conduct business abroad, to manage and to direct the specific business'.[3] This study confirms that this is a valid model for a majority of British free-standing companies in Russia; however, as will be shown, in some cases a free-standing company was an 'umbrella structure' for other organizational forms.

One of the main reasons for the existence of free-standing companies was the different nature of the relationship between industrial enterprises and banks in Great Britain and Continental Europe. On the Continent, banks accompanied an industrial venture, as Alexander

Gerschenkron put it, 'from the cradle to the grave, from establishment to liquidation throughout all the vicissitudes of its existence'.[4] German banks, for example, were known to invest both their deposits and their own capital in industrial enterprises since the mid-nineteenth century. They also readily formed syndicates, which in conjunction with the large size of German banks significantly minimized investment risk.[5] Besides financial control over industrial undertakings by means of long- and short-term lending, European, and especially German, banks developed the practice of participating in companies' entrepreneurial decisions through the institution of the supervisory boards. Banks often placed their representatives on the boards of directors of companies with which they were involved: for example, in the year 1913 the Deutsche Bank held seats on 161 corporate boards.[6] British banks, on the other hand, tended to avoid long-term industrial investment, especially in new ventures. According to Emile Burns, 'most of the underwriting of new issues was undertaken, not by banks in the restricted sense, but by specialized financial houses'.[7] If British banks agreed to provide capital for new undertakings, they tried to sell the shares left in their hands as quickly as possible.

The literature on both British banking and overseas investment in the nineteenth and early twentieth centuries is enormous. The same can be said of the economic history of Tsarist Russia. Yet the role of both British and Russian financial institutions in relation to British companies conducting business in Russia has not been given due attention and no detailed work exists in this area. This chapter attempts to provide answers to the following questions:

- What was the mechanism of financing British-Russian undertakings? Who financed these undertakings? In which country was the money raised?
- What were the relationships between British and Russian financial institutions and the companies being financed? Were there any connections between organizational patterns and the type of financial mechanism?

The first part of this chapter examines the nature of functional relationships in a typical business cluster, including the participation of investment trust companies that acted as intermediaries as well as intermediary and core free-standing companies. The distinction between intermediaries and core free-standing companies is unique to my research. The second part analyses examples at variance with the typical pattern. The third part summarizes the most important findings of the research.

The Typical Business Cluster

A typical model of a 'core' free-standing company's functional connections is provided by British investment in non-ferrous metals production and oil extraction. The first British entrepreneurs involved in these industries took the form of 'intermediary' free-standing companies with comparatively small capital bases. These companies purchased concessions for the exploration and development of mines in Russia; subsequently they would sell options either to a British company set up to acquire capital stock of a Russian mining enterprise, or to a British company directly involved in the development of ore deposits in the Russian Empire. Among these intermediary companies was the Anglo-Siberian Corporation.

The Anglo-Siberian Corporation belonged to a group of ventures associated with the Scottish entrepreneur Leslie Urquhart, one of the major promoters of British investment in the mining industry of the Urals and Siberia. Urquhart's name appears as a director of all the companies in this group. The Anglo-Siberian Corporation was launched in London in December 1906 with a share capital of £500,000 in order to buy the option to exploit the mineral wealth in the Kyshtim District.[8] Although this mining property ('estate') had been worked profitably since the beginning of the nineteenth century and was well known in Russia, it had been neglected because of mismanagement and a lack of capital.[9]

The results of the Kyshtim mining estate's examination, arranged in 1907 by the Anglo-Siberian Corporation and conducted by two British engineers, were successful. Exploratory drilling confirmed the presence of rich deposits of iron, copper, and sulphur, as well as promising gold veins and alluvial gold in the Soymonovsk Valley.[10] However, the technical condition of the mines and plants was far from satisfactory.[11]

It soon became clear that the programme of works which the Anglo-Siberian Corporation intended to pursue at the Kyshtim estate would require more capital than had been put up initially. To raise additional financial resources, the promoters decided to launch a new company to assume direct control of the Kyshtim option. The new venture was named the Perm Corporation. More than three-quarters of its shares were allotted to the Anglo-Siberian Corporation.[12] By the end of 1907 the Perm Corporation had invested about £200,000 in the Kyshtim Mining Works Company.[13] More funds were needed, and in October 1908 the Perm Corporation sold the option to a newly created 'core' free-standing company, the Kyshtim Corporation, whose issued equity capital was £1 million.[14]

By 1910 the group of companies involved in the development of the

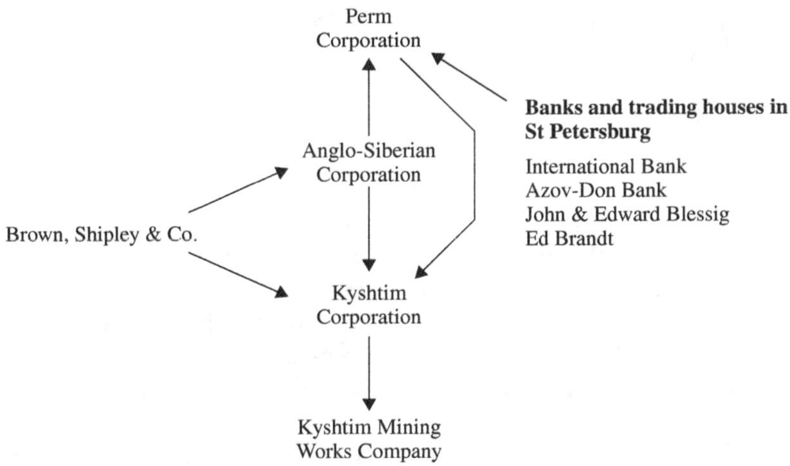

Fig. 6.1. The ownership structure of the Kyshtim cluster, 1910
Sources: GL Brown, Shipley & Co: L 64.22, MS 20.122, pp. 1717, 1734, 1781; RGIA, f. 61, op. 1, d. 11: pp. 130, 132, 138, 163, 195, 388, 421, 450, 476; f. 62, op. 1, d. 13: pp. 6, 7; f. 62, op. 1, d. 24: pp. 2, 3; f. 62, op. 1, d. 34: p. 3; f. 62, op. 1, d. 38, pp. 134, 165, 166; f. 62, op. 1, d. 44: pp. 115, 401, 544; f. 62, op. 1, d. 48: p. 102; f. 62, op. 1, d. 49: p. 3; f. 62, op. 1, d. 55: pp. 2, 3.

Kyshtim option had the following ownership structure (Fig. 6.1). The Anglo-Siberian Corporation held 243,710 shares in the Perm Corporation and 502,045 shares in the Kyshtim Corporation.[15] Most of the remaining shares of the Kyshtim Corporation were divided between the Perm Corporation and the London merchant bank Brown, Shipley & Co.[16] This bank also had holdings in the equity capital of the Anglo-Siberian Corporation.[17] The Azov-Don Bank, the International Commercial Bank of St Petersburg, and the trading houses John & Edward Blessig and Ed Brandt were among the shareholders of the Perm Corporation.[18] The Kyshtim Mining Works Company was the wholly owned affiliate of the Kyshtim Corporation.[19]

This complex structure did not last long. At the end of 1910, the first year that the Kyshtim Mining Works made profits, the Anglo-Siberian Corporation took over the assets of the Perm Corporation and the latter ceased to exist. Two years later, the board of the Anglo-Siberian Corporation decided to dissolve the company. Most of its shares (200,000) were exchanged for the shares of a newly established venture, the Russo-Asiatic Corporation.[20]

Having looked at the ownership structure of the Kyshtim cluster, we need to investigate the other aspect of the financial links within this group—namely, the provision of capital for operating purposes. One possible way of approaching this problem is to analyse the functional relationships between the intermediaries and the core free-standing companies. In a straightforward (ideal) model, one might assume that an intermediary company and a core one would undertake the following functions:

Intermediary free-standing company	Core free-standing company
Search for suitable concessions in the Russian Empire, afterwards selling concessions to core British free-standing companies, thus aborting any further contacts with Russian enterprises.	Pursuit of a particular business opportunity abroad to provide more efficient use of British investors' capital. These British free-standing companies would assume all the responsibilities connected with long-term and short-term financing of Russian ventures.

In reality, however, relationships between members of the same cluster were not so straightforward. The structure of financial transactions within the Kyshtim group (Fig. 6.2) shows that the British free-standing

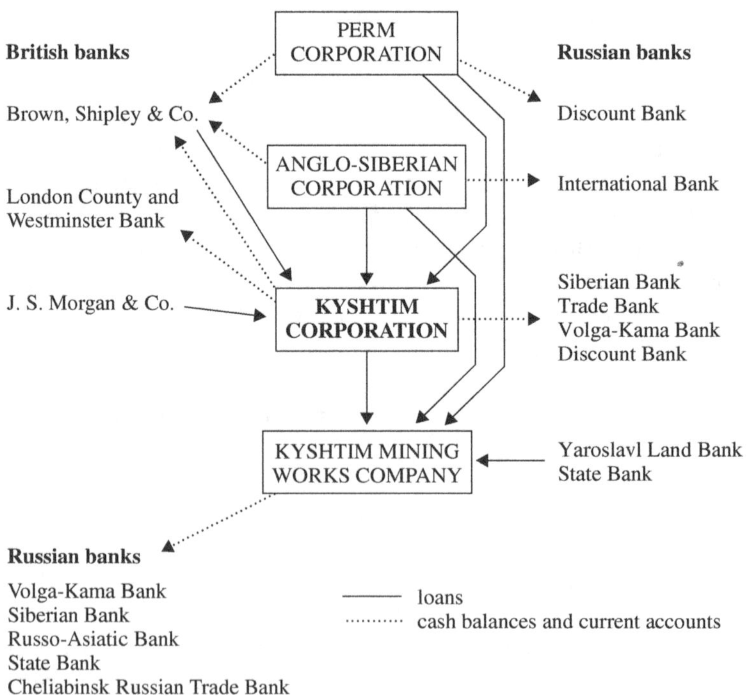

Fig. 6.2. Financial transactions within the Kyshtim cluster, 1907–1910
Source: See Fig. 6.1.

TABLE 6.1. *Advances to the Kyshtim Corporation, 1907–1908 (£)*

Lender	1907	1908
1. Perm Corporation	97,104	55,000
2. The Anglo-Siberian Corporation	35,980	a
3. Brown, Shipley & Co.	a	100,000
4. J. S. Morgan	a	b

Notes:
a = information not available.
b = amount of loans unknown.
Sources: 1907 (rows 1, 2): RGIA, f. 62, op. 1, d. 11: 450; 1908 (row 1): RGIA, f. 62, op. 1, d. 11: 138; 1908 (row 3): RGIA, f. 62, op. 1, d. 11: 388; 1908 (row 4): RGIA, f. 62, op. 1, d. 11: 163.

companies were not the only creditors of Russian enterprises. The Kyshtim Mining Works Company, for example, enjoyed direct loans provided by two Russian banks, the Yaroslavl Land Bank and the State Bank. Both intermediary companies, the Perm Corporation and the Anglo-Siberian Corporation, were among the creditors of the Russian enterprise. Furthermore, the Perm Corporation and the Anglo-Siberian Corporation also took part in financing the Kyshtim Corporation itself. Particulars of these financial transactions are given in Tables 6.1 and 6.2.

Fig. 6.2 and Tables 6.1 and 6.2 bring out an important but hitherto unnoticed feature of the relationships between British-financed enterprises that conducted business in the Russian Empire and banks. In historical studies the traditional way to describe links between a company and a bank was by saying that 'a certain company was financed by/connected with a certain bank or a group of banks'. This expression, however, lacks precision and prompts a further question of what *exactly* is meant by the words 'financed' and 'connected'. A major finding of the present research is that we are now able to identify and specify various

TABLE 6.2. *Advances to the Kyshtim Mining Works Company, 1906–1913 (£)*

Year	(1) Yaroslavl Land Bank	(2) Kyshtim Corporation	(3) Anglo-Siberian Corporation	(4) Perm Corporation	(5) Russian Government
1906	528,304	a	a	133,082	93,465
1907	a	a	a	a	a
1908	a	a	a	a	a
1909	584,596	a	a	98,865	582,047
1910	571,840	153,260	a	64,260	99,280
1911	a	31,143	88,000	b	a
1912	a	222,492	c	b	a
1913	a	305,103	b	b	a

a = information not available.
b = no loans.
c = amount of loans unknown.
Sources: 1906 (cols. 1, 4, 5): RGIA, f. 62, op. 1, d. 13: 6, 7; 1909 (cols. 1, 4, 5). RGIA, f. 62, op. 1, d. 24: 2, 3; 1910 (cols. 1, 4, 5): RGIA, f. 62, op. 1, d. 35: 2; 1910 (col. 2): RGIA, f. 62, op. 1, d. 34: 3; 1911 (col. 2): RGIA, f. 62, op. 1, d. 44: 544; 1911 (col. 3): RGIA, f. 62, op. 1, d. 38: 134, 165, 166; 1912 (col. 2): RGIA, f. 62, op. 1, d. 49: 3; 1912 (col. 3): RGIA, f. 62, op. 1, d. 44: 401; 1913 (col 2): RGIA, f. 62, op. 1, d. 55: 8.

types of financial connections between British–Russian companies and banks, such as holding of equities, floating debenture issues, providing long-term and short-term loans, and operating accounts on which companies drew to cover current expenditures (or current accounts). Only some of these transactions led to the actual provision of capital for ventures in Russia.

The British free-standing company called the Irtysh Corporation was another brainchild of Leslie Urquhart. This company financed the activity of two Russian enterprises (using the phrase 'Russian enterprises' to refer to those registered in Russia), the Ridder Company and the Kirghiz Company, which developed lead, zinc, and coal mines in the Kirghiz Steppe. The Irtysh Corporation was launched in London in 1914. Its formation was mediated by the Anglo-Siberian Corporation's successor, the Russo-Asiatic Corporation.[21] According to the agreement between the two companies, the Russo-Asiatic Corporation was allotted 1.1 million shares in the newly established free-standing company.[22] The Irtysh Corporation, in turn, accepted the responsibility to pay off a £33,000 debt owed by the Ridder and Kirghiz Companies to the Russo-Asiatic Corporation.[23]

The Russo-Asiatic Corporation and the Irtysh Corporation had interlocking directorates: Leslie Urquhart and R. Gilman Brown were on the boards of both companies. The directors of the Irtysh Corporation also included the Chairman of the Private Commercial Bank of Petrograd, A. A. Davidoff; the Chairman of the Kyshtim Mining Works Company, Baron V. V. Meller-Zakomelski; the director of the Kyshtim Corporation, American mining engineer Herbert Hoover; the director of the Tanalyk Corporation, A. Scott; and mining engineer D. Mitchell.[24]

The Irtysh Corporation was the principal shareholder in both the Ridder Company and the Kirghiz Company and provided them with advances of working capital.[25] In 1917 the free-standing company advanced a total of Rs.11,996,115 (£339,871)[26] for the conduct of business in Russia.[27] The total share capital of the Kirghiz and Ridder Companies at that time being Rs.24.5 million, the sum advanced was equivalent to 42 per cent of the recipients' equity liabilities.[28]

Although the official banker of the Irtysh Corporation was the London County and Westminster Bank, two Russian banks, the Azov-Don Bank and the Siberian Bank, played a very substantial role in the development of the company's properties in Russia.[29] In December 1916 the board of the Kirghiz Company asked the Azov-Don Bank to open a credit line valued at Rs.1,996,000 (£133,512).[30] A year later the total of direct loans outstanding from the Siberian Bank to this enterprise was recorded as Rs.1,800,000 (£60,000).[31] The Ridder Company for its part reached an agreement with the Siberian Bank in March 1917

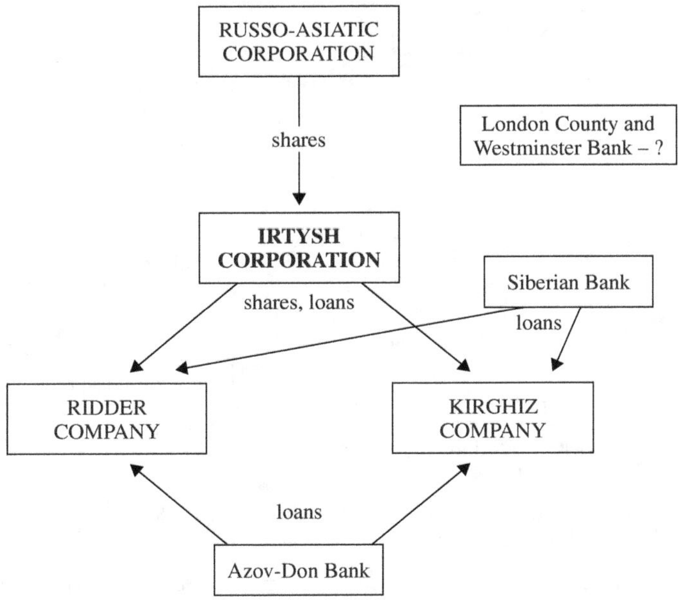

Fig. 6.3. The structure of ownership and other financial transactions in the Irtysh cluster, 1914–1917
Sources: RGIA, f. 1427, op. 1, d. 2: 18, 21; RGIA, f. 1427, op. 1, d. 24: 7; RGIA, f. 1427, op. 1, d. 49: 2, 4: RGIA, f. 1423, op. 1, d. 7: 4.

to extend its credit up to Rs.4,500,000 (£150,000).[32] By May 1917 the Ridder Company's credits at the Azov-Don Bank totalled Rs.1,978,505 (£65,950).[33] The structure of shareholding and other financial transactions in the Irtysh cluster are shown in Fig. 6.3.

Regarding the relationship between the Irtysh Corporation and its official banker, the London County and Westminster Bank, available documentary evidence is inconclusive. The Bank's prospective loans and investment were discussed at the meetings of its Daily Committee. Although the name of the Irtysh Corporation does not appear in the Committee's Reports, one cannot be absolutely sure that the Bank did not act as the company's creditor, since the available documents concentrate on large loans and ignore smaller advances.[34]

The Sissert Company, a free-standing company set up to develop copper deposits in Imperial Russia, did not belong to the ventures grouped around the activities of Urquhart. It was launched in London in 1912 to purchase the entire equity capital of the Russian enterprise, the Sissert Mining District Company, from its promoter, the Russian Trust and Finance Company.[35] The board of the Sissert Company had among its members Sir James B. Dale, director of the Consett Iron Company and of Pease and Partners Company; William Selkirk, a

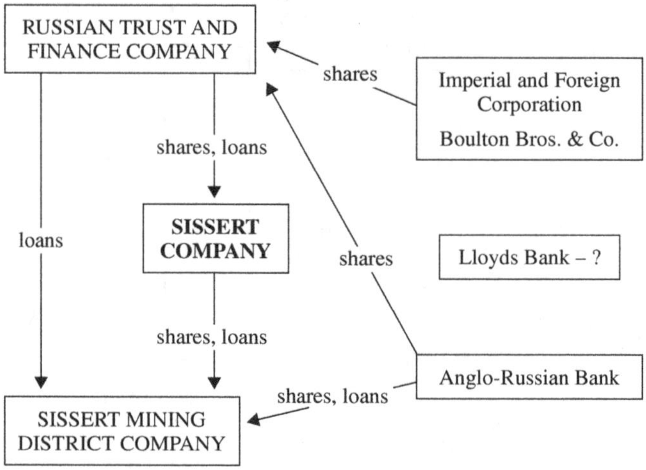

Fig. 6.4. Functional relationships within the Sissert cluster, 1912–1916
Sources: RGIA, f. 86, op. 1, d. 5: 2, 3; RGIA, f. 86, op. 1, d. 9: 2, 20; PRO BT 31: 20239/120885, 1, 33, 45.

member of the Royal Geological Society and the Institute of Mining and Metallurgy; Prince Alexander Golitsin and Prince Alexander Urusov, members of the State Duma and directors of the Sissert Mining District Company; and Grigori Benenson, the director of the Anglo-Russian Bank in St Petersburg.[36] In 1915 the Sissert Company's board was extended to include two new members: Mr Kiaer, manager of the London branch of the Anglo-Russian Bank; and Herbert Guedalla, representative of the Imperial and Foreign Corporation.[37]

The pattern of functional relationships within the Sissert cluster (Figure 6.4) was very similar to that of Urquhart's ventures. Table 6.3 shows that the free-standing company (the Sissert Company) bore the brunt of the financing costs of the Russian enterprise (the Sissert Mining District Company), although some loans were made by the intermediary, the Russian Trust and Finance Company, and one of the Sissert Company's bankers, the Anglo-Russian Bank.

TABLE 6.3. *'Cash' indebtedness of the Sissert Mining District Company, 1912–1916 (£)*

Year	Local bank	Anglo-Russian Bank	Russian Trust and Finance Company	Sissert Company
1912	—	—	—	75,600
1913	—	—	—	75,600
1914	—	—	—	79,050
1915	—	—	—	70,037
1916	7,883	33,780	13,378	64,509

Notes: In the original document the amount was given in roubles. We converted the figures from roubles into pounds using the following offical exchange rates: 1912/13: £1 = Rs.9.45; 1914: £1 = Rs.12.20; 1915: £1 = Rs.13.77; 1916: £1 = Rs.14.95.
A dash means no loans.
Source: RGIA, f. 86, op. 1, d. 63: 156.

Little is known of the functional relationship between the Russian Trust and Finance Company and the Sissert Company. However, in the documents of the Sissert Company the former is often referred to not only as the promoter but as the free-standing company's financier as well.[38] Since one of the objectives of the present research is to investigate the functional relationships among the members of each cluster, the links between these two companies need more thorough examination.

In March 1912 the representatives of the Anglo-Russian Bank of St Petersburg, Grigori Benenson (the Bank's agent in England), and Frederick Cripps, along with the delegates of two British companies, Messrs Boulton Bros. & Co. and the Imperial and Foreign Corporation,[39] launched a new enterprise with a view to 'seeking business in the Empire of Russia' and 'in particular to form, constitute, lend money to, assist and control any company'.[40] The venture was named the Russian Trust and Finance Company. Most of its equities were allotted to the nominees of the Anglo-Russian Bank, the Imperial and Foreign Corporation, and Messrs Boulton Bros. & Co. (Table 6.4).

The relationships between the Russian Trust and Finance Company and the Anglo-Russian Bank (and its director, Benenson) were not limited to a mere shareholding. In May 1912 the company and the Anglo-Russian Bank made an agreement by which the bank undertook to 'give its services and its best endeavours to assist the Company in connection with any business which may be offered to the Company by any person, firm or corporation in the Empire of Russia'.[41] In February 1913 a similar agreement was made between the Russian Trust and Finance Company and Benenson.[42]

Unfortunately, available archival documents are insufficient to reveal fully the nature of the financial relationships between the Russian Trust and Finance Company and the Sissert Company. Nevertheless, it is

TABLE 6.4. *Ownership structure of the Russian Trust and Finance Company, 1912–1917 (%)*

Shareholders	As at 1 May 1912		As at 9 April 1917	
	Preference shares	Ordinary shares	Preference shares	Ordinary shares
The Anglo-Russian Bank total	50.0	13.5	67.0	34.0
of which Grigori Benenson	—	13.5	—	34.0
Representatives of the Imperial and Foreign Corporation	50.0	27.0	33.0	20.2
Representatives of Messrs Boulton Bros. & Co.	—	13.5	—	36.0
Other British shareholders	—	46.0	0.0	9.8
TOTAL	100.0	100.0	100.0	100.0

Note: A dash means no interest.
Source: PRO BT 31: 20239/120885, 1, 33.

possible to trace some details showing that the role of the intermediary company was more substantial than acting merely as a mediator and coordinator between British and Russian enterprises.

It is known, for example, that, when the Sissert Company was formed in the year 1912, the Russian Trust and Finance Company was allotted 23 per cent of its equity.[43] Another interesting fact is that Guedalla, one of the Russian Trust and Finance Company's directors and principal shareholders, had 'a very large holding' in the Sissert Company.[44] It is also likely that the promoting company acted as the Sissert Company's creditor.

Our analysis would be incomplete without considering another aspect of functional connections within the Sissert cluster—namely, the links between banks and the free-standing company. The Anglo-Russian Bank, which played such an important role in the activity of the Russian Trust and Finance Company, in this case merely carried out current transactions for the company.[45] It, however, did not preclude the Bank's involvement in directly financing the Sissert Mining District Company. In 1916, for example, the Bank provided the Russian enterprise with a loan valued at Rs.505,000.[46] Furthermore, the Anglo-Russian Bank was one of the Sissert Mining District Company's shareholders.[47]

The other bank which secondary sources indicate financed the activity of the Sissert Company in Russia is Lloyds Bank.[48] Research in the archives of Lloyds Bank in London has not brought to light any documents to confirm the Bank's interest in the equity capital of the Sissert Company or that the Bank acted as the company's creditor.[49] If financial links between the Sissert Company and Lloyds Bank existed, the Bank would probably have operated the Sissert Company's current accounts.

Another sector of the late imperial Russian economy with a high concentration of British free-standing companies was the petroleum industry. Organizationally and financially the majority of these companies followed the pattern of the typical model described earlier. Among these ventures were the Bibi-Eybat Petroleum Company and the Emba Caspian Oil Company.

The Bibi-Eybat Petroleum Company was floated in London in 1900 with an authorized capital of £460,000.[50] This free-standing company acquired all the equity capital of the Russian enterprise, the Bibi-Eybat Naphtha Company. As is shown in Table 6.5, the British company was the major source of financial support for the Russian venture. Occasionally, as, for example, in 1910, the International Commercial Bank of St Petersburg provided credits. Although, in this particular case, the free-standing company's promoter, the London Trust Company, did

TABLE 6.5. *Creditors of the Bibi-Eybat Naphtha Company, 1909–1917 (£)*

Year	Bibi-Eybat Petroleum Company	International Commercial Bank of St Petersburg
1909	53,537*	a
1910	55,515*	54,693*
1911	b	a
1912	b	a
1913	61,250	a
1914	62,542	a
1915	82,395	a
1916	94,727	a
1917	109,537	a

* These figures were originally given in roubles (1909/10 £1 = Rs. 9.64).
a = no loans.
b = amount of loans unknown.
Source: GL SEAR, Nitrate and Oil Reports, 1909/10, 1910/11, 1913/14, 1914/15, 1915/16, 1916/17, 1917/18.

not have an interest in the equity capital, it was one of its principal debenture holders.[51] I can find no definite indications of the position of British financial institutions in this cluster.

The Emba Caspian Oil Company was incorporated in July 1912 in London to acquire a part of the equity capital of the Russian company, the Emba Caspian Naphtha Industrial Company.[52] Similar to many other British free-standing companies operating in Late Imperial Russia, the Emba Caspian Oil Company had financial responsibilities towards

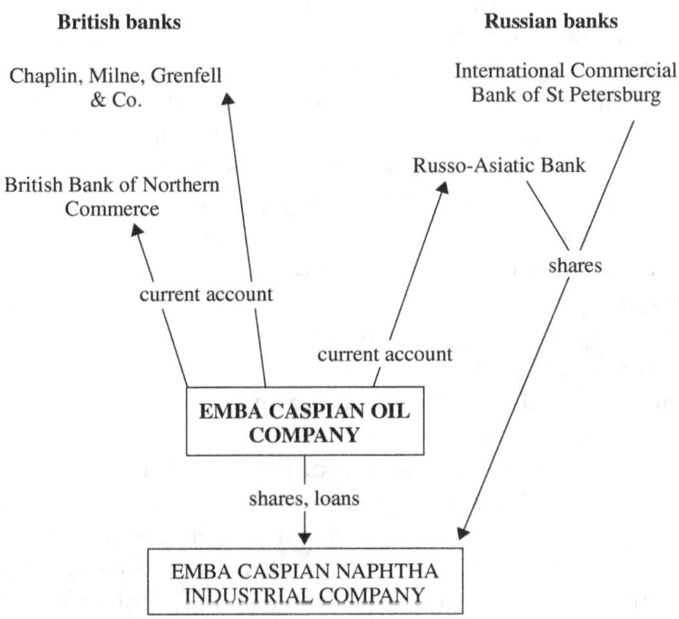

Fig. 6.5. Functional relationships within the Emba Caspian cluster, 1912–1917
Sources: GL SEAR, Nitrate and Oil Reports, 1912/13, 1913/14, 1914/15, 1915/16; *Monopolisticheski kapital v neftyanoi promyshlennosti Rossii, 1914–1917* (1973), 156–7.

its subsidiary which included the provision of working capital. In 1914/15 the Emba Caspian Oil Company provided the Russian enterprise with a loan valued at £138,172. A year later the Emba Caspian's direct advances totalled £143,808.[53]

The documents of the Emba Caspian Oil Company reveal that it had four official bankers: two British banks, Chaplin, Milne, Grenfell & Co. and the British Bank of Northern Commerce, and two Russian, the International Commercial Bank of St Petersburg and the Russo-Asiatic Bank. Chairmen of the Russian banks, Alexander Wyshnegradski and Alexei Poutiloff, and a representative of Chaplin, Milne, Grenfell & Co., Arthur Morton Grenfell, were members of the Emba Caspian Oil Company's board. The Russo-Asiatic Bank and the two British banks carried out current transactions for the free-standing company.[54] However, relations between Chaplin, Milne, Grenfell & Co. and the Emba Caspian Oil Company were rather short-lived: by 1914 the bank had invested too much of its capital in real estate in Canada and was declared bankrupt.[55]

In addition to their role as official bankers of the free-standing company, both Russian banks were also involved in financing the activity of the Emba Caspian Naphtha Industrial Company. In 1916 the International Commercial Bank and the Russo-Asiatic Bank held 99,455 shares of the Russian company.[56] Fig. 6.5 indicates the functional relationships within the Emba Caspian cluster.

After all that has been said, there may be a question as to why this rather lengthy discussion about functional relations within business clusters with the participation of British free-standing companies is of any importance. I believe that this analysis may help us to understand what type of overseas investment, direct or portfolio, was represented by free-standing companies. Wilkins argued that this type of capital exports should be regarded as a direct investment.[57] By contrast, Mark Casson, whose arguments are based on the different nature of competitive advantages in property development and manufacturing industries, suggests that free-standing companies should rather be included in the foreign portfolio investment statistics.[58] Casson maintained that in a free-standing firm significant control was exercised only during the initial development phase.[59] This is the view that I would like to challenge.

As was shown earlier in this section, one of the most important functions of British free-standing companies was not only providing Russian enterprises with equity capital during the investment phase but also supplying working capital during the operating phase. This was a response to the constant problem of undercapitalization faced by many British-financed companies in Russia, especially in the mining industry and textiles. Archival documents show that a substantial proportion of the first issue of British free-standing companies' equities was typically associated with the acquisition of property rights in Russia. These equities were not paid in cash, but were rather taken 'for considerations other than cash', i.e. allotted to the former owners of properties in the Russian Empire. This share was especially high, usually more than 50 per cent of the initial issue, in the mining industry. The case of the Yenisei Copper Company, set up in April 1902 in London to acquire and develop copper-mining concessions in the District of Minusinsk and Achinsk in Siberia, represents one of the most remarkable examples of this phenomenon.[60] Out of 167,007 equity shares of this company allotted by August 1902, only 20,007, or 12 per cent, were paid wholly in cash.[61] In the textile industry the 'undercapitalization' problem started to occur at the end of the nineteenth century when the low concentration of capital in the retail trade forced many textile companies to develop their own sales network. In this way companies were able to obtain additional profits. However, these factors also contributed to higher production costs, leaving many companies short of capital for operating purposes.[62]

Although my findings show that both British and Russian banks took part in financing British–Russian enterprises, it was free-standing companies that played the pivotal role in attracting funds of the British public into Russian ventures during the operating phase. I would also suggest that raising funds for highly risky ventures overseas in a situation when banks' response was often far from adequate would require very similar entrepreneurial skills and equally strong determination at both the initial investment stage and operational stage.

The fact that the majority of British free-standing companies and their Russian subsidiaries had interlocking directorates should also be considered as an indicator of free-standing firms' managerial control during the operational phase. For example, the directors of the Kyshtim Corporation, Urquhart and Charles Frederick Henry Leslie, were also members of the board of the Kyshtim Mining Works Company.[63] Urquhart was on the boards of the Irtysh Corporation and its subsidiaries, the Kirghiz Company and the Ridder Company.[64] He was also a director of another British free-standing company, the Tanalyk Corporation, and the South-Urals Mining Company, which it controlled.[65]

Variations in Business Cluster Patterns

The foregoing typical models of functional relationships between British and Russian industrial ventures and financial institutions do not represent the whole variety of financial connections between Russian companies, their British owners, and banks. In this section I consider a number of examples to illustrate the complexity and sometimes peculiar interplay of financial and organizational patterns of business clusters involving the participation of British free-standing companies. I begin the analysis with the history of a free-standing company called the Anglo-Russian Cotton Factories, set up in London in 1896.

In the past, most research on British investment in the Russian textile industry has focused on the companies situated in the Central region and allied with De Jersey & Co. of Manchester and Baron Ludwig Knoop. Even though the bulk of British capital in textiles was invested in St Petersburg and the surrounding region, the enterprises concerned have attracted little attention. No attempts, moreover, have been made to investigate financial relationships between Russian textile factories and their British owners.

As has been pointed out by many scholars, on the eve of the First World War the Russian textile industry was almost entirely outside the sphere of influence of Russian banks.[66] On the one hand, according to V. Ya. Laverychev, 'St. Petersburg's banks did not seriously attempt to penetrate the textile industry because they were unable to mobilize the substantial funds invested in other industries', whereas 'Moscow capitalists . . . did not need their [the banks'] financial support' since they 'had a very strong financial foundation' built during the pre-capitalist period.[67] On the other hand, before the outbreak of the war only a few Russian textile companies resorted to issuing debt to obtain fresh funds.[68] Usually the companies would increase capital by borrowing from their shareholders.[69]

What type of financial mechanism was used by Russian textile companies with British participation? One of the best-documented case studies is that of the Anglo-Russian Cotton Factories, whose activity in Russia was associated with the merchant houses of the Hubbard family.

At the beginning of the nineteenth century, the Hubbard family was one of a small number of mercantile families that dominated British textile trade with Russia through the Baltic. In 1816 the founder of the dynasty, John Hubbard, opened a merchant house in St Petersburg. Later on one of his sons, William Egerton Hubbard, became a leading partner in this concern.[70] In 1842 the Hubbards launched their first company in Russia, the Petroffsky Cotton Spinning and Weaving Manufacturing Company. Their second enterprise, a cotton-print factory, was acquired twenty-two years later in 1864. The Spassky Cotton Mills (built in 1839 in a suburb of St Petersburg) were taken over by the Hubbard family in 1869.[71]

Before 1896 the financial arrangements between the Russian factories and their British owners were quite simple and straightforward. The

Hubbard family held all the shares in the three Russian textile factories.[72] Messrs John Hubbard & Co. of London acted as the creditor of the Russian companies. This London house was run by the descendants of John Hubbard, initially by his son John Gellibrand Hubbard, who became a partner in 1821. When John Gellibrand died in 1889, the leadership was taken over by his heir Evelyn Hubbard (1852–1934).[73]

In the middle of the nineteenth century this financial arrangement had worked smoothly; the textile factories in Russia 'very rapidly earned large profits', which could be reinvested.[74] By the end of the century, however, the business situation in the Russian textile industry, as well as the financial position of the Hubbard house in London, had changed: 'every year after 1880 saw increasing competition and increasing demand for more difficult and varied work. This necessitated greater investment of capital, more than the founders of the business had at their own command.'[75]

Another explanation for the financial difficulties of the Hubbard business at that time has been suggested by M. J. Daunton. The crisis, he argued, was precipitated by two factors. One was that both of the founder's sons, John Gellibrand Hubbard and William Egerton Hubbard, at their deaths failed to clarify the relationship between the family and the firms, and mishandled the question of inheritance and succession. The second reason was business incompetence of the next generation, the cousins Evelyn Hubbard and Egerton Hubbard, who took over their fathers' positions in London and St Petersburg.[76]

In 1889 the beneficiaries of John Gellibrand Hubbard deposited their money in the London partnership and agreed not to withdraw it without the company's permission. Even so, funds were still inadequate to sustain business in Russia.[77] An attempt to reorganize the companies and give an impetus to business both in Russia and England was made in 1896, when the Hubbards launched a new enterprise called the Anglo-Russian Cotton Factories in London. The new company was to acquire the stock of the three Russian textile factories owned by the Hubbard family.[78]

Although the Anglo-Russian Cotton Factories was now responsible for financing the Russian companies, it was decided that Messrs Egerton Hubbard of St Petersburg would continue to manage and control the factories in Russia.[79] The Russian shareholders in the three textile companies were told that the main reason for setting up the Anglo-Russian Cotton Factories was the need 'to arrange for a permanent provision of working capital, and to take advantage of the cheaper rates current for money in England. . . . It is clearly more advantageous to English Shareholders to possess Shares in an English Company which can be dealt with in England than to hold Shares in Russian Companies, for which there is no market in this country.'[80]

One may question the validity of the final part of this passage, because, according to Evelyn Hubbard's remark at one of the annual meetings, 'in the case of this company . . . there was practically no market for shares . . . it was mostly a family concern, and sales were by private treaty'.[81] More likely, it was the company's ability to issue debentures in England and use the lending facilities of British banks which made the formation of the Anglo-Russian Cotton Factories 'clearly more advantageous to English Shareholders'.

The first issue of debentures valued at £500,000 was floated by the Anglo-Russian Cotton Factories at the end of 1896. A substantial part of the issue (£300,000) was offered for public subscription. The remainder was taken up privately by the members of the Hubbard family. The proceeds of the issue were used to increase the amount of capital the company intended to employ in Russia from £470,320 to £970,000.[82] Contrary to the Board's expectations, the funds did not prove sufficient to meet the permanent needs for working capital for the Russian factories and make them independent of the St Petersburg discount market. In 1899 the Hubbards were impelled to ask an industrialist, Stuart Rendel, who had married into the family, for financial assistance. Rendel, who lived in England, continued to support the Hubbard enterprises until 1913.[83]

What was the nature of financial relationships in the Hubbard cluster? The Anglo-Russian Cotton Factories was launched (in 1896) by the Hubbard family, which also stood behind one of the leading British-based investment groups that included, apart from textile companies, banking, petroleum, and forestry interests.[84] The Anglo-Russian Cotton Factories was a free-standing company; it did not originate from a manufacturing base in the UK.

One could assume that, as a free-standing company, the Anglo-Russian Cotton Factories would raise capital for investment in Russia by public flotation of equities and debentures. Instead, the actual financial mechanism it adopted was rather similar to that of a family-based investment group, which rarely resorted to the provision of capital from outside the family. This combination of the financial pattern of an investment group and the organizational pattern of a free-standing company resulted in a very peculiar form of financial arrangement in the Hubbard cluster. During the first twelve years of the Anglo-Russian Cotton Factories' existence, from 1896 to 1908, debenture issues and financial support by the family members were the primary source of fresh funds for this free-standing company. The role of its banker, the Bank of England, was confined mainly to handling current-account transactions.[85]

The turning point in the relationship between British financial institutions and the Hubbards' enterprises came in 1908. At the beginning of that year there had been a rise in Russian demand, particularly for high-quality cotton goods. The Board of the Anglo-Russian Cotton Factories decided to increase the weaving capacity of the Petroffsky and Spassky Mills and install new machinery to produce the finer classes of textile.[86] The successful implementation of this programme, however, was threatened by the still unsatisfactory financial position of the Russian factories. Once again the Hubbards needed additional financial resources from outside.

A part of these funds was raised by the issue of 1,500 6 per cent debentures of £100 each. The issue was floated by the banking house Glyn, Mills, Currie & Co., who themselves bought most of the debentures.[87] The remaining sum was obtained by the Anglo-Russian Cotton Factories in a totally new fashion. It reached an agreement with the London and County Banking House to open a line of credit valued at £40,000.[88] The loan was secured against 500 newly created debentures deposited by the Anglo-Russian Cotton Factories at the Banking House.[89]

In 1914–16 the London County and Westminster Bank made another series of advances to the Anglo-Russian Cotton Factories. These advances were secured by Russian Government Bonds placed by the company with the State Bank in St Petersburg at the London County and Westminster Bank's disposal. In 1915, to secure further advances, the Anglo-Russian Cotton Factories made a deposit of Rs.240,000 in cash at another St Petersburg bank, the Azov-Don Bank, and a deposit of Russian Treasury Bills worth Rs.900,000 at the State Bank.[90] By 1917 the company's short-term credits from the London County and Westminster Bank totalled £181,900 (Table 6.6).[91]

The importance of external financing of the Hubbard business in Russia grew after the formation of the Anglo-Russian Cotton Factories in 1896. Nevertheless, John Hubbard & Co., previously the principal supplier of working capital to the Russian factories, continued its

TABLE 6.6. *The Anglo-Russian Cotton Factories' cash credits from the London County and Westminster Bank, 1914–1916 (£)*

Year	Value of the loan
1914	62,400
1915	95,500
1916	24,000
TOTAL	181,900

Source: GL ARCF, L 69.55, MS 11.760.

activity as the London agent of Messrs Egerton Hubbard & Co. of St Petersburg. Cotton acceptances undertaken for the St Petersburg house became the main part of its business.[92]

The structure of the Hubbard business and the general scheme of financial transactions between its Russian and British divisions and British financial institutions are shown in Fig. 6.6. The pivotal role in the whole system was played by the Anglo-Russian Cotton Factories. The company was the major link between funds in Britain and its recipients in Russia. Money raised by the Anglo-Russian Cotton Factories in Britain was transferred to St Petersburg and put at the disposal of its General Agent and Manager in Russia, Messrs Egerton Hubbard & Co.[93] Each of the three Russian companies belonging to the Hubbard family had in its books an account 'Anglo-Russian Cotton Factories, Ltd', and the British company's advances were listed under that account.[94]

Throughout the period 1900–17 advances outstanding at the year end by the Anglo-Russian Cotton Factories to its subsidiaries in Russia exceeded its investment in the Russian companies' equity capital valued at £470,320. The most interesting figures are those for the period 1909–16, when the amount of outstanding credits was one and a half times greater than the capital employed in the Russian companies' equities (Table 6.7).[95]

The price the Russian cotton factories had to pay for the credits was high. Interest rates charged by the Anglo-Russian Cotton Factories for

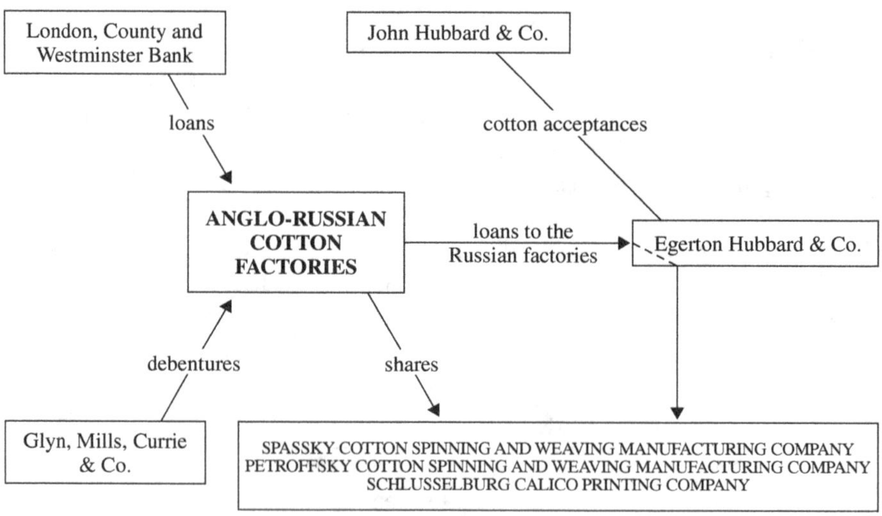

Fig. 6.6. Financial transactions between the Hubbard textile enterprises and outside institutions, 1897–1917
Sources: GL ARCF, MS 11.760, Minute Book of Ordinary and Extraordinary General Meeting of Shareholders, 1897–1948.

TABLE 6.7. *Outstanding advances of the Anglo-Russian Cotton Factories to Schlusselburg Calico Printing Company and the Petroffsky and Spassky Spinning and Weaving Companies, as at the year-end, 1897–1917 (£)*

Year-end	Schlusselburg Calico Printing Company	Petroffsky Cotton Spinning and Weaving Manufacturing Company	Spassky Cotton Spinning and Weaving Manufacturing Company	Total
1897	380,000	45,000	45,000	470,000
1898	380,000	45,000	45,000	470,000
1899	380,000	45,000	45,000	470,000
1900	380,000	90,000	45,000	515,000
1901	380,000	90,000	45,000	515,000
1902	380,000	90,000	45,000	515,000
1903	380,000	90,000	45,000	515,000
1904	380,000	90,000	45,000	515,000
1905	380,000	90,000	45,000	515,000
1906	385,692	93,000	56,277	534,969
1907	385,692	93,000	66,523	545,216
1908	385,692	93,000	66,523	545,216
1909	422,431	141,349	148,597	712,377
1910	417,144	146,634	148,597	712,377
1911	417,144	146,634	148,597	712,377
1912	417,144	146,634	148,597	712,377
1913	417,144	146,634	148,597	712,377
1914	467,259	136,046	119,589	722,895
1915	467,259	136,046	119,589	722,895
1916	467,259	136,046	119,589	722,895
1917	229,934	136,046	119,589	485,570

Source: GL ARCF, L 69.55, MS 11.760, Minute Book of Ordinary and Extraordinary General Meetings of Shareholders, 1897–1948.

its advances were well in excess of current discount rates both in Russia and Britain.[96] Moreover, the Russian factories were 'expressly forbidden to raise moneys or borrow in any way which will prejudice the security of the English Company [i.e. Anglo-Russian Cotton Factories]'.[97] A resolution passed at the Second Meeting of the Anglo-Russian Cotton Factories' Board of Directors declared:

[it was resolved] to inform them [i.e. each of the Directors of the three Russian Companies] that such advances are made upon the distinct understanding that the Directors of the Russian Companies will not in any way allow any other creditor by any means to become in a better position than the English Company as a creditor of the Russian Companies, and it is hereby clearly explained to each Director that the English Company as a holder of the controlling interest in the shares in the Russian Companies desires this to be a standing instruction to the Directors of the Russian Companies.[98]

The financial arrangements between the Anglo-Russian Cotton Factories and its affiliated companies were so rigid and apparently biased in favour of the British side that Stuart Rendel called the Russian factories a 'milch cow' for the Hubbards.[99] Incidentally, the content and the tone of the above quote also demonstrate that the Anglo-Russian Cotton Factories was a true direct investor exercising both financial and operational control over the affiliated textile companies.

Other variants on the free-standing companies' typical organizational and financial patterns are the cases of two petroleum concerns, the Schibaieff Petroleum Company and the Ural Caspian Oil Corporation, and the gold-mining company, the Lena Goldfields. The distinctive feature of the activity of the Schibaieff Petroleum Company and the Ural Caspian Oil Corporation was that one was from the start and the other quickly became part of Royal Dutch Shell's network in the Russian Empire. On the surface, they looked like free-standing companies, but they fit the classic multinational enterprise model.

The Schibaieff Petroleum Company was set up in February 1898 by the Shell Transport and Trading Company in order to take over the enterprise belonging to the Baku merchant, S. M. Schibaieff. Shell's role in the Schibaieff Company's affairs became more prominent after its reconstruction under the name of the New Schibaieff Petroleum Company at the beginning of 1913, when the Anglo-Saxon Petroleum Company, representing the Royal Dutch Shell Group, acquired about one-third of its equity capital (Fig. 6.7). The management of the whole Schibaieff cluster was entrusted to the Anglo-Saxon Company. It also had the right to appoint the majority of the New Schibaieff Petroleum Company's directors.[100]

The Shell Group also controlled the operations of the Russian

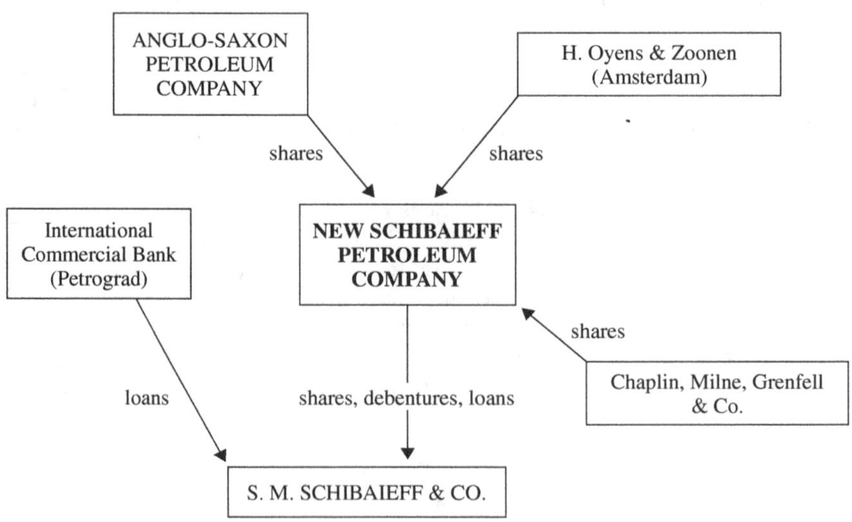

Fig. 6.7. Functional relationships within the Schibaieff cluster, 1912–1916
Sources: GL SEAR, Nitrate and Oil Reports, 1912/13, 1913/14, 1914/15, 1915/16.

enterprise, S. M. Schibaieff & Co. Its products in Russia were distributed by the Mazout Company in which Shell held the majority of equity capital.[101] All other administrative arrangements concerning the activity of S. M. Schibaieff & Co. were carried out in association with other companies under the management of the Royal Dutch Shell Group—as happened, for example, in May 1916, when the Russian company sold its refinery in order to enable the formation of a new venture which would combine certain refineries in the Baku region.[102]

The Ural Caspian Oil Corporation was floated in London in April 1910.[103] It was for a very brief period a free-standing company. In May 1911 its Russian subsidiary, the Ural Caspian Petroleum Company, struck a substantial gusher of oil near the Dos-Sol salt lake. The result of this success was a rise in the price of the Corporation's shares in London.[104] In June 1911 the Corporation accepted the offer to buy a part of its shares by a syndicate consisting of H. W. A. Deterding, C. S. Gulbenkian, and F. Lane of the Royal Dutch Shell Group, and W. Ritter von Ofenheim of Ofenheim & Co. This group was described as being 'second to none, not only from the commercial point of view in dealing with oil propositions, but from their financial standing in the City of London'.[105] By the end of 1913 the syndicate held about 39 per cent of the Corporation's equities, and in order to provide for the further financial requirements of the Corporation it agreed to subscribe for, when required, 200,000 shares of £1 each.[106] Deterding, Gulbenkian, Lane, and Ofenheim joined the Corporation's board, thus exercising not only financial but also administrative control over the activity of the former free-standing company and its Russian subsidiary.[107] Fig. 6.8 indicates the functional relationships within the Ural Caspian cluster.

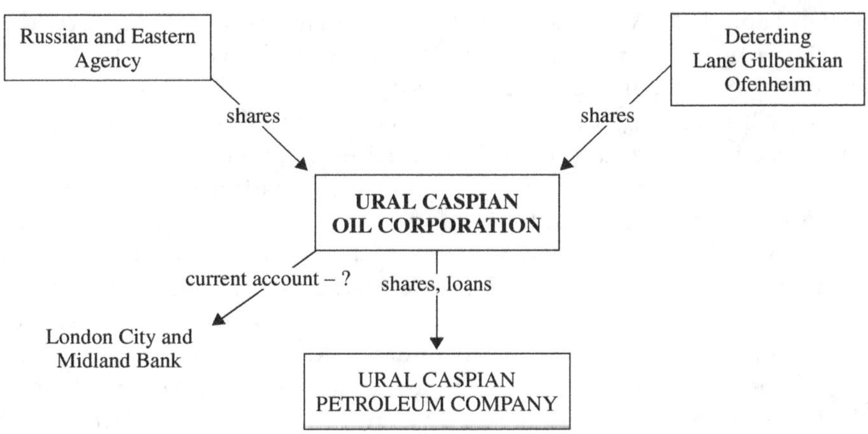

Fig. 6.8. Functional relationships within the Ural Caspian cluster, 1911–1916
Sources: GL SEAR, Nitrate and Oil Reports, 1910/11, 1911/12, 1912/13, 1913/14, 1914/15, 1915/16.

The literature on British participation in the Russian gold-mining industry pre-1917 in general, and on the Lena Goldfields company in particular, is not extensive. Furthermore, researchers' interest has usually been focused on whether the Lena Goldfields were British, Russian, or mixed venture capital. The question of financial links between the Lena Goldfields, the Lenskoie Company, and British and Russian banks has hitherto attracted no attention. Yet it was the nature of financial connections in the Lena group that made it so different from other clusters with the participation of free-standing companies.

The Lena Goldmining Partnership (the Lenskoie Company) was one of the oldest gold-mining companies in Russia. Set up at the end of the 1850s by Siberian merchants, it was soon taken over by the St Petersburg banking house of the Ginzburgs and E. Meyer & Co.[108] The company flourished for most of the second half of the nineteenth century, but in the 1890s its financial position worsened. In St Petersburg Lenskoie shares, whose nominal value was Rs.800, were quoted at as low as Rs.60,[109] and the company's losses reached a total of Rs.4.1 million.[110] Although the authorized capital of the Lenskoie Company was Rs.11 million, only Rs.2.1 million was actually issued.[111]

In 1906 the owners of the Lenskoie began to explore the possibility of reconstructing the company by getting financial and technical assistance from the UK. In the second half of 1906 one of the Lenskoie's principal shareholders, Baron Alfred Ginzburg, and the company's manager I. N. Belozerov travelled to London to negotiate a proposition to incorporate some of the largest gold-mining ventures in the Prilensky District in Siberia—namely, the Lenskoie Company, the Industrial Company, and gold-mining properties belonging to the Siberian merchant Ratkov-Rozhnov—into one large joint-stock company with the participation of British capital.[112] As a result of these negotiations, a new venture, the Russian Mining Corporation, was launched in November 1906. The objectives of the company were broadly defined as the acquisition and dealing with mining properties and concessions in Russia. The company was registered in London with an authorized capital of £153,750.[113]

The Directors of the Russian Mining Corporation included several representatives of important mining concerns: Frederick William Baker, Chairman of the Venture Corporation; Henry D. Boyle, Director of the Consolidated African Trust, Ltd; Stanley Christopherson, Director of the Consolidated Gold Fields of South Africa, Ltd; and Walter McDermott, Director of the Consolidated Mines Selection Company, Ltd. Other members of the company's Board were Arthur Balfour Haig; Zigfrid Aschkenazy (banker); Henry Champagnier (Director of the Commercial Bank of Warsaw in St Petersburg); Basil Timiriazeff (the Russian Privy Councillor); Baron Alfred Ginzburg (Lenskoie

Company); and William Edward Smith (General Manager of the Westinghouse Company, Ltd).[114]

Although the Russian Mining Corporation was registered in London and had a majority of British shareholders at its launch in 1906, part of its capital was raised in countries other than Britain. The companies whose representatives were on the Corporation's Board—the Venture Corporation, the Consolidated Gold Fields of South Africa, the South African Gold Trust, and the Gold Mines Investment Company—were allotted about 20 per cent of its equity. Another 23 per cent was held by Russian shareholders, and 9 per cent by French and other nationals. This structure remained unchanged for four years. Changes started to

TABLE 6.8. *The distribution of the Russian Mining Corporation equity capital, 1906–1912*

Shareholders	1906 The number of shares	%	1910 The number of shares	%	1912 The number of shares	%
British shareholders, total out of which:	101,938	68.1	39,772	26.5	93,304	41.4
The Venture Corporation	16,249	10.8	—	—	—	—
The Consolidated Gold Fields of South Africa	9,250	6.2	19,555	13.0	45,089	20.0
The South African Gold Trust	6,250	4.2	10,694	7.1	—	—
The Gold Mines Investment Company	2.625	1.8	6,523	4.4	—	—
The International Financial Society	—	—	500	0.3	—	—
The Scottish National and Gold Mining Company	—	—	1,000	0.7	—	—
Other shareholders	67,564	45.1	1,500	1.0	48,215	21.4
Russian shareholders, total out of which:	33,875	22.6	36,711	24.5	56,445	25.1
Russo-Asiatic Bank	—	—	300	0.2	1,656	0.7
Commercial Bank of Siberia	—	—	2,000	1.3	7,750	3.5
International Bank [a]	—	—	—	—	300	0.1
Other shareholders	33,875	22.6	34,411	23.0	46,739	20.8
French shareholders, total	6,562	4.4	24,547	16.4	24,249	10.8
German shareholders, total out of which:	—	—	15,875	10.6	47,840	21.3
Dresden Bank	—	—	680	0.4	5,852	2.6
Deutsche Bank	—	—	6,415	4.3	20,722	9.2
Direction der Disconto Gesellschaft	—	—	1,930	1.3	2,967	1.3
Other shareholders	—	—	6,850	4.6	18,299	8.2
Other nationals	7,265	4.9	1,250	0.8	3,162	1.4
The nationality of shareholders is unknown	—	—	31,845	21.2	—	—
TOTAL	149,640	100.0	150,000	100.0	225,000	100.0

[a] The full name of this bank was International Commercial Bank of St Petersburg (later Petrograd).
Sources: 1906: PRO BT 31, 11728/90881, 301; 1910: ibid. 86; 1912: ibid. 58.

occur soon after 1910. The overall role of British shareholders was reduced, although Consolidated Gold Fields (and its affiliated companies) continued to be important; the holdings of the Russian and especially German banks began to grow (Table 6.8).

In 1908 the Russian Mining Corporation (RMC) signed a contract to purchase 74.5 per cent of the Lenskoie Company's assets for Rs.700,000.[115] By that time the Lenskoie Company was in deep financial difficulty, and the majority of its shareholders in Russia, anxious to save at least some of their investment, were eager to sell out to the foreigners. Later in the same year, RMC sold the 74.5 per cent option for £85,000 to another British company, the Lena Goldfields, formed in July 1908 to acquire the Lenskoie properties and to develop them 'by advances of additional working capital'.[116] Twenty per cent of the equity in the Lena Goldfields was allotted to the Russian Mining Corporation.[117]

After 1908 the Russian Mining Corporation continued to show interest in the activity of the Lena Goldfields in Russia. The two companies had interlocking boards of directors, and RMC acted as the Lena Goldfields 'agency' in the Russian Empire.[118] Through the years 1908–16 the Lena Goldfields remained the key provider of funds for the Lenskoie Company, by way both of equity and of working capital (Fig. 6.9 and Table 6.9).

The Lena Goldfields, claimed the *Financial Times* on 8 December 1910,

has secured, and continues to secure, to this enterprise [the Lenskoie Company] an easy and constant form of credit for working capital and

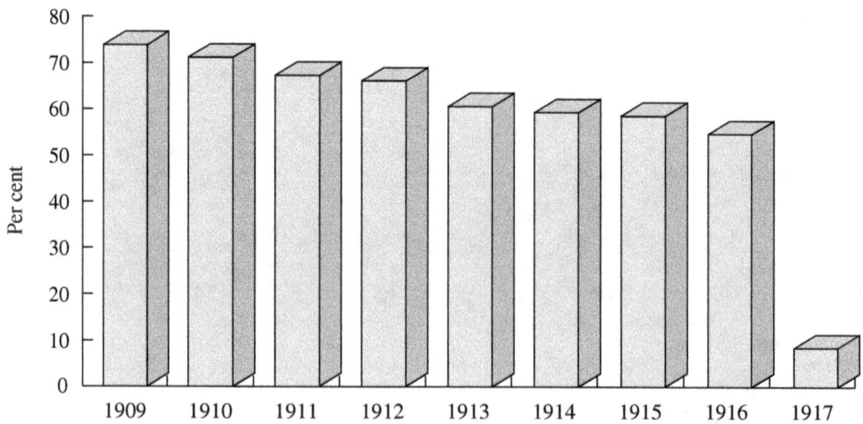

Fig. 6.9. Lena Goldfields' holding in the Lenskoie Company equity capital, 1909–1917
Sources: GL SEAR, Mining Reports, 1910–1917, the Lena Goldfields.

TABLE 6.9. *Cash transactions between the Lena Goldfields and the Lenskoie Company, 1908–1918 (£)*

Financial year	Advances from the Lena Goldfields to the Lenskoie Company during the financial year	Repayment of the Lena Goldfields' advances by the Lenskoie Company during the financial year
1908/9	113,011	—
1909/10	not recorded	
1910/11	301,648	—
1911/12	—	301,648
1912/13	—	—
1913/14	1,039,098	948,671
1914/15	1,148,019	1,192,519
1915/16	32,877	102,598
1916/17	396,543	18,787
1917/18	—	394,409

Note: A dash means no cash transactions.
Source: GL Mining Reports, 1908–1918, the Lena Goldfields.

development purposes. Thanks to the Lena Goldfields the Russian Company [the Lenskoie Company] was able to get rid of dependence on the State Bank, which, although furnishing in the past a very effective help to the Lenskoie undertaking, had, owing to its organisation, to demand conditions of credit which proved to be hindering. It is to our company [the Lena Goldfields] and to the parent company [of the Lena Goldfields], the Russian Mining Corporation, Ltd., that Lenskoie is indebted for having been able, without difficulty and at the propitious moment, to enlarge its region of activity by the purchase of the mines of the Industrial Company, owing to which the gold reserve has been largely increased and the life of the mines at present rate of working may be considered as almost doubled.[119]

The organizational pattern of the cluster of companies and banks connected with the Lena Goldfields corresponded to the typical model described above (Fig. 6.10 *a*, *b*).[120] However, as regards the provision of working capital, there is a striking difference between the nature of

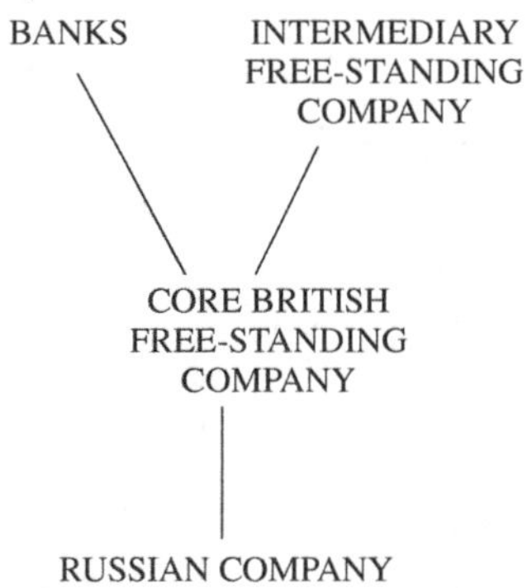

Fig. 6.10*a*. The typical organizational structure of a British-financed business in Russia

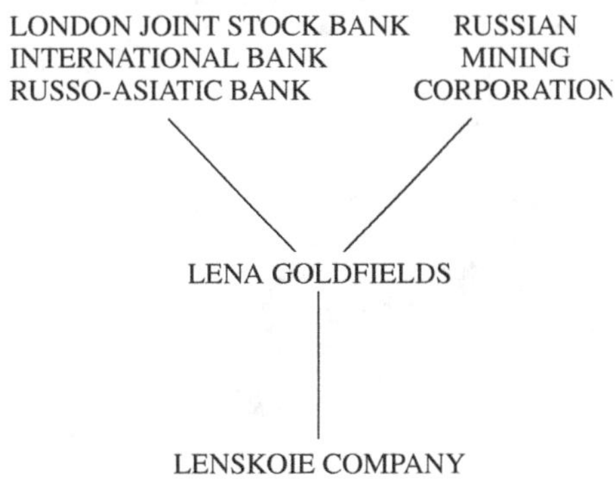

Fig. 6.10*b*. The organizational structure of the Lena cluster, 1908–1917
Source: See text.

financial transactions in the typical model and in the Lena group. The characteristic feature of the typical model (Fig. 6.11*a*) was the existence of active and reciprocal relationships between all the members of a cluster. If a British free-standing company wanted to make a loan to a Russian enterprise, it in turn would try to raise money either by borrowing from an intermediary company or banks, or by floating a debenture issue. Often the role of the Russian company's creditor was played directly by an intermediary company. In the case of the Lena group, however (Fig. 6.11*b*), the Lena Goldfields did not create debt or borrow money from banks. Instead it exploited the fact that the prices both of its own shares and of the shares of the Lenskoie Company rose very rapidly, and it raised the necessary liquid capital through the realization of the Lenskoie shares on the St Petersburg Stock Exchange.[121] The Lena Goldfields resorted to a bank loan only once, in the financial year 1914/15. This loan amounting to £52,000 was secured on shares in the Lenskoie Company. The need to get the loan in the UK was caused by 'the drop in the value of the rouble' which made it unreasonable 'to withdraw, at a considerable loss, cash from Petrograd to London'.[122] It is not clear from which British bank the Lena Goldfields borrowed.[123] Possibly it was the London Joint Stock Bank, the London banker of the company.[124]

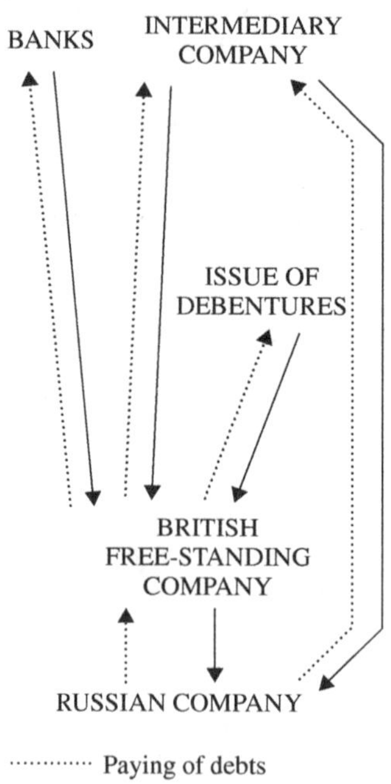

Fig. 6.11*a*. Financial transactions in the typical model

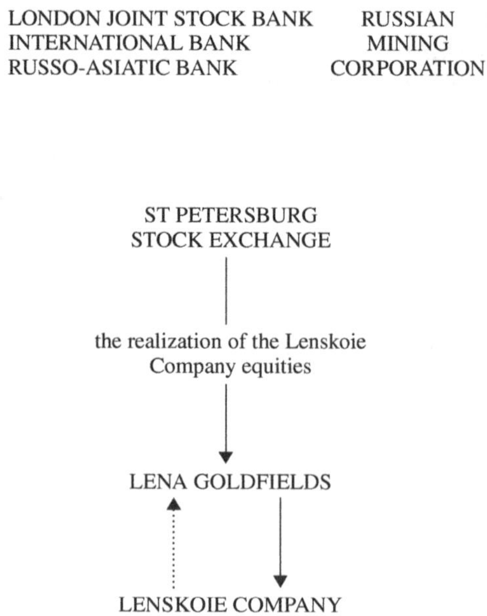

Fig. 6.11*b*. Financial transactions in the Lena cluster, 1908–1917
Source: See text.

Unfortunately for the Lena Goldfields, 'the rapidity of the rise' of the Lenskoie equities in 1910 'had all the appearance of gambling'. As a result, in Russia, the British company was accused of being a 'superfluous institution and likewise antipatriotic'. The St Petersburg press made allegations that the liquid assets of the Lena Goldfields were not used to assist the Lenskoie Company.[125] When the Russian media expressed doubts regarding the role of the British enterprise, the Chairman of the Lena Goldfields, Lord Harris, responded by praising Basil Timiriazeff, one of the company's Russian directors, for holding 'a distinguished position . . . in commercial circles of St. Petersburg', as well as in 'the political field'.[126] This press campaign marked the beginning of a long conflict within the Lena Goldfields which in 1916 resulted in 'a struggle' and 'fight' on the company's board.[127]

At the end of 1910 the Lena Goldfields underwent a major organizational restructuring. A group of Russian banks led by the Russo-Asiatic Bank and the International Commercial Bank of St Petersburg took over most of the equity in Lena Goldfields. Some of the Russian holders of the company's equities organized themselves into a separate group, with a representative committee, in order better to assert Russian interests.[128] At the beginning of 1911 this committee raised the question of the liquidation of the Lena Goldfields, whose existence, it argued, was 'unnecessary' because the company was no longer performing its assigned functions.[129] The Russian shareholders also requested the addition of three Russian directors to the company's board.[130] In 1911, prominent and influential representatives of the Russian financial circles, Alexander Wyshnegradski and Alexei Poutiloff (who would soon join the board of Emba Caspian Oil Company—see above), together with the Financial Agent of the Russian Empire in London, Mieczilas de Routkowsky, were appointed Directors of the Lena Goldfields.[131]

In the same year the holders of the Lenskoie Company elected a new, 'pro-Russian', board of directors consisting primarily of the delegates of two St Petersburg banks (the Russo-Asiatic Bank and the International Bank): N. S. Avdakov, H. D. Boyle, A. W. Eropkin, L. F. Graumann, A. E. Kalistratoff, and I. C. Ozeroff.[132] One of the first decisions made by the new board was to repay the company's debts to the Lena Goldfields and to seek its own ways and means for finance. To achieve this it was decided to increase the nominal capital of the Lenskoie Company from Rs.10,980,000 to Rs.16,500,000 by a corresponding issue of new shares.[133] The Lena Goldfields responded to this decision coolly:

> up to now the Lenskoie has required considerable financial assistance during the non-washing period of the year, and by keeping a large liquid

balance we [the Lena Goldfields] have been able to effect this purpose easily. During the course of the year . . . we at one time had lent as much as £667,000 to Lenskoie. . . . Now if the issue of capital proposed by Lenskoie is approved by the Russian Government, Lenskoie will not require the same amount of financial assistance from this company [the Lena Goldfields] as it did in the past year.[134]

After the Russian government sanctioned the capital increase of the Lenskoie Company, that company's financial position improved. In the years 1911–12 the company repaid its debt of the previous year to the Lena Goldfields. In 1913–18 the Lena Goldfields' loans to the Lenskoie Company were usually repaid within the financial year (see Table 6.9).

Let us now turn to the question of whether and how these organizational upheavals affected the financial relationships between the Lena Goldfields and the Lenskoie Company, especially the Lena Goldfields' equity holding in the Russian enterprise. Information on this subject appears to be contradictory. There are two broad categories of documentary sources. The first category includes the book by Ya. I. Livshin *Monopolii v ekonomike Rossii* (*Monopolies in the Russian Economy*) and *Sbornik svedenii o deistvuyuschikh v Rossii aktsionernykh obschestvakh i tovarischestvakh na payakh* (*A Collection of Documents on Joint-Stock Companies and Partnerships in Russia*), published in St Petersburg in 1914.

According to these publications, in a three-year period from 1911 to 1914 the proportion of the Lenskoie Company shares in the possession of the Lena Goldfields had decreased dramatically. By 1914 only a tiny fraction—1.6 per cent—were owned by the British free-standing company. At the same time, the proportion of equities held by the Russo-Asiatic Bank's group and the International Bank's group was stated to have risen to 30.6 per cent and 34.1 per cent respectively (Table 6.10).

These data, in conjunction with changes in the composition of the two companies' boards and in the perceptions of Russian shareholders considered earlier in this section, suggest that by 1914 the nature of the Lena Goldfields' participation in the development of the Siberian gold-mining had entirely changed. The British company no longer had either

TABLE 6.10. *The Lenskoie Company's shareholders, 1914 (according to Russian sources)*

Shareholders	Number of shares	%
Lena Goldfields	1,760	1.6
Russo-Asiatic Bank's group	33,653	30.6
International Bank's group	37,474	34.1
Other shareholders	37,113	33.7
TOTAL	110,000	100.0

Sources: Ya. I. Livshin, *Monopolii v ekonomike Rossii* (Moscow, 1961), 60; *Sbornik svedenii o deistvuyuschikh v Rossii aktsionernykh obschestvakh i tovarischestvakh na payakh* (1914), 146.

organizational or financial influence on affairs in the Lenskoie Company. In short, according to the documents of the first group, the Lena Goldfields' investment in Russia ceased to be a *direct* investment. Instead it became the type of investment made by 'wealthy individuals or firms seeking optimum returns from diversified share holding'—that is, *portfolio* investment.[135]

The documents in the second group are the accounts of the Lena Goldfields Ordinary General Meetings during the period 1908–18 in the collection of mining reports compiled by the staff of the London Stock Exchange. They tell a different story. These documents state that the dramatic change in the number of the Lenskoie shares held by the Lena Goldfields occurred only at the very end of 1916, when the British company sold 50,950 Lenskoie equities, reducing its holding from 55.2 per cent to 8.94 per cent. The shares were bought by 'a powerful Group' formed in 1915, the members of which were the Imperial and Foreign Corporation and the Anglo-Russian Bank and its director, Grigori Benenson. The Lena Goldfields reserved the right to retain the voting rights attached to the shares until the moment of their actual delivery to the buyers. The Group made it a condition of its offer to purchase the Lenskoie Company shares that the Lena Goldfields board consent to allot to the Group or its nominees the balance of the unissued 246,703 Lena Goldfields shares of £1 each at a favourable price of 32*s.* 6*d.* per share.[136] The Group also authorized Sir Ian Amory, Grigori Benenson, and Herbert Guedalla, the Chairman of the Imperial and Foreign Corporation, to represent its interests on the Lena Goldfields' board.[137] In 1916–17 they were duly appointed directors of the company.[138]

Although the Lena Goldfields had ceased by the end of 1916 to hold the majority of the Lenskoie equities, at least up to the start of 1917 it continued to be closely involved in the management of the Russian company. In 1916 the Lena Goldfields board had appointed an engineer, Charles Purington, to report on the prospects of the Lenskoie Company, and pressed the Lenskoie board to appoint a committee of experts to investigate the weaknesses in management.[139] The only possible interpretation of these facts is that within the whole period from 1908 to 1917 the Lena Goldfields remained involved in the Lenskoie Company's activity. This was possible because, under the terms of the agreement on the sale of the Lenskoie's equities, until the moment of the *actual* delivery of shares the voting rights associated with them were retained 'absolutely by Lena Goldfields'.[140] This also confirms that the Lena Goldfields' investment in the Lenskoie Company was a *direct* investment. It seems likely that the Russian sources assumed the

Russian banks were principals, when in fact they were acting on behalf of the Lena Goldfields.[141]

My final case study is the history of the Russian Tobacco Company, which provides an interesting example of a venture, apparently launched as a free-standing company, that within a year or two was transformed into one of the most powerful investment groups in Imperial Russia. It provides an opportunity to discuss the question of whether British-registered free-standing companies always represented *British* direct investment.

The Russian Tobacco Company (RTC) was set up in London in September 1913 by a group of Russian banks led by the Russo-Asiatic Bank of St Petersburg. These banks—the Russo-Asiatic Bank, the Private Commercial Bank, the Trading and Industrial Bank, Petrograd Discount and Loan Bank, the Siberian Bank, the Russian Bank for Foreign Trade, and the Rostov-Don Merchant Bank—provided almost the entire share capital of the new venture. A mere 0.04 per cent of RTC equities was held by the British merchant house H. Higgins & Co. and other British individuals. According to my calculations, the overall non-Russian holding in RTC was slightly less than 2 per cent (Fig. 6.12).[142]

This figure is a little smaller than that given by S. Kalmykov, who, in his 1992 thesis, argued that non-Russians held 6.5 per cent of the Russian Tobacco Company's equity capital.[143] It is, however, at odds with a statement of E. Kruze, who claimed in an article published in 1959 that up to 30 per cent of the company's equities belonged to British shareholders.[144] Indeed, a figure showing a higher proportion of British capital could be found in the text of one of the initial versions of the agreement on the formation of a tobacco syndicate. This agreement, however, was never consummated.[145]

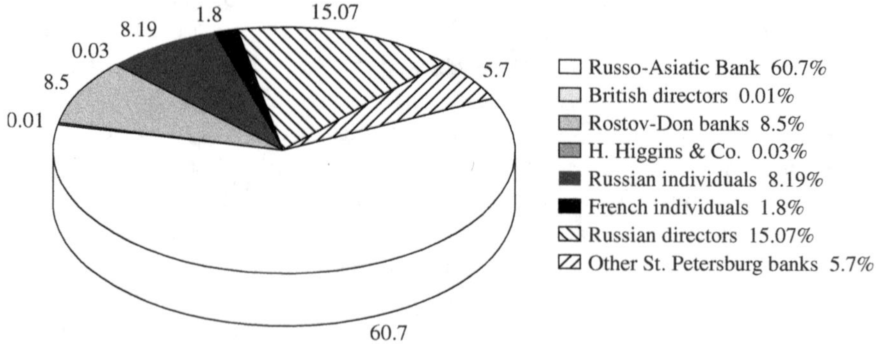

Fig. 6.12. Ownership structure of the Russian Tobacco Company, 1913
Source: PRO BT 31: 41067/130881, vol. A, 4–8.

The Russian Tobacco Company was formed to buy between 31 and 50 per cent of the shares of eleven Russian tobacco-producing factories:

in St Petersburg	Laferm
	Bogdanov & Co.
	Ottoman
	Shaposhnikov & Co.
	Bros. Shapshal
	Kolobov & Bobrov
in Moscow	Dukat
	Ghabay
in Rostov-na-Donu	Kushnarev & Co.
	Asmolov & Co.
	Bros. Aslanidi.

A few months later, in March 1914, the Russo-Asiatic Bank acquired the rest of the Russian factories' equity. Subsequently, this was exchanged for shares of the Russian Tobacco Company, the issued capital of which equalled £2.5 million.[146] The Russo-Asiatic Bank took full responsibility for financing this enterprise and for providing the affiliated Russian factories with advances of working capital. In October 1913 the Russian Tobacco Company reached an agreement with the bank to open a line of credit totaling Rs.1,480,000 (£156,614). In January 1917 the bank's directors made a decision to provide another series of loans to the value of Rs.10 million (£333,333).[147] The Russo-Asiatic Bank also floated new share issues of both the affiliated Russian factories and the free-standing company itself. This occurred, for example, in November 1916, when the acquisition of two more factories—Dunaeff in Moscow and Stamboli in Pheodosia—led to an increase of the Russian Tobacco Company's equity capital to £3.5 million.[148]

When the Russian Tobacco Company was launched in 1913, it seemed to satisfy the definition of a free-standing company. It 'did *not* grow out of domestic operations of existing enterprises that had head-quarters in Britain'; it was 'set up to conduct business abroad' and 'was registered in England . . . as a joint-stock, limited liability company'; and it 'had a board of directors . . . who might or might not be British'; 'a memorandum of association and articles of association defined corporate objectives and functions'. Its 'capital was denominated in sterling'; and it was intended to operate 'directly abroad'.[149] The Russian Tobacco Company also possessed another very important characteristic of a free-standing company—namely, it operated in only a single economic sector, in the tobacco industry. The only criterion that it did *not* satisfy was that it was *not* British 'owned and controlled'.

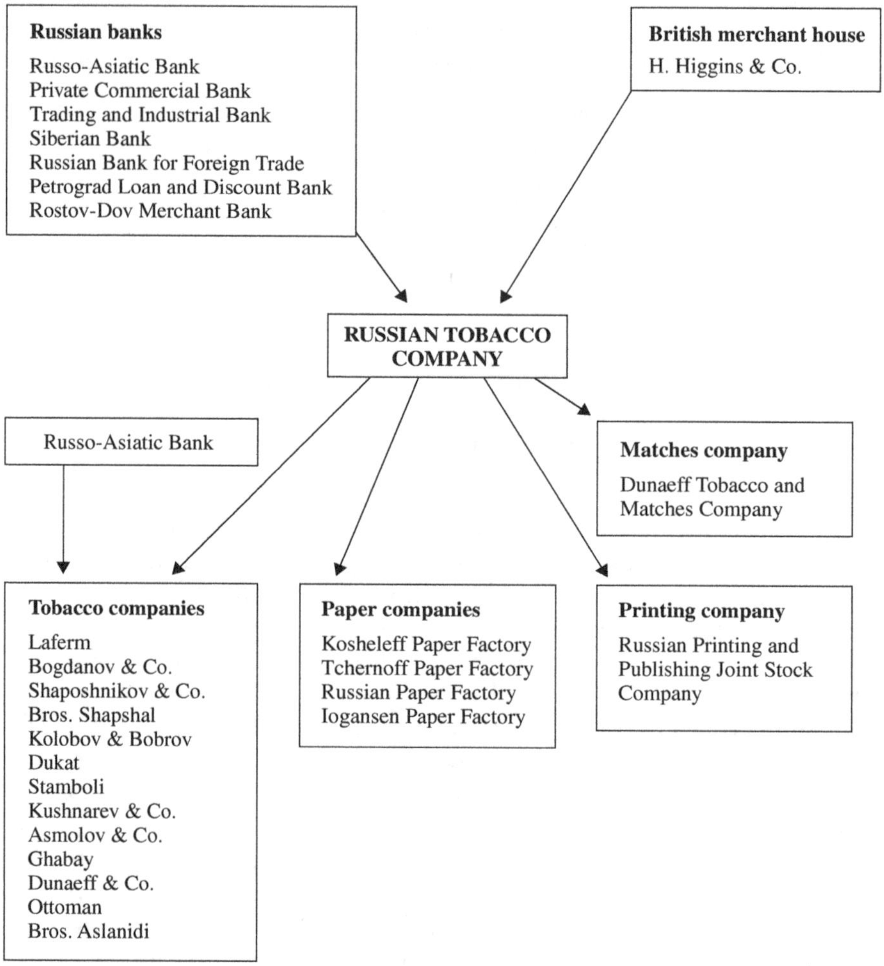

Fig. 6.13. The structure of investment in the Russian Tobacco factories cluster, 1917
Source: See Fig. 6.12.

In the year 1915 the investment policy of the company changed. It established a sugar-trade department, whose turnover during the year reached Rs.5 million.[150] At the beginning of 1916, RTC acquired 13,810 shares of Rs.100 in the Russian Paper Mills Company of Petrograd.[151] In October 1916 it bought most of the equity capital of the Russian Paper Manufactory. By September 1917 the Russian Tobacco Company had also become the principal shareholder in the Kosheleff Paper Factory, the Tchernoff Paper Factories Partnership in Moscow, and the Iogansen Paper Factory in Revel.[152]

The Russian Tobacco Company further widened its interests to include some Russian printing companies and manufacturers of

TABLE 6.11. *The structure of the Russian Tobacco Company's investment, 1914 and 1916*

Investment at cost	As at 31 October 1914		As at 4 October 1916	
	£	%	£	%
In tobacco companies	2,526,067	96.8	2,238,525	87.0
In other companies	84,210	3.2	333,849	13.0
TOTAL	2,610,277	100.0	2,572,374	100.0

Source: PRO BT 31: 41067/130881, vol. A, 2 and the balance sheet as at 4 Oct. 1916.

matches. In 1916 it became a stockholder in the Russian Printing and Publishing Joint-Stock Company in Petrograd. In 1917 it bought Dunaeff Tobacco and Matches Factory in Yaroslavl.[153] The structure of the Russian Tobacco Company's investment by the year 1917 is shown in Fig. 6.13 and Table 6.11.

The account of the Russian Tobacco Company's activity raises the question whether a free-standing company should always be considered as a form of direct *British* overseas investment? I suggest that, although the RTC was a British-registered company, it was from the financial point of view a Russian enterprise. The arguments in favour of this proposition are as follows.

First, the amount of capital invested by British individuals and the merchant house H. Higgins & Co. in the company's stock was almost negligible. The second reason is that advances of additional working capital for the development of the Russian Tobacco Company's properties in Russia were made exclusively by the Russo-Asiatic Bank of St Petersburg. Thirdly, one of the main reasons for the formation of RTC in London was not the want of capital or the technical backwardness of the tobacco industry in Russia, but rather the fact that Russian tobacco manufacturers were trying to avoid certain regulations of the Commercial Code discouraging the creation of monopolies in the Russian Empire.[154] In short, what might look like a British free-standing company was not one at all.

Conclusion

The most important findings of the present study can be summarized as follows:

- The majority of British free-standing companies in Late Imperial Russia represented direct capital exports. Their managerial and financial involvement in the activity of affiliated Russian enterprises went beyond the initial investment phase. However, in a small number of cases, such as the Russian Tobacco Company (and the Russian General Oil Corporation, not discussed herein), although companies were registered in the UK, the majority of their shares were held by Russian financial institutions, which also provided the affiliated Russian enterprises with operating capital and exercised managerial control over them. These companies do not meet Wilkins's definition of *British* free-standing ones (see Chapter 1 herein).

- Intermediary companies—some intermediary free-standing companies and other trust companies—took an active part in financing both affiliated Russian companies and British core free-standing companies.
- Russian banks often acted as both short- and long-term lenders to companies with British participation. Moreover, in some cases (e.g. the Russian Tobacco Company) Russian banks were the major shareholders in British registered companies.
- The participation of British banks in the equity capital of free-standing companies was quite rare. However, they commonly provided long- and short-term loans to free-standing companies.
- Although both Russian and British banks took part in financing British-Russian enterprises, it was free-standing companies that played the most important role in attracting funds of the British public into Russian ventures. The area in which the activity of free-standing companies was especially noticeable and successful was the provision of working capital for the needs of affiliated Russian enterprises.

NOTES

1. M. Wilkins, 'The Free-Standing Company, 1870–1914: An Important Type of British Foreign Direct Investment', *Economic History Review*, 2nd ser., 41 (May 1988), 262–3.
2. Ibid.
3. Ibid. 261.
4. A. Gerschenkron, *Economic Backwardness in Historical Perspective* (Cambridge, Mass., 1966), 14.
5. F. B. Tipton and R. Aldrich, *An Economic and Social History of Europe, 1890–1939* (Baltimore, 1987), 20–1.
6. Ibid. 21.
7. E. Burns, *Modern Finance* (London, 1920), 22.
8. M. Yu. Lachaeva, 'Angliiskii kapital v mednorudnoi promyshlennosti Urala i Sibiri v nachale XX v', *Istoricheskie zapiski*, 108 (1982), 77.
9. Russkii Gosudarstvennyi Istoricheskii Arkhiv (RGIA) (Russian State Historical Archive in St Petersburg), f. (record group) 62, op. (inventory) 1, d. (file) 20: 6; RGIA, f. 62, op. 1, d. 11: Urquhart to MacPherson, 25 Dec. 1907, 145.
10. RGIA, f. 62, op. 1, d. 10: 3–31.
11. Ibid.

12. The issued capital of the Perm Corporation at that time was £250,000. See RGIA, f. 62, op. 1, d. 11: 137.
13. Ibid.
14. Ibid. 138.
15. *Russian Year-Book for 1912* (London, 1912), 679.
16. A. D. Breiterman, *Mednaya promyshlennost SSSR i mirovoi rynok*, pt. 3 (Leningrad, 1930), 48.
17. Guildhall Library, London (GL), Brown, Shipley & Co., L 64.22, MS 20.146, 13–15, 189–92.
18. RGIA, f. 62, op. 1, d. 11: 141. Both the Blessigs and Brandts were deeply involved in other Russian businesses. S. D. Chapman, *Merchant Enterprise in Britain* (Cambridge, 1992), 207, 316.
19. RGIA, f. 62, op. 1, d. 44: 543.
20. Lachaeva, 'Angliiskii kapital v mednorudnoi promyshlennosti Urala i Sibiri v nachale XX v', 82–3.
21. RGIA, f. 1427, op. 1, d. 10: 3.
22. The equity capital of the Irtysh Corporation was £2m divided into 2m shares of £1 each. See RGIA, f. 1427, op. 1, d. 10: 1, 3.
23. Ibid.
24. Ibid. Herbert Hoover would later become President of the USA.
25. RGIA, f. 1427, op. 1, d. 38: 34.
26. The official exchange rate for the year 1917 was £1 = Rs.30.
27. RGIA, f. 1427, op. 1, d. 49: 2.
28. Ibid. 8.
29. RGIA, f. 1427, op. 2, d. 10: 1.
30. RGIA, f. 1423, op. 1, d. 7: 4. The official exchange rate for the year 1916 was £1 = Rs.14.95.
31. RGIA, f. 1427, op. 1, d. 49: 2. The official exchange rate for the year 1917 was £1 = Rs.30.
32. RGIA, f. 1427, op. 1, d. 10: 7.
33. RGIA, f. 1423, op. 1, d. 7: 4.
34. The Archive of the National Westminster Bank in London, London County and Westminster Bank/1, Daily Committee—Reports to the Board, Books Nos. 10046–10049.
35. RGIA, f. 86, op. 1, d. 9: 2.
36. RGIA, f. 86, op. 1, d. 5: 2.
37. RGIA, f. 86, op. 1, d. 9: 7; Public Record Office, London (PRO), BT 31: 20239/120885, Register of Directors of the Russian Trust and Finance Company, 1.
38. RGIA, f. 86, op. 1, d. 5: 2; RGIA, f. 86, op. 1, d. 9: 10.
39. PRO BT 31: 20239/120885, 134, 224.
40. Ibid. 45, 323.
41. Ibid. 45.
42. Ibid., Register of Directors of the Russian Trust and Finance Company, 90.
43. RGIA, f. 86, op. 1, d. 5: 2.
44. RGIA, f. 86, op. 1, d. 9: 7; PRO BT 31: 20239/120885.
45. Lachaeva, 'Angliiskii kapital v mednorudnoi promyshlennosti Urala i Sibiri v nachale XX v', 95.
46. RGIA, f. 86, op. 1, d. 63: 156.
47. RGIA, f. 86, op. 1, d. 231: 6.
48. Lachaeva, 'Angliiskii kapital v mednorudnoi promyshlennosti Urala i Sibiri v nachale XX v', 95.
49. The Lloyds Bank Archive in London, Investment Ledgers, HO/CA/Inv.2–4 (1902–22), Books Nos. 5155–5157; Memorandum Book, HO/CH/Phi.2

(1901–21), Book No. 5337; Investment Committee Minute Book, HO/D/Inv.5–7 (1907–20), Books Nos. 497–499; Annual Reports of Lloyds Bank's investment in other companies, HO/T/Gen.11 (1910–1925), File No. 5227.
50. *Stock Exchange Yearbook for 1901*, 1402.
51. GL, Stock Exchange Annual Reports (SEAR), Nitrate and Oil Reports, 1910–1911, the Bibi-Eybat Petroleum Company, Letter to Debenture Holders, 1 July 1911.
52. The equity capital of the Emba Caspian Naphtha Industrial Company was Rs.30m in 300,000 shares of Rs.100 each. The British company held 100,000 shares worth £420,720. The issued equity capital of the Emba Caspian Oil Company was £1.14m. GL SEAR, Nitrate and Oil Reports, 1912/13, the Emba Caspian Oil Company, Directors' Report for the year ending 31 Oct. 1913.
53. GL SEAR, Nitrate and Oil Reports, 1914/15, the Emba Caspian Oil Company, balance sheet as at 31 Oct. 1915; Nitrate and Oil Reports, 1915/16, the Emba Caspian Oil Company, balance sheet as at 31 Oct. 1916.
54. GL SEAR, Nitrate and Oil Reports, 1912/13, the Emba Caspian Oil Company, balance sheet as at 31 Oct. 1913.
55. S. D. Chapman, *The Rise of Merchant Banking* (London, 1984), 80.
56. *Monopolisticheskii kapital v neftyanoi promyshlennosti Rossii, 1914–1917* (Leningrad, 1973), 156.
57. Wilkins, 'The Free-Standing Company', 261.
58. M. Casson, 'Institutional Diversity in Overseas Enterprise: Explaining the Free-Standing Company', *Business History*, 36 (Oct. 1994), 95–108.
59. Ibid. 103. In Chapter 3 herein, he modifies his original argument.
60. PRO BT 31: 33767/73502, 213.
61. Ibid. 104.
62. S. V. Ilyin, 'Torgovyi dom "L.Knop", N.A. Vtorov i tekstilnaya promyshlennost' Rossii v kontse XIX—nachale XX veka', in V. I. Bovykin (ed.), *Monopolisticheskii kapitalizm v Rossii* (Moscow, 1989), 127–8.
63. RGIA, f. 62, op. 1, d. 227: 102; *Russian Year-Book for 1912*, 681.
64. RGIA, f. 1427, op. 1, d. 4: 51; RGIA, f. 1423, op. 1, d. 3: 93.
65. RGIA, f. 1423, op. 1, d. 47: 10.
66. I. F. Gindin, *Banki i promyshlennost v Rossii. K voprosu o finansovom kapitale v Rossii* (Moscow, 1927), 164–5; V. Ya. Laverychev, *Monopolisticheskii kapital v tekstilnoi promyshlennosti Rossii (1900–1917 gg.)* (Moscow, 1963), 32; S. V. Ilyin, *Formirovanie kapitalisticheskikh grupp v khlopchatobumazhnoi promyshlennosti tsentralno-promyshlennogo raiona Rossii (90–e g. XIX v.–1914 g.)* (Moscow, 1990), 9–11.
67. V. Ya. Laverychev, *Monopolisticheskii kapital v tekstilnoi promyshlennosti Rossii (1900–1917 gg.)*, 32.
68. In 1914 only 9 of 289 manufacturing companies in the Russian Empire floated debenture issues: N. N. Konshin Manufactories Partnership in Serpukhov; P. V. Berg Rozhdestvenskaya Manufactory Partnership; A. Gubner Calico Manufactory Partnership; Bros. Krestovnikov Manufacturing and Commercial Partnership; The Partnership of Manufactories founded by I. I. Skvortsov; L. Rabenek Manufactories Partnership; Yasyuninskie Manufactories Partnership in Kokhma; Bolshaya Kineshemskaya Manufactory Partnership; Prokhorovskaya Trekhgornaya Manufactory Partnership. See Ilyin, *Formirovanie kapitalisticheskikh grupp v khlopchatobumazhnoi promyshlennosti tsentralno-promyshlennogo raiona Rossii (90–e g. XIX v.–1914 g.)*, 10. The data on the total number of manufacturing companies in Russia are taken from Ch. M. Ioksimovich, *Zabastovki, nalogi i dokhodnost' u manufakturistov i neftepromyshlennikov (v svyazi s tamozhennym tarifom)* (Moscow, 1915), 9.

69. Gindin, *Banki i promyshlennost v Rossii. K voprosu o finansovom kapitale v Rossii*, 164–5; Ilyin, *Formirovanie kapitalisticheskikh grupp v khlopchatobumazhnoi promyshlennosti tsentralno-promyshlennogo raiona Rossii (90–e g. XIX v.–1914 g.)*, 11.
70. S. D. Chapman, 'British-Based Investment Groups before 1914', *Economic History Review*, 2nd ser., 38 (May 1985), 248.
71. GL, Anglo-Russian Cotton Factories (ARCF), L 69.55, MS 11.760, Report of Proceedings of an extraordinary General Meeting of Shareholders, held on 24 Apr. 1917, p. 1; GL ARCF, L 69.55, MS 11.762, Russian Statutes of Petroffsky Cotton Spinning and Weaving Manufacturing Company, Schlusselburg Cotton Print Manufacturing Company, and Spassky Cotton Spinning and Weaving Manufacturing Company.
72. GL ARCF, L 69.55, MS 11.762, Agreement for Allotment of Shares credited as fully paid-up between Messrs. Egerton Hubbard & Co. on behalf of the shareholders of the Petroffsky and Spassky Spinning and Weaving Companies and Schlusselburg Calico Printing Company and the Anglo-Russian Cotton Factories, Ltd., 21 Jan. 1897, 4–6.
73. M. J. Daunton, 'Inheritance and Succession in the City of London in the Nineteenth Century', *Business History*, 30 (July 1988), 272.
74. GL ARCF, L 69.55, MS 11.760, 2.
75. Ibid.
76. Daunton, 'Inheritance and Succession in the City of London', 272–6.
77. GL ARCF, L 69.55, MS 10.364, file 1 (1874–1900), E. Hubbard to S. Rendel, 27 Feb. 1900, pages unnumbered.
78. GL ARCF, L 69.55, MS 11.762, Agreement for Allotment of Shares, 1.
79. GL ARCF, L 69.55, MS 11.762, Issue of First Charge 4½% Debentures, Prospectus.
80. GL ARCF, L 69.55, MS 11.762, Letter to the shareholders of the Petroffsky and Spassky Spinning and Weaving Companies and Schlusselburg Calico Printing Company, 10 Nov. 1896.
81. GL ARCF, L 69.55, MS 11.760, the Nineteenth Annual General Meeting, 23 Mar. 1916, pages unnumbered.
82. GL ARCF, L 69.55, MS 11.760, Minute books of ordinary and extraordinary General Meetings of Shareholders, 1897–1948, Directors' Report for the year ended 31 Dec. 1897. An authorized capital of the Anglo-Russian Cotton Factories was £502,000 divided into £50,200 shares of £10 each. 47,032 shares were issued and fully paid.
83. Daunton, 'Inheritance and Succession in the City of London', 273.
84. Chapman, 'British-Based Investment Groups before 1914', 248.
85. GL ARCF, L 69.55, MS 11.759, vol. 1, 132nd Meeting of the Board of the Directors, 20 Jan. 1909, 313.
86. GL ARCF, L 69.55, MS 11.759, vol. 1, 112th Meeting of the Board of the Directors, 28 Oct. 1907, 262; GL ARCF, L 69.55, MS 11.760, the Eleventh Annual General Meeting of Shareholders, 7 May 1908; Directors' Report.
87. GL ARCF, L 69.55, MS 11.762, the Anglo-Russian Cotton Factories Prospectus of 16 Dec. 1908; GL ARCF, L 69.55, MS 11.759, vol. 1, 135th Meeting of the Board of the Directors, 17 Feb. 1909, 320.
88. In 1909 the London and County Banking House changed its name to the London County and Westminster Bank.
89. GL ARCF, L 69.55, MS 11.759, vol. 1, 132nd Meeting of the Board of the Directors, 20 Jan. 1909, 314.
90. GL ARCF, L 69.55, MS 11.759, vol. 2, 261st, 265th, and 277th Meetings of the Board of the Directors, 243, 244, 248, 283, 284.
91. According to the report of the Chairman of the Anglo-Russian Cotton

Factories W. E. Hubbard, the value of the loan made to the company by the London County and Westminster Bank for the first six months of 1916 was £120,000. However, this credit was drawn only partially. See GL ARCF, L 69.55, MS 11.759, vol. 2, 291st Meeting of the Board of the Directors, 8 Feb. 1916, 322.

92. GL ARCF, L 69.55, MS 11.759, vol. 1, 130th Meeting of the Board of the Directors, 22 Dec. 1908, 304–5.
93. Messrs Egerton Hubbard & Co. were appointed the General Agent and Manager of the Anglo-Russian Cotton Factories in Russia in Jan. 1897. See GL ARCF, L 69.55, MS 11.759, vol. 1, 8, 12, 22, 26, 28.
94. GL ARCF, L 69.55, MS 11.759, vol. 1, 369.
95. These findings are in line with Fred Carstensen's suggestion that the financing of working capital was one of the most important areas for foreign financial resources in Russia. See F. Carstensen, 'Numbers and Reality: A Critique of Foreign Investment Estimates in Tsarist Russia', in M. Lévy-Leboyer (ed.), *La Position internationale de la France* (Paris, 1977), 281.
96. The Schlusselburg Calico Printing Company repeatedly asked to lighten the burden of interest rates on advances made by the Anglo-Russian Cotton Factories. See GL ARCF, GL 69.55, MS 11.759, vol. 1, 69.
97. Ibid. 10.
98. Ibid. 11, 12.
99. Daunton, 'Inheritance and Succession in the City of London', 275.
100. GL SEAR, Nitrate and Oil Reports, 1912–1913, Schibaieff Petroleum Company, letter to the shareholders, 13 Mar. 1913.
101. Ibid.
102. *Stock Exchange Official Intelligence for 1916*, 1468.
103. *Stock Exchange Official Intelligence for 1911*, 1491.
104. F. C. Gerretson, *History of the Royal Dutch*, iv (Leiden, 1957), 143.
105. GL SEAR, Nitrate and Oil Reports, 1910/11, the Ural Caspian Oil Corporation, repr. from the *Financial Times*, 13 June 1911.
106. GL SEAR, Nitrate and Oil Reports, 1912/12, the Ural Caspian Oil Corporation, Directors' Report, Dec. 1913.
107. GL SEAR, Nitrate and Oil Reports, 1910/11, the Ural Caspian Oil Corporation, repr. from the *Financial Times*, 13 June 1911.
108. Ya. I. Livshin, *Monopolii v ekonomike Rossii* (Moscow, 1961), 57.
109. *Gornye i zolotopromyshlennye izvestiya*, 19 (1909), 181.
110. Livshin, *Monopolii v ekonomike Rossii*, 57.
111. V. A. Dmitriev-Mamonov (ed.), *Ukazatel' deistvuyuschikh v Imperii aktsionernykh predpriyatii* (St Petersburg, 1907), 370.
112. *Gornye i zolotopromyshlennye izvestiya*, 8 (1907), 100.
113. PRO BT 31:11728/90881, 209.
114. Ibid. 149.
115. Ibid.
116. A. Lukin, 'Proniknovenie angliiskogo kapitala v gornoe delo Sibiri (1900–1914)', *Materialy po istorii Sibiri. Sibir perioda kapitalizma. Issue 2: Ekonomicheskoe i obschestvenno-politicheskoe razvitie Sibiri v 1861–1917 gg.* (Novosibirsk, 1965), 119; GL SEAR, Mining Reports, 1908–1909, K-L, the Lena Goldfields' 1st Ordinary General Meeting, 25 Nov. 1909, 3; *The Russian Year-Book for 1912*, 681.
117. The Lena Goldfields was formed with an authorized capital of £1,405,000 divided into 1,405,000 shares of £1 each. By June 1909 989,958 shares were issued and fully paid (See GL SEAR, Mining Reports, 1908–1909, K-L, the Lena Goldfields' 1st Ordinary General Meeting, 25 Nov. 1909, 8–9). The

Russian Mining Corporation was allotted at least 195,000 shares. See PRO BT 31: 11728/90881, the Mortgage Deed, 23 Oct. 1908.

118. GL SEAR, Mining Reports, 1908/9, K-L, the Lena Goldfields' 1st Ordinary General Meeting, 25 Nov. 1909, 1; GL SEAR, Mining Reports, 1909/10, K-M, the Lena Goldfields' 2nd Ordinary General Meeting, 7 Dec. 1910, 1; PRO BT 31: 11728/90881, 112, 149, 254, 263.
119. GL SEAR, Mining Reports, 1909/10, K-M, the Lena Goldfields' 2nd Ordinary General Meeting, 7 Dec. 1910. Exhaustive Statement of the Position and Prospects (repr. from *Financial Times*, 8 Dec.1910), 18.
120. In 1908–10 some of the Lena Goldfields' shares were held by the Consolidated Gold Fields of South Africa, one of the shareholders in the Russian Mining Corporation. GL SEAR, Mining Reports, 1908/9, Bro-Co.
121. GL SEAR, Mining Reports, 1908/9, Bro-Co. Before 1908 the market price of the Lenskoie equities had never exceeded their nominal value. However, in 1909 the company's equities whose nominal value was Rs.450 were quoted at the St Petersburg Exchange at Rs.1,850. In 1910 the selling price rose sharply to Rs.6,075, but at the beginning of 1911 dropped almost twofold to Rs.3,100. In the second half of 1911 the market value of the Lenskoie Company shares rose again and reached Rs.5,500. At the end of 1911 the prices fell down to the level of Rs.3,300–3,400. See P. Pospelov, *Lenskie priiski* (Moscow, 1937), 29.
122. GL SEAR, Mining Reports, 1914/15, K-Mor, the Lena Goldfields' 7th Ordinary General Meeting, 21 Mar. 1916, balance sheet, 3, 8, 9.
123. The fact that it was a British bank is confirmed in the proceedings of the 7th Ordinary General Meeting of the Lena Goldfields in London which say that 'it has been necessary. . . to contract a loan in this country [i.e. the UK]'. See GL SEAR, Mining Reports, 1914/15, K-Mor, the Lena Goldfields' 7th Ordinary General Meeting, 21 Mar. 1916, balance sheet, 33.
124. GL SEAR, Mining Reports, 1910/11, K-Mor, the letter of Mr H. Richards, the secretary of the Lena Goldfields, 9 Aug. 1911, London.
125. *Birzha*, 2 (1911), 5–6; 5 (1911), 6; 6 (1911), 4–5; 8 (1911), 5; 11 (1911), 3–4; GL SEAR, Mining Reports, 1910/11, K-Mor, the Lena Goldfields, repr. from *Financial Times*, 11 Nov. 1911.
126. GL SEAR, Mining Reports, 1910/11, K-M, the Lena Goldfields, Exhaustive Statement of the Position and Prospects (repr. from *Financial Times*, 8 Dec. 1910).
127. GL SEAR, Mining Reports, 1915/16, J-Ni, the Lena Goldfields, Minutes of the Proceedings of the 8th Ordinary General Meeting, 13 June 1917, 4, 5.
128. GL SEAR, Mining Reports, 1909/10, K-M, the Lena Goldfields, Exhaustive Statement of the Position and Prospects (repr. from *Financial Times*, 8 Dec. 1910).
129. Livshin, *Monopolii v ekonomike Rossii*, 60.
130. GL SEAR, Mining Reports, 1910/11, K-Mor, the Lena Goldfields' 3rd Annual Report, 10 Nov. 1911, 5.
131. GL SEAR, Mining Reports, 1911/12, K-Mor, the Lena Goldfields' 4th Ordinary General Meeting, 3 Dec. 1912, 1.
132. Ibid. 5.
133. GL SEAR, Mining Reports, 1910/11, K-Mor, the Lena Goldfields' 3rd Annual Report, 10 Nov. 1911, 3.
134. GL SEAR, Mining Reports, 1910/11, K-Mor, the Lena Goldfields, repr. from *Financial Times*, 11 Nov. 1911.
135. Chapman, 'British-Based Investment Groups before 1914', 232.
136. GL SEAR, Mining Reports 1916/17, J-Ni, the Lena Goldfields' 8th Ordinary General Meeting, 13 June 1917, 4. As was shown earlier in this chapter, the

members of the Group—the Anglo-Russian Bank, its director Grigori Benenson, and the Imperial and Foreign Corporation—were also involved in the formation of the Russian Trust and Finance Company. The Russian Trust and Finance Company was one of the shareholders and financiers of the Sissert Company and its Russian subsidiary, the Sissert Mining District Company.

137. '. . . the Group pointed out . . . that if they were to take a large interest in Lenskoie, it was but reasonable that they should have also a large interest in Lena Goldfields and a proportionate voice in the management of Lena Goldfields affairs' (GL SEAR, Mining Reports, 1916/17, J-Ni, the Lena Goldfields' 8th Ordinary General Meeting, 13 June 1917, 12).
138. GL SEAR, Mining Reports, 1916/17, J-Ni, the Lena Goldfields' 8th Ordinary General Meeting, 13 June 1917, 1; GL SEAR, Mining Reports, 1917/18, I-M, the Lena Goldfields' 9th Ordinary General Meeting, 26 May 1919, 1.
139. GL SEAR, Mining Reports, 1916/17, J-Ni, the Lena Goldfields' 8th Ordinary General Meeting, 13 June 1917, 10.
140. Ibid. 4.
141. A plausible explanation of the contradiction between the two sources of information about the ownership structure of the Lenskoie Company can be found in V. S. Ziv's 1917 study on foreign investment in the Russian mining industry. He argued that 'due to the fact that "Lena Goldfields" was a financial syndicate and, as such, was not registered in Russia, its name was not in the register of shareholders of the Lenskoie Goldmining Partnership. In recent years, the Russo-Asiatic Bank and Petrograd International Bank represented the syndicate's interests at the general meetings of the Lenskoie Goldmining Partnership. For example, at the general meeting of the Lenskoie Goldmining Partnership's shareholders held on the 30th September 1916 . . . the majority of shares was presented by: the Chairman of the Petrograd International Commercial Bank, A. I. Wyshnegradski—29,641 shares, and the Chairman of the Russo-Asiatic Bank, A. I. Poutiloff—also 29,641 shares' (V. S. Ziv, *Inostrannye kapitaly v russkoi gornozavodskoi promyshlennosti* (Petrograd, 1917), 106).
142. PRO BT 31: 41067/130881, vol. A, 4–8.
143. S. V. Kalmykov, 'Russko-Aziatskii bank i obrazovanie monopolii na osnove holding-kompanii nakanune i v gody pervoi mirovoi voiny', unpublished Ph.D. Thesis (Moscow, 1992), 174.
144. E. Kruze, 'Tabachnyi i nitochnyi tresty. (Iz istorii monopolii v obrabatyvayuschei promyshlennosti Rossii)', in M. P. Vyatkin (ed.), *Iz istorii imperializma v Rossii* (Moscow, 1959), 64.
145. Kalmykov, 'Russko-Aziatskii bank i obrazovanie monopolii na osnove holding-kompanii nakanune i v gody pervoi mirovoi voiny', 154.
146. Ibid.
147. Ibid. 175–6.
148. PRO BT 31: 41068/130881, vol. F, 178–9.
149. Wilkins, 'The Free-Standing Company', 261–2.
150. Kalmykov, 'Russko-Aziatskii bank i obrazovanie monopolii na osnove holding-kompanii nakanune i v gody pervoi mirovoi voiny', 167.
151. In 1916 the rate of exchange between the rouble and pound was £1 = Rs.14.95. The seller of the equities, the Russo-Asiatic Bank, was paid Rs.776,250 (approx. £52,000) in cash and allotted 100,000 shares of £1 each in the capital of the Russian Tobacco Company. See PRO BT 31: 41068/130881, vol. F, 41.
152. Revel is a pre-1918 name of Tallinn.
153. Kruze, 'Tabachnyi i nitochnyi tresty. (Iz istorii monopolii v obrabatyvayuschei

promyshlennosti Rossii)', 64–5; G. Tsiperovich, *Sindikaty i tresty* (Leningrad, 1927), 251.

154. As Harm Schröter has pointed out in correspondence with the author, most of the literature emphasizes 'the other way round (make FDI look Russian in order to get through)'. In point of fact, British company law could be used to the advantage of domestic Russian investors.

7

British Free-Standing Companies and Investment Groups in India and the Far East

Stanley Chapman

The literature on British overseas investment has demonstrated that free-standing companies (FSCs) were by no means the only vehicle for the transmission of capital to imperial and foreign countries. The enterprise of merchant partnerships setting up companies and private ventures was evidently no less significant. Merchant investment certainly pre-dated FSCs by several generations, while merchants' investment groups were among the biggest in the whole British economy, several times the size of the major FSCs.[1] In India and the Far East, if not elsewhere, investment groups were the most important form of organization in the various national economies, as well as in the international movements of capital. The reasons for this continuing mercantile supremacy form the subject matter of this chapter.

All the economic historians of British India have, without exception, been in no doubt that mercantile capitalism, or what was widely known as 'the agency house system', was the principal force in the commercial, financial, and industrial development of India and South-East Asia in the long nineteenth century (1815–1914). Naturally, some historians make the point more explicitly than others. P. S. Lokanathan's *Industrial Organisation in India* (1935) provides one of the best-informed and most balanced accounts, free of the nationalist anti-British sourness that mars some academic writing of the post-Second World War years. 'Industrial development in India has been up to the present entirely bound up with the managing agency system of organisation and control, and except in regard to joint-stock banking, no important industrial activity has been carried on independently of that system', he wrote.[2] We shall see that by this date there were several agency-house investment groups owned and run by indigenous (mainly Parsi) enterprise, but they were clearly modelled on the British mercantile system. Mercantile dominance in Western investment was, of course, nothing new in 1935. Palmers, Cruttendons, and the string of leading merchant houses that became insolvent in India in the early 1830s paid the penalty of illiquidity following heavy investment in docks, harbours, warehouses, plantations, and other fixed capital commitments in India.[3] Of course, the main opportunities for company formation came following the favourable British legislation in the early 1860s, and the subsequent joint-stock boom. The dominance of the agency-house system is already clear from this period. 'Of all the companies included in the *Times of India Directory*, 1872, there were only three companies [in Bombay] excluding banks which functioned without a managing agent', R. S. Rungta records in his valuable *Rise of Business Corporations in India*.[4] The numerous business histories of the agency houses chronicle the competitive struggle of the various mercantile partnerships for control of more companies, and a greater variety of them; from about 1860 to 1914, the system appeared to follow something like an exponential growth curve.[5]

For the benefit of those not familiar with the economic history of India and South-East Asia, the essence of the mercantile agency house must be explained. In the eighteenth century, the underdeveloped condition of the economies of the states of India, the Malayan archipelago, and the treaty ports of China compelled Western merchants to invest in transport and warehousing. The insatiable European demand for oriental textiles motivated the East India Company, and then the successor merchant partnerships, to build 'factories' (i.e. compounds to assemble native craftsmen so as to direct them to the specific needs of Western consumers), and from this followed the promotion of production of better quality dyestuffs and, in due course, indigo plantations. Capital was not too difficult to come by, for expatriate civil servants were pleased to deposit their savings and Indian merchants were often willing to lend to their white connections. However, the merchants always felt vulnerable to illiquidity, for financial crises in the Far Eastern sector were no less frequent or severe than in other sectors of the international economy. The East India Company was a large joint-stock company, and its directors enjoyed the privileges of control without ownership—that is, inducing shareholders to provide most of the capital—and merchant partnerships searched for a comparable advantage.[6] They stumbled across a device by which they exchanged their name (reputation) and marketing expertise for 'agency' (in fact control) of local companies, often taking a small or token shareholding. Beginning in a tentative way, merchant partnerships built up strings of agencies, often specializing in two or three lines, such as indigo plantations, jute or cotton mills, tea gardens or teak forests, river transport or shipping agencies. To expand their businesses, merchant houses floated new companies as well as competed for the management of established ones, and the practice became so general that, as management superseded their traditional import–export business, British merchant houses in the Far East assumed the name of agency houses.[7]

Intimate local knowledge was united with the maintenance of close links with Britain—or, rather, with the home port (London, Glasgow, Liverpool, or Manchester). In the early years, partners expected to make their fortunes in a few years of overseas residence (if they did not succumb to tropical disease first), so there was no shortage of recruits from the families or (failing that) the 'super cargoes' (superintendents of cargoes) who sailed on each of the partners' ships. Senior partners returned to Britain to maintain the business in the home port, and to provide a continuous flow of information and advice to the men grappling with the local buying and selling situation. In later years, as the mercantile partnerships continued to grow, the Scottish and the ancient universities (Oxford and Cambridge) provided a flow of young gentlemen anxious to win their fortunes in India, which was always regarded as the most exciting and challenging part of the British Empire. Thus the home connection ensured a flow of capital (if needed) and of young management recruits.[8]

While the origins of the agency-house system can be traced back to the late eighteenth or early nineteenth century, its most vigorous development was reserved for the last thirty or forty years of the Victorian age. Most of the houses were originally based on the cotton and silk trade (exporting from Britain cotton piece goods, importing silks), but, as competition sharpened following the Cobden free trade treaty with France (1860), the opening of the Suez Canal (1869), and the laying of the submarine cable to India, there was a pressing need to diversify. Connections with new industries (coal, iron, gold, hardwoods, tea, rubber, and petroleum) were sought, and the system extended from Calcutta, Bombay, and Madras to Burma, Persia, Malaya, Borneo, Java, Siam, Japan, and other countries of South-East Asia.[9] In other words, the agency houses were a dynamic economic movement that were in the vanguard of exploitation of global opportunities, having the strongest representation at the hub of the international economy, London.

The Supremacy of the Agency-House System

It is now easy to understand why free-standing companies played a minimal or insignificant role in the migration of British capital to India and South East Asia. British merchant houses not only pioneered the trade to this major sector of the international economy; they also pioneered and built up much of the basic modern industries and economic infrastructure there. The leading houses were well established before the imperial and state banks were founded, and they often formed the boards of directors of the former; in one way or another, they were the chief creditors to innumerable oriental business enterprises, and this position helped them to maintain control.[10] In London, twenty out of the thirty leading agency houses also appeared as merchant banks by the end of the nineteenth century. By the early part of the twentieth century, they had grown so big that a third of the top (£4m. + capital) British-based companies were operating a form of agency-house system in India, South Africa, Russia, or Latin America. Clearly it was not easy for new businesses to compete with such formidable financial strength and local managerial expertise.[11]

In the context of the eighteenth and early nineteenth centuries, it is not strictly correct to speak of India as an underdeveloped economy. Numerous industrial products were recognized to represent craft techniques superior to those known to Europe, while trading networks had been established for centuries and capital accumulated in the hands of a mercantile class. European contacts were initially with this group, and during the course of several generations they learned much from each other. This strong indigenous enterprise gave rise to major industrial developments in some important sectors, notably cotton, coal, and iron. The relative importance of British and Indian business in some of the main sectors of the economy is summarized in Table 7.1.[12]

Cotton mill production was begun in India in 1854 by Parsi merchants and bankers, advised and financially supported by Platt Bros. of Oldham, one of the leading British machine builders. The machinery was worked under the supervision of overlookers sent to India by Lancashire machine-makers. Other north of England machine-builders soon made their own connections with Parsi entrepreneurs, and by 1915 ninety-six mills had been opened. The third such venture, a huge complex of 50,000 spindles and 1,000 looms, was incorporated in 1858 and adopted the agency-house system, thus inaugurating the

TABLE 7.1. *European and Indian enterprise in some leading sectors of the Indian economy, 1911*

Sectors	Production units	Company directors			Private firms' partners	
		All European	All Indian	Both	All European	All Indian
Cotton mills	167	14	98	25	0	30
Jute mills	50	49	0	0	1	0
Jute presses	109	50	16	0	7	36
Cotton presses	630	18	180	14	0	418
Collieries	331	133	17	26	13	142
Tea plantations	927	681	32	0	116	98

Source: Indian Industrial Commission, cited in N. Z. Ahmed, 'Some Aspects of the History of British Investments in the Private Sector of the Indian Economy 1875–1914', M.Sc. Econ. thesis (London School of Economics, 1955).

system in cotton mill management which prospered well into the twentieth century. The agents usually had a substantial stake in these mills and an intimate knowledge of cotton-marketing, just as British merchants did. In 1925 ninety-five out of a total of 175 directors of ninety-seven Indian cotton mills were representatives of agency houses, and that was after a considerable shake-out of the slothful at the turn of the century. These figures serve to underline the ubiquity of the system, not restrained by any ethnic tradition.[13]

Similarly, the Indian iron industry was started in Bombay in 1871 by a Parsi merchant family, the Tatas. Tata & Co., at first in cotton exports and mill production, operated the agency-house system from an early period. In 1906 Tatas tried to raise British support for an Indian iron and steel plant and spent over a year in unsuccessful negotiations in England. Returning to India, they raised the required capital of £1.63 million in three weeks. Another historian of the Indian cotton industry records that 'There was plenty of money in Bombay awaiting fruitful investment. The capital required for starting an efficient and viable mill was not exorbitant . . . '.[14] Quite so, and the most expensive projects were evidently not beyond the reach of Indian enterprise, who were not, of course, inhibited by any feelings about protecting British domestic producers.

The story of the coal industry in India is not so well documented. The main reason for including indigenous enterprise is that the much-quoted *Investor's India Year Book* for 1912 (the first year of publication) recorded that 'practically the whole of the capital [was] drawn from investors in India'. The big companies were evidently of European origin, and most of the well-known agency houses had colliery interests, but there was a larger number of small private concerns owned and run by Indian entrepreneurs (Table 7.1).[15]

If new enterprise was to break into this established system, it most probably had to be at periods of inauguration of new industries, or at periods of crisis in the old.[16] In India, as elsewhere, the nineteenth century was punctuated by the cycle of boom and bust, but none with sufficient power, it seems, to break the grip of the inherited system. Thus the tea plantation boom of the early 1860s attracted a motley corps of entrepreneurs, but long before the end of the century the whole of this huge investment was controlled by a relatively small number of agency houses.[17] The end of the century saw a crisis in cotton mill profits and a few agency houses lost control of their companies, but the basic system continued.[18] Jute mills were introduced to India when the Borneo Company had 'a huge amount of capital on their hands' and the Company's agents (George Henderson & Co.) persuaded the directors to start the Borneo Jute Co. in India (1859).

Managers and superintendents were recruited in Dundee, Scotland. The early Indian jute mills 'simply coined money' so that other agency houses were quickly drawn in, and dominated the industry into the twentieth century.[19]

Another reason for agency houses controlling so much *private* investment was that there was a much larger *public* sector of investment, controlled and guaranteed by the British government, giving a safe return to small shareholders and trustees for whom security was the first priority. By 1914–15, Indian railways represented a total investment of £346 million, which dwarfed the £23 million in tea plantations, £14 million in cotton mills, £11 million in jute mills, and £5 million in coal-mining companies. Indeed, railways represented nearly two-thirds (65.5 per cent) of all company investment in India during the period.[20] When Indian investment was in vogue, there was no problem for the fallible investor. Of course, the railways provided the essential and high-cost infrastructure which gave the agency houses the opportunity to exploit the economic potential of a newly united country.

The imperial government also benefited the agency houses, principally by the laxity of company law, which enabled the merchant partnerships to control vast enterprises with minimal capital outlay. (Perhaps the most striking example is Andrew Yule & Co., which had a capital of £1.3 million in 1917, but controlled sixty companies and directly or indirectly employed 200,000 people.[21]) There is a large literature on the techniques by which company articles of association ensured that the managing agents were permanent, well paid (whatever the company profitability), and constitutionally more powerful than the united shareholders.[22] Some agency-house companies (such as those of Jardine Skinner, one of the biggest houses) did not even bother to appoint boards of directors, simply treating them as subsidiaries of the merchant partnership.[23] The result was that the agency houses were able to control much of the economy at astonishingly low capital cost, using their names to recruit capital in India, and lax company law to keep control. If they had a problem, it was that of retaining good managers from recruitment by rival houses, but of course this was a problem faced by overseas business in general.

Yet another reason for the lack of serious rivalry to the agency houses was the inexperience of company promoters and the extraordinarily high cost of public flotations in England. Quite a lot is known of the careers of the early London company promoters—particularly Baron Grant, David Chadwick, John Bunting, H. Osborne O'Hagan, and E. T. Hooley—but none of them had any experience with India and the Far East, and evidently did not care to dabble in oriental affairs.[24] When the merchant banks were belatedly drawn into company promotion, they showed no more interest in this sector.[25] No doubt they met the nabobs of Indian economic enterprise at London clubs, in Parliament, and on the London social round of rowing and horse-racing events (Henley, Goodwood, etc.), and agreed to respect the territories of their peers. Certainly the period is well known for a generous measure of 'give and take' among leading City of London financiers, many of whom were drawn from similar social backgrounds.[26]

The overhead costs of floating public companies were so high that it was uneconomical to raise less than £500,000 at the end of the nineteenth century. In the early twentieth century (especially in the 1920s and 1930s), some strenuous efforts were made to cut the high cost of launching a new company, but the ideal of one of the most successful advocates of small-company flotations was 'to raise as little as £100,000 at a cost of £10,000, and yet contrive to produce a modest profit'.[27] The cost was so high as a result of the company promoter's fee (steep because he had to assess scores of applicants before identifying one suitable case for flotation) and because of legal, advertising, underwriting, and broker's fees. By contrast, the cost of a smaller tea plantation or cotton or jute mill was nearer to £50,000 and rarely exceeded £100,000. It was, of course, possible in principle to group several tea gardens or textile mills, but in practice business opportunities came singly and, in any event, Indian investors did not care to have too many eggs in one basket.

The problems of raising capital in London by company flotation is illustrated by the experience of Jardine Skinner & Co., one of the largest agency-house investment groups. The group's early interests were in indigo plantations, silk filatures, tea gardens, and jute mills; by the 1880s the first two were losing money and the partners in London and Calcutta were searching for new opportunities (although, like all merchants, they were wary of 'lock-ups' of their capital). The Calcutta partner wrote in 1890 that

> under present conditions of mercantile business so few opportunities now occur for the profitable employment of capital in trading operations. In fact, outside of the employment we now find in the various producing industries in which we are employed, there is practically no direction in which we may obtain, even with all the advantages of our position, safe, steady & remunerative occupation [for our capital] except in the enlargement of our Agency business, and that is not always to be had for the wishing . . .

The partners never succeeded in picking up an agency for a cotton mill, and had to struggle to get into coal. They were worried about committing to gold mining: 'The gold craze will I dare say be followed before long by a gold crash in which many reputations as well as fortunes will be wrecked,' they fairly surmised.[28] The senior partner in London hit on the idea of raising £5 million in London (£3 million in shares and £2 million in debentures) to acquire another jute mill, a large cotton mill, a paper mill, and a jute press. 'The idea of having the interest spread in four industries would, I am sure, be appreciated,' he wrote.[29] At the end of 1890 the Baring crisis led to rumours about the soundness of Jardine Matheson (the famous British merchant house in China and Japan), with whom Jardine Skinner had long-standing links, and the project had to be reduced and then dropped, as, it was conceded in 1892, 'there is practically no market at home just now for Indian investments'.[30] Instead, the partnership closed down its silk manufacture, curtailed indigo manufacture, and acquired a paper mill and a colliery. Nevertheless, the £5 million project was never revived by Jardine Skinner, and nothing similar was, so far as is known, projected by any other Indian-based investment group. Instead, the group began to 'practise the habit now so common . . . of financing outside [i.e. through banks] and using our own capital largely as margin'.[31] It is astonishing that the group lived entirely on its own capital for so long, but this must be attributed to the traditional financial autonomy of the agency houses. One of the rival houses that Jardines had in mind was Finlays (of Glasgow and Calcutta), which at the end of the century had running credits with at least a dozen imperial and Anglo-German banks, and appeared to have no difficulty at all in opening new accounts. Such connections are worth separate consideration.

Methods of Raising Capital

Apart from retained profits and bank facilities, the Indian investment groups developed several techniques of raising capital. One or two of them ran pretty close to free-standing company-type development, so the whole range of options is worth reviewing in a little detail.

The recruitment of expatriate capital in India was a marked feature of the agency houses from their early years. Already in the eighteenth century, it became the practice of larger houses to receive deposits from their many friends and connections in the East India Company service, and this increased after 1822 when interest on the Company's debts was reduced from 8 to 4 or 5 per cent. There were no European banks in the Far East at this time, so expatriates had the opportunity to leave their savings on deposit at better interest than they could have earned at home. The conspicuous wealth of the early partners returning to Britain persuaded people that the agency houses were as solid as the Company. This image was severely dented by the collapse of the 'big six' houses in 1830–5, and several other houses in 1847–8, but confidence quickly returned, and the houses never lost the respect of the Indian commercial community.[32]

The only problem is to discover the extent of this lending. The agency houses were, until a late date, all private partnerships, and normally published nothing of their finances. The most that can be done is to consider the position of one firm that disclosed details to a public inquiry. The position of Bird & Co. of Calcutta, one of whose partners considered their finances fairly typical of the agency houses as a whole, is set out in Table 7.2. The European interest included a large percentage held by Bird & Co., 'almost two-thirds of the capital in some cases'. The Indian shareholding was nearly 12 per cent of the total in the companies, but it does not by any means tell the whole story of this large investment group. The group also controlled two large paper mills, representing an investment of £0.7 million in 1917, an engineering works, a fire clay and silica works, a coke manufacturing company, and an electric supply company.[33] The data in Table 7.2 are, however, sufficient to make the point that, by the early part of the twentieth century, Birds attracted extensive expatriate shareholdings, and fragments of evidence suggest that these were fairly typical of the sectors in which they were involved.

There is also evidence to suggest that the banks in India were more involved in long-term finance than those in Britain. The clearest statement of the position comes from a partner (W. A. Lee) in one of the smaller houses, giving evidence to the Indian Industrial Commission in 1916:

> There is plenty of Indian capital available for enterprises but the capitalists . . . distrust industrial proposals. . . . The European banks do not exist for the purpose of providing funds for expenditure on capital account. Their business is to finance trade, not the construction of factories. . . . This is the theory upon which the British banks have always based their operations. [But] the joint stock banks domiciled in India do not in all cases

TABLE 7.2. *Shareholdings in Bird & Co.'s agencies in 1917*

Shareholdings	Shareholders		Share capital	
	European (no.)	Indian (no.)	European (lakhs of rupees)	Indian (lakhs of rupees)
Ten coal companies	1,551	464	97	8
Eight jute companies	2,471	423	148	25
	4,022	887	245	33
Sterling equivalent			£1.63m.	£0.22m.

Note: Sterling conversion at one rupee = 1*s*. 4*d*.
Source: *Report of the Indian Industrial Commission* (Parliamentary Papers, 1919), xvii, evidence of W. A. Ironside of Bird & Co., 869.

employ their whole funds for financing trade, and they are able to use part of their funds for loans which represent capital expenditure.[34]

Lee was not more specific than this, but Finlays' records show that they borrowed extensively from Scottish, London, and imperial banks to help with their acquisitions. Sometimes these facilities were huge: when Finlays acquired North & South Sylhet Tea Companies, the Royal Bank of Scotland lent £870,000 to cover the acquisition.[35] The agency houses were well represented on the boards of the imperial banks. Thus, partners in Ogilvy Gillanders & Co. (the Gladstone family) were directors of the Bank of Bengal from 1842 to 1910, while partners in the Planters' Stores & Agency Co. (the Warren family) were directors of National & Grindlays Bank from its inception. The Mercantile Bank of India kept Yule (ultimately the most successful Calcutta agency house) and Guthrie (a leading Malayan house) partners on its board for many years. Such connections must have granted more financial security and easier access to capital for new developments.[36]

Several of the largest Anglo-Indian investment groups were big enough to run their own financial division, rather like a private investment bank. Birds established an Investment and Finance Company in 1896, originally at the suggestion of the Bank of Bengal, which was not allowed to subscribe to debenture issues. In 1908 Birds set up the General Trust and Investment Company to operate outside (as well as for) Birds' agencies. The two investment companies soon ceased to confine themselves to guaranteeing transactions for the Bank of Bengal and began to underwrite on their own account issues for jute mills.[37] Similarly, Finlays' merchant banking wing existed primarily to provide capital to finance their jute and tea companies.[38] Such organizations also benefited from strong connections with powerful financial interests in Britain. Sir Ernest Cable, a partner in Birds from 1886 to 1927, was closely associated with C. S. Cox (Cox, McEwen & Co.), who had influential connections in the City of London, and was particularly concerned with the floating, financing, and underwriting of companies in India and Egypt.[39] Sir Alexander Muir, the key figure in Finlays for many years, worked closely with Samuel Smith MP, the senior partner in Liverpool's most successful firm of cotton brokers.[40] And Sir David Yule, the head of Andrew Yule & Co., had a long-standing connection with Vivian Hugh Smith of Morgan Grenfell, the leading Anglo-American merchant bank.[41] If the records of the agency houses had been better preserved, it must be expected that a lot more connections of this kind would be uncovered. It appears that this combination of financial muscle (in London, Liverpool, and Glasgow) with intimate local knowledge and representation did not leave much room for outsiders.

In general, then, British financial interests could find their way into India only through the agency houses. The point is well illustrated by the examples of two strong Indian industries. We have seen that jute was monopolized by the agency houses, who competed fiercely for business with one another. In the early years of the Indian industry (1868–73), 'it was only necessary to issue a prospectus for a jute mill to have all the shares snapped up in a forenoon'.[42] Where competition with Dundee became significant, some Scottish interests tried to find their way directly into the Indian industry, but without success. The Indian cotton industry, as already noticed, was largely an area of indigenous enterprise, though dependent in the early years (down to about 1914) on Lancashire built machinery. Platts and other machine-builders evidently made some investments in the development of the Indian cotton industry, but managed to do so only through Indian and British agency houses. However, 'outsiders' put their greatest efforts to break into investment in tea gardens and rubber plantations, an important subject to which the final part of this chapter must be devoted.

Tea Gardens and Rubber Plantations

The directories of the late nineteenth and early twentieth centuries indicate that the colossal British investment in tea plantations (often called 'gardens' at the time) was as dominated by the agency-house investment groups as any other sector (Table 7.3). Indeed, such sources may even underestimate the huge British interest in this area: the largest British investment group in tea, the Glasgow-based James Finlay & Co., is not fully represented. Early in the twentieth century, Finlay had tea estates in Assam, Sylhet, Cachar, Dooars, Darjeeling, Travancore, and Ceylon, with 77,000 acres planted and an investment of over £5 million. The firm employed about 70,000 Indian workers as well as a staff of 300–400 superintendents, managers, and assistants sent out to India from Scotland. The second largest firm in tea plantations, Duncan Macneill & Co. with an investment of £1.6 million, is even more short-changed on Table 7.3; it is not listed as an agent for one or more of the biggest tea companies.[43]

The distinguishing feature of tea gardens and (later) rubber plantations was that they were a 'new-frontier' kind of development, open to adventurers, new settlers, unemployed expatriates, and anyone who could acquire a plot of suitable land and afford to pay local labour during the period of clearing and initial planting. The tea mania of the early 1860s produced an avalanche of capital and a scramble to recruit

TABLE 7.3. *The leading (£100,000+ capital) sterling tea companies in India, 1899–1901*

Tea company	Issued capital (£000s)	Agents (investment group)
Consolidated Tea & Lands Co.	1,760	James Finlay & Co.
Amalgamated Tea Estates	705	James Finlay & Co.
Empire of India	600	Gillanders Arbuthnot & Co.
Imperial Tea Co.	488	McLeod & Co.
Nedeem Co.	450	Octavius Steel & Co.
Jokai (Assam) Co.	350	Balmer Lawrie & Co.
Singlo Tea Co.	300	Gillanders Arbuthnot & Co.
Assam Frontier Tea Co.	285	Shaw Wallace & Co.
Assam Co.	200	Kilburn & Co.
Lungla (Sifhet) Tea Co.	200	Octavius Steel & Co.
Cachar & Dooars Tea Co.	200	Jardine Skinner & Co.
Doom Dooma Tea Co.	157	Planters' Stores
Jetinga Valley	150	Begg Dunlop & Co.
Brahmahputra	120	James Finlay & Co.
Makum (Assam) Tea Co.	100	Balmer Lawrie & Co.

Source: compiled from Thacker, Spink & Co., *Thacker's Directory of the Chief Industries of India including Tea and other Estates in Ceylon* (Calcutta, 1899), 51–8, and later *Thacker's Directories*.

anyone offering to manage an estate. One contemporary authority recorded:

> People who have failed in everything else were thought quite competent to make plantations . . . tea planters in those days were a strange medley of retired or cashiered Army or Navy officers, medical men, engineers, veterinary surgeons, steamer captains, chemists, shop keepers of all kinds, stable keepers, used-up policemen, clerks, and Goodness knows who besides. Is it strange the enterprise failed in their hands?[44]

Land bought at inflated prices and planted by managers with scant knowledge of tea cultivation soon ran into financial difficulties and thereby fell into the hands of the principal creditors, the merchants and the banks. Even the earliest and at one time the biggest company, the pioneer Assam Company, established in 1839 by a group of thirteen merchant houses with a projected capital of £500,000, was shortly compelled to delegate its marketing to one of the agency houses (Larpents, then Kilburn & Co.) and scale down its ambitions.[45]

A list of the tea companies floated in London—most in the 1860s and early 1870s—is assembled in Table 7.4. Information on capital usually refers to the actual issued capital, but in a few instances may be authorized capital that was never reached; even the pioneer Assam Company, initially very profitable, never attained more than 40 per cent (i.e. £200,000) of its authorized shareholding. Firm information is available on fifteen companies, eleven of which survived until the end of the century, but all in the hands of the agency houses. Their capitals were lower than the later companies and increased little if at all (Table 7.4).

TABLE 7.4. *Free-standing tea companies formed 1839–1875*

Tea company	At formation		In 1900	
	Date	Capital (£000s)	Investment group	Capital (£000s)
Ceylon Company Ltd.	1864	384	no record	—
British India Tea Co.	1863	239	Balmer Lawrie & Co.	61
Assam Co.	1839	193	Kilburn & Co.	200
Upper Assam Co.	1862	189	Macneill & Co.	80
Darjeeling Co. Ltd.	1864	135	Begg Dunlop & Co.	135
Tea Co. Ltd.	1875	125	no record	—
Eastern Assam Co.	1864	122	Barry & Co.	—
India Tea Co. of Cachar	1863	94	Shaw Wallace & Co.	95
Jorehaut Tea Co.	1859	90	Begg Dunlop & Co.	100
Tarrapore Tea Co.	1875	90	Macneill & Co.	90
Luckimpore (Assam) Co.	1865	71	no record	—
Lower Assam Co.	1861	58	Williamson Magor & Co.	90
Borokai Tea Co.	1864	44	Shaw Wallace & Co.	44
Leboug Tea Co.	?	10	Balmer Lawrie & Co.	—
India & China Co.	1872	10	no record	—

Note: Several companies appear in a list of liquidations, suspensions etc., but with no capital recorded.
Source: *Seyd's London Commerical List, 1877 III Miscellaneous Companies* (copy at West Yorks Record Office, Wakefield, C 149/958); Estell & Co, *Directory of Joint-Stock Companies* (1876); Thacker, Spink & Co., *Directory of the Chief Industries of India . . . and . . . Ceylon* (Calcutta, 1899), tea companies, 51–8.

Despite such early setbacks, British imports of Indian tea advanced by leaps and bounds, from £4.6 million in 1865 to £96 million in 1889.[46] This gave opportunity for new entrepreneurs to find their way into the plantation business, numbers of them financed by connections in the City of London. The London Stock Exchange files of company reports reveal a handful of smaller tea companies that had been launched during the 1890s or the next decade directly from London and were apparently independent of the managing-agency system. Their annual reports are not particularly revealing, but it is possible to venture a few generalizations. The owners appear to have been men who had spent their careers in India and, with a few friends, invested their savings in an estate. Control was maintained by the appointment of 'visiting agents', inspectors who visited the estate three or four times a year and reported to the owners. As steamship services became regular and more luxurious, the Chairman might make an occasional visit. Such free-standing companies, if that is what we must call them, were evidently very much on the margins of the system by this time.[47]

The experience of the rubber plantation business was very similar to that of tea, except that it began some forty years later, and largely focused on Malaya and Java rather than on India. The industry quickly became dominated by a small number of investment groups, notably Guthrie, Harrisons & Crosfield, Barlow Boustead, and Sime Darby.[48] The main difference was that there was less indigenous capital in

Malaya than in India, so Harrisons & Crosfield at first raised capital in London by floating new companies, beginning in 1903.[49] Their success encouraged others, so that on the eve of the First World War there were still a lot of smaller rubber companies quoted on the London Stock Exchange. Reading their reports, it is clear that several of them were floundering, destined for early absorption into the larger groups. Thus we read that the Batang Malaka Rubber Estates (1,250 acres) was bought for £28,000 in 1909, and that the directors had invested a further £19,000, but the concern was still short of working capital. The Bandjarsarie (Java) Rubber Co. was formed in 1907 with an initial capital of £25,000, but 'the property was neither properly worked nor efficiently supervised' and a hundred acres had reverted to jungle; a further £17,000 had been invested but the company was still losing money. The Baru (Java) Estates Ltd. was established in 1910 to acquire an estate for £50,000, but, a visiting director reported, 'the system and method of management left much to be desired' and 'the working capital provided was insufficient'. The last two were already appointing local managing agents and thus were in the process of being absorbed into the traditional British investment system.[50]

Conclusion

The dominance of the agency houses in European mercantile and industrial enterprise in India, and of indigenous entrepreneurs in all other sectors, appears so complete that it is difficult to locate significant numbers of firms that can (or might) be identified as truly free-standing companies, and even fewer that lasted any significant amount of time. At the end of the nineteenth century, commercial and investors' directories, crammed with detailed information, were common, but they are uninformative on FSCs as an identifiable category. The well-known *Investor's India Year Book* (Calcutta, 1911 onwards) has chapters listing the railway companies and banks, then jute, tea, coal, cotton, and miscellaneous companies, but the introduction explains that these are 'companies which are of sufficient importance for their shares to be quoted on the Stock Exchanges of Calcutta, Bombay, Madras and Rangoon', but evidently not London. Thacker, Spink & Co's *Directory of the Chief Industries of India . . . and . . . Tea, Coffee and other Estates* (Calcutta, 1899 onwards) is no less detailed, but no more informative on the present subject. The *Indian Industrial Census Report* of 1911 is heavy with tabulations and meticulously gathered evidence, but the divisions of business identified are concerned with European, Indian, and 'mixed' enterprises, rather than with the location of capital raising or the origins of white entrepreneurs. The obvious lack of interest in today's academic categories was surely not just blindness or perversity; the category we now seek was clearly of little (if any) significance to people actively involved in business at the period in India.

The weaknesses of free-standing companies, so evident in several chapters of this book, were such that they were overwhelmed by the established mercantile investment groups in Britain's major imperial territory. Even at the end of the nineteenth century, international communications were still slow and control was difficult to maintain over long distances, while good management was difficult to recruit and retain. The combination of central direction with local expertise and control that was the essence of the mercantile investment group system evidently gave them an easy lead over the remote control of the free-standing company.

NOTES

1. S. D. Chapman, *Merchant Enterprise in Britain* (Cambridge, 1992), chs. 4, 8.
2. P. S. Lokanathan, *Industrial Organisation in India* (London, 1935), 309.
3. Chapman, *Merchant Enterprise*, 111–12.
4. R. S. Rungta, *Rise of Business Corporations in India* (Calcutta, 1970), 240–1.
5. A list of house histories is contained in Chapman, *Merchant Enterprise*, 257–61, 313–16. Most of these histories were privately published in the 1960s; none of the major London libraries has anything like a complete holding. A few of the best are included in the references contained in this chapter.
6. K. N. Chaudhuri, 'The East India Co. in the 17th and 18th Centuries', in L. Blussé and F. Gaastra (eds.), *Companies and Trade* (Leiden, 1981).
7. Chapman, *Merchant Enterprise*, ch. 4.
8. Ibid. The most revealing set of London–Calcutta correspondence is in the Jardine Skinner MSS, Cambridge University Library (CUL).
9. Chapman, *Merchant Enterprise*, 237–41, and the various house histories.
10. Lokanathan, *Industrial Organisation in India*, ch. 8.
11. Chapman, *Merchant Enterprise*, 252–4.
12. There is a strong bibliography on indigenous enterprise; see in particular B. B. Kling and M. N. Pearson (eds.), *The Age of Partnership: Europeans in Asia before Dominion* (Honolulu, 1979); S. Subrahmanyam (ed.), *Merchants, Markets and the State in Early Modern India* (Bombay, 1990); R. J. Ray (ed.), *Entrepreneurship and Industry in India 1800–1947* (Bombay, 1992).
13. S. M. Rutnagur, *Bombay Industries: The Cotton Mills* (Bombay, 1927), 9, 23, 46–7, 249.
14. S. K. Sen, *The House of Tata 1839–1939* (Calcutta, 1975). A. K. Sen, 'The Pattern of British Enterprise in India 1854–1914', in Ray (ed.), *Entrepreneurship and Industry in India*.
15. G. H. Le Maistre, *Investor's India Year Book* (Calcutta, 1912), 213.
16. See C. Erickson, *British Industrialists 1850–1950* (Cambridge, 1959).
17. Later in this chapter, I will discuss the investments in tea plantations.
18. Rutnagur, *Bombay Industries*, 49, 52.
19. D. R. Wallace, *The Romance of Jute* (London, 1928), 15, 29–30, 33–64.
20. N. Z. Ahmed, 'Some Aspects of the History of British Investments in the

Private Sector of the Indian Economy 1875–1914', M.Sc. Econ. thesis (London School of Economics, 1955), 25.
21. Chapman, *Merchant Enterprise*, 125.
22. For an excellent analytical case study, see R. E. Stewart, 'Scottish Company Accounting 1870–1920', unpublished Ph.D. thesis (University of Glasgow, 1986), ch. 8.
23. CUL Jardine Skinner MSS, Guard Books XVII, 18 Mar. 1913.
24. *Dictionary of Business Biography* (London, 1984–6); P. L. Cottrell, *Industrial Finance 1830–1914* (London, 1980), ch. 2.
25. S. D. Chapman, *The Rise of Merchant Banking* (London, 1984).
26. Y. Cassis, *La City de Londres 1870–1914* (Paris, 1987). On 'give and take', see, for example, Sir Lawrence Jones, *Georgian Afternoon* (London, 1958), 143–4.
27. J. Kinross, *Fifty Years in the City* (London, 1982), 70. For the nineteenth century, see H. O. O'Hagan, *Leaves from my Life* (2 vols.; London, 1929).
28. CUL Jardine Skinner MSS, John Steuart to W. O. B. Irving (London), 11 Sept. 1890.
29. Ibid. Irving to Calcutta, 19 Aug. 1890.
30. Ibid. Irving to Calcutta, 6 May 1892.
31. Ibid. Steuart to London, 9 June and 22 Sept. 1892, 28 June 1894; see also J. Keswick to Sir A.Wilson, 26 July 1886, referring to the system of capital recruitment at Finlays and Gillanders Arbuthnot & Co.
32. Chapman, *Merchant Enterprise*, 111–13.
33. G. Harrison, *Bird & Co. of Calcutta . . . 1864–1964* (Calcutta, 1964).
34. *Report of the Indian Industrial Commission*, *Parliamentary Papers*, 1919, XVII, 747.
35. Glasgow University Library, Finlay MSS D91/23.
36. J. S. Gladstone, *History of Gillanders, Arbuthnot & Co. and Ogilvy Gillanders & Co.* (London, 1910), 75; India Office Library, London, taped memoirs of Kenneth Warren; Mercantile Bank records from Stuart Muirhead, company historian.
37. Harrison, *Bird & Co.*, 63, 87.
38. Stewart, 'Scottish Company Accounting', 146.
39. Harrison, *Bird & Co.*, 71–2.
40. Chapman, *Merchant Enterprise*, 196–7.
41. *Andrew Yule & Co. Ltd. 1863–1963* (London, 1963), 13; *Thomas Sivewright Catto 1879–1959: A Personal Memoir* (Edinburgh, 1962), 67.
42. Wallace, *Romance of Jute*, 30.
43. Glasgow University Library, Finlay MSS D91/141; Sen, *House of Tata*, app. B, Tea Gardens and Agents in 1902, 73. *Thacker's Directories*.
44. Quoted in H. A. Antrobus, *History of the Assam Company* (Edinburgh, 1957), 144–5.
45. Ibid. 154, 172, and ch. 6.
46. P. Griffiths, *History of the Indian Tea Industry* (London, 1967), 125.
47. GL SEAR (1880–1965), Series inscribed 'Tea, Coffee and Rubber'.
48. J. H. Drabble, *Rubber in Malaya 1876–1922* (Kuala Lumpur, 1973).
49. G. Nickalls (ed.), *Great Enterprise: A History of Harrisons & Crosfield* (London, 1990), ch. 3.
50. GL SEAR.

8

British Free-Standing Companies on the West Coast of South America

Rory Miller

The historiography of British investment in Latin America has experienced some revision since 1980, when Alfred Chandler emphasized the retarded development and poor performance of British multinational firms compared with their US equivalents.[1] Already, in the late 1970s, Irving Stone and Peter Svedberg had independently argued, on the basis of published data on British investment in Latin America, that a large component of this capital flow had taken the form of direct investments in which the British had maintained control of the assets established with their funds.[2] Company histories also began to indicate that a number of leading British multinational companies, including ICI, Lever Brothers, J. & P. Coats, BAT, and Glaxo, established significant operations in Latin America early in the twentieth century.[3] However, most of the British direct investments in the region before the First World War did not take the form of the classic multinational company, but rather consisted of hundreds of apparently independent enterprises separately registered on the Stock Exchange and operating in one or two contiguous countries. Analysing British direct investment in Latin America before 1914 thus required concepts which drew a distinction between the typical British firm and the multinational corporation, the normal vehicle for US direct investment in the region.

In the search for appropriate analytical tools recognizing the distinction between British and US patterns of direct investment, two contributions to the literature stand out: the concept of 'investment groups' developed by Stanley Chapman, and that of the 'free-standing company' pioneered by Mira Wilkins. These concepts allowed specialists on Britain's economic relationship with Latin America to make

The arguments here owe much to frequent discussions over twenty years with Robert Greenhill of London Guildhall University, and particularly to joint papers which we prepared for the Development Studies Association Annual Conference in 1980 and the International Congress of Americanists in 1988. I am grateful for his comments on this chapter, and for those of Mira Wilkins. I have also gained much from exchanges of draft papers and ideas with Charles Jones. None of these, of course, is responsible for the final content of this chapter.

much more sense of the firms and investment flows they were studying. While their primary interests lay in other parts of the globe, both Chapman and Wilkins briefly mentioned examples drawn from the experience of British companies in South America in support of their arguments. In fact, Latin America is a crucial test for their concepts. As Charles Jones has pointed out, the fact that the region received between a fifth and a quarter of Britain's overseas investment before 1914 makes it central to the evaluation both of these ideas and of the other revisions which have begun to occur in areas such as the growth of multinational companies and the classification and measurement of British overseas investment.[4]

The concept of the free-standing company, which Wilkins argued was 'probably the most typical mode of British direct investment abroad' before 1914, is of direct relevance.[5] Wilkins, apparently with the experience of foreign investment in North America in mind, seems to have been concerned principally with finding a means of describing companies which, unlike the usual industrial multinational enterprises, were not outgrowths of existing firms wishing to develop access to supplies or to markets. To specialists on Latin America this concept seemed obviously to fit the British-owned railway companies or the early British banks in countries such as Argentina, Brazil, or Chile. Indeed, at the end of her 1988 paper Wilkins explicitly emphasized its potential utility for understanding British companies in South America, mentioning the example of British nitrate firms in Chile, among others, but without taking the analysis much further.[6]

The fact of the British domicile of a free-standing company was, for Wilkins, crucial, since this registration made it subject to British laws and thus gave investors the confidence to subscribe its capital. However, in most cases, she argued, the governance structure of such companies was extremely weak, and they relied heavily upon the services supplied by a range of individuals and firms who were often represented among the shareholders and on the board of directors. Such people might have interests in several different free-standing companies, forming loosely connected and overlapping clusters of firms based on a particular company promoter, a financial group, professionals in law, accounting or engineering, trading companies, or merchant banks.[7] The development of adequate middle managerial structures was, she argued, critical to the survival of free-standing companies; continued reliance on outside agents for such important functions might well explain the fairly rapid disappearance of many of those registered in Britain between 1870 and 1914.[8]

The idea of clusters brought Wilkins close to Chapman's concept of the investment group, defined as 'an entrepreneurial or family concern whose name and reputation was used to float a variety of subsidiary trading, manufacturing, mining or financial enterprises'.[9] Historians of the merchant houses which had operated on the west coast of South America were well accustomed to the type of business organization he defined in this way. One of the principal features of British business in Chile and Peru had been the longevity and continuing significance of trading firms headquartered in Liverpool or London and possessing a diverse range of interests in these two economies and elsewhere on the Pacific Rim. Chapman himself cited the examples of Antony Gibbs & Sons and Balfour, Williamson & Co., two of the best known, as merchant partnerships which, in response to declining margins in their staple trades after the advent of the transatlantic cable in the 1870s, had developed a range of geographically dispersed companies reflecting their particular interests. Specialists could have added another two important Liverpool merchant houses, Duncan Fox and Graham Rowe, to his list of investment groups. They also considered applying the label to these firms' principal US competitor, W. R. Grace & Co.[10]

Peru and Chile (and to a lesser extent Bolivia), neighbouring and interconnected economies on the west coast of South America, thus provide a useful arena in which to examine these concepts. Of the approximately 2,000 British free-standing companies which Wilkins estimated to have been in existence in 1914, between 80 and 100 (about 5 per cent of the total) operated in these three countries.[11] Although not on the scale of Britain's investments in the River Plate or Brazil, Chile still ranked third and Peru fifth as destinations for British capital exports to South America in the half-century preceding the First World War.[12] They acted as hosts to what at first sight look like significant and long-lived free-standing railway companies, the Peruvian Corporation and the Antofagasta (Chili) and Bolivia Railway Company (henceforth called the Antofagasta Railway), as well as some obvious groups of smaller firms based either on merchant houses like Gibbs and Balfour, Williamson or else on company promoters like Colonel John Thomas North, whose activities in the 1880s earned him the appellation of the 'Nitrate King'. All three countries had dynamic local business élites with whom the British formed complex relationships. Domestic entrepreneurs developed copper-mining and agriculture in Chile, the production of silver, sugar, and cotton in Peru, and silver- and tin-mining in Bolivia.[13] Finally, in all three economies there was a clear transition from Britain to the USA as the predominant foreign partner during the first half of the twentieth century, when US firms moved into mining, oil, and industry. This may confirm some of Wilkins's ideas about the shortcomings of free-standing companies. It also raises questions about the contrast, implicit in Chapman's work, between the eventual failure of British 'investment groups' in Latin America and the consolidation of conglomerates such as Jardine Matheson and Butterfield & Swire in the Far East.

The Development of Free-Standing Companies on the West Coast

British investors in Peru and Chile, as in other independent Latin American countries, initially concentrated on the making of government loans and the formation of mining associations to exploit the supposed riches of the former Spanish colonies. By the end of the 1820s these ventures had failed, leaving the mining firms in dissolution and the government bonds in default.[14] However, the renegotiation of the post-independence debts, Chile's in 1842 and Peru's in 1849, permitted the resumption of investment. Portfolio investment, in the form of loans to governments, became the dominant mode in the mid-nineteenth century, preparing the ground for the later surge in direct investment. The Peruvian state, on the back of its guano income, became a major borrower. This culminated in the issue of two massive loans jointly in Paris and London in 1870 and 1872 for a total nominal amount of £32.7 million, intended primarily for the construction of railways into the Andes, but quickly followed by default at the beginning of 1876.[15] Chile also contracted loans for public-works projects, but state finances there, except for a period in the late 1870s, were generally in much better health than Peru's, and it did not default until the Depression of the 1930s.[16]

In both countries British merchant houses epitomized the foreign presence in the mid-nineteenth century, for they handled much of the republics' foreign trade, normally on a consignment basis. Gibbs, Graham Rowe, and Huth Grüning had all arrived with independence, while Duncan Fox and Balfour, Williamson & Co. made their appearance in the 1850s and 1860s.[17] By then some of these firms were beginning to undertake direct investments of their own, frequently as a result of foreclosure on debts. The most significant of these was probably Gibbs's development of the Tarapacá Nitrate Company in southern Peru after 1865.[18] Trading began on the London Stock Exchange in the shares of some of the short railways constructed in the 1850s and 1860s which the British had purchased from the original local proprietors. They included the Lima Railways Co. and the Arica and Tacna Railway in Peru, and the Caldera–Copiapó and Coquimbo–La Serena lines in Chile, all of which were in British hands by the end of the 1870s.[19]

The Pacific War of 1879–83, in which Chile defeated Peru and Bolivia, capturing a monopoly of the nitrate fields as a consequence, coincided with the beginnings of a period of rapid growth in British direct investment in Latin America.[20] Once it had seized power in 1885–6, therefore, the Cáceres government in Peru renegotiated the debt incurred by its predecessors in an attempt to regain access to British capital markets. Under the Grace Contract of 1889 it ceded to the bondholders a lease on the state railways, freehold land concessions, and a monopoly of guano export in return for the cancellation of the loans. To operate these concessions the bondholders formed a major free-standing company, the Peruvian Corporation; by 1895 it had issued £20.2 million in stock and debentures.[21] Taking advantage of the temporary revival of interest in Peru, several other small public companies, including the Caylloma Silver Mining Co., the Backus & Johnston Brewery Co., and the Peruvian Cotton Manufacturing Co., were formed to purchase and develop assets there. William Keswick of Jardine Matheson also organized a private firm, the London & Pacific Petroleum Co., to exploit oilfields in the north. However, the economic crisis of the early 1890s and the failure of the Peruvian Corporation to maintain interest payments on its debt soon curtailed this enthusiasm. Shaken by these disappointments and the wider consequences of the Baring Crisis, British investors did not regain their interest in Peru until the decade before the First World War. Then, however, they floated two other railway companies, two more petroleum firms, and a raft of mining enterprises. In addition both the Banco del Perú y Londres and the Lima Light, Power & Tramways Co. (known in Peru as Empresas Eléctricas Asociadas) sought capital on the London Stock Exchange and Paris Bourse. The organization of free-standing companies for Peru was not confined to London. In New York an important US free-standing firm, the Cerro de Pasco Copper Corporation, was formed in 1901; within twenty years it had established its dominance over other mineral producers in the central sierra.[22]

While default and defeat deterred many British capitalists from investing in Peru until the Grace Contract had been finalized, their interest and enthusiasm for Chile was, if anything, enhanced by its victory and the government's obvious desire to accommodate foreign interests. Following the 1882 decision to return the nitrate deposits in the captured Peruvian territory to private hands, several free-standing companies were formed in Britain.[23] During the following decade promoters like Colonel John Thomas North and the merchant house of Antony Gibbs & Sons floated a series of nitrate companies, together with associated enterprises such as railways, waterworks, financial, and shipping companies.[24] Enthusiasm for Chile also stimulated other investments. By 1914 these included the Chili Telephone Co., the Valparaiso Drainage Co., a number of small mining firms in the north and centre, sheep-farming companies in the south, and various manufacturing and food-processing interests.

British (and French) investors also showed some interest in Bolivia after the Pacific War. The Antofagasta Railway was purchased from its Chilean owners in 1888, and floated by Schroders on the London Stock Exchange. The capital raised financed the extension of the line into Bolivia in 1889–92.[25] The Antofagasta Railway's record of profits, helped by the growth of the Chilean nitrate and Bolivian tin industries, allowed it to purchase a controlling interest in the Bolivia Railway Co. in 1908, a move which consolidated its dominance of that country's rail network. European investors also bought locally controlled mining interests and later, during the Amazon rubber frenzy of 1907–10, formed a handful of free-standing companies to acquire concessions in the Bolivian *selva*. In addition they traded in the stock of companies registered in Chile but operating in Bolivia, and also subscribed for debentures issued by firms under Bolivian control.

Table 8.1 provides an indication of the number and capitalization of British-controlled free-standing companies in Bolivia, Chile, and Peru on the eve of the First World War. The starting point for its compilation was the 1916 report of the US Federal Trade Commission (FTC) listing 'British organized or controlled companies' with properties over-

TABLE 8.1. *British free-standing companies in Bolivia, Chile, and Peru on the eve of the First World War*

Sector	Bolivia		Chile		Peru		Total	
	Paid-up capital (£m.)	No.	Paid-up capital (£m.)	No.	Paid-up capital (£m.)	No.	Paid-up capital (£m.)	No.
Finance	—		0.100	1	0.500	1	0.600	2
Land	—		2.731	4	0.497	1	3.228	5
Manufacturing	0.152	1	0.719	3	0.353	2	1.224	6
Mining	1.404	3	2.318	7	1.234	10	4.956	20
Nitrate	—		9.377	32	—		9.377	32
Petroleum	—		—		0.400	1	0.400	1
Railways	—		23.720	9	24.020	4	47.740	13
Retail	—		0.331	1	—		0.331	1
Rubber	0.356	3	—		0.335	1	0.691	4
Utilities	—		0.876	3	2.241	1	3.117	4
TOTAL	1.912	7	40.172	60	29.580	21	71.664	88

Notes: Companies with assets in two or more countries have been attributed to that where the majority was held: the Santa Rosa Milling Co. and Antofagasta (Chili) and Bolivia Railway Co. to Chile, and the Peruvian Corporation to Peru.

Although they appeared in the FTC list, the following companies have been excluded since most of their equity is known to have been held in Latin America, their debentures being the primary British interest: Agua Santa Nitrate & Railway Co., Antofagasta Nitrate Co., Banco de Chile, Electric Light & Power Co. of Cochabamba, Junín Nitrate and Railway Co., Loa Nitrate Co.

The following companies have been excluded because it is clear from lists of directors and other information that control of the company lay outside Britain: Anglo-French Ticapampa Silver Co. (France), Chilean Electric Tramway & Light Co. (Germany), Lagunitos Oil Co. and London & Pacific Petroleum Co. (USA). The Keswick family had sold control of the latter to Standard Oil of New Jersey in 1913.

Source: See text.

seas, but some amendments have been made in the light of information in other contemporary sources and in later business histories.[26] Both the Anglo-South American Bank (which by 1914 possessed a network of branches in Argentina and Europe as well as Chile), and the Pacific Steam Navigation Co. have been considered multinational enterprises rather than free-standing companies and thus excluded. Other firms on the FTC list have been left out where the paper traded on the London Stock Exchange consisted of debentures rather than equity stock.[27] The table also excludes a number of private companies which did not have a Stock Exchange listing; into this category fall several enterprises organized by individuals or merchant houses which had not been developed to the point where a market flotation was justified.

Categorizing Free-Standing Companies

Taking the 'free-standing company' to be an enterprise primarily owned and controlled by UK interests, with a small headquarters in the UK but the bulk of its assets in one or at most two contiguous overseas countries, the firms of this type operating on the west coast of South America seem to fall into three groups: autonomous free-standing companies, free-standing companies controlled by 'investment groups', and free-standing companies of mixed ownership. Categorizing an individual company into these groups is occasionally problematic. Several firms moved from one category to another or were transformed from free-standing companies into multinational firms. On the other hand, exploring some of these difficulties may help to refine the concept, as well as indicating some possible explanations for the survival of some companies and the disappearance of others.

This analysis depends on two kinds of sources. First, a number of business archives have survived, in particular those of two major railway companies (the Peruvian Corporation and the Antofagasta Railway), two of the most important banks (the Anglo-South American Bank and the Banco del Perú y Londres), and some of the largest merchant houses (Antony Gibbs & Sons, Balfour, Williamson & Co., and the New York house of W. R. Grace & Co.).[28] Secondly, the *Stock Exchange Yearbook*, a standard business history source, has been used to provide a census of directors of firms on the west coast at roughly twenty-year intervals (1895, 1913, 1935).[29] Interpreting such lists is, of course, problematic. Overlapping directorships do not necessarily indicate that nominally independent firms behaved as a group, for individual directors could be recruited in order to facilitate access to finance and other services or because of their specialized regional knowledge.[30] The assumption here is that a majority of directors in common and the use of the same company secretary and registered office imply the existence of an investment group. The availability of company archives and histories provides a means of checking these judgements, as well as offering evidence on the autonomy, adequacy, and efficiency of the companies' governance structures.

The most obvious firms falling into the category of autonomous free-standing companies are the large railway enterprises, the Peruvian Corporation and the Antofagasta Railway.[31] Although they had both developed international interests by 1914, in the sense that both operated lines in Bolivia, they do not fit the standard pattern of a multinational enterprise growing outwards from its home base: they had little connection with the British economy except through the City of London and the engineering firms with whom they placed orders. Nor did they form part of larger investment groups, judging from their internal correspondence and lists of directors, few of whom held similar posts in other companies on the west coast.[32] Both the major railway firms operated, for most of their lives, as independent entities. However, they differ from Wilkins's archetypal short-lived free-standing company in that while their governance structure in London remained lean they soon internalized almost all the major technological and financial functions, developing, like railway companies everywhere, complex and professional managerial hierarchies.[33] Their consulting engineers were precisely that—professionals who could provide advice drawn from wider experience whenever key strategic decisions such as the development of a new kind of motive power were required. Such engineering partnerships, however, played virtually no role in the daily management of the company.[34] Although the Peruvian Corporation, early in its history, suffered from some extremely poor-quality management, its governance structure was from the beginning designed to meet the needs of administering a set of disconnected railways. The professionalism of both companies' management by the time of the First World War is evident from their internal correspondence. By then both habitually filled key positions, in London and South America, with career railwaymen who possessed wide experience of local conditions and a good knowledge of Spanish.[35]

Much the same could be said of most, if not all, the other independent railway enterprises like the Taltal or the Lima Railways, the major exceptions being two poorly engineered and loss-making minor companies in Peru which appear to have been promoted for speculative reasons.[36] Apart from the other railway companies such as the Chilean Eastern Central and the Chilean Northern, the evidence of the *Stock Exchange Yearbooks* would suggest a number of other autonomous British free-standing companies of some longevity. These include

Chilean Mills Co., Chilean National Ammunition Co., Chili Telephone Co., the Backus & Johnston Brewery in Lima, the Valparaiso Drainage Co., and some small mining and land companies, in particular in Chile.[37]

The Nitrate Railways Co. was a distinct case, for it had initially been part of a larger investment group but had become an autonomous free-standing company by 1913. Colonel North had purchased this railway from its Peruvian owners in 1887. Its monopoly of transport on the nitrate *pampa* immediately exacerbated the rivalries between North and other British nitrate interests, notably Gibbs and Campbell Outram. Both the Santiago government and the other nitrate firms feared, with some justification, that North intended to use the railway to achieve a monopoly of the industry.[38] However, North had relinquished many of his Nitrate Railways shares by the time of his death in 1896. It certainly seems to have become independent of the remnants of the North empire thereafter, judging from the membership of its board. Although it continued to be chaired by Sir Robert Harvey, North's former associate, only one of the other seven directors in 1913 had any formal links with a nitrate firm.[39] By then it seems to have attracted significant French or Belgian interests, while in the inter-war period the Graces were also represented on the board.[40] This seems, however, to have reflected changes in shareholdings rather than undermining the autonomy of the company's management.

This example illustrates how components of an investment group (in Chapman's words) or a cluster (in Wilkins's) could be spun off into autonomous free-standing companies with a specialized and independent management. They could also pass through this stage and become fully-fledged multinational companies. The case of Sir Robert Harvey, who chaired seven companies operating in Chile in 1913 as well as sitting on the board of the Antofagasta Railway, illustrates this well.[41] Like the Nitrate Railways, the Anglo-South American Bank, the largest of the companies Harvey chaired, had become independent after North's death. It had started life in 1888 as the Bank of Tarapacá and London and a very obvious part of the North group, but it had long operated independently while retaining Harvey as chairman. Indeed, as early as the mid-1890s, when North died, the company's internal correspondence shows that it was acting as an orthodox and independent Anglo-Chilean bank rather than an adjunct to North's nitrate firms, although its business clearly benefited from its links with them.[42] In 1900 it expanded into Argentina by purchasing a small British bank there, and renamed itself the Bank of Tarapacá and Argentina. A further change in 1906 turned it into the Anglo-South American Bank, and it acquired partial control of several other banks operating in South America, including, for a time, the Banco del Perú y Londres.[43] Thus it became, in essence, a multinational bank independent of any larger group until its absorption into the Bank of London and South America, by then itself controlled by Lloyds Bank, in 1936. The leading figure in its expansion was not Harvey, despite the links he possessed with many other west-coast companies, but R. J. Hose, a career banker, who had joined the bank as secretary in 1896, ascended to the post of managing director in 1911, and eventually succeeded Harvey as chairman in 1918.[44]

To sum up thus far, a number of the British firms on the west coast of South America in 1913, including the majority of the most heavily capitalized, were autonomous free-standing companies. In some cases they had evolved out of investment groups. The key to differentiating them is their managerial independence from other firms. The archives of companies such as the Peruvian Corporation, the Antofagasta Railway, and the Anglo-South American Bank provide no indication, for example, of behaviour like the granting of preferences to their directors' other companies, or pressure on middle management to favour one client rather than another. There is also little indication that they contracted out administrative or technical functions that should have been internal to the firm, or that, by the standards of the time, their governance structures were inadequate for the task. Management may at times have been of low quality, unable to seize opportunities or adapt to an alien environment, but that is a different issue. Even in the case of the Peruvian Corporation, probably the best-documented example of such shortcomings, these problems had been largely overcome by 1913.

Our second group of free-standing companies are those controlled by investment groups. The continued significance of British merchant houses in the commodity trades of the west coast meant that by the early twentieth century there were also several clusters of free-standing companies based around them. The production and processing of raw materials, such as nitrate or cotton, the trade along the coast in Chilean wheat, Peruvian sugar, and later Peruvian oil, and the growth of local manufacturing gave the merchants opportunities to profit from their specialized expertise and to utilize spare capital. Their hope was that by developing an enterprise to the point where it could be transformed into a public company they could regain their initial investment, secure a worthwhile profit from the flotation, offload the risk onto the shareholders, and yet retain for their houses the lucrative commissions on sales, supplies, shipping, and insurance that the company would provide. In certain cases they might also continue to act as management agents for the outwardly independent firm. The two British west-coast houses which stand out in this regard are Antony Gibbs & Sons and Balfour, Williamson & Co.

Gibbs's direct investments on the west coast concentrated on nitrate and they pre-dated Chile's capture of Tarapacá and Antofagasta during the Pacific War. During the 1880s Gibbs was second only to Colonel North as a promoter of nitrate enterprises, floating the Alianza, Tamarugal, Salar del Carmen, and Pan de Azúcar companies, and later taking over the Fortuna Nitrate Co.[45] Even though it began to sell some of these interests to Chilean businessmen immediately before the First World War, it frequently retained its agencies, and its position in the trade was such that it was the obvious firm for the British government to appoint as purchasing agents for nitrate during the war.[46] By 1913 Gibbs's partners and associates dominated the boards of the Alianza, Fortuna, New Tamarugal, and Santa Catalina companies, while acting alongside Balfour Williamson representatives on the boards of Angela and Salar del Carmen.[47] Gibbs was also, as Chapman shows, very active in promoting companies in Argentina.[48]

Balfour, Williamson was in some ways even more successful as an investment group, less vulnerable to liquidity crises than Gibbs (at least until 1920–1), and with a more diversified range of companies associated with it.[49] Like Gibbs it possessed nitrate interests of its own, in Agua Santa and Taltal, but it also controlled some public companies of impressive profitability in other sectors, in particular the Santa Rosa Milling Co., which had interests in both Chile and Peru, and Lobitos Oilfields, which, having been floated on the Stock Exchange in 1908, became the second largest producer in Peru and, through its offshoot, Anglo-Ecuadorian Oilfields, the largest in that country as well. It is clear from the private correspondence of Sir Archibald Williamson (Lord Forres) that these companies worked in close cooperation with each other, at least until the early 1920s. Judging from the reduced volume of Williamson's personal correspondence relating to oil matters, the Lobitos management then became more independent of its chairman, although for some time the primary object of the firm's strategy in Peru remained the protection of the interests of Balfour, Williamson & Co. and Milne & Co., its Lima associate.[50]

Merchant houses were the main, but not the only, source of investment groups controlling apparently free-standing companies. Despite the separation of the Nitrate Railways and the Bank of Tarapacá and London from the North cluster, a rump of North's original investment group still remained intact in 1913 under the chairmanship of Sir Robert Harvey. These firms included the Tarapacá Waterworks Co., the Arauco Co. (which operated a railway and coal mine in the south of Chile), and the Colorado and Liverpool nitrate companies.[51] The alliance which North had formed in the 1880s with Wm. & Jno. Lockett, a Liverpool merchant house, and W. R. Grace & Co., the most important New York house trading on the west coast, had also continued, at least to an extent, after his death.[52] The cooperation among these three houses was, by 1913, most evident in the Lagunas Syndicate. Wm. & Jno. Lockett meanwhile had developed its personal interests in the privately owned British Sugar Co. (which it had formed in 1900 to take control of estates indebted to it), and in the San Lorenzo Nitrate Co.

Wilkins makes the point that London was not the only focus for British free-standing companies, and that provincial stock exchanges such as Edinburgh and Glasgow might also provide a conduit for such capital.[53] The example of the Lockett firm suggests that for the west coast of South America Liverpool should not be ignored. Despite its connections with the North interests in London, this firm was firmly rooted in the Liverpool business community, and even in 1913 the Liverpool, London, and Colorado nitrate companies, remnants of the North group, remained registered there. Although it eventually moved its headquarters from Merseyside to London in 1909, largely because of its senior partner's political career, Balfour, Williamson & Co. had also long been known as a 'first-class Liverpool house', and it undoubtedly benefited from its contacts and reputation in both cities in floating its companies.[54] A third example of a Liverpool merchant who had promoted free-standing companies operating on the west coast is J. Lionel Barber, whose trading firm eventually went into liquidation in 1921. Barber chaired the Lampa Mining Co. (a Peruvian silver venture), which had been registered in Liverpool in 1906, and also sat on the board of the Corocoro United Copper Mines, which he had formed in 1909 to acquire and consolidate properties in Bolivia's principal copper-mining centre.[55]

It may be, however, that the growing disparity between the resources of London and Liverpool was making it more difficult for merchants based in the north to float companies. It is noticeable, for example, that, while Duncan Fox and Graham Rowe both made substantial direct investments of their own after the turn of the century, neither seems to have wished to form them into British-registered companies. In Peru Duncan Fox possessed interests in cotton-processing facilities and two cotton mills, El Progreso and La Unión, which together were valued at £p200,000 in 1922, and in Chile they had invested in a paper mill and sheep farms in the south. For a time they also owned livestock estates in central Peru.[56] Graham Rowe, which went into liquidation in 1931, had interests in sugar refining in Chile, and was a major distributor of machinery and vehicles in Peru. It is difficult to be sure about the reasons for these strategies, since these firms' archives have disappeared, but they clearly chose not to follow the path of Gibbs, Balfour, Williamson & Co., or North, and float their direct investment interests on the London Stock Exchange.[57] Graham Rowe, Duncan Fox, and Cockbain & Edmondson had all been jointly or separately involved in a number of enterprises in Chile in the late nineteenth century, but the only one apparently registered in London in 1895 was Chilean Manganese Mines, which was linked with Duncan Fox. The other Chilean interests of these firms, largely in railways, seem to have remained capitalized in pesos and domiciled in Valparaiso, with biannual meetings of the British shareholders in Liverpool.[58] This may have been because, once completed to the mining zones, these railways required little new capital. However, registration of their companies in Latin America continued to be the path the Liverpool houses tended to follow after the turn of the century.

The other important investment group that had a long association with the City of London and extensive interests on the west coast of South America was the New York house of W. R. Grace & Co. Beginning as ship's chandlers during the guano age, this house, formed by Irish emigrants, subsequently became a leading multinational firm. One of its two leading figures, Michael P. Grace, the younger brother of the founder, nurtured his contacts with the City of London while negotiating on behalf of the Peruvian bondholders in the 1880s, and he then became closely associated with Colonel North. He subsequently made his home in England, and controlled the British branch of the firm with his cousins, Edward and William S. Eyre.[59] The Graces were involved in a succession of enterprises on the west coast. For a brief period in the early 1890s they were, according to the Gibbs, influential in the affairs of the Peruvian Corporation, and they also floated in London the Cartavio Sugar Co., which owned plantations in northern Peru, at the same time as they were working with North on nitrate flotations.[60] In 1900–1, a few years after North's death, they took the decision to invest on their own account in nitrate, and in 1909 they consolidated their trading interests in northern Chile into the wholly owned Nitrate Agencies Ltd., which acted as managing agents for other firms.[61] By 1913 their nitrate business was structured around twelve London-registered nitrate companies, eight of them chaired by H. W. Lowe, two by Edward Eyre, and two by R. E. Morris.[62] Grace, more than any other west-coast investment group, became a prototype multinational conglomerate along the lines of the Far East agency houses, but the declining capacity of the City to mobilize funds for Latin America and the collapse of the Chilean nitrate industry in the 1920s meant that by the mid-1930s its London interests had become restricted to a couple of directorships (the Peruvian Corporation and the Nitrate Railways), and a moribund investment trust incorporating the rump of its nitrate activities.

These examples raise a number of issues about both the nationality and the independence of free-standing companies and, more broadly, about the role of the City of London in international finance. These nitrate companies have always been considered as British firms with major British shareholders, but they were at least partially controlled by a US investment group, as was the Peruvian Corporation for short periods in its history.[63] On the other hand, some British merchant houses, especially in Liverpool, preferred to establish some of their direct investments under Latin American commercial laws rather than in Britain, perhaps for reasons of commercial confidentiality, perhaps because they saw little advantage in using the stock market for these particular ventures.[64] Wilkins seems to regard registration as the most significant factor in determining the nationality of a company.[65] Yet how British were supposedly British free-standing companies, particularly during the decade before the First World War? At least ten of the companies which the US Federal Trade Commission considered 'British organized or controlled' firms with interests in Chile, Peru, or Bolivia in 1916 should not in fact be described as such.[66] There are several cases on the west coast where ownership and control of a free-standing company nominally registered in London were international or indeterminate.

Our third category of free-standing companies is thus those of 'mixed ownership'. The formation of free-standing companies in London to operate businesses on the west coast of South America reached a peak in the two decades before 1914 and it reflected a number of factors: the long-standing interests of British merchants in the region, the continued importance of the British market for certain of these countries' exports, and the ability of the City of London to act as a conduit for savings not only from within Britain but also from other countries. As a result businesses originally begun by British expatriates or by Latin Americans might be registered as British companies. Once London lost its capacity to channel capital to Latin America, few new free-standing companies were formed, while existing ones began to dissolve or migrate, although it took over sixty years for this process to be completed. These points can be illustrated by some examples of firms which were only temporarily or partially British in terms of their registration, ownership, or management.

In the 1880s and 1890s the shares of certain Chilean-registered companies became quite widely known in Europe, allowing merchants and bankers like Gibbs to conduct arbitrage operations on their own account between *bolsas* in Latin America, especially Valparaiso, and stock exchanges in Europe, or else as agents for other investors by taking orders to carry out share transactions in Latin American companies. In the 1890s, for example, Gibbs was trading on the Valparaiso market, for itself and for others, in the shares of both the Huanchaca and the Copiapó mining companies and remitting the stock to Europe.[67] The Chilean owners of the Huanchaca company had already hived off their railway interests to British investors in 1888.[68] Continued trading in the mining shares might have been a preliminary to further 'denationalization'; that it did not come to that in the case of the Huanchaca company was probably due more to the flooding of the mines in 1895 than anything else.[69] Indeed, the Huanchaca example clearly illustrates one means by which British free-standing companies were established to operate in Latin America. During investment booms Latin American entrepreneurs found it worthwhile to sell assets at attractive prices to British entrepreneurs, either to take windfall profits or to finance their own expansion elsewhere. Many of the South American rubber properties floated on the London Stock Exchange between 1907 and 1910 probably also fall into this category.

Investment booms also gave Latin American entrepreneurs the opportunity to move their companies to London in order to raise fresh capital, at the risk of diluting ownership, but not control. One notorious example is the Peruvian Amazon Company of Julio C. Arana, the firm implicated in the Putumayo rubber atrocities, which had been registered in London in 1907 with a capital of £1 million and three British directors. The latter freely confessed to a parliamentary inquiry a few years later that they had no acquaintance whatsoever with the Amazon region. One possessed no knowledge of Spanish, the language in which much of the board's business was conducted.[70] Another example is the registration of Aramayo Francke Mines in London in 1906. This firm was controlled by Francisco A. Aramayo, one of the three major tin-producers in Bolivia, who had been Bolivian minister in London from 1897 until 1903 and who then resided frequently in Paris. In 1912 Aramayo promoted another company, Porco Tin Mines, in London.[71] However, both these cases also illustrate the footloose nature of such Latin American-inspired free-standing companies: by 1913 the Peruvian Amazon Co. had gone into liquidation following the Putumayo affair (though Arana, the liquidator, continued to operate his company in Peru), and in 1916 Aramayo transferred his companies to Switzerland.[72]

The example of Aramayo, a Bolivian living in Paris and carrying on business in London, suggests that determining the ownership of mining companies, and the extent to which they should be considered British, can become a real problem. Many French investors bought stock in companies registered in London: in these cases neither control, nor the outward flow of capital, could really be considered British. The *Stock Exchange Yearbook* of 1913 provides several examples: the Anglo-French Ticapampa Silver Mining Co., which was registered in England and operated in Peru, had its accounts made up in francs and all but one of its directors resident in Paris; half the board of Aporama Goldfields and a similar proportion of Barber's Corocoro United Copper Mines were French; and Inambari Gold Dredging Concessions had an even more international aspect with a German as well as two Frenchmen on the board.[73] So little is known about the fate of these companies, however, that it is difficult to be more precise.[74]

In practice the extent to which British-registered free-standing companies really were British ran along a spectrum from the truly British to the international. It also varied from one moment to another. It has been too easy for historians brought up in an age of exchange controls to forget just how international a capital market the City of London was before 1914. This has become evident from research on Latin American government loans before the First World War, which has shown the extent to which bonds issued in London were held in Continental European countries as well as in Latin America itself.[75] Company finance has been relatively neglected, yet it is clear that many free-standing companies had mixed ownership and only partial British control, even if they were registered in London. The legacy of the Peruvian bond issues of the 1870s and their renegotiation meant that the Peruvian Corporation retained enough of a European minority shareholding for it deliberately to recruit French and Dutch directors to its board. This does not stop it being considered a British free-standing company, at least until it moved to Canada in 1956, but it does suggest that the company's nationality was by no means secure, a feature enhanced by the sorry fact that it never paid a dividend on its ordinary shares and they were thus traded at nominal prices, making it relatively cheap to purchase influence in a firm with superficially attractive assets.[76] Struggles for control took place on at least two occasions before the First World War—in 1906–7, when New York interests (Grace and Speyer) suddenly acquired influence in its management, and in 1910, when there was substantial French buying of its stock.[77] Outside observers also found it difficult to categorize the Santiago Electric Light & Power Co., which was registered in London but in which the Compañía Alemana Transatlántica de Electricidad held a large block of shares until they were sequestered by the British authorities in 1919 and transferred to a new company controlled by S. Pearson and Son.[78]

Perhaps the two greatest problems of definition on the west coast just before the First World War, however, relate to the Banco del Perú y Londres and the Lima Light, Power & Tramways Co. The first was not registered as a British company but the Anglo-South American Bank obtained, for a time, the controlling voice in it; the latter was, but was never fully under British control. The case of the bank showed, first, another example of the partial denationalization of Latin American business, and, secondly, a struggle for control between British and French investors between 1907 and 1912. The decisive factor in resolving this was the fusion in 1912 of the London Bank of Mexico and South America (whose branch in Lima had been a predecessor of the Banco del Perú y Londres and which had held a minority shareholding in the Lima bank since its foundation in 1897) and the more aggressive Anglo-South American Bank. The merger gave Anglo-South American Bank effective control over the Banco del Perú y Londres, until it sold blocks of shares to Peruvian investors at the end of the war.[79] Lima Light, Power & Tramways Co. is even more complex, because the company's need to issue debentures in London in 1910 led to a restructuring which put the bondholders into a majority on the board. The US house of Grace, the London merchant bank of Schroders, and the Banco del Perú y Londres then together attempted to support the market in the bonds of what was essentially a very poorly managed and capital-short enterprise. By 1923 the Banco del Perú y Londres had had enough: the light and power company was again refinanced, but this time it came under the control of Italian and Swiss interests, aided by a new issue of £1.5 million in debentures in London by Schroders.[80]

The evidence of British companies on the west coast suggests therefore that the label 'free-standing companies' appears to cover several different classes of firms: quite long-lived and relatively successful companies which were autonomous of any single dominant interest and envisaged their growth largely in terms of consolidating and extending their existing activities; companies clustered around company promoters or a particular merchant partnership and operated in accordance largely with the group's short or long-term interests; and a mixture of companies with an international and often volatile ownership. While the mining companies tended to be relatively small and speculative, a handful of large and poorly managed firms contained a considerable amount of water in their balance sheets. Whatever the quality of their management, such firms, because of their frequent need for restructuring and the attraction of the assets they owned, were open to attempts by larger companies or investment groups to acquire a controlling interest in them. This is beginning to hint at some of the possible reasons for success and failure.

The Survival of Free-Standing Companies

Mira Wilkins, drawing on her own research in the USA and that of D. G. Paterson on Canada, suggests that free-standing companies were generally short-lived. Her explanation rests largely on the quality of management and the inability of many such companies to escape dependence on the battery of financiers, advisers, and consultants that surrounded them. This meant that they failed to develop their own governance structures. She does recognize, however, that the problems may not have been so acute in companies operating in less developed economies, where, despite their deficiencies, British free-standing companies may have possessed an edge in management skills.[81]

How short is short-lived? None of the companies on the west coast now survives in British hands, but many had an existence of thirty, forty, or fifty years before going into liquidation, or being transferred to Latin American or other foreign ownership. Table 8.2 shows the survival rate of the forty-five free-standing companies registered in London and operating in these three countries in 1895. The data do not suggest a total failure. The problems are concentrated in metals-mining and nitrate (the decline in the number of railway companies before the First World War reflects the voluntary transfer of some lines to the Chilean state). Other companies in Chile survived until the 1940s, when, like their counterparts in Argentina, Brazil, and Uruguay, they were expropriated or sold to local investors. These included the Taltal and Nitrate railways, Tarapacá Waterworks, the Valparaiso Drainage Co., and the Patagonian Sheep Farming Co.[82] The Peruvian Corporation and Antofagasta Railway both retained their autonomy for even longer. Nevertheless, it is also true that none of the independent free-standing companies diversified, and none of the investment groups based on the merchant houses developed into a multinational conglomerate on

TABLE 8.2. *The longevity of British free-standing companies in Bolivia, Chile, and Peru*

Sector	Number in 1895	1895 companies still existing in 1913	1895 companies still existing in 1935
Finance	1	1	1
Land	1	0	0
Manufacturing	2	2	1
Mining	8	2	0
Nitrate	19	10	1
Railways	10	7	6
Utilities	4	3	2
TOTAL FOUNDED BEFORE 1895	45	25	11
TOTAL COMPANIES	45	88	32

Source: *Stock Exchange Yearbooks*.

the scale of the British houses in the Far East or Grace in Latin America. What are the explanations for this record?

First, there are several cases where insufficient capital or deficient technical preparation created a legacy of problems. Inadequate finance may seem an improbable explanation in view of the apparent ease of raising funds for overseas ventures in London before 1914, or the common view that many such companies watered their stock. Yet both could hinder a company. Too high a price paid for assets in Latin America meant that often the flotation supplied too little in the way of working capital, and no reserve for emergencies. Too much water in the stock often meant low dividends and therefore difficulties in raising loan finance on reasonable terms, especially in countries such as Peru and Bolivia which were less well regarded in London than Chile or Argentina. Such problems were summed up in a plaintive letter to the Foreign Office from the ill-fated Chimbote Coal & Harbour Syndicate in 1910. It had been impossible, it claimed (even during a boom in Latin American securities), to float a company in London to complete and operate the rail concession the syndicate had acquired 'owing to the fact that Peruvian stocks were not favourably looked upon by London Financial Houses and Underwriters, unless such issue was in the form of Bonds, and interest on same guaranteed by the Peruvian government "backed" by a good and solid tax'.[83] To be successful a company needed the support of a highly regarded merchant house such as Gibbs or Balfour, Williamson & Co., or else, like the Antofagasta Railway or some of the nitrate firms, to have the backing of a resourceful merchant bank like Schroders.[84]

The need for adequate technical preparation is evident in the contrasting experience of the two British oil companies in Peru, the London & Pacific, headed by William Keswick, and Lobitos, headed by Sir Archibald Williamson. 'It has been a sink of money and never paid,' Williamson wrote of the London & Pacific when Keswick offered it to him in 1908.[85] When the firm was eventually sold to Standard Oil of New Jersey in 1913 after Keswick's death, the purchasers bought it on the basis of its potential rather than its existing installations. The property was then professionally surveyed for the first time and the capital supplied not only to increase new drilling but also to ensure that the company could store and transport sufficient oil to meet its sales contracts; previous failures were ascribed by Jersey Standard's consultant to the inexperience of the entrepreneurs and engineers.[86] Williamson, in contrast, already had experience of the oil industry in California. He thus ensured that Lobitos was properly surveyed at an early stage by Sir Boverton Redwood, the leading British oil consultant; contracted C. T. Bowring & Co., the Liverpool specialists in oil-tanker charters, to organize the company's shipping; and took care to develop adequate markets; as well as conserving the company's precious working capital through excessive depreciation allowances and passed dividends.[87] Once businesses like the oil industry, which required capital resources on a major scale, became the most dynamic areas of expansion, old attitudes and techniques could not suffice. 'The oil business is not all beer and skittles', Weetman Pearson wrote after his major discovery in Mexico. 'I entered into it lightly, not realising its many problems. . . . Now I know that it would have been wise to surround myself with proven oil men . . . and not to rely, as I did, upon commercial knowledge and hard work, coupled with a superficial knowledge of the trade.'[88]

Lack of local expertise could also be a problem, given the difficulty of adequately assessing potential business in an unfamiliar environment and the political sensitivity of many concessions. Most vulnerable in this respect were the British entrepreneurs who were sold concessions by visiting Latin American businessmen or by foreign intermediaries who had negotiated them in Latin America, and who did not take the trouble properly to evaluate the business. It is this that probably explains the failure of the two minor railway companies in Peru, one of which was beset with enormous engineering problems in order to reach the intermontane valleys that might have provided some traffic, while the other sought to obtain profits from a line meandering through the coastal desert and competing with well-established steamship lines. Neither, significantly, had any directors on their boards who held similar posts with other companies operating in Peru.

Many of the small mining companies floated on the market before 1914 suffered, in some combination, from all of these factors: inadequate working capital due to the excessive price paid for concessions, insufficient technical preparation, and lack of knowledge of Latin American conditions. While silver and gold mining could be carried out on a relatively small scale in the Andes, even in the early part of the twentieth century, such firms were never likely to excite the City. On the other hand, small copper deposits could no longer be developed in the way they had been before 1900. Cerro de Pasco, though a free-standing company, paid out over £1,000,000 for its concessions and a further £600,000 to settle the legal claims of rival Peruvian entrepreneurs, in addition to its investments in smelting facilities and a railway. Rosemary Thorp and Geoffrey Bertram estimate its overall expenditure between 1901 and 1907 alone at over £3,000,000.[89] The problems of raising sufficient capital to develop low-quality copper deposits are illustrated also by the fact that the initial US entrepreneurs in Chile in the early twentieth century, William Braden and the Guggenheims, were each in the end forced to relinquish their holdings, for lack of capital, to other US multinational firms, Kennecott and Anaconda.[90]

Another point evident from Table 8.1 is how many of the British companies in these countries in 1913 were in sectors with only a limited technological future. The first collapse was the Amazon rubber industry, where the primitive technique of using labourers to gather rubber by periodically walking trails in the jungle was undercut around 1910 by the organized plantations in the Far East. One US observer reported in the early 1920s that, of the twenty-two foreign companies with concessions in the Amazon (including Brazil), only ten were still operating (six of these were in Bolivia and one in Peru).[91] Nitrate was next. Its production technology had hardly changed since the 1880s, apart from the substitution of oil for coal in some *oficinas*, and labour productivity showed a steady downward trend. The nitrate companies attempted several times to form combinations to support prices, but in the long term this aided the growth of competition from atmospheric and synthetic nitrates, a trend exacerbated by German technological advances during the First World War. In the 1920s many of the British firms sold out as the Guggenheims attempted to consolidate the industry and introduce capital-intensive processes, a move in which the leading British nitrate interests like Gibbs refused to participate (wisely as it turned out). The outcome, in rapid succession, was the liquidation of several long-standing British nitrate firms, the collapse of the Guggenheims' poorly costed scheme, and the loss of independence of the Anglo-South American Bank, which had played a leading role in financing the Guggenheims.[92]

Railways were the third main area in which the technology used by British free-standing companies became outdated. Urban passenger services were hit in the 1920s by the development of road competition, followed later by the creaming-off of their most valuable freight traffic as long-distance highways were constructed and trucks purchased by local entrepreneurs. By the 1950s the only viable railways on the west coast (and even in these cases there were acute financial problems caused by frozen tariffs and exchange depreciation) were the lines which could depend, like the Peruvian Corporation's Central Railway or the Antofagasta Railway, on a high and steady volume of mineral traffic.

The growth of competition and technological obsolescence, in rubber, nitrate, and railways, thus explains the eventual disappearance of many of the British free-standing companies in these countries. It does not, however, explain why the merchant houses suddenly seem to have lost their ability to seek out and finance new ventures, or what happened to free-standing companies in other sectors, in land, manufacturing, and public utilities. For this other explanations are required.

As the history of the Peruvian oil industry implies, a merchant base was not sufficient for the development of modern industries. The merchant needed to acquire, either from within the firm or from outside consultants, the technical knowledge needed for success. Balfour, Williamson & Co.'s prosperous ventures in Peru, in flour-milling and petroleum, depended heavily on the expertise of Alexander Milne, its partner in Peru, and his sons, who later took over day-to-day control of the businesses. 'The management of Mr Milne and his sons has been excellent,' Sir Archibald Williamson wrote ten years after investing in the flour-milling business. 'Their devotion to their work and to the interests of the mill have been exemplary, and contributed, of course, the chief elements of its success.'[93] However, more sophisticated technology, especially that which required scientific knowledge and experience, left the ordinary merchant floundering. In 1923 Milnes began to investigate the possibility of investing in a plant in Lima to produce bleach and caustic soda. 'We are quite ignorant about the industry,' Fred Milne confessed to Williamson, 'and since enquiring about the effect of the fumes, it has struck us also that there may be [liquid] waste products to be disposed of. . . . We are quite sure that we would not be allowed to run it into the river.'[94]

The financial base of British merchant houses also hindered continued growth after the First World War. Greater fluctuations in commodity prices, especially the steep falls of the early 1920s, hit them hard.[95] Their fundamental problem, though, was the partnership organization which kept their financial affairs confidential but which they believed was also vital to their credibility, since it exposed each partner to unlimited liability. Unlike the Graces, who incorporated in 1894, the British houses remained partnerships.[96] The dangers were that as ventures became increasingly complex it would become more difficult to raise seedcorn finance from within the firm, and that the retirement or death of a senior partner would mean a massive withdrawal of capital, suddenly curtailing the merchants' activities. These problems hit Balfour, Williamson & Co. especially hard at the end of the 1920s. While their rivals were coping with similar hazards by selling their fixed investments or else issuing debentures to finance them, the firm took the radical step (for a South American house) of deciding to incorporate as a limited liability company. The achievement of this status at the beginning of 1930 made it possible to overcome the financial difficulties for the firm which would otherwise have arisen from the death of Lord Forres, the senior partner, the following year.[97] These financial and legal problems, however, together with the general difficulties of the commodity trades, must have severely affected the merchants' ability to initiate and float new ventures. Even before the crash of 1929–31, the atmosphere in their British headquarters was pessimistic. 'One is tempted to sit down and ask one's self why not put everything in War Loans and cease to maintain this costly organisation, which after all its risks makes only a small return,' Forres himself wrote in June 1928.[98] Such attitudes in London must have helped to impede the development of any business suggested by more dynamic middle management in Latin America.

The informal controls which the Bank of England exercised over the issue of capital for ventures in Latin America during the 1920s also curtailed ambition. During the early part of the decade the maximum that could be issued in shares and bonds for any one company was £1 million, and raising money for enterprises in countries outside the Empire was particularly difficult.[99] This did not prevent small ventures, or indeed limited increases in an existing company's capital, but it did impede more far-reaching schemes. Guggenheims' nitrate consolidation, for example, simply could not have been financed on the London Stock Exchange, except, perhaps, briefly, towards the end of the decade.[100] As a result there were very few new issues for free-standing companies operating on the west coast: an increase of £600,000 in Lobitos' issued capital in 1925–7; and a new debenture issue of £300,000 for the Peruvian Corporation in 1928 following the renegotiation of its contract with the Peruvian government.[101] Schroders also brought out debentures in the 1920s for Lima Light, Power & Tramways Co. (although managerial control of the company was simultaneously transferred to Continental Europe) and the Antofagasta Railway.[102] However, only four new firms, two in Bolivia and two in Peru, appear to have been founded in the 1920s, and the largest of these, the Bolivia and General Tin Trust, was capitalized at only £500,000.[103] The result of these difficulties in raising new finance for ventures in Latin America was that existing companies were forced to depend either on the reinvestment of profits or on commercial bank loans.[104] Difficulties in raising new finance to expand facilities may have lain behind some of the decisions taken at the end of the 1920s to sell assets in Latin America to US businessmen—for example, the transfer to ITT of the Chili Telephone Co. in 1927 and the Peruvian Telephone Co. in 1930.[105] In this way one of the advantages that British firms had enjoyed before 1914, access to the savings mobilized by City institutions, disappeared. Moreover, with the informal exchange controls in the 1920s, firms with interests in Latin America were more seriously affected than those in the Empire.

The restrictions on capital exports were not the only problems facing existing British free-standing companies in the 1920s. Increasing income tax in Britain began to outweigh the advantages of registering in London and indeed encouraged both British and Latin American entrepreneurs to move companies overseas in order to control the amounts they declared to the Inland Revenue.[106] Thus Gibbs in 1915 recommended to the Chilean purchasers of the Alianza and Pan de Azúcar nitrate companies that they should transfer their domicile to Chile rather than remain in London, and Gibbs itself floated another company in Chile in 1917.[107] However, as the countries in which they were operating also introduced income taxes, especially in the Depression, holding companies in London found it necessary to make critical decisions about the optimal place to locate the registration of the companies they controlled. Sir Archibald Williamson (Lord Forres) complained at the end of his life that after five decades of intense expansion he had spent the last few years of his career worrying about incorporation and taxation.[108]

These factors—the increasing inability of British capital markets to raise funds for ventures in South America, British company taxation, and British exchange controls—came to a head again after the Second World War, when many of the remaining British companies were sold to Latin American investors or wound up. The Backus & Johnston Brewery, for example, was purchased by Peruvian interests in the early 1950s, largely, it seems, due to the problems the British owners faced in transferring new capital overseas.[109] At much the same time the assets of the financially troubled Peruvian Corporation were transferred to a Canadian holding company which would be free both of British and Canadian income tax.[110]

Changes in Latin America tended towards the same result. The British companies on the west coast had, from the early twentieth century, often found it difficult to deal with labour problems, but firms like the railways or public utilities also faced increasing financial difficulties as governments found it politically impossible to accede to requests for the tariff increases required to cover higher labour and social-security costs and the depreciation of Latin American currencies. Continued disputes with the regulatory authorities in Chile persuaded Whitehall Electrical Investments to sell its electricity and tramway interests to US investors in 1928.[111] The exchange controls imposed in every Latin American country in the early 1930s further worsened the problems by making it more difficult to obtain the sterling required to pay debenture-holders and other creditors in Britain. The stunted development of local capital markets compared, for example, with those in the Dominions and Asia must also have hindered British merchants and free-standing companies in Latin America, since this exaggerated their dependence on the willingness of the Treasury and Bank of England to permit capital flows to the region.[112] In addition, the Anglo communities in Latin America were diminishing in size and the region becoming less attractive to emigrants from the UK, further exacerbating the difficulties of management.

Conclusion

The concepts of the free-standing company and the investment group, taken together, offer historians of British business in Latin America useful tools to analyse both individual firms and the overall dynamics of British direct investment. It is essential to have a means of distinguishing enterprises such as the railway, mining, and utility companies which operated in one country from the 'classic' multinational mining, oil, or manufacturing firms of European or US parentage. However, this chapter departs from Wilkins's original formulation of the concept in three principal respects. First, free-standing companies, at least in this region, have to be categorized into those which were autonomous and those which formed part of investment groups. Secondly, defining the nationality of a firm solely in terms of registration may be misleading: this region provides several examples of 'international' or footloose firms registered in London but with relatively little British influence in management. Thirdly, many free-standing companies survived beyond infancy. A lean headquarters in London did not always imply weakness. Railways and banks in particular developed appropriate managerial hierarchies to operate their businesses overseas; the smaller autonomous firms, as well as those which formed part of investment groups, also acquired and internalized the necessary specialized knowledge, albeit on a lesser scale.

The evidence from the west coast of South America also provides some indications of why the free-standing company became such an important component of British direct investment. In part it arose as merchants responded to the revolution in communications and the commodity trades which occurred after the 1870s by developing fixed investments where they had previously avoided them.[113] The growth of business also stimulated an increase in the size and expertise of the British communities on the coast, giving birth to entrepreneurs such as North and Harvey, both of whom returned from the west coast after the Pacific War to become leading businessmen in the City. Once the capacity of the City of London to raise finance for such overseas ventures became obvious in the 1880s, it encouraged the sale of assets originally developed by Latin American entrepreneurs and the development of new concessions and new businesses.[114] However, once

British financial policy marginalized Latin America, after the First World War, these attractions disappeared. Few new free-standing companies were formed, while the existing ones found the business environment turning against them both in Latin America and Europe. The poor development of Latin American stock markets and the growing alienation of Anglo business communities from their host economies removed an option for transforming free-standing companies which remained open elsewhere, especially in Asia and the Dominions. In the end most free-standing companies were sold to the state or local investment groups.

Thus the explanations for the career of the free-standing companies here are rather different from those proposed by Wilkins. Some of the reasons which she identified in order to explain their apparently short life, in particular the watering of capital by company promoters and poor management structures, are certainly evident amongst British firms on the west coast, but their significance is limited. The short life of many mining companies, speculative propositions subject to poor evaluation beforehand and deliberate scams by promoters, distorts the broader picture by providing an impression of instability which did not apply elsewhere. Many British firms on the west coast did survive for long periods, either as autonomous free-standing companies or as part of larger investment groups. In these cases governance structures seem much less of a problem. At times the quality of management may have been poor, but over the long run these firms went out of existence for other reasons. Some merchant houses found it more profitable to keep their ventures out of the London financial markets, especially after 1914, while Latin American entrepreneurs, who had floated companies of their own in London in the long pre-1914 boom, also found that the disadvantages of registration in London began to outweigh the benefits. However, the real problems for these firms seem to lie deeper: in the technological and financial shortcomings of the British economy after 1914, the vulnerability of the merchant houses to commercial crises, and the difficulties created by increasing economic nationalism and exchange controls in Latin America itself. Together, the interaction of these factors ensured that few of the British free-standing companies on the west coast survived beyond the 1950s. Probably the last to disappear was the Antofagasta Railway, whose Bolivian assets had been nationalized in the early 1960s. In 1979, nine years before its centenary, control of this firm, which had survived the Allende years in Chile without expropriation, passed to a Chilean entrepreneur.[115]

NOTES

1. A. D. Chandler, 'The Growth of the Transnational Industrial Firm in the United States and the United Kingdom: A Comparative Analysis', *Economic History Review*, 2nd ser., 33 (1980), 396–410.
2. I. Stone, 'British Direct and Portfolio Investment in Latin America before 1914', *Journal of Economic History*, 37 (1977), 690–722; P. Svedberg, 'The Portfolio Direct Composition of Private Foreign Investment in 1914 Revisited', *Economic Journal*, 88 (1978), 763–77.
3. By 1935 at least twenty British industrials possessed subsidiaries in Latin America. When ICI was formed in 1926 it took over an explosives firm in Chile and later founded joint companies with Du Pont in Brazil and Argentina. Lever Brothers established factories in Argentina (1927) and Brazil (1930). J. & P. Coats was manufacturing in Brazil from 1905 and in Mexico from 1913. By the time BAT became truly British in the early 1920s, it already had plants in Mexico, Brazil, Argentina, and Chile. Glaxo established a plant in Argentina in 1933. These, and other British industrial firms in South America, are the subject of my own current research, financed by the Nuffield Foundation. For a preliminary survey, see Miller, 'Multinational Manufacturing Firms', in C. M. Lewis and R. Miller (eds.), *British Business in Latin America, 1850–1950* (forthcoming).
4. C. Jones, 'The Origins of Modern Multinational Corporations: British Firms in Latin America, 1850–1930', in C. Marichal (ed.), *Foreign Investment in Latin America* (Milan, 1994), 28–39; a longer version of this paper has been published as C. Jones, 'Los antecedentes de la moderna corporación transnacional: Los grupos de inversión británicos en América Latina', in C. Marichal (ed.), *Las inversiones extranjeras en América Latina, 1850–1930* (Mexico City, 1995), 70–95. See also Charles Jones, 'Institutional Forms of British Foreign Direct Investment in South America', *Business History*, 39 (Apr. 1997), esp. 23. On multinational companies, see G. Jones, 'The Expansion of British Multinational Manufacturing, 1890–1939', in A. Okochi and T. Inoue (eds.), *Overseas Business Activities* (Tokyo, 1984), 125–53; G. Jones, 'The Performance of British Multinational Enterprise, 1890–1945', in P. Hertner and G. Jones (eds.), *Multinationals: Theory and History* (Aldershot, 1986), 96–112; G. Jones, 'Origins, Management, Performance', in G. Jones (ed.), *British Multinationals: Origins, Management and Performance* (Aldershot, 1986), 1–23. On the measurement of British investment, see T. A. B. Corley, 'Britain's Overseas Investments in 1914 Revisited', *Business History*, 36 (Jan. 1994), 71–88.
5. M. Wilkins, 'The Free-Standing Company, 1870–1914: An Important Type of British Foreign Direct Investment', *Economic History Review*, 2nd ser., 41 (May 1988), 261.
6. Ibid. 278.
7. Wilkins identifies ten different types of cluster-sets: I have included here only those most relevant to the British experience in Peru and Chile. See Wilkins, 'The Free-Standing Company', 265–9.
8. Ibid. 274–5, 279.
9. S. D. Chapman, 'British-Based Investment Groups before 1914', *Economic History Review*, 2nd ser., 38 (1985), 231.
10. The concept of investment groups also had obvious relevance for the analysis of domestic business organization in Latin America, much of which was based on extended family networks. In fact it was soon utilized by Alfonso Quiroz as a means of analysing Peruvian business structures between 1880 and 1930: see A. W. Quiroz, 'Financial Leadership and the Formation of Peruvian Élite Groups, 1884–1930', *Journal of Latin American Studies*, 20 (1988), 49–81.

11. The figure of 2,000 is provided by Wilkins, 'The Free-Standing Company', 270. The US Federal Trade Commission report of 1916, which is frequently cited as an accessible list of British companies operating in South America at the beginning of the First World War, counted ninety-three firms in these three countries, but this list, which was presumably compiled from Stock Exchange publications, needs some revision in the light of other data on registration and ownership. See US Federal Trade Commission, *Report on Cooperation in American Export Trade* (Washington, 1916), ii. 541–74 (henceforth cited as FTC, *Report*).
12. Stone, 'British Direct and Portfolio Investment', 695.
13. It was not until the early years of the twentieth century that mining came under foreign control in any of these countries; agriculture and much of the manufacturing sector remained under the control of local capitalists. For economic histories, see R. Thorp and G. Bertram, *Peru, 1890–1977: Growth and Policy in an Open Economy* (New York, 1978); and M. J. Mamalakis, *The Growth and Structure of the Chilean Economy from Independence to Allende* (New Haven, Conn., 1976).
14. C. Marichal, *A Century of Debt Crises in Latin America: From Independence to the Great Depression, 1820–1930* (Princeton, 1989); F. G. Dawson, *The First Latin American Debt Crisis: The City of London and the 1822–1825 Loan Bubble* (New Haven, Conn., 1990); C. Veliz, 'Egaña, Lambert, and the Chilean Mining Associations of 1825', *Hispanic American Historical Review*, 55 (1975), 637–63; C. Veliz, 'The Irisarri Loan', *Boletín de Estudios Latinoamericanos y del Caribe*, 23 (1977), 320; C. Palacios Moreyra, *La deuda anglo-peruana, 1822–1890* (Lima, 1983); J. Deustua, 'The Socavón of Quiulacocha and the Steam Engine Company: Technology and Capital Investment in Cerro de Pasco, 1820–1840', in R. Miller (ed.), *Region and Class in Modern Peruvian History* (Liverpool, 1987), 35–75; J. Deustua, 'Mining Markets, Peasants and Power in 19th-Century Peru', *Latin American Research Review*, 29 (1994), 29–54.
15. Marichal, *A Century of Debt Crises in Latin America*; Palacios Moreyra, *La deuda anglo-peruana*.
16. Chile issued eighteen loans in Europe between 1885 and 1911, sixteen of them lead-managed by London merchant banks; of these, twelve were organized by Rothschilds. See F. M. Halsey, *Investments in Latin America and the British West Indies* (Washington, 1918), 219. There were also a number of municipal issues and government-guaranteed bonds—for example, for some of the railway companies.
17. The best summary of their activities in Chile can be found in J. Mayo, 'Before the Nitrate Era: British Commission Houses and the Chilean Economy, 1851–1880', *Journal of Latin American Studies*, 11 (1979), 283–302. See also E. Cavieres, *Comercio chileno y comerciantes ingleses, 1820–1880* (Valparaiso, 1988). There were also a host of smaller British merchant houses operating in both economies, often from a base in Liverpool. These included firms like Nicholson Green in the middle of the nineteenth century, and Bates Stokes & Co. and H. M. Beausire & Co. towards the end.
18. O. Bermúdez Miral, *Historia del salitre desde sus orígenes hasta la Guerra del Pacífico* (Santiago, 1963), 168–70; T. F. O'Brien, 'The Antofagasta Company: A Case Study of Peripheral Capitalism', *Hispanic American Historical Review*, 60 (1980), 5–6; J. Mayo, 'La Compañía de Salitres de Antofagasta y la Guerra del Pacífico', *Historia* (Santiago), 14 (1979), 76–7.
19. Report by Consul-General Thomas Hutchinson, *Parliamentary Papers* (1872), lvii. 176; R. N. Oppenheimer, 'National Capital and National Development: Financing Chile's Central Valley Railroads', *Business History Review*, 56 (1982),

61. The latter two, though owned by British interests, remained registered as Chilean companies whose shares were traded in Britain.

20. Marichal, *A Century of Debt Crises in Latin America*, 126–48; on one of the most important destinations, Argentine railways, see C. M. Lewis, *British Railways in Argentina, 1857–1914: A Case Study of Foreign Investment* (London, 1983), 45–72.
21. R. Miller, 'The Making of the Grace Contract: British Bondholders and the Peruvian Government, 1885–1890', *Journal of Latin American Studies*, 8 (1976), 73–100. The original equity of the Peruvian Corporation comprised £9.0m. in ordinary stock and £7.5m. in preference stock. By 1895 £3.7m. 6% debentures had been issued: Memorandum by W. H. Hall, 27 Apr. 1950, found loose in 'The First Forty Years of the Peruvian Corporation, 1890–1930', UCL, Peruvian Corporation Archive, file G2/A.
22. Cerro de Pasco remained effectively a free-standing company operating in one overseas country until it purchased assets in Chile in the 1950s. See D. G. Becker, *The New Bourgeoisie and the Limits of Dependency: Mining, Class, and Power in 'Revolutionary' Peru* (Princeton, 1983), 139. This distinguished it from the US multinational mining firms such as Anaconda and ASARCO (American Smelting and Refining Co.), which also purchased assets in Peru during the First World War. For further discussion of the growth of the Cerro de Pasco Corporation, see T. F. O'Brien, *The Revolutionary Mission: American Enterprise in Latin America, 1900–1945* (Cambridge, 1996), 114–16, 121–7.
23. In an attempt to stabilize the industry, the Peruvian government had begun to expropriate nitrate *oficinas* in 1875. See R. G. Greenhill and R. M. Miller, 'The Peruvian Government and the Nitrate Trade, 1873–1879', *Journal of Latin American Studies*, 5 (1973), 107–31; T. F. O'Brien, *The Nitrate Industry and Chile's Crucial Transition, 1870–1891* (New York, 1982).
24. On the North empire, see especially H. Blakemore, *British Nitrates and Chilean Politics, 1886–1896: Balmaceda and North* (London, 1973).
25. H. Blakemore, *From the Pacific to La Paz: The Antofagasta (Chili) and Bolivia Railway Company, 1888–1988* (London, 1989), 27–8; R. Roberts, *Schroders: Merchants and Bankers* (London, 1992), 101–4.
26. FTC, *Report*, 541–74. The other main US source used was Halsey, *Investments in Latin America*.
27. The Lima Light, Power & Tramways Co., whose debenture-holders had control of the board, presents particular problems of categorization and is discussed later.
28. There are excellent monographs on some of these firms. See Blakemore, *From the Pacific to La Paz*; A. W. Quiroz, *Banqueros en conflicto: Estructura financiera y economía peruana, 1884–1930* (Lima, 1989); W. Hunt, *Heirs of Great Adventure: The History of Balfour, Williamson and Company Limited* (2 vols.; London, 1951, 1960); Lawrence A. Clayton, *Grace: W. R. Grace & Co., the Formative Years, 1850–1930* (Ottawa, Ill., 1985); M. James, *Merchant Adventurer: The Story of W. R. Grace* (Wilmington, Del., 1993).
29. Much of the argument that follows is based on a database of directors drawn from the 1895, 1913, and 1935 *Stock Exchange Yearbooks*. I am happy to provide a disk containing this database to other researchers.
30. This, of course, internalizes a firm's information costs.
31. The Peruvian Corporation is characterized as a railway company because, although it had other assets, the bulk of its income was generated by the railways it operated: between 1910/11 and 1914/15 21.2% of its net income came from guano, while its land concessions made a loss (Peruvian Corporation, *Annual Reports*).
32. In 1913 members of the board of the Antofagasta Railway held directorships

with other British railway companies operating in Argentina, Uruguay, Brazil, and Venezuela, but there is no indication that their interests in these countries were interdependent with those in the Antofagasta. This was a very different situation from the grouping of railway and other companies which Percival Farquhar attempted to put together in southern Brazil, Paraguay, and Argentina on the eve of the First World War. At various times too the Antofagasta board also included businessmen from the Anglo-South American Bank, Schroders, and the stockbrokers Walpole Greenwell: this reflected a business link between the firms, but does not mean that the Antofagasta was controlled by them or even that it depended on their services.

33. Because of their engineering needs and the number of employees handling cash, railways were among the pioneers in developing systems of line management and internal control. See A. D. Chandler and S. Salsbury, 'The Railroads: Innovators in Modern Business Administration', in Alfred D. Chandler *et al.* (eds.), *The Changing Economic Order: Readings in American Business and Economic History* (New York, 1968), 231–4. Banks, for much the same reasons, also possessed complex managerial hierarchies and career structures.
34. On railway engineering and management on the west coast of South America, see R. Miller, 'Transferencia de técnicas: La construcción y administración de ferrocarriles en la costa occidental de Sudamérica', *Siglo XIX: Cuadernos de historia*, 7 (1993), 65–102. Associations such as the Institution of Civil Engineers were central to the diffusion of knowledge of railway-engineering practices in overseas conditions, as was the development of specialist consultancy firms such as Livesey Son & Duncan (later Livesey Son & Henderson).
35. On the poor management of the Peruvian Corporation in its early years, see R. Miller, 'The Grace Contract, the Peruvian Corporation, and Peruvian History', *Ibero-Amerikanisches Archiv*, 9 (1983), 319–48. There are many indications that when these firms needed to recruit senior managers from outside they deliberately looked for personnel with experience on other British-owned railways in Latin America.
36. The North Western Railway of Peru and the Chimbote Coal and Harbour Syndicate (which was in fact a railway company). The North Western, having been given a government guarantee on a kilometre basis, built a serpentine line through the coastal desert north of Lima.
37. The one doubt about the Backus & Johnston Brewery is that in 1913 it shared its company secretary, F. W. Bishop, with three nitrate companies and the Poderosa Mining Co. H. W. Sillem, a director of the brewery and associate of Antony Gibbs & Sons, also sat on the board of six nitrate companies, as well as being managing director of Lobitos Oilfields Ltd., a Balfour, Williamson & Co. firm. This seems to be more a case of a businessman with expertise in the region sitting on several boards rather than one of interlocking company interests; in 1935 none of the brewery's directors sat on the boards of other west-coast firms. What possible business connection could there be between a brewery and a nitrate firm?
38. Blakemore, *British Nitrates and Chilean Politics*, 48–51, 151–2, 221.
39. G. T. Symons was also on the board of the Lagunas Nitrate Co.
40. On the changing investment interests of the US house of Grace, see more later in this chapter. In 1935 the Nitrate Railways Company was chaired by A. W. Bolden, who also presided over the Antofagasta Railway (where he had begun his career) as well as sitting on the board of the Anglo-South American Bank.
41. Harvey was chairman of three nitrate firms, a railway company, a bank, a coal-mining company, and a water company.
42. The bank's papers are part of the Bank of London and South America archive

in University College London. In its early years the bank used its links with the nitrate firms, which provided the majority of the sterling bills available in Chile, to manipulate foreign exchange markets (GL Gibbs Archive 11470/15, Daubeny to Miller, 8 Feb. 1894). Judging from the bank's correspondence, Harvey's main intervention in the day-to-day management of the business was to offer his personal views on the creditworthiness of leading Chileans.

43. For the complicated story, see D. M. Joslin, *A Century of Banking in Latin America: To Commemorate the Centenary in 1962 of the Bank of London and South America Ltd.* (London, 1963), 174–201, 254–73. The Banco del Perú y Londres (BPL) was formed in 1897 as a result of a merger between the only two Peruvian banks that had survived the Pacific War with Chile, the Banco del Callao and the more than three-decades-old Lima branch of the London Bank of Mexico and South America. BPL was never a British free-standing company, despite its name and the minority financial interest of British investors (for further discussion, see later in this chapter). Its strategy was dominated by José Payán, a Cuban immigrant to Peru, and the leading figure in the Lima business world during the quarter century before 1914. For more on its history and the events which led to its collapse in 1930, see Quiroz, *Banqueros en conflicto*, and A. W. Quiroz, *Domestic and Foreign Finance in Modern Peru, 1850–1950: Financing Visions of Development*, (London, 1993). For its counterpart in Mexico, the Banco de Londres y México, which was also not a free-standing company, see Reinhard Liehr and Mariano E. Torres Bautista, Chapter 9 herein.
44. G. Jones, *British Multinational Banking, 1830–1990* (Oxford, 1993), 159. Charles Jones makes a similar point about the independence of the London and River Plate Bank from the other business interests of George Drabble, even though he remained its chairman. See C. Jones, 'The Origins of Modern Multinational Corporations: British Firms in Latin America, 1850–1930', in C. Marichal (ed.), *Foreign Investment in Latin America* (Milan, 1994), 27–39.
45. R. G. Greenhill, 'The Nitrate and Iodine Trades, 1880–1914', in D. C. M. Platt (ed.), *Business Imperialism, 1840–1930* (Oxford, 1977), 238–9, 243–4.
46. J. R. Couyoumdjian, 'El mercado del salitre durante la primera guerra y la posguerra, 1914–1921', *Historia* (Santiago), 12 (1974–5), 22, 29.
47. *Stock Exchange Yearbook* (1913).
48. S. D. Chapman, *The Rise of Merchant Banking* (London, 1984), 104, 159.
49. Chapman notes that Gibbs faced liquidity crises in 1876, 1884, 1890, 1894, and 1920, and that as the partners moved into the aristocracy their individual drawings on the firm's capital substantially weakened its financial base. See Chapman, 'British-Based Investment Groups', 235.
50. The Balfour Williamson Archive is in University College London. In 1910 Balfour Williamson acquired a controlling interest in the Lima house of Milne & Co., whose founder had taken the initiative in developing first flour-milling and then oil exploration in Peru. Milnes remained managing agents for Lobitos. On Balfour, Williamson & Co.'s history, see Hunt, *Heirs of Great Adventure*. On Lobitos, see R. Miller, 'Small Business in the Peruvian Oil Industry: Lobitos Oilfields Limited before 1934', *Business History Review*, 56 (1982), 400–23.
51. One interesting link on these boards was the presence of H. and W. Shield of Fawcett Preston, the Birkenhead engineering firm. The Tarapacá Waterworks Co. and the Arauco Co. shared the same company secretary, as did the Colorado and Liverpool nitrate companies.
52. Blakemore, *British Nitrates and Chilean Politics*, 32–3; Greenhill, 'The Nitrate and Iodine Trades', 236–7; James, *Merchant Adventurer*, 241; Bill Albert, *An Essay on the Peruvian Sugar Industry, 1880–1920* (Norwich, 1976), 225*a*–26*a*. Wm. & Jno. Lockett had originally given North the entrée to Liverpool business

circles which permitted the flotation of his first nitrate company in 1883; apart from its own profits from company flotations and share speculation it also acted as agent for the North companies in Chile. The importance of the Lockett firm to the development of the North empire is indicated by the fact that in 1895 three members of the Lockett family between them held fourteen directorships in North's companies.

53. Wilkins, 'The Free-Standing Company', 261.
54. Hunt, *Heirs of Great Adventure*, i. 66. The phrase comes from 1893 and is that of the Gibbs partners in Valparaiso, who clearly differentiated 'first-class London' houses (themselves; Huth Grüning; Weber Vorwerk; Browne Beeche & Co.) from 'first-class Liverpool' houses (Balfour, Williamson; Duncan Fox; Graham Rowe; Cockbain & Edmondson) (GL Gibbs Archive 11470/15, Valparaiso to London, 12 Dec. 1893).
55. *Stock Exchange Yearbook* (1913); *West Coast Leader* (Lima), 18 Mar. 1924.
56. C. Jiménez, 'Estadística industrial del Perú', *Boletín del Cuerpo de Ingenieros de Minas y Aguas* (1922), 105; H. W. Kirsch, *Industrial Development in a Traditional Society: The Conflict of Entrepreneurship and Modernization in Chile* (Gainesville, Fla., 1977). A brief history of the firm is provided in H. H. Davies, 'Short History of Duncan Fox', unpublished manuscript (1966).
57. The Agua Santa Nitrate and Railway Co., with which Balfour, Williamson was closely associated, issuing debentures for it in London in 1896 and 1908, also remained registered in Chile (*Stock Exchange Yearbook* (1913), 1610).
58. *Stock Exchange Yearbook* (1895), 167, 188, 364. The Callao Dock Co. fell into the same category.
59. For histories of Grace, see Clayton, *Grace*, and James, *Merchant Adventurer.*
60. GL Gibbs Archive 11040/2, Herbert Gibbs to Harry L. Gibbs, 8 Dec. 1893.
61. Clayton, *Grace*, 263.
62. The total capitalization of these firms was approximately £2.7m. See *Stock Exchange Yearbook* (1913), and FTC, *Report.*
63. It was hardly surprising that Michael Grace had influence in the Corporation immediately after its formation under the contract he had negotiated with Peru. There was also a brief period, between 1906 and 1908, when Grace, along with Speyer & Co. (New York), appeared to be using the Peruvian Corporation as a means of building up its position in the Bolivian railway network. At that time William S. Eyre went to Lima to negotiate a settlement of a dispute with the Peruvian government and report on the company's properties. Peruvian Corporation, *Annual Reports*, 1906 and 1907.
64. In contrast to quoted companies, firms which remained partnerships, private companies, and undertakings registered in Latin America did not have to publish financial information which might have affected the credit of the parent merchant house. See R. Roberts, 'What's in a Name?', *Business History*, 35 (July 1993), 28.
65. Wilkins, 'The Free-Standing Company', 261–2. For qualifications, see her Chapter 1 herein.
66. These companies were omitted from the figures in Table 8.1 and are listed in the notes to that table. In Chapter 1 herein, Wilkins omits non-British owned and controlled companies from the category of British free-standing companies.
67. The evidence runs through the Gibbs correspondence in the 1890s, when every mail from Valparaiso included an account of its dealings in both these companies' shares.
68. Blakemore, *From the Pacific to La Paz*, 27–9; Roberts, 'What's in a Name?', 103–4.
69. A. Mitre, *Los patriarcas de la plata: Estructura socioeconómica de la minería boliviana en el siglo XIX* (Lima, 1977), 135–6.

70. House of Commons, 'Report from the Select Committee on the Putumayo', *Parliamentary Papers* (1913), xiv. 1–16.
71. The example of Aramayo is mentioned by J. Hillman, 'The Emergence of the Tin Industry in Bolivia', *Journal of Latin American Studies*, 16 (1984), 429. Hennart offers the same case as a warning against assuming that the initiative for free-standing companies always came from capital-rich countries. See J.-F. Hennart, 'International Financial Capital Transfers', *Business History*, 36 (Jan. 1994), 70. On the Aramayo family, see A. Crespo, *Los Aramayo de Chichas: Tres generaciones de mineros bolivianos* (Barcelona, 1981), 186–8. For some examples in Argentina, see D. J. Guy, 'Dependency, the Credit Market, and Argentine Industrialization, 1873–1906', *Business History Review*, 58 (1984), 532–61; the classic one there is Pedro Vasena's iron and steel interests.
72. J. F. Rippy, *British Investments in Latin America, 1822–1949* (Minneapolis, 1959), 127.
73. *Stock Exchange Yearbook*, (1913). Ferrobamba Ltd., a London-registered mining company operating in Peru and capitalized at £1.5m., was chaired by A. C. Burrage of Boston, who had bought out the original British owners in 1911 for £670,000 in shares and cash. Representatives of the latter remained in a majority on the board. See *Peru Today*, 2/10 (Dec. 1910) and 3/5 (July 1911). For Burrage and his activities in Chile, see M. Wilkins, *The Emergence of Multinational Enterprise: American Business Abroad from the Colonial Era to 1914* (Cambridge, Mass., 1970), 181.
74. The case of Mexico, where many British-registered free-standing mining companies operated, may shed more light on this issue. For more on the City of London's role in mining finance, see C. E. Harvey and J. Press, 'The City and International Mining, 1870–1914', *Business History*, 32 (July 1990), 98–119.
75. D. C. M. Platt, 'British Portfolio Investment before 1870: Some Doubts', *Economic History Review*, 2nd ser., 33 (1980), 1–16; D. C. M. Platt, *Britain's Investment Overseas on the Eve of the First World War: The Use and Abuse of Numbers* (London, 1986); R. Miller, 'The London Capital Market and Latin American Public Debt, 1860–1930', in R. Liehr (ed.), *La deuda pública en América Latina en perspectiva histórica* (Frankfurt, 1995), 91–116.
76. I was told by a former director in 1971 that the Canadian purchase of the firm in the 1950s was motivated by the feeling that its land concessions had never been properly developed rather than the attractions of its railways.
77. On Grace interests in the Peruvian Corporation in 1906 see UCL, Lobitos Papers, Balfour Williamson Archive, Mathieson to Williamson, 12 Dec. 1906, File 6; on Speyers' interest, UCL, Peruvian Corporation Archive, File B1/9. Speyer & Co. had recently taken the lead in the organization of the Bolivia Railway Co. in New York which was later, in 1908, sold to the Antofagasta Railway. On the French interest, see *The Economist*, 19 Feb. 1910.
78. Halsey, *Investments in Latin America*, 243; L. Jones, C. Jones, and R. Greenhill, 'Public Utility Companies', in D. C. M. Platt (ed.), *Business Imperialism, 1840–1930* (Oxford, 1977), 95.
79. Quiroz, *Banqueros en conflicto*, 215–73; Quiroz, *Domestic and Foreign Finance in Modern Peru*, 77.
80. Quiroz, *Banqueros en conflicto*, 243–6, 290–1; Quiroz, *Domestic and Foreign Finance in Modern Peru*, 85; Thorp and Bertram, *Peru, 1890–1977*, 131; Roberts, *Schroders*, 205. Of the £1.5m., £250,000 was taken by Swiss interests: *Stock Exchange Yearbook, 1935*, ii. 1892. The debenture-holders continued to control the majority of appointments to the board: in 1935 these included Sir Bernard Greenwell and A. W. Bolden (director and chairman respectively of the Antofagasta Railway), and H. W. B. Schroder of the merchant bank.

81. Wilkins, 'The Free-Standing Company', 271, 275–6, 279.
82. The details of negotiation can be followed in Bank of England Archives, File OV 160/40.
83. PRO FO 371/970/A34245/10, Huxley to Foreign Office, 19 Sept. 1910.
84. The close links that Schroder developed with Chile before 1914, and the importance of their name in raising finance for companies, is evident in Roberts, *Schroders*, 101–4, 137–9.
85. UCL, Balfour Williamson Archive, Archibald Williamson to Harry Williamson, 9 July 1908, Archibald Williamson's personal letterbook No. 1.
86. G. S. Gibb and E. H. Knowlton, *The Resurgent Years, 1911–1927: The History of the Standard Oil Company (New Jersey)* (New York, 1956), 94–5. See also J. C. Brown, 'Jersey Standard and the Politics of Latin American Oil Production, 1911–1930', in J. D. Wirth (ed.), *Latin American Oil Companies and the Politics of Energy* (Lincoln, Nebr., 1985), 16–17.
87. Miller, 'Small Business in the Peruvian Oil Industry'. Lobitos, founded in 1908, did not pay its maiden dividend until 1912.
88. Quoted in D. Young, *Member for Mexico: A Biography of Weetman Pearson, First Viscount Cowdray* (London, 1966), 119.
89. Thorp and Bertram, *Peru, 1890–1977*, 81–91.
90. In the case of the Guggenheims this was a deliberate decision undertaken in order to finance their attempt to reorganize the Chilean nitrate industry. See T. F. O'Brien, '"Rich beyond the Dreams of Avarice": The Guggenheims in Chile', *Business History Review*, 63 (1989), 142–3.
91. W. L. Schurz, *Rubber Production in the Amazon Valley* (Washington, 1925), 7–8. Since there were only three British ones in Bolivia in 1913–14 (see Table 8.1), three of the six were either not British or were founded after 1913–14.
92. On this see O'Brien, '"Rich beyond the Dreams of Avarice"'. O'Brien seems to work on the assumption that, because the Guggenheims were more technically advanced than the British, their scheme must have been inherently sensible, but he never costs out the sales and prices needed to secure a return on their investment nor questions the political and economic assumptions on which they were working. It could be argued that the labour-intensive industry of the pre-1914 years at least gave producers the option of shutting down production, temporarily laying off workers, and passing dividends in response to falling demand; the Guggenheims instead made a majority of workers in the industry redundant in one blow while never making a profit themselves.
93. Quoted in Hunt, *Heirs of Great Adventure*, ii. 70. It was Alexander Milne, not the Williamsons, who had taken the initiative in investigating the Lobitos concession; in 1903 he brought in Balfour, Williamson & Co. and (for a brief period) the Peruvian Corporation in order to secure further exploration finance.
94. Compañía Petrolera Lobitos Archive, Callao, Milne to Forres, 23 Mar. 1923, private correspondence. This archive has now disappeared.
95. All the Liverpool houses were caught holding stocks of Peruvian cotton in 1921, although only J. Lionel Barber went into liquidation. Graham Rowe collapsed in 1931 owing huge sums to Martins Bank.
96. Clayton, *Grace*, 255–6.
97. Hunt, *Heirs of Great Adventure*, ii. 173–82.
98. UCL, Balfour Williamson Archive, Forres to Henderson, 1 June 1928, Archibald Williamson, personal letterbook No. 9.
99. D. E. Moggridge, 'British Controls on Long-Term Capital Movements, 1924–1931', in D. N. McCloskey (ed.), *Essays on a Mature Economy: Britain after 1840* (London, 1971), 117–18.

100. O'Brien estimates that Guggenheims raised $130m. (£26.7m.) in New York for their nitrate enterprises.
101. Burmah Oil Archive, Swindon, Lobitos Oilfields Limited, *Proceedings of Extraordinary General Meeting, 10 Feb. 1925*; UCL, Peruvian Corporation Archive, Peruvian Corporation, *Annual Report, 1930*, 9.
102. Roberts, *Schroders*, 205.
103. *Stock Exchange Yearbook* (1935) ii. 1983.
104. The latter needs much more research, especially in the archives of the Anglo-South American Bank. The ASAB lent huge sums to the Guggenheims, but also made loans to some British-owned railways in Argentina. See Joslin, *A Century of Banking in Latin America*, 265–73; R. S. Sayers, *The Bank of England, 1891–1944* (Cambridge, 1976), 263–7; R. García Heras, 'Las companías ferroviarias británicas y el control de cambios en la Argentina durante la Gran Depresión', *Desarrollo Económico*, 29 (1990), 477–505. It would not be unreasonable to suppose that ASAB was making commercial loans to other companies on the west coast, but for want of research there is little evidence on this except for Joslin's comment that the bank had provided accommodation for several nitrate firms.
105. Jones, Jones, and Greenhill, 'Public Utility Companies', 111; Quiroz, *Domestic and Foreign Finance in Modern Peru*, 210.
106. Wilkins quotes Sir Robert Kindersley's comments on this in 1929: see Chapter 1 herein. For the case of Forestal in Argentina, see Michael Cowen, 'Capital, Nation and Commodities: The Case of Forestal Land, Timber and Railway Company in Argentina and Africa, 1900–1945', in J. J. van Helten and Y. Cassis (eds.), *Capitalism in a Mature Economy: Financial Institutions, Capital Exports and British Industry, 1870–1939* (London, 1990), 203–4.
107. Couyoumdjian, 'El mercado del salitre durante la primera guerra y la posguerra', 52–3.
108. Hunt, *Heirs of Great Adventure*, i. 111–13, ii. 194–5.
109. L. A. Sánchez, *Historia de una industria peruana: Cervecería Backus y Johnston S.A.* (Lima, 1978), 179–82.
110. Janet Percival, *The Archives of the Peruvian Corporation* (London, 1980), 4.
111. Jones, Jones, and Greenhill, 'Public Utility Companies', 111–13.
112. I owe this point to Professor Frank King.
113. The cable, of course, also facilitated management of subsidiaries at a distance, accelerated the flow of information to investors in Britain, and made possible the kind of arbitrage operations in shares which the merchant houses developed and which often led to acquisitions of companies by the British.
114. Many of the free-standing firms on the west coast bear out Jean-François Hennart's contention that such companies were frequently formed in London to take over and extend existing enterprises rather than initiate new ones. See J.-F. Hennart, 'Free Standing Firms and the Internalisation of Markets for Financial Capital: A Response to Casson', *Business History*, 36 (Oct. 1994), 121–2.
115. Blakemore, *From the Pacific to La Paz*, 287.

9

British Free-Standing Companies in Mexico, 1884–1911

Reinhard Liehr and Mariano E. Torres Bautista

Mira Wilkins has described the most common type of British direct investment abroad in the period 1870–1914 as the 'free-standing company'.[1] Earlier chapters in this volume have analysed the characteristics of this form of investment. This chapter examines the British free-standing company as it operated in Mexico during the era of President Porfirio Díaz (1876–1911). Most of our data commence in 1884, the year of the start of British–Mexican negotiations to resume long-severed diplomatic relations, and include the period up to Díaz's resignation from the Mexican presidency in 1911. The first part of this chapter provides a general overview of foreign investment in Mexico from the 1820s to 1913, with emphasis on Porfirian Mexico. Then we specifically consider free-standing companies, based on a sample that we have developed of such Anglo-Mexican enterprises.

An Overview

In the decade after independence (1821), Mexico experienced an investment boom with an influx of British capital. Mexico's fabulous riches, especially its mineral resources, attracted much British direct investment in mines. Nevertheless, in the 1820s portfolio investments, especially the two British loans of 1824 and 1825 to Mexico's federal government, were much more important than direct investments. Soon, failures of mining companies and, above all, the periodically occurring defaults and renegotiations of the two British loans, destroyed the reputation of Mexico and its companies among investors.[2] In August 1867, after the end of French intervention (for several years, the French had run Mexico), diplomatic relations between Mexico and Britain were completely severed.[3] From 1867 to about

Research for this chapter has been made possible by funds of the Consejo Nacional de Ciencia y Tecnología, Mexico, and the Freie Universitat Berlin. We thank Heike Dorit Gruhn and Bernardo Ibarrola for assistance in collecting and processing the data.

1880, Mexico's standing as a host to both foreign portfolio and direct investments was low; relations between Mexico and the financial centres of Europe were at an all-time nadir.

In August 1884 Britain and Mexico signed a preliminary agreement to re-establish diplomatic relations.[4] Mexico had already restored relations with France in 1880, and the USA and Germany had received most-favoured-nation status in 1883. In the preliminary agreement between Mexico and Britain and in the ensuing official and private negotiations, the Mexican government agreed to settle the claims of British subjects within the Republic and, most importantly, to arrange the conversion of the long-outstanding old debt of the British bondholders. The settlement of these claims and the ratification of a new treaty of commerce were Britain's conditions for the official renewal of diplomatic relations, which occurred in 1888. The Anglo-Mexican commercial treaty and the restoration of relations, as well as the already re-established relations with the USA, Germany, and France, provided a new political and judicial security for foreign investments in Mexico.

Porfirio Díaz, President of Mexico, had renegotiated the claims of the British bondholders, and, finally, redeemed these claims through the proceeds of an 1888 loan, floated by a newcomer in European financial markets, the Berlin-based merchant bank, S. Bleichröder. At the same time, Díaz did everything to renew and to strengthen Mexican relations with the major European countries, especially Britain, France, and Germany, as a way to counterbalance the growing American influence.[5]

Porfirio Díaz, a successful commander of the Liberal army, had assumed power in 1876 and ruled Mexico directly or indirectly for the next thirty-four years. His authoritarian regime led to a strengthening of the federal government and the institutions of the central state at the expense of the caudillos and élites in the different regions. At the end of his era the total income of the federal government was more than five times what it had been before. Development was no longer restrained by the internal and external wars that had been so endemic during the first fifty-five years of Mexico's postcolonial history. As a prime priority, Díaz's *pax porfiriana* guaranteed internal political stability for economic ventures, repressing all political opposition, using the paramilitary rural guard (the *rurales*) and the army to prevent the rise of an organized labour movement, and putting down Indian and campesino rebellions.[6]

From 1884 to 1911 a new British investment boom occurred, in particular channelled by free-standing companies, though from 1888 on also through loans. British capital flowed into Porfirian Mexico. The two and a half decades before the outbreak of the Mexican Revolution and the resignation of Díaz in May 1911 were the golden age of British companies in, and of foreign loans to, Mexico. British direct and portfolio investments in Mexico soared in the 1880s, and, although they slowed in the 1890s, they expanded again in the first decade of this century, reaching an all-time peak in 1911. There followed a stagnation in inward capital flows as a consequence of the Mexican Revolution.[7] The capital outflow from Britain to Mexico correlated positively with the long swing of total British capital exports in the years 1884–1911.[8]

During 1884–1911 information on companies and business opportunities in Mexico was published in Britain in books, booklets, and the press, and was widely discussed there. In 1900 Mexico set up a Mexican Information Bureau in London. Mexico began to shed its former reputation as a lawless, violent nation with a weak and backward economy. It acquired a new image as a politically stable, diplomatically recognized country, with huge, untapped natural resources.[9] Direct investments from gold-backed currency countries, such as Britain, the USA, and France, were increasingly at an advantage in Mexico, because of that country's depreciating silver currency. From 1875 onwards the Mexican silver peso slowly began to drop to about half its former gold value, until finally in 1905 the Mexican government also went on the gold standard.[10]

Although Porfirian Mexico was a low-income country with only modest improvements in standards of living, the population and the internal market grew rapidly. The Mexican population rose from ten million in 1882 to more than fifteen million in 1910.[11] The railway boom further expanded markets; the construction of a national railway system led to a fall in freight rates, which dropped to between a fifth and a tenth of what they had been before. Mexico's water transport was limited to some local traffic on highland lakes and to insignificant coastal shipping.[12] The central government was able to reduce transport costs even further by using the rural guard and the army to suppress banditry. The Díaz administration abolished inland duties (*alcabalas*) in order to widen the internal market and to aid in the formation of a national economy. Mexico continued to be protected by high, even increasing import tariffs. Nearly all major industries enjoyed some kind of tariff protection or federal aid. Import tariffs were the most important source of income for the federal government.[13] Before 1905, in addition to high import tariffs, the depreciated silver peso also contributed to Mexico's protective wall. At the same time, the central government sought to attract foreign investment and the transfer of new technology by exempting from tariffs and other federal taxes imported machinery needed to set up major factories. Once established, many factories that enjoyed these concessions benefited from a further tax-exempt status for a period of up to thirty years.[14] On the export side, while there was a levy on silver and gold (an obligation to pass the mints and pay mintage), there were no restrictions on transferring earnings on investment.[15]

There were also problems. Mexican manufacturers were not competitive in foreign markets, because, even after the massive railway construction, internal transport costs were higher than those in Europe and the USA. In addition, Mexico lacked experience in seafaring and shipbuilding, possessing no merchant fleet or shipping company to move the goods cheaply to less industrialized Central or South American countries. Finally, Mexican banking and financial institutions were in their infancy and interest rates were higher than those in Europe and the USA.[16]

Mexico did enact mining legislation favourable to foreign mine-owners. The colonial mining laws had been amended in 1823 to allow foreign participation. A new Mining Code (*Código Minero*) of 22 November 1884 transferred subsoil property rights in mining, petroleum, and gas resources from the nation to the private surface owners, including foreign investors. A law of 6 June 1887 relaxed and in some instances even abolished earlier taxes on mines and petroleum deposits.[17] The Congressional Commission for the new mine law of 4 June 1892 openly declared the law's objective as: 'Facility to acquire, liberty to exploit, and security to retain'.[18]

Thus far, research on British companies and British direct investment in Porfirian Mexico has been limited to diplomatic and economic relations studies, typified by an outstanding monograph and an earlier article by Alfred Tischendorf on British–Mexican relations.[19] A book on the same topic by Lorenzo Meyer is weak on the business history of the Anglo-Mexican companies.[20] Moreover, an intense controversy has arisen on the extent of *total* British investment overseas, including the Latin American countries and Mexico. Estimates vary due to differences in sources and methods. The most important assemblers of figures were Herbert Feis (1930),[21] who based his data on earlier estimates of George Paish;[22] J. Fred Rippy (1959);[23] Irving Stone (1977),[24] who inherited the database accumulated by Matthew Simon; and Lance Davis and Robert Huttenback (1986).[25] Rory Miller summarized the results of these efforts: 'All that can be said with certainty about the level of Britain's assets there [in Latin America] is that they had a nominal value in 1913 of between £700 million and £950 million.'[26] D. C. M. Platt criticized earlier calculations by Feis, Rippy, and Stone as far too high.[27] Davis and Huttenback published lower estimates for Latin America, excluding Mexico.[28] We believe the best total is the lower one of £700 million, or perhaps T. A. B. Corley's even lower figure of £546 million. But Corley's figure is only for British foreign *direct* investment in Latin America—not *total* British investment.[29]

Although we agree with Platt that Stone overestimated the flow of British capital to Latin America, Stone's figures still offer the best survey of its geographical distribution within Latin America. His data (based on stock-exchange manuals) show that, after Argentina and Brazil, Mexico held third place as a recipient of total British investment from the 1880s to 1913. Mexico's share of all British assets in Latin America expanded from 16 per cent in 1885 to more than 17 per cent in 1905, but after the outbreak of the Mexican Revolution fell back to 11 per cent in 1913, while the respective shares of Argentina and Brazil continued to rise. Argentina, the most important recipient, experienced from the 1880s onward a much bigger inflow of British capital than Mexico, rising from 18 per cent of the total in 1885 to 41 per cent in 1913. The share of Brazil grew from 19 per cent in 1885 to 22 per cent in 1913.[30] These figures cover all British assets in Latin America, not only direct investments.

During the three decades before 1913, Mexico, in common with other Latin American countries, witnessed a rise in British *direct* investments. For 1913, Stone estimated that direct investment constituted 33 per cent of all British assets in Mexico. Over the years there had been a corresponding decline in the share of the portfolio investments (government bonds, railway, public utility, and a few other company debentures).[31] British (and American) direct investments in Mexico flowed from the 1870s to 1913 primarily into railways and, to a lesser extent, into mining and land companies.[32] Much of the British direct investment was in the form of free-standing companies.

The best research on foreign, including British, investment in Porfirian Mexico by a Mexican is the study by Luis Nicolau D'Olwer. He and others emphasized that Britain, although by far the biggest investor in Latin America, was surpassed in Mexico from the 1880s and 1890s by the USA. This movement of American capital to Porfirian Mexico began earlier and in a broader way than similar US capital flows to nearby Canada and the Caribbean. In 1911 American assets, with 38 per cent of Mexico's total foreign investment, undoubtedly were the highest, followed by British assets with 29 and French with 27 per cent.[33]

The influx of foreign capital into Mexico after the 1880s helped the national income to grow at unprecedented annual rates—rates that had not been seen subsequent to independence and were not to be repeated after the Revolution, up to the present. Mexico's per capita national income (expressed in 1950 US dollars) more than doubled from \$62 in 1877 to \$132 in 1910.[34] This rapid growth, even by international standards, led to extreme social disparities and tensions that exploded in the Mexican Revolution. Growth was most pronounced in the export-oriented sectors of the economy and fastest in the mining sector. The latter was substantially aided by the new availability of railway lines. Furthermore, electric power and cyanide processing helped to more than triple the production of silver and gold. There was also a widening of the mining sector to include copper, lead, zinc, and subsequently the drilling for oil; Mexico could provide these minerals to the industrial markets of the Atlantic Rim. The cultivation of plantation cash crops for export—first of all *henequén* (sisal)—also expanded in a spectacular way.[35] It was, however, the mining of silver and gold, using modern technology, that (after railways) attracted the most foreign investment.[36] On the rivalry between British and American interests, especially in Mexican railways and mines, Friedrich Katz maintains that 'a kind of division of labour between them had developed, with the British concentrating essentially on central and southern Mexico while American investment tended to be directed above all into the north of the country'.[37] We shall see if our data verify this conclusion.

British Free-Standing Companies in Porfirian Mexico

Following the definition of the free-standing company proposed by Wilkins, we searched for this type of firm (one which maintained only minimal headquarters in Britain—often in the City of London—but at the same time conducted as an independent, but fully controlled company all its business overseas in Porfirian Mexico). On the basis of British[38] and Mexican[39] publications, we found that most British companies that were established and active in Porfirian Mexico conformed to this pattern. We will consider companies set up between early 1884 and the end of 1910.

Information gathered from the *Stock Exchange Yearbooks* and the Company Prospectuses in the Archives of the London Stock Exchange led us to the identification of 154 free-standing companies active in Mexico and quoted on the stock markets of the UK between 1884 and 1910. In any single year only a small portion of that group were quoted.

The 154 includes five important free-standing companies registered in Canada under Canadian law, with minimal headquarter offices in Toronto or Montreal; three of them maintained additional office facilities in London for the promotion of their securities.[40] The shares and bonds of these five firms were traded on the stock exchanges of London and the other markets of the UK in the same way as those of other Anglo-Mexican free-standing companies. If, as some historians have argued,[41] a firm with direct investments only in its empire should not be defined as a multinational enterprise, we can consider these Canadian–Mexican firms as a special category of Anglo-Mexican free-standing companies, special because they maintained legal headquarters in the dependent Dominion of Canada. The minimal head offices of such a parent company operated financially as a kind of British offshore enterprise, which was well connected to London, the centre of British imperial (and world) capitalism. They had access to the capital markets of both the UK and Continental Europe and, at the same time, to modern technology and capital goods, mostly from the USA and European countries, including Britain.

These five Canadian–Mexican firms were electrical utility companies set up from 1902 on by the dynamic American promoter and engineer Fred Stark Pearson of New York, together with Canadian promoters, lawyers, engineers, and bankers, who had earlier acquired experience in the USA and Canada. Pearson's group included other free-standing companies established at the same time for electricity services in Brazil and Spain. They all belonged to a wider and growing cluster of Canada-based Latin American electricity firms. Pearson's Canadian–Mexican free-standing enterprises were electric light and tramway companies for the cities of Mexico and Puebla, which included a huge hydroelectric power plant at the Necaxa River in the north of the State of Puebla. During the decade and a half before the first World War, American competitors were preoccupied with modernizing their own cities. This gave the chance for the Canada-based, free-standing utility companies of Pearson and other US and Canadian promoters to enter the major Latin American markets, which after the war came to be dominated by American multinational enterprises.[42] Pearson, in his capacity as an experienced hydroelectric engineer and property scout, was president or member of the board of each of the firms he promoted. Through his own New York-based Pearson Engineering Company, he acquired for them (in return for stiff fees) all capital goods, including modern technology, mainly from the USA, Britain, and Germany.[43] The capital he relied on as a promoter was initially raised by Canadian banks, investment funds, and brokers. At the beginning of his ventures, Canada's growing financial élite retained control of the common stock and took part of the company's debentures. The Canadian capital market, however, soon proved too narrow for substantial bond issues. After 1906, banks in London and other European centres filled the gap and placed large amounts of company bonds and also some stock, so that control finally shifted to Britain. Armstrong and Nelles estimate that in 1910 only one-third of the capital invested in Canadian–Mexican utilities came from Canada and two-thirds from Britain and the European Continent.[44] Businessmen knew that the Canadian company law treated these firms with more laxity than the British Company Act. They also 'were aware that Canadian companies were usually regarded as British firms in all but name. British investors might be persuaded to put money into them in due course, and the companies might expect to enjoy whatever diplomatic and commercial protection the government of the United Kingdom could provide in foreign parts.'[45] During the Mexican Revolution, the local directors of Pearson's cluster of Canada-based utility firms did receive the active support of the British government and British diplomats. Pearson also asked the US government for assistance, since he and his Pearson Engineering Company were American. He flew either flag when it suited him, although in many cases diplomatic help was of limited value.[46] The internalized managerial knowledge of Pearson's cluster of free-standing companies was based on placing headquarter facilities in the Dominion of Canada (with its lax company law), relying on the capital markets of the UK, and using superior electrical technology (mostly from the USA).

In the Mexican financial magazines that we scrutinized, we found, in addition to the aforementioned 154 Anglo-Mexican free-standing companies, information on a further 135 British firms in the country. We did not, however, include them in our statistics on British free-standing companies active in Mexico, because up to now we have been unable to find any further details about them to classify them as such. Most of these additional firms probably were registered as joint-stock companies in London or Edinburgh, but after registration their shares were not offered to a broader public on the stock exchanges of the UK. Possibly some of them, often in the form of a partnership, did not register. For all of these firms, raising capital seemed to have been less difficult or less necessary. It is assumed that most of them were established as small companies, the shares of which were owned by family members or by small groups of business partners. These additional Anglo-Mexican companies were not quoted on the stock exchanges of the UK and, therefore, are not part of our sample.

Alfred Tischendorf went through company registration files in London and culled a total of 304 British firms, which during the years 1876–1910 conducted business activities in Mexico; most of these would fit our definition of free-standing companies. He included in this number railway companies, one bank that clearly was not a free-standing company, some factories, many small companies, and even (by mistake) a few companies not active in Mexico. He noted that his figures did not cover a further twenty-three Anglo-Mexican companies registered in Edinburgh.[47]

For our sample of 154 British free-standing companies in Mexico that were traded on stock exchanges in the UK, we made the decision not to include the one bank and the railway companies on Tischendorf's list. The bank was omitted for the following reasons: the Banco de Londres,

México y Sudamérica was established in 1864 as a fully owned and controlled branch of a British multinational bank, the London Bank of Mexico and South America, founded in 1863 in London and specializing in business on the west coast of Latin America. Its London headquarters maintained other branches: one in Lima and, though only for some years, one each in Callao and in Bogotá. These four branches in Mexico, Peru, and Colombia were supplemented by six agencies in Mexico and another three in Colombia as well as correspondents in the USA and Continental Europe. The London Bank was not a bilateral free-standing company. Under Mexico's new Commercial Code of 1884, which initiated the evolution of a national banking system, the Mexico City branch of the London Bank, in order to maintain its concession to issue notes, had to be transformed into an independent Mexican bank, the Banco de Londres y México (this occurred in 1889). Initially the London Bank retained control, keeping two-thirds of the stock. However, after an increase in the capital, in 1896 the London headquarters lost control, even though it continued to hold a substantial block of shares. The Banco de Londres y México, with its headquarters in Mexico City, maintained branches in Veracruz, Puebla, and Querétaro. It became the second largest private bank in Porfirian Mexico; it operated under Mexican law. The largest one was its rival, the Banco Nacional de México, established in 1884. Although included in Tischendorf's figures, the Banco de Londres y México was not a free-standing company.[48] Neither was the Banco Nacional de México, which was said to be two-fifths British-owned; it had no British parent.[49]

Our sample also excludes the railway companies, in this case because our data are as yet insufficient to analyse their evolution and mergers, as well as their different share and, especially, bond issues. However, it seems clear that the railways were the most efficient of all the British free-standing companies in Mexico, channelling to the host country until 1913 more than half the quoted British direct and portfolio investments.[50] The Mexican railway system was built predominantly in the era of Porfirio Díaz, in the early stages mostly by British companies (which were later outstripped for first place by American capital and enterprises). The system grew with extraordinary speed from 640 kilometres in 1877, when Díaz seized power, to more than 19,000 kilometres in 1910, shortly before the outbreak of the Revolution.[51] The economic savings achieved by the railways, especially in freight transport, were much higher in mountainous Mexico than in lowland countries such as the USA, England and Wales, or Tsarist Russia.[52] The railway system strengthened the export-led growth of the economy and, most importantly, the expansion of the mining sector.[53]

American firms built the two major railways between Mexico City and the US border, while British companies constructed the lines in central and southern Mexico. In addition to some short British side-lines and mineral railways,[54] there were basically three big British-controlled companies: the Mexican Railway Company Ltd. (Mexico City–Veracruz), the first of the major ones in the country; the Inter-oceanic Railway of Mexico Ltd. (Acapulco–Veracruz, uncompleted); and the Mexican Southern Railway Ltd. (Puebla–Oaxaca). There were also two small railway firms registered in London and traded on the stock exchanges of the UK; their main purpose was to organize British holders of US–Mexican railway bonds and their interests in these companies.[55]

Of all the Anglo-Mexican free-standing companies, the British railway firms sold the largest amounts of stock and bonds. Unlike mining companies, they could raise capital not only through stock, but also through bond issues, because alongside their lines they owned land, which provided the necessary collateral.[56] The shares and bonds of the Anglo-Mexican railway companies were mainly held by British, but also (though to a lesser degree) by Continental European and Mexican investors. The same groups of investors also owned large blocks of shares and bonds of the US–Mexican railways.[57] The British railways were costly mountain lines in the central highlands of Mexico. They were operated under federal concessions with high annual subsidies and under supervision by two or three board members appointed by the federal government to act in Mexico City or London. With normally insufficient traffic (minerals and railway materials being the most important freight), only the Mexican Railway Company Ltd., operating between Mexico City and Veracruz on the country's traditional main route for exports, made profits and could pay dividends to its shareholders over a long period of time.[58] Finance Minister José Yves Limantour (1893–1911), the first to achieve a balanced budget in the country's national history, on the basis of the 1899 railway law began a 'Mexicanization' programme of the foreign-owned railways. In a series of measures the federal government purchased between 1903 and 1910 a controlling interest in Mexico's largest British and American railways and absorbed a series of smaller lines. Beginning in the last decade of the *Porfiriato*, all the foreign railway companies gradually ended up forming part of the National Railways of Mexico (Ferrocarriles Nacionales de México), established in 1907. 'By 1910 . . . more than two thirds of Mexico's steam railroads under federal concession had been Mexicanized.'[59]

An exceptionally long-standing venture, which is included in our 154 Anglo-Mexican free-standing companies, was the United Mexican Mining Company Ltd. This enterprise operated silver mines it had purchased in 1827 from the then-bankrupt British company United Mexican Mining Association, established in 1823 and active in the famous silver mining area of Guanajuato.[60] After a reregistration in 1862, it continued its activities for another thirty-three years, until 1895. A third reregistration of the company under the name United Mexican Mines Ltd. followed, and the enterprise finally failed in 1896.[61] After 1884 control of this London-based mining firm passed to a group of German shareholders from Bremen. In 1898, two years after its failure as a free-standing company, it was reopened once again under the name United Mexican Mines Association as a joint venture, including Mexican owners. In 1905 New York investors purchased the property.[62]

After registration in London (or Edinburgh) and following the establishment of the firm in Britain, most free-standing companies, especially in the mining sector, began activities in Mexico by purchasing the already existing properties of an older, generally smaller, often bankrupt enterprise. Only a few companies commenced their activities in this host country without such an existing basis. So far we have been unable to identify very clearly the vendors of properties to the newly established Anglo-Mexican companies. The *Stock Exchange Yearbooks* do not provide this information. Thus, it has proved difficult to name experienced promoters of clusters of companies, who probably bought existing properties from Mexican, American, or British expatriate owners to sell them at a profit to a free-standing company formed by them for that purpose and for further development. The Mexican government encouraged such takeovers to attract additional capital as well as modern technology from abroad, in order to expand the economy and to increase tax revenue. According to the *Stock Exchange Yearbooks*, vendors were generally paid partly in cash, to cover their expenses, and partly in shares of the new free-standing company. After the acquisition, the new company would continue to operate the property on the basis of the increased capital stock, which generally consisted of imported modern machinery, including chemical-processing and electrical-power technology.[63]

In reference to promoters and their clusters of Anglo-Mexican free-standing companies, we have already mentioned the group of Canadian–Mexican enterprises set up by the American engineer and promoter Fred Stark Pearson and his New York-based Pearson Engineering Company. In addition, we analysed the board members of our sample of Anglo-Mexican free-standing companies for the years 1893 and 1909. The years were chosen arbitrarily. In 1893 there were thirty-three Anglo-Mexican free-standing companies quoted on the stock exchanges of the UK; by 1909 the number had fallen to thirty-one (see Fig. 9.1).

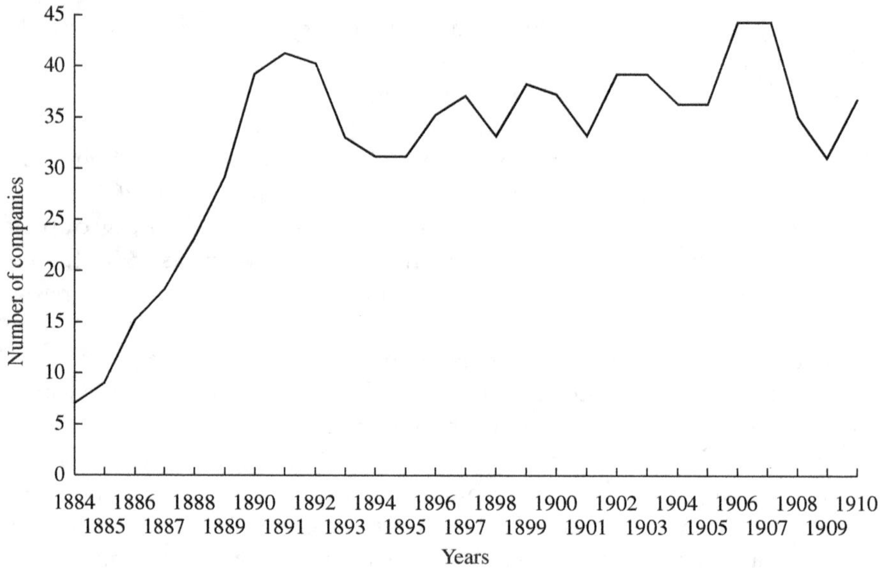

Fig. 9.1. Number of British free-standing companies active in Mexico, 1884–1910
Source: See text.

For the year 1893 we discovered only two experienced promoters: George Hopkins, a London-based civil engineer and promoter, who acted not only as chairman of two Anglo-Mexican gold and silver mining enterprises (the Princesa Gold Mining Company Ltd. and the Anglo-Mexican Mining Company Ltd.), but also as chairman of twelve and as director of another two British free-standing companies active in Australia, South Africa, Canada, the USA, Peru, and Uruguay. Hopkins's companies were mostly gold and silver mines, but also included a lead-mining and a land-development enterprise. The second promoter, James Whittall, of the London-based firm J. Whittall & Company, general merchants, was in 1893 not only chairman and board member of two Anglo-Mexican gold and silver mines (New Imuris Mines Ltd. and Mesquital del Oro Mining Company Ltd.), but also acted as chairman of an Anglo-British Columbian salmon-fishing company, as board member of two British overseas banks, and as member of the London committee of a Paris-based Franco-Spanish railway line.[64] Consequently these few promoters of British free-standing companies were active not only in Mexico, but also in other parts of the world.

For 1909 we identified fourteen directors who served at the same time on two (three of them on three) boards of Anglo-Mexican free-standing companies.[65] The triple board members were Chandos S. Stanhope, along with Pablo de Escandón and J. B. Body (both of

Mexico City). Stanhope was a British engineer who began his career in Mexico City as a technical troubleshooter for the Anglo-Mexican free-standing firm Mexico Electric Tramways Ltd. After the takeover of this company by a Canadian–Mexican enterprise, organized by Fred Stark Pearson, Stanhope returned to London to serve as director on the boards of the following Anglo-Mexican free-standing companies: Salinas of Mexico Ltd. (a salt-producing firm) and Anglo-Mexican Oilfields Ltd. (an oil-drilling firm), as well as the Interoceanic Railway of Mexico Ltd. and the Mexican Eastern Railway Company Ltd., both controlled in 1909 by the Mexican federal government. Stanhope seemed to be an experienced specialist, not a promoter.[66] Escandón was a politically influential Mexican entrepreneur and investor close to the federal government, who acted in 1909 as a director of the Mexican Railway Company Ltd., the Veracruz Terminal Company Ltd., and the Canada-based Puebla Tramway, Light & Power Company. Body lived in Mexico City from 1895 to 1919 and was the local director of the construction works and the Mexican enterprises organized by Weetman D. Pearson, the famous British contractor, oil magnate, and personal friend of Porfirio Díaz. In 1909 Body was a board member of the Veracruz Terminal Company Ltd., the Canada-based Puebla Tramway, Light & Power Company, and managing director of the Veracruz (Mexico) Railways Ltd., in the last two enterprises along with W. D. Pearson as chairman. Body also served in 1909 as director in Pearson's home-based company S. Pearson & Son Ltd. as well as in Mexican enterprises (registered in Mexico, but controlled by Pearson and his family) such as the Compañía Mexicana de Petroleo El Aguila, S.A., a big oil firm which clearly was not a free-standing company.[67] When Pearson established El Aguila and included Mexican politicians as board members, he argued that 'the Mexican company would be assured of Government support much more than a foreign company and I should feel that our investment would be on a much safer basis than if entirely owned by us'.[68]

Weetman D. Pearson (1856–1927) was the most prominent of the remaining fourteen directors in 1909. As mentioned, together with Body, he was chairman of two Anglo-Mexican free-standing railway and tramway enterprises, and, together with Stanhope, director on the board of the Interoceanic Railway of Mexico Ltd., controlled in 1909 by the federal government. Furthermore, he acted as director of an Anglo-Spanish railway company, as chairman of an English cement firm, and as board member of another English land-development company. Most importantly, he was president of S. Pearson & Son Ltd., the family firm of builders and contractors which he continued and expanded into a multinational enterprise, through which he controlled until 1919 the Mexican Eagle Oil Company and the related oil-transport and oil-marketing companies registered in the UK.[69] Pearson was a dynamic international entrepreneur.

Of the other directors of 1909, Stanley Clay was probably a mining specialist and promoter; he served as board member of two Anglo-Mexican and another six free-standing mining companies in Africa and Norway, owning mainly gold and silver mines. Robert J. Price acted as chairman and board member of two Anglo-Mexican gold- and silver-mining enterprises, as well as of another five free-standing firms active in Mexico, Colombia, and Spain. He was a member of the British Parliament, as were C. G. Hyde and Henry W. Forster. It was very typical of free-standing companies to have British MPs decorate their boards.[70] Forster and Edward Nettlefold both served as board members of two Anglo-Mexican firms as well as of other British banking, insurance, investment, land, steel, and railway companies. L. Camacho and Enrique Camacho-Guisasola were Mexico's financial agents in London and were board members mainly in those Anglo-Mexican companies in which the Mexican federal government had an interest. Thus we did not find for 1893 and 1909 many repetitions of the names of the board members of the analysed Anglo-Mexican free-standing companies.

Another result of our research is a very simple figure (see Fig. 9.2) representing the number of free-standing companies registered every

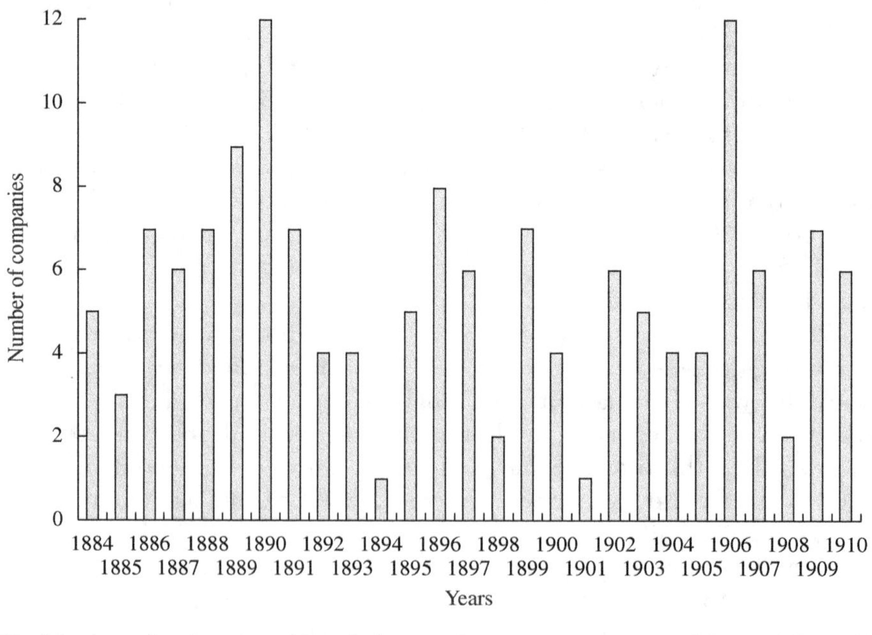

Fig. 9.2. Annual registration of British free-standing companies active in Mexico, 1884–1910
Source: See text.

year from 1884 to 1910. The figure is based on our sample of 154 firms. The data include both new British enterprises, often ones that acquired Mexican firms, as well as reregistrations of previously bankrupt British free-standing companies with existing assets in Mexico. Following registration, each of these companies would be established and later their shares would be offered on the stock exchanges of the UK, especially in London. There was normally a time lag between the registration date, the first offering of the shares on the stock exchanges, and the year when the company was first mentioned in the *Stock Exchange Yearbooks.* There exists a significant coincidence between, on the one hand, the first two dates of the re-election of Díaz (1884, 1888) and the consequent rise of an obviously stable and friendly climate for foreign direct investment in Mexico, the beginning of negotiations to re-establish Anglo-Mexican relations in 1884, and finally the ratification of the trade agreement and the renewal of diplomatic relations in 1888, and, on the other hand, the steep rise and the first peak in 1890 relating to the registration of free-standing companies. A second peak in 1906 followed the introduction of the gold standard in 1905, another confidence-building measure designed to attract additional capital to the Mexican economy.[71] There was, moreover, a major British push factor for the capital exports: the mounting number of new registrations in the late 1880s and the soaring number in 1906 coincided with the boom of British capital export and the downswing in the 1890s.[72] The annual rate at which companies were registered and launched was low, but of a remarkable continuity throughout the period studied, the aforementioned two steep increases being the only major exceptions. However, annual registrations also included reregistrations, especially of short-lived mining enterprises. We would sum up by stating that, after 1884, the country became open to sizeable British free-standing company investment.

Of great importance to this development were the Mexican 'pull factors', such as the depreciated silver currency (initially), the stable and friendly conditions for foreign capital, including the new mining legislation, and the proverbial Mexican mining bonanzas which, as in the 1820s, became once again important to British investors. Of our sample of 154 British free-standing companies in Mexico between 1884–1910 73.4 per cent were mining companies (see Table 9.1), followed some way behind by real-estate companies, with 15.6 per cent. The rest were public utilities and financial-services enterprises, including those organized from Canada, with 9.1 per cent, as well as petroleum companies, with 1.9 per cent.

How do our results compare with those of other researchers? Tischendorf, who included for the period 1876–1910 small registered

TABLE 9.1. *Anglo-Mexican free-standing companies, 1876–1910*

Type of company	1884–1910		1876–1910	
	Traded on the stock exchanges of the UK		Registered in London	
	No.	%	No.	%
Mining companies	113	73.4	224	73.7
Real-estate companies	24	15.6	32	10.5
Railway companies	Not included		17	5.6
Factories	None		11	3.6
Public utilities (and financial services)	14	9.1	10	3.3
Petroleum companies	3	1.9	9	3.0
Banks	Not included		1	0.3
SUBTOTAL	154	100.0	304	100.0
Registered in Scotland	Unknown		23	
Additional unspecified firms	135		None	
TOTAL BRITISH COMPANIES	289		327	

Sources: Columns 1 and 2: *The Stock Exchange Yearbook* (1884–1911); microform copy of the Company Prospectuses (1884–1900), Archives of the Royal Stock Exchange, GL; *El economista mexicano* (Mexico City, 1886–1914); *La Semana Mercantil* (Mexico City, 1891–1911). Columns 3 and 4: A. Tischendorf, *Great Britain and Mexico in the Era of Porfirio Díaz* (Durham, NC, 1961), 141.

firms as well as the limited number of railway companies and the one bank, identified 73.7 per cent of a total of 304 London-registered Anglo-Mexican companies as being mines, 10.5 per cent as real-estate companies, and 5.6 per cent as railway companies. The remaining 10.2 per cent were in manufacturing, public utilities, petroleum, and banking. He too found that mining companies numerically occupied a dominant position, while railway companies were way ahead in paid-in capital. If we put railway companies aside, the mining industry (followed by land-owning companies) was clearly the sector in which British free-standing enterprises were predominantly active in Porfirian Mexico.[73] Our results are confirmed by Tischendorf's figures. It is worth noting that none of the few manufacturing and only three of the petroleum companies found by Tischendorf to have been registered as free-standing companies in London floated their shares on the stock exchanges of the UK. We assume that their equities were held by small groups of shareholders not in need of raising capital.

If the dream of profit from the British mining firms in Porfirian Mexico was constant, so were the high risks and the ensuing disillusionment suffered by most of them. Our research shows that the average lifespan of Anglo-Mexican free-standing mining companies between 1884 and 1910 was six and a half years. With the exception of the aforementioned United Mexican Mining Company Ltd., with a record of thirty-three years of existence after reregistration in 1862, most of the companies lasted only a few years. Longevity of mining enterprises among the British free-standing companies in Porfirian Mexico was fairly rare. Briefness was characteristic, as was the continuous rate of reregistration for further operations. Before 1914, British free-standing companies active in the USA in precious metal mining ran similarly high risks of bankruptcy, as Wilkins observed. Both in the USA and in Mexico, the marketing of industrial minerals gave mining an additional possibility of income and expansion.[74] Yet free-standing companies—whether in precious metals or in industrial minerals—were still short-lived.

British free-standing companies sought to overcome the high risks and costs of mining enterprises in the Mexican highland regions. Mining companies, especially pit-mining ventures, offered (contrary to railway, land, and plantation companies) little collateral for debenture issues. The sale of shares of a foreign-based free-standing company provided, in a less-developed capital market, the only form of long-term venture capital that could be channelled to risky investments with little collateral. This was the reason why in Mexico most British free-standing companies were risky, short-lived mining companies. By the same token the few free-standing railway firms were able to channel more than half of total British capital invested in Mexico through both share and bond issues, because they had land that could serve as collateral.[75] For exactly the same reasons, the most prominent British free-standing companies in Mexico after railway and mining enterprises were real-estate companies, including land-development firms and plantations. However, in other sectors, such as oil drilling, banking, and especially manufacturing, branches of classic multinational enterprises with experience in the home market, or national firms (often run by experienced expatriates), were more in evidence than British free-standing companies.

In late Porfirian Mexico, as Tischendorf maintains, control of many British free-standing companies (including the small, unquoted ones, especially in the mining, railway, utility, manufacturing, and petroleum sectors) was centralized in the hands of a dozen or even fewer investors. This minority, represented on the board, was mostly British.[76] In some cases, however, a notable or even controlling influence would be exercised by other nationals, such as wealthy Mexicans, Americans, French, or Germans. These non-British nationals used London-based free-standing companies mainly to organize and channel capital for the use of their business abroad.[77]

Tischendorf also draws attention to a remarkable management disadvantage on the part of Anglo-Mexican mines. The small British staff of the Mexican extensions, which often included American engineers, tended to face unexpected obstacles that Mexican managers could handle more skilfully. Apart from the normal mining risks such as cave-ins, floods, and fires, British executives experienced difficulties in dealings with their workers, in coping with inadequate transportation facilities, and in operating without government assistance. Communication problems with the parent board in Britain often postponed important decisions. Mexican pit-mining required large amounts of capital before profits could be made and the delays compounded the difficulties. Communication chasms between local British managers and the head office in Britain also led to disadvantages in public-utilities enterprises (for example, in the case of the Mexican Gas & Electric Light Company, Ltd). Indeed, the vast majority of labour-intensive cotton textile and tobacco factories in Porfirian Mexico (which did not need to call on British capital markets) were Mexican companies, organized under Mexican law, and run by Mexicans.[78] During and after the Mexican Revolution, many British free-standing companies apparently passed into Mexican hands, becoming Mexican firms with no parent board in Britain.

The abridged annual reports on British free-standing companies in the *Stock Exchange Yearbooks* do not allow for an assessment of the British capital flows to Porfirian Mexico. The difficulty of making a precise calculation on the amounts has been described by Nicolau D'Olwer.[79] We do not intend to revise his figures. Nevertheless, analysing the *Yearbook* reports on our 154 Anglo-Mexican free-standing companies, we were able to gather interesting information for the years 1884–1910 on the ratios of called-up and paid-in share capital after the companies' introduction into the stock exchanges of the UK. Shares of new British free-standing companies working in Mexico were regularly offered in Britain. Every time a new company was established, more capital was mobilized; we assume that much of the capital was exported to Mexico. There were peaks of raising British capital for export to Mexico. The outstanding years were 1887–9, when the companies started calling up capital. The other time periods when paid-in capital reached a high level were the years 1896–7, 1902–3, and 1906. Share sales depended on data on the company's performance, on the availability of information on the companies, and on the attractiveness of their expected profits. The raising of capital also depended on the situation in the London capital market—that is, on the interest rates paid there, which always moved capital towards better yields. The average of share sales of these free-standing companies—that is, the average paid-in share capital—was 71 per cent, a relatively low figure, which perhaps related to the short life expectancy of the companies.

Our data do indicate a poor profit performance on the part of free-standing companies. Between 1884 and 1910, only thirty-six (23.4 per cent) of the 154 Anglo-Mexican and Canadian–Mexican free-standing companies analysed by us reported profits at least in one year, and only thirty-eight (24.7 per cent) paid any interest on bonds and/or dividends.[80] Apparently, companies often used the first pay-out of interest or dividends as a selling manœuvre to boost their bond or share prices. Founders could then exit. Tischendorf reported that during the entire Porfirian era there were in Mexico only twenty-six dividend-paying British enterprises (8.6 per cent of the 304 British companies he monitored).

The depreciation of the silver peso resulting from an expanding world production of this metal had encouraged new British free-standing companies to buy up assets cheaply in Porfirian Mexico. Before 1905 labour costs, although already low, tended to be even lower in Mexico than in gold-currency countries. Yet higher import expenses (because of the depreciated currency) and the difficulty of transforming silver-currency profits back home into sterling meant that the same companies often struggled under a disadvantage in order to produce profits and pay dividends. Many of the few dividend-paying firms were lead, copper, zinc, gold, or mercury mines, and the Canadian–Mexican electrical power-supply and tramway companies. The most prosperous mining companies had sufficient ore stocks and mined gold. No real-estate company reported continuous profits. Only very few of them and none of the early petroleum companies paid a dividend.[81]

These data once again raise the question: what was the reason for the sustained capital flow to Mexico? While our earlier analysis indicated a continuous presence of British free-standing enterprises, Figure 9.1 showed how many of our 154 companies were (between 1884 and 1910) each year active in this host country. From 1884 onwards the number of companies rose, reaching a clear peak between 1890 and 1892. In 1893 a decline set in, but after 1901 the number of registered Anglo-Mexican free-standing companies was once again on the increase. After 1905 the number rose more steeply, reaching its highest point in 1906 and 1907, only to decline once again in the final years of our period.

Luis Nicolau D'Olwer[82] and Lorenzo Meyer[83] both argue that direct investments from abroad, including British direct investment, in general operated in a speculative and rapacious manner, leaving little to Mexico. We would counter that it is hard to find any capital altruistically invested abroad. However, the short lifespan of Anglo-Mexican free-standing companies was partly due to the high risks of long-term ventures in pit-mining. Most of these companies did not reach their expected goals. Some of the entrepreneurs abandoned activities in Mexico simply to move to better mining or land-development investments in South Africa, Australia, or the European peripheries.[84] In some cases, the registration and establishment of free-standing enterprises in London for investment in Mexico merely served as a means of making a living for clever promoters, who as chairmen or members of the board of directors started, closed, and reopened companies, each time attracting new funds, which partly would serve to maintain their London offices, before beginning business abroad.

The very small number of Anglo-Mexican companies which paid interest on their debt and made profits to pay dividends confirms a picture of their poor performance. While the main objective of the invested capital of a company ostensibly was to obtain a return higher than that available in the London capital market, the performance of these enterprises often seemed to be of a secondary priority. The returns to the promoters were perhaps the first priority. Yet, the dissolved British free-standing companies seem to have left productive assets in Mexico, a real contribution to economic growth in this period. The high risks and costs of Mexican pit-mining forced British companies out of business, giving way to national firms, which was a repetition of the British experience in Mexican mining in the first decades after 1821.[85]

Fig. 9.3. British free-standing mining companies in Mexican states, 1884–1911
Note: The numbers indicate the number of British free-standing companies in each state.
Source: See text.

The British presence in Mexico and its contribution was strongest in Mexico's area of fastest growth: the north. Seventy-one per cent of the mining companies and 42 per cent of the real-estate companies analysed by us settled in this region, which accounted for the major part of the invested capital (see Fig. 9.3 on the geographical location of British free-standing mining companies). The statement by Friedrich Katz that British companies were concentrating in central and southern Mexico, while American firms dominated the north of the country, might well apply to the railways, but not to mining, real estate, or other sectors of the Mexican economy.

Conclusion

This chapter, which presents initial results from a broader research effort, addressed the difficulty of calculating the amount of British direct investment in Porfirian Mexico. We found little new to add to the debate. However, the concept of the free-standing company did permit us to identify, classify, and analyse the characteristics of an important part of British direct investment in Mexico. Although the profits these free-standing companies earned from their activities in Porfirian Mexico were limited, we believe that the capital invested did make an important contribution to Mexican economic and social development. The growth rates of this period were impressive. The Mexican economy depended, on the one hand, on the import of foreign capital in combination with foreign technology and engineering skills, and, on the other hand, to a large extent on the export of raw materials to foreign markets. Mexico as a host country could retain this capital only if foreign investors had confidence in its long-term stability and favourable conditions for investment prevailed. When a new free-standing company bought a mining property or land, it usually introduced new methods of exploitation or improved on existing ones; this applied even when the enterprise had to be liquidated a few years later without ever having paid any dividends. Often, it left behind a monetary or capital injection in the shape of paid wages, taxes, and installed equipment, mostly of a new technology. In this manner foreign direct investment by British free-standing companies served to expand the local industrial capacity of production as well as to widen the national market.

In common with other foreign enterprises, British free-standing companies in Porfirian Mexico were favoured by the general policies of the federal government and also, before 1905, to a certain degree by the impact of the depreciated silver currency. For a time, they seem to have channelled long-term venture capital from Britain and other countries into risky Mexican enterprises, which were unable to obtain funds in the less developed national capital market. However, they failed, with few exceptions, to earn a profit. The majority of our sample of Anglo-Mexican free-standing companies went bankrupt. The British management of their Mexican extensions seems to have laboured under a disadvantage compared with Mexican companies. In the long run, many of these companies, after several reregistrations and reorganizations, changed their legal status into that of a local enterprise operating under Mexican law with a Mexican management and free of any ties to a parent board of directors in faraway Britain.

NOTES

1. See several articles by M. Wilkins, especially 'Defining a Firm: History and Theory', in P. Hertner and G. Jones (eds.), *Multinationals: Theory and History* (Aldershot, 1986), 80–95; 'The Free-Standing Company, 1870–1914: An Important Type of British Foreign Direct Investment', *Economic History Review*, 2nd ser., 41 (May 1988), 259–82; 'European and North American Multinationals, 1870–1914: Comparisons and Contrasts', *Business History*, 30 (Jan. 1988), 8–45. Also see Chapter 1 herein.
2. J. F. Rippy, 'Latin America and the British Investment "Boom" of the 1820's', *Journal of Modern History*, 19 (1947), 122–9; H. J. Heath, 'Los primeros escarceos del imperialismo en México: Las casas comerciales británicas, 1821–1867', *Historias* (Mexico City), 22 (1989), 77–89; H. J. Heath, 'British Merchant Houses in Mexico, 1821–1860: Conforming Business Practices and Ethics', *Hispanic American Historical Review*, 73 (1993), 261–90.
3. 'Papers Relating to the Withdrawal of the British Mission from Mexico, 1867–68', in Great Britain, *Parliamentary Papers, House of Commons* (1867–8), xxiii.
4. 'Papers Respecting the Renewal of Diplomatic Relations with Mexico', in Great Britain, *Parliamentary Papers, House of Commons* (1884), xxxvii; A. Tischendorf, *Great Britain and Mexico in the Era of Porfirio Díaz* (Durham, NC, 1961), 3–20.
5. C. Marichal, 'Foreign Loans, Banks and Capital Markets in Mexico, 1880–1910', in R. Liehr (ed.), *La deuda pública en América Latina en perspectiva histórica* (Frankfurt, 1995); F. Katz, *The Secret War in Mexico: Europe, the USA and the Mexican Revolution* (Chicago, 1981), 50–9; F. Katz, 'Mexico: Restored Republic and Porfiriato, 1867–1910', in L. Bethell (ed.), *The Cambridge History of Latin America*, v (Cambridge, 1986), 24–7.
6. S. H. Haber, *Industry and Underdevelopment: The Industrialization of Mexico, 1890–1940* (Stanford, Calif., 1989), 12, 18–25; El Colegio de México, *Estadísticas económicas del Porfiriato: Fuerza de trabajo y actividad económica por sectores* (Mexico City, 1960), 199.
7. J. F. Rippy, 'The Peak of British Investment in Latin American Mines', *Inter-American Economic Affairs*, 2 (1948), 41–8.
8. M. Edelstein, *Overseas Investment in the Age of High Imperialism: The UK, 1850–1914* (London, 1982), 30.
9. Tischendorf, *Great Britain*, 71–7; L. Nicolau D'Olwer, 'Las inversiones extranjeras', in D. Cosío Villegas (ed.), *Historia moderna de México*, vii. *El Porfiriato: La vida económica*, pt. 2 (Mexico City, 1965), 982–4.
10. J. Schneider, O. Schwarzer, and F. Zellfelder (eds.), *Währungen der Welt*, i.

Europäische und nordamerikanische Devisenkurse 1777–1914 (Stuttgart, 1991), 395–7; D. M. Pletcher, 'The Fall of Silver in Mexico, 1870–1910, and its Effect on American Investments', *Journal of Economic History*, 18 (1958), 33–55.

11. Instituto Nacional de Estadística, Geografía e Informática (INEGI), *Estadísticas históricas de Mexico* (2 vols; 2nd edn., Aguascalientes, 1990), i. 9, 177–9; El Colegio de México, *Estadísticas económicas*, 25, 147–54.
12. J. H. Coatsworth, *Growth against Development: The Economic Impact of Railroads in Porfirian Mexico* (DeKalb, Ill., 1981), 25–6, 103; Haber, *Industry*, 13–16.
13. Haber, *Industry*, 21, 38; D. Cosío Villegas, *La cuestión arancelaria en México* (Mexico City, 1932; repr. 1989), 38–61.
14. Haber, *Industry*, 38.
15. G. Nava Oteo, 'La Minería', in D. Cosío Villegas (ed.), *Historia moderna de México*, vii. *El Porfiriato: La vida económica*, pt. 1 (Mexico City, 1965), 238–9; Nicolau D'Olwer, 'Las inversiones extranjeras', 978.
16. Haber, *Industry*, 39–42.
17. H. K. Wright, *Foreign Enterprise in Mexico: Laws and Politics* (Chapel Hill, NC, 1971), 51–61; M. Bernstein, *The Mexican Mining Industry, 1890–1950: A Study of the Interaction of Politics, Economics, and Technology* (New York, 1964), 18–19; F. J. Munch, 'The Anglo-Dutch–American Petroleum Industry in Mexico: The Formative Years during the Porfiriato 1900–1910', *Revista de Historia de América* (Mexico City), 84 (1977), 135–8; D. M. Coerver, 'The Perils of Progress: The Mexican Department of Fomento during the Boom Years 1880–1884', *Inter-American Economic Affairs*, 31 (1977), 55–6.
18. Bernstein, *The Mexican Mining Industry*, 27.
19. Tischendorf, *Great Britain*, and his earlier 'British Investments in Latin American and African Mines', *Inter-American Economic Affairs*, 6 (1953), 29–37.
20. L. Meyer, *Su Majestad británica contra la Revolución Mexicana, 1900–1950: El fin de un imperio informal* (Mexico City, 1991).
21. H. Feis, *Europe: the World's Banker, 1870–1914* (New York, 1965: repr. of 1930. edn.).
22. They are reprinted in M. Wilkins (ed.), *British Overseas Investments, 1907–1948* (New York, 1977).
23. J. F. Rippy, *British Investments in Latin America, 1822–1949* (Minneapolis, 1959).
24. I. Stone, 'British Direct and Portfolio Investment in Latin America before 1914', *Journal of Economic History*, 37 (1977), 690–722, and his 1962 Ph.D. dissertation from Columbia University, *The Composition and Distribution of British Investment in Latin America, 1865 to 1913* (New York, 1987).
25. L. E. Davis and R. A. Huttenback, *Mammon and the Pursuit of Empire: The Political Economy of British Imperialism, 1860–1912* (Cambridge, 1986).
26. R. Miller, *Britain and Latin America in the Nineteenth and Twentieth Centuries* (London, 1993), 120–1.
27. D. C. M. Platt, *Britain's Investment Overseas on the Eve of the First World War: The Use and Abuse of Numbers* (London, 1986), 87–92.
28. Davis and Huttenback, *Mammon*, 49.
29. T. A. B. Corley, 'Britain's Overseas Investments in 1914 Revisited', *Business History*, 36 (Jan. 1994), 81.
30. Stone, 'British Direct and Portfolio Investment', 695.
31. Ibid. 706; C. Armstrong and H. V. Nelles, 'A Curious Capital Flow: Canadian Investment in Mexico, 1902–1910', *Business History Review*, 58 (1984), 180; C. Armstrong and H. V. Nelles, *Southern Exposure: Canadian Promoters in Latin America and the Caribbean, 1896–1930* (Toronto, 1988), 188.
32. Stone, *The Composition*, 153F, 161–2, 166–7, 169.
33. Nicolau D'Olwer, 'Las inversiones extranjeras', 1154; M. Wilkins, *The Emergence*

of Multinational Enterprise: American Business Abroad from the Colonial Era to 1914 (Cambridge, Mass., 1970), 110, 125–7. The figures of Nicolau D'Olwer have been often used—for example, by Armstrong and Nelles, *Southern Exposure*, 188, and C. A. Aguirre Rojas, 'Mercado interno, guerra y revolución en México: 1870–1920', *Revista Mexicana de Sociología* (Mexico City), 52 (1990), 216. They need reconsideration.

34. J. H. Coatsworth, 'Obstacles to Economic Growth in Nineteenth-Century Mexico', *American Historical Review*, 83 (1978), 82.
35. Katz, 'Mexico: Restored Republic and Porfiriato', 28–9; INEGI, *Estadísticas históricas*, 402, 449–54, 469; El Colegio de México, *Estadísticas económicas*, 77–8, 135–45; Bernstein, *The Mexican Mining Industry*, 51.
36. F. Rosenzweig, 'El desarrollo económico de México de 1877 a 1911', *El Trimestre Económico* (Mexico City), 32 (1965), 432–4.
37. Katz, 'Mexico: Restored Republic and Porfiriato', 32.
38. We consulted in London: *The Stock Exchange Yearbook* (1884–1911), as well as the microform copy of the Company Prospectuses (1884–1900), Archives of the London Stock Exchange, GL.
39. In Mexico City, we went through the following financial magazines of the Porfirian era for further information: *El Economista Mexicano* (Mexico, 1886–1914) and *Semana Mercantil* (Mexico, 1891–1911).
40. On the Canadian–Mexican free-standing companies, see Armstrong and Nelles, *Southern Exposure*, 85–104, 185–205, 282–3; Armstrong and Nelles, 'A Curious Capital Flow', 182–95, 199–203; C. Armstrong and H. V. Nelles, 'Corporate Enterprise in the Public Service Sector: The Performance of Canadian Firms in Mexico and Brazil, 1896–1930', in C. Marichal (ed.), *Foreign Investment in Latin America: Impact on Economic Development, 1850–1930* (Milan, 1994), 71. See also Gregory Marchildon, Chapter 15 herein, for a different approach to these same Canadian–Mexican companies. Marchildon considers them as Canadian rather than 'British'.
41. G. Jones, 'The Making of Global Enterprise', *Business History*, 36 (Jan. 1994), 7, referring to several articles and the *Habilitationsschrift* of Harm Schröter.
42. Armstrong and Nelles, *Southern Exposure*, 34, 44.
43. *The Stock Exchange Yearbook* (1884–1911); Mexico, Ministerio de Hacienda, *The Mexican Yearbook: A Statistical, Financial, and Economic Annual, Compiled from Official and Other Returns. Issued Under the Auspices of the Department of Finance*, iii. *1909–10* (London, 1909), 316–26A; Armstrong and Nelles, 'A Curious Capital Flow', 183, 199; Armstrong and Nelles, *Southern Exposure*, 280–1; Armstrong and Nelles, 'Corporate Enterprise', 72–4.
44. Armstrong and Nelles, 'A Curious Capital Flow', 184–5, 187, 194–7, 202; Armstrong and Nelles, *Southern Exposure*, 37, 47, 74–80, 91, 94–5, 276.
45. Ibid. 48.
46. Ibid. 190–208, also 66, 71–3, 272–3, 277–9, 283–7; Armstrong and Nelles, 'Corporate Enterprise', 75–6.
47. Tischendorf, *Great Britain*, 21–3, 141.
48. D. Joslin, *A Century of Banking in Latin America: To Commemorate the Centenary in 1962 of the Bank of London and South America Ltd.* (London, 1963), 85–9, 207–11; L. Ludlow and C. Marichal (eds.), *Banca y poder en México (1800–1925)* (Mexico, 1986), 209–345; C. Jones, 'Commercial Banks and Mortgage Companies', in D. C. M. Platt (ed.), *Business Imperialism, 1840–1930: An Inquiry Based on British Experience in Latin America* (Oxford, 1977), 17–25; W. F. McCaleb, *Present and Past Banking in Mexico* (New York, 1920), 12–24, 52–8, 63–6; Tischendorf, *Great Britain*, 23n., 139–41. For more on the London Bank, see Rory Miller, Chapter 8 herein.

49. C. Jones, 'Commercial Banks', 25.
50. Stone, *The Composition*, 160–2.
51. Coatsworth, *Growth*, 35–37; Nicolau D'Olwer, 'Las inversiones extranjeras', 1085–6.
52. Coatsworth, *Growth*, 179–80.
53. Ibid. 132–3, 181.
54. For example, the Mexican Eastern Railway Company Ltd., the Michoacan Railway and Mining Company Ltd., and the Mexican Mineral Railway Company Ltd., all with headquarters in London.
55. The Mexican Central Railway Securities Ltd., and the Mexican National Railway Company Ltd.; see also Nicolau D'Olwer, 'Las inversiones extranjeras', 1066–7; *The Stock Exchange Yearbook* (1897–1911).
56. *The Stock Exchange Yearbook* (1884–1911); Mexico, Ministerio de Hacienda, *The Mexican Yearbook*, iii. *1909–10*, 298–329; see also J.-F. Hennart, 'International Financial Capital Transfers: A Transaction Cost Framework', *Business History*, 36 (Jan. 1994), 60–3.
57. *The Stock Exchange Yearbook* (1884–1911); Nicolau D'Olwer, 'Las inversiones extranjeras', 1064–8.
58. *The Stock Exchange Yearbook* (1884–1911); Nicolau D'Olwer, 'Las inversiones extranjeras', 1081–4; Tischendorf, *Great Britain*, 31–70.
59. Coatsworth, *Growth*, 45–6.
60. Tischendorf, *Great Britain*, 24; Nicolau D'Olwer, 'Las inversiones extranjeras', 988.
61. *The Stock Exchange Yearbook* (1884–1897).
62. R. Gibbs (ed.), *Dos siglos de cooperación México—Gran Bretaña* (Mexico City, 1983), 30; Tischendorf, *Great Britain*, 77–8.
63. *The Stock Exchange Yearbook* (1884–1911).
64. *The Stock Exchange Yearbook* (1893); *The Directory of Directors* (1893). Whittall & Co. was, or became, also involved as a British agency house in Malaya. See S. D. Chapman, *Merchant Enterprise in Britain* (Cambridge, 1992), 271.
65. The fourteen (in alphabetical order) were J. B. Body (Mexico); L. Camacho; Enrique Camacho-Guisasola (Mexico); Stanley Clay; J. W. DeKay; Pablo de Escandón (Mexico); Henry W. Forster, MP; C. G. Hyde, MP; L. Méndez; Edward Nettlefold; Sir Weetman D. Pearson, Bart., MP; Sir Robert J. Price, Kt., MP; Chandos S. Stanhope; F. G. Steuart; see *The Stock Exchange Yearbook* (1909–11); Skinner, *The Directory of Directors* (1909).
66. See also Armstrong and Nelles, *Southern Exposure*, 95–6; Tischendorf, *Great Britain*, 142.
67. On J. B. Body and Weetman D. Pearson's construction works and oil business interests in Mexico, see J. C. Brown, *Oil and Revolution in Mexico* (Berkeley, Calif., 1993), 49–51, 166; and D. Young, *Member for Mexico: A Biography of Weetman Pearson, First Viscount Cowdray* (London, 1966), 171, 189–91.
68. Ibid. 135.
69. *Dictionary of Business Biography* (London, 1985), iv. 582–94; Young, *Member for Mexico*, 135–6, 189.
70. Wilkins, 'The Free-Standing Company', 266.
71. This seems counter to the argument that a depreciating currency attracted new investment.
72. See Edelstein, *Overseas Investment*, 30.
73. Tischendorf, *Great Britain*, 21–3, 120–7, 141.
74. M. Wilkins, *The History of Foreign Investment in the United States to 1914* (Cambridge, Mass., 1989), 126–9, 237–46.

75. Stone, *The Composition*, 160–2; Hennart, 'International Financial Capital Transfers', 60–3.
76. Tischendorf, *Great Britain*, 27–8, 34, 126, 142–3; Armstrong and Nelles, 'A Curious Capital Flow', 194.
77. Tischendorf, *Great Britain*, 77–8, 90, 113–14, 142–3.
78. Ibid. 28–9, 77–94, 112–14, 126–7. See also R. W. Randall, *Real del Monte: A British Mining Venture in Mexico* (Austin, Tex., 1972), 213–19.
79. Nicolau D'Olwer, 'Las inversiones extranjeras', 973–7.
80. *The Stock Exchange Yearbook* (1884–1911).
81. Tischendorf, *Great Britain*, 29–30, 72, 92–4, 141; Pletcher, 'The Fall of Silver in Mexico', 40–55; Armstrong and Nelles, 'A Curious Capital Flow', 194–7.
82. Nicolau D'Olwer, 'Las inversiones extranjeras', 1168–85.
83. Meyer, *Su Majestad británica*, 18–25, 71–100.
84. See also Tischendorf, 'British Investments', 29, 37.
85. Randall, *Real del Monte*, 213–19.

10

A French Free-Standing Company in Brazil's Sugar Industry: A Case Study of the Société de Sucreries Brésiliennes, 1907–1922

Tamás Szmrecsányi

This chapter provides a preliminary review of the first fifteen years of the history of the Société de Sucreries Brésiliennes, a holding company of five sugar manufacturing enterprises owned by the same French economic group and, with the exception of one, all located in the state of São Paulo. The company, which remained in foreign hands until the late 1960s, was at the time considered one of the largest and best-organized firms within the Brazilian sugar industry. Its origins go back to the last decades of the nineteenth century, when Brazil's central government, still under the monarchy, attempted to establish the central sugar-milling system.

That system, based on a division of labour and on a separation of ownership and control between agriculture and manufacturing, was already prevailing in beet-sugar-producing countries and had been successfully introduced in several cane-sugar-producing regions of the world. In the case of Brazil, however, it did not take root. The failure of that attempt and the subsequent piecemeal and partial nature of the Brazilian sugar industry's modernization were undoubtedly among the main factors underlying the ease and rapidity of the French group's entry. But, the decisive reasons for the French group's investment lay elsewhere—namely, in the fast growth and increasing prosperity of Brazil's emerging internal market, which by the start of the twentieth century had already absorbed the greatest part of the country's sugar production. Brazil's growth and prosperity were, in turn, largely related to the fast and sustained expansion of the coffee export economy, concentrated in and around the states (former provinces) and cities of São Paulo and Rio de Janeiro, and, especially in the former, increasingly based on the free labour provided by European immigrants and their descendants.

From the mid-1870s to the end of the following decade, mainly owing to the fiscal and financial incentives of the Brazilian government, no less than eighty-seven central sugar factories (*engenhos centrais*) obtained official support for their installation and operation. Yet only a dozen or so were in operation at the beginning of the Republican regime (1889). One half or more of these were located in the states of São Paulo and Rio de Janeiro, despite the fact that the bulk of Brazil's sugar continued to come—as in colonial times—from the north-eastern region.[1] The four central mills authorized to function in the state of São Paulo, those of Porto Feliz (founded in 1878), Piracicaba and Lorena (both installed in 1881), and Villa Raffard (created in 1882), were, after several vicissitudes, sold between 1899 and 1901 to the French entrepreneurial group which would later found and control the Sucreries Brésiliennes.[2] The same occurred with the sugar mill of Cupim, which had been founded in 1881 near the city of Campos, in the state of Rio de Janeiro.[3]

At the time of their purchase by the French group, all of these sugar mills had ceased to be central mills, in the technical sense of the expression; they had become *usinas*, regular sugar mills with attached cane plantations, some of which were already quite large. Although most of the mills were still far from self-sufficient with regard to the supply of their raw material, each tried to reduce to a minimum its dependency on local, independent, sugar-cane growers. It was precisely for this reason that Cupim, shortly after its acquisition by the French group, took over the fields and industrial installations of the neighbouring mill of Tocos.[4] At least from that time on, increasing concentration of landownership became a well-known feature and objective of Brazilian sugar-milling companies.[5]

The French buyers of the five enterprises, even before the 1907 merger and consolidation into a holding company, were the same group of individuals and had their headquarters at the same address: 25 Boulevard Poissonière in the city of Paris.[6] The names which appeared as directors were: Maurice Allain, businessman domiciled at the aforementioned address; Fernand Doré, manufacturer in the city of Troyes; Lucien Mellier, *rentier* living in Paris; Edmond Steinheil, industrial engineer also resident in Paris; and Léon de Bertier de Sauvigny, proprietor in the same city. All these men would later continue, until their death or retirement, to figure in the Société's Board reports. To this list we may add, among others, Edmond Avisse, engineer and later director and vice-president at the Compagnie Fives-Lille (an important producer of sugar-mill machinery), Alfred Marsenet, an engineer, and Georges Hemmenier, a manufacturer.

How did these French men become interested in and come into the possession of these five Brazilian sugar mills? What were the economic and/or financial relationships of this group of persons with other firms and organizations within the French economy, or, eventually, within any other economy? The evidence that I have been able to gather to answer these questions is scant and impressionistic; definite answers will be arrived at only through archival research in France. Meanwhile, we shall have to satisfy ourselves with some plausible hypotheses. One of these, which I have been considering from the very beginning of my research, relates to the nationality of the mills' machinery. With the partial exception of Villa-Raffard, all of the mills were equipped with machines of French origin. Therefore, the suppliers might well have been, directly or indirectly, the main source of information and, perhaps, even the main source of incentives for the entrepreneurs' interest in acquiring the Brazilian mills. This hypothesis, up to now, has been supported only by a reference which I found in a 1969 secondary source, linking the Société de Sucreries Brésiliennes to the Compagnie Fives-Lille-Cail, one of the main manufacturers of equipment for sugar mills; to the Banque de Paris et des Pays Bas; and to one of the most important associates of the latter—the Banque Française et Italienne pour l'Amérique du Sud (better known internationally as SUDAMERIS).[7] Although this information has not been repeated or confirmed in more recent publications, either Brazilian or foreign,[8] I am inclined to retain my hypothesis, based on other evidence uncovered.[9]

There can be no doubt that the basic decisions with regard to the activities of the holding company and of its component sugar enterprises were made in Paris. The management in Brazil was mostly, if not exclusively, foreign expatriate personnel, particularly (but not exclusively) of French origin. These men reported directly to the headquarters in Paris, from where they received instructions and, whenever needed, financial advances and other production inputs (including, for example, spare parts and some chemicals). On all these aspects, the Société de Sucreries Brésiliennes (and its French-owned predecessors) conformed entirely to Mira Wilkins's model of the free-standing company.[10] The Société's main characteristics can easily be grasped by reading its Statutes of 1907 and the subsequent yearly reports of its administrative board (*conseil d'administration*) to its shareholders.

Before analysing the contents of these documents, it may be useful to stress that the Statutes were not the first or sole formal indication of the common ownership of the five sugar mills. Four years before the Statutes were enacted, the directors of the then 'separate' five enterprises sent an expert to Brazil, in order to assess the productive capability of their industrial installations and respective cane fields; the report of his visit was, at least to my knowledge, the first document to mention them all together.[11] This important report, which only now is being published (in Portuguese), is the best starting point for an in-depth study of the Société's evolution, something which transcends the scope and objectives of the present chapter.

Here we are concerned only with the Société's performance during the first fifteen years of its existence. We base our work on primary sources, which include the forenamed Statutes, their modification in 1918, and a series of yearly reports and accounts. Owing to the unavailability of the third of the latter (relative to the crop-year 1909/10), it was found useful to extend the period under observation by one year, to keep a total of fifteen accounts (see Tables 10.1 and 10.2).[12]

The Société de Sucreries Brésiliennes, although formally created in June 1907 as a new and specific entity,[13] had (as indicated above) already been functioning for several years in its component parts. The owners of these earlier companies remained and, in the period under review, the efficiency and profitability of those separate enterprises were expected to improve under their new and more coordinated central administration. This in fact occurred, as can be seen in the figures provided in the two tables.

These fifteen yearly accounts show that the Société's total assets grew much more and much faster than its liabilities: while the former more than doubled in ten years, increasing by 109 per cent, the latter grew only 58 per cent in the same period. This difference gave rise not only to sizeable and sometimes growing profits, but also to the expansion of financial assets *vis-à-vis* fixed capital. Current profits in 1917/18 were more than five times larger than those of ten years earlier, having increased by 433 per cent. Until 1915/16, depreciated fixed capital had always had a greater participation in the accounts than financial assets, but this changed radically and definitely from then on.

The growing availability of financial resources enabled the Société to contribute to France's military expenditures during and after the First World War, through the acquisition of sizeable amounts of *Bons de la Défense Nationale*. These French public securities appeared for the first time in the accounts of crop-year 1915/16, representing no less than 16.9 per cent of total assets, and increased almost continuously in value until the crop-year 1919/20, when they represented 24.9 per cent of total assets. The highest participation in these was reached in crop-years 1916/17 and 1917/18, when they amounted to 29.2 and 27.8 per cent of total assets respectively. During the 1920s they still appeared in the yearly accounts, although showing decreasing values and participation rates in total assets. The latter reached 17.2 per cent in crop-year 1920/1 and 8.5 per cent in 1922/3.

A good part of the sudden prosperity can be attributed to the effect of the First World War on sugar prices, whose increase in Brazil had no equivalent counterpart in the labour and other costs of producing that

TABLE 10.1. *Yearly accounts of the Société de Sucreries Brésiliennes, modalities of investments*

Crop-year	(1) Total assets (FF)	(2) Depreciated fixed capital[a] (%)	(3) Productive inventories[b] (%)	(4) Sugar and alcohol stocks (%)	(5) Financial assets[c] (%)	(6) Total liabilities (FF)	(7) Capital shares (%)	(8) Share-holders' bonds (%)	(9) Various creditors (%)	(10) Financial provisions[d] (%)
1907/8	12.319.399	71.8	4.5	4.7	19.0	10.645.067	65.8	21.5	12.7	—
1908/9	11.649.515	65.2	8.7	4.4	21.7	10.035.061	69.7	20.5	5.6	4.2
1910/11	11.504.857	68.0	8.3	4.7	19.0	10.426.395	67.1	17.0	6.3	9.6
1911/12	12.498.385	70.4	7.8	3.1	18.7	10.938.984	64.0	16.2	10.1	9.7
1912/13	12.205.628	53.2	9.7	7.0	30.1	10.304.308	67.9	16.7	4.4	11.0
1913/14	12.408.789	57.6	12.7	6.4	23.3	11.115.669	62.9	15.0	6.7	15.4
1914/15	13.241.932	63.1	7.5	7.7	21.7	11.516.666	60.8	13.9	2.9	22.4
1915/16	15.089.720	43.6	7.2	8.4	40.8	11.393.786	61.4	13.5	2.7	22.4
1916/17	18.975.746	27.2	7.6	3.7	61.5	11.765.950	59.5	—	4.0	36.5
1917/18	25.802.497	22.3	6.4	2.9	68.4	16.817.126	83.3	—	6.6	10.1
1918/19	24.789.807	28.8	9.1	2.7	59.4	19.086.357	73.3	—	3.1	23.6
1919/20	36.026.270	14.4	6.2	4.4	75.0	23.709.118	59.1	—	1.7	39.2
1920/1	36.365.245	14.3	13.5	10.2	62.0	25.433.104	55.0	—	3.3	41.7
1921/2	28.382.316	34.3	16.3	8.5	40.9	24.217.230	57.8	—	6.7	35.5
1922/3	30.134.770	29.0	9.5	4.3	57.2	23.144.112	60.5	—	2.3	37.2

[a] Land, installations and equipment, animals for traction.
[b] Inputs for processing, fuels, packing material, cultures on the fields.
[c] Cash, bills, deposits, bonds, foreign currencies, debtors, advancement to suppliers.
[d] Legal, extraordinary and special reserves, provisions for insurance against fire and accidents.
Source: See text.

TABLE 10.2. *Yearly accounts of the Société de Sucreries Brésiliennes, financial flows*

Crop-year	(1) Credits (FF)	(2) Sales (%)	(3) Stocks (%)	(4) Debit (FF)	(5) Costs[a] (%)	(6) Depreciation (%)	(7) Current Profits (FF)	(8) Carry-over (FF)	(9) Total profits on credits (%)	(10) Current profits on sales (%)
1907/8	9.075.836	93.2	6.3	7.401.504	71.3	22.8	1.674.331	—	18.4	19.8
1908/9	8.186.649	93.2	6.2	6.597.217	77.6	19.2	1.589.431	25.023	19.7	20.8
1910/11	7.283.870	92.5	7.5	6.275.058	95.1	2.6	1.008.812	69.650	14.8	15.0
1911/12	8.575.432	95.5	4.5	7.087.695	88.0	9.7	1.487.737	71.664	18.2	18.2
1912/13	10.964.288	92.2	7.8	9.138.980	75.5	22.2	1.825.308	76.012	17.3	18.1
1913/14	8.902.054	91.1	8.9	8.034.945	84.2	14.4	867.109	426.012	14.5	10.7
1914/15	6.953.721	85.2	14.8	5.654.467	94.6	3.6	1.299.255	426.012	24.8	21.9
1915/16	12.504.751	89.5	10.0	9.237.667	74.1	24.1	3.267.084	428.849	29.6	29.2
1916/17	16.600.096	93.7	4.3	9.531.006	79.4	19.4	7.069.089	140.707	43.4	45.4
1917/18	19.910.316	93.7	3.7	10.987.378	83.7	15.9	8.922.938	62.433	45.1	47.8
1918/19	14.444.587	90.7	4.4	9.305.910	88.7	10.7	5.138.677	554.772	39.5	39.2
1919/20	39.129.174	94.4	4.0	27.142.070	72.0	11.6	11.987.104	330.048	31.5	32.5
1920/1	30.026.892	85.6	12.2	19.342.637	86.5	12.2	10.684.255	247.886	36.4	41.6
1921/2	15.349.319	82.9	15.7	11.776.735	99.6	0.2	3.572.584	592.503	27.1	28.1
1922/3	25.957.267	94.3	5.0	19.158.808	80.2	19.7	6.798.459	192.199	26.9	27.8

[a] Raw material, maintenance, processing, and overhead.
Source: See text.

commodity. The values of both profits and financial assets began to rise dramatically only from the crop-year 1915/16 on. To be sure, the values in themselves are not the most significant aspect of the company's evolution; accounts in general were less in real terms, owing to wartime inflation and the devaluation of the French franc. Much more important in this respect were the yearly profit rates (which appear in the last two columns of Table 10.2) and the rates of participation of financial in total assets (fifth column of Table 10.1).

With regard to the former, we can see that the take-off began, not in 1915/16, but one crop-year earlier. The profit rates of the Société had been more than satisfactory from the very beginning of its activities, before the First World War averaging 17.1 per cent *vis-à-vis* both total credit and current sales. From the war on, however, there was a substantial rise in the level, which averaged 36.5 per cent in relation to total credit and 36.7 per cent in relation to current sales between 1914/15 and 1918/19, decreasing thereafter to 30.5 and to 32.5 per cent respectively.

The percentage of financial assets in total assets had also been quite sizeable from the very beginning of the Société's existence, averaging 21.9 per cent in the period between crop-years 1907/8 and 1914/15. The highest rate in that period (30.1 per cent) had been attained in 1912/13. But it was only in 1915/16 that these proportions changed drastically, reaching an overall average of 58.1 per cent during the subsequent eight crop-years. And in this case, no decrease occurred after the war was over; quite on the contrary, the average rate went up from 57.5 per cent between 1915/16 and 1918/19, and to 58.8 per cent thereafter.

At least in relation to these percentages, the company's new situation does not seem to have originated predominantly from the windfall gains during the war. And even in the case of the profit rates, the data fail to show a return to the pre-war situation. We are apparently confronted with an instance of structural change, rather than a mere cyclical fluctuation.

To what extent was the change due to the market (that is, to increased demand for and to higher prices of the product), or rather to improved productivity and the cost structure within the company itself? This is a question not only of historical, but also of theoretical interest. On the theoretical level, it was successfully addressed and solved almost forty years ago by Edith Penrose.[14] According to Penrose, for whom firms are historical entities and not merely theoretical constructs, changes in market conditions are external factors that influence both the speed and the direction of the firms' growth. Their importance, however, cannot be precisely assessed without a previous knowledge of the nature and the conditions of the firm itself. For this reason she was more interested in formulating an 'internal' theory of the growth of the firm, a theory unrelated to fortuitous external events.

One of her assumptions (confirmed by practice) is that all successful expansion tends to be preceded by planning, and that firms do not grow automatically, but rather in response to human decisions. Because of this, while there are always limits to the amounts of expansion that can be undertaken (or digested) at any given time, continuous expansion through time remains an open possibility. Firms are complex economic institutions; their growth through time, according to Penrose, can be thought of as having three components: (*a*) constant returns to scale in the long run, (*b*) the possibility of diversification, and (*c*) increasing costs of growth that apply to both diversification and up-scaling. One of these increasing costs is represented by the need to reinvest ever larger amounts of accumulated profit; in the long run, higher growth rates always require higher levels of retained profits.

To all this we may still add that the external inducements to a firm's expansion will never be put to good use if the firm in question is not 'ready' or has not been 'prepared' for it. Going back to the data in the tables, we can see that something of the sort seems to have happened with the Société de Sucreries Brésiliennes during the period under analysis. This company had a very low external indebtedness (column nine of Table 10.1) and practised a deliberate and systematic depreciation policy *vis-à-vis* its fixed capital (as can be observed in the second column of Table 10.1 and in the sixth column of Table 10.2), a policy which enabled it to accumulate, year after year, quite sizeable financial provisions (last column of Table 10.1) or reserves, of which some were effectively reinvested (also yearly) in productive facilities or fixed capital (mostly industrial equipment and installations).[15]

These reinvestments do not appear in the tables; nevertheless, they were always quite substantial, averaging 7.6 per cent of total assets in the five years before the First World War, 6.8 per cent during the war years, and 12.6 per cent at the beginning of the 1920s. They not only increased the company's productive capacity, but also (and more importantly) reduced its costs of production and/or improved considerably the productivity of its labour force and capital, especially in the manufacture of sugar and alcohol. Production of the latter from the molasses derived from the manufacturing of sugar was practically the only output diversification of the Société. As can be seen in the second and third columns of Table 10.2, sales and stocks of these two products were virtually the only sources of the company's annual revenues.

We need next to turn to the more qualitative information provided by the Statutes and the yearly reports to shareholders of the Société administrative board. According to the former, the new company, created in June 1907, resulted from the incorporation and consolidation of all the assets belonging to five sugar-producing enterprises already in operation: the S. A. Sucrerie de Villa Raffard, founded in February 1899; the S. A. Sucrerie de Piracicaba, created in March of that same year; the S. A. Sucrerie de Cupim, the only one located in the state of Rio de Janeiro, and founded in February 1900; the S. A. Sucrerie de Porto Feliz, created in January of the following year; and the S. A. Sucrerie de Lorena, founded in March 1901. The new holding company's capital was divided into 70,000 shares of 100 francs each; 69,500 of these were distributed to the shareholders of the former five enterprises, and 500 were new ones to be purchased by the main shareholders. The latter were to form a board of seven to eleven members entrusted with the administration of the Société.[16]

The company's yearly reports can be grouped, for analytical purposes, into three blocs comprising respectively: (*a*) those of the years before the First World War, (*b*) those of the war years, and (*c*) those of the early 1920s. The first period, with its six available reports out of seven, was the longest one and corresponded to the time of the organization of the new company's joint and centrally coordinated activities.[17] The second was the most lucrative and saw a doubling of the Société's registered capital.[18] Finally, the third marked the start of a further process of expansion and modernization of the Société's productive capacity.

Ordinary assemblies of shareholders were always held in October, having as their main task an appreciation statement, followed by a discussion and approval of the Board's and the Trustees' reports. These covered annual periods ending at 31 March each year. On the basis of them, decisions were taken with regard to the yearly dividends to be distributed, and on other administrative matters, including the election or re-election of the trustees and members of the Board.

During the early years of its activities, up to the First World War, the Société increased its cane-crushing and sugar-manufacturing capacities by 50 per cent. It was this increase in the scale of production through the acquisition of newer and more productive machinery, plus the beginning of large-scale alcohol production, that enabled the company to face with tranquillity a stiffening of competition and widely fluctuating prices on the São Paulo and Rio markets, as well as to maintain its yearly payments of dividends to the shareholders on an average level of 7 francs per share. The only problem in this regard occurred on the eve of the war; mainly because of Brazil's financial crisis, the dividends dropped to 5 francs per share in 1913/14, from a level of 10 francs in the previous crop-year.

This level, however, was again attained in 1914/15, doubling the following crop-year and going up to 25 francs per share in 1916/17. The war years were a golden age in terms of the Société's profitability. This was not only due to the higher prices then prevailing. The company's five mills also increased their joint cane-crushing and sugar production, respectively from average levels of 179,000 tons and 255,000 bags (of 60 kilos each) per year before the war to 220,000 tons and 284,000 bags in wartime. This increase was not larger because the averages for the war years were distorted by the bad crop of 1918/19 (owing to climatic conditions, whose effects persisted in the subsequent crop-year).

Dividends did not decrease in the post-war years, but grew again by 70 per cent in nominal terms. In this case, however, we have to take into account both the high sugar prices still prevailing at the beginning of the 1920s and the devaluation of the French franc. Nevertheless, precisely at that stage, taking advantage of its retained wartime profits, the Société was again involved in the augmentation and modernization of its equipment and installations. The company's production did not grow in those years, but its further expansion was already under way.

While our study—based on company accounts—goes only to 1922, the company continued on. During the mid- and late 1920s, however, a sugar-cane plant disease called *mosaico* reduced output considerably. Owing to the lack of profits, payment of dividends was temporarily interrupted. These difficulties were overcome in the early 1930s, when the production rose. But at that time, because of the Depression, demand and sugar prices were very low. The Lorena mill was closed down in 1933, with its machinery being distributed among the three other São Paulo mills. Simultaneously, the French company expanded its ethanol production for fuel. With this, profits returned, yet remittances to France remained difficult because of Brazil's balance-of-payments problems.

Until the end of the 1940s, the Société remained the premier sugar producer in the state of São Paulo.[19] From the early 1930s to the end of the 1940s, the joint production of its three mills there went up from a yearly average of 482.7 thousand bags (of 60 kilos each) to 829.5 thousand; this represented 28.2 per cent of the state's total production at the beginning of the 1930s, but only 14.1 per cent at the end of the 1940s. The output of its local competitors was increasing even faster. During the 1950s, the Société was reduced to third rank among *paulista* producers, with its participation decreasing from 9.3 to 7.3 per cent of total production, despite an increase in output from 1,027.5 to 1,477.3 thousand bags. And finally, in the 1960s, its production represented only 5 per cent of the state's total, with 1,539.8 thousand bags at the beginning of the decade and 1,689.9 thousand at the end. By that time, the company had become the fifth-ranking producer in the state. In

1969, its French owners sold its assets to the Silva Gordo group, which controlled the Banco Português do Brasil and which already owned three other sugar mills, two in São Paulo and one in the state of Goiás. This financial group soon went bankrupt, selling the Porto Feliz and Villa Raffard Mills to COPERSUCAR in 1973, and closing the Piracicaba mill two years later.

NOTES

1. A. P. Canabrava, 'A Grande Lavoura', in S. Buarque de Holanda and P. Moacyr Campos (eds.), *O Brasil Monarquico: 4. Declínio e Queda do Império*, vol. vi of the *História Geral da Civilização Brasileira* (São Paulo, 1971), 109.
2. These purchases were authorized by the Brazilian government through the following decrees: Piracicaba, no. 3330, 4 July 1899; Villa-Raffard, no. 3333 of the same date; Porto Feliz, no. 4090 of 22 July 1901; and Lorena, no. 4092 of the same date. The decrees give the initial capital of those firms, respectively, as FF 2.2m., 1.6m., 1.0m., and 1.5m.
3. The acquisition of the Cupim sugar mill was authorized by the decree no. 3663, 28 May 1900; the initial capital of the resulting new firm amounted to FF 1.25m. The foundation year of that mill is provided in G. Dé Carli, *A evolução do problema canavieiro fluminense* (Rio de Janeiro, 1942), 52.
4. The purchase of the Tocos mill, probably founded in the 1890s, appears in the report Sucreries de Piracicaba, Villa-Raffard, Porto Feliz, Lorena et Cupim, *Mission d'Inspection de Monsieur J. Picard, Ingénieur, du 1er Mars au 15 Juillet 1903* (Paris, Sept. 1903), 159–60. My access to this and to all other documents of the Sucreries has been provided by Dr Einar Alberto Kok, whose kind support of my research activities I herewith wish to acknowledge and thank.
5. T. Szmrecsányi, 'Growth and Crisis of the Brazilian Sugar Industry, 1914–1939', *Rivista di storia economica*, 5 (June 1988), 193–219, 268–70.
6. It was only one year after the formation of the holding company that these headquarters were moved to a new address. This place, however, seems to have been too small for sheltering the shareholders' assemblies. During the whole period under analysis, only one of these assemblies, held in October 1914, did take place there. See Société de Sucreries Brésiliennes (Sucreries de Villa-Raffard, Piracicaba, Cupim, Porto Feliz et Lorena réunies), Société Anonyme au capital de 7,000,000 de francs; Siège Social à Paris: 13 rue Henner et 17 rue Chaptal, *Assemblée Générale Ordinaire tenue le 26 Octobre 1909, à 3 heures de l'après-midi, à la Salle de la Société des Anciens Elèves des Ecoles d'Arts et Métiers: Rapport du Conseil d'Administration, Exercice 1908* (Paris, 1909).
7. See H. Claude, *Histoire, réalité et destin d'un monopole: La Banque des Pays Bas et son groupe, 1872–1968* (Paris, 1969), 29, 211–13.
8. See, for example, M. Marianno, *SUDAMERIS Brasil: 80 anos de trabalho* (São Paulo, 1991); E. Bussière, *PARIBAS: 1872–1992, Europe and the World* (Antwerp, 1992).
9. Thus, in 1913, the Société's retiring Board chairman Lucien Mellier was replaced by Alfred Allain, described as a 'member of the Board of important French sugar companies'. See Société de Sucreries Brésiliennes, *Assemblée Générale Ordinaire tenue le 28 Octobre 1913, à 2 heures et ½ de l'après-midi, à la Salle de la Société des Ingénieurs Civils de France: Rapport du Conseil d'Administration, Exercice 1912* (Paris, 1913), 4. In 1920 there was the substitution on the board,

post mortem, of Edmond Avisse by Albert Louppe, general-director of the Cie. Fives Lille. See Société de Sucreries Brésiliennes, *Assemblée Générale Ordinaire tenue le 26 Octobre 1921, à 14 heures et ½, à la Salle de la Société des Ingénieurs Civils de France: Rapport du Conseil d'Administration, Exercice 1920* (Paris, 1921), 5.

10. M. Wilkins, 'The Free-Standing Company, 1870–1914: An Important Type of British Foreign Direct Investment', *Economic History Review*, 2nd ser., 41 (May 1988), 259–82.
11. See n. 4 for the complete reference.
12. The computational systematization of the raw data for these tables was done by my former student and young colleague, Dr Nelson Prado Alves Pinto, to whom I wish to extend my gratitude. The responsibility for their aggregation and interpretation is all mine and, therefore, I am the only one to be blamed for any errors and mistakes.
13. Its operation in Brazil, with an initial capital of FF 7m., was authorized by the decree no. 6699, 24 Oct. 1907.
14. See E. T. Penrose, 'Limits to the Size and Growth of Firms', originally published in the *American Economic Review*, 45 (May 1955), 531–43, and reissued in E. T. Penrose, *The Growth of Firms, Middle East Oil and Other Essays* (London, 1971), 30–42; and more particularly chapters IV and V of her famous *The Theory of the Growth of the Firm* (Oxford, 1959) 43–87. See also the foreword by Martin Slater to the second edition (1980) of this book.
15. In the crop-years 1911/12, 1917/18, and 1918/19 the Société also made important acquisitions of cultivable land. Société de Sucreries Brésiliennes, *Assemblée Générale Ordinaire tenue le 25 Octobre 1912, à 2 heures et ½ de l'après-midi, à la Salle de La Société des Ingénieurs Civils de France: Rapport du Conseil d'Administration, Exercice 1917* (Paris, 1918), 4; Société de Sucreries Brésiliennes, *Assemblée Générale Ordinaire tenue le 14 Octobre 1919, à 2 heures et ½ de l'après-midi, à la Salle de La Société des Ingénieurs Civils de France: Rapport du Conseil d'Administration, Exercice 1918* (Paris, 1919), 4.
16. Société de Sucreries Brésiliennes, *Statuts* (Paris, 1907).
17. One of the first measures taken by the administration of the new company was the centralization in the city of São Paulo of all the Brazilian commercial and financial operations. Société de Sucreries Brésiliennes, *Assemblée Générale Ordinaire tenue le 11 Octobre 1918, à 2 heures et ½ de l'après-midi, à la Salle des Anciens Elèves des Ecoles d'Arts et Métiers: Rapport du Conseil d'Administration, Exercice 1907* (Paris, 1908), 4.
18. Société de Sucreries Brésiliennes, *Assemblée Générale Extraordinaire tenue le 22 Février 1918, à 10 heures et ½ du matin, à la Salle de la Société des Ingénieurs Civils de France: Rapport du Conseil d'Administration* (Paris, 1918).
19. The information on the Société after 1933 covers only the São Paulo mills and was extracted from an unpublished MA dissertation by Pedro Ramos, completed in 1983 at the School of Business Administration of the Fundação Getulio Vargas in São Paulo: 'Um estudo da evolução e da estrutura da agroindústria canavieira do Estado de São Paulo (1930–1982)', 72–92.

Part III

Countries that were Homes to Free-Standing Companies: General and by Sector

11

Dutch Free-Standing Companies, 1870–1940

Ben P. A. Gales and Keetie E. Sluyterman

Mira Wilkins coined the term 'free-standing company', identifying it as a typical mode of British direct investment abroad. Describing the British situation between 1870 and 1914, Wilkins concluded that free-standing companies were to be found as investors in many different countries and in such widely differing activities as agriculture, timber, cattle-raising, mining, oil production, manufacturing, transportation, public utilities, mortgage banking, and land development. In many instances, the free-standing company served as an alternative to the extension abroad of the British home-based operating companies. Free-standing companies were often part of networks of promoters, bankers, financiers, solicitors, accountants, engineers, politicians, and traders. These networks provided the services the home office could not give because of its smallness. Wilkins supposed that the mortality rate was high among the free-standing companies, because the headquarters and networks failed to provide the necessary financial and managerial services. For this reason, the British free-standing companies were inferior to US multinational companies.[1]

But what about free-standing companies with headquarters in other European countries? Did free-standing companies exist in the Netherlands? How important were they and where and in which industries did they operate? This chapter analyses the relationship between the Dutch free-standing companies and the Dutch business community between 1870 and 1940. In this relationship, there are several central questions. Who took the initiative to found free-standing companies and who provided the financial and managerial services?[2] Were free-standing companies indeed short-lived?

We would like to thank Mark Casson, Geoffrey Jones, Thomas Lindblad, August Veenendaal, and especially Mira Wilkins for their stimulating discussions on this subject.

A Quantitative Overview

How many free-standing companies were headquartered in the Netherlands on the eve of the First World War? Of all the Dutch companies listed in *Van Oss' Effectenboek*, the Dutch directory of companies quoted on the Amsterdam Stock Exchange, 184 would qualify as free-standing in 1913. However, there were many more unlisted free-standing companies. This group was traced with the help of *Mrs Van Nierop & Baak's Naamlooze Vennootschappen*. This source surveyed the formation of new companies with limited liability. Every other year, the authors gave a complete overview of the firms in existence. In this chapter, the edition of 1912 is used.[3] The advantage of *Van Nierop & Baak* is that it includes all Dutch limited-liability companies. It is therefore more complete than *Van Oss*. On the other hand, *Van Oss* gives more information on each listed company and that sample could be followed more easily through the years up to 1939.

In which sectors and countries did the Dutch free-standing companies operate? Table 11.1 gives a breakdown of the Dutch free-standing companies listed by *Van Oss*. Nearly 60 per cent were active in the field of tropical agriculture (sugar, coffee, tea, tobacco, rubber). Other activities were mining, oil exploration and exploitation, mortgage banking, and tramways. The vast majority of the listed free-standing companies operated in colonial Indonesia (Netherlands East Indies). In 1913, 76 per cent of the Dutch free-standing companies worked there, and in 1937, 86 per cent.[4]

The larger number in *Van Nierop & Baak* allows a more detailed breakdown. Table 11.2 is based on total assets of 846 companies.[5] The book value of the 846 companies amounted to 1,225 million guilders, while the assets of the 184 companies listed in *Van Oss* was 895 million guilders. (Before the First World War the exchange rate was roughly 12.10 guilders to the pound and 2.44 guilders to the dollar.) The smaller

TABLE 11.1. *Classification of Dutch-listed free-standing companies, by activity and region, 1913* (in numbers)

Sector	Netherlands East Indies	Other countries	Total
Tropical agriculture	100	5	105
Mining	6	6	12
Oil	7	4	11
Rail- and tramways	15	—	15
Industry	7	2	9
Mortgage banks	—	25	25
Banks	5	2	7
TOTAL	140	44	184

Source: *Van Oss' Effectenboek* (1915/16).

TABLE 11.2. *Classification of Dutch free-standing companies, by activity and region, 1912* (share of total assets in percentages)

Sector	Netherlands East Indies	Netherlands West Indies	Europe	North America	South America, Asia, Africa	Other	All
Agriculture, incl. sugar mills	37	1	0	2	0	0	40
Mining	7	1	2	1	0	1	12
Oil	3	0	1	1	0	0	5
Industry, construction, utilities	2	0	1	0	0	0	3
Infrastructure	14	0	0	0	0	0	14
Banking, insurance	1.5	0.5	0	0	1	0	3
Mortgage banks	0	0	0.5	9.5	2	0	12
Shipping	3	0	0	0	0	0	3
Trade, other	6	0	0.5	0	0	0.5	7
ALL	73.5	2	5	13.5	3	1.5	99

Note: The sample comprised the book value of the assets of 846 companies. Numbers do not add up to 100 per cent because of rounding.
Source: *Mrs Van Nierop & Baak's Naamlooze Vennootschappen* (1912).

Van Oss sample thus included the larger and more important free-standing companies.

Table 11.2 also demonstrates the high concentration of the activities of the Dutch free-standing companies. Agriculture dominates again with 40 per cent. The structure is roughly similar to the one in Table 11.1 in other respects as well. Even though the Royal Dutch was left out of the sample, mining and oil amounted to about one fifth. Infrastructure (mainly tramways) and mortgage banks remain important groups. The widening scope did not diminish the importance of colonial Indonesia.[6] At the time, foreign observers already pointed out the 'extraordinary large sums' invested by the Dutch in their East Indies.[7] (The other Dutch colonies were host to only a few Dutch free-standing companies.) Comparisons justify their amazement. By 1910, a recent estimate suggests that Belgium had invested less than one-tenth of its foreign direct investment in Africa, while all non-European countries together received 40 per cent of Belgian foreign direct investment.[8] The British Empire—according to one source—attracted 56 per cent of all British foreign direct investment. In this context, the Dutch figure is truly striking.[9]

From the perspective of the home economy, free-standing companies were a phenomenon concentrated within a few sectors. This is clearly demonstrated by Table 11.3. In agriculture, mining, oil, and mortgage banking, free-standing companies constituted a substantial portion of all Dutch limited-liability companies. The total of 846 in 1912 was only 9 per cent of all such companies in existence in that year. Numbers of companies, however, are a poor indicator. The institutions designed to

TABLE 11.3. *The importance of free-standing companies relative to all Dutch limited-liability companies, by sector, 1912*

Sector	(1) Free-standing companies (number)	(2) All limited liability companies (number)	(3) Col. 1 as share of col. 2 (%)
Land reclamation	0	11	0
Agriculture, estates, fishing	425	730	58
Sugar	19	41	46
Mining	67	90	74
Oil	40	46	87
Industry	41	1,502	3
Construction	11	2,067	1
Utilities	5	79	6
Infrastructure, transport	21	246	9
Banking, administration, insurance	42	673	5
Mortgage banking	23	92	25
Trade	29	1,014	3
Shipping	100	1,823	5
Other	23	943	2
TOTAL	846	9,357	9

Source: *Van Nierop & Baak* (1912).

operate abroad were capital intensive. According to the official *Statistiek der Rijksinkomsten*, capital paid in by all companies registered in the Netherlands came to 1,900 million guilders. Capital of the companies in our sample was 627 million guilders.[10] The share, therefore, was nearly one-third.

How important was investment in free-standing companies in comparison to total Dutch foreign direct investment? In a previous publication, we estimated total Dutch foreign direct investment at almost 2,300 million guilders in 1914, of which 1,680 million was invested in the East Indies and 329 million in the USA.[11] These estimates can serve as a rough point of reference. The estimated total assets of free-standing companies in 1912 was 1,225 million guilders. Presumably about half of all Dutch foreign direct investment was free-standing. One cannot attribute the other half to multinationals or companies working within several parts of the Empire. Most of the remainder consisted of investment by companies registered in the East Indies and managed by expatriates.

Is Investment in the Colonies Foreign Investment or Not?

It has become British custom to treat colonial and foreign investment on a par. In his recent study on multinationals from small countries, Harm Schröter excluded all investment in colonies, because the colonies had the same legal system, currency, and official language as their

European mother countries. In his analysis of non-colonial business, Schröter found that the 'nearby-factor' was strong. Multinationals preferred markets that were both geographically and mentally close to the home market. How nearby then were the colonies?[12] Schröter probably would agree that to start a business overseas in completely different surroundings required a far greater entrepreneurial effort than to open another production unit a few miles across the national border. He, however, might argue that the Dutch had nevertheless significant advantages relative to non-Dutch subjects. Colonies were distant, but more familiar territories for some than others.

Was entry into Dutch East Indian markets relatively easy for Dutch entrepreneurs? Mental nearness of the colonies is difficult to assess, but institutional nearness is easier. In this respect, the differences between the Netherlands and its colonies were large. Mining is an illuminating case. The national character of the mining industries became a widespread preoccupation of European governments during the last quarter of the nineteenth century. One might, therefore, expect that in this sector nationals had the largest institutionally guaranteed competitive advantage or that the barriers for foreigners were largest.

Mining in the Netherlands itself was regulated by the Napoleonic mining law of 1810. In the East Indies, the Royal Decrees of 1873 were in force; they were replaced by a special Indian mining law, which passed parliament in 1899. In the West Indies, mining became regulated only on the eve of the First World War. Crucial principles of the colonial regulations were often the opposite of those in Dutch law. The historical evolution was for some time different as well. In the 1890s the prescribed registration of new companies in the Kingdom was abandoned in the East Indies; in Surinam only nationals could acquire new concessions for gold-mining after 1902.

Neither the legal framework nor more informal policy discriminating against foreigners was a major handicap. Businessmen would not hesitate long to transfer control to the Hottentots if that would increase security and dividends, as Robert Waley Cohen of Shell declared when the 'Britishness' of that company was under discussion.[13] So-called 'transfer investments' were a cheap alternative. Some French or Belgian entrepreneurs decided to transfer investments to the Dutch colonies, through a firm registered in the Netherlands, but they did not give up control. Some of the free-standing companies in our sample were part of the business empire of Adrien Hallet, the pioneer of palm-oil cultivation in the East and renowned for his Belgian firm's elaborate supervisory service to the plantation companies in the tropics. In other companies, French and Belgian investors were only involved passively.[14] We did not try to identify transfer investments.[15]

Neither law nor currency nor language were endowments which conveyed substantial competitive advantages specifically to citizens during the last quarter of the nineteenth and the first decades of the twentieth centuries. According to James Foreman-Peck, 'there is little evidence of the exclusion of one European country's traders from another's colonies'.[16] That was also true for investors. Nevertheless, we decided to treat the companies operating in the colonies as a special category in order to make our analysis transparent.

The Founding of Free-Standing Companies

The great majority of the listed Dutch free-standing companies operated in colonial Indonesia. They aimed to profit from the natural richness of Indonesia. Private foreign investment was closely linked to the spectacular expansion of export-oriented production, which took place in the Indonesian archipelago. The real value of exported agricultural produce and oil grew annually by 4.3 per cent between 1880 and 1900, while the gross value added by estates grew by 5.2 per cent. Between 1900 and 1913 the rate of growth declined somewhat, exports to 3.8 per cent annually, gross value added to 4.3. Between 1913 and 1929 growth figures increased to 5.7 per cent for exports and 5.4 for the estates. During the following decade, the depression notwithstanding, exports still grew, 0.22 per cent, but the value added by the estates declined to 0.7 per cent average per annum. In exports, the emphasis shifted from traditional commodities such as sugar, coffee, and tobacco, to new products such as rubber, oil, and copra.[17]

When one considers the founding of individual free-standing companies in colonial Indonesia, two principal patterns emerge. Traders, colonial officers, or planters already working in the colony discerned promising new opportunities to grow coffee, tea, or tobacco, or to exploit a mine or oilfield. Sometimes they made a beginning by acquiring land or a licence. For real headway, however, their financial means were often inadequate. Therefore, they applied to the home country for money. A Dutch association or limited company was founded to raise capital. If the official headquarters of the new company was located in a Dutch city, a free-standing company was born. Oil companies and some mining companies especially followed this course, but so did the tobacco company Deli-Batavia Maatschappij.[18] Royal Dutch had such a start. A. J. Zijlker, who went to the Dutch East Indies as a tobacco planter, realized the possibilities of petroleum production over there. A beginning was made with small-scale exploration in 1884. When the results proved promising, the production of crude oil was undertaken. To obtain money, a Dutch registered limited company, Royal Dutch, was floated in 1890; it succeeded in raising the necessary capital in the Amsterdam capital market.[19] Royal Dutch had no operations in the Netherlands until 1902 and was therefore in its origin a free-standing company.

A second pattern was that firms already in existence—for instance, sugar factories or tea plantations—needed more capital. Their owners/managers would participate in founding a limited company to take over the existing plantation or factory. As the money came from the Netherlands, the official headquarters was often changed from colonial Indonesia to the Netherlands, much to the chagrin of the people working in Indonesia.[20] Not only individuals, but existing free-standing companies might take the initiative to found a new free-standing company. The tramway company Samarang-Joana Stoomtram-Maatschappij set up three more independent tramway companies, headquartered in the Netherlands but operating in Java. The four companies had the same board of directors, but were financially independent.[21] Investment in railways, tramways, and utilities was to a large extent associated with investment in primary products. Therefore, the larger free-standing companies in agriculture and mining were also active in promoting investment in infrastructure. What all above-mentioned patterns have in common is the fact that the decision to set up a free-standing company was made in the host country.

In only a minority of cases, the initiative for founding a free-standing company lay in the Netherlands. This was true of the Tabakmaatschappij Arendsburg, which was founded by the Rotterdam wholesale trader in tobacco and cigars, P. van den Arend, who was interested in the cultivation of tobacco as a separate source of profit. Even if the tobacco would turn out to be unsuited for the Rotterdam tobacco market and had to be sold somewhere else, he was still interested in starting a plantation in Java or Deli. His firm became the pioneer in the cultivation of the Deli tobacco, later made into a success by the Deli Maatschappij.[22] Rubber estates, which were set up in the twentieth century, were mostly initiated from outside the Netherlands East Indies, but often also from outside the Netherlands.[23]

The Dutch colony Surinam hosted only a handful of Dutch free-standing companies; most were agricultural, and a few specialized in forestry and mining. Surinam had long ceased to attract much interest from Dutch non-resident investors. The abolition of slavery in 1863 only accelerated the decline of the cotton, coffee, cocoa, and mainly the sugar estates set up in decades before. There was a gradual shift from large estates to small farms; the share of the latter increased dramatically after 1910. At the margin of these export crops, small entrepreneurs operated more profitably than large agricultural companies. In gold-mining the same was true. Likewise in the Caribbean West Indies, exporting estates were local companies. Outside capital was involved only in phosphate-mining, hemp, and the breeding of ostriches, but ambitions, grand designs, and capital did not guarantee success.[24]

The non-colonial free-standing companies were clustered both geographically and in terms of activity. Agriculture, mining and oil extraction, and banking were the three clusters of viable activities. In all three the USA was the most important host country. Agricultural companies were partially similar to the colonial estates (albeit not in tropical products), but there were also firms specializing in the purchase and sale of land frequently connected either with mortgage activities or mining.

Since the American Revolution, Dutch capitalists had shown a great interest in portfolio investments in that country. In the nineteenth century, Dutch money found its way into state loans, railway securities, and mortgage banks. In the twentieth century, the USA also became the object of direct investment by multinational companies. One might expect that the Dutch also founded many free-standing companies operating there. However, their number was relatively small, especially in comparison with the huge opportunities provided by this country. A huge Dutch investment went into the Maxwell Land Grant Company, headquartered in Amsterdam and set up officially in 1880 to reorganize the Maxwell Land Grant & Railway Company, established in the USA in 1867 and declared bankrupt in 1877. From the Dutch perspective, the Maxwell was mainly a financial venture, a long-lasting attempt to minimize losses.[25] A. J. Veenendaal, the authority on Dutch investment in American railways,[26] concludes that the large Dutch interest in railways was an almost perfect example of portfolio investment. Only in the case of the Kansas City, Pittsburgh & Gulf Railroad in East Texas was the Dutch participation more marked.[27]

The Dutch connection with railways in Texas led to the founding of three Dutch free-standing companies in the oil industry. The Dutch journalist and stockbroker, S. F. van Oss, was a great promoter of American railway securities, among them the Kansas City, Pittsburgh & Gulf Railroad and the less successful Oklahoma Central Railway. Through his connections there he heard about the Oklahoma oilfields. Together with the brothers E. and H. Deen and D. A. J. Kessler,[28] he set up three free-standing companies, headquartered in The Hague: the Oklahoma Petroleum Compagnie (1907), the Union Petroleum Compagnie (1909), and the Tulsa Petroleum Compagnie (1909).[29] Kessler and the Deen brothers had been active in the oil business in colonial Indonesia. After having acquired several existing companies and new leases, they started negotiations to sell their US properties in 1910, as they were not prepared to put up more money for further exploration and exploitation. Royal Dutch Shell was not interested, but a combination of French financiers took over the three free-standing companies in 1911 and founded the Union des Pétroles d'Oklahoma, with headquarters in Paris.[30]

The third cluster of activities in non-colonial free-standing companies consisted of those in mortgage banking. The roots of international activities in this field went back to 1861. During the last decades of the nineteenth century the number of national mortgage banks increased, reaching a peak after the turn of the century. The peak of the banks going abroad came just before the beginning of the First World War. In 1912 the mortgages owned by the twenty-three banks operating abroad had a value of 104 million guilders. That was a substantial amount. The portfolio of the sixty banks which operated within the Netherlands was worth 430 million guilders. As Table 11.2 shows, the USA and Canada were the major foreign markets. As of year-end 1913, the mortgage bonds outstanding of thirteen Dutch free-standing mortgage banks in the USA came to 73 million guilders.[31]

The first initiative to found the mortgage banks doing business in America lay in the USA and not in the Netherlands. The Holland Texas Hypotheekbank was closely linked with Dutch investment in the Kansas City, Pittsburgh & Gulf Railroad and its connected construction companies. The Dutch investors showed a marked interest in the state of Washington, especially Spokane, where no less than five free-standing mortgage banks worked on the eve of the First World War. A small Dutch community lived in and around Spokane. In the wake of the banks, some industrial free-standing companies emerged: the Houtzaagmolen Phoenix founded in 1898 and the Spokane Meelmolens of 1903, both operating in Spokane and based in Amsterdam. In both cases the initiative to set up the company lay with Dutchmen already in America. But, overall, with the mortgage banks the links with immigration were weak and non-banking free-standing initiative was not stimulated.[32] The Dutch banks were mainly in the American West, which had relatively high interest rates. The American West was, however, not a captive market. Competition among mortgage banks and life-insurance companies supplying savings from the American Northeast had become intense by the late 1880s. Capital there was more expensive than in Amsterdam, but not much more. After a wave of failures in the early 1890s, many US mortgage companies collapsed. Under these conditions, there was a niche for the international mortgage companies, which mobilized the savings of foreign investors accustomed to this type of banking and with a different perception of risk.[33]

This short survey on the founding of free-standing companies shows that the initiative lay frequently in the host countries. In this respect, free-standing companies were different from multinational companies from the very beginning, because for the latter the decision to establish foreign subsidiaries was nearly always taken in the home country.

Which Sectors in the Dutch Economy were Involved in Free-Standing Companies?

As we learnt from Table 11.3, the Dutch free-standing companies were no reflection of Dutch business in general, but were concentrated in agriculture, mining, and oil. Why then did people setting up free-standing companies turn to the Netherlands? This question may be approached in two ways: by unravelling the personal networks and by analysing the flow of resources (goods, services).

Jan Korsten looked at the networks linking directors and managing directors of about 200 listed free-standing companies between the years 1920 and 1928, mainly in colonial Indonesia.[34] He found that in the first place the free-standing companies provided each other with directors. There was some specialization. The managing director of one tobacco company would often be a director of several other tobacco companies. The same held true for sugar factories and oil companies. There was also a regional specialization. The managing director of the Deli Company, growing tobacco, was director of a Deli rubber plantation and a Deli railway company.

Financial institutions formed the second group of interested parties. Often bankers, stockbrokers, merchant bankers, and trustees sat on the board of free-standing companies, representing the interests of the moneylenders. Their involvement with free-standing companies was sometimes forced by circumstances, when a firm could not pay back large sums of money advanced on crops. Generally, their participation in free-standing companies was not very different from their role in providing short-term credit or portfolio investment.

The third group, partly interwoven with the second, was the large trading houses and the so-called 'culture banks', peculiar colonial Indonesian institutions specializing in agricultural finance and administration. Their interest in free-standing companies was two sided. First, they often gave advances on a crop and, secondly, they handled the marketing of the same crop. Their interest in free-standing companies can be seen as a way of integrating backwards. These trading houses and culture banks come nearest to the modern multinational company. One house, Handelsvereeniging Amsterdam (Trading Society Amsterdam), even ended its trading activities and concentrated solely on the management of agricultural companies. Most of latter were once expatriate or separate free-standing companies, but became now part of one big free-standing company. Smaller trading houses, such as the Amsterdam firm H. G. Crone and the Rotterdam firm A. van Hoboken & Co., specialized in administering free-standing companies and marketing their products.[35]

A few politicians had seats on the boards of free-standing companies, but there is little evidence that 'ornamental' persons figured largely on these boards, in contrast to what seems to have been the case in Britain. While most free-standing companies were headquartered in the large Dutch cities of Amsterdam, Rotterdam, and The Hague, several mortgage banks operating in the USA were headquartered in rural Dutch towns. This may be an indication that the investors were Dutch landowners with faith in the agrarian development of the USA or that the investors knew of opportunities from family members who had emigrated to America.

The absent party was the Dutch industrial companies. Almost no managing directors of Dutch industrial companies were represented on the boards of the free-standing companies. The absence is interesting. A recent analysis of the Dutch economic and financial élite at the end of the nineteenth century revealed that traders were the most prominent group, followed by bankers. Industrialists had a rather marginal position in the Dutch élite.[36] It seems that the situation remained the same throughout the 1920s as far as international business in the colonies was concerned.

To understand fully the lack of integration of the Dutch industrial companies in the network of free-standing companies, it is useful to study the flow of goods and services. The most important Dutch free-standing companies in the USA were concerned with financial transactions (mortgage banking), and it is understandable that only the financial sector in the Netherlands was involved. More amazing is the lack of integration of the Dutch industrial companies in the colonial Indonesian network. Which firms could have had a potential advantage from a linkage with Indonesia? And which firms could have used the relationship with a free-standing company as an alternative to vertical integration?

The sugar refineries in Amsterdam might have been interested in sugar production in the colonies. However, cane sugar from the colonies had to compete with European beet sugar. As beet-sugar production was protected in most European countries, the competition was very unequal. Moreover, the transportation costs were prohibitive for colonial crude cane sugar; it was cheaper to buy crude beet sugar in Europe. The largest Dutch sugar refinery, Wester Suikerraffinaderij, did indeed follow a policy of integrating backwards, but opted for Dutch beet-sugar factories and showed no interest in colonial mills.[37]

The Dutch cigar-making factories used large quantities of Java and Sumatra tobacco. Yet, there was no more than an occasional or incidental link between Dutch cigar factories and tobacco cultivation in the colony or somewhere else.[38] The explanation is quite simple: the Dutch cigar-making firms were too small to integrate backwards. One of the largest and most well-known (at that time) Dutch cigar manufacturers, Ribbius Peletier, had a share capital of only *f* 700,000 in 1913, while the largest tobacco growing company in Indonesia, Deli Maatschappij, had a share capital of *f* 9,000,000.[39] The size of the cigar-making firms had another consequence. The cigar factories needed a mix of tobacco from various countries, not only Java and Sumatra, but also from South America. Even large firms could never take all tobacco produced by a single tobacco-growing company. It was more efficient to wait for the tobacco to be brought to the Amsterdam tobacco market, where the cigar manufacturers could make their choice from tobacco from different countries and companies. It was logical that the manufacturers were not involved with tobacco-growing in the colonies, while the trading companies were.[40]

The Dutch plated tin-can manufacturers might have been interested in the exploitation of tin mines. However, they preferred to import tin plate from Germany instead of processing tin ore.[41] During the First World War, international markets became disturbed, which was the most important reason why Jurgens tried to obtain a foothold in the Indonesian copra oil industry. As we will see further on, this policy was not successful and was abandoned after the post-war boom had ended. There were no Dutch tyre-makers and thus none integrated backwards into rubber plantations.

In conclusion, it is apparent that Dutch industrial companies had little inclination to dominate, much less to monopolize, the products of colonial Indonesia. The Royal Dutch seems an exception. That company, however, was at origin not a Dutch 'industrial company'. It had no operations in the Netherlands until 1902 and its trade was global. Our results coincide with those of Thomas Lindblad. Studying the relationship between the Netherlands and colonial Indonesia, he concludes that the growth of exports from colonial Indonesia was not accompanied by an increase in trade between the colony and the mother country; quite the contrary: less mutual trade was accompanied by more investment.[42] Wilkins's conclusion—that in many instances the free-standing company served as an alternative to the extension of the British home-based operating enterprises abroad—is certainly not true for the Dutch case as far as industry was concerned. Dutch trading houses, banks, and brokers, however, were closely connected with the network of free-standing companies.[43] What had these sectors to offer the free-standing companies and how essential was their contribution?

Financial Services

J.-F. Hennart recently revived an explanation of enterprise across borders concentrating upon international flows of capital. He uses a transactional framework to explain the specific nature of flows of capital to regions with underdeveloped capital markets.[44] Hennart discerns two dimensions, which create four options: first, the capital transfers might be intermediated or not, and, second, capital might be transferred through price or through hierarchical mechanisms. Investors and savers might deal directly or through intermediaries. Banks making loans to foreigners intermediate, as do firms taking equity in foreign firms. The former is a contractual, the latter a hierarchical coordination of savers and borrowers. Loans or bonds are considered price or contractual modes of transfer in contrast to equity, the hierarchical mode. A free-standing company is one possibility out of these four: it is a hierarchical, but not intermediated transfer of capital. Free-standing companies are in fact 'foreigners' selling stocks to the public.

Equity and therefore hierarchical relations are chosen if the costs of information and enforcement are high. High risks do not allow the use of collateral instead of equity. That is one aspect which explains why foreigners might sell stocks, thus set up free-standing companies, and cannot attract capital through bonds or loans or through intermediation. The absence of intermediation is a function of the projects for which capital is demanded. In Hennart's view, free-standing companies are used to finance highly risky, but small-scale ventures with standard technology. New technology will stimulate intermediation. International bank lending is preferred to finance large-scale, complex projects offering good collateral.

Multinationals will arise if it pays to internalize particular markets, technical or managerial know-how, services in distribution or marketing, and reputation—all the intangible assets associated with market failure, which explains the advantage of placing similar plants under common administrative control. Vertical integration is usually seen as internalization of markets for raw materials or intermediate products where investments are specific and switching costs high. In contrast to classic multinationals, free-standing firms would internalize only one market, the capital market. In short, free-standing firms arose to bypass international capital markets and reduce transaction costs by hierarchical coordination.[45]

There is something to be said for Hennart's argument that free-standing companies were a capital market phenomenon. Free-standing companies were relatively capital intensive. From the perspective of the colonial economy and thus the 'foreign' borrower, the free-standing company was an option, but not the only one. Sugar mills or rubber plantations might be organized as either free-standing or genuine colonial companies. In either case they operated within the same markets. Generally, companies registered in the Netherlands, but operating in the Indies, were only a small percentage of the companies registered in the Indies and working there. Furthermore, the share of the former decreased over time, as can be seen from Table 11.4.[46] However, capital issued by individual free-standing companies was on the average substantially larger than capital issued by the Indonesian companies. Registration in the mother country was preferred if links with the capital market were important.

The Hennart model is not easily reconciled with the common consensus on the colonial economy, although his model was devised with rubber plantations or tin-mining and smelting firms expressly in mind. His choice of dimensions in particular causes problems. Dutch free-standing companies in the Dutch East Indies were concentrated within agriculture or mining. Most contemporaries would agree that these investments were relatively risky. It seems, however, odd to qualify plantations and oil or mining companies as small-scale ventures with standard technology.

The major problem, however, lies in his views on the nature of the capital market. Hennart suggests that free-standing companies were 'foreigners' who, so to speak, raided the European capital markets once, at the beginning of their venture. In principle, a firm was set up

TABLE 11.4. *New companies starting operations in the Netherlands East Indies, 1885–1925*

Year	Registered in the Netherlands		Registered in the Netherlands East Indies	
	Share of all new companies (%)	Capital issued per firm (*f* 1,000)	Share of all new companies (%)	Capital issued per firm (*f* 1,000)
1885	36	970	64	320
1890	48	600	52	214
1895	42	548	58	187
1900	27	477	73	155
1905	21	787	79	99
1910	19	582	81	182
1915	13	402	87	160
1920	4	471	96	217
1925	11	349	89	157

Note: Year is a five-year average.
Source: W. L. Korthals Altes, 'De betalingsbalans van Nederlandsch-Indië 1822–1939', diss. (Rotterdam, 1986), table 6.

for a single project. The sale of equity was a mechanism to create reputation; shares, after all, give 'lenders' a general right to direct the behaviour of 'borrowers'.[47] These elements are crucial in Hennart's characterization because they explain why free-standing companies were not intermediated capital transfers. Intermediation by banks or similar institutions is likely if there is a mismatch between the average size of savings and investments at home and abroad. The same is likely if, because of the technology involved or market conditions, a lot of information is required, which furthermore is continuously changing. The absence of intermediation or of non-hierarchical coordination is difficult to explain if borrowers turn to a capital market regularly or if overseas projects are not unique, but integrated with others overseas. Colonial free-standing companies, however, were not small scale; they needed information, and they did not turn to mother-country capital markets only once.

Plantations, by far the most important part of Dutch overseas investment, had to be embedded in a financial network, and transfers to them were and remained to a large extent intermediated. The culture banks and the trading houses, providing credit, had a central position in the network of both the plantations, trading houses, and so forth registered in the Indies and those plantations and trading houses operating as Dutch free-standing companies. Free-standing companies did not substitute for such a network; instead they were an integral part of it. Both colonial and free-standing companies required short-term credit and long-term capital on a regular basis. The relations between plantations and trading houses or culture banks were continuously cemented by the use of registered pledges on crops, a revolving type of credit. In 1914, probably 60 per cent of the Indonesian estates had issued bonds besides equity. Plantations as a whole or parts were bought and sold regularly. The position of the intermediaries changed over time. From the 1880s, banks and trading houses assuming banking functions became involved more deeply in the agricultural sector. Gradually, they usurped management functions. Intermediaries became responsible for the administration of legally independent companies or became owners. One, therefore, cannot say that within the colonial context free-standing companies were not intermediated capital transfers.

Problematic too is Hennart's proposition that free-standing companies operated where there were underdeveloped capital markets. At least, he argues, that is the reason why they disappeared in the USA by the 1920s, but survived in Malaya until the 1960s. What, however, is an underdeveloped capital market? It is not obvious that international markets were particularly imperfect around 1900. Institutionally, the Indonesian capital market differed radically from the Dutch one;

demand and supply conditions were different too. But underdevelopment implies substantial market imperfections. Such imperfections should show up in interest-rate differentials. Greater riskiness would, however, increase interest rates as well. The interest rates in colonial Indonesia were substantially above the Dutch or American ones. The differential, however, continuously declined. In the first decade of the twentieth century, Indonesian interest rates came close to the Dutch level and more capital was raised locally than in Europe. One might argue that, before the first decade of the twentieth century, free-standing companies were a means to repair international capital-market imperfections, and, in time, in the same way as commercial-paper houses and mortgage companies integrated the regions within the USA, they served to integrate international capital markets. At best, however, free-standing companies were bypasses needed for relatively large investments. The need for such bypasses of the capital markets disappeared soon after the turn of the century. The ratio of new free-standing companies declined, as new establishments in Indonesia accelerated. The colonial economy became more Indonesian. In 1898 there were 1,075 corporations operating there: 423 companies (or 39 per cent) had a seat in the Netherlands and had shared the colonial economy with 622 corporations with a colonial base and thirty with their residence elsewhere. In 1913, there were 2,708 corporations doing business in the East Indies, of which 1,909 were colonial corporations, 632 (or 23 per cent) had a Dutch mother economy seat, and 167 were rest-of-the-world-based ones.[48]

The structure which embedded the free-standing companies itself started to change. The network became looser; hierarchy became less important, intermediation became restricted to the beginning of operations, and European investment became more of the portfolio type. The contrast between rubber-growing and the older cultures is illuminating.[49] Contemporary observers were fascinated by what they called the English rubber trusts, London-based companies backed by the great merchant houses of Singapore or managing agencies. British trusts such as the Java Investment Loan & Agency Limited or the Rubber Plantations Investment Trust were active in colonial Indonesia. These trusts prepared, promoted, and financed the start of rubber-growing companies; they were a mechanism to transfer agricultural know-how. Usually, the trusts relinquished control after some time and kept only a small part of equity, in contrast to what had happened in other crops. Rubber trusts did not exist within the Netherlands, but so called culture syndicates had a similar function. Most had a Dutch base, even though an Indonesian managing house was at the centre of one group.

Although investment groups became less important when rubber-growing matured and although investments of these groups soon had a portfolio character, loose groups kept some advantages. The links within existing networks were specific and the bonds were lasting. British trusts confined themselves to Indonesian estates that were a British initiative and did not broaden their portfolio to estates registered in the Netherlands. The Dutch syndicates confined themselves to estates registered in the Netherlands or Indonesia. The capital market acknowledged successful development and attributed continuity in performance to membership in a network. In Amsterdam, equity of rubber estates belonging to the syndicates was labelled as 'current'; stock of other estates was considered as difficult to market.

While rubber estates were embedded in a loose structure, other plantations continued to operate within a more integrated network, at least in colonial Indonesia. Culture banks and the prominent Dutch trading houses were and remained actively involved in sugar and tea, as they operated more 'passively' in rubber. The Indonesian free-standing structure, as it had emerged during the 1880s and the following decades, which was a mix of free-standing estates and closely interested financial or commercial groups, remained confined to the older crops. In these, the structure remained largely as it was. Both in the old and in the newer markets, free-standing companies did not disappear.

Managerial Services

Analysing the contribution of the Dutch headquarters to their free-standing companies is useful in two respects. First, to decide whether free-standing companies are to be classified as direct or as portfolio investment. Secondly, to figure out whether or not the headquarters added value. Little is known about the management of the free-standing companies that invested outside colonial Indonesia. The Dutch owners of the three gold mines in Surinam were certainly not active industrialists. They held the mining rights and left the actual working of the mines to British and American companies. It is doubtful whether the Van Oss/Deen group ever had the intention of establishing a permanent oil company in the USA. While in the colonies, entrepreneurship was scarce, in the USA Dutch entrepreneurs had little special to offer. Therefore, Dutch investors probably reasoned that they could invest their money just as well, probably even better, in an American company than in a Dutch free-standing company. The Dutch mortgage banks operating in America were an exception. They certainly were managed from the Netherlands. The banks worked with agents in the USA, in Canada often with trust companies, or they tried to set up a local organization of their own. Before the end of the First World War, financial turbulence and fiscal pressures stimulated a shift of management to the markets where property was mortgaged. Most, but not all banks kept their Dutch registration.

Enough is known about the management of free-standing companies in colonial Indonesia to allow for some generalizations.[50] In the preceding paragraphs we described how many free-standing companies in colonial Indonesia were the result of colonial (expatriate) initiatives, in combination with Dutch capital. Furthermore, these free-standing companies were in most cases part of a network. Which party was actually the controlling one? In all cases, the board of directors in the home country held the purse strings and in that way had a large influence over the free-standing companies. In the nineteenth century communications were slow. An exchange of letters took weeks. The cable was fine for short instructions, but unsuited for an exchange of ideas and the forming of a common policy. Sometimes, the board in Holland appointed representatives of banks or trading companies in colonial Indonesia to keep an eye on the operations. The board in Holland seldom had up-to-date information about what happened in Indonesia. On the other hand, the Dutch board was well informed about world market prices and the financial aspects of the operations. The directors in Holland certainly tried to instruct their employees in the colonies; they introduced early budgets and asked for financial estimates from overseas; but they had little control over what was going on there from day to day. They could write angry letters if they felt that their money was being squandered and when no profits were generated. The exchange of letters occasionally showed a certain helplessness on the part of the directors. Sometimes they felt they had lost all control, and one of them could decide to visit the colony in person to take matters in hand. A common complaint was that the local managers were spending too much money on side projects. On the other hand, when new capital was needed to expand the business or to make improvements in buildings and machinery, the local management was completely dependent on the board in Holland. Was it possible to convince them of the necessity of improvement or expansion? The directors in Holland were often considered overcautious and hard to convince.

While in the nineteenth century the directors in Holland had to rely on their local representatives, in the twentieth century monitoring from Holland became easier. Communications improved and the information available to Dutch directors increased. It became common practice to appoint as managing director in Holland someone who had led the company overseas and wanted to return to live in Holland. These were very knowledgeable men. In Holland all decisions were still being made on financial matters. The marketing of the product was sometimes decided in the colony and sometimes at home. The Dutch headquarters were often active in the acquisition of capital goods. European personnel was recruited in Holland.

In the daily management of the free-standing companies, the representatives of Dutch trading houses in Indonesia played an important role. The most spectacular example was the Handelsvereeniging Amsterdam (HVA). The HVA changed from a trading house into an administrator and financial intermediary. Contemporaries found it difficult to decide whether the firm was a culture bank or a very big estate company. The differences were vague, because financing tropical agriculture, the supply of managerial skills in production and marketing, and assistance with the provision of capital or its supply were often closely intertwined. The company owned and managed legally independent plantations, but it took integration further. Before 1910 the HVA had laid out the largest sugar estate and factory in Java and one of the largest in the world, an estate administered directly and not as a legally separate limited company. The HVA combined decentralization with rigidly standardized budgets and a strict system of information for the main offices in the Indies. The Dutch headquarters concentrated upon strategic allocations of capital and the marketing of the produce. By 1930 the HVA had thirty-six plantations, produced and marketed a large range of tropical products—tobacco, coffee, cinchona, rubber, sisal—and employed a stunning number of 170,000 labourers besides a staff of 800 in the Dutch East Indies. About 200 people were working at the Dutch headquarters in Amsterdam.[51] The Rotterdam trading house Internationale Crediet en Handels-Vereeniging combined the trading of primary products with the administration of plantations. Some plantations were owned, others only managed.[52] In the management of rubber plantations the trading houses H. G. Crone and Geo Wehry & Co. were well-known names. Occasionally, the larger agricultural companies acted as administrators of smaller plantation companies. Java tobacco came from forty estates in 1904, but was brought to the Netherlands by nine importers. The five banks that specialized in financing plantations were interested in seventy-six sugar companies, seventy-three coffee plantations, and fifty-nine other companies. They controlled 44 per cent of the sugar production in 1884, and 57 per cent in 1904. Their share was a few per cent less in the mid-1930s.[53] In more or less the same way, Royal Dutch worked oil concessions of several free-standing oil companies, until these companies were gradually bought up completely. Already in 1913, nearly all Dutch free-standing oil companies were somehow linked to Royal Dutch.[54] Table

TABLE 11.5. *Concentration of management in the estates in the Netherlands East Indies around 1937*

Product	Number of estates	Number of managements
Sugar	81	13
Coffee	383	14
Tea	327	17
Rubber	1,226	24
Cinchona	101	15
Tobacco	80	8
Oil palm	43	3

Source: J. F. Haccoû, *Management of Direct Investments in Less Developed Countries* (Leiden, 1957), 194.

11.5 gives an indication of the concentration of management in the plantations in the 1930s.

At the beginning of the century, the Netherlands was the primary location of top management. All culture banks and most trading houses were registered there. Managerial skills were less expensive in Europe. More importantly, economies of scale, and particularly economies of scope, pulled top management to Europe by combining several managerial functions. Information on markets and finance were the primary ones. In time, tropical agriculture became more science-based. The headquarters in Europe adapted easily to that change. Initially, commercial and financial skills dominated. Gradually, more and more planters were promoted from local administrators or advisers to the higher ranks of management. In the course of the twentieth century, the mother country became a less dominant location for top management, although the culture banks and trading houses, and thus the centres of the networks, were still directed from the Netherlands. J. F. Haccoû tried to quantify the location of actual top management around 1937, isolated from the estates' legal seat of residence. He concluded that almost 80 per cent of the sugar production was managed from the Netherlands, but only 47 per cent of the coffee, 39 per cent in the case of tea, and 31 per cent of the rubber production.[55]

Within the colonial economy specialization increased. After the First World War, the importance of contracts of consignment waned. Plantations also relied less upon debenture capital. Finance, on the one hand, and the sale or marketing of produce, on the other, grew apart. There were two opposing trends among the producers. Within some firms, the level of integration increased. Financial supervision at a distance changed into more strict management from Europe. Higher economic turbulence stimulated the transfer of control. It was resented and made contentious by other forces. Geographical shifts in the consuming markets and better communications stimulated companies to transfer managerial functions from the Netherlands to the Indies. The shift to the producing areas was most marked for the smaller plantations and for a product like rubber. In tea and quinine also, the managerial hierarchy became more locally based, by Dutch or other European expatriates, who settled in Indonesia. By contrast, the relatively capital-intensive sugar companies kept the essentials of policy-making in the Netherlands, but they too transferred part of commercial policy to the producers' organizations established in the Indies. Despite these changes, throughout the inter-war years the Netherlands remained the primary location of top management. The links with the capital market, but even more the importance of managing sales and recruitment and of processing information, were the basis of the value added of the headquarters. The headquarters in the Netherlands were far more than 'brass nameplates' in the city.

Were the Free-Standing Companies Doomed to Disappear?

According to Mira Wilkins, the management structure of the free-standing companies was weak and therefore inferior to the multinational company. In her view, at least in her *Economic History Review* article, the free-standing companies were doomed to disappear.

The short but stirring history of the Oliefabrieken Insulinde seems a perfect illustration of the weakness of the free-standing company. In 1903 a small vegetable-oil mill was set up in Blitar, Indonesia, working with primitive machinery. In 1907 the firm was changed into a limited company. The newly appointed manager, B. Streefland, had high aspirations. He installed new processes and new machinery and hoped to serve expanding markets. More capital, therefore, was needed, which was sought in the Netherlands. The Oliefabrieken Insulinde became a company quoted at the Amsterdam Stock Exchange. It had a head office in Amsterdam, but no other business activity there. During the First World War it expanded enormously, building new factories and taking over others. Reluctantly, the board of directors in Holland went along with seven issues of new capital. In 1920 the Oliefabrieken Insulinde was among the ten largest Dutch industrial companies measured in assets. The company had the misfortune that its two most senior managers in the colony died, one soon after the other. The board in Amsterdam was unable to provide the right management quickly enough. It was not convinced that the supply of information was defective and remedies seemed unnecessary. When copra oil prices started to go down from 1920 onwards, the company went adrift and had to be liquidated in 1922.[56]

Would a multinational company have fared better? By chance, we can compare the fortunes of Insulinde with those of a multinational. During the First World War, A. Jurgens, one of the Dutch predecessors of Unilever, acquired and constructed oil mills in Indonesia. Shortages in copra, entry of Indonesian oil-millers in the copra market, and transportation problems stimulated Jurgens to go into oil-milling himself. Jurgens spent large sums of money on the modernization and enlargement of the factories until 1920. The overall lavish expansion left the company very short of capital. When vegetable-oil prices went down and transportation costs for copra diminished greatly, no other solution remained than to close down the four factories at a great loss.[57] The multinational Jurgens, therefore, did not manage its overseas factories much better than the board of directors which managed the free-standing company Insulinde from Amsterdam. In both cases the activities in colonial Indonesia were ended.

A characterization of the free-standing company as a kind of multinational *manqué* is difficult to assess because so little systematic information is available on the unsuccessful ventures of traditional multinationals. Moreover, free-standing companies should be compared not with multinational companies as such, but with individual projects undertaken by these. Also, a short life cycle and failure are not necessarily identical. Within the Dutch insurance industry, trials ending within three or four years preceded successful multinational expansion. Most of the efforts were calculated risks, not outright failures. At the moment we can analyse only overall patterns within the free-standing companies as a group. The case of the Oliefabrieken Insulinde was not representative. The life cycle of the free-standing companies in the colonies was not very different from the companies registered overseas. We collected stock data. Comparative statistics might give an impression of the evolution between benchmark years. We followed such a procedure for the period after 1912. For the decades before 1912 we used a different methodology.

We have an overview of the free-standing companies still in existence in 1912. It is possible to construct backwards a time series of the number of firms established in each year for those companies which survived until 1912. Fig. 11.1 shows the series from 1855 onwards for the colonial free-standing companies in the *Van Nierop & Baak* sample. Fig. 11.2 contains a similar time series for all Dutch free-standing companies working outside the colonies. In order to interpret these series one must either know how many firms did not survive or have an idea of the mortality pattern. Annually, the colonial authorities published how many new companies were registered in the Netherlands with the aim to do business in the East Indies. The incoming stream therefore is known for that region. In Fig. 11.1 we confronted the time

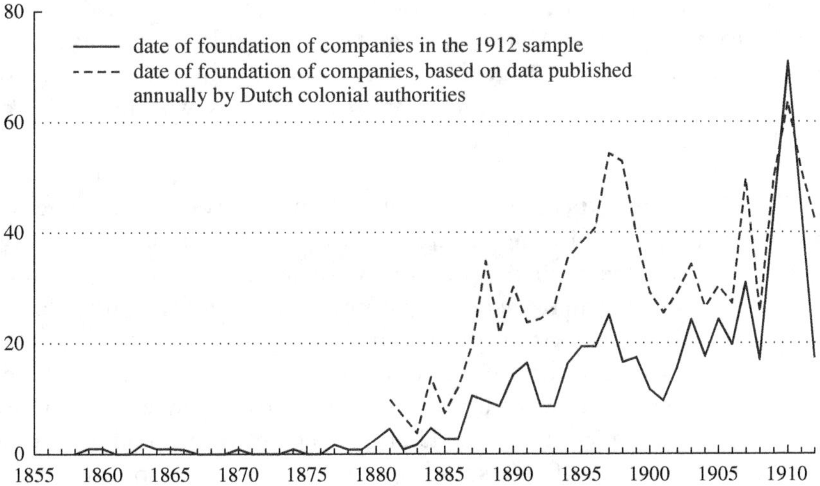

Fig. 11.1. Persistence of Dutch free-standing companies working in the Dutch colonies
Source: *Mrs Van Nierop & Baak's Naamlooze Vennootschappen* (1912); J. N. F. M. à Campo, 'Strength, Survival and Success: A Statistical Profile of Corporate Enterprise in Colonial Indonesia 1883–1913', in *Jahrbuch für Wirtschaftsgeschichte* (1995).

series based upon these data with the time series constructed from the stock of 1912. The sample gives a reasonably correct impression of past developments. Firm-mortality caused a gap between both series, as was to be expected, but more than half of the companies were survivors. The analysis is crude, but sufficient to conclude that the life cycle of the

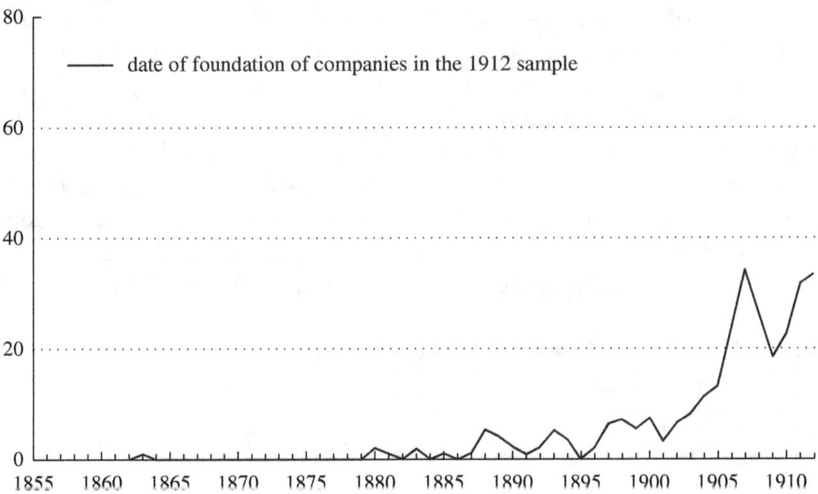

Fig. 11.2. Persistence of Dutch free-standing companies working outside the Dutch colonies
Source: *Mrs Van Nierop & Baak's Naamlooze Vennootschappen* (1912).

colonial free-standing companies was not extraordinarily short in the years before the First World War and comparable to the expatriate firms. J. à Campo found that the survival rate of the Dutch-registered free-standing companies operating in the colonies was not different from those registered in colonial Indonesia.[58]

The environment was different outside the colonies. A pattern as in Fig. 11.2 is to be expected if the rate of mortality is high. The vast majority of the free-standing companies were ten years old at the most. Most of them were young; true survivors were an oddity. The non-colonial segment of the free-standing companies therefore came close to Wilkins's characterization of the group.

How many free-standing companies, active in 1913, survived until 1937? Table 11.6 gives more information about the longevity of Dutch listed free-standing companies. There is, again, a marked difference between the fortunes of free-standing companies in colonial Indonesia and elsewhere. From the free-standing companies in colonial Indonesia 23 per cent disappeared, against 59 per cent of those operating in other countries. Of the 18 per cent of free-standing companies in other countries that still survived in 1937, many were no more than struggling along. The foreign portfolio of the mortgage banks, 104 million guilders in 1912, reached a peak in 1917 and then declined steadily to 13 million guilders in the mid-1930s.

Of course, not all free-standing companies in Indonesia were successful. Crises and war, bad management and over-optimism frequently led to the liquidation of free-standing companies which had begun in great hopes. The liquidation of a company, however, did not necessarily mean the end of operations. The First World War caused upheaval. New channels for products had to be found. Prices went up until 1920, and then down again suddenly. This led to a series of mergers. From 1922 onwards, many companies were prospering again. In the 1920s free-standing companies were able to pay high dividends, in fact higher than the average Dutch company. The companies active in colonial Indonesia but with a residence in the Netherlands also paid much higher dividends than the firms seated in the colony itself—12 and 6 per cent respectively.[59] However, the Depression years were difficult for

TABLE 11.6. *Longevity of Dutch-listed free-standing companies* (%)

From the 1913 sample	Netherlands East Indies	Other countries
Still active in 1937	61	18
Merged or taken over	16	23
Disappeared	23	59
TOTAL	100	100

Source: *Van Oss' Effectenboek* (1915/16, 1939).

most agricultural enterprises. Worldwide the growing of agricultural products had to be limited. Plantations had to be closed down and companies were forced into liquidation. Most sugar, tobacco, tea, and rubber companies paid no dividend between 1930 and 1936. These were particularly difficult years for the sugar companies. Nearly half of the sugar companies in the 1913 sample either merged or liquidated. Losses due to reorganizations were estimated at 50 million guilders on a capital of 90 million. Not only the plantations had problems; domestic Dutch sugar enterprises had to reduce capital too. In comparison, the rubber companies fared better. After 1936 the situation cleared and company results improved.[60] As a whole, the Indonesian economy was on its way towards recovery when the Second World War started. After the war, the relationship between the Netherlands and Indonesia changed fundamentally. In this new situation there was no longer room for the Dutch free-standing companies.

The non-colonial free-standing companies were perhaps the 'true' free-standing companies, especially those outside the networks. But these were not very important in terms of capital. It is not surprising that there were so few 'true' free-standing companies. Their rarity is a sign that market failure was not widespread. It would have been a substantial signal of failure in the capital market if free-standing companies were important and at the same time failed often.

Conclusion

In the Dutch case, free-standing companies were an important form of direct foreign investment. They were also nearly synonymous with investment in colonial Indonesia. Here the free-standing companies were embedded in a comfortable network of Dutch trading houses, merchant banks, and an active community of Dutchmen and other Europeans. Dutch industrial companies seldom acted as promoters. The free-standing companies were not portfolio investment, because the directors in the Netherlands tried hard to keep control over the company. During the nineteenth century this was made difficult by poor communications. In the twentieth century, poor communications were no longer a major problem, but now the business community in colonial Indonesia felt less inclined to take orders from Holland. This self-esteem was very understandable, as many companies had prospered over the years, sending attractive profits to the Netherlands. Several very large companies had developed out of the Indonesian activities. Not economic factors, but the Second World War and the policies of decolonization after 1945 brought the era of Dutch free-standing companies in Indonesia to an end.

The free-standing companies outside colonial Indonesia were much less successful. Many were short-lived or paid only very moderate dividends, if dividends were paid at all. These free-standing companies were probably too isolated, so that the directors in the Netherlands could not build up the necessary know-how to establish a competitive business. Only in the colony of Indonesia was the network of supporting firms and activities strong enough to make the free-standing companies successful. By combining Dutch entrepreneurship and capital with chances of profit in foreign countries, the free-standing company could indeed be an efficient way to exploit the richness of the colony.

In the end the question remains whether colonial investment is foreign investment. We demonstrated that it is worthwhile to study the colonial free-standing company as a special category. Instead of arguing, as Wilkins did, that the free-standing company was inferior to the multinational company and therefore doomed to disappear, one might argue that the free-standing company could function very well as long as it was part of a colonial framework. In the Dutch case the free-standing company ended when colonialism ended, because the special relationship that provided a viable setting for free-standing companies disappeared.

NOTES

1. M. Wilkins, 'The Free-Standing Company, 1870–1914: An Important Type of British Foreign Direct Investment', *Economic History Review*, 2nd ser., 41 (May 1988), 259–82.
2. Mark Casson, Chapter 3 herein.
3. *Mrs Van Nierop & Baak's Naamlooze Vennootschappen* (1912); *Van Oss' Effectenboek* (1915/1916). The different base years of the two sources had only negligible effects on our results.
4. Of the 159 Dutch FSCs in 1937, 139 were operating in the Netherlands East Indies: *Van Oss' Effectenboek* (1939).
5. Capital issued by free-standing companies is known. The capital value of all investments was estimated by using the balances published in the source. For each category a ratio between capital issued and the balance total excluding obligations of shareholders was calculated. A ratio of 2 is a common rule of thumb; in agriculture, however, the ratio was lower. The estimated book value of the free-standing companies was 1,225 million guilders.
6. We identified 583 free-standing companies operating in the Netherlands East Indies before the First World War. A recent analysis of the major colonial business directory by J. à Campo showed 632 corporations with a seat in the Netherlands, but mainly active in Indonesia in 1913. The number based upon an authoritative source from the host country instead of the home country is surprisingly close to ours, considering that in our count trade and shipping companies were likely to be excluded (J. N. F. M. à Campo, 'Strength, Survival and Success: A Statistical Profile of Corporate Enterprise in Colonial Indonesia 1883–1913', in *Jahrbuch für Wirtschaftsgeschichte* (1995), 51).

7. B. Harms, *Volkswirtschaft und Weltwirtschaft: Versuch der Begründung einer Weltwirtschaftslehre* (Jena, 1912), 237.
8. W. Peeters, 'Belgische Investeringen in het Buitenland 1873–1914. Deel I. Directe Private Investeringen. Het nominaal kapitaal van Naamloze Vennootschappen werkzaam in het buitenland', Paper for the Workshop on Quantitative Economic History (K. U. Leuven, Feb. 1994), 21. We classified Russia as European.
9. T. A. B. Corley, 'Britain's Overseas Investments in 1914 Revisited', *Business History*, 36 (Jan. 1994), 81. That the Dutch invested much more than other European countries in their colonies is, however, denied by H. Baudet, 'Nederland en de rang van Denemarken', *Bijdragen en Mededelingen betreffende de Geschiedenis der Nederlanden*, 90 (1975), 439.
10. *Van Nierop & Baak* does not specify for each company capital paid in; capital issued is always known. In services the difference might be large, sometimes only 10% being actually paid. For this comparison we used capital paid in and, if not known, capital issued. The source is not free from typing errors. In the summary table, *Van Nierop & Baak* indicated a total of 464 banks and administration offices; in fact the total came to 364.
11. B. P. A. Gales and K. E. Sluyterman, 'Outward Bound: The Rise of Dutch Multinationals', in G. Jones and H. G. Schröter (eds.), *The Rise of Multinationals in Continental Europe* (Aldershot, 1993), 65.
12. H. G. Schröter, *Aufstieg der Kleinen: Multinationale Unternehmen aus fünf kleinen Staaten vor 1914* (Berlin, 1993).
13. D. Yergin, *The Prize: The Epic Quest for Oil, Money and Power* (New York, 1993), 192.
14. On Adrien Hallet's Société Financière des Caoutchoucs, later Socfin, see G. C. Allen and A. G. Donnithorne, *Western Enterprise in Indonesia and Malaya* (London, 1957), 114, 119, 140–2.
15. Nor did we try to identify so-called bypass investments, those originating from Germany and transferred back to that country through a firm registered in the Netherlands. Our focus was on *Dutch* owned and controlled free-standing companies.
16. J. Foreman-Peck, 'Foreign Trade and Economic Growth', in D. H. Aldcroft and S. P. Ville (eds.), *The European Economy 1750–1914: A Thematic Approach* (Manchester, 1994), 244.
17. Calculations made on the basis of the export figures of J. Th. Lindblad, 'De handel tussen Nederland en Nederlands-Indië, 1874–1939', *Economisch-en sociaal-historisch jaarboek*, 41 (1988), 253–61. Real gross value added was estimated by P. J. van der Eng, *Agricultural Growth in Indonesia since 1880: Productivity Change and the Impact of Government Policy* (Groningen, 1993), 302–5. In 'The Real Domestic Product of Indonesia, 1880–1989', *Explorations in Economic History*, 29 (1992), 343–73, Van der Eng published slightly different figures. Total domestic product grew 1.9% between 1880 and 1900 and subsequently around 2.6% till the 1930s.
18. J. Baks, 'Steenkolenmaatschappij "Poeloe Laoet" in Zuidoost-Borneo, 1903–1913', in A. P. H. Clemens and J. Th. Lindblad (eds.), *Het belang van de buitengewesten, 1870–1942* (Amsterdam, 1989); P. T. Scholte, 'Mijnbouwmaatschappij "Salida" in West-Sumatra, 1910–1933', in ibid. 151–74; F. C. Gerretson, *History of the Royal Dutch* (4 vols.; Leiden, 1953–7); *Deli-Batavia Maatschappij 1875–1925* (Amsterdam, 1925).
19. Gerretson, *History of the Royal Dutch*, i. 58–67, 93–102.
20. N. C. van Gheel Gildemeester, *Gedenkboek van de suikeronderneming 'Poerwodadi', 1833–1933* (Poerwodadi, 1933); 'Landbouw Maatschappij "Ketanen"

1898–1938 (typescript, 1938); *Javasche Cultuur Maatschappij 1890–1940* (Amsterdam, 1940); *Senembah Maatschappij 1889–1939* (Amsterdam, 1939); W. J. P. van den Bosch, *Cultuur-Maatschappij Pondok-Gedeh, 1887–1912* (The Hague, 1912).

21. *De tramwegen op Java: Gedenkboek samengesteld ter gelegenheid van het vijf en twintig-bestaan der Samarang-Joana Stoomtram-Maatschappij* (The Hague, 1907).
22. A. Hoynck van Papendrecht, *Tabak Maatschappij Arendsburg, 1877–1927* (Rotterdam, 1927).
23. J. F. Haccoû, *Management of Direct Investments in Less Developed Countries* (Leiden, 1957), 197.
24. C. Ch. Goslinga, *The Dutch in the Caribbean and in Surinam 1791–1942* (Assen, 1990), 461–7, 481–6, 659–64; J. Van Soest, *Olie als water: De Curaçaose economie in de eerste helft van de twintigste eeuw* (Zutphen, 1977), 29–32, 54–6, 74–82, 124–7, 138–45.
25. K. D. Bosch, *Nederlandse beleggingen in de Verenigde Staten* (Amsterdam, 1948), 180, 182, 349, 521.
26. A. J. Veenendaal, Jr., *Slow Train to Paradise: How Dutch Investment Helped Build American Railroads* (Stanford, Calif., 1996).
27. A. J. Veenendaal, Jr., 'An Example of "Other People's Money": Dutch Capital in American Railroads', *Business and Economic History*, 2nd ser., 21 (1992), 147–57.
28. D. A. J. Kessler was the brother of J. B. A. Kessler, who headed the Royal Dutch in the crucial years 1890–1900.
29. Gerretson, *History of the Royal Dutch*, iv. 233–6.
30. A. J. Veenendaal, Jr., 'The Dutch Connection: Salomon Frederik van Oss and Dutch Investment in Oklahoma', *The Chronicles of Oklahoma*, 65 (1987), 252–67.
31. J. C. J. Kempees, 'De Nederlandsche Hypotheekbanken in de Verenigde Staten van Noord-Amerika en in Canada', *De Economist* (1919), 666; Bosch, *Nederlandse beleggingen in de Verenigde Staten*, 439; M. Wilkins, *The History of Foreign Investment in the United States to 1914* (Cambridge, Mass., 1989), 514–15.
32. J. van Hinte, *Nederlanders in Amerika: Een studie over landverhuizers en volkplanters in de 19e en 20ste eeuw in de Vereenigde Staten van Amerika* (Groningen, 1928), ii. 242–4; Bosch, *Nederlandse beleggingen in de Verenigde Staten*, 186–7, 201, 448–9.
33. On the American market, see K. A. Snowden, 'Mortgage Rates and American Capital Market Development in the Late Nineteenth Century', *Journal of Economic History*, 47 (1987), 688; L. E. Davis and R.E. Gallman, 'Savings, Investment, and Economic Growth: The United States in the Nineteenth Century', in J. A. James and M. Thomas (eds.), *Capitalism in Context: Essays on Economic Development and Cultural Change in Honor of R. M. Hartwell* (Chicago, 1994), 216–26; and Wilkins, *The History of Foreign Investment*, 508–10.
34. J. Korsten, '"Little More than a Brass Nameplate Someplace in the City": De Free-standing company in Nederland 1910–1928', MA thesis (Nijmegen, 1992).
35. G. C. E. Crone, *H. G. Th. Crone, 1790–1940: Gedenkboek uitgegeven ter gelegenheid van het 150-jarige bestaan der firma op 2 juni 1940* (Haarlem, 1940), 70–4; A. Hoynck van Papendrecht, *Gedenkboek A. van Hoboken & Co, 1774–1924* (Rotterdam, 1924), 147–51.
36. H. Schijf, *Netwerken van een financieel-economische elite: Personele verbindingen in het Nederlandse bedrijfsleven aan het eind van de negentiende eeuw* (Amsterdam, 1993), 44–9.
37. K. E. Sluyterman, *Driekwart eeuw CSM: Cash flow, Strategie en Mensen* (Diemen, 1995), 12–44.
38. The Rotterdam firm Van Nelle tried not very successfully to cultivate tobacco in colonial Indonesia in the nineteenth century. At that moment, the firm was

more a trading than an industrial company as it became in later years. H. F. W. Bantje, *Twee eeuwen met de weduwe. Geschiedenis van De Erven de Wed. J. van Nelle N.V., 1782–1982* (Rotterdam, 1981), 58–62.

39. *Van Oss' Effectenboek* (1915/16).
40. K. E. Sluyterman, *Ondernemen in sigaren: Analyse van bedrijfsbeleid in vijf Nederlandse sigarenfabrieken in de perioden 1856–1865 en 1925–1934* (Tilburg, 1983), 78–108.
41. J. A. de Jonge, *De industrialisatie in Nederland tussen 1850 en 1914* (Nijmegen, 1968), 186.
42. J. Th. Lindblad, 'Foreign Investment in Late-Colonial and Post-Colonial Indonesia', *Economic and Social History in the Netherlands*, 3 (1991), 193.
43. In his magisterial study on the colonial transport company Koninklijke Paketvaart Maatschappij (KPM), J. à Campo recently demonstrated how the KPM created a maritime infrastructure, which positively interacted with the political and economic expansion in colonial Indonesia. By offering transport and communication the KPM strengthened the state formation and the economic infrastructure (J. N. F. M. à Campo, *Koninklijke Paketvaart Maatschappij: Stoomvaart en staatsvorming in de Indonesische archipel, 1888–1914* (Hilversum, 1992), 635–41).
44. J.-F. Hennart, 'International Financial Capital Transfers: A Transaction Cost Framework', *Business History*, 36 (Jan, 1994), 51–70.
45. See also Jean-François Hennart, Chapter 2 herein; J.-F. Hennart, 'The Transaction Cost Theory of the Multinational Enterprise', in C. Pitelis and R. Sugden (eds.), *The Nature of the Transnational Firm* (London, 1991), 96. General discussions of the transaction-cost interpretation of multinational enterprise abound. See R. K. Caves, *Multinational Enterprise and Economic Analysis* (1st edn., Cambridge, 1982).
46. Unfortunately, the data used in Table 11.4 do not allow us to control statistically for type of activity. It is, therefore, difficult to tell whether sugar or tobacco plantations, for example, registered in the Netherlands were more capital intensive than firms in the same industry registered in the Indies. This, however, seems to be suggested in the data.
47. The function then of the headquarters in Europe was to transmit funds and in particular to market equity. See Casson, Chapter 3 herein.
48. À Campo, 'Strength, Survival and Success', 51.
49. Rubber plantations are regularly used by Hennart as an illustrative example. Hennart, 'Transaction Cost Theory', 96; and 'International Financial Capital Transfers', 61. We mainly used W. Tervooren, *Die Finanzierung von Kautchukplantagen* (The Hague, 1930), 71–95, 114–19.
50. Our generalizations are based on the various company histories mentioned in the notes.
51. J. van der Zwaag, *Verloren tropische zaken: De opkomst en ondergang van de Nederlandse handel- & cultuurmaatschappijen in het voormalige Nederlands-Indië* (Meppel, 1991), 102–3; [W. Brand], *1879 HVA 1979: Honderd jaar geschiedenis der Verenigde HVA Maatschappijen NV* (Amsterdam, 1979), 13–16, 47.
52. A. C. Mees, *NV Internationale Crediet- en Handels-Vereeniging 'Rotterdam': Gedenkboek uitgegeven bij het vijf- en zeventig jarig bestaan op 28 augustus 1938* (Rotterdam, 1938), 8–31.
53. C. Eisfeld, *Das Niederländische Bankwesen* (The Hague, 1916), 203; Crone, *H. G. Th. Crone, 1790–1940*, 93; Haccoû, *Management*, 192–5.
54. *Van Oss' Effectenboek* (1915/16).
55. Haccoû, *Management*, 195–200. The following is based upon pp. 139–52, and J. F. Haccoû, *De Indische exportproducten: Hun beteekenis voor Indië en Nederland*

(Leiden, 1947), 31–43; Haccoû, 'Nederlands-Indië economisch: Een beeld van groei en strijd', in H. Baudet and I. J. Brugmans (eds.), *Balans van Beleid: Terugblik op de laatste halve eeuw van Nederlands-Indië* (Assen, 1961), 265–6.

56. R. N. J. Kamerling, *De N.V. Oliefabrieken Insulinde in Nederlands-Indië: Bedrijfsvoering in het onbekende* (Franeker, 1982), 42–50, 53–85.
57. Ç. Wilson, *The History of Unilever* (New York, 1968), ii, chs. 10, 13.
58. À Campo, 'Strength, Survival and Success', 51.
59. Korsten, '"Little More than a Brass Nameplate"', 66–8; J. Th. Lindblad, 'Ondernemen in Nederlands-Indië, 1900–1940', *Bijdragen en Mededelingen betreffende de geschiedenis der Nederlanden*, 108 (1993), 710.
60. In the *Kroniek van mr. dr. A. Sternheim*, annual surveys are given based on published annual accounts of sugar, tea, coffee, and rubber companies between 1930 and 1940.

12

Continental European Free-Standing Companies: The Case of Belgium, Germany, and Switzerland

Harm Schröter

The free-standing company (FSC) was studied initially in the context of British economic history.[1] Soon the question was raised, to what extent were FSCs headquartered in other states? In Chapter 11, Ben Gales and Keetie Sluyterman considered Holland as home to FSCs; my interest is in Belgium, Germany, and Switzerland. I have noted in an earlier book that the majority of Belgian foreign direct investment (FDI) was carried out through FSCs.[2] In Chapter 5 herein, Peter Hertner showed that Belgian FSCs' investment in Italy was substantial, second only to the British interest. By contrast, other nations with a sizeable share of the FDI in Italy, such as Switzerland or Germany, played a small or even insignificant role there in foreign investments made by FSCs.

My opening question is, to what extent are my prior findings on Belgium and Peter Hertner's evidence, which was gathered for one major host nation, confirmed by further research? Thus, my first section will offer data on FSCs headquartered in Belgium, Germany, and Switzerland, providing information on numbers, destinations, periods of foundation, branches of industries, finance, and so forth. The second part of this chapter will be devoted to special problems that arose during my research and also the association of my empirical materials with the emerging theory on the FSC.

A multinational enterprise (MNE) is often defined as an enterprise that owns and directs income generating assets in more than one country. The FSC was initially perceived as an MNE which owns and directs income generating assets abroad, but which, in contrast to the common MNE, has no such business operations at home. One point of contention between Jean-François Hennart and Mark Casson is whether all FSCs are to be seen as MNEs. In this chapter, I define an FSC as an enterprise set up and registered in one state which carries out its ordinary business activities (such as production, service, and so forth) not in the nation of registration but abroad. With this definition I do not confront the Casson–Hennart dispute; I will, however, try to find arguments (based on empirical evidence) which in the end may contribute to that debate.

Quantitative Information on Free-Standing Companies

My earlier finding that the FSC headquartered in Belgium was important is right. I have now identified 257 FSCs headquartered in Belgium in selected years from 1890 to 1930 (see Table 12.1).[3] Corresponding figures for Switzerland and Germany were much lower, with merely twenty-nine and forty-nine firms respectively. I found only one such enterprise registered in Austria. The figures for Belgium were considerable, even when compared with the over 700 for Scotland (see Mira Wilkins, Chapter 1 herein) and the roughly 200 for the Netherlands (see the *Van Oss* sample in Gales and Sluyterman's Chapter 11).[4]

My first pass revealed that the picture presented of Italy as a large host nation for FSCs was partially representative as an approximation for the ranking of FSCs by nationality. The principal exception was the Netherlands, which, in contrast with other home nations, allocated little to Italy and an astonishing part of its FSCs' investments within its own colonies, especially the Dutch East Indies.

Throughout this volume, contributors have found the free-standing company to have had its main extension before the First World War. Corresponding figures for the inter-war period were substantial, but smaller. Indeed, the world wars led to deep reductions in this form of company, and the second war was a watershed. Similar results are found in my research: the most FSCs were active between the turn of the century and 1914 (see Table 12.2). Before 1890 less than three dozen such firms were founded, while in the twenty-four years up to the First World War there was a rush to use this form of organization. Then the pace slackened. In order to have additional proof for the slowdown in the employment of this form, I looked into the financial manuals for

TABLE 12.1. *Number of registered free-standing companies, 1890–1930*

Year	Belgium	Germany	Switzerland	Total
1890	23	8	1	32
1900	113	24	8	145
1914	220	38	16	274
1930	169	16	12	197
TOTAL[a]	257	49	29	335

[a] In each year there were duplications. The 'total' indicates the number of individual companies recorded.

Sources: Calculated from *Recueil Financier* (1903, 1915, 1931); *Salings Börsen-Jahrbuch* (1902/3, 1914/15, and 1931/2); *Schweizerisches Jahrbuch für Finanz-, Bank-, Transport', und Versicherungswesen* (1901, 1915, 1931).

TABLE 12.2. *Period of foundation of free-standing companies* (numbers of companies)

Period	Belgium	Germany	Switzerland	Total
Up to and including 1890	23	8	1	32
1891–1900	90	20	7	117
1900–14	107	14	11	132
1915–30	34	2	9	45

Sources: See Table 12.1. Where information was lacking (e.g. on the year of the founding of a particular FSC), I was unable to include it in this table.

1960 and 1990 for Switzerland and Germany. Indeed, there was very little indication of FSCs after 1945. In Switzerland, only nine FSCs were registered in 1960; the corresponding figure for Germany was four, and it shrank to two in 1990. It seems that FSCs did indeed die out after the Second World War.[5] However, I wonder if today's offshore companies, registered in Liechtenstein, the Cayman Islands, and so forth, do not meet, to a certain extent, the definition of the free-standing company.[6]

There remains the question of why so many FSCs were situated in Belgium. Up to now there has been no comprehensive answer. However, light can be cast on this issue by considering Belgian institutions and 'mentality'. First, Belgian corporate law was one of the most liberal in Europe.[7] Secondly, corporate taxes were relatively low (for example, compared with those in France; thus Belgium became a channel for French foreign investment). Thirdly, the Belgian financial market was far more developed than that in Germany or, even, in Switzerland. For the same amount of assets, the Belgian capital market was prepared to provide larger credits than either the Swiss or the German one. Up to 1914 in the German-speaking states, a ratio of share capital to credits of 2 : 1 was seen as good; a ratio of 1 : 1 or 1 : 1.5 was possible, but very few firms sought credit under such conditions, fearing questioning by banks and suppliers. An enterprise whose customers, suppliers, and bankers thought it might fail found it impossible to get credit.

Belgian firms had the advantage of much larger credit ratios. The Compagnie d'Éclairage de Bahia, incorporated in Brussels and active in Brazil, in 1914 employed a share capital of 1 million BFr. and credits of 12.7 million BFr. while it had a turnover of 13.7 million BFr.;[8] the ratio between share capital and turnover was 1 : 13.7. Similarly, in 1913 the Auxiliaire d'Éclairage et Tramways de Force de Kolozvar, another FSC, employed 1 million BFr. of credits. With a share capital of only 60,000 BFr., it achieved a turnover of 1.1 million BFr.;[9] this meant a ratio of 1 : 18.3.

The Brussels FSC, Tramways de Madrid et d'Espagne, which was founded in 1886, had paid back all its share capital. With a share capital of virtually zero, it had obtained credits of 3.9 million BFr. and had a turnover of 4.7 million BFr.[10] The FSC Société Immobilière de Tientsin, registered in Brussels in 1912, had a balance-sheet sum of 626 million BFr. and a share capital of zero.[11] Other Belgian FSCs also operated with a share capital of zero BFr.;[12] no German or Swiss firm could do the same. 'The golden rule of balance' (*Goldene Bilanzregel*) of German and Swiss firms meant that share capital and long-term credits should be larger than investment. A survey of the financial behaviour of typical MNEs from small states (including Belgium) showed such firms applied this golden rule to a large extent.[13] However, after the First World War there is no evidence for the same construction of the balance sheet in Belgium.

Indeed, the possibility of obtaining in Belgium large amounts of credits on little or no share capital may have been one reason why this particular country headquartered so many FSCs. But clearly other reasons worked in the same direction, since, as will become evident, many Belgian FSCs used little or no credits, but instead operated with their own capital. In 1914 Belgian FSCs commanded a capital of about $540 million (current US dollars), while in 1930 this sum had risen to about $2.2 billion (current US dollars). See Table 12.5 below.

The aforementioned rush to adopt the free-standing company form in the period preceding the First World War was summarized in Table 12.2, showing periods of formation. While in 1890 fewer than three dozen FSCs had been founded in Belgium, Germany, and Switzerland, in the last decade of the nineteenth century the number more than tripled. Interestingly, the growth took place in all three countries. The next period, from the turn of the century to the First World War, showed a considerable rise in number. The numbers then drop. Because Germany suffered from a lack of capital (and had lost all its outward foreign investments), it is not surprising to find only two FSCs floated there.[14]

Of major interest is the destination of free-standing companies. It has been suggested by Gales and Sluyterman and by Casson that the FSC is a typical colonial form of investment. This, of course, is the picture in the Dutch case. Belgium, too, had a bias towards investment into the Belgian Congo. Out of its sixty-nine FSCs active in Africa, forty-one were situated there (see Table 12.3). However, almost as many Belgian FSCs were placed in Latin America, and more than three times as many were placed in Europe. Europe, not Africa, was the main destination for Belgian FSCs.

The same pattern was true in the German case. As many FSCs as in the German colonies in Africa were in Europe, while almost twice as many were active in Latin America. Like Belgium, Switzerland (a nation without colonies) had the greatest number of FSCs in Europe. Our

TABLE 12.3. *Destinations of free-standing companies* (numbers of companies)

Destination	Belgium	Germany	Switzerland	Total
Europe	148	9	10	167
Africa, incl. Congo	69	10	4	83
Belgian Congo	41	0	0	41
Latin America	36	18	4	58
Asia	29	9	6	44
North America	10	0	3	13
Rest of the world	1	3	0	4

Sources: See Table 12.1. The column totals do not correspond to those in Table 12.1 for Belgium and Switzerland because of differences in available information.

findings on destinations are consistent with the material in Hertner's and Gurushina's contributions to this volume (Chapters 5 and 6): Europe was an important host area for FSCs—especially the underdeveloped southern and eastern parts of Europe. Only a handful of FSCs went to industrially developed host states in Europe. In this sense, the free-standing company seems different from the 'classic' multinational enterprise. The large majority of outward FDI made by traditional MNEs (that from the UK possibly excepted) was placed in industrialized states.[15] International comparisons show that the FSC was directed not so much at colonies, but towards less developed countries. Looked at by destinations, the FSC served as a supplement to traditional FDI.

Data on financial allocation provides us with the same picture as that of numbers of companies: in 1914 less than 10 per cent of the capital of all Belgian FSCs was employed in the Belgian Congo. The First World War and tax considerations raised this share to 14 per cent by 1930 (see Table 12.5 later in this chapter). Yet this was still but a small portion of the whole. Not only the majority of FSCs, but the bulk of Belgian capital abroad was invested outside colonial territory.

The branches of industry in which FSCs from Belgium, Switzerland, and Germany were active differed greatly from that within the respective home nations' economy, as well as that represented by exports and by the direct investment of the nations' 'classic' MNEs. Concerning the number of FSCs, infrastructure (railroads, tramways, power and light, gas, and so forth) was the principal branch of activity for this form of enterprise (see Table 12.4). This was, of course, influenced by the fact that a substantial amount of European outward investment in infrastructure was channelled through Belgium. The number of mining firms was second. This is in line with the evidence presented on Scottish FSCs (see Mira Wilkins, Chapter 1 herein). Finance (mainly banks and real estate) was third. Agriculture, with roughly 12 per cent of all firms, was curiously underrepresented. For Scotland, agriculture had a share

TABLE 12.4. *Branches of industry of free-standing companies* (numbers of companies)

Branch	Belgium	Germany	Switzerland	Total
Mining	55	10	7	72
Infrastructure	109	6	5	120
Finance	42	9	7	58
Agriculture	20	18	3	41
Manufacture	39	0	3	42
Trade	8	3	1	12
Others	7	3	3	13

Sources: See Table 12.1. The column totals do not correspond with those in Table 12.1 and 12.3 for Belgium and Switzerland because of differences in available information.

of 16 per cent, while in the case of the Netherlands it added up to more than one half of all FSCs. Since our table includes Belgium, with its important Congo colony, this result seems strange. By contrast, manufacturing is overrepresented, compared with Scotland. Interestingly, not a single German FSC was to be found in manufacturing, although there were many traditional MNEs in this sector. The large German FDI in manufacturing was all connected with German-headquartered industrial enterprises. Agriculture *was*, however, important for German FSCs.

My 1914 'guestimates' on the amount of capital of all FSCs (including private and joint-stock companies not listed on stock exchanges, in millions of current US dollars) would be for Belgium $400 (assets $850), for Germany $180 (assets $260), and for Switzerland $240 (assets $470).

While the financial data on Germany and Switzerland are limited (too small a sample of companies distorts the percentages), our Belgian data are very useful. In 1914 more than half of the total assets employed by Belgian FSCs was allocated to infrastructure (see Table 12.5, which contains only stock-exchange listed companies). The financial sector was second (this includes banks, insurance companies, and real-estate property). While the most important Belgian FSCs for infrastructure were active in the southern and eastern parts of Europe, the FSCs active in the financial sector invested most of their capital in Latin America and Canada. The Belgian mining companies, although considerable in number, raised comparatively small amounts of capital. This is surprising, because modern mines typically require heavy investment for their development. The relatively small amount of capital invested by free-standing mining companies suggests that they were modest firms. This is quite similar to findings on 'classic' Belgian multinationals in this sector.[16] The average amount of capital employed by manufacturing or agricultural FSCs was also small, in most cases below $US200,000.

TABLE 12.5. *Assets of free-standing companies headquartered in Belgium* (current $USm.)

Sector	1914	1930
Infrastructure	274	478
Finance	115	902
Mining	55	490
Other	93	374
TOTAL	537	2,244
Within colony	41	311

Note: Table contains only stock-exchange listed companies.
Source: Calculated from *Recueil Financier* (1915, 1931).

In 1930, however, the structure of Belgian FSCs was different from that before the First World War. More than 40 per cent of all capital was concentrated in the financial sector. In this sector, Banque Italo-Belge was the largest firm, employing 2.8 billion BFr. in 1930. With a headquarters in Brussels, this bank was active in Argentina, Brazil, and Uruguay.[17] The capital employed in infrastructure had been reduced in relative terms, even though the Société Nationale de Chemins de Fer en Colombie raised sizeable amounts of fresh capital during the 1920s.[18] In the shift towards the financial sector, the expropriations by the Soviet Union and the takeovers of such FSCs by Belgian holding companies, such as SOFINA, played an important role. (As indicated later in this chapter, I have not classified SOFINA as an FSC; like most of the public-utility holding companies discussed by William J. Hausman and John Neufeld (Chapter 14 herein), the traditional MNE model seems a better fit.) The most important change between 1914 and 1930 took place by growth in investment in the mining sector, in spite of the fact that here, too, expropriations had occurred in Russia. This sector grew sixteenfold in size of assets employed compared with the average quadrupling principally because of new investments in oil (oil is classified under 'mining'). None the less, the single largest FSC in this sector continued to be the Compagnie Royale Asturienne des Mines.[19]

The financing of Belgian FSCs varied. As noted, some companies used enormous amounts of credits, while others worked with their own (in most cases equity) capital. With mining and manufacturing, in 1914 the average of 'own capital' employed was two-thirds of the total. The First World War did not change this ratio very much; the average was about 60 per cent in 1930.[20] Other sectors were different. In 1914 the average of Belgian FSCs with investment in infrastructure employed 50 per cent of own capital; in the financial sector the share was 39 per cent. All these are substantial ratios. Over time, these ratios altered dramatically. In 1930 FSCs in the infrastructure sector provided only 9 per cent of their own capital, while in the case of financial institutions the ratio had fallen to 11 per cent. I would interpret this to be a consequence of the First World War, during which Belgium, although among the victors, suffered intensively. The impact of the war on Belgian finances was mirrored generally by the changing ratio of own capital to credits; while, in 1914, 48 per cent of all capital employed by Belgian FSCs was owned, this had dropped to only 9 per cent in 1930. The total assets of stock-exchange listed Belgian FSCs had more than quadrupled from $537 million to $2,244 million (current US dollars), but the financial structure of the firms had deteriorated dramatically.

It is interesting that those FSCs active in Belgian colonies followed the general trend. While the percentage of own capital employed by colonial FSCs in 1914 was at 66 per cent, it was down to 20 per cent in 1930; yet in 1914 and in 1930 it remained above the overall average. Unfortunately the *Recueil Financier* provides no information on where the credits were obtained. However, the difference in financial structure between colonial (in own colonies) and general FDI suggests the idea that outside the colonies a development similar to that in pre-Revolutionary Russia might have taken place: additional capital might have been obtained from indigenous host-country sources.[21]

While in 1914 no especially large FSCs dominated, the Belgian picture had changed by 1930. The three largest financial firms held over 72 per cent of all assets of FSCs in this sector,[22] while the share of the three largest ones in infrastructure amounted to 28 per cent.[23]

One consequence of the First World War was that a couple of FSCs moved from incorporation abroad to that in Belgium. Apparently they no longer felt secure with a foreign registration. A second possible reason, plans for expansion at home (better profit chances inside Belgium), can be ruled out.[24]

In Belgium two-thirds of all FSCs were registered in a single place, in Brussels, the capital and main financial centre of the country. Antwerp and Liège came second and third. Registration in the Congo occurred only after the First World War (no FSC was registered in Africa before 1914). Since the Belgian Congo stayed with Belgium in the inter-war period, free-standing companies registered in this colony have been counted as Belgian FSCs (see below). Most of these firms were FSCs

TABLE 12.6. *Place of registration of Belgian free-standing companies* (number of companies)

Brussels	Antwerp	Liège	Congo	Others
167	34	9	35	11

Source: Calculated from *Recueil Financier* (1915, 1931).

TABLE 12.7. *Place of registration of Swiss free-standing companies* (number of companies)

Geneva	Zurich	Basle	Others
10	9	5	5

Source: *Schweizerisches Jahrbuch für Finanz-, Bank-, Transport-, und Versicherungswesen* (1901, 1915, 1931).

that had been set up in Belgium earlier, sometimes under the same name. The change in registration meant little besides a legal step, because all such FSCs retained their administrative head office in their Belgian home country. There was virtually no transfer of administrative know-how when the change in place of registration occurred. The reallocation of the registration was probably a result of tax legislation; however, since this issue has not been discussed in the literature and the stock-exchange handbooks were not explicit, I am still uncertain on the rationale. In any case, such a movement of registration causes problems for theory and definition, which are addressed later in this chapter.

While in Belgium the location of registration was heavily concentrated in one city (Brussels), this was not true in Germany and Switzerland. In Germany most FSCs were registered in Berlin and in the two main cities for overseas trade, Hamburg and Bremen. In Switzerland the three cities with stock exchanges were preferred (see Table 12.7). Although Zurich had the largest stock exchange, Geneva was as important as a place for registration. In both Germany and Switzerland, cities with no stock exchanges attracted few FSCs. This suggests a link between stock markets and FSCs. In order to obtain a greater supply of capital, FSCs were typically set up in cities with a flourishing stock market.

Problems and Methodological Questions

The numbers on FSCs presented above tell only a part of the story. All the information on FSCs collected for this chapter comes from stock-exchange handbooks. It is well known, however, that many FSCs were founded as private, not traded enterprises. Many were never formally incorporated. Yet they would be registered and some of them later floated on a stock exchange. Not all incorporated firms were floated. We do not know the ratio of firms with or without floated stock. Thus, in the *Recueil Financier* for 1931, some firms which had been founded before the turn of the century are listed for the first time. Of course, other FSCs were never traded on the stock exchange and we have no specific information on such firms. Therefore, we do not know the relation between listed (on the stock exchange) and non-listed firms, nor how this relationship changed over time. The dependence on stock-exchange manuals creates a methodological bias that exists for most contributions in this volume. Presumably the number of FSCs was much greater than presented here—and in our 'guestimates' on amounts of capital, given earlier in this chapter, we did raise our numbers accordingly.

However, these were truly 'guestimates', for we have no information on how much to enlarge our totals. In any case, the ratio of stock exchange listed and personally owned FSCs was probably very different in different states. In countries with experienced know-how on foreign markets and a surplus of capital, such as the UK or Switzerland, the usual thing to do would probably be to establish a personal firm.[25] By contrast, in states with a lack of capital and an established capital market, such as Sweden, firms quite commonly tapped capital markets from the start.[26] In the case of Belgium I would expect a lot of FSCs that were not listed on the stock exchange; in Switzerland and Germany I would expect a certain amount, and in Sweden between none and a few. In some cases, even foreign-headquartered FSCs were listed on the stock exchange. Thus, the Société Houilière d'Irmino (Donetz) and the Compagnie Française des Mines de Bor (both French FSCs, registered in Paris) were listed on the stock exchanges of Brussels and Zurich respectively, as well as on the Paris stock exchange.[27] On the Zurich stock exchange, the FSC Charbonnages du Bassin de Budapest, founded in Brussels in 1925, was listed.[28]

For the first half of the ninteenth century, we have little information on FSCs, but I would expect some such firms were active during that period. If they were liquidated, there is no information. The major source up to now has been stock-exchange handbooks. An example of an old-established FSC is the Compagnie Royale Asturienne des Mines. It was founded in Belgium in 1833 to mine coal in Spain; later it concentrated on zinc and lead mines in Spain. After the First World War it remained active, still as an FSC, in Spain, but also in Morocco, Tunisia, and France.[29] Some might argue that, with the geographical diversification, it no longer qualified as an FSC.

A number of enterprises which in the handbooks appear as FSCs I did not count as such. Thus, the Aktiengesellschaft der Moskauer Textilmanufaktur in Glarus and the Aktiengesellschaft für Schappe, both active in Russia, were owned by Swiss 'classic' multinational enterprises.[30] In the case of Russia, compared with the rest of the world, these Swiss multinationals chose a unique strategy. While in most cases Swiss multinationals preferred for their foreign investments an ownership of about 100 per cent, this was not so for Russia. There joint ventures were preferred (the names of the joint ventures gave no indication which Swiss firm owned a particular enterprise). These companies were not FSCs; each relied on the experienced know-how of its Swiss parent. The same applies to firms such as Motor Columbus and others, which, though at first glance they looked free-standing, were in fact owned and directed by Swiss electrotechnical enterprises such as Brown, Boveri & Cie.

Some firms that appeared to be FSCs were owned by holding companies such as Electrobel or SOFINA. Electrobel and SOFINA were not owned and directed by an electric concern, as was Motor Columbus by BBC. They were owned jointly by several foreign and Belgian electric companies and investment groups. However, since they owned and managed tramway companies and power and light firms inside Belgium, as well as outside, I considered them to be traditional MNEs. Their legally independent subsidiaries have not been counted as FSCs.

Other groups of firms, such as those associated with Electrobel and SOFINA, have been identified. This is no surprise: various scholars have pointed to clusters of Belgian firms, similar to those clusters in the UK.[31] The following companies, for example, had the same address in Brussels: Compagnie du Selangor, founded in 1906; Plantations de Hallet, founded in 1909; Plantations de Fauconnier et Posth, founded in 1910; and Plantations de Tennamaram, founded in 1912. These four were counted as FSCs; they were, however, all headed by the same president, G. Dochen, and the same vice-president, Adrien Hallet.

No similar clusters of companies were found to be headquartered in Switzerland or Germany. Clusters of firms did exist in Sweden, but only in one branch of industry. Many Swedish timber firms, small and medium-sized enterprise by tradition, owned forest concessions in Finland and Russia.[32] Of these, the most important group involved the speculator William Olsson.[33] Olsson bought, merged, and sold saw mills, timber firms, and forest concessions on a large scale within the Nordic countries. In his trading in companies, it may well have happened that he temporarily owned no such firm in Sweden, retaining only headquarters in Stockholm. This then would have turned his investments abroad into FSCs and back into a common cluster with mixed investments at home and abroad, when he bought anew a Swedish firm. In such cases the definition of free-standing companies needs to be applied with flexibility; it would be arbitrary if his firms were counted as FSCs.[34]

The examples of Olsson and other Swedish timber firms reveal the need for more consensus as to what extent firms in clusters are to be understood as FSCs. If one firm in a cluster was active at home, would this affect the definition of all others as being FSCs? To complicate matters, if the 'home-active' firm were sold, there would be no effect on the other firms. Another question arises: are firms within the same cluster and active at home, but in different branches of industry, 'allowed' for other ones to be of an FSC character? Furthermore, should the traditional branches of industry, or alternatively Michael Porter's clusters of related industries, be taken into account?[35] There are a set of theoretical and definitional questions that need to be addressed on the FSC character of firms in clusters and of holding companies.

A certain group of 'organizations' were active as FSCs. However, it is to be questioned as to what extent they were 'firms'.[36] Usually a firm is set up with the goal of earning profits. However, the Société Anonyme du Village Suisse en Genève had another focus. Village Suisse was an exhibit that was shown at the World Exhibition in Paris in 1900, and subsequently in various cities around the world to enhance goodwill for Swiss products and to attract foreign tourists to Switzerland. The Missions-Handlungs-Gesellschaft AG, set up in Bern in 1859, was special as well. In the case of the Missions-Handlungs-Gesellschaft, Swiss missionaries wanted to provide the group in which they were active with cheap goods. In Switzerland these two organizations were set up as joint-stock companies, which acted as FSCs. But their task was different from ordinary firms, since their primary purpose was not to earn money. I have counted these firms as FSCs, because they fit the definition (and, of course, the purpose of an organization can change over time). There might have been more such cases, but I did not include non-listed enterprises.

A major problem arose concerning 'nationality'. Free-standing firms, especially those established in Belgium, were sometimes not of Belgian origin. Such cases are similar to that of Russian Tobacco, discussed by Natalia Gurushina in Chapter 6. In 1898 a man by the name of Stein from Wetzlar in Germany founded the Société Internationale des Ciments et Brevets Stein in Tilleur in Belgium. Eighty-six per cent of the shares were taken by Stein, who in return brought into this enterprise his cement factory at Wetzlar as well as his patents. Only 14 per cent of the shares were taken by Belgian investors.[37] Because the Belgian capital market was tapped only marginally and what Mark Casson has called 'competence' (in Chapter 3) rested totally in Germany, the Belgian enterprise, Internationale des Ciments et Brevets Stein, can hardly be presented as a Belgian foreign direct investment. The 14 per cent of it which was Belgian owned should be assumed to be a portfolio investment abroad. Was it a Belgian enterprise? If yes, what made it a 'Belgian' firm? Only registration.

The question is to what extent does the formal registration in a particular country create a national enterprise? In 1887 the company Mines et Chemins des Fer de Bacarès-Almeria was registered in Brussels and Paris at the same time. Other companies, such as Compagnie Générale des Charbonnages, founded in 1900,[38] Compagnie des Charbonnages de Podbédenko, founded in 1898,[39] and Phosphates d'Ain-Kerma, founded in 1899,[40] were registered solely in Brussels, while their seat of administration was in Paris only. No staff was employed permanently in Brussels by these companies. There were other cases wherein Belgian-registered FSCs were owned and directed from abroad. Ninety-nine per cent of the shares of the Companie d'Éclairage de Galatz (Poland, then part of Russia), registered in Brussels in 1904, were owned by the Société Internationale d'Éclairage à Paris.[41] Such connections were by no means exclusive to the French-speaking world. The Usines à Zinc de Hambourg, Germany, registered in Brussels in 1911, was about two-thirds owned by the International Metal Company, London, and 21 per cent owned by Aron Hirsch & Sohn and other German firms, and only 12.7 per cent of the share capital was held in Belgium.[42] The company Gaz de Rio de Janeiro was founded in Brussels in 1887. Two decades later, in 1905, nearly 100 per cent of its shares were acquired during a hostile takeover by the Canadian-owned Rio de Janeiro Tramway, Light & Power. Although the management nearly all became Canadian and British subjects, the enterprise itself remained registered in Brussels (even after the First World War). To what extent was this firm 'Belgian'? Belgium was the registration site, but after 1905 it was only the legal domicile.

One firm moved its nation of registration three times in the years before the First World War. To what extent was its national character changed by these transfers? On 11 January 1870 the Companie Générale pour L'Exploitation des Chemins de Fer de la Turquie en Europe was founded as an FSC in Paris. Nine years later the enterprise was transformed into Betriebsgesellschaft der Orientalischen Eisenbahnen, an Austrian FSC, set up and registered in Vienna. In 1910 the place of registration was again moved, this time to Constantinople. Nothing is known of the ownership or management of the French FSC. However, the ownership under Austrian and under Turkish registration was mainly Austrian, although part of the share capital was owned by Swiss and German banks. During its time of registration in Vienna, this company was an Austrian FSC. More interesting is the question of whether it should be called Austrian or Turkish after the seat was transferred to Constantinople. The direction after 1879 and after 1910 remained in Austrian hands; in 1910 the capital did not become Turkish. Yet no parent company existed in Austria. From a legal point of view and from the way statistics are assembled today, this would be a Turkish enterprise, owned from abroad.[43]

There is a set of firms for which the question of nationality gets even more complex. Nearly all scholars have considered investment in a nation's own colonies as foreign direct investment. This is a totally ex-post approach, since contemporaries rarely thought of colonies as separate from the 'mother country', much less as 'foreign' states. For the sake of comparability, I have counted investment in a country's own colonies as 'foreign investment', however controversial I believe the concept to be. Thirty-five FSCs included in Table 12.6 were registered in the Belgian Congo. Without exception their administration was situated in Belgium. In most cases, as noted, the registration had been transferred from Belgium into the Congo colony after the First World War. If the investment in a country's own colony is to be counted as a 'foreign' one, and registration is the criterion for identifying the 'home' country, such companies were transferred from one country to another. In the theoretical contributions to this volume by Casson and Hennart, administrative direction is presented as an important aspect of a firm. In these Belgian Congo cases, the administration was left in Brussels, while the registration and principal business activity were in the Congo. These operations were clearly run not by expatriates—even Europeans active in European colonies did not consider themselves to be expatriates—but by Belgians headquartered in Belgium. Would such facts turn these FSCs, active and registered in the Congo, into Congolese multinationals, because they maintained an investment 'abroad' in Belgium? This is, of course, bizarre. There was no direction from the Congo, which is a necessity for any FDI. There was no Congolese portfolio investment either, because income generated abroad was not transferred into the Congo, but in the opposite direction; it was taken from there. What this reveals is that registration cannot be the only criterion for a 'headquarters'. While registration is often useful, clearly we must go beyond 'registration' in this case. Our theory must take this into account. The suggestion here is not to create a new category of foreign investment, but rather to note that, if we apply the definitions very precisely, sometimes we lose sight of reality. There are, in short, two questions: first, should the 'headquarters' of a firm—irrespective of registration—be fundamental to defining the home country for outward FDI? And secondly, if contemporaries perceived a colony as 'not foreign' if the investment was made in the context of the same legal institutions (as in the case of some colonies), is it appropriate ex-post to call this foreign investment?

International political developments were important for all enterprises. For some FSCs, they were the reason for existence or for liquidation. Take the case of the Comptoir d'Escompte de Mulhouse, a bank, founded in 1848. In 1871, after France had lost the war, Alsace became German. Subsequently, the bank, while keeping its seat in Mulhouse, was active only in various parts of France.[44]

The redrawing of Germany's borders after the First World War also created FSCs. These were exactly the FSCs that had been founded in Germany during the inter-war period. The Vereinigte Königs- und Laurahütte AG was founded in 1871 for a combined production of coal, iron, and steel in Upper Silesia. After this area became Polish, the company was refounded as a German FSC under its established name and ownership.[45] The same process was carried out by 'Oberbedarf'.[46] Oberbedarf was founded in 1871 and produced coal, iron, steel, and machinery. Its main plant was in Kattowitz. When this town became the Polish Katowice in 1919, Oberbedarf was turned into an FSC in 1922, which owned several firms and plants in Poland.[47]

Other FSCs, such as the Deutsch-Österreichische Bergwerksgesellschaft, founded in 1895, and the Duxer Kohlenverein, established in 1872, both of which mined lignite deposits in Bohemia, retired into Germany after the area in which they were active became part of the newly established state of Czechoslovakia. A parallel movement was carried out by the Belgian FSC Charbonnages Nord-Ouest de Bohême (Falkenau), a competitor of the German firms. Founded in 1899, it stopped mining in Bohemia during the First World War. Both the German and the Belgian firms lost their character as FSCs, but survived as firms. After selling out in Bohemia, they acquired coalfields in their home country and continued within their branch of business. Insecurity, based on possible political events in the unknown future, caused such firms to retreat from business abroad. Such decisions made on the basis of possible future events were tied to managerial risk assessment. Other FSCs made different choices. The Charbonnages Tchécho-Slovakique, with its headquarters in Brussels, was founded in 1921 to run four Bohemian lignite mines near Usti.

The expropriation without reimbursement of the many FSCs in Russia caused a different set of problems. Because the foreign owners objected to this procedure, they continued to assert their rights. During the inter-war period, Switzerland never accepted the expropriation of its investments. However, the quotations on the stock exchanges of Swiss FSCs with investments in what had become the Soviet Union eventually ceased.

On the Brussels stock exchange, shares of FSCs that had operated in Russia, such as Les Tramways de Kiev and the Société Belge des Tramways de Moscou, were traded throughout the inter-war period. In some cases such shares were acquired by holding companies (especially those established for electric power supply and railway or tram investments). Thus, the shares of the Belgian FSC Tramways d'Iekatérinoslaw were bought by Compagnie Centrale de Chemin de Fer in Paris. Electrobel, a major Belgian holding company for electric enterprises, acquired the shares of Tramways et Électricité en Russie,[48] Société d'Électricité d'Odessa, and others. Most of these expropriated Russian assets had no value, their quotations on Western stock exchanges notwithstanding. Only in those cases where the investment was in regions lost by the Russian Empire after 1919 (Poland, Finland, Latvia, Lithuania, Estonia, and Bessarabia, an area which became part of Romania) did business go on relatively undisturbed.[49] In these nations, a couple of Belgian FSCs continued, including Tramways de Bialystock, established in 1895. Few FSCs were as lucky as Compagnie des Glaces du Midi de la Russie à Novocielofka, founded in Brussels in 1899. This enterprise lost only one of its former four investments in Russia, since three of them were situated in what became the independent Polish state.[50]

Although many of the problems of determining FSC nationality are the same as those for the more traditional MNE, it has been discussions of the FSC that have revealed the questions in all their facets. My contribution at this point is not to solve the dilemma; perhaps the only solution is to take legal institutions into account—that is, to count as 'foreign' what contemporary statistics judged as foreign and which can be established in the trade statistics. Another approach would be to see as 'foreign' those countries that used legal structures and institutions that were markedly different from those of the home state. This is a difficult approach, for over time colonies often established varying degrees of 'separate' legal structures. The line between identical legal structures and 'markedly different' ones can be hard to determine.

Conclusions

What has become clear through comparisons of European national data is that there were two groups of countries that were homes to FSCs. The first group, with many FSCs, consisted of the UK, the Netherlands, Belgium, and France, while the second one included the rest of the developed European states. Less or newly developed states were not usually headquarters for FSCs. A characteristic of the first group of nations was, first of all, a very well-developed capital market; secondly, an abundance or even a surplus of capital; and, thirdly, relatively low rates of growth. Parenthetically, this last point suggests why the USA developed comparatively few FSCs. Mira Wilkins notes the equal relevance of the second criterion in the pre-1914 years (the USA was a debtor nation in world accounts).[51] The other group of

European countries was more heterogeneous. States with a lack of capital, such as Sweden, are included, but so are those with a tradition of capital export, such as Switzerland. It seems that all the three conditions mentioned for the first group of states had to be met in order to generate a substantial amount of FSCs.

As important as their numbers was the amount of capital employed by FSCs (and in most cases transferred over borders). Unfortunately, we still have no solid statistics on the size of outward foreign direct investment by small but important countries such as Belgium or Switzerland in the period up to the Second World War. If we accept the figures provided by John Dunning on FDI,[52] I calculate the share of FSCs from Belgium and Switzerland out of all FDI by the nations combined by Dunning (Belgium, Italy, the Netherlands, Sweden, and Switzerland) was in 1914 about 40 per cent of the FDI total. Since FSC investment from the Netherlands was not included in my figures, the above-mentioned percentage would be substantially higher. My estimate on FSCs exceeds that of Corley's, provided in Chapter 4. In the case of the UK free-standing investment, much of it was previously not counted as FDI; after consideration, the figures on British FDI have recently been raised substantially.[53] We need a closer review of the figures for the small Continental European states, especially Belgium, the Netherlands, and Switzerland. I am certain the results will be a still larger total amount of FDI, perhaps more than 40 per cent greater than that given in the Dunning estimates.

Another result of my research is that the FSC, which a few scholars thought to have been strictly a colonial matter, cannot be reduced to that, nor to colonial times. With Belgian, Swiss, and German FSCs, colonies as hosts played only a minor role. Especially in the case of Belgium, where the figures are large enough to draw legitimate conclusions, only one-quarter of all FSCs were active in the Congo, while most did business abroad, in Europe. The same finding is forthcoming when the amount of the FSC investment is the measure. Less than 15 per cent of all Belgian FSC investment was allocated to the Congo; the bulk went to Latin America and Europe.

An unsolved problem, which applies to all FDI, relates to the question of nationality. Differences in treatment of changing borders, moving headquarters, plus the issue of whether colonies are 'foreign' mean that figures cannot be satisfactorily compared as long as different authors use different definitions.[54] Perhaps some of the differences could be solved by an institutional approach: only investment in countries with a distinct set of legal institutions or structures should be counted as 'foreign'; yet, as noted, such an approach has limitations, for it is sometimes hard to decide what is a 'distinct set of legal institutions'.

One final point to be addressed is on the very nature of the free-standing company. We have many examples of enterprises that fit our definition of FSCs and clearly made foreign direct investments. However, we also discovered cases of enterprises that were not directed from the state of their legal registration. But direction, or rather competence (in Casson's terms), is necessary for FDI (otherwise the investment concerned would be a portfolio one). In some instances, such as the Belgian-registered Société Internationale des Ciments et Brevets Stein in Tilleur, direction never was intended to come from Belgium. Furthermore, we have cases where there was little or even no investment from the state of registration. Gurushina has presented similar evidence in Chapter 6. As mentioned above, I think there is no need for a new category apart from portfolio and foreign direct investments. In the example given, the Belgian investment in the Stein firm was a portfolio one. In consequence, this seems to provide evidence for the view Casson provided theoretically: free-standing companies can be either foreign direct or portfolio investment. Wilkins, however, takes exception to this. She argues that the Belgian investment in the Stein firm was indeed a portfolio one, yet it is not the investor but the firm that does business abroad; the firm makes the foreign direct investments. In my view, however, although most of the examples of FSCs fell into the category of FDI, some did not.

Often, the FSC seems to furnish a bridge between the two forms of foreign investment, direct and portfolio. Even though these two types of foreign investment have often been presented as theoretically distinct, economists and historians know that reality always turns out more variation than theory can foresee or capture. Indeed, I am convinced that the free-standing company is a theoretical 'tool' that provides a unique opportunity to understand better the characteristics of both portfolio and direct foreign investment.

NOTES

1. M. Wilkins, 'The Free-Standing Company, 1870–1914: An Important Type of British Foreign Direct Investment', *Economic History Review*, 2nd ser., 41 (May 1988), 259–82.
2. H. G. Schröter, *Aufstieg der Kleinen: Multinationale Unternehmen aus fünf kleinen Staaten vor 1914* (Berlin, 1993), 258.
3. Later on in this chapter, I will discuss my methodology in identifications.
4. A second sample (from *Van Nierop & Baak*), presented by Ben Gales and Keetie Sluyterman, Chapter 11 herein, contained 846 companies.
5. A special case of an FSC was the Wismut SDAG (Sowjetisch-Deutsche Aktiengesellschaft). Wismut was probably the largest single supplier of uranium ore (yellow-cake) in the world. It was set up by the Soviets in 1945 in the

southern part of their occupied zone of Germany. Its capitalistic form of a share company was quite strange to both communist states. However, Wismut was indispensable for the Soviet atomic programme. Later Wismut was owned jointly by the Soviets and the German Democratic Republic, but the general direction remained in Moscow, which qualifies Wismut as an FSC.

6. Boehringer, Mannheim, a renown German pharmaceutical firm with a turnover of $US1.65 billion in 1994, set up a holding company called Corange Ltd. in Hamilton, Bermuda. This holding company is the owner of all assets of this group of firms. Today's FSCs have been set up largely for reasons of tax avoidance. Therefore, it is little wonder that this form of enterprise died out in major states.
7. H. Veulemans, 'Gemengde Banken en Holdings in Belgie Tijdens de 19e en Begin 20e Eeuw', unpublished manuscript (Leuwen, 1974); G. Kurgan van Hentenrijk, 'Un aspect de l'exportation des capiteaux en Chine: Les Entreprises Franco-Belges, 1896–1914', in M. Lévy-Leboyer (ed.), *La Position internationale de la France* (Paris, 1977), 203–13; H. van der Wee, 'Large Firms in Belgium, 1892–1974: An Analysis of their Structure and Growth', in D. C. Coleman and P. Mathias (eds.), *Enterprise and History* (Cambridge, 1984), 199–211.
8. *Recueil Financier* (1915), i. 599.
9. Ibid. 608.
10. Ibid. 304.
11. *Recueil Financier* (1931), iii. 50.
12. For example, Société des Tramways de Rostoff-sur-le-Don (share capital 0, credits 9 million BFr., turnover 10 million BFr.). See *Recueil Financier* (1931), iii. 342.
13. The average out of forty typical pre-First World War MNEs based in Denmark, Belgium, the Netherlands, Sweden, and Switzerland showed a ratio between share capital and long-term credits and investment of 1.4:1 (Schröter, *Aufstieg der Kleinen*, 43ff). Belgian MNEs surpassed even this ratio (Schröter, *Aufstieg der Kleinen*, 259).
14. On those two, see text of chapter.
15. J. H. Dunning, *Explaining International Production* (London, 1988); M. Wilkins, *The Emergence of Multinational Enterprise: American Business Abroad from the Colonial Era to 1914* (Cambridge, Mass., 1970); M. Wilkins, *The Maturing of Multinational Enterprise: American Business Abroad from 1914 to 1970* (Cambridge, Mass., 1974); H. G. Schröter, 'Die Auslandsinvestitionen der deutschen chemischen Industrie 1870 bis 1930', in *Zeitschrift für Unternehmensgeschichte*, 35 (1990), 1–22; Schröter, *Aufstieg der Kleinen*, 64ff.
16. Schröter, *Aufstieg der Kleinen*, 246, table 76.
17. *Recueil Financier* (1931), i. 25.
18. This company, set up in 1923, employed a capital of 184m. BFrs. in 1930. That was more than two-thirds of all investment by Belgian FSCs in infrastructure (*Recueil Financier* (1931), i. 63).
19. *Recueil Financier* (1931), ii. 835.
20. Calculated on information provided by the *Recueil Financier* (1915), i–ii, and (1931), i–iii.
21. See Natalia Gurushina, Chapter 6 herein.
22. These three firms were: Banque Italo-Belge, Banque du Congo Belge, and Société Immobilière de Tientsin.
23. Gaz de Rio de Janeiro, Union Nationale des Transports, and Tramways du Caire.
24. Among those companies that announced they would transfer all their activities into Belgium and actually carried this out were: Charbonnages Nord-Ouest de

Bohême, Société Industrielle et Pastorale Belge–Sud-Amérique, and Compagnie Foncière et Hypothecaire Belgo-Argentine. All these were FSCs incorporated in Belgium *before* they decided to become active in the domestic market.

25. See A. D. Chandler, *Scale and Scope: The Dynamics of Industrial Capitalism* (Cambridge, Mass., 1990) on family firms. In a survey on similarities between small European nations and the three Chandlerian types of capitalism, Belgium seemed closest to the British type of personal capitalism. H. G. Schröter, 'Small European States and Cooperative Capitalism 1900–1980', in A. Chandler, F. Amatori, and T. Hikino (eds.), *Big Business and the Wealth of Nations, 1880s–1980s* (Cambridge, 1997). Studies of British FSCs that have included data from the registration records, as distinct from data from stock-exchange manuals, reveal how very many companies were excluded from the manuals.
26. In 1914 the stock-exchange handbook for Stockholm included more firms than all stock-exchange handbooks in Switzerland. In most cases, the companies listed in Sweden employed very little capital, between 100,000 and 200,000 SKr. ($US25,000–50,000). Similar amounts were usually raised privately in Switzerland.
27. *Recueil Financier* (1931), iii. 292 (Société Houilière); *Schweizerisches Börsen-Handbuch* (1937), 382 (Mines de Bor).
28. *Schweizerisches Börsenjahrbuch* (1937), 379.
29. In 1930 its turnover was 713 million BFr. ($US99.46m.) and it employed a share capital of 279 million BFr. (*Recueil Financier* (1931), ii. 835).
30. Schröter, *Aufstieg der Kleinen.*
31. H. Daems, *The Holding Company and Corporate Control* (Leiden, 1978); G. Kurgan van Hentenrijk, *Rail, finance et politique: Les Entreprises Philippart (1865–1890)* (Brussels, 1982); G. Kurgan van Hentenrijk, 'The Groupe Philippart: An Experience of Multinational Enterprise in Railway and Banking in Western Europe, 1865–1880', in A. Teichova, M. Lévy-Leboyer, and H. Nussbaum (eds.), *Multinational Enterprise in Historical Perspective* (Cambridge, 1986), 65–73; H. van der Wee, 'Investment Strategy of Belgian Industrial Enterprise between 1830 and 1980 and its Influence on the Economic Development of Europe', in G. Verbeke (ed.), *Belgium and Europe* (Brussels, 1981), 81–4; Veulemans, 'Gemengde Banken'; H. van der Wee, 'La Politique d'investissement de la Société Générale de Belgique 1822–1913', *Histoire Economie et Société* (1982), 603–20.
32. J. Glete, *Ägande och industriell omvandling: Ägarsgrupper, skogsindustri, verkstadsindustri 1850–1950* (Stockholm, 1987).
33. H. G. Schröter, 'On the Specific Freedom of Manœuvre of Small States and their Businessmen: Economic Mediation between Great Britain and Soviet Russia in 1921', in C. Due-Nielsen, H. Kirchhoff, K. C. Lammers, and T. Nybom (eds.), *Konflikt od samarbejde: Festskrift til Carl-Axel Gemzell* (Copenhagen, 1993), 53–66.
34. However, with Olsson the question of nationality is open, because he transferred the legal seat of his enterprise to London. There he set up a small administration and a timber-importing enterprise. His main headquarters remained in Stockholm. There is no indication that British capital entered the firm, and Olsson himself remained a Swedish subject. Did the transfer of registration create a British FSC? Much depends on the definition of the FSC.
35. M. Porter, *The Competitive Advantage of Nations* (London, 1990).
36. M. Casson, *The Firm and the Market* (Cambridge, Mass., 1987); M. Wilkins, 'Defining a Firm: Theory and History', in P. Hertner and G. Jones (eds.), *Multinationals: Theory and History* (Aldershot, 1986), 80–95.
37. *Recueil Financier* (1915), i. 697.
38. Ibid. 438.
39. Ibid. 507.

40. Ibid. 557.
41. Ibid. 601.
42. Ibid. 566.
43. Many Swiss firms owned from abroad are counted by some authors as part of Swiss-owned FDI, because of their Swiss registration (e.g. Pirelli, Kühne & Nagel, Wienerwald, Merck, Triumph, etc). See S. Borner and F. Wehrle, *Die Sechste Schweiz* (Zurich, 1984), 131. Furthermore, compilers do not identify the ownership; FDI by such firms appears in Swiss statistics as Swiss.
44. It established subsidiaries in Paris, Lyon, Marseille, Troyes, Saint-Dié, Besançon, Belfort, Le Havre, Plombiers-Les-Bains, Remiremont, Dijon, and Lure (*Salings Börsen-Jahrbuch* 1910/11, ii. 128).
45. The Polish state in most cases did not expropriate German owners.
46. 'Oberbedarf' was the official abbreviation for Oberschlesische Eisenbahnbedarfs Actien-Gesellschaft.
47. Above all Spolka Akcyjna Friedenshütte Katowice. Acquisitions of the Donnersmarkhütte and others in Germany turned this FSC-by-chance into a typical multinational enterprise, active in both Germany and Poland.
48. This company changed its name into Électricité et Tramways de l'Est de l'Europe (*Recueil Financier* (1931), iii. 873).
49. Foreign investment was not nationalized in these territories, but the economic upswing that Imperial Russia experienced before 1914 was broken. Except for Finland, all these states stagnated economically.
50. However, most of the assets had to be written off. In 1930 the share capital of the three Polish firms together figured at 8.3m. BFr., while the Russian investment (on its books) remained unchanged since the expropriation at 17.3m. BFr. (*Recueil Financier* (1931), i. 427).
51. M. Wilkins, *The History of Foreign Investment in the United States to 1914* (Cambridge, Mass., 1989).
52. Dunning, *Explaining International Production*, 74, table 3.1.
53. T. A. B. Corley, 'Britain's Overseas Investments in 1914 Revisited', *Business History*, 36 (Jan. 1994), 71–88, and Chapter 4 herein.
54. In France the most important colony, Algeria, was always counted as home, since the country had no intention to withdraw from that territory up to the late 1950s. In contrast, Dutch scholars (see, e.g., discussion in Chapter 11 herein) count Dutch investment in the Dutch colonies as 'foreign'. Despite such differences, figures on FDI are assembled and presented without mentioning details on definitions and the fragility of the comparisons.

13

British Overseas Banks as Free-Standing Companies, 1830–1996

Geoffrey Jones

The British overseas banks represent one of the earliest, most important, and long-lived variants of the 'free-standing' corporate form. Beginning in the 1830s, British-owned banks were established to operate branches in both the Empire and in sovereign countries. By 1913 some twenty-eight British overseas banks controlled 1,286 branches outside Britain. They operated dense branch networks in the settler economies of Australasia and southern Africa, and less dense branch networks covering the major ports and commercial towns of Latin America, Africa, and Asia. There were outposts in the USA, Canada, and the Mediterranean. The banks varied widely in their size and significance. However, it can be said with confidence that some of the banks were substantial business institutions for their time—in 1913 the nine largest banks had assets ranging from £19 million to almost £40 million—and that between them they financed a considerable proportion of British (and other) foreign trade flows and held substantial shares of the domestic banking markets of the southern-hemisphere economies, as well as parts of Asia.[1]

The overseas banks fitted Mira Wilkins's benchmark definition of free-standing firms as companies which, 'unlike the American model, did not grow out of the domestic operations of existing enterprises that had headquarters in Britain'. They did not conduct domestic banking in the UK, nor did domestic (clearing) banks establish foreign branches or subsidiaries. The first case of the latter came only in 1911. The overseas banks conformed to another feature of the Wilkins model in that they were largely bi-national—i.e. Anglo-Australian, Anglo-South African, etc.—although a number were or became bi-regional. Their corporate governance structures were also those of the Wilkins free-standing company. Their British-based head offices comprised 'a corporate secretary and . . . board of directors (whose members participated in other activities in Britain), and little else'.[2] It was in their longevity that the overseas banks differed most sharply from the Wilkins model. Although a dual process of consolidation and acquisition by domestic banks began after the First World War, overseas banks of the free-standing type were still much in evidence in the 1950s and 1960s, and one survivor of the genre remained an important British bank in 1998.

This chapter has two main sections. The first section considers the extent to which these banks should be called free-standing companies. This necessitates a closer examination of what the term really means. The second section explains the longevity of the banks.

Overseas Banks and the Concept of Free-Standing Companies

There are two particularly worrying elements of the free-standing-company concept. These are, first, the external relationships between the companies and wider enterprise groups, and, secondly, their internal governance structure, which includes the question of how much managerial 'control' was exercised from Britain over the overseas activities of the firms. Both these matters are of central concern for explaining the existence of the free-standing firm, and for evaluating whether it should be truly regarded as engaging in foreign direct investment (FDI).

It has always been evident that the term free-standing company is a misnomer, at least in the British case, because a considerable number of firms were not 'free-standing' but part of wider enterprise groups. Stanley Chapman drew attention to the diversified 'investment groups' which linked the many nominally independent British companies active in Asia, Latin America, Africa, and Russia. Trading and shipping companies were often at the core of these groups, though mining companies were more in evidence in Africa. The clusters of firms in these groups were joined by a mixture of interlocking directorships, equity investments, and long-term business relationships.[3] The scale of some of these enterprise groups was truly remarkable. The Mackinnon Group constructed a diversified intercontinental enterprise between the 1840s and 1890s which was based around its extensive steamship operations, which extended over four continents. Beyond shipping, the Group had investments in trading firms in the Arabian Gulf and East Africa, as well as in the production of commodities to be carried on its steamers—including tea estates in Bengal and Assam, coal-mining in Bengal, jute mills and a cotton mill in Calcutta, and a meat-freezing factory in Queensland. This business empire lacked a central headquarters, but was in reality closely controlled by two Scottish families active in three partnerships in Glasgow, London, and Calcutta.[4]

It has become clear that the business networks in which free-standing companies operated differed greatly between different host regions. Corporate interlock was widespread among British business in Latin America,[5] and also common elsewhere. In South-East Asia, the trading companies were at the centre of the business networks. In Russia, recent remarkable research by Natalia Gurushina has found British free-standing companies embedded in networks with Russian and British banks as well as Russian investors.[6]

Wilkins developed and extended Chapman's investment groups by observing that free-standing companies—including the large numbers active in the USA before 1914—were 'clustered'. The clusters formed around promoters, investment-trust companies, solicitors, accountants, 'ornamental' directors, geographical locations, and mining engineers, trading companies, and merchant banks. 'Common to all clusters, because of the free-standing companies' limited head office facilities and absence of internal 'know-how', was the provision of services.'[7]

A striking feature of the British overseas banks before 1914 was the modest extent of their involvement with these wider business groups. The investment groups identified by Chapman rarely included a bank, although the overseas banks typically had members of major British commercial interests active in their host regions on their boards. The trading companies sometimes opposed the foundation of banks, as in the case of Jardine, Matheson & Co. and the Hongkong Bank. It was not until thirteen years after that bank's foundation in 1864 that a representative of Jardine's joined its Board, though subsequently the trading company and the bank became involved in a number of joint projects.[8] When members of an investment group were also involved with a bank, an effort was made to preserve the latter's autonomy. An example was the London and River Plate Bank, one of the most important of the British-owned banks in nineteenth-century Latin America.[9] The Chairman of the bank for many years was George Drabble. The Drabble family controlled one of the more important Latin American 'investment groups' which have been identified by Charles Jones: their interests included land, meat, rails, refrigerated transport and storage, and butchers. Yet Jones concludes that it is quite clear that the London and River Plate Bank was run as a truly autonomous business and 'not the kind of back-pocket bank that acts as the creature of a broadly based mercantile investment group'.[10]

It was late in the history of the British overseas banks that a number of institutions appeared that were very closely identified with, and controlled by, investment groups. The Bank of British West Africa (1894) was created and controlled by Alfred Jones, the principal owner of the Elder Dempster Steamship Line, a large shipping concern with diversified investments in West Africa. Jones owned more than a third of the bank's capital on his death in 1901, and its head office was at Liverpool, the centre of the shipping group, until shortly before the First World War.[11] The Eastern Bank (1909) was an outgrowth of E. D. Sassoon, one of Chapman's Far East 'investment groups'. The bank's first London offices were in the premises of E. D. Sassoon.[12] Finally, the P&O Banking Corporation (1920) was the creation of the Inchcape shipping group (the successor to the Mackinnon Group discussed above). These three banks never grew to any great size: the P&O Banking Corporation lasted a mere seven years before coming under the control of Chartered Bank, one of the old established British overseas banks.[13]

In addition, a number of other connections between investment groups and banks can be identified. There were some cases of British business interests active abroad forming banks which were registered in the colonies rather than in the UK. Thus the Yule family, which had large business activities in Calcutta, set up its own bank—the Bank of Calcutta. This was acquired and absorbed by the Mercantile Bank of India in 1906, with a member of Andrew Yule & Co. joining the British bank's board.[14] There is also at least one important case of an investment group becoming involved in domestic British banking. The Mackinnon Group had a long-term relationship with the City of Glasgow Bank. Group companies were customers of the bank and had shareholdings in it, while the owning families had seats on the board. The bank's failure in 1878—a landmark event in British banking history—caused serious problems for the Mackinnon Group, causing it to switch its banking business from Scotland to the City of London, where it also had a large interest in a leading discount house.[15]

The British overseas banks fit more comfortably into Wilkins's looser 'cluster' concept. There was a considerable overlap among the promoters and directors of the first (1830s) generation of overseas banks, despite the fact that they covered completely different geographical regions (i.e. Australia, Canada, and the Ionian Islands in the Mediterranean).[16] Subsequently, there was the striking example of the role played by the London private bank Glyn, Mills in British overseas banking from the 1850s. Members of these banking families sat on a range of overseas bank boards and also actively promoted the foundation of new banks. A Glyn became a member of the board of the Union Bank of Australia in 1854, and thereafter there was either a Glyn or a Mill on the board until it merged with another Anglo-Australian bank a century later. Between the 1850s and the 1880s Glyn, Mills was involved in the promotion of a number of new overseas banks, including the Bank of Egypt, the Ottoman Bank, the London and Brazilian Bank, the Anglo-Austrian Bank, the English Bank of the River Plate, and the Imperial Bank of Persia. Usually family members were appointed to the boards of these banks, though Glyn, Mills did not provide significant amounts of equity, or seek to coordinate the different banks.[17] There were echoes of the inclusion of banks in other clusters.

The Imperial Bank of Persia's promoters included the merchant bank Schroders and the stockbroking firm Walpole Greenwell & Co., who were in turn associated in various overseas ventures.[18] It is likely that detailed research on the promotion of the overseas banks would find further evidence of clustering at that stage, but there is remarkably little evidence of any *sustained* influence of clusters beyond the foundation stage of the banks.

Overall, the British overseas banks can be regarded as more genuinely 'free-standing' than many other examples of this corporate genre active in other sectors. A number of industry-specific factors help to explain their autonomy. An obvious problem was that any bank which was closely associated with a major investment group was unlikely to attract the custom of that group's competitors. This was not only because of the risk that they might be denied credit facilities at a critical time, but crucially because of the danger that confidential business information would leak into the hands of rivals. The establishment of 'in-house' banks was, therefore, rarely an attractive commercial proposition. The preferable strategy was for a bank to have a spectrum of different commercial interests represented on its boards. In many cases these connections were long term and sometimes lasted several generations.

There was also little incentive for investment groups to own their own banks when, even before 1914, the activities of commercial banks tended to be more regulated than those of other commercial enterprises. This was particularly so in the USA—such an important host economy for free-standing companies in other industries—where extremely restrictive regulations were in force on the activities of foreign banks (as well as on local banks).[19]

Conversely, the trading companies at the heart of many investment groups could and did undertake many financial activities of direct relevance to their core business while avoiding the regulatory and other costs and drawbacks of establishing a separate bank. Both in Asia and Africa British trading companies provided credit and performed other quasi-banking functions on a very large scale indeed. In West Africa, the British trading companies provided much more credit than the British banks in the inter-war years and through the post-Second World War period. They, rather than the overseas banks, were the real providers of retail banking services, a situation which changed only when their roles were altered with the creation of produce-marketing boards in the 1950s.[20] The trading companies were extensively involved in a wide range of other financial services which might, in different contexts, have been performed by a bank. Balfour, Williamson & Co., for example, began its US trading activities as an exporter of grain from the

Pacific Coast, developed regular contacts with farmers, and then diversified into mortgage lending.[21]

If the overseas banks were genuinely 'free-standing' in their external relationships with other business enterprises, examination of their internal governance structures poses real problems for a central element in Wilkins's concept of free-standing firms. Wilkins was particularly impressed by the small size of the London corporate headquarters of the free-standing companies, which consisted of a part-time board of directors and little else. This lean governance structure was regarded as a crucial constraint for it meant that the free-standing firms lacked organizational capability. It ruled out their participation in industrial sectors involving advanced technology. More generally, their 'inherently weak managerial structure was responsible for the short life or failure of many of the British businesses operating overseas'.[22]

The evidence from the British overseas banks shows clearly that this argument has to be treated on an industry-by-industry basis. The London head offices of the banks were small. They consisted of part-time directors, who met once or more a week, supported by a handful of clerks. In most cases a chief executive post existed, which might be located with the board in London (as in the case of the British banks active in Asia and Latin America) or alternatively in the region of operation (as in the case of banks active in Australia and South Africa). In either case, the London staff amounted to a mere handful. In the 1900s the London office of the Imperial Bank of Persia—which was the state bank of issue in Iran, and operated around twenty branches spread over the whole country—functioned with its part-time directors, four or five permanent staff, and a changing population of young men receiving a few months on-the-job training before transfer to the overseas branches.[23] Nevertheless, such smallness did not mean that the London head offices were not both important and effective.

The London offices, despite their modest size, added significant value to the operations of the banks. In part, this added value was in the form of entrepreneurial and managerial judgements. These included the overall strategic direction of the bank and the recruitment of managerial staff. The directors performed an invaluable role in providing contacts with important customers, and as a source of business information. As the banks were so heavily involved in the finance of commodities, accurate information about markets and conditions was vital. For banks active in countries which were the subject of international diplomatic rivalries (such as nineteenth-century Iran), directors would also be appointed with contacts with the British government.

As in the case of Japanese companies in the 1990s, the recruitment of managerial staff with the right character and ability was regarded as a critical activity in which the highest level of management—in the British banks' case, the directors—was involved. The board of directors subsequently supervised the careers of all the British staff, including deciding on individual salary levels, awarding or denying permission to marry, and congratulating or administering individual performance. The London offices also supervised and monitored the business of the overseas branches. In a typical bank, each branch would be required to send very full half-yearly reports and accounts to London, as well as less detailed weekly or fortnightly returns. The smallest items of expenditure (i.e. down to postage costs) would be recorded and examined. Often subcommittees of directors would be formed to undertake specific functions, such as supervising bad debts, examining customers' securities, and considering loans. Nor was the role of London offices restricted to retrospective checking. Loans over a certain amount would typically be referred to London for approval. The successful performance of these management functions was a critical factor in the success of banks.

The London offices of the overseas banks also performed important banking functions in Britain. In simple terms, they were 'free-standing' firms because they did not engage in domestic British banking. Nor were they the outgrowth of domestic banks, nor (before 1918) did they have significant equity links with domestic banks. Yet it is misleading to say that they did not engage in banking in Britain, for their core business—foreign-trade finance and related foreign-exchange operations—required banking activities to be conducted in London. These included the discounting of bills, the continuous confirmation of letters of credit opened to cover shipments, and dealings in bullion and in securities. Central to the liquidity and cash flow of the overseas banks was the discounting of bills on the London money market. The London offices of the banks were continuously receiving bills of exchange from overseas which they could discount for cash to increase their liquidity. This cash in turn would be used to meet sterling telegraphic transfers and drafts on London sold by overseas branches. The London office would also purchase outward bills (i.e. bills of exchange drawn on importers abroad) representing mainly manufactured goods. The discounting of bills involved continuous discretionary judgements about the most profitable use of funds at a particular time, for it was up to each bank, depending on its own need for funds, to decide whether or not to discount its bills and, if so, what amount.[24]

The London offices of the overseas banks also worked closely with their 'correspondent' London bank. This relationship was critical to the effective operation of a bank. The principal facilities the overseas banks received from their London banks were cash advances, acceptance of bills, and overdraft facilities. The ability of the overseas banks to borrow large sums from their London banks played an important role in routine trade finance, and sometimes a vital role at times of crisis.[25] It is striking that extremely long-term and stable relationships were formed between the overseas banks and their London bankers, which usually lasted until one or other bank passed out of existence.

In the case of the overseas banks, therefore, the lean management structure did not mean that the London offices were not crucial to the business of the banks. Their main contributions lay in their physical proximity to London's agglomeration of financial institutions and markets; in managerial judgements—about staff, customers, the movement of foreign exchanges, the appropriate level of liquidity; and in skills in maintaining relationships. These things did not demand a large managerial hierarchy, and could be successfully performed by part-time directors, provided they had the right mix of accumulated experience, business contacts, and judgemental ability. Conceptually, this raises the question whether the overseas banks should be included in the free-standing category at all. Moreover, as the London head offices of other free-standing companies in other sectors were also likely to have performed strategically important activities, albeit not ones requiring extensive managerial hierarchies, there is surely a need to rethink the free-standing concept in this area.

In addition to undertaking important value-added activities, the London offices of the overseas banks were successful in controlling the overseas operations of their banks. Elsewhere, it has been shown that the lean governance structures of the overseas banks were effective in controlling their overseas operations through the use of socialization strategies. Each bank developed a specific corporate culture which was based on the recruitment of a culturally and socially homogenous managerial corps, which enjoyed lifelong employment, and was given on-the-job training. At a time when transport and communication difficulties made ineffective the use of a hierarchical control system over managers in distant branches, socialization strategies enabled the British overseas banks to manage effectively their branch networks, to limit losses from poor lending decisions, and to overcome principal–agent problems between head offices and their branch managers.[26]

There was a distinction between the strategies employed by British banks in their employment policies. In host economies that were settled by white Anglo-Saxons, the management of the overseas branches was entrusted to 'locals' very early on. In the nineteenth century, some of the British banks in Australia recruited staff in Britain and transferred them to Australia, but this became unusual, although the tradition survived in one bank until the inter-war years.[27] The structure of these banks came to consist of a British board and staff in London, and a local staff (including senior management) in the host country. The local staff was, however, treated like the expatriate British staff, with lifetime employment and strong corporate loyalties. In other host regions, British staff always managed each branch, supported by a large permanent local staff, whose recruitment into the managerial cadre did not even begin to be debated until the 1930s.

The lean organizational structure, in which many business decisions were made in the overseas markets by branch managers—albeit monitored in London—made sense given the environments faced by the overseas banks. Firms that operate across borders face the problem of how best to ensure that managers of foreign subsidiaries respond effectively to the directives of the parent company. In economic theory this is a principal/agent problem. The principal is the parent company and the subsidiary is the agent which agrees to act on the parent's behalf. Bounded rationality, opportunism, and moral hazard mean that transactions between agent and principal involve problems of policing and enforcement. The firm can be regarded as a highly developed mechanism of contract enforcement, or—in Oliver Williamson's terminology—a governance structure. The problems of enforcing contracts and monitoring behaviour (or governance costs) are particularly acute in firms operating across borders. The organizational design of a multinational enterprise can be regarded as an attempt to minimize the cost of contracting and monitoring these contracts.

While an extensive managerial hierarchy has often been regarded as providing the most appropriate organizational structure for multinationals, there are in reality a considerable number of organizational choices open to a multinational. The bureaucratic mode of control does not represent the only alternative to market relationships. Using a transaction-cost framework, W. G. Ouchi and others have argued that types of corporate culture or *clans* could do better than bureaucracies in certain circumstances.[28] Bureaucratic hierarchies resolve the problems of monitoring their employees by means of rules and other policing methods. The clan—whose members are heavily socialized and share common goals and understandings—can be regarded as offering a superior organizational form in situations in which there are considerable problems of monitoring and far too great uncertainty exists for prices or rule systems to be able to function well. The clan form has less need for formalized and sophisticated flows of information, for common ideas, beliefs, and values instead function as information carriers and provide sufficient guidance for management action.[29]

The market conditions faced by the British overseas banks resemble those for which Ouchi argues that the clan rather than the bureaucratic mode would work best. In many host economies in which the British overseas banks operated before 1914, the market was unpredictable and volatile. This unpredictability arose from diverse causes, including the problems of assessing risk in alien business cultures, which colonial rule only partly reduced, and the volatility of exchange rates and primary commodity prices.

The experience of the British overseas banks suggests that no direct correlation exists between the size of the London head offices of free-standing companies and their effectiveness as controllers of direct investments overseas. Large managerial hierarchies provided only one means of controlling overseas assets, and probably not the best one in many cases before 1914. The appropriate size of a managerial hierarchy needs to be related to the environment in which a firm operated. It follows that the British free-standing companies must be examined on an industry-by-industry (and region-by-region) basis in order to reach a judgement if their lean management structures were a handicap or an advantage. Given that most of the companies operated in alien business cultures or else 'frontier' conditions, and were engaged in either service or primary industries which were subject to greater volatility than manufacturing, there would appear good grounds for arguing that their managerial structures were appropriate to their time and place.

It might be necessary to push some of these arguments further, and extend them to free-standing firms in all industries. A recent contribution by James Markusen emphasizes the importance of knowledge-based, firm-specific assets (FSAs) in MNEs. These are the proprietary assets of the firm that are embodied in such things as the human capital of the employees, 'or even more intangible assets such as management "know-how" or the reputation of the firm'. MNEs, he argues, 'are in the business of supplying the services of the firms' FSAs to foreign subsidiaries'.[30] The London head offices of the free-standing companies—though small—were precisely engaged in supplying such management and other services to their overseas operation, as well as reputation factors. What is the real distinction between free-standing companies and a conventional MNE?

Longevity

There remains uncertainty about the exact fate of the British free-standing companies. As Mark Casson has argued, there were numerous transient free-standing companies,[31] but there were also instances of longer-lived firms, and in some cases underlying continuities were disguised by a change of legal structure for one reason or another. It would appear that the number of free-standing firms floated in Britain to operate in the USA declined after 1900, and that most of the existing free-standing firms had failed or had been taken over by Americans by the end of the First World War. By contrast, as Jean-François Hennart has shown, British free-standing tin mining firms in Malaya and Nigeria prospered until the late 1960s.[32] This issue is complicated by the incorporation of British free-standing firms outside the USA into wider groups, either the post-1914 successors to Chapman's investment groups or new corporate creations. An example was the London Tin Corporation (LTC), which was formed in the 1920s. It secured control of twenty ostensibly free-standing tin companies accounting for about a third of Malaya's production, and by the 1930s it also controlled sufficient British tin companies in Nigeria to account for half that country's tin output. As with the investment groups, LTC rarely took majority ownership of these enterprises, but exercised control through a combination of management and interlocking directorships.[33]

The fates of the British overseas banks after 1914 were significantly different from those of these free-standing companies. No bank was absorbed into a wider investment group, while only in a few exceptional cases did control pass into the hands of their host economies. This latter fate was confined to the handful of British banks which had operated branches in the USA. The last of the Anglo-North American overseas banks was the Bank of British North America, founded in 1836, which survived until 1918, when it and its ninety-two branches in Canada were absorbed by the Bank of Montreal. The next significant example of this phenomenon did not occur until 1976, when the Australian and New Zealand Banking Group (ANZ), which had absorbed by merger all the British 'free-standing' banks active in Australia, shifted its domicile from the UK to Australia.

In general, there were two fates awaiting the overseas banks founded in the nineteenth century. The first was the acquisition of control (or, more exactly, partial ownership) by the large domestic (i.e. clearing) banks, which had avoided multinational banking until shortly before the First World War. Two of the clearing banks made substantial investments in multinational banking. After the First World War Barclays Bank acquired British banks active in the West Indies and Egypt and merged them with a South African registered bank to form, in 1926, Barclays (DCO), a large multinational bank partially owned by Barclays Bank. This autonomous bank lasted as a new kind of semi-free-standing company until it was fully integrated into Barclays in 1971. Another larger clearer, Lloyds, took equity interests in a number of British banks, including the Bank of London and South America, which by 1936 had absorbed all British banking interests in

Latin America. However, these banks effectively continued to function as autonomous free-standing units until 1973, by which time a process of integration into Lloyds was finally completed.[34]

A significant number of the British overseas banks remained free of any domestic bank shareholder and continued to operate through the inter-war years and beyond. After the Second World War a process of mergers took place, usually involving banks in the same region. In 1955 twelve British overseas banks continued to function without a clearing bank as a major shareholder, together with the special case of the Hongkong Bank, which was British managed but registered in Hong Kong. In 1970 the number was down to three British-registered banks—ANZ (with 1,549 branches in Australia and New Zealand), Standard Chartered (with 400 branches in Asia and Africa), and National and Grindlays (with 117 branches in Asia and Africa). ANZ's shift of domicile in 1976, and its acquisition of National and Grindlays in 1984, left Standard Chartered as the sole remaining free-standing overseas bank, which it remained in 1998. The anomalous position of the Hongkong Bank was resolved in the early 1990s when it shifted domicile to Britain and acquired Midland Bank, one of the Big Four clearing banks. As HSBC Holdings, it was in 1994 Europe's largest bank by market capitalization, the UK's third largest company by the same measure, and the thirteenth largest bank in the world by total assets. It is the only European equivalent to Citibank as a truly global bank with a retail deposit base spread over Asia, the Middle East, Europe, and the USA.

Why did the free-standing form last so long in British overseas banking? Three reasons will be considered. First, that it remained a viable governance structure. Secondly, the advantages of incumbency. Thirdly, the role of the British regulatory authorities.

The first reason has already been discussed: it was an appropriate and efficient governance structure for the kind of business being undertaken. With the exception of a single bank in Latin America, the British overseas banks survived the Great Depression as well as the disruption of the two world wars. They were also sufficiently flexible to adjust lending and other strategies to changing circumstances. The banks evolved from trade finance into greater involvement with their host economies. While they emphasized their image as respectable and orthodox 'British'-style banks, they progressively modified the terms on which they would lend. Short-term lending gave way to the provision of longer-term credit, and in regions where collateral was hard to obtain, large amounts of credit were made available on the basis of trust rather than conventional Western banking criteria.[35] The lean governance structures and the socialization strategies arguably made possible a degree of flexibility which a more complicated bureaucratic structure would have found hard to achieve.

An interesting comparison can be made in the inter-war years between the survival of the overseas banks and the direct investments made by the clearing banks in Continental Europe. After 1911 four of England's then Big Five clearing banks established banking subsidiaries in France, Spain, Italy, Switzerland, and elsewhere. These efforts were highly unsuccessful, resulting in heavy and sustained financial losses, as well as a number of farcical episodes, as in the case of Barclays' attempts to secure the Pope's bank account.[36] This episode provides little support for any argument that more modern styles of FDI were more successful than the free-standing companies.

A second important reason for the survival of the free-standing British banks was the advantages of incumbency. In many cases the banks had been 'first movers', or at least had the opportunity to establish substantial franchises alongside locally owned banks. The British banks had substantial physical assets in their host markets in the shape of imposing branch buildings—which conveyed important signals about stability and security. At least as important was their knowledge of local conditions and long-standing relationships with customers based on trust and mutual knowledge. These incumbency advantages were re-enforced by the extensive web of regulations which host governments applied to banking between the 1920s and 1970s. In Australia, New Zealand, and elsewhere, the entry of new foreign banks was effectively blocked from the 1920s. The established British banks found themselves protected from new entrants alongside the local banks.

The incumbency advantages of the overseas banks were partially undermined by two influences after the Second World War. First, from the 1950s, the end of European colonialism and the spread of economic nationalism led many African, Asian, and Latin American governments to restrict the activities of foreign banks in their countries. The British banks which survived and flourished were those whose business interests were in havens where governments continued to pursue liberal, market-oriented policies, such as Singapore and Hong Kong. Secondly, the growth of the global capital and money markets from the 1960s resulted in a fundamental change in the nature of multinational banking, despite continuities with older forms of activity. In the new environment, the organizational structures of the overseas banks were no longer so effective. A much greater degree of professionalism was needed to take part in the new markets, which the British overseas banks (and other British banks) were very short of compared to the large US banks.[37]

Nevertheless the incumbency advantages of the overseas banks could be substantial. The case of Standard Chartered, which tried hard (but failed) to overcome its free-standing heritage in the 1970s and 1980s, is illustrative of this point. Standard Chartered was created in 1970 by the merger of Standard Bank (whose operations covered South Africa and the rest of Africa) and Chartered Bank (whose operations were spread over Asia and the Middle East). Both banks were free-standing in the sense that they still had no domestic banking business in the UK. The new bank adopted a strategy of globalization, which included the purchase of a large California bank in 1979, and it also sought to develop a domestic banking business in Britain. There was a logic to this latter strategy. Standard Chartered's structure meant that its overseas branches had long-term relationships with the subsidiaries of British companies in particular foreign markets, but it had few contacts with the headquarters of large British multinationals, which had traditional relationships with the large clearing banks. As British multinationals began to handle their banking and treasury positions on a worldwide basis, Standard Chartered was at a disadvantage. These banks also had no British deposit base, which meant that Standard Chartered had to buy all of its deposits on the London money markets. This meant, in turn, that the cost of funds, and hence the profit margins of foreign trade-financing, fluctuated with interest rate movements outside the bank's control. A further problem was that the British clearing banks competed ever-more energetically for foreign-trade finance—Standard Chartered's core business.[38]

Through the 1970s and 1980s Standard Chartered sought to overcome its free-standing heritage. In 1973 it acquired a British retail finance company, which turned out to have numerous bad-debt and other problems. In 1975 it began to open a number of branches in Britain in an attempt to start to build a retail deposit base. By 1979 the bank had a definite strategy of competing for 'good quality domestic business'. The problem was that the bank's past meant that its 'name in the UK is not well known'.[39] In 1981 it attempted to take over one of the three big Scottish domestic banks, the Royal Bank of Scotland. This bid was rejected by the British regulatory authorities—primarily in order to protect the autonomy of the Scottish banking system. The failure of this bid weakened the bank. In 1986 it was the target of a takeover bid by Lloyds Bank. This was defeated only when major Far Eastern and Australian customers of the bank took a 40 per cent shareholding in the bank. But by this time the bank was so weakened that it had to dispose of its recently acquired US affiliates and other assets.

The striking feature of Standard Chartered's subsequent recovery was its reversion to its original free-standing structure. The bank had made large losses when it attempted to penetrate markets with which it was not familiar, demonstrating the importance of experience and local knowledge as a source of competitive advantage in multinational banking. As one executive commented retrospectively, 'old colonial boys from Malaysia or Nairobi were planted in Zurich or New York and they couldn't cope'.[40] However, within its traditional Asian and African markets, Standard Chartered had long-established franchises that were potentially very valuable. During the 1990s the bank's profits and reputation recovered as it reverted to a focus on its core markets. As these included the world's fastest-growing economies, such as Malaysia, Singapore and Hong Kong, they offered some of the most profitable opportunities in multinational banking anywhere in the world.

A third reason for the survival of the free-standing British overseas bank was the role of the regulatory authorities. From the First World War onwards, the Bank of England and the British government would not allow a British bank to fail. The high priority given to maintaining the stability of the banking system meant that banks that were endangered—as in the case of Cox & Co. and the Anglo-South American Bank in the interwar years—were prevented from actually failing, and ushered into the safer hands of other banks.[41] In other words, the barriers to exit by failure were made extremely high by the regulators.

In addition, between the 1920s and the 1980s the Bank of England prohibited the acquisition of British overseas banks by foreign banks and even sought hard (though less successfully) to block clearing bank acquisition of them also. During the 1950s and 1960s large US banks, which were starting large-scale multinational growth, were greatly attracted by the prospects of acquiring British overseas banks, which offered ready-made branch networks in attractive markets. The Bank of England was active in the thwarting or the outright blocking of US attempts to acquire several of the overseas banks, a number of which would undoubtedly otherwise have passed into American ownership in the 1950s and 1960s.[42]

Conclusions

Further research on the free-standing company needs to establish a typology of the range of different types of organizational structure covered by this umbrella description. This chapter has suggested that the rationale, performance, effectiveness, and strategies of these types of company need to be analysed on an industry basis.

There are no doubt important similarities across industries—for example, the importance of capital availability in the origins of these firms—but there are also acute dangers in excessive generalization. Certainly banking has a number of idiosyncratic industry-specific characteristics which have to be taken into account when discussing the free-standing British overseas banks. In banking, a modest managerial hierarchy in London did not prevent their London offices from performing essential banking services and providing ongoing strategic managerial functions. In crude terms, a 'brass plate' headquarters could add substantial value. The critical importance of trust and information in banking shaped the way the overseas banks functioned. Their relations with other enterprises—customers, correspondents, and so forth—were based on trust rather than equity, and were typically long term. First-mover and incumbency advantages were particularly important in banking. They help to explain the longevity of the overseas banks. The industry-specific regulatory conditions were also critical. They provide part of the explanation why the overseas banks were only loosely connected with the wider 'investment groups'. They are also important in explaining the longevity of the banks, for formidable barriers to exit were erected by the Bank of England.

NOTES

1. G. Jones, *British Multinational Banking* (Oxford, 1993).
2. M. Wilkins, 'The Free-Standing Company, 1870–1914: An Important Type of British Foreign Direct Investment', *Economic History Review*, 2nd ser., 41 (May 1988), 262–4.
3. S. Chapman, 'British-based Investment Groups before 1914', *Economic History Review*, 2nd ser., 38 (May 1985), 230–51.
4. J. F. Munro, 'Shipping Subsidies and Railway Guarantees: William Mackinnon, Eastern Africa and the Indian Ocean, 1860–93', *Journal of African History*, 28 (1987), 209–30; J. F. Munro, 'Scottish Overseas Enterprise and the Lure of London: The Mackinnon Shipping Group, 1847–1893', *Scottish Economic and Social History*, 8 (1988), 73–87.
5. G. Stang, 'Entrepreneurs and Managers: The Establishment and Organisation of British Firms in Latin America in the Nineteenth and Twentieth Centuries', *Historisk Tidskriff*, 1 (1982), 40–60.
6. Natalia Gurushina, Chapter 6 herein.
7. Wilkins, 'The Free-Standing Company', 265–70.
8. F. H. H. King, *The History of the Hongkong and Shanghai Banking Corporation*, i (Cambridge, 1987).
9. D. Joslin, *A Century of Banking in Latin America: To Commemorate the Centenary in 1962 of the Bank of London and South America Ltd.* (London, 1963).
10. C. Jones, 'Institutional Forms of British Foreign Direct Investment in South America', *Business History*, 39 (Apr. 1997), 31.
11. R. Fry, *Bankers in West Africa* (London, 1976), G. Jones, *British Multinational Banking*, 76.
12. Ibid. 77.

13. Ibid. 158.
14. Ibid. 80.
15. Munro, 'Scottish Overseas Enterprise'.
16. G. Jones, *British Multinational Banking*, 15.
17. P. L. Cottrell, 'The Coalescence of a Cluster of Corporate International Banks, 1855–75', *Business History*, 33 (July 1991), 31–52; G. Jones, *British Multinational Banking*, 17.
18. G. Jones, *Banking and Empire in Iran* (Cambridge, 1986), 26; R. Roberts, *Schroders: Merchants and Bankers* (London, 1992), 104.
19. M. Wilkins, *The History of Foreign Investment in the United States to 1914* (Cambridge, Mass., 1989), 454–63.
20. Fry, *Bankers in West Africa*, 184–6.
21. Wilkins, *The History of Foreign Investment*, 506–7.
22. Wilkins, 'The Free-Standing Company', 279.
23. G. Jones, *Banking and Empire in Iran*, 158–9.
24. S. Muirhead, *Crisis Banking in the East: The History of the Chartered Mercantile Bank of India, London and China 1853–1893* (Aldershot, 1996).
25. G. Jones, *Banking and Empire in Iran*, 70–1.
26. G. Jones, *British Multinational Banking*, 46–53.
27. S. J. Butlin, *Australia and New Zealand Bank* (London, 1961), 334.
28. W. G. Ouchi, 'Markets, Bureaucracies and Clans', *Administrative Science Quarterly*, 25 (1980), 129–41.
29. M. Alvesson and L. Lindkvist, 'Transactions Costs, Clans and Corporate Culture', *Journal of Management Studies*, 30 (1993), 427–52.
30. J. R. Markusen, *Service Trade by the Multinational Enterprise* (Vancouver, 1990), 2.
31. M. Casson, 'Institutional Diversity in Overseas Enterprise: Explaining the Free-Standing Company', *Business History*, 36 (Oct. 1994), 95–108.
32. J.-F. Hennart, 'Free-Standing Firms and the Internalisation of Markets for Financial Capital: A Response to Casson', *Business History*, 36 (Oct. 1994), 118–31.
33. J.-J. van Helten and G. Jones, 'British Business in Malaysia and Singapore since the 1870s', in R. P. T. Davenport-Hines and G. Jones (eds.), *British Business in Asia since 1860* (Cambridge, 1989), 168–9.
34. G. Jones, *British Multinational Banking*.
35. Ibid. 294–315.
36. G. Jones, 'Lombard Street on the Riviera: The British Clearing Banks and Europe 1900–1960', *Business History*, 24 (Apr. 1982), 199–200.
37. G. Jones, *British Multinational Banking*.
38. Ibid. 340–1.
39. Corporate Strategy Conference, 15–17 Nov. 1979, Standard Chartered Archives.
40. 'Standard Shifts into Recovery', *Independent*, 12 Aug. 1993.
41. G. Jones, *British Multinational Banking*, 239–44.
42. Ibid. 260–1, 274–5; G. Jones, 'Competition and Competitiveness in British Banking, 1918–71', in G. Jones and M. Kirby (eds.), *Competitiveness and the State* (Manchester, 1991), 120–40.

14

US Foreign Direct Investment in Electric Utilities in the 1920s

William J. Hausman and John L. Neufeld

Considerable attention has been devoted to 'researching the determinants of the growth of multinational enterprise over the last century'.[1] Yet much more attention has been devoted to manufacturing, trading, and banking than to public utilities. This is certainly the case for US foreign investment in electric utilities, which has been a relatively neglected topic in the history of multinational enterprise. This is unfortunate for a number of reasons: (1) direct investment in electric utilities comprised a substantial component of US foreign direct investment in the period under study here; (2) these foreign investments were related, albeit indirectly, to an event of momentous significance in US economic history, the stock market boom and crash of the late 1920s; and (3) direct investment in electric utilities has again become a topic of discussion and action in the industry because of political and structural changes in the 1990s both in the USA and abroad.[2] The purposes of this chapter are to establish the quantitative importance of US foreign direct investment in electric utilities, which was especially vigorous in the last half of the 1920s, to identify the businesses that made these investments, and to discuss the structure of these multinational businesses, including the extent to which they could be described as 'free-standing companies'.

The concept of the free-standing company was developed by Mira Wilkins to describe a previously misunderstood form of British foreign investment that occurred in Britain's heyday as an international financial leader from the 1870s to the First World War.[3] An open question is whether this institutional form of foreign investment existed in a meaningful sense in other places and times. The vast majority of the foreign direct investments described in this chapter were not made by companies that were free-standing, although in a few cases the entities created to invest in foreign electric utilities could be described as having some of the attributes of free-standing companies. The reasons for this can be

The research on which this paper is based was partially funded by a summer research grant from the College of William & Mary.

explained by drawing on Jean-François Hennart's model of international financial capital transfers. Hennart categorizes foreign investment by whether it was contractual (loans) or hierarchical (equity) and whether the capital transfer was intermediated or not. The structural form of the capital transfer depends on information and enforcement costs in the choice between loans and equity and on the existence of asymmetry between savers and borrowers in determining whether or not the transfer will be intermediated. Hennart argues that free-standing companies were hierarchical without intermediation because they arose 'to finance highly risky foreign projects offering no collateral (hence the need for equity) but when the scale of investment is low and the technology relatively well known (hence no pay-off from intermediation)'.[4] The investments discussed in this chapter were hierarchical and intermediated. They were intermediated because of the relatively large scale of the investments and were hierarchical most likely because the rapid technical and organizational changes occurring in the industry raised transactions costs to the point that hierarchical coordination was more cost effective than contracting.[5]

US Foreign Direct Investment in the 1920s

Around the turn of the twentieth century the USA became a persistent net exporter of goods and services for the first time in its history. Between 1896 and 1914 the positive US trade balance averaged $270 million per year (versus deficits averaging $70 million per year over the previous fifteen years). During the First World War and immediately thereafter, the positive trade balance rose to unprecedented heights, averaging $3.5 billion per year from 1916 to 1920. After a rather rocky return to 'normalcy', the trade balance declined but remained positive during the following decade, averaging $1.3 billion per year from 1921 to 1925 and $1.1 billion per year from 1926 to 1930.[6]

The positive trade balance gave Americans foreign-currency balances and substantial claims on assets. This position reinforced desire on the part of maturing US firms to expand into foreign markets. The result was that the USA, for the first time in its history, became a net investor in foreign countries. From the beginning of the century until the outbreak of war in Europe, the majority of this foreign investment was direct.[7] The huge war surpluses changed the character of foreign investment, which during the war was dominated by government lending, with portfolio investment comprising most of the rest. Between 1914 and 1919 total net USA foreign investment increased by $7.4 billion and the US became a net creditor nation, but only $1.2 billion (16 per cent) of the increase was direct investment. Most of the foreign investment in the first

TABLE 14.1. *US foreign direct investment, 1919–1929*

Sector	FDI 1919 ($m.)	FDI 1924 ($m.)	% change 1919–24	FDI 1929 ($m.)	% change 1924–9	% change 1919–29
Public utilities	138	224	+62	1,025	+358	+643
Manufacturing	795	1,252	+57	1,821	+45	+129
Oil production and distribution	604	967	+60	1,341	+39	+122
Sales and purchasing organizations	255	314	+23	378	+20	+48
Banking	125	125	0	125	0	0
Mining	876	967	+10	1,227	+27	+40
Agriculture	587	918	+56	986	+7	+68
Railroads	297	347	+17	309	−11	+4
Miscellaneous	203	276	+36	342	+24	+68
TOTAL FDI	3,880	5,389	+39	7,553	+40	+95

Sources: M. Wilkins, *The Maturing of Multinational Enterprise: American Business Abroad from 1914 to 1970* (Cambridge, Mass., 1974), 55; C. Lewis, *America's Stake in International Investments* (Washington, 1938), 605.

half of the 1920s was portfolio investment. During the second half of the decade the share going to direct investment gradually rose, with dramatic increases occurring in 1928 and 1929.[8]

The components of US foreign direct investment in the 1920s are presented in Table 14.1. Investment in public utilities played an important role in the decade.[9] Between 1914 and 1919, investment in public utilities increased only slightly, from $133 million to $138 million. This changed dramatically during the 1920s. Public-utility investment was the fastest-growing component of foreign direct investment throughout the 1920s. Especially striking is the increase in public-utility investment that occurred in the last half of the decade, when it comprised nearly 40 per cent of the increase in total foreign direct investment.[10] This investment boom coincided with the rise in the US stock market, and occurred in the midst of a major restructuring of the domestic electric power industry, which was being driven by a vigorous utility holding company movement (assisted by investment bankers). The stocks of electric utility holding companies were among the highest of the high flyers in the stock-market frenzy of the late 1920s. The importance of the USA as a source of foreign investment in the 1920s is a significant aspect of the larger role the country was then playing in the world economy. The fact that such a large and growing share of direct investment was in the public-utility sector was intimately related to events in the domestic industry.

The US Electric Utility Industry in the 1920s

The 1920s was an era of expansion in the domestic electric utility industry. The proportion of urban homes with electricity increased from less than half at the beginning of the decade to nearly 90 per cent by the end, and electricity equally replaced steam as a source of power in factories. Installed generating capacity of investor-owned utilities more than doubled from 12 million kW in 1920 to 28 million kW in 1929; likewise output increased from 38 billion kWh in 1920 to 88 billion kWh in 1929.[11] The expansion was accompanied by rapid technological change, which resulted in increases in the optimum size of electric utilities. Between 1912 and 1929 the maximum size of turbine generators grew by over tenfold.[12] The use of larger generators led electric utilities to expand their service areas, and improvements in transmission capability supported this expansion. In addition, important economic advantages existed if electricity could be provided within a *network* which combined multiple generating stations and diverse users within an interconnected grid owned and controlled by a single company. The result was that the increased demand for electricity was supplied by a decreasing number of utilities. Between 1917 and 1932 the number of privately owned operating utilities in the USA declined by 61 per cent, from 4,224 to 1,627.[13]

The rise of holding companies was impressive in its scope. The share of electricity generated by the ten largest utility companies increased from 25 per cent in 1916 to 71 per cent in 1929. By 1929 the three largest holding companies (United Corporation, Electric Bond & Share, and the Insull interests) alone controlled 45 per cent of total electricity generated in the USA.[14] Holding companies dominated electric and gas utility-financing in the USA, and it is not surprising that they functioned as a conduit for most of the US financing of foreign utilities as well. Their role in foreign investment was a logical extension of their activities in the US electric utility industry.

The Utility Holding Company as an Organizational Structure

The typical US utility holding company owned a minority but controlling interest in a large number of other companies.[15] It was common for holding companies to have a 'pyramid' structure where a top-level holding company would control intermediate-level holding companies, with those at the bottom owning controlling interests in operating utilities. In this way the top-level holding company could exert effective control over the operating companies at the base of the pyramid even though its share of the operating companies' equity might be quite small. Holding companies increased their financial leverage over operating utilities by having intermediate-level companies finance their ownership of stock by issuing bonds or debentures. Such leverage could multiply the profits of top-level holding companies so long as the dividends of operating companies were growing, but made them vulnerable to bankruptcy if operating-company dividends declined, even slightly.

Several factors were responsible for the rise of holding companies. Perhaps the most important factor was the voracious capital requirements of the industry. Much of the total cost of operating an electric utility consists of the costs of generation, transmission, and distribution equipment. The rapid growth of the industry meant that most utilities were permanently in the position of having to spend more on equipment than was received in income. Outside financing was both a necessity and a major concern for operating utilities. Some of the oldest holding companies (United Electric Securities Co., for example) were created by electrical equipment manufacturers, because operating utilities often paid for equipment with stocks or bonds, and a mechanism was needed to turn these securities into cash. Holding companies reduced transaction (information) costs by operating on a national scale. Investors were willing to invest in holding companies, whereas they had been reluctant to invest directly in the smaller operating companies. Holding companies also came to offer the operating companies in their systems access to technical and managerial expertise. As holding companies began to dominate the industry in the 1920s, a number of engineering consulting firms (such as Stone & Webster) adopted the structure, in part to ensure continued access to their clientele. As a result, most of the holding companies maintained a technical staff and provided technical services to their operating company subsidiaries, both domestic and foreign.

As holding companies grew in importance, the financial activity of the industry became an important component of the business of investment bankers. By the late 1920s, some holding companies were formed by investment bankers, at least in part for the underwriting fees that they would provide.[16] The United Corporation is a prime example. By the end of the decade, holding companies had acquired the great majority of the operating utilities in the USA. Later acquisitions often came at very high prices because existing systems found themselves bidding against one another for properties. It is not surprising in such a situation that some companies turned their attention to foreign countries. Foreign operating companies would have seemed inexpensive to American holding companies, managerial and technical expertise was needed, and the potential for expansion of electric service was great.

By at least one measure, holding companies were spectacularly successful in the 1920s. Figure 14.1 presents stock price indexes for utility holding companies, utility operating companies, and industrial companies from 1925 to 1933. The figure forcefully demonstrates the

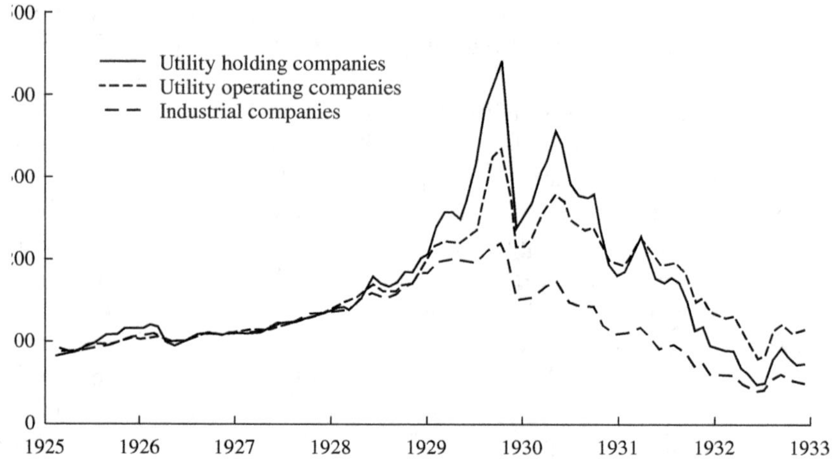

Fig. 14.1. Price indexes of utility and industrial stocks, 1925–1933
Note: Utility indexes include gas and electric companies.
Source: Alfred Cowles 3d and Associates, *Common Stock Indexes* (Bloomington, Ind., 1939), 68–9, 86–7, 96–7.

contribution of utilities to the stock-market boom of the late 1920s.[17] An initial, brief escalation in the price of utility holding company stocks lasted from mid-1924 through 1925. There was a setback in early 1926, and from then until the spring of 1928, utility stocks generally kept pace with industrials. Beginning in the spring of 1928 utility stocks surged, especially those of holding companies, and dramatically outpaced the market until the crash in September and October of 1929. Between June 1928 and September 1929 utility holding company stocks rose in value by 170 per cent, utility operating company stocks by 114 per cent, and industrials by 46 per cent. They maintained their position relatively well for the next few years, but eventually faded badly as a number of prominent holding companies went bankrupt.

Was this a purely speculative bubble or were there underlying fundamentals that might help explain this performance? In addition to the real developments taking place in the industry during the 1920s there is evidence that investors perceived the relative risk of investing in electric utilities to be falling during the 1920s. Figure 14.2 demonstrates that bond yields on a sample of electric light and power companies were falling faster than yields on a comparable sample of industrial bonds. After 1922 the yield on electric light and power bonds was less than the yield on industrial bonds (although this was not true for electric railway bonds, a declining subsector of the industry). Thus there is some evidence that the superior performance of electric utility stocks was warranted.[18] Finally, in the critical period from 1926 to 1929 yields on

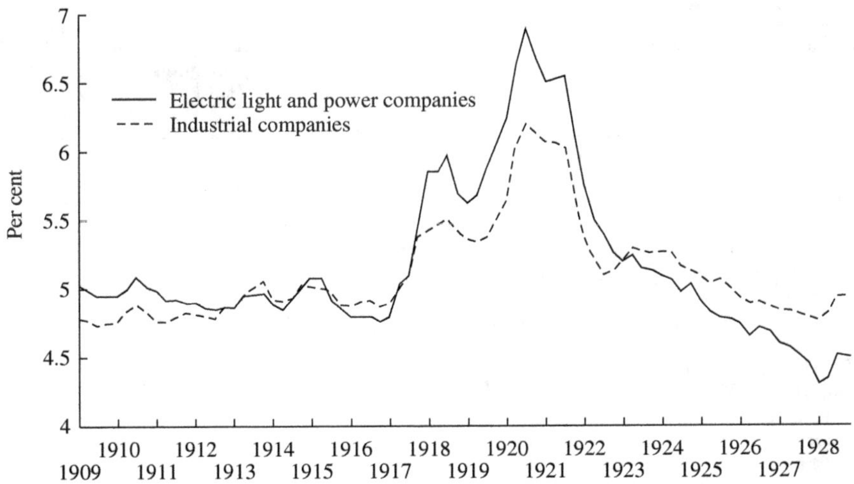

Fig. 14.2. Quarterly bond yields, 1909–1928
Source: J. F. Reinboth, 'Measurement of Risk in Public Utility Industries', *Journal of Land and Public Utility Economics*, 6 (1930), 83–93.

newly issued utility holding company bonds fell faster than yields on newly issued operating company bonds.[19]

Investments in Foreign Electric Utilities at the End of the 1920s

We have attempted to identify, classify, and estimate the relative magnitude of US investments in foreign electric utilities up to the end of the 1920s. The data are based primarily on US sources and there are undoubtedly omissions.[20] The results are presented in Table 14.2. Any such listing is fraught with difficulties. The book value of total assets does not measure the actual amount of US capital transferred, but it does give a sense of the size of the foreign enterprise controlled and permits the major investors to be identified. We have divided the investing firms into several categories based on the following characteristics: whether or not their primary interest was in foreign investing, whether or not they were a utility holding company or a non-utility firm primarily interested in obtaining a source of power, and whether or not they were a utility or an investment trust. We believe that this taxonomy is reasonable, although the lines may be blurred, especially between utility holding companies and trusts and entities created by investment bankers heavily involved in the industry. It is possible to question the extent of 'control' intended in some of these investments, and in some cases it is not clear whether the US holding

TABLE 14.2. *US foreign direct investments in electric utilities, 1929/30*

Foreign direct investors	Book value of foreign assets ($m.)	Installed generating capacity (kW)
Large holding companies or interests with substantial foreign holdings		
Electric Bond & Share Co.		
American & Foreign Power Co. (investments in Argentina, Brazil, Chile, China, Costa Rica, Cuba, Ecuador, Guatemala, India, Mexico, Panama, and Venezuela; minority interests in Europe and Japan)	756[a]	883,000[a]
Electric Investors Inc. (minority interests in Canada, France, Germany, Italy, and Japan)	—	—
J. E. Aldred interests		
Shawinigan Water & Power Co. (Canada)	146	600,000
International Power Securities Corp. (minority interests, especially Italy and France)	42	—
Aldred Investment Trust (minority interests in Canada, Italy, other European countries)	—	—
Aldred Investment Corp. (Canada) (holdings not specified)	—	—
Smaller holding companies or interests primarily with foreign holdings		
Intercontinents Power Co. (American Equities Co.) (Argentina, Chile, and Brazil)	20	24,000
Morrison–McCall interests	20[b]	22,400[c]
Compañia Eléctrica Chapala, Guadalajara (Mexico)		
Large holding companies with foreign holdings		
United Corporation		
(minority interests in France and other holding companies with foreign interests)	—	—
Niagara Hudson Power Corp.		
Canadian Niagara Power Co. Ltd. (Canada)	17	70,100
St Lawrence Securities Co. (Canada)	—	—
Middle West Utilities (Insull interests)		
Great Lakes Power Co. Ltd. (Canada)	7	21,600
Central & Southwest (Matamoras, Mexico)	—	—
Stone & Webster Inc. (Engineers Public Service)		
Ponce Electric Co. (Puerto Rico)	1.4	4,000
Jamaica Public Service Ltd. (Jamaica, BWI)	3.4	3,700
El Paso Electric Co. (Juarez, Mexico)	—	—
(minority interests in Canada, Mexico, Poland, etc.)	—	—
Public Utilities Consolidated (W. B. Foshay & Co.)		
Central American Power (Nicaragua)	2.0[d]	—
Planta Electrica (Honduras)	0.5[d]	—

TABLE 14.2. *(Continued)*

Foreign direct investors	Book value of foreign assets ($m.)	Installed generating capacity (kW)
Central Public Service		
Islands Gas & Electric (Haiti, Dominican Republic, and Mallorca)	22	—
Maine & New Brunswick Power Co. (Central Gas & Electric) (Canada)	—	6,600
(several small Canadian interests)	—	—
Cities Service		
New Brunswick Power Co. (Federal Light & Traction Co.) (New Brunswick, Canada)	7.6	—
North American Gas & Electric Co. (Saskatchewan, Canada)	—	3,600
National Power & Light Co. Ltd. (Iowa Southern Utilities Co.) (Saskatchewan, Canada)	3	10,500
Utilities Power & Light		
Greater London & Counties Trust (UK)	83	—
Maritime Coal, Railway & Power Co. (Nova Scotia, Canada)	—	—
Associated Gas & Electric		
Manila Electric Co. (Manila, Philippines)	—	22,000
Associated International Electric Corp. (provincial Philippine utilities)	—	—
Maritime Electric Co. Ltd. (New England Gas & Electric) (Nova Scotia, New Brunswick, PEI, Canada)	—	4,250
Standard Gas & Electric (Byllesby interests)		
Empresa de Servicios do los Estados Mexicanos, SA (Nogales, Sonora)	—	—
(other properties in Hermosillo, Culican, and Guayamas)	—	—
International Utilities Corporation (registered in Canada)		
Canadian Utilities Corp. (Alberta and Saskatchewan, Canada)	—	—
(investments in Canada, Spain, Europe, and South America)	—	—
United Utilities and Service Corporation (several utilities serving Canary Islands)	9	—
General Power & Light Co.		
Arizona Edison Co. (small holdings in Mexico)	—	—
Industrial or trading firms with foreign utility holdings		
International Paper & Power Co.		
Canadian Hydro-Electric Corp. Ltd. (Canada)	134	465,000
Aluminum Company of America		
Duke–Price Power Co. (Canada)	64	370,000
Union Carbide and Carbon Co.		
Sauda Falls Co., Ltd. (Norway)	8	44,800[e]
Meraker Smelting (Norway)	—	—

TABLE 14.2. *(Continued)*

Foreign direct investors	Book value of foreign assets ($m.)	Installed generating capacity (kW)
Mexican Candaleria Mining Co. (proposed development)	—	—
W. R. Grace & Co. (several plants in Chile and Peru)	—	—
International Combustion Engineering Corp. (built and operated plant in Spain)	—	—
Utility investment trusts with significant foreign holdings		
Public Utility Holding Corporation of America		
South Am. Ry. Co. (Buenos Aires Lacroze Lt. & Power Co.) (Argentina)	—	16,000
Union Électrique Rurale (one-third interest in French utility)	—	—
Westphalia United Electric Corp. (one-half interest in German utility)	85	233,000

Notes: A dash indicates that information cannot be determined or foreign investment cannot be segregated.
Sources: Moody's (1930), unless otherwise noted.
[a] Annual Report of the company (includes some non-utility assets)
[b] *Electrical World* (6 May 1926).
[c] *Electrical World* (4 Sept. 1926).
[d] FTC, part 25, 196, 291.
[e] *Public Utility Compendium* (May 1930).

company actually exerted control, sought input into the decision-making process, or merely viewed foreign utility holdings as risk-spreading portfolio investments.

Electric Bond & Share, one of the venerable firms in the industry, was the company by far most heavily committed to the acquisition and management of foreign utilities, and it operated on a near-global basis. At the end of 1929 it controlled around half, and possibly substantially more, of the total assets of US-controlled foreign electric utilities, and it had clear intentions of expanding.[21] But it did not stand alone as a major foreign investor. The investments of John Edward Aldred, an important but overlooked utility executive and financier, were substantial (especially in Canada) and were also growing at the end of the decade. The investments of the non-utility companies were impressive in their scale, although much of the power generated was used for industrial purposes. Still, this represented a substantial commitment of capital. A large number of holding companies were making foreign investments, some of them quite large (Utilities Power & Light's investment in Greater London & Counties Trust, for example). Although most of their foreign investments would have been small relative to the domestic holdings of these companies, foreign investments most likely would have continued to grow given conditions in the domestic industry at the end of the 1920s. There also were a few smaller holding companies and at least one investment trust that specialized in foreign utilities.

In order better to understand the process by which the strategy of direct investment in foreign electric utilities was undertaken by the somewhat disparate firms discussed above, we intend to discuss in more detail several of the companies in the table. We will discuss Electric Bond & Share because of its obvious importance, Stone & Webster because of its early and deep interest in foreign investment, J. E. Aldred's interests because little has previously been written about him, the non-utility firms because of the scale of their investments, Morrison-McCall interests because they are an example of a smaller holding company, and the Public Utility Holding Corporation of America because it was an important and expansive investment trust formed at the height of the boom and was one of the few entities that could be described as having some of the attributes of the free-standing company.

Electric Bond & Share Company (American & Foreign Power Company)

The Electric Bond & Share Company traces its origins to the earliest days of the industry. In order to sell their electrical systems, the equipment manufacturers encouraged the establishment of local electric-lighting companies. But the early lighting companies were small, strictly local enterprises, and financing them was sometimes difficult. In order to help promote these local companies, the manufacturers would accept the securities (both stocks and bonds) of these companies as partial payment for equipment. The problem was what to do with these securities. Charles A. Coffin of the Thomson–Houston Company devised a way to turn the bonds that the company held into cash. Thomson–Houston organized the United Electric Securities Company, which then issued its own bonds and debentures. With its superior reputation, and backed by a diverse portfolio of operating company utilities, the bonds were successfully sold to the public. When the Edison General Electric Company merged with Thomson–Houston in 1892, the newly formed General Electric Company absorbed the subsidiary.[22]

General Electric continued to hold the capital stock in a number of electric utilities. To turn these stocks into cash it formed the Electric Bond & Share Company in 1905. Control of Electric Bond & Share was put in the hands of Sidney Z. Mitchell, who demanded and received considerable independence from General Electric, even though General Electric held all of the common stock of Electric Bond & Share.[23] The strategy developed by Electric Bond & Share was to form a series of holding companies to take control of a large number of diverse operating companies by accepting the common stocks previously held by General Electric, to merge as many as possible of the operating companies in a region into a single operating company which would then be large enough to have an identity with the investing public (and which might entail interconnections and rationalizations to reduce costs), to refinance these companies by selling bonds, debentures, and preferred stock to the public, and to maintain effective control by holding a sufficient amount of the common stock.[24] The funds raised were then used to pay for improvements and expansion in the business. Although local consolidation was one of the strategic goals, each holding company also pursued territorial diversification. Active management of properties was also a part of the strategy. Construction, engineering, and operating management were provided. The first holding company created was American Gas & Electric Company in 1906, followed by American Power & Light Company in 1909, National Power & Light Company in 1921, and American & Foreign Power Company in 1923. At least partly in response to an impending federal investigation of a 'power trust' (and partly because their interests had diverged), General Electric spun off Electric Bond & Share in February 1925.[25]

Electric Bond & Share was to become by far the largest single US investor in foreign electric utilities.[26] The strategy began during the First World War when Electric Bond & Share was approached by the US government about the possibility of purchasing electrical properties in Panama. The government was concerned about the war's effects on the Panama Canal and suggested to Electric Bond & Share that it purchase the electric systems in Panama City and Colón. After a careful study, the company purchased the properties in 1917. As a publication of the company stated,

> An important consideration which made the projected venture of Bond and Share seem desirable from the standpoint of broad public policy was the knowledge that the remodeling and expansion of these Latin-American utility plants would lead to the purchase of machinery and equipment in this country (instead of in Europe as had previously been the practice) and materially help to sustain employment in the United States. Furthermore, it was reasonable to assume that the investment of large amounts of American capital in Latin America would help to maintain a better understanding between the United States and the Latin-American republics.[27]

In 1919 the State Department contacted Electric Bond & Share about obtaining properties seized from the Germans by the Guatemalan government. A temporary lease was arranged and in 1920 the electric utility was purchased. In 1920 Electric Bond & Share and International

General Electric built an electric railway and hydroelectric plant for the government of Santa Catarina in Brazil, which was the first of a series of investments in that country.[28] The first Cuban property was acquired in 1922 in Santiago, which was the genesis of the Cuban Electric Company. Electric Bond & Share sought to expand in Cuba by adding the utility operating in Havana. This was ostensibly controlled by German capital represented in New York by Speyer & Company. Sidney Mitchell quietly bought enough of the stock to gain control and brought it into the system.[29] By 1923 Bond & Share had invested over $17 million in Central and South America.

In December 1923 Electric Bond & Share created the American & Foreign Power Company to serve as a vehicle for further foreign expansion. The first annual report of the company asserted that, if domestic diversification was a profitable strategy, then it made sense to diversify internationally, citing as justification the principle followed by Lloyds for over 200 years.[30] Over the next six years American & Foreign Power expanded rapidly, with total assets rising eventually to nearly a billion dollars (see Figure 14.3). It acquired properties (from national interests as well as from Canadian and British companies, some of which could be characterized as free-standing) in Ecuador, Costa Rica, Chile,[31] Argentina, Mexico,[32] India, and Brazil.[33] In 1927 the industry trade journal *Electrical World* took notice, commenting that

America's capital surplus is finding an attractive market in the development of public utilities abroad. By the proposed acquisition of a group of utilities in South America, France and Japan, The American & Foreign

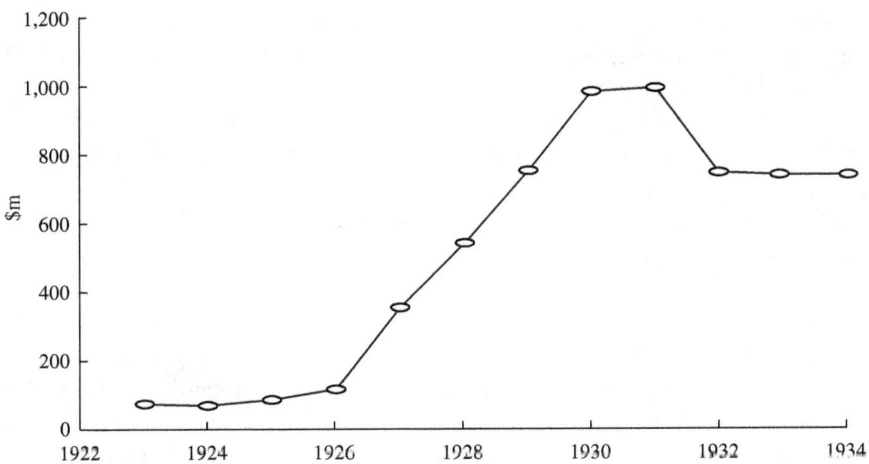

Fig. 14.3. American & Foreign Power Company (total assets)
Source: American & Foreign Power Company, *Annual Reports* (1924–35).

Power Company moves forward to first place in the control of public utility companies in the foreign field. The properties referred to have already been acquired by Electric Bond & Share Company under a specially established subsidiary, the South American Power Company.[34]

American & Foreign Power purchased the Shanghai Power Company in 1929. The Shanghai Municipal Council had decided to sell the company and solicited bids. This was the oldest and largest electric utility in China, established by foreign investors in the foreign settlement of Shanghai in 1882. The Municipal Council purchased the company in 1893 and had once previously tried to sell it. American & Foreign Power made the highest of three offers and purchased the company for $32 million. This was the largest single American investment in China at the time.[35]

Electric Bond & Share used related holding companies to purchase minority interests in foreign utilities. Electric Investors Inc. was organized in 1909 for the purpose of trading, dealing, and underwriting securities. By the late 1920s it held cross-interests in American & Foreign Power Company and a large stake in the Great Consolidated Electric Power Company Ltd. (Daido Denryoku Kabushiki Kaisha) of Japan. It also held interests not exceeding 6 per cent in the Canadian firm, Shawinigan Water & Power (see below), British Columbia Power Corporation Ltd., Toho Electric Power Company Ltd., and the Italian Superpower Corporation.[36] Italian Superpower was formed in January 1928 'to acquire substantial interests, but in no case a majority of stock of a number of important electric power and light companies in Italy'.[37] It held interests in fourteen Italian companies plus Società Nazionale per lo Sviluppo delle Imprese Elettriche. In January 1929 American Superpower, an investment company with $223 million in assets created by the investment bankers Bonbright & Company (which had links to Electric Bond & Share), acquired 50 per cent of the voting stock of Italian Superpower.[38]

Electric Bond & Share maintained a special relationship with American & Foreign Power. It was the only holding company in the system in which it claimed to hold a majority interest.[39] Mitchell's biographer, quoting the Securities and Exchange Commission, noted that 'between 1925 and 1931 Bond and Share realized $288,580,000 from the sale of its own securities and the greater portion was invested in American & Foreign Power'.[40] When Electric Bond & Share was reorganized on 13 March 1929, it increased its investment account overnight from $93 million to $493 million.[41] The $400 million write-up was entirely attributed to an increase in the 'market' value of the holdings of American & Foreign Power.[42]

Stone & Webster (Engineers Public Service)

The story of Stone & Webster offers a contrast to that of Electric Bond & Share. Although Stone & Webster was a quite sophisticated participant in international endeavours, the company was much more conservative than Bond & Share, both in its corporate structure and in its acquisition of foreign electric utilities. Perhaps this derived from the engineering as opposed to financial origins of the company.

Charles Stone and Edwin Webster began as consulting and designing engineers in the pioneering days of the electric utility industry. Their technical expertise gave them a good sense of the value of electrical properties, which they eventually sought to manage and control. Not until the mid-1920s, however, did they form a holding company, Engineers Public Service, to serve as the vehicle to control the utilities for which they had been providing services.[43] Stone & Webster was also one of the pioneer firms in the industry in terms of its interest in foreign projects, but it did not become a dominant foreign investor during the boom of the 1920s.

Stone and Webster were classmates and friends at the Massachusetts Institute of Technology. Shortly after graduation they formed a partnership, Massachusetts Electrical Engineering Company (1889) with a capitalization of $2,600. They started by designing and installing electrical generation and transmission systems and street railways. For finance they could draw on a family connection with the banking house Kidder, Peabody (where Webster's father was a partner), and for engineering advice and staffing they cultivated existing ties with MIT. According to the company's historian, the Panic of 1893 had a profound effect on the young electrical industry but an ironically positive effect on Stone & Webster, as the firm had come to be known by then. When the electrical manufacturers found themselves in financial difficulty, they had to dispose of the securities of many of the operating companies they had accepted as payment for electrical equipment: 'To solve the problem, hastily organized financial syndicates purchased the operating-company securities, moving control of electrical operating properties from manufacturers to investment bankers, some of which were in Boston.'[44] Much of Stone & Webster's early business was in evaluating and appraising electrical properties so that an accurate value could be put on them. 'Stone & Webster was called upon to make hundreds of appraisals throughout the United States and Canada.'[45] This led them to expand into managing and owning electrical properties. The first property acquired was Cumberland Electric Light & Power Company of Nashville, which they bought from Morgan interests in 1894 after having been asked to appraise the property by the investment bankers.[46]

The first indication that Stone & Webster might be interested in foreign endeavours was when the firm's financial officer, Cameron Forbes, was reported in April 1898 to have been 'in Mexico investigating a business possibility there'.[47] Nothing apparently came of this visit. Stone & Webster continued to collect domestic properties, including the Savannah Electric Company, which engaged them for the first time with the Boston financiers Lee, Higginson & Company, which was to become a leader in utility financing. Corporate reorganizations occurred as growth continued. A securities department was established in 1902 and the following year its first major underwriting operation was the initial public offering of the Philadelphia Electric Company. In July 1906 Stone & Webster Engineering Corporation was formed, followed in 1907 by Stone & Webster Management Association.[48]

The first substantial foreign direct investment was made in 1901 when Stone & Webster organized and became general manager of the Ponce Electric Company in Puerto Rico. Ponce Electric owned the securities of Ponce Railway & Light Company, which operated an electric railway between Ponce and its port and provided power for the lighting systems of both.[49] In 1903 Stone & Webster served as transfer agent and became general manager of the Cape Breton Electric Company Ltd. in Sydney, Nova Scotia, but it never gained control of the company, which provided electric lighting and street-car service in Sydney and North Sydney.[50] Stone & Webster also organized the El Paso Electric Company in 1903, which operated an interurban railway to Juarez, Mexico, and did the electric lighting, power, and traction business in El Paso and Juarez.[51] The company continued to expand its activities, undertaking a number of large construction projects and even venturing into manufacturing. On the eve of the First World War Stone & Webster had offices in twenty-five states, Canada, and the West Indies.[52]

Stone & Webster provides an excellent example of the effect the war had on the way some American businessmen felt about investing in the rest of the world. Although Stone & Webster had a large presence in Canada, and had casually investigated investment possibilities in Britain, the war served as a catalyst for action. As Stone told a group of industrialists

> London has been for generations the financial and commercial center of the world, but at the moment, she needs assistance. We have become a rich nation and have as yet not developed our own internal resources. Assisting in the development of these resources, and at the same time holding out a helping hand to the other nations of the world, is the essence of great

opportunity which now presents itself to us. After this war is at an end, all the nations involved will need help.[53]

The ambiguity evident in the statement (domestic needs, perceived opportunities, a tinge of altruism) was to become evident after the war.

When Frank Vanderlip of National City Bank organized the American International Corporation in 1915[54] and raised $50 million in seed money to provide an investment vehicle for businessmen interested in pursuing foreign investments, he hired Charles A. Stone to be the company's president. Stone moved to New York, and American International's and Stone & Webster's New York offices became one and the same. George J. Baldwin, a long-time associate of Stone & Webster experienced in electric railway management, became vice-president of American International, and several other Stone & Webster employees were transferred from Boston to New York.[55]

In January 1916 Stone & Webster significantly bolstered its international presence by purchasing a half-interest in the Ulen Contracting Corporation. American International and Marshall Field held the other half-interest as an investment. Stone & Webster engaged in a number of major construction projects, both domestic and foreign, during the war.

At the close of the war Stone & Webster reconsidered its commitment to foreign investment:

The company eyed a global market but the more immediate opportunities lay at its own doorstep, and there was good reason to move cautiously beyond American borders. US utility companies were ready for improvements and expansions postponed during the war. Moreover, the feeling of international involvement began to shrink back into isolationism, as Americans shunned the League of Nations and took up a new cause labeled 'a return to normalcy'.[56]

Stone & Webster did not rule out expanding overseas, but remained 'attuned primarily to engineering and construction needs in this country'.[57] Stone remained as president of American International until 1923.

The 1920s was an era of domestic expansion and for Stone & Webster a more modest movement than might have been expected into foreign electric utilities. Webster visited Japan shortly after the war, and Stone & Webster was subsequently awarded a contract to design and construct a $10 million plant for the Shō River Hydroelectric Company on Honshu, but the project was discontinued and the contract cancelled when a financial crisis struck Japan.[58] In 1923 Stone & Webster combined with Russell Bell, a Canadian industrialist, to purchase the West India Electric Company in Kingston, reorganized as Jamaica Public Service Ltd.[59]

In 1924 there was renewed interest in Japan. Stone & Webster engineers made two studies of Japanese power companies on assignment for Lee, Higginson & Co. and Guaranty Co. of New York. While there, they also visited some electric properties on their own behalf. The decision was made to maintain contacts but for the present to limit attention to making appraisals for the investment bankers. George Muhlfeld, who headed Stone & Webster's construction and engineering division, remained optimistic about prospects for electric investments in Japan: 'It cannot feed its people, so to continue to grow, and really to exist, it has to become an industrial nation, and what coal has done for Britain, water power can do for Japan.'[60] A later visit to China by Webster and Muhlfeld resulted in a much less optimistic assessment.

From 1925 to the end of the decade, Stone & Webster jockeyed for position in the domestic market with other utility holding companies.[61] It did not pursue a vigorous strategy of acquiring and managing foreign electric utilities, although its construction and banking activities led it to acquire significant minority holdings in a number of foreign companies, including Utilities Corporation (Poland) Ltd. (12 per cent of voting stock), Idroelettrica Piemonte (18,702 shares), International Power Securities Corporation (4,500 shares), Devonshire Investing Corporation, and the Russian Finance & Construction Company.[62]

J. E. Aldred's Electrical Investments

John Edward Aldred was a major but largely overlooked participant in international electric utility investments. Described as 'an active and imaginative banker of Boston',[63] Aldred, with the support of the Aluminum Company of America (then the Pittsburgh Reduction Company, later known as Alcoa), established the Shawinigan Water & Power Company (which by the mid-1920s had constructed the third-largest hydroelectric installation in Canada).[64] Aldred later became president of the Consolidated Gas, Electric Light & Power Company of Baltimore (which he used as a forum vigorously to promote foreign investment in that city), and in the 1920s formed several international investment companies that participated in the financing of numerous foreign electric utilities.

The Shawinigan Water & Power Company was incorporated in 1898 and three years later began producing power from a 10,000 hp hydroelectric installation. Alcoa had been searching for an appropriate hydroelectric site to locate its energy-intensive process, and, according to the company's historian, they acquired the rights to develop Shawinigan Falls on the St Maurice River in 1899. The

Shawinigan Water & Power Company was incorporated in Canada, with the US financier J. E. Aldred as president and apparently exerting control. The power company established a contractual relationship with Alcoa, dedicating a portion of its output to Alcoa through contracts that guaranteed that they would not sell power to any other aluminum producers.[65] The power company also benefited from this relationship, because Alcoa's rolling mill at Shawinigan supplied the aluminum wires that permitted construction of a transmission line to Montreal.[66]

Aldred soon became involved in other projects. He was appointed receiver of an uncompleted hydroelectric project on the Susquehanna River in 1909 because of his reputation for developing Shawinigan and he brought with him Shawinigan's chief engineer.[67] In 1910 Aldred and Herbert A. Wagner took control of the Consolidated Gas, Electric Light & Power Company of Baltimore. Aldred became one of the city's greatest boosters, using his Canadian as well as English connections to attract capital to Baltimore.[68]

During the 1920s Aldred's activities in international finance increased dramatically. He remained president of Shawinigan Water & Power and of Consolidated Gas of Baltimore, and formed investment firms in New York (40 Wall St), London (Lombard St), Paris (20 Place Vendôme), and Canada. Aldred continued to expand his interests in foreign utilities throughout the decade.[69]

In January 1927 Shawinigan purchased all the common stock of Eastern Canada Power Company, which served Huntington, Quebec.[70] Shawinigan also owned a substantial interest in the stock of the Laurentide Power Company, which in turn controlled several other Canadian utilities serving Quebec.[71] Aldred had complicated joint interests in other Canadian utilities. Shawinigan held a substantial stake in Montreal Heat, Light & Power and they jointly controlled Montreal Tramways (through ownership of another holding company, United Securities Ltd.). Aldred also had an interest in Canadian Light & Power Company, Ltd.[72]

The Aldred Investment Trust (organized in Massachusetts in 1927) held minority interests in the Adamello General Electric Company of Italy, Edison General Italian Electric Company of Milan, Shawinigan Water & Power, and the International Power Securities Company, along with US holdings.[73]

International Power Securities Corporation was controlled by Aldred. Incorporated in Delaware in April 1923 as the Italian Power Company, the name was changed to International Power Securities Corporation in 1924. The stated purpose of the company was to 'acquire securities of public utility companies operating in the United

States and foreign countries'. In 1929 the company had assets of $42 million ($36 million in securities), with substantial interests in Italy, including 57,894 shares of Edison General Italian Electric Company valued at $1.6 million.[74]

In a talk given in New York in the summer of 1926, Professor Gian Giacomo Ponti, a member of the Italian Parliament and head of an electric light and power company in Turin (Società Idroelettrica Piemonte) extolled the skills of the Italian engineers and noted the recent contributions of American capital to Italian electrical developments:

> American capital had joined in the financing of these useful enterprises, and we note its presence in the most important undertakings, such as the Milan Edison Company, the Piedmont, the Roman and the Venetian groups. It would be difficult to overestimate the significance of this union of Italian electrical and American financial genius in the development of electricity and its application to industry in Italy.[75]

J. E. Aldred was both a utility executive and a financier, and was a major participant in foreign utility investments, but he did not appear to have created a full-scale firm providing engineering and managerial services. The precise extent of control he exerted is not known, but it was almost certainly substantial for his Canadian interests, probably less so for his European interests. So little is known about the technical sources on which he could draw that it is impossible to categorize his interrelated interests, but they did not have the characteristics of a free-standing company.

Non-Utility Companies with Electrical Holdings

Companies using energy-intensive processes frequently participated in the development of foreign electric power sites. The case of Shawinigan Water & Power has already been discussed, but other Americans were to become interested in Canadian electric power. Early in the twentieth century James B. Duke, president of the American Tobacco Company, had been diversifying into electric power, electric railways, and textiles and was considering entering the aluminum business. He initially sought a source of bauxite but had also been looking for hydroelectric sites. The Saguenay region of Quebec captured his attention and he purchased several properties in the area in 1913. He did not immediately pursue the project, but again became interested after the war. In 1922 he approached Sir William Price, whose family had developed the pulp and paper industry in the area and who had connections with Royal Trust, Bank of Montreal, and Royal Bank. At about the same time, Duke was approached by J. E. Aldred, who wanted to expand his own power operations. Duke ultimately failed to obtain a source of bauxite and ended up merging his properties with Alcoa in 1925. Duke died shortly after the merger and Alcoa ended up with slightly over 50 per cent ownership of the Duke–Price Power Company, with Shawinigan Water & Power and Duke–Price interests holding about a quarter each.[76]

Other companies purchased or developed foreign power sites. A major producer of power that obtained substantial interests in Canada in the late 1920s was the International Paper & Power Company. The International Paper Company was incorporated in New York in 1898 as an amalgamation of a large number of north-eastern paper companies and by the 1920s was the largest manufacturer of paper in the world. International Paper & Power Company was organized as a holding company in November 1928. In March 1929 the company organized another holding company, International Hydro-Electric System, which controlled the New England Power Association and the Canadian Hydro-Electric Corporation Ltd. During 1929 the company purchased the entire common stock of International Power & Paper Company of Newfoundland Ltd.[77] The Union Carbide company owned the entire stock of the Sauda Falls Company Ltd. (Aktieselskabet Saudefaldene) of Norway. The company was organized in 1913 for the purpose of developing the power resources of the Storelven in the district of Rogoland; it had installed generating capacity of 60,000 hp and supplied around 40 per cent of its output under contract to Union Carbide's Electric Furnace Products Company Ltd.[78] In 1929 Union Carbide also purchased Aktieselskabet Meraker Smelteverk, a Norwegian smelter with some hydroelectric plants.[79] W. R. Grace & Company, in conjunction with its foreign operations, owned some traction, light, and power properties in Chile and Peru.[80] The Mexican Candelaria Mining Company, an American enterprise led by Charles Dunphy of San Francisco, operated mines, timberlands, and plantations in western Mexico. In 1925 the company announced plans to construct a hydroelectric plant in the Sierra Madres, near the historic mining town of San Dimas. The plant was expected to have an ultimate capacity of 250,000 hp, with one-half anticipated in eighteen months, the rest in three years. The company intended to run transmission lines to the mining districts of Durango and Sinaloa and into the borders of the states of Sonora and Jalisco and eventually to Mazatlan.[81] Finally, International Combustion Engineering Corporation constructed electric plants in England and Italy and then turned them over to local interests. According to *Electrical World*, the company intended 'to build and operate' a plant of the same type in southern Spain.[82]

Morrison–McCall Interests

Central Power & Light was organized in 1916 by R. W. Morrison and W. S. McCall. They had developed a number of properties, the most important of which was the Central Texas Power Company, but also had some foreign holdings. In 1922 they had acquired the Compañia Eléctrica Matamoras, SA, serving the border town across the Rio Grande from Brownsville. They also owed a Chilean steamship company, Compañia de Vapores de Chili. In August 1925 Middle West Utilities Company bought out most of the US properties of Morrison–McCall and organized the Central & South West Utilities Company.[83] The following year Morrison–McCall expanded in Mexico. As *Electrical World* reported, 'One of the largest industrial transactions that have taken place in Mexico for several years was the purchase several months ago of the electric and rapid transit holdings of the Compañia Eléctrica Chapala of Guadalajara by R. W. Morrison of San Antonio.'[84] The company was purchased from the Banco Nacional of Mexico City. The property consisted of three hydroelectric plants with 30,000 hp capacity situated on Santiago River. Morrison anticipated spending around a million dollars enlarging and improving the electrical properties, increasing capacity to 38,000 hp. He also expressed the belief that the Santiago River had a potential for development nearly equal to that of Niagara Falls, and contemplated serving a market with a 300-mile radius: 'Within that radius are many important mining districts where low-grade ore properties cannot now be successfully worked because of high fuel costs, as well as a number of cities and towns of considerable size with splendid future prospects [including Manzanillo, Colima, and Tepic].'[85] The largest customer of the Compañia Eléctrica Chapala at the time of the purchase was the Compañia Cinco Minas, an American company using 6,000 hp at its mines which were located sixty miles north-west of Guadalajara. Morrison expressed great confidence in the future of Mexico and praised its workers. E. J. Puig, the former manager of the electric light and power plant at Laredo, Texas, was to be president and general manager. This may well have been a case where utility-owners saw an opportunity to sell a domestic utility, taking the profit and searching for opportunities in a foreign nation.

Public Utility Holding Corporation of America

The Public Utility Holding Corporation of America was organized in September 1929 by Harris, Forbes & Company, American Founders Corporation, and United Founders Corporation. Its stated purpose was:

The primary objective of the management will continue, for the present at least, to be the acquisition of large minority interests in various public utility companies where the management of our corporation is represented on the board of directors and where our holdings, together with those of our associates who are in charge of the management, represent control of the company.[86]

The company proposed investing in companies that would benefit from a capital restructuring, which in turn would increase earning power and hence the value of the capital stock. This echoed the initial purpose of Electric Bond & Share, except that it was to be applied primarily to foreign utilities. With only fifteen employees, it definitely had characteristics of a free-standing company. One of its major holdings was the South American Railways Company, established to develop and extend railroad and terminal facilities in Argentina. A subsidiary, Buenos Aires Central Railroad and Terminal Company, had been formed in 1928 to finance underground terminal facilities in central Buenos Aires to be connected to a terminal outside town by subway (probably electric). In addition, Buenos Aires Lacroze Light & Power Company was acquired as part of the deal.[87]

The holding company moved aggressively and had total assets by May 1930 of $67.2 million. It was one of the small number of holding companies pursuing utility investments in Europe. It held a one-third interest in Union Électrique Rurale (France) and had contracted jointly with Deutsche Bank and Disconto Gesellschaft for the acquisition of securities convertible into a one-half interest in the voting stock of Westphalia United Electric Corporation, a major German electric utility.[88] It also held an interest in International Paper & Power, as well as in several domestic utilities.

Conclusion

US foreign direct investment in electric utilities has been a relatively neglected topic in the history of multinational enterprise, yet it comprised nearly 40 per cent of total foreign direct investment in the last half of the 1920s. Investment in foreign electric utilities was intimately connected with conditions in the domestic industry. During the stock-market boom at the end of the decade the investing public had a nearly insatiable appetite for utility securities of all types, and some of these funds were used to invest in foreign utilities. The nature of the firms making these investments varied. Utility holding companies, especially Electric Bond & Share (through its subsidiary American & Foreign Power), led the way, and most of the major US holding companies acquired some foreign properties. Some smaller companies entered foreign markets when their domestic properties were bought out. Energy-intensive industrial firms also made substantial investments as part of a strategy of vertical integration of their foreign operations. At the height of the stock-market frenzy, investment bankers became active in restructuring the domestic electric utility industry,[89] and a number of investment trusts were formed to acquire interests in foreign utilities.

Most of the companies identified in this chapter were not free-standing, and this exposition serves to delimit the application of the concept. The substantial size of the investments involved, combined with the complexity of the technology, necessitated control of the acquired properties; thus, using Hennart's terminology, the capital transfer was hierarchical and intermediated. The larger holding companies had professional staffs that provided construction, engineering, managerial, and financial services to their constituent operating utilities. The holding company form of organization was also transferred quite often to foreign utilities. This facilitated the strategy of creating networks, thus lowering costs, improving and expanding service, and raising profits and, hence, the value of the properties. As an executive of American & Foreign Power noted, these investments also could have a positive effect on the host country: 'The Americans revolutionized the power business in Latin America, generalizing the use of electricity by vastly improved service and lower rates, with consequent effects on the social and economic life of the communities served.'[90]

The investment boom in foreign electric utilities was brought to a halt by the stock-market crash, subsequent Depression, foreign political events, and the passage of the Public Utility Holding Company Act in 1935.[91] American & Foreign Power, technically separated from Electric Bond & Share in 1935, survived but struggled as currency depreciation, exchange controls, and confiscations of property affected its operations. A number of other utility holding companies went bankrupt or into receivership. Despite the capital and expertise transferred, most of the US investments in foreign electric utilities made in the late 1920s provided disappointing returns.

NOTES

1. G. Jones, 'The Making of Global Enterprise', *Business History*, 36 (Jan. 1994), 1.
2. A 1993 article in a major industry trade journal describes foreign investment in electric utilities as 'among the most exciting new frontiers' confronting the industry. There is no mention of previous experience at the frontier (E. R. Anthony, 'Toward a Global Paradigm', *Electric Perspectives*, 17 (1993), 20–7). See also T. W. Lippman, 'An Electrifying Opportunity', *Washington Post*, 20 Apr. 1993.

3. M. Wilkins, 'The Free-Standing Company, 1870–1914: An Important Type of British Foreign Direct Investment', *Economic History Review*, 2nd ser., 41 (May 1988), 259–82. Corley has confirmed the quantitative importance of this form of British foreign investment (T. A. B. Corley, 'Britain's Overseas Investments in 1914 Revisited', *Business History*, 36 (Jan. 1994), 71–88).
4. J.-F. Hennart, 'International Financial Capital Transfers: A Transaction Cost Framework', *Business History*, 36 (Jan. 1994), 52. See also Chapter 2 herein.
5. Hennart, 'International Financial Capital Transfers', 56. Foreign investment in electric utilities does not fit Hennart's model perfectly because there was also a substantial amount of non-intermediated lending during this period. From 1914 to 1928, $723m. worth of foreign public utility bonds were issued in the USA: 40% of the total were of European origin (with German companies being the largest single borrowers at $149m.), 26% were Canadian, 18% were Latin American, and 14% were Japanese (*Electrical World*, 92 (6 Oct. 1928), 710).
6. US Bureau of the Census, *Historical Statistics of the United States, Part 2* (Washington, 1975), 867.
7. For a discussion of US foreign direct investment in this era, see M. Wilkins, *The Emergence of Multinational Enterprise: American Business Abroad from the Colonial Era to 1914* (Cambridge, Mass., 1970).
8. US Bureau of the Census, *Historical Statistics of the United States, Part 2*, 867.
9. Data in the table are from M. Wilkins, *The Maturing of Multinational Enterprise: American Business Abroad from 1914 to 1970* (Cambridge, Mass., 1974), 55, and C. Lewis, *America's Stake in International Investments* (Washington, 1938), 605. It is not possible to separate precisely electric utility investments from other types of public-utility investments. Electric plants were often operated in conjunction with tramways (which declined in importance during the 1920s), inter-urban railroads, gas works, ice plants, and waterworks. There may be some telephone investments in these figures. But it is clear that the bulk of public-utility investment during the 1920s was in electric generating plants, high-voltage transmission lines, and distribution networks. By 1936 electric and gas utilities comprised 84% of total foreign 'public-utility' investments (US Department of Commerce, *American Direct Investments in Foreign Countries—1936* (Washington, 1938), 18).
10. The Bureau of Foreign and Domestic Commerce identified 119 foreign public utility investments (including transportation in the case of Canada) between 1925 and 1929, versus 21 in the previous five years (US Department of Commerce, *American Direct Investments in Foreign Countries—1936* (Washington, 1938), 47–9).
11. Edison Electric Institute, *Historical Statistics of the Electric Utility Industry* (New York, 1974), 1, 24.
12. C. E. Neil, 'Entering the Seventh Decade of Electric Power', *Edison Electric Bulletin*, 10 (Sept. 1942), 325.
13. US Bureau of the Census, *Census of Electrical Industries 1932: Central Electric Light and Power Stations* (Washington, 1934), 4.
14. US Federal Trade Commission, *Utility Corporations: Summary Report of the Federal Trade Commission to the Senate of the United States*, US Sen., 70th Cong., 1st sess. (Washington, 1935), doc. 92, part 72A, 38–9. The same consolidation movement was not taking place in the gas industry. The top ten firms (some of which were holding companies) produced only 13.3% of total gas output in 1930 (*Summary Report of the Federal Trade Commission to the Senate of the United States*, 48). (This source is a multi-volume report on the

electric utility industry that commenced in 1929 and continued into the 1930s. It focused exclusively on the domestic industry and firms were not asked to report on their foreign activities. Fortunately, many firms included information on these activities in their testimony and exhibits. It will be cited hereafter as FTC, followed by part and page numbers.)

15. FTC 72A, 83–4. Much of the information in this section draws on the final report of the FTC investigation. Also see N. S. Buchanan, 'The Origin and Development of the Public Utility Holding Company', *Journal of Political Economy*, 44 (Feb. 1936), 31–53.
16. See V. Carosso, *Investment Banking in America* (Cambridge, Mass., 1970), 294–8.
17. White also made this point, although he did not distinguish between holding companies and operating companies. See E. White, 'The Stock Market Boom and Crash of 1929 Revisited', *Journal of Economic Perspectives*, 4 (Spring 1990), 71.
18. The data are from J. F. Reinboth, 'Measurement of Risk in Public Utility Industries', *Journal of Land and Public Utility Economics*, 6 (1930), 83–93.
19. The yield differential fell from +0.66% in 1926 to +0.18% in 1929. *Moody's Manual of Public Utility Securities* (1954), a3. (The manual is cited hereafter as *Moody's*).
20. Only a systematic and detailed examination of sources in host countries would allow a census of US foreign direct investment in electric utilities around the world.
21. Electric Bond & Share controlled a substantially smaller share of installed generating capacity. Many of the large Canadian hydroelectric installations, for example, were essentially wholesale suppliers and did not have extensive distribution systems.
22. For a recent discussion of the merger between Edison General Electric and Thomson–Houston, see W. B. Carlson, *Innovation as a Social Process: Elihu Thomson and the Rise of General Electric, 1870–1900* (Cambridge, 1991), 292–301.
23. The original portfolio of Electric Bond & Share contained a number of foreign stocks: Ateliers Thomson–Houston, Paris, with a book value of $233,000; Chatham & District Light Railways, preferred and common, $113,000; Compagnie Française pour L'Exploitation des Procédés Thomson–Houston, Paris, $59,000; Cie d'Électricité Thomson–Houston de la Méditerranée, Paris, $159,000; Lanarkshire Tramways Co., $131,000. The combined value of the foreign stocks was $349,000 or 18% of the total value of stocks in the portfolio. As an indication of the risk involved, the total value of all stocks in the portfolio had a combined book value 32% below par value. None of the $1.2m. in bonds held by the company was foreign. S. A. Mitchell, *S. Z. Mitchell and the Electrical Industry* (New York, 1960), 62–4. See also Carlson, *Innovation*, 224.
24. Electric Bond & Share later claimed not to be a holding company but rather 'an investment engineer and banker' (Mitchell, *S. Z. Mitchell*, 102).
25. FTC 72A, 86–7; US Federal Trade Commission, *Control of Power Companies* (Washington, 1927), pp. xxvi–xxvii, 17 (cited hereafter as FTC (1927)).
26. This section draws heavily on W. J. Hausman and J. L. Neufeld, 'The Rise and Fall of The American & Foreign Power Company: A Lesson from the Past?', *Electricity Journal*, 10 (1997), 46–53.
27. American & Foreign Power Company Inc., *The Foreign Power System* (New York, 1953), 8. Mitchell had apparently approached the Royal Securities Corporation in 1915 with a proposal to purchase (in exchange for preferred stock of Electric Bond & Share) the Canadian, Latin American, and Caribbean properties with which Max Aitken had been involved, along with several other Latin American utilities. No agreement was reached, but much later American

& Foreign Power gained control of the Cuban properties under discussion. See C. Armstrong and H. V. Nelles, *Southern Exposure: Canadian Promoters in Latin America and the Caribbean, 1896–1930* (Toronto, 1988), 250–1, and Gregory Marchildon, Chapter 15 herein.

28. Mitchell, *S.Z. Mitchell*, 106–7.
29. Ibid. 107–8.
30. Ibid. 110.
31. The Chilean Tramway & Light Company Ltd., which served Santiago, was financed in 1897 with British capital. Some time thereafter Deutsche Übersee Elektrizitätsgesellschaft gained control. In 1918 the British government sold at auction the shares of Chilean Tramway held by the German company. The British firm Whitehall Securities Corporation purchased a controlling interest, reorganized the company in 1921 (Compañía Chilena de Electricidad), and further developed the property. When they were purchased in 1928 by South American Power (a subsidiary of Electric Bond & Share later transferred to American and Foreign Power), the total capitalization of the companies included in the group was £20m. See R. Simpson, 'Organization of Private Gas and Electric Utilities', *Transactions of the Third World Power Conference*, v (Washington, 1938), 58–9.
32. On the acquisition of Northern Mexican Power, see Marchildon, Chapter 15 herein.
33. In December 1928 Electric Bond & Share invested $500,000 in ordinary shares of Brazilian Traction, Light & Power Co. (Ltd.) (FTC 24 and 25, 474). The book value of Brazilian Traction, Light & Power Co.'s assets was $377m. in 1930 (Armstrong and Nelles, *Southern Exposure*, 252).
34. *Electrical World*, 90 (8 Oct. 1927), 761. There is no mention of European or Japanese investments in the annual reports of American & Foreign Power, although they are noted, along with Canadian investments, in *Moody's* (1928, 1929, 1930). A table presented by Luciano Segreto indicates that American & Foreign Power held interests (along with Zurich-based Elektrobank) in Iberian Electric Corp. Ltd. (Montreal), European Electric Corp. of Canada (Montreal), and British & International Utilities Ltd. In addition, Electric Bond & Share held an interest in the Belgian utility holding company, Société Financière de Transports et d'Industries Électriques (Sofina). See L. Segreto, 'Du "Made in Germany" au "Made in Switzerland": Les Sociétés financières suisses pour l'industrie électrique dans l'entre-deux-guerres', in M. Trédé (ed.), *Électricité et électrification dans le monde* (Paris, 1992), 360.
35. See Electric Utility Regulation Board, National Construction Commission, Nanking, 'Electric Power Development in China', *Transactions of the Third World Power Conference*, ii (Washington, 1938), 105–30, and Electric Utility Regulation Board, National Construction Commission, Nanking, 'Organization of Private Electric Utilities in China', *Transactions of the Third World Power Conference*, v (Washington, 1938), 69–75. The first source also lists the Western District Power Co. as 'Chinese–American', although the value of the investment is not given. F. H. H. King also discusses the purchase of the Shanghai property in *The History of the Hongkong and Shanghai Banking Corporation* (Cambridge, 1987), iii. 388. The bank held a substantial amount of the debentures of Shanghai Power.
36. In 1930 Electric Investors merged with Electric Bond & Share. By this time the investments in other US holding companies were becoming increasingly interrelated. Electric Bond & Share held interests in Stone & Webster, Insull Utility Investors, Middle West Utilities, Niagara Hudson Power, and Westinghouse Electric (*Moody's* (1925, 1928, 1930)).

37. *Moody's* (1930), 635.
38. Ibid. 1870. American Superpower was one of the companies controlled by the United Corporation when it was organized later in 1929.
39. *Moody's* (1930). In 1929, 22% of the gross revenues of the companies supervised by Electric Bond & Share originated outside the USA (FTC 23 and 24, 410).
40. Mitchell, S. Z. *Mitchell*, 110–11. By the mid-1940s American & Foreign Power produced 30% of the electrical power in Mexico, 15% in Brazil, 13% in Argentina, 75% in Chile, and 90% in Cuba. Since there was little foreign direct investment in utilities in the 1930s, these numbers closely reflect their position at the beginning of the decade (S. G. Hanson, *Economic Development in Latin America* (Washington, 1951), 292–315).
41. The $400m. showed up on the liability side as an increase in surplus, which could have been used to pay dividends. Mitchell's obituary in the *New York Times*, 19 Jan. 1944, claims that he may at one time have been the wealthiest man in the world; if so, this would most likely have been true only between March and September 1929.
42. Electric Bond & Share wrote down the value of these investments by $400m. in December 1931 (FTC 66, 1266, 1274). The 'artificial' write-up of utility properties was subsequently considered to be one of the major abuses of the holding companies (FTC 72A, 298–301, 845–8). Another of the charges levelled against the holding companies, and specifically against Electric Bond & Share, was that they overcharged their constituent companies for services. Bond & Share charged its highest supervision fees to the operating companies of American & Foreign Power (an average of 2.83% of operating revenues, versus an overall average of 1.51%), although this might have reflected higher real costs (Norman S. Buchanan, 'Service Contracts in the Electric Bond and Share Company: A Further Note', *Journal of Land and Public Utility Economics*, 7 (May 1935), 209–10). For a discussion of the amount and structure of service fees charged in 1927 by Electric Bond & Share, see FTC 23 and 24, 670–81.
43. This may have been a defensive move to gain more formal control of the operating companies Stone & Webster had been supervising in order to protect the company from having these firms purchased by rival holding companies (D. N. Keller, *Stone & Webster, 1889–1989: A Century of Integrity and Service* (New York, 1989), 154). See also T. P. Hughes, *Networks of Power: Electrification in Western Society, 1880–1930* (Baltimore, 1983), 386–90.
44. Keller, *Stone & Webster*, 21–2. J. P. Morgan was also involved in this process ('Stone & Webster', *Fortune*, 2 (Nov. 1930), 92–4).
45. Keller, *Stone & Webster*, 22.
46. The company was later sold at a profit.
47. Forbes resigned from the company in 1902 and went on to become Governor-General of the Philippines (1909) and later US Ambassador to Japan. His assistant, Guy Tripp, later became president of Westinghouse Electric Company, with which Stone & Webster maintained a close relationship (Keller, *Stone & Webster*, 27–8, 94).
48. Keller, *Stone & Webster*, 37–45.
49. Ibid. 45. Ponce later became part of Engineers Public Service, indicating that it was under the management and *control* of Stone & Webster (Keller, *Stone & Webster*, 132).
50. The company also operated a ferry and had a half-interest in a railroad. As of December 1929, Stone & Webster owned only 2% of the outstanding shares (FTC 67, 1206). The company was foreclosed in 1931 (*Public Utility Compendium*, Oct. 1931) and is listed as being owned by the Island Electric Co. in 1932 (*Public Utility Compendium*, Apr. 1932).

51. In 1929 El Paso Electric was listed as a 'constituent company' of Engineers Public Service with total assets of $17m. All of its generating stations were located in the USA (*Moody's* (1930)).
52. Keller, *Stone & Webster*, 79.
53. Ibid. 88.
54. See also the discussion in Wilkins, *Maturing of Multinational Enterprise*, 19–23.
55. This move did not appear to create conflict in the partnership with Webster, who eventually joined the board of American International (Keller, *Stone & Webster*, 90–4).
56. Keller, *Stone & Webster*, 111.
57. Ibid. 113.
58. Ibid. 115.
59. The company was incorporated in Canada, but Stone & Webster owned one-third of the voting stock and managed the utility (Keller, *Stone & Webster*, 126–9; *Public Utility Compendium* (Apr. 1931); FTC 67, 1206).
60. Keller, *Stone & Webster*, 130–1. There were, however, restrictions on foreign direct investment in public utilities in Japan that were severely to inhibit the activity of US firms there. See M. Mason, *American Multinationals and Japan: The Political Economy of Japanese Capital Controls, 1899–1980* (Cambridge, Mass., 1992), 24.
61. Stone & Webster and four banking houses formed a syndicate in 1925 to finance its largest utility purchase ever, Virginia Railway & Power Co. (reorganized as Virginia Electric & Power Co.). This syndicate, after several paper transactions, became Engineers Public Service, the holding company through which Stone & Webster asserted control over its operating companies. In January 1927 Stone & Webster's securities department merged with the investment banking house of Blodgett & Co. to form Stone & Webster and Blodgett Inc., which was a major participant in the roughly billion dollar per year utility security market over the next three years (Keller, *Stone & Webster*, 139–40).
62. FTC 67, 1206.
63. T. King, *Consolidated of Baltimore, 1816–1950* (Baltimore, 1950), 169.
64. The Niagara system at this time was by far the largest (700,000+ hp), followed by Montreal Heat, Light, & Power's installation at Cedar Rapids, and Shawinigan with 192,000 hp (J. B. Challies, 'Water Powers of Canada: Their Nature, Extent and Administration', *The Transactions of the First World Power Conference*, i (London, 1924), map opp. p. 172).
65. G. D. Smith, *From Monopoly to Competition: The Transformation of Alcoa, 1888–1986* (Cambridge, 1988), 96. For a history of Shawinigan, see C. Bellavance, *Shawinigan Water and Power 1898–1963: Formation et déclin d'un groupe industriel au Québec* (Quebec, 1994).
66. J. E. Igartua, '"Corporate" Strategy and Locational Decision-Making: The Duke-Price Alcoa Merger, 1925', *Journal of Canadian Studies*, 20 (1985), 86.
67. King, *Consolidated of Baltimore*, 169.
68. Ibid. 191–2.
69. Aldred actively pursued other business interests. In 1917 Aldred & Co. purchased controlling interest in the Gillette Safety Razor Co., with Aldred serving as Chairman of the Board (R. Adams, *King Gillette: The Man and his Wonderful Shaving Device* (Boston, 1978), 93–4).
70. The purchase price was $146,000 (FTC 65, 476).
71. *Public Utility Compendium* (May 1928), 310.
72. Ibid. 306–9.
73. *Moody's Banking and Finance Manual* (1930), 2308–9.
74. *Moody's* (1930), 1668–71. In 1925 International Power Securities offered

through Aldred & Co., Harris, Forbes & Co., and others $10m. in secured gold bonds to finance extensions for the Edison General Italian Electric Co. of Milan (*Electrical World*, 86 (1925), 1286). In 1926 Aldred participated in the acquisition of the Società Anonima per Imprese Elettriche Conti by Edison General Italian Electric Company. Aldred described Edison General Italian Electric as both an operating and holding company that with its affiliates forms an 'interconnected and co-ordinated Edison group' with installed generating capacity of over 912,000 hp (*Electrical World*, 88 (18 Dec. 1926), 1293).

75. *Electrical World*, 88 (31 July 1926), 237. International Power Securities also participated in the financing of a French electric utility, Union d'Électricité, Paris, by issuing $4m. in collateral trust gold bonds secured by the French and Italian properties (*Public Utility Compendium* (May 1928), 321–2).
76. For a discussion of the Duke–Alcoa merger, see Igartua, '"Corporate Strategy"', 82–101; Smith, *From Monopoly to Competition*, 142–5, 154–9; H. Marshall, F. A. Southard, Jr., and K. W. Taylor, *Canadian–American Industry* (New Haven, Conn., 1936), 103–5. This was a substantial project that increased hydroelectric capacity in Canada by 20%. The project comprised ten generators with a capacity of 450,000 hp and an investment of $30m.–35m. See Challies, 'Water Powers of Canada', 173. The company also controlled the Alma & Jonquiere Ry. Co. and Saguenay Transmission Co. The name was changed to Saguenay Power Co., Ltd. in 1935 (*Public Utility Compendium* (Apr. 1936), 295).
77. The Canadian subsidiary controlled the Gatineau Power Co., Gatineau Electric Light Co., St John River Power Co., Ottawa & Hull Power Co., and Ottawa River Power Co. It had over 620,000 hp of developed power (*Moody's* (1930), 1886, 3108). See also FTC 31 and 32, 938–45.
78. *Public Utility Compendium* (May 1928), 323.
79. *Moody's Manual of Industrial Securities* (1930).
80. Ibid.
81. *Electrical World*, 85 (14 Feb. 1925), 368–9.
82. *Electrical World*, 86 (1 Aug. 1925), 239.
83. FTC 68, 336.
84. W. D. Hornaday, 'Guadalajara Hydro-Electric Development', *Electrical World*, 88 (4 Sept. 1926), 469.
85. Ibid. 470.
86. *Moody's* (1930), 2416.
87. The company had a 16,000 kW oil generator to supply the tramway (*Public Utility Compendium* (May 1930), 334).
88. *Moody's* (1930), 2417. In the *Public Utility Compendium* (Apr. 1931), 329, Vereinigte Elektrizitätswerke Weslfalen G.m.b.H. is listed as half-owned by municipalities served and the Free State of Prussia and half by Public Utility Holding Corporation of America and Deutsche Bank of Berlin. By 1933 the company was listed as entirely German owned.
89. There was some speculation during this time that the United Corporation and Electric Bond & Share were moving toward creation of a giant utility that would cover the entire eastern USA (FTC 72A, 111–15).
90. J. S. Carson, 'The Power Industry', in L. J. Hughlett (ed.), *Industrialization of Latin America* (Westport, Conn., 1970; repr. of 1946 edn.), 319.
91. This act led eventually to massive divestiture of operating companies by the holding companies that survived the Depression. In 1988, for example, the ten largest generators of electricity produced 29% of total US generation compared with 71% in 1929 (Energy Information Administration, *Financial Statistics of Selected Electric Utilities 1988* (Washington, 1990), tables 42, 61, 67).

15

The Montreal Engineering Company and International Power: Overcoming the Limitations of the Free-Standing Utility

Gregory P. Marchildon

Mira Wilkins has proposed that, because of its unique attributes, the free-standing company (FSC) should be thought of as a separate subcategory of the multinational enterprise (MNE).[1] While the analytical value of the FSC concept continues to be debated, it has already established its heuristic value by helping us think about foreign investment more clearly.[2] Between the polar opposites of portfolio investment implying little or no control, on the one hand, and direct investment accompanied by almost complete control, on the other, lies a grey area inhabited by a striking variety of corporate vehicles of investment involving varying degrees of control and types of governance. At a very minimum, the concept of the FSC invites us to probe the mysteries that lie within this grey area.

Between 1870 and 1914 British FSCs may have been the single most important corporate conduit for foreign investment in the world.[3] Based upon Wilkins's pioneering study, their characteristics can be summarized briefly. FSCs were established to operate in a foreign nation[4] without any corresponding domestic operation. Unlike the typical American MNE, they did not grow organically from well-established domestic operations whose operations 'spilled over' political boundaries. As a consequence, FSC head offices were skeletal affairs compared to the head-office operations of the American-style MNE, often 'little more than a brass nameplate in the City'.[5]

Wilkins's FSC owed its existence to the highly developed financial markets of Britain, vast pools of family wealth, and relatively slow domestic economic growth, all of which conspired to produce low rates of return on domestic investments. The potential profitability of FSCs seemed much greater than the traditional type of direct or portfolio investment available to investors at this time. FSCs were also much riskier investments. Their speculative nature could be observed in the promotional costs associated with FSCs, ranging from 17 to 33 per cent of the total capital raised, often leading to the recurrent charge that they were nothing more than 'financial scams'.[6]

Part of this risk related to the expense and tardiness of communication between the head office, directors, and shareholders in Britain, and the managers of the FSC's operations thousands of miles away. In fact once the FSC began operating, distance forced the directors to devolve most of the decision-making upon the individual(s) directly at the scene of the FSC's operations. At times, local management even assumed the more general long-term policy-making function for the FSC, at least until interruptions in the flow of dividends and interest prodded the British board members into action.[7] There was tremendous variation among FSCs, however, and generalizations concerning the activities of directors and officers may be impossible.

British FSC investments declined precipitously after the First World War, in part because of the increasing number of bankruptcies. Wilkins suggests that the main problem was the absence of a 'real home office' which could transfer hard-won experience in decision-making.[8] There is some empirical support for this observation. In his study of early British direct investment in Canada, D. G. Paterson also found that the geographical separation between head office and operations, combined with the FSC's (defined as the board of directors and shareholders) lack of knowledge of local conditions, resulted in relatively poor decision-making and consequent failure of many of the British FSCs with operations in Canada.[9]

There were exceptions, however, to the otherwise dismal record of British FSCs, and from these successes Wilkins draws more general conclusions as to the characteristics necessary for survival. Those firms which were able to develop effective managerial organizations (moving closer to the structure of the 'typical' MNE), or those firms which remained or were placed within the managerial structure of a holding company, be it a mining engineering company or a trading company, better weathered the storm of time.[10] In other words, only those FSCs which adopted some of the strategies and structures of Chandlerian MNEs were capable of competing with them.[11]

The purpose of the following study is to determine to what extent the first Canadian utility FSCs possessed the characteristics described above. The article combines new research on the group of FSCs associated with one Canadian investment house, the Royal Securities Corporation, with previously published work on Canadian utility FSCs.[12] Finally, the activities of the Montreal Engineering Company and its relationship with the Royal Securities group of utilities are examined in more detail. From its creation in 1907, through its expansion during the utility holding company rage of the 1920s and its consolidation during the Depression years of the 1930s, Montreal Engineering was the most significant attempt by Canadians to overcome the limitations of the utility type of FSC.[13]

Canadian Utility FSCs, 1896–1939

Like Americans, Canadians embraced the revolution wrought by electrical power in the final decades of the nineteenth century, rapidly establishing integrated utility networks in which electricity generated by water (hydro) and coal-fired (thermal) plants lit streets and houses and powered factories and streetcars.[14] When utility opportunities began to be exhausted in Canada, and when increasing municipal restrictions threatened the future profitability of private ventures, Canadian utility entrepreneurs began setting up operations in rapidly developing urban centres abroad, and soon 'developed an internationally recognized specialization in the finance and operation of utilities'.[15]

Two main factors account for this specialization: (1) Canada's strategic position between the USA, the main source of technological, organizational, managerial, and financial innovations in the utility business, and Britain, the main source of surplus capital in the world, to which Canadian access was privileged by ties of culture, language, and empire; and (2) the technological, managerial, and financial capability of domestic utility entrepreneurs who were responsible for converting Canadian cities and urban transportation systems to electrical power in the early 1890s.

Table 15.1 summarizes the most basic data on almost all Canadian utility FSCs operating before the First World War.[16] All were Canadian in the sense that they were domiciled in Canada, and remained so during the inter-war years, in part because of Canada's lax corporate reporting and security laws. At least initially their boards were dominated by Canadians who held the majority of their voting stock. Later, Europeans would increasingly invest in the larger FSCs and eventually dilute, but never entirely displace, Canadian ownership. Management of the FSC's operations fell to expatriate Canadians, Americans, Englishmen, and others, while almost all of the engineers originally hailed from the USA. None of the FSCs listed in Table 15.1 ever had an operational head office in Canada. Most were run with little reference to their Canadian directors and officers (and the utilities domiciled in Canada with which they were sometimes connected), although Canadians played the critical role in raising new capital for the enterprises.

These FSCs constituted a significant share of total Canadian investment in utilities, soaking up, according to one estimate, approximately double the capital invested in domestic utilities by approximately 1905.[17]

TABLE 15.1. *Canadian utility free-standing companies established before 1914*

Canadian Utility FSC	Incorporated (head office)	Locus of operations (country, colony, etc.)	Power source	Services	Gross assets (Can. $000)	Gross earnings (Can. $000)	Ultimate disposition
City of Birmingham Tramways Company	1896 (Toronto)	Birmingham (Britain)	thermal	power, tram	2,500 (1896)[a]		sold in 1902
West India Electric Company	1897 (Montreal)	Kingston region (Jamaica)	hydroelectric	power, lighting tram	1,590 (1906)	148 (1906)	sold in 1971
São Paulo Tramway, Light & Power Company	1899 (Toronto)	São Paulo region (Brazil)	hydroelectric	power, lighting tram	14,780 (1906)	963 (1906)	sold in 1978
Demerara Electric Company	1899 (Montreal)	Georgetown (British Guiana)	thermal	power, lighting tram	1,569 (1907)	127 (1907)	sold in 1960
Trinidad Electric Company	1901 (Halifax)	Port of Spain (Trinidad)	thermal	power, lighting tram	2,041 (1907)	205 (1907)	operating in 1939
Mexican Light & Power Company	1902 (Montreal)	Mexico City region (Mexico)	hydroelectric	power, lighting	32,901 (1908)	2,938 (1908)	operating in 1939
Rio de Janeiro Tramway, Light & Power Company	1905 (Toronto)	Rio de Janeiro region (Brazil)	hydroelectric	power, lighting tram, telephone	98,177 (1912)	3,742 (1912)	sold in 1978
Monterey Railway, Light & Power Company	1905 (Toronto)	Monterey region (Mexico)	thermal	power, tram lighting, gas	10,335 (1909)	122 (1909)	sold in 1950
Mexico Tramways Company	1906 (Montreal)	Mexico City (Mexico)	thermal	tram			operating in 1939
The Camagüey Company	1906 (Montreal)	Camagüey (Cuba)	thermal	power, lighting tram	1,661 (1911)	161 (1911)	sold in 1926
Porto Rico Railways	1906 (Montreal)	San Juan region (Puerto Rico)	hydroelectric	power, lighting tram, railway	7,904 (1912)	828 (1912)	sold in 1944
Mexican Northern Power Company	1909 (Montreal)	State of Chihuahua (Mexico)	hydroelectric	power	22,600 (1909)		sold in 1929
Barcelona Traction, Light & Power Company	1911 (Toronto)	Barcelona region (Spain)	hydroelectric	power, lighting tram			bankrupt by 1914

[a] Estimate based upon cost of properties.

Sources: Derived from *Annual Financial Review (Canadian)*; D. McDowall, *The Light: Brazilian Traction, Light and Power Company Limited* (Toronto, 1988); C. Armstrong and H. V. Nelles, *Southern Exposure: Canadian Promoters in Latin America and the Caribbean, 1896–1930* (Toronto, 1988); G. P. Marchildon, *Profits and Politics: Beaverbrook and the Gilded Age of Canadian Finance* (Toronto, 1996); J. Sexton, *Monenco: The First 75 Years* (n.p., 1982).

By the mid-1890s, utility entrepreneurs such as William Mackenzie, James Ross, and B. F. Pearson, having already established electrical lighting and tramway systems in cities such as Montreal, Toronto, and Halifax, began to invest in street railway systems in cities close to the border such as Minneapolis, Detroit, and Toledo. As they could never become more than mere rentiers (with correspondingly lower profits) in the American projects, however, they began to search out opportunities that they could control in areas where integrated electrical utilities were not yet well established.

The first such opportunity appeared to present itself in Britain, where integrated electrical utility networks were just in the planning stage. After their proposal for greater London was turned down, in 1896 Mackenzie and Ross purchased the existing horse, steam, cable, and battery powered transportation companies in Birmingham, and the City of Birmingham Tramways Company was incorporated to take over the properties and transform them into a integrated overhead cable trolley system. Mackenzie and Ross soon discovered, however, that they had moved too quickly. Birmingham's council was not prepared to have their city marred by unsightly overhead wires. Unwilling to install expensive and inefficient underground conduit wiring, they decided to cut their losses by running the existing system until a willing buyer could be found, and they sold out six years later.

By this time Mackenzie and Ross had begun to focus on the Caribbean and Latin America, where there was little concern about the aesthetic quality of overhead wiring and much eagerness to gain the benefits of electrification. They were joined by a stampede of other utility promoters from Canada hoping to get in on the ground floor of what was still a brand new business in the tropics. The first venture to materialize was the West India Electric Company (in 1897), where a small hydroelectric plant was built to electrify a tramway being constructed to serve Kingston, Jamaica. This was followed in rapid succession by new utilities in British Guiana, Brazil, Trinidad, and Mexico.

After constructing an electric railway to replace the mule-powered tram in Georgetown, British Guiana, the Demerara Electric Company's system was described in the trade press as the first 'up-to-date trolley road and electric plant in northern South America'.[18] The Trinidad Electric Company in Port of Spain, Trinidad, involved an almost identical conversion project, and both railways were in operation by 1901.[19] A much larger project, the São Paulo Tramway, Light and Power Company was conceived by F. S. Pearson, a brilliant but erratic electrical engineer who was one of the pioneers in the science of integrated utility engineering in the USA. Unable to find financial backers at home, Pearson turned to the Canadian associates he had first met while giving advice on the electrification of the Halifax trolley system in 1895. A group of wealthy Canadians including William Mackenzie and B. F. Pearson enthusiastically backed the project.

São Paulo Tramway made money virtually from the day the tram began operating, and convinced a wider circle of Canadian utility promoters to try their luck, including a small group of financiers associated with the Royal Securities Corporation, a combination investment bank and securities dealer that specialized in new capital issues. Royal Securities had been established in 1903. In 1906 this group went to Cuba and purchased the city of Camagüey's thermal power and lighting plant. The plant was then enlarged and improved, transmission lines were extended, and an electric railway was constructed which began operating in early 1908.[20] In 1906 Royal Securities, in conjunction with New York engineering consultants J. G. White & Company, launched a larger hydroelectric power, tramway, and interurban railway connecting the most populous towns and suburbs in Puerto Rico with the capital of San Juan in one integrated electrical transmission grid.[21]

F. S. Pearson was the mastermind behind the biggest project of all—an immense hydroelectric enterprise servicing Rio de Janeiro and the suburbs and towns near it. This FSC did not live up to Pearson's or his Canadian associates' expectations, however, and by 1912 Rio de Janeiro Tramway, Light & Power was barely covering its operating expenses, and had to be rescued by funnelling it some of São Paulo Tramway's cash flow through a merger of the two FSCs under a holding company known as the Brazilian Traction, Light & Power Company.[22]

The Mexican Light & Power Company—formed in 1902—was also Pearson-inspired. Before the company began operating, Mexico City was receiving electricity from a number of small thermal companies, and Pearson convinced his Canadian friends that, by constructing a hydroelectric plant at a site on the Necaxa River almost 160 kilometres from Mexico City, they could deliver power through their transmission lines much more cheaply to the industries, street railways, and population (nearly 800,000) in the valley of Mexico.[23] Pearson and a slightly different group of Canadian financiers then formed the Mexico Tramways Company (in 1906). The plan was to acquire, consolidate, and expand the existing tramways of Mexico City, and eventually become Mexican Light & Power's best customer. In 1909, however, after years of operating well below capacity owing to chronic drought conditions, the hydroelectric company was taken over by the street railway firm in order to increase the former's cash flow. Both parent and subsidiary would soon suffer from the political earthquake of the Mexican Revolution, dampening their prospects for years and cutting short new investment. A similar fate awaited other Canadian FSCs in Mexico.[24]

One such FSC was the Monterey[25] Railway, Light & Power Company (set up in 1905), which claimed 5.1 million pesos for the damages it sustained during the Revolution.[26] Another was the Mexican Northern Power Company (formed in 1909), which had just constructed a hydroelectric dam on the Conchos River to service the mining towns and cities of Chihuahua when the Revolution broke out. To avoid defaulting on its bond interest, this firm was reorganized as the Northern Mexican Power & Development Company in 1919. It hobbled along until bought out ten years later by the American & Foreign Power Company, a subsidiary holding company of the US-controlled Electric Bond & Share Company.[27]

Barcelona Traction, Light & Power Company was the last sizeable FSC utility launched before the First World War. Created towards the end of 1911 by Pearson and his Canadian friends, along with some European investors, the plan was to replace a number of small thermal power companies with one large and integrated hydroelectric and streetcar system for Barcelona and surrounding Catalonia. Owing to expensive changes to the original engineering design and the sharp recession of 1913, however, the venture went into receivership at the end of 1914.[28]

After the war, Canadian utility FSCs faced mounting pressure from the governments of the host countries to reduce rates and improve and extend services, as well as criticism from domestic élites beginning to question the benefits of foreign-controlled investment.[29] They were also the target of acquisition attempts by new US and European utility conglomerates, some of which were true MNEs with links to electrical equipment manufacturers, which had moved into adjacent markets.[30] FSCs such as Trinidad Electric and West India Electric, now reorganized as Jamaica Public Service Limited, a holding company with three tiny operating companies, managed to keep their autonomy but at the price of stagnant growth, in part a product of not having access to the capital resources of holding companies. A few FSCs such as the Camagüey Company and Mexican Northern Power were sold outright to American utilities.

The largest companies, Brazilian Traction and Mexico Tramways, barely remained Canadian-controlled after large blocks of voting shares were purchased by the Belgian holding company Société Financière de Transports et d'Entreprises Industrielles (SOFINA), during the 1920s. They were also under threat by the Electric Bond & Share Company, a US-based MNE that was acquiring new utilities throughout the Americas. In response, Mexico Tramways and Brazilian Traction consolidated their positions within their respective markets through a few

TABLE 15.2. *Canadian utility free-standing companies and holding companies by 1930* (Can.$m.)

Canadian utility group	Book value of assets
Brazilian Traction, Light & Power Company[a]	376.6
Rio de Janeiro Tramway, Light & Power Company[a]	
Brazilian Telephone Company	
São Paulo Tramway, Light & Power Company	
São Paulo Electric Company	
City of Santos Improvement Company	
Brazilian Hydro-Electric Company	
Mexico Tramways Company[a]	105.6
Mexican Light & Power Company[a]	
Mexican Electric Light Company	
Pachuca Light & Power Company	
Mexican Southern Power Company	
South West Power Company of Mexico	
Toluca Electric Light & Power	
International Power Company[a]	32.8
Venezuela Power Company	
Tocayo Electric Company	
San Salvador Electric Light Company	
Oriente Electric Light Company	
Newfoundland Light & Power Company	
Oruro Light & Power Company	
Bolivia Power Company	
Demerara Electric Company	
Porto Rico Railways Company	
Trinidad Electric Company	4.0
Jamaica Public Service Limited[a]	0.8
West India Electric Company	
Jamaica Light & Power Company	
Jamaica Hydro-Electric Company	

[a] Holding company.
Sources: Armstrong and Nelles, *Southern Exposure*, 252–3. Although included in their table, Northern Mexican Power & Development Company and its subsidiaries are excluded from the above because this group of companies had come under US ownership and control by 1929. Although SOFINA held a controlling interest in Brazilian Traction and Mexico Tramways, these companies remained under Canadian control; see McDowall, *The Light*.

strategic acquisitions, and hunkered down to defend themselves against any possible hostile takeovers.[31]

International Power and the Royal Securities Group of FSCs

There was an important exception to the overall defensive posture of Canadian utility FSCs during the inter-war period. During and after the First World War, the Royal Securities Corporation investigated new possibilities for ventures in Central and South America through teams of engineers belonging to the Montreal Engineering Company, a firm controlled by Royal Securities.[32] These same engineers then rationalized existing and new utility services into integrated plants and built the power plants and distribution systems that supported the services. By the early 1920s, Royal Securities and Montreal Engineering had established integrated utilities in Bolivia, Venezuela, El Salvador, and Newfoundland (then still a British colony), and in the process challenged the vigorous utility MNEs such as Electric Bond & Share on their own ground.

In 1926 the International Power Company was established by Izaak Walton Killam, the man who had succeeded Max Aitken (later Lord Beaverbrook) as president and chief shareholder of the Royal Securities Corporation. The new holding company purchased the shares of its pre-war utility companies such as Demerara Electric and Porto[33] Rico Railways, as well as the many new FSCs being rapidly added to Killam's new foreign utilities empire.[34]

International Power resembled the utility holding companies that were springing up in the USA during the roaring Twenties. These were largely financial creations intended to take advantage of the rapid rise in utility share prices and the public's seemingly insatiable appetite for utility holding company shares. This phenomenon was paralleled by the emergence and expansion of European holding companies, such as SOFINA, which were domiciled in Belgium or Switzerland where corporate laws were among the most relaxed in Europe.

Utility financiers, such as Killam, obtained a number of advantages from the holding company structure. For one, he could exert control over his operating companies with less investment than would be required through direct control. International Power was in fact the middle tier between Killam's investment house, the Royal Securities Corporation, and the individual operating companies in the Caribbean, Central America, South America, and Newfoundland.[35] For example, if Royal Securities held 51 per cent of the voting shares of International Power, which in turn held 51 per cent of the voting stock in the individual operating companies, Killam could exercise control in the operating companies with an investment of only one-half of the amount that would normally be required. As can be seen in Table 15.3, in 1939 International Power actually held 100 per cent of the shares in three of its operating subsidiaries, 51 per cent or slightly more in three others, and a less than 51 per cent but none the less controlling share of three further FSCs.

This type of pyramiding also allowed Killam to increase his financial leverage. If the stock in the operating companies was purchased by the holding company through issuing its own shares, International Power could magnify its potential return.[36] By the same token, however, any operating company losses were amplified in the decline of earnings for

TABLE 15.3. *International Power Company's subsidiaries, 1939*

Location	Subsidiary
Venezuela	Venezuela Power Company (wholly owned) Tocayo Electric Light & Power Company (wholly owned)
Bolivia	Bolivian Power Company (wholly owned) Oruro Light & Power Company (controlling interest)
El Salvador	San Salvador Electric Light Company (majority interest) Oriente Electric Light Company (majority interest)
Puerto Rico	Porto Rico Power Company[a] (controlling interest)
Mexico	Monterey Railway Light & Power Company (controlling interest)
Newfoundland	Newfoundland Light & Power Company (majority interest)

[a] The successor to the Porto Rico Railways Company.
Source: *Annual Financial Review (Canadian)*, 40 (July 1940), 704–5.

holding companies. The instability of this structure directly increased the risk to operating companies as well. While an operating company might easily survive a mild downturn even if this resulted in a major reduction of income for the holding company, the failure of a holding company during a more turbulent period could also bring down an otherwise healthy operating company. This point was driven home to the world during the stock-market crash of 1929 when the share values of American utility companies fell harder than virtually any other class of security, forcing bankruptcy and receivership on operating as well as holding companies.

In other words, while operating FSCs gained little benefit from the holding company structure, they faced greater risk. When various holding company 'service' charges are taken into consideration, the whole system seemed like an ingenious scheme for promoters to divert profits from operating company treasuries into their own pockets. To some extent, this was true of many of the utility holding companies created during the 1920s, but those companies must be distinguished from others that returned some value to the operating companies.

To better understand the nature of Killam's utility organization, a point of comparison can be provided through a very brief examination of the structure of the Electric Bond & Share Company (EBASCO[37]), the company that other Canadian FSCs found so threatening during the inter-war years. In 1905 EBASCO was created by General Electric to perform three functions: it was to be a holding company for dozens of operating utilities; it was to act as an investment bank; and it was to give operational support by providing engineering, supervisory, accounting, and construction services to these same enterprises. Technical and engineering services were substantially aided by EBASCO's direct tie to General Electric.[38] This 'full-service' structure was only slightly altered when EBASCO transferred its foreign utilities to the care of American & Foreign Power, a subholding company EBASCO incorporated in 1923 for this purpose.[39]

Armstrong and Nelles suggest that EBASCO's technical and engineering services as well as its linkage with General Electric gave the company a tremendous competitive advantage over the Canadian FSCs.[40] While any definitive test of their proposition would require further detailed research on EBASCO and its group of companies, a task beyond the purview of this chapter, the limited evidence available does suggest that EBASCO did provide its operating subsidiaries with, in Wilkins's words, 'a real home office' capable of transferring technical-engineering, accounting, and construction knowledge, and perhaps even valuable managerial experience, gathered from years of dealing with numerous geographically separated FSCs.

Similarly, Killam's head office in Montreal transferred both knowledge and skills to his small empire of operating utilities, and this may have been a key element in the survival and success of the Royal Securities–International Power group of FSCs. Unlike EBASCO, however, International Power was not a 'full-service' utility company; its role was limited to that of a financial holding company. The two other classes of services provided by EBASCO—investment banking and operational support—were divided between the Royal Securities Corporation and the Montreal Engineering Company.

Like International Power, Montreal Engineering was an offspring of Royal Securities, and the majority of its voting stock was held by Royal Securities for most of its existence. Although living separate corporate existences, Royal Securities, International Power, and Montreal Engineering must be seen as part of a single organization—a single brain lodged on St James Street, the heart of Montreal's (and Canada's) financial district during the first half of the twentieth century.[41] In the words of Montreal Engineering's founder, the organizations had originally been 'tied together' so that the operating companies would 'derive great economies from the system' thus created.[42]

The Montreal Engineering Company, 1907–1939

Montreal Engineering was the first organized effort by Canadian utility entrepreneurs to overcome the shortcomings of enterprises whose financial and legal head offices were geographically detached from their operating bodies by providing cost-accounting, purchasing, construction, and engineering advisory services. When asked to investigate utility propositions abroad by Royal Securities, Montreal Engineering sent teams of engineers to examine conditions in the countries in question and prepare feasibility reports. When Royal Securities decided to proceed with an individual proposal, Montreal Engineering designed and constructed the utility project. Once the utilities were up and running, Montreal Engineering's main task was to collect systematic operating data from the FSCs, so that their diverse experiences could be accumulated and general lessons learned and used as a basis for suggesting operational changes.

Knowledge of the science of electrical engineering was a rare commodity at the turn of the century, and, not surprisingly, almost all of the engineers that initially worked for the Canadian FSCs were Americans who had studied with, or under, individuals such as F. S. Pearson in the 1880s and 1890s, and had then gone on to work for the new electrical utility companies beginning to service the urban centres of America. During these years, Canada provided ambitious corporate lawyers, utility entrepreneurs willing to operate outside familiar environments, lax incorporation and financial reporting laws, and even good utility managers on occasion, but before 1914 it was not yet producing a cadre of knowledgeable and well-trained electrical engineers. This 'imported' expertise was essential to the initial success of all of the Canadian FSCs. It was Royal Securities' desire to enhance this expertise that led to the creation of Montreal Engineering.

When Montreal Engineering was incorporated in 1907, the Royal Securities group controlled four of the FSCs listed in Table 15.1: Trinidad Electric; Demerara Electric; the Camagüey Company; and Porto Rico Railways. All, with the exception of Porto Rico Railways, were relatively small thermal-powered utility operations, with tram income providing their main source of revenue. One company—Demerara Electric—was on the verge of bankruptcy when taken over and reorganized by the Royal Securities group in 1905. All were supervised at some point by Fred Teele, a talented American electrical engineer who managed Trinidad Electric from its inception in 1901, reconstructed Demerara Electric, and initially supervised the Cuban and Puerto Rican projects.[43]

Not long after Trinidad Electric began operating, Teele complained to his Canadian directors about the excessive prices being charged for operating equipment by F. S. Pearson's engineering and purchasing agency in New York, a middleman between the Canadian FSCs and the major electrical equipment manufacturers in the USA such as General Electric and Westinghouse. Trinidad Electric, for example, would place its orders for new equipment and components to repair existing facilities through Pearson's agency in New York, which would then obtain the equipment from the most appropriate and (presumably) lowest-cost manufacturer, and arrange to have it shipped south. All service and consulting fees were hidden in the invoice that accompanied the equipment to Port of Spain, including the fees for engineering advice on new equipment.

While he was reconstructing Demerara Electric, Teele's criticism of W. P. Plummer (F. S. Pearson's main partner) intensified as equipment began arriving late and in damaged condition.[44] In response to the difficulties, the Royal Securities Corporation set up its own purchasing and engineering department as an experiment in 1906. The investment house was responsible for financing all of the equipment acquired by the West Indian utilities; if Royal Securities could exert greater control over construction and repair costs, then the corporation could more precisely estimate the funds that needed to be raised over time. When the department was converted into the Montreal Engineering Company the following year, Pearson's purchasing and engineering agency in New York was dropped permanently.[45]

Fred Clarke, the organization's new accountant, had once been chief accountant of Trinidad Electric, and had introduced the innovative accounting system developed at Trinidad Electric to Demerara Electric when it was reorganized by Royal Securities in 1905. Clarke's duties included promptly responding to purchase orders and auditing the accounts submitted by construction contractors and subcontractors. When the Camagüey and Porto Rico companies began operating in 1906, Montreal Engineering took over the main accounting responsibilities, with the companies sending weekly and monthly statistical reports to Montreal. In addition, Clarke personally ran the competitions for the new engineering and accounting positions created by the new companies in Cuba and Puerto Rico from Montreal Engineering's office in Canada.

To give Montreal Engineering privileged access to administrative, financial, and operating information from the FSCs, Clarke was appointed secretary of the Demerara, Camagüey, and Porto Rico companies. The operating FSCs forwarded all data directly to Montreal Engineering, including copies of all inter-office correspondence. With this information, Montreal Engineering began to provide an extensive array of managerial services for its FSCs, including developing a policy to deal with corrupt government officials which eventually reduced the amount of money being lost to bribes.[46]

Owing to an internal dispute between the Halifax and Montreal factions of Royal Securities Corporation, however, Clarke was not appointed secretary of the Trinidad Electric Company. As a consequence, Montreal Engineering had greater difficulty in obtaining detailed information from Trinidad Electric, with Halifax directors and Port of Spain managers jealously guarding their autonomy. From

1907 until the end of 1910, Montreal Engineering provided purchasing, engineering, and accounting services to Trinidad Electric on a fee-for-service basis, but it was never permitted to run the firm in the same way that it managed the other FSCs. Trinidad Electric would in fact remain permanently outside the control of the Royal Securities group after the Montreal Engineering contract was terminated in 1910.[47]

Montreal Engineering's first president and chief consulting engineer was Carl C. Giles. An electrical engineer originally from the USA, Giles had been in charge of running the thermal power plant and lighting system in Camagüey, Cuba, before it was purchased by Royal Securities.[48] His main job was to train engineers capable of providing high-quality reports on new utility propositions brought forward by Royal Securities, often travelling abroad himself to examine the feasibility of the proposals.[49] From Montreal and periodically on-site, Giles and his staff provided engineering advice to all of Royal Securities' FSCs, as well as some of the new utilities that the investment house was then establishing in Canada.[50]

By 1908 Montreal Engineering had already succeeded in speeding up delivery and reducing the cost of most of the equipment and other accoutrements shipped from North America to the tropics. The new firm had also provided a valuable service in supervising the building of the tramway system in Cuba as well as the hydroelectric plant and electric railway in Puerto Rico. The latter was particularly important in that the cost overruns of the chief contractor, J. G. White & Company, were almost double the original estimates and threatened to bring down both the project and the Royal Securities Corporation, since the 'cost-plus' basis of the original contract put all of the risk on the Canadians. Montreal Engineering played a central role in identifying discrepancies in the accounts submitted by J. G. White & Company, ultimately forcing the New York firm to accept a renegotiation of the original contract. Carl Giles was then appointed as the Royal Securities group's expert in the final adjustment of differences, and, along with Teele and the other members of the Montreal Engineering staff, closely supervised the completion of the project according to the new terms.[51]

When a further dispute arose between J. G. White & Company and Royal Securities, Montreal Engineering stepped in and finished the hydroelectric construction project in Puerto Rico. This was the beginning of a series of construction projects for which Montreal Engineering would eventually become famous both inside and outside Canada. The foreign projects included building a hydroelectric dam high in the Andes to service the tin industry of Bolivia, as well as power dam projects that delivered electricity to the emerging petro-chemical industries of Venezuela.[52]

Between 1910 and 1914, however, Montreal Engineering was virtually mothballed as the two principals behind the Royal Securities Corporation, Max Aitken and Izaak Walton Killam, concentrated on issuing and selling Canadian industrial securities in Great Britain. During these years, Royal Securities let control over its FSCs slip into the hands of investment cliques in Halifax and Toronto, and temporarily lost Carl Giles.[53] Then, just months before the First World War began, Aitken and Killam decided to revive Montreal Engineering and regain control of the FSCs. Giles was brought back in as president, and he immediately opened negotiations with the FSCs on new service contracts for the engineering company.

Two of the FSCs—the Camagüey Company and Demerara Electric—had been performing so badly since leaving the Royal Securities' fold that dividends had to be discontinued in one case and were about to be suspended in the second. While the management of both companies wanted Montreal Engineering's assistance in rooting out the causes of their difficulties, they were reluctant to accept Aitken's and Killam's demand that management be placed entirely in the hands of the Montreal company's engineers and accountants.[54] The war temporarily suspended these negotiations, but, in April 1915, Aitken, Killam, and Giles were approached by S. Z. Mitchell, the president of EBASCO, who proposed a joint venture in which EBASCO and Royal Securities would consolidate a number of Canadian and US-controlled FSCs in the Caribbean (as well as the Canadian power companies controlled by Royal Securities) under one enormous holding company.[55] Although EBASCO and Royal Securities seemed to agree on the basic elements of the new organization, the deal was never consummated, and surviving Montreal Engineering documentation does not disclose the reason why the scheme was dropped.[56] It was clear, however, that EBASCO expected Royal Securities to convince the Canadian FSCs to sell their shares to the new consortium, and this may have been impossible to do at the time, given the unwillingness of certain operating firms such as Trinidad Electric to give up their managerial autonomy.

Whatever the reason for the failure in the EBASCO negotiations, by June 1915 Aitken, Killam, and Giles had agreed to begin a programme of foreign utility expansion on their own, and soon Montreal Engineering personnel were being sent to Venezuela, Bolivia, and other Latin American countries to investigate new hydroelectric and integrated utility possibilities.[57] This expansion overseas was accompanied by very large electrical engineering projects in Canada, and Montreal Engineering soon became a training school for perhaps the most talented group of hydroelectric utility engineers and managers in the country. Giles soon retired from Montreal Engineering but he was replaced by prominent Canadian engineers and managers such as Geoffrey A. Gaherty and Dennis Stairs.[58]

After the war, Izaak Walton Killam, now in sole control of Royal Securities with Lord Beaverbrook's retirement from the firm, continued his campaign to regain control of the firm's old FSCs. It would be a long and difficult process, but by the mid-1920s the Camagüey Company, Demerara Electric, and Porto Rico Railways were again subject to Royal Securities and Montreal Engineering, with control effected through the use of the International Power holding company. With the exception of the Camagüey Company, which was sold by Killam to an American utility in 1926, these companies would remain within the Royal Securities group well into the post-war era.

Preliminary Assessment of Montreal Engineering's Performance

The critical issue is whether the operating companies, particularly those FSCs which were functionally autonomous for fifteen years, were actually better off as part of the group before 1911 and after 1925. Unfortunately, the limited evidence available concerning Montreal Engineering's activities after the First World War will permit only a preliminary and partial response to that critical question.[59] This is important to keep in mind, given the fact that there were both tangible and intangible costs associated with accepting Montreal Engineering services, including engineering consulting fees and the loss of managerial autonomy. These costs were high enough for the Halifax directors of Demerara Electric and the Camagüey Company to fight off the Royal Securities group for fifteen years before rejoining 'the system', and Trinidad Electric never rejoined the St James Street 'gang' after its departure in 1910.

Table 15.4 summarizes the financial performance of the Royal Securities FSCs created before the First World War. To permit comparison with FSCs outside the Royal Securities circle, the financial performance indicators used here are identical to those used by Christopher Armstrong and H. V. Nelles in estimating the performance of (1) the São Paulo and Rio de Janeiro utilities whose balance sheets were consolidated under those of Brazilian Traction, Light & Power after 1912; (2) Mexico Tramways; and (3) Mexican Light & Power, which continued to issue a separate set of accounts despite its status as a subsidiary of Mexico Tramways after 1909.[60] Since accounting practices, particularly those related to depreciation, varied considerably among companies and over time, the resulting calculations concerning operating ratios and returns on incomes are at best extremely crude (and sometimes misleading) indicators of relative performance. In reality, share-price data might actually be superior indicators of relative performance.[61] Unfortunately the smaller Royal Securities' utilities rarely had their shares publicly listed (with the exception of Porto Rico Railways and Trinidad Electric, and then only for a few years), and these data are consequently not available.

The operating-ratio and excess-revenue figures indicate the ratio of the FSC's variable costs (operating expenses) to its total income (operating revenue), and the potential income thus available (excess revenue) to cover interest and dividend payments and for reinvestment in the utility. The operating-ratio figure can, however, be used as an extremely rough approximation of the efficiency of the FSC in question, keeping in mind that thermal operations were bound to have proportionately higher operating costs than hydroelectric utilities: burning imported coal was simply more expensive than using geographically proximate water power.

Electrical engineers and utility financiers such as F. S. Pearson put great emphasis on operating ratios. For his hydroelectric utilities, Pearson's rule of thumb was to get operating expenses down to, or below, the 50 per cent mark. In fact, this involved precise calculations concerning the upkeep, improvement, and extension of power plants, the replacement of big ticket items such as generators and transformers, as well as carefully improving scheduling, maintenance, and routing of tram cars and track, and selecting the optimal time to enlarge lighting and tram systems.[62]

Carl Giles and his successors at Montreal Engineering were equally adamant about operating ratios. During the Royal Securities' 1914 negotiations to regain control of the Camagüey Company, for example, Giles sent a circular to all of the principal Halifax director-shareholders pointing out how hard Montreal Engineering had worked to reduce the FSC's operating ratio from 56 per cent in 1908 to 51 per cent in 1911. He then pointed out the fact that, after Montreal Engineering's services were discontinued, Camagüey's operating expenses had climbed to 59 per cent by 1914, drastically reducing net income, and forcing the company to suspend dividends.[63]

From 1914 until approximately 1923, the years that Montreal Engineering did not manage the FSCs in question, operating ratios did deteriorate dramatically. Although some decline over time could have been expected as plant and equipment aged, an active programme of reinvestment guided by a team of expert engineers should have been able to prevent the degree of deterioration illustrated in Table 15.4. Unfortunately, the absence of individual company data for Camagüey after 1922, for Porto Rico after 1923, and Demerara after 1924, prevents

TABLE 15.4. *Financial performance of Royal Securities group of free-standing companies, 1909–1924*

Year	(1) Book value of assets (Can.$)	(2) Operating revenues (Can.$)	(3) Operating expenses (Can.$)	(4) Operating ratio (%)	(5) Excess revenue (Can.$)	(6) Net incomes (Can.$)	(7) Private rate of return on investment (%)	(8) Net rate of return on investment (%)	(9) Share price (Can.$)
Camagüey Company									
1906[a]	—	59,005	31,214	52.9	27,791	14,458	—	—	—
1907[a]	—	77,887	39,106	50.2	38,781	21,281	—	—	—
1908[a]	—	119,652	67,804	56.7	51,848	26,016	3.8	1.9	—
1909[a]	1,382,622	133,667	75,174	56.2	58,493	28,493	4.2	2.1	—
1910[a]	1,382,622	142,893	78,904	55.2	63,989	28,173	4.6	2.0	—
1911[a]	1,661,089	161,166	83,211	51.6	77,955	42,174	4.7	2.5	—
1912	1,721,459	182,857	102,305	55.9	80,552	44,584	4.7	2.6	—
1913	1,733,778	195,626	116,316	59.5	79,310	43,500	4.6	2.5	—
1914	1,775,991	207,066	128,438	62.0	78,628	50,145	4.4	2.8	—
1915	—	—	—	—	—	—	—	—	—
1916	—	—	—	—	—	—	—	—	—
1917	—	—	—	—	—	—	—	—	—
1918	—	—	—	—	—	—	—	—	—
1919	—	496,983	302,171	60.8	194,812	—	—	—	—
1920	—	621,790	306,206	49.2	315,584	—	—	—	—
1921	—	708,584	328,586	46.4	379,998	—	—	—	—
1922[a]	—	705,551	353,351	50.1	352,200	—	—	—	—
Demerara Electric									
1906[a]	—	120,438	70,690	58.7	49,748	—	—	—	—
1907[a]	—	120,909	69,108	57.2	51,801	—	—	—	—
1908[a]	1,568,821	127,016	70,825	55.8	56,191	23,151	3.6	1.5	—
1909[a]	1,060,905	135,378	72,548	53.6	62,830	29,743	5.9	2.8	—
1910[a]	1,063,406	132,603	75,548	57.2	56,803	23,316	5.3	2.2	—
1911[a]	1,130,844	139,112	73,262	52.7	65,850	31,560	5.8	2.8	—

TABLE 15.4. *(continued)*

Year	(1) Book value of assets (Can.$)	(2) Operating revenues (Can.$)	(3) Operating expenses (Can.$)	(4) Operating ratio (%)	(5) Excess revenue (Can.$)	(6) Net incomes (Can.$)	(7) Private rate of return on investment (%)	(8) Net rate of return on investment (%)	(9) Share price (Can.$)
1912	1,132,166	143,985	82,894	57.6	61,091	22,362	5.4	2.0	—
1913	1,124,455	143,616	86,460	60.2	57,156	18,441	5.1	1.6	—
1914	1,113,674	141,237	84,531	59.9	56,706	26,350	5.1	2.4	—
1915	—	—	—	—	—	—	—	—	—
1916	1,108,043	135,978	90,708	66.7	45,270	16,239	4.1	1.5	—
1917	1,121,282	160,676	108,274	67.4	52,402	23,167	4.7	2.1	—
1918	1,147,241	183,673	127,811	69.6	55,862	26,627	4.9	2.3	—
1919	1,145,284	197,909	144,133	72.8	53,776	25,008	4.7	2.2	—
1920	1,167,827	237,151	195,183	82.3	41,968	13,433	3.6	1.2	—
1921	1,192,145	271,349	223,630	82.4	47,719	19,184	4.0	1.6	—
1922	1,146,840	261,062	208,833	80.0	52,229	23,871	4.6	1.6	—
1923[a]	1,142,779	282,460	216,368	76.6	66,092	39,288	4.6	2.1	—
1924[a]	1,178,721	278,911	204,649	73.4	74,262	46,455	6.3	3.9	—
Porto Rico Railways									
1906[a]	—	298,803	199,648	66.8	99,155	47,646	—	—	—
1907[a]	6,015,038	349,868	206,301	59.0	143,567	97,622	2.4	1.6	—
1908[a]	6,135,891	376,244	203,645	54.1	172,599	122,176	2.8	2.0	—
1909[a]	6,650,886	409,031	214,687	52.5	194,344	—	2.9	—	—
1910[a]	6,679,225	561,662	293,903	52.3	267,759	120,956	4.0	1.8	—
1911[a]	7,134,025	748,802	400,120	53.4	348,682	199,559	4.9	2.8	—
1912[a]	7,903,655	828,084	524,772	63.4	303,312	134,061	3.8	1.7	—
1913[a]	8,359,929	850,121	449,853	52.9	400,268	175,847	4.8	2.1	—
1914[a]	8,453,427	772,905	404,071	52.3	368,834	173,023	4.4	2.0	101
1915	8,391,374	747,181	369,819	49.5	377,362	—	4.5	—	—
1916	8,257,702	829,057	412,431	49.8	416,626	—	5.1	—	90

TABLE 15.4. (*continued*)

Year	(1) Book value of assets (Can.$)	(2) Operating revenues (Can.$)	(3) Operating expenses (Can.$)	(4) Operating ratio (%)	(5) Excess revenue (Can.$)	(6) Net incomes (Can.$)	(7) Private rate of return on investment (%)	(8) Net rate of return on investment (%)	(9) Share price (Can.$)
1917	8,313,405	902,393	505,981	56.1	396,412	—	4.8	—	80
1918	8,282,382	1,035,955	605,864	58.5	430,091	250,429	5.2	3.0	—
1919	8,341,431	1,129,782	693,843	61.4	435,939	265,660	5.2	3.2	—
1920	8,537,980	1,402,736	839,666	60.0	563,070	—	6.6	—	—
1921	8,663,074	1,332,486	866,770	65.1	465,716	—	5.4	—	73
1922	8,691,686	1,330,446	813,607	61.2	516,839	557,405	6.0	—	78
1923	8,615,318	1,324,798	891,444	67.2	433,354	—	5.0	—	67
Trinidad Electric									
1903[a]	1,732,761	158,096	66,502	42.1	91,594	—	5.3	—	77
1904[a]	2,003,515	201,842	83,120	41.9	118,722	82,723	5.9	4.1	81
1905[a]	2,012,874	205,286	84,997	41.4	120,289	84,290	6.0	4.2	92
1906[a]	2,030,727	202,739	88,242	43.5	114,497	78,497	5.6	3.9	80
1907[a]	2,041,376	205,043	89,302	43.6	115,741	79,741	5.7	3.9	—
1908[a]	2,050,392	210,210	94,732	45.1	115,478	79,478	5.6	3.9	—
1909[a]	2,076,366	208,643	93,378	44.8	115,265	79,265	5.6	3.8	—
1910[a]	2,064,751	206,901	101,366	49.0	105,535	69,534	5.1	3.4	—
1911[a]	2,073,840	222,277	108,621	48.9	113,656	77,656	5.5	3.7	—
1912	2,114,192	224,548	115,956	51.6	108,592	72,592	5.1	3.4	—
1913	2,140,311	225,216	126,869	56.3	98,347	62,347	4.6	2.9	—
1914	2,144,327	225,873	126,281	55.9	99,592	63,591	4.6	3.0	—
1915	2,143,932	228,140	137,675	60.3	90,465	54,465	4.2	2.5	—
1916	2,196,958	242,657	137,127	56.5	105,530	69,529	4.8	3.2	—
1917	2,209,830	252,379	113,861	45.1	138,518	75,518	6.3	3.4	—
1918	2,252,460	265,125	176,909	66.7	88,216	52,216	3.9	2.3	—
1919	2,166,446	327,487	262,185	80.1	63,302	26,302	3.0	1.2	—

TABLE 15.4. (*continued*)

Year	(1) Book value of assets (Can.$)	(2) Operating revenues (Can.$)	(3) Operating expenses (Can.$)	(4) Operating ratio (%)	(5) Excess revenue (Can.$)	(6) Net incomes (Can.$)	(7) Private rate of return on investment (%)	(8) Net rate of return on investment (%)	(9) Share price (Can.$)
1920	2,285,073	423,611	294,735	69.6	128,876	66,451	5.6	2.9	—
1921	2,300,000	502,214	392,813	78.2	109,401	73,401	4.8	3.2	—
1922	2,342,806	506,113	414,459	81.9	91,654	55,655	3.9	2.4	—
1923	2,353,480	435,355	304,457	69.9	130,898	94,897	5.6	4.0	—
1924	2,407,515	391,561	260,966	66.6	130,595	94,595	5.4	3.9	—

[a] Years in which the utility was controlled by Royal Securities and/or serviced by the Montreal Engineering Company.

Source: Derived from *Annual Financial Review (Canadian)*, 10 (1910)–25 (1925).

a more penetrating analysis concerning the impact of Montreal Engineering on the performance of the operating utilities.[64]

Net income is what is left over after operating and business expenses as well as bond interest have been met. The private rate of return on investment is the gross rate of return before capital costs, sinking fund contributions, depreciation, and dividends are deducted.[65] The net rate of return on investment indicates percentage of total assets (book value of assets) available for stock dividends, sinking fund payments, and reinvestment.

As can be seen in Table 15.4, private and net rates of return fluctuate so much over these same years that no consistent pattern emerges. This may be a product of the accounting conventions of the day, which included valuing the plant, equipment, and other property at the time of assembly or purchase with no adjustments for depreciation. The problems which this creates, when combined with valuing common and preference stock liabilities listed at par rather than market value on the debit side of the balance sheet, means that the total-asset figures produced at this time were less than accurate proxies for the underlying value of the companies. Included here because they are useful for examining an individual firm's profit performance over time, private and net rates of return may be misleading in any comparisons *among* firms.

Finally, it is difficult to compare the financial performance of Royal Securities' FSCs with those covered by Armstrong and Nelles in their study in part because of the impact of exogenous shocks, such as the Mexican Revolution, which severely damaged the earning power of the FSCs in Mexico. For this reason, higher operating ratios and lower rates of return for the Mexican companies than for Royal Securities' Caribbean utilities should not be a surprise. As for the Brazilian FSCs, São Paulo Tramway, Light & Power consistently outperforms all Canadian FSCs, including the Royal Securities group. On the other hand, Rio de Janeiro Tramway, Light & Power was a poor performer relative to the Royal Securities group.

Unfortunately, after the organization of International Power in 1926, separate accounting data for the individual operating companies were no longer available, and we are forced to use an even more indirect and aggregate measure of performance—that of share prices for the holding companies. As International Power was publicly listed on the Montreal and Toronto stock-exchanges in 1928, share price data are summarized and compared with the Brazilian and Mexican holding companies in Table 15.5. The results are unambiguous. International Power's share value survived the 1929 stock market crash much better than the other holding companies, a reflection of the company's perceived strength

TABLE 15.5. *Comparative preference share prices, 1928–1930*

Utility holding company	1928 (Can.$)	1929 (Can.$)	1930 (Can.$)	decline (1928–30) (%)
Brazilian Traction, Light & Power Company	59	57	38	35.6
Mexico Tramways Company	41	43	19	53.7
International Power Company	98	83	87	11.2

Note: Share prices are recorded at year-ends, midway between bid and asked price.
Sources: Armstrong and Nelles, *Southern Exposure*, 358–9, and *Annual Financial Review (Canadian)*, 30 (July 1930), 695.

among investors, some of which was due to Killam's head-office organization, with Montreal Engineering serving as the lynchpin for the Royal Securities family of operating FSCs.

Conclusion

British FSCs were often regarded as highly speculative promotions that sometimes bordered on the fraudulent. While the majority were not financial scams, the Canadian utility FSCs covered here were none the less highly speculative ventures designed to generate very high rates of return to their promoters. In the case of the Royal Securities Corporation, these companies invariably began as vehicles to create new share issues for the investment house. Similarly, the utility holding company schemes of the 1920s were innovative attempts to increase both profits and control without necessarily investing more in the operating companies. Pyramided holding companies not only were capable of draining profits away from operating companies; they also lessened their chances for survival by making the operating companies the foundation for a rickety house of cards, all of which could fall together during a downturn like the 1929 stock-market crash.

This speculative side could be offset only by holding companies providing real value to the operating companies in return for their assumption of greater risk. In the case of EBASCO, this came in the form of providing investment banking, engineering, management consulting, accounting, legal, and other services. In the case of International Power, value added came in the form of Royal Securities raising new capital at lower cost than could be obtained from an arm's-length investment bank, and most significantly through Montreal Engineering, which planned, constructed, managed, supervised, and improved the operating facilities of the FSCs.

Utility promoters such as Max Aitken and Izaak Walton Killam created such a system because their utilities were highly location-specific investments with assets not easily moved into other uses. Once capital was raised and then sunk in a utility project abroad, the only way for Royal Securities to protect the value of the shares it had issued, and continue making successful utility issues in the future, was to run the integrated utility system as efficiently as possible.

Why was the Royal Securities system not emulated by other utility groupings in Canada? There are at least two possible answers. First, the need was not as pressing. The Royal Securities FSCs were among the smallest foreign utilities established by Canadians. They did not benefit from the same economies of scale and therefore had to be more concerned about their operating ratio of costs to revenues. Three of the first four were coal-fired thermal plants whose operating expenses were proportionately higher than the larger, hydroelectric-based FSCs. None alone could afford the large engineering staffs directly employed by Brazilian Traction and Mexico Tramways companies.

Secondly, the Royal Securities' FSCs were far-flung operations that could never have been integrated into a single market. Both the Mexico Tramways and Brazilian Traction groups were within markets that could be (and were) unified over time, with the staffs of the various operating subsidiaries able to share knowledge and experience. This contrasts sharply with the situation of the small and geographically dispersed West Indian utilities whose skeletal staffs were necessarily limited in terms of experience and knowledge.

According to the operating ratios over time as well as the share performance of International Power, the Royal Securities' group of utilities performed better than average because of Montreal Engineering. At the same time, the survival rate of the Canadian utility FSCs, even among those without strong head-office support, was far higher than the British FSCs studied by Wilkins. None the less, with the exception of the Royal Securities group, Canadian utility FSC expansion essentially halted after the First World War. A few were sold to the new utility MNEs with head offices in Europe and the USA that were swiftly moving into foreign countries during the 1920s. Without a head-office structure that delivered some value to the FSCs operating abroad, it was difficult to challenge companies such as EBASCO.

NOTES

1. See M. Wilkins, 'The Free-Standing Company, 1870–1914: An Important Type of British Foreign Direct Investment', *Economic History Review*, 2nd ser., 41 (May 1988), 259–82; M. Wilkins, 'Defining a Firm: History and Theory', in P. Hertner and G. Jones (eds.), *Multinationals: Theory and History* (Aldershot, 1986), 80–95. For a description of the American model of the MNE, see M. Wilkins, *The Maturing of Multinational Enterprise: American Business Abroad from 1914 to 1970* (Cambridge, Mass., 1974), 414–22.

2. See D. K. Fieldhouse, 'The Multinational: A Critique of a Concept', in A. Teichova, M. Lévy-Leboyer, and H. Nussbaum (eds.), *Multinational Enterprise in Historical Perspective* (Cambridge, 1986), 9–29, for a critique of the very concept of an MNE.
3. Given the speculative nature of many FSCs, this belies the predominant image of the British investor as a passive, risk-eschewing 'coupon clipper' as portrayed by many scholars. See G. P. Marchildon, 'British Investment Banking and Industrial Decline before the Great War: A Case Study of Capital Outflow to Canadian Industry', *Business History*, 33 (July 1991), 72–92.
4. Defined as an independent state or a dependent colony that is culturally and geographically separated from the mother country. This is in accord with Wilkins's inclusion as FSCs those enterprises with British head offices operating in the British colonies and with Ben P. A. Gales and Keetie E. Sluyterman's treatment of Dutch FSCs in Chapter 11 herein.
5. S. J. Nicholas says this was originally Leslie Hannah's observation: 'British Multinational Investment before 1939', *Journal of European Economic History*, 11 (Winter 1982), 606. See P. Payne, *The Early Scottish Limited Companies, 1856–1896* (Edinburgh, 1980) for examples of Glasgow-based FSCs.
6. Wilkins, 'The Free-Standing Company', 263.
7. For an instructive example of the interaction between the FSC's local management and its board of directors, see M. Gerriets, 'The Rise and Fall of a Free-Standing Company in Nova Scotia: The General Mining Association', *Business History*, 34 (July 1992), 16–48.
8. Wilkins, 'The Free-Standing Company', 276.
9. D. G. Paterson, *British Direct Investment in Canada, 1890–1914: Estimates and Determinants* (Toronto, 1976), 80–102.
10. Wilkins, 'The Free-Standing Company', 271.
11. See A. D. Chandler, Jr., *Scale and Scope: The Dynamics of Industrial Capitalism* (Cambridge, Mass., 1990). Also see M. Wilkins, *The Emergence of Multinational Enterprise: American Business Abroad from the Colonial Era to 1914* (Cambridge, Mass., 1970); Wilkins, *The Maturing of Multinational Enterprise*, 414–22.
12. D. McDowall, *The Light: Brazilian Traction, Light and Power Company Limited, 1899–1945* (Toronto, 1988). C. Armstrong and H. V. Nelles, *Southern Exposure: Canadian Promoters in Latin America and the Caribbean, 1896–1930* (Toronto, 1988).
13. On the history of Montreal Engineering, see G. P. Marchildon, *Profits and Politics: Beaverbrook and the Gilded Age of Canadian Finance* (Toronto, 1996), and J. Sexton, *Monenco: The First 75 Years* (n.p., 1982).
14. In 1888 Richmond, Virginia, became the first city in the world to replace its horse-car system with an overhead trolley (tram) car system, powered by electricity generated by a thermal plant. On the nature and implications of the electrical revolution, see T. P. Hughes, *Networks of Power: Electrification in Western Society, 1880–1930* (Baltimore, 1982). On specific aspects of electric systems, see C. W. Cheape, *Moving the Masses: Urban Public Transit in New York, Boston, and Philadelphia, 1880–1912* (Cambridge, Mass., 1980); C. Armstrong and H. V. Nelles, *Monopoly's Moment: The Organization and Regulation of Canadian Utilities, 1830–1930* (Philadelphia, 1986); H. Passer, *The Electrical Manufacturers, 1875–1900* (Cambridge, Mass., 1953).
15. Armstrong and Nelles, *Southern Exposure*, p. ix.
16. Small, non-publicly-listed FSCs may be excluded from this survey: one example was the International Light & Power Company, which owned a small thermal generating plant in Mexico and claimed compensation from the Mexican government in 1926 for 300,000 pesos worth of losses it suffered during

the revolutionary upheavals following the overthrow of Porfirio Díaz's government in 1911 (Armstrong and Nelles, *Southern Exposure*, 210).

17. Armstrong and Nelles, *Southern Exposure*, 25.
18. *Street Railway Journal*, 1 Dec. 1900, 1151.
19. Ibid. 13 Jan. 1900, 491; 17 Feb. 1900, 198; 12 May 1900, 491; 27 Oct. 1900, pp. v–vi; 1 Dec. 1900, 1151; 16 Mar. 1901, p. v; 6 Apr. 1901, 417–19; 8 June 1901, p. viii. Also see Armstrong and Nelles, *Southern Exposure*, 38–40, 108–19.
20. *Cuba Review* (Jan. 1908), 20–1. House of Lords Record Office, London, Beaverbrook Papers (hereafter HLBP), A/10/Teele, 1906 correspondence between F. Teele and M. Aitken.
21. HLBP, A/10/Ross, 1906 correspondence between W. D. Ross and W. M. Aitken. *Porto Rico Review*, 12 Oct. 1907, 8; 21 Dec. 1907, 9; 6 June 1908, 9.
22. McDowall, *The Light*, chs. 1–4.
23. *Annual Financial Review (Canadian)*, 10 (Apr. 1910), 292–3. Existing thermal plant operators were dependent on coal imported thousands of miles, often from Britain, and this expense was passed on to power consumers.
24. Armstrong and Nelles, *Southern Exposure*, chs. 5, 10.
25. An anglicized and incorrect spelling of 'Monterrey'.
26. *Annual Financial Review (Canadian)*, 10 (Apr. 1910), 512–16. Armstrong and Nelles, *Southern Exposure*, 210.
27. *Annual Financial Review (Canadian)*, 10 (Apr. 1910), 285. W. J. Hausman and J. L. Neufeld, 'The Rise and Fall of Public Utility Holding Companies', unpublished working paper (Feb. 1992). Armstrong and Nelles, *Southern Exposure*, 253.
28. Armstrong and Nelles, *Southern Exposure*, 163–8.
29. On Porto Rico Railways' numerous difficulties, see S. J. Randall, 'The Development of Canadian Business in Puerto Rico', *Revista/Review Interamericana*, 7 (1977), 16–20. Brazilian Traction's inter-war problems are dissected by McDowall in *The Light*.
30. On the links between utility holding companies and Siemens and other manufacturers, see P. Hertner, 'Financial Strategies and Adaptation to Foreign Markets: The German Electro-Technical Industry and its Multinational Activities, 1890s to 1939', in A. Teichova, M. Lévy-Leboyer, and H. Nussbaum (eds.), *Multinational Enterprise in Historical Perspective* (Cambridge, 1986), 145–59.
31. McDowall, *The Light*; Armstrong and Nelles, *Southern Exposure*, ch. 13. Hausman and Neufeld, 'Public Utility Holding Companies', and their Chapter 14 herein.
32. From its creation in 1907 until the early 1950s, Royal Securities held a controlling block of shares in Montreal Engineering. None of Montreal Engineering's shares was sold publicly, nor was the company publicly listed. See Sexton, *Monenco*, 265–72.
33. 'Porto' is an Americanization of 'Puerto' that was adopted when the USA took possession of the island following the Spanish–American War, and 'Porto' Rico remained its official name until 1932 (J. L. Dietz, *Economic History of Puerto Rico: Institutional Change and Capitalist Development* (Princeton, 1986), 85).
34. The Royal Securities group had lost control of the Camagüey Company, Trinidad Electric, Demerara Electric, and Porto Rico Railways by 1912. By the early 1920s, Killam was beginning to re-exert control over all of the companies (except Trinidad Electric), a process completed by about 1926, the year he sold the Camagüey Company to an American company (National Archives of Canada, Ottawa, Beaverbrook Papers, MG27/II/G1 (hereafter NABP), Reel A1776, Montreal Engineering correspondence, 1910–1913; Sexton, *Monenco*, ch. 3).

35. A colony of Great Britain, Newfoundland did not join the Canadian federation until 1949.
36. See Hausman and Neufeld, 'Public Utility Holding Companies', for the following example: if operating company A raises $100 by issuing $50 of bonds (6% rate of interest) and $50 of preference stock (10% dividend), and thus pays $8 for its capital, then subholding company B can purchase the $50 shares, paying less than $4 for it by issuing $25 of preference stock (10% dividend), and $25 common shares (paying 5% dividend) to holding company C.
37. This acronym is used here only for the sake of convenience, and should be distinguished from Ebasco Industries, the name which Electric Bond & Share assumed in 1968 (Hausman and Neufeld, 'Public Utility Holding Companies').
38. There is some dispute over whether the connection continued after General Electric formally divested itself of EBASCO, in the midst of a Federal Trade Commission investigation, in 1924. See Hausman and Neufeld, 'Public Utility Holding Companies'; Armstrong and Nelles, *Southern Exposure*, 254; Hausman and Neufeld, Chapter 14 herein; Wilkins, *The Maturing of Multinational Enterprise*, 131.
39. S. A. Mitchell, *S. Z. Mitchell and the Electrical Industry* (New York, 1960), 62–5, 109.
40. Armstrong and Nelles, *Southern Exposure*, chs. 13, 14.
41. Montreal Engineering shared the same building at 164 St James Street with Royal Securities until 1909, when Royal Securities left Montreal Engineering to take up more capacious offices a short distance away at 179 St James Street (NABP, Reel A1776, Montreal Engineering correspondence, 1910).
42. NABP, Reel A1776, letter, Aitken to Clarke, 30 Aug. 1911.
43. Before he joined Trinidad Electric in 1901, Teele had been the chief engineer of the Boston Elevated Railroad Company's power station. As such, he was part of the emerging corps of American engineers educated and trained in electric power generating and transmitting (*Street Railway Journal*, 6 Apr. 1901, 419).
44. McDowall, *The Light*, 66. Plummer's New York letterhead advertised that he was a general export and commission agent, as well as the *principal* agent for the São Paulo, Rio de Janeiro, Trinidad, and other companies (HLBP, A/6/N-P, letter, W. P. Plummer to Aitken, 29 Dec. 1905).
45. Marchildon, *Profits and Politics*, ch. 5.
46. Bribes had been a regular part of the FSC business in Latin America and the Caribbean, but Clarke devised a scheme in which feigning indifference when threatened, combined with the Montreal office directly negotiating with the council or government officials responsible, often over the head of the individual attempting to extract a bribe, reduced outlays by the company over time (NABP, Reel A1776, letter, Vander Voort (general manager of the Camagüey Company) to Teele, 23 July 1911).
47. HLBP, A/16/W. B. Ross, letter, Ross to Trinidad Electric Company, Trinidad, BWI, Oct. 1907. Armstrong and Nelles, *Southern Exposure*, 251–3.
48. HLBP, A/9/R, letter, Aitken to W. B. Ross, 4 Dec. 1906.
49. NABP, Reel A1776, letter, Giles to Aitken, 6 Aug. 1910.
50. HLBP, A/14/Giles, A/22/Giles, and A/19/Abbott, Montreal Engineering correspondence, 1907 and 1908. NABP, Reel A1776, letter, Clarke to Aitken, 15 Aug. 1911.
51. HLBP, A/22/Giles, A/16/W. B. Ross, and A/13/Clarke, correspondence, 1908.
52. Killam's biographer romantically describes how Montreal Engineering became 'his tool for construction projects', including the 'production of power for the tin of Bolivia' and 'the oil of Venezuela'. In the first case, Montreal Engineering apparently obtained 'a contract to service all tin production' after it 'surveyed

the Andes for power sites'. It then built the power plant and transmission lines through the mountainous terrain, an engineering accomplishment described by some as 'remarkable'. See D. How, *Canada's Mystery Man of High Finance: The Story of Izaak Walton Killam and his Glittering Wife Dorothy* (Huntsport, NS, 1986), 58.

53. NABP, Reel A1776, correspondence with Giles and Clarke, 1910–11. By 1911, the head offices of Demerara Electric and the Camagüey Company had been moved to Halifax, and the contracts with Montreal Engineering discontinued and F. S. Pearson's New York agency was reappointed the purchasing agent for the FSCs. Porto Rico Railways was moved to Toronto that same year, and Montreal Engineering could continue servicing that company only if Clarke agreed to move to Toronto. Giles vacated the presidency that same year.
54. NABP, Reel A1776, Montreal Engineering correspondence, 1914.
55. The companies included: Calgary Power, St John Railway, Porto Rico Railways, the Camagüey Company, Santiago Electric Light & Traction, West India Electric, Trinidad Electric, Demerara Electric, Panama Tramway, and the Matanzas, Cardenas, and Cienfuegos utility companies in Cuba (NABP, Reel A1776, letter, Giles to Aitken, 1 Apr. 1915).
56. NABP, Reel A1776, letters, Giles to Aitken, 1 and 27 Apr. 1915, and Teele to Aitken, 13 Apr. 1915.
57. NABP, Reel A1776, letters, Aitken to Giles, 15 and 16 June 1915.
58. NABP, MG/27/G1, Reel A1776, Montreal Engineering Company correspondence, 1910–15. M. Baker, R. D. Pitt, and J. M. Pitt, *The Illustrated History of Newfoundland Light & Power* (St John's, 1990), 95–103. Sexton, *Monenco*, ch. 4.
59. How, *Canada's Mystery Man*, 57. In this popular biography, the author refers to Killam's records being destroyed in a 1969 fire at Royal Securities head office in Montreal; these records presumably included the files of the International Power and Montreal Engineering companies.
60. See appendix in Armstrong and Nelles, *Southern Exposure*, 351–9.
61. This refers specifically to preference shares since most utilities generally waited a decade or longer to list common shares, which were generally given to insiders as 'promoters' profit' when the FSC was first created. Armstrong and Nelles calculated prices per share as the average between the bid and asked prices at year-end, and the same procedure is adopted here.
62. Armstrong and Nelles, *Southern Exposure*, 98.
63. NABP, Reel A1776, letter, Giles (Montreal Engineering) to T. G. McMullen (Camagüey Company, Halifax), 1 Sept. 1914.
64. After International Power's incorporation, the FSC's financial accounts were consolidated under the holding company.
65. The private rate of return on investment might have given a clearer picture of an FSC's potential if it had not been weighted down by the overcapitalized structure (involving high interest and dividend obligations) often imposed by utility promoters.

Part IV

Conclusion

16

The Significance of the Concept and a Future Agenda

Mira Wilkins

In the years from 1830 to 1870 the world economy became more integrated. By 1870–1914 numerous companies were crossing national frontiers. If any reader had doubts, the chapters in this volume should be convincing. The First World War interrupted the globalization pattern. The 1920s saw, however, a revival of business over borders, only to be tempered by the heightened nationalism of the 1930s. Then came the Second World War and the cold war. Yet in the 1950s and 1960s, and to an even greater extent in the 1970s, 1980s, and 1990s, there was a renewal of internationalization, initially including principally non-communist countries and then extending to cover once more the entire world.

The free-standing company was a major participant in pre-First World War globalization; its role in the 1920s and 1930s was muted (there were, however, continuities and the establishment of new free-standing companies); by the end of the Second World War, far better—more appropriate to the then existing conditions—channels for the internationalization of business existed. In the 1990s there are still free-standing companies but their role is trivial in the overall story. Many free-standing companies that did business in the USA were assimilated and became domestic entities before the First World War; the Russian Revolution ended the existing free-standing companies there; post-Second World War decolonization and Third-World nationalism were other crowning blows. Even more important, as the world economy has evolved, international direct investments in relatively 'low' technology activities have been increasingly replaced by those in 'high' technology fields for which the free-standing company form was unsuitable. The free-standing company as a conduit was never associated with investments in differentiated products that required trademarks, follow-up service, ongoing complex technical assistance, and/or sizeable flows of research and development from a parent. The form was inappropriate in modern knowledge-intensive economic activities. The free-standing company had its time and place.

The concept of the free-standing firm has helped scholars in examining in an analytically informed manner the principal characteristics of business over borders—financing, strategies, structures, performance, and impact. This has been (and will continue to be) useful for economic and business historians (generalists and those concentrating on a particular country or region), banking historians, students of modern global history, as well as for economists, political scientists, sociologists, economic geographers, and experts on multinational enterprise—albeit in some of these fields the concept has as yet had little influence. None the less, the resulting cross-disciplinary insights supplement and fortify the research of the specialists. As is evident in the preceding chapters, the concept has served as a tool to clarify a number of different conundrums. In my view, the concept of the free-standing company has both analytic and heuristic value. What then in summary has been its significance, and what are the gaps in our knowledge that still need to be filled?

One set of issues on which insights from the concept of the free-standing company has cast light relates to the flows of capital that moved internationally. The concept has aided scholars in delineating new frameworks for understanding the size of (re-examining old numbers) and the types of (portfolio/direct, debt/equity, short-term/long-term, private/public) capital flows.[1] Through the exploration of the key features of the free-standing company (and the various clusters associated with it), existing capital-flow data have been reconsidered and new perspectives have been unveiled about the financing of business over borders. The concept has illuminated both the complexities of the capital flows in single years and over time. Different types of capital flows have unique consequences, so the distinctions have broad implications. Studies of free-standing companies have contributed to the growing awareness that there is a long history of foreign direct investment and that the latter was historically much more important than many earlier scholars had realized.[2] There has, however, at the same time arisen a realization that merely defining and tracing capital flows (or for that matter determining the level of FDI) by quantities, types, industries, and direction are insufficient to a study of business's role in global integration. Numbers can only go so far.

Thus, the second set of issues has focused more specifically on the institutional conduit *per se* (the business form) and its use. Considerations of the free-standing company as one actor engaged in international transactions give the basis for comparisons and contrasts with alternative forms of doing business in foreign countries. The chapters in this volume make it evident that the free-standing company was an important kind of organizational structure, with sub-typologies. I am struck by how many free-standing companies have been identified.

Free-standing companies facilitated the transfer of capital over borders and, in most instances, provided more than capital to the economic activity abroad. Like the well-studied 'classic' multinational enterprise, like all other foreign direct investments, it superimposed on the foreign operations an administrative structure, designed to facilitate the pursuit of business strategies. Capital was not exported by itself (in a vacuum), but rather it was embodied in a business organization. The business was—at least formally—managed from afar. Managers obtained, furnished, and diffused diverse services. Studies of why the free-standing company existed, the longevity of a company (which survived, which did not, and why), the functions of a head office, the relations between the head office and the operations abroad, the manner in which the company was managed, the extent of and rationale behind the delegation of managerial and technical competencies, the free-standing company's associations over time with wider enterprise groups and other clusters, and, most crucial, how and what kinds of changes occurred through time in the business and its relationships have helped clarify key facets of globalization by business entities. One of the principal additions of the free-standing-company concept to the historical literature is its insistence that the administration of a business matters and that management is firm- (and often sector/industry-) specific. What this means is that management cannot be assumed away and must be considered as we write on capital moving over borders. The focus on the firm enables the consideration of a tissue of business relationships—within and exterior to the firm.

While the chapters in this book establish that the free-standing company was an important actor in the decades before the First World War, far more research is required to determine its activities relative to other conduits in the international movements of capital, personnel, information, and added tangible and intangible assets (including management). Also, in certain economic activities the free-standing company proved efficient and in others inadequate. There seem to be substantial variations between and among international investment conduits, by sector and over time by geographical direction. As for sectors, the free-standing-company form of multinational-enterprise activity contributed to the start of many basic infrastructure-type investments (railroads, ports, canals, banking facilities) and to the development of a number of primary products that entered into foreign commerce. Yet free-standing companies did not always mine or cultivate primary products for export; the long-lasting and sizeable French free-standing company in Brazil's sugar industry—described so well by Tamás Szmrecsányi (Chapter 10)—served the domestic Brazilian market (it may have been more important to the export of French sugar machinery than to the export of Brazilian primary commodities). In the formation of infrastructure, it is highly significant that free-standing companies assisted in the diffusion of modern British banking methods on a global scale, as Geoffrey Jones (Chapter 13) has shown. These British banking facilities served as a foundation for domestic banking as well as international trade finance. The free-standing company was present in certain manufacturing industries from flour-milling to textiles to breweries, albeit it was markedly absent in high-technology (science- and knowledge-intensive) industries (e.g. chemicals and electrical/electronics), which required a different type of business organization. As for geographical direction, we need more studies on whether the places for the investments (the host countries or regions) varied in a systematic fashion over the years from those of other business conduits and specifically from those of the classic multinationals. Scattered evidence suggests this, and that the direction was closely linked with the sector of the investments.

A third set of insights that has emerged from the study of free-standing companies concerns those associated with the history and theory of multinational enterprise. It has long been known that the growth and contraction of business over borders through time has not been a neat nor steady process. Complexity reigns. Research on the free-standing company confirms such findings. Once, much of the vast literature on multinationals concentrated on industrials, and much of the research is still 'locked into a goods production mind-set'.[3] Now more scholars pay attention to service multinationals.[4] Current writings on multinational enterprise consider alliances and partial associations.[5] Scholarship on the differing paths of free-standing companies (the ones that did not exit rapidly) makes us ever more conscious of the long history of intricate intra-firm and inter-firm associations in primary commodities, manufacturing, and services over extended space and through time. In keeping with the new attention to services and to alliances in multinational-enterprise theory, the free-standing-company concept encourages us to depart from the goods production mind-set and to consider business enterprises in terms of goods and services and particularly in terms of the services essential in carrying out economic activities (whether at home or abroad). The clusters surrounding free-standing companies press us to ask new questions on hierarchy, contract, and market relationships.[6] My work on free-standing companies has been interpreted as confirming the illegitimacy of a theory of multinationals that sees them merely as 'arbitragers of finance'.[7] I think this is an appropriate conclusion. In this connection, however, a student of foreign direct investment in the USA has argued that a theory that assumes the investing firm possesses superior abilities at the time of its foreign direct investment does not explain the late 1980s foreign corporate takeovers in the USA, and that 'foreign acquisitions may reflect changes in world markets that require foreign firms to acquire abilities, technologies, or firm structures which they need for effective worldwide competition but which are more costly to develop internally'.[8] Leaving aside whether this analysis is correct, the study of the history of the free-standing firm tells us that, were it true of the late 1980s, the absence of initial superior abilities within the parent firm has precedent. The historical data do reveal—along the lines of the widely accepted traditional theory—that ultimately, however, to sustain operations the multinational enterprise must be able to acquire those abilities, find the managerial and technical capabilities, and internalize at least a core competency. The process and pace of that internalization seem basic to an understanding of the growth and success of the firm. I am convinced (albeit this is not shared by all the contributors to this volume) that a firm must have some kind of advantage beyond the existence of integration over borders in order to survive.[9]

To a large extent the theory of multinational enterprise has become associated in the economics literature with industrial-organization theory, and in that context with a theory of the firm; in both the economics and the business literature, it has become linked with John Dunning's eclectic paradigm, which drew on many theoretical foundations, including industrial-organization theory.[10] As I introduced the free-standing-company concept, some critics perceived it as a step backward, because the rationale within the home country for raising the capital and investing abroad was that of seeking higher returns. One critic saw my rendition as a reversion to pre-Hymer times.[11] The free-standing-company approach is, however, a step forward. It does not refute but rather adds body to the existing widely accepted theory of the multinational firm.[12] Because free-standing companies were set up to meet new individual investment opportunities, they were identified directly with profit prospects. Then, as the firm evolved, I treat the enterprise no differently from an approach within the prevailing framework of multinational-enterprise theory. And, indeed, the interpretation of my work, as cited above, which sees it as a refutation of the *post*-Hymer reversion to theories of the firm as a capital arbitrageur is far more on target than this criticism.

The importance of the free-standing-company concept lies in its demonstrating that the 'classic' American model was not universal; it was not the only form of foreign direct investment. The 'classic' multinational-enterprise description—based principally on the evolution of US industrial enterprise—does not conform to what historically was the dominant mode of British (and probably Dutch and Belgian) multinational enterprise type investments in the late nineteenth and early twentieth centuries. Thus, the free-standing-company concept has pushed both Jean-François Hennart and Mark Casson to extend and to amplify the theory of multinational enterprise to take into account the historical realities. Both make, within this volume, important contributions to the theory of multinational enterprise. In particular, I think that Hennart's discussion of the role of minority interests by the wider enterprise groupings is a major step forward in the literature. The free-standing-company concept compels us to study the different organizational forms (and different degrees of internalization) that firms take over time as they move over borders, both at origin and then subsequently. Here Rory Miller's sub-topologies are very helpful.[13]

Mark Casson once wrote that the modern theory of the multinational enterprise has the potential to become a general theory of the firm.[14] I perceive the research on free-standing companies as contributing to this endeavour. The research is consistent with the academic interest in what is internalized within the firm (and why) and what are the external, partial alliances, and relationships (and why). The free-standing-company paradigm pays special attention to the governance requirements of international businesses, by economic activity, through time. Internalization issues are seen in economic terms with the insistence on the nature of managerial requirements and their limits. This does not mean, however, that we ignore the political issues, for business over borders by definition involves operating under diverse political regimes (see below). Yet, the aim is to study organizational structures in their complexities, taking into account all the relevant circumstances, including the dynamics of change through time.

As the free-standing-company concept has undermined the universality of the 'American model', it impels us to study other forms of foreign direct investments—and not only the free-standing-company form. The concept has thus opened up opportunities to enlarge theory to comprise different types of managed multinational-enterprise behaviour in diverse periods of history and in separate economic sectors. Research on free-standing companies reinforces conclusions that different sectors (different industries) are associated with distinct business needs and structures. I believe the core of accepted theories of multinational-enterprise behaviour is sound, but that the free-standing-company concept has revealed the need to enlarge that core and focus on a closer analysis of how various kinds of economic activities are established and administered over borders. Why have a head office abroad? Is 'control' synonymous with management? What do we mean by control? As I have pointed out in Chapter 1, and as has been well accepted in the literature, often ownership does not define 'control' (ownership and control may not coincide).[15] We require more studies in depth on how business strategies relate to the structure and performance of business in different sectors over time—and how this is associated with managerial extensions over borders. This must be done based on company archives.

The theory of multinational enterprise has long recognized that firms did not simply manage money over borders, they managed personnel, products, processes, inputs into the production process, trade (domestic and international), and information. The free-standing-company concept challenged us to scrutinize added forms of international-resource allocation within the firm beyond the familiar 'classic' American multinational enterprise model. Stanley Chapman's work on merchant enterprise has, I believe, nourished and been nourished by the introduction of the free-standing-company concept. Just as with the classic American multinational enterprise where there were firms within firms, so too with the newer work on free-standing companies we are seeing firms within firms albeit now the interrelationships seem looser and less well defined. The merchant enterprise can be perceived as a multinational one, with minority interests in a number of firms. That some firms within the grouping had British head offices and others did not contributes to our understanding of the structure of conduits for overseas investments and the nature of global integration.[16]

Research on the international spread of public utilities—particularly in the 1920s—suggests that neither the classic model of multinational enterprise nor the free-standing one fits very comfortably and that, while both approaches offer valuable insights into an agenda for analysis (including the questions on business relationships that need addressing), it is essential that there be a deeper study of multinational enterprise in public utilities through time. The chapters of William Hausman and John Neufeld and of Gregory Marchildon are marvellous beginnings in this endeavour; Jean-François Hennart adds context; but we require more applications of theories of multinational enterprise, including that of the concept of the free-standing company, to German, French, British, Swiss, and Belgian holdings abroad in electric light and power. The free-standing company and, subsequently, the classic model of multinational enterprise seem to conform better to studies of the global history of telephones than to those in power and light.[17]

An added aspect of history and theory to pursue is that of the historical role of international networks of banks—especially those banks with headquarters on the European Continent—in facilitating foreign direct investments. Here, too, my current thinking is that neither the free-standing model nor the classic one of multinational enterprise is fully explanatory. What Natalia Gurushina (Chapter 6 herein) has attempted in the British/Russian case sorely needs to be done *vis-à-vis* free-standing companies headquartered on the Continent—and the host countries should be extended beyond Russia. She finds the free-standing-company approach appropriate, but will this be the case with German, French, and Swedish banking relationships?[18]

This book has added little on the inherent and multiple information asymmetries (adverse selection and moral hazard problems) involved in all business over borders. It would, I believe, be most useful to consider the free-standing company, the classic multinational enterprise, and other forms of foreign direct investment in the context not merely of bilateral information asymmetries but rather of a coterie of information relationships that by definition lack balance. Is there anything systematic on the way information asymmetries are offset by these different types of multinational enterprise?[19]

We need to analyse with a historical perspective both *intra-* and non-arm's-length partial *inter-*firm relations, with our attention going beyond information asymmetries to the specifics of company and industry, with concentration on the process of change. Indeed, one central contribution of the research on the free-standing company to theory is that it stimulates us to look at history so as to study dynamic processes. A good theory of multinationals has to recognize major changes in individual firms over time.[20]

Theories of multinational enterprise need to look carefully at management. If a company internalized a workable professional management structure and if it moved from a single function, single plant, single product, single locale operation to a giant multifunction, multiplant, multiproduct, multilocale business, I see little value in retaining the free-standing-company designation. These companies can then be studied as 'classic' multinational enterprises. Some companies, however, stayed for decades as basically single-product, dual-country (home and host) entities; in these situations, it is probably useful to retain the concept. In any case, the concept remains extremely valuable in understanding and deciphering the genesis of, the starting requirements of, and the early growth of the business. It seems less viable in considering the firm once substantial expansion has occurred and once managerial and other talents are internalized (and there is a core competence of experience and learning within the firm). In our theories, we have to pay more attention to the *loci* of management, the structure of management, the management needs, and the limits on management. More must be done on headquarters and their functions through time. What functions do head offices serve? What kinds of headquarters services are provided to the overseas operations? Similarly, how much middle management exists? The size, activities, and evolution of home offices—by sector—seem to differ substantially. Continuities, and also discontinuities, of businesses as well as new businesses over borders need to be explored in the context of free-standing companies. There has been sizeable research done on the pre-1914 years; far more needs to be done on subsequent years. Registration was an imperfect handle in defining headquarters in the era before the First World War, as we have pointed out. As Liechtenstein, Luxembourg, Panama, Bermuda, the Cayman Islands, and the Netherlands Antilles became the nominal headquarters for businesses, there is much more necessity to deal with ultimate beneficial owners (UBOs) and, even more important, the real centres of overall administrative direction.[21]

Over the years, there have been many valuable studies of the multinational enterprise's role in international trade.[22] Such studies need to be done on a historical basis *vis-à-vis* the classic multinational as compared with the free-standing company. Because a number of free-standing companies were associated with merchant groups, with making infrastructure investments, and with clusters that involved machinery exports from the home country, they may have been truly trade-creating—to a far larger extent than the classic multinational. From tea to rubber, from tin to oil, these companies opened new resources that were brought into international trade. The role of free-standing companies in domestic and international trade in inputs, as well as trade in outputs, needs more scrutiny.[23]

In short, there should be much more testing of historical experience against theory and vice versa. The present research broadens our historical insights on business over borders and results in the clear injunction not to be fettered by the restraints of (the shackles of) the classic model of multinationals. A theory of multinationals must be broad enough to encompass and to explain our empirical findings.

A fourth set of issues has homed in on the performance of the business over borders over time. Did the classic multinational enterprise perform better than the free-standing company? How do we evaluate success? As noted in Chapter 1, in the initial rendition of the concept, many of my readers assumed that free-standing firms by definition did not perform well, had a high failure rate, and because of lean governance at home were unable to give effective guidance to the business abroad. My introduction to the present volume and the other chapters herein have refined this discussion. Clearly, some firms that began as free-standing ones performed very well: had good profits, did not fail, and coped effectively with the problems of lean governance. By contrast, others did exit rapidly.

First, let us briefly consider the poor performers. There were 'scams' (albeit it is not clear what proportion of the companies fit in this category; the suggestion is that there were more mining frauds than in any other sector). Research shows that in some sectors—those where core competencies at home could be transferred abroad at low cost—it could be predicted that the free-standing firm would not be a satisfactory mode. In other sectors, failure was caused by the absence of finding oil or a mineral product (a more experienced international oil or mining company might have had success, but there were no guarantees). Rory Miller writes—in Chapter 8—that certain free-standing companies (his example was a coal and harbour company) never got started, because they could not obtain the backing of the appropriate external services (the right cluster). In Chapter 9, Reinhold Liehr and Mariano E. Torres Bautista state that most of the Anglo-Mexican mining companies were not successful in corporate terms (returns to shareholders), but they still left a satisfactory legacy (see below). Gregory P. Marchildon (Chapter 15) documents how Montreal Engineering Company, International Power Company, and Royal Securities Corporation could serve free-standing public utilities in overcoming the limitations of this mode. As pointed out in the original rendition of the concept (in 1988), sometimes, however, the head office was just too distant and too ignorant to be able to function effectively. It did not have within, nor could it obtain, the appropriate headquarters services to assist the business abroad.

By contrast, in some cases, by all definitions, the performance of free-standing companies proved equal to or even superior to that of the 'classic' multinational enterprise (in tea and rubber plantations, for example). And, in these cases, the 'cluster' was—as in Marchildon's story of the public utilities—typically key not only to the success in financing, but to the subsequent profitable performance of the company. I am convinced that governance mattered, and we need to study how the firm was able to provide suitable management and sector-specific technical skills that served the company in its operations abroad (other contributors are not as certain that management mattered).

A company could have a small head office or a not so small one could emerge. The free-standing-company concept has, to repeat, made us ponder what a head office abroad contributes to the performance of a business over borders. We knew the answers to this question with the classic multinational. We now have a body of knowledge on how head offices assist free-standing companies' business abroad. In my revisiting, I focused on those companies with continuities. If we judge performance by longevity (i.e. remaining in business over a long period of time), there were indeed quite a number of 'successful' free-standing firms—and it is useful to observe what their head offices did. Usually, in those cases, the rationale for the head office was not simply raising capital, but acquiring supplies for the business abroad (from machinery to other tangible and intangible inputs), finding personnel, making contacts, obtaining information on markets, offering both general and specific knowledge. The head office, however small, became the channel for resources mobilized at first from *outside* the free-standing company. This was true at the start for overseas banks, which then internalized many activities, still retaining the small head office. Once they did this, I am inclined no longer to label such firms free-standing ones. In certain ventures, the calling on the clusters—frequently, but not always, from broader enterprise groups—proved highly satisfactory. The nuclei of financial, commercial, client, and other services provided in the City of London (and other financial capitals) could be critical to the successful performance of a free-standing company. The professionalization of management might take place in the host country (countries) with lean, but again entirely adequate management from the home country. On the other hand, if the business needed firm-specific engineering services, these for all practical purposes probably required internalization.

Lance Davis and Robert A. Huttenback have done excellent work on profits by British firms, by sectors, domestically, within empire, and foreign (outside empire).[24] It would be extremely useful to mesh their findings with the free-standing-company concept and decipher whether the form of business abroad related to its 'success', as measured by profitability. Were the returns to firms that remained single-product, single-country entities superior or inferior to those of the classic multinational enterprise?[25]

A fifth set of insights that has arisen from the free-standing-company investigations lies in the impact of free-standing companies on home-country economic growth. Where do these companies fit in the course of national (source-of-capital country) economic histories? The study prompts us to explore changing home-country comparative advantages. Thus far, research on free-standing companies and home-country economic growth has been unsystematic.[26] There have been hints that free-standing companies echoed decline and counter suggestions that, instead, they demonstrated vitality (and competitiveness). Those who have emphasized the high failure rate of free-standing companies argue, as John Maynard Keynes did, that a bankrupt railroad abroad was of no value to the home economy.[27] Others have been impressed that the taxable British profits of these free-standing companies well into the twentieth century far exceeded the number of overseas assessments as a share of the British domestic and overseas total.[28] These figures, however, tell us little about the size of the investments, and nothing on the return on investments. Also, failed companies do not have profits. The average capital of free-standing companies appears to be larger than that of domestic companies (but is an average meaningful and does this matter?). The free-standing company's impact on home-country economic growth needs to be segregated from other conduits of foreign investments. Where specifically do such companies fit in terms of capital exports and alternative domestic investments, exports and imports of different categories of goods and services, applications of talent (where entrepreneurial and managerial energies are deployed), and domestic employment? Free-standing companies served as a connector between the home country and locales abroad; as noted, their activities generated substantial trade. Prices of foodstuffs and raw materials declined in source-of-capital countries, raising real incomes in the consuming countries. It has been argued that British overseas investments 'translated directly into foreign purchases of British goods, by providing importers with the credits they required'.[29] I would like to see documentation of this specifically in relationship to free-standing companies. Indeed this could be done in connection with more theoretical studies of free-standing companies and trade. Many questions remain unresolved in evaluating their benefits and costs to the home country.

In my mind, the jury is still out on the extent to which the rise and fall of free-standing companies were 'causes of', 'reflections of', or 'caused by' prevailing economic conditions in the home nations. Most authors tend to see gradations: they were 'causes' in that they provided important conduits for international economic integration in the nineteenth and early twentieth centuries. They were 'reflections of', in that they evolved at a time when economic conditions made them highly appropriate. And they were 'caused by', in that, as economic conditions over which they had no impact changed, their role diminished; as new high-technology industries evolved, they were not efficient generators or transmitters of such activities. Perhaps measures of 'extent' (or weighing) are impossible and we should settle simply for a notion of interaction.

A sixth set of impacts considers those on particular host countries' economic growth patterns, and here there has to be a different framework of analysis from that of the impact on the home country. Many free-standing companies were associated with broadly defined infrastructure investments (from railroads to basic banking facilities) as well as with primary commodity output. Everywhere there was the introduction of something new—a demonstration effect. This was even true when existing companies in host countries were taken over. In some host countries, the economic activity generated by free-standing companies was large enough to affect aggregate growth. It was a free-standing company that opened up the potential for oil production in Iran. The free-standing companies of Leslie Urquhart in Russia by 1916 (by one estimate) produced most of that nation's silver and lead, 60 per cent of its copper, and a sizeable proportion of its gold.[30] In many other nations around the world, free-standing companies had an equally profound impact.[31] They stimulated change. The research casts extraordinary new light on foreign-owned business structures, particularly in less developed countries. There seems no question but that the consequences were jarring. In that machinery—whether in mining, for sugar mills, or for textile factories—embodied process technologies, the existence of free-standing companies in these sectors provided for technology transfers.

Were these foreign companies instruments of growth (or 'exploitation')? Were their profits excessive, or (as Reinhard Liehr and Mariano E. Torres Bautista suggest in Chapter 9) were they often unprofitable to shareholders, but highly useful in economic growth? Just what were their contributions? Can we determine their role in raising productivity? What types of host nation linkage effects emerge?[32] Did these companies complement (or substitute for) domestic investment? Did they spur within host countries the creation of a wide variety of specialized inputs? Did they mobilize domestic (as well as foreign) capital for productive purposes? Were they able to attract the needed technical (engineering, for example) services? What impact did they have on host-country domestic and international trade? Did they provide host-country consumers with the desired goods and services? Were they more important in certain commodities than in others (and why)? What were their consequences *vis-à-vis* the quantity, wage, and quality of host-country employment? Did they add to host-government income? Did they supply a foundation for future economic development? Did their small (albeit often 'expensive') head office abroad serve a constructive purpose in the economic growth of the host nation, or was it a locale for superfluous cost (did the benefits exceed the costs)? How in terms of the host-country economy did free-standing companies compare with other conduits of capital, technology, managerial methods, and modes of doing business?

There need to be more studies of entrepreneurial initiative. Typically with the free-standing companies, one or several entrepreneurs (expatriates or 'locals' in the host-country, home-country individuals, or third-country nationals) would identify an opportunity within a particular host country. The free-standing-company form provided a means—not otherwise available—to pursue and to develop that prospect.[33] Thus, new economic activity could be undertaken—and resources made productive and brought into trade. But, once established, were these companies from the host country's standpoint an inferior form of foreign direct investment (as some have perceived them), or a different form that filled needs that would have otherwise been neglected?[34] Essays in this volume offer some answers to these questions, but we lack solid conclusions. Systematic research on the specific and distinctive impacts of free-standing companies on the economy of host countries would be highly fruitful. We need to do this research in a calm and detached fashion, shedding many stereotypes and preconceptions.[35]

A seventh set of insights appraises world growth rates, global integration, and where the free-standing company lies in the overall story of global economic history. Its role seems fundamental. We are struck by how cosmopolitan the involvements were—whether we talk about ownership, finance, direction, technical needs, trade, or personnel requirements. The international relationships are difficult to study, for we are often bound by a national or regional focus. Yet, it is useful to delve into how these businesses blended home, host, and third-country capital and talents; how they spread technology; how they assisted in the integration of commodity markets; and, in this analysis, the clusters are crucial, as is the position of stock markets. There are many clues in these chapters that the size, characteristics, and vitality of national (in both home and host countries) stock markets had a major impact on the beginnings and continuities of free-standing companies. More historical research needs to take place on overlapping and non-overlapping listings on stock exchanges and the reasons for listings on particular exchanges. Home-country biases in investments (by currency denominations) are well worth contemplating.[36]

One feature that distinguished the free-standing company from the classic multinational enterprise was its country (or region) focus. The classic multinational enterprise, with some noted exceptions, seems to have spread its investments more broadly—to more countries and regions. I am not, however, convinced that the classic multinational enterprise made a greater contribution to global integration than the free-standing company. Each classic multinational firm may have done so through its broader geographical span, but, aggregating the free-standing companies together, they could easily have had wider consequences in the pre-First World War years—especially as we deal with trade along with investment in our global integration stories—and as we deal with change through time.

In terms of a global economy, we know only the most rudimentary amount about the relationship between the free-standing companies and international trade in goods and services. In some instances, machinery manufacturers participated in setting up these companies (and machinery moved in trade), but the market for the final output was local. In other instances, free-standing companies produced commodities that were exported and the exports were handled by a wider enterprise group. In still different circumstances, they or others in the wider enterprise group provided trade finance. By contrast, there appear to have been free-standing companies that were not in any manner involved in international trade transactions. As noted earlier, our current findings are that free-standing companies tended to be trade-creating but these results require far more verification.

Finally, an eighth interest is political. Free-standing companies were most visible in the age of high imperialism. Was there a relationship, or relationships? If so, what were the associations? A number of chapters bring out the nuanced links between expatriates in the colonies and access to home capital markets and home 'services'. While the patterns described were not necessarily distinctive to empire, 'imperial' aspects require more investigations. In the Dutch case, there was from the start a heavy concentration of free-standing companies within the Netherlands East Indies, which concentration increased over time. In the British case, the free-standing companies that persisted were frequently those within the Empire. By contrast, in the case of Belgium, in terms of the amount of foreign direct investment in 1910, a sizeable percentage of which was that of free-standing companies, less than one-tenth was within the Empire.[37] Perhaps discussions of free-standing companies within empires should be considered in the context of reduced information asymmetries by virtue of expatriate presence and colonial administration.

In sum, the free-standing-company concept has become a guide in asking numerous questions and seeking answers. The findings do not fit neatly. The 'model' of the free-standing company, as has been shown in the chapters herein, is not tidy; it is not mathematical; we might call it an 'existential model', using Graeme Donald Snooks's term (an empirical model of reality, a model of existence, that can be contrasted with the deductive model).[38] Yet it does help us in our understanding of the history of business over borders. It does reveal the dynamics of microeconomic structures. There are still ambiguities requiring clarification. We need many more archival studies, using business archives. There is much evidence that remains untapped. We do need more systematic treatment—by home-country nationality—of the various wider enterprise groups and of clusters, particularly those that were 'cosmopolitan' in nature. We need more studies through time of what happened to these enterprises (and to headquarters functions). And, as we learn about the nature of free-standing companies, we can in a more systematic fashion study their impact. This book has, hopefully, opened up many research horizons. The chapters have also given us new insights and evidence to enrich our knowledge of fundamental aspects of the history of the world economy.

NOTES

1. We have not discussed private sector/public sector capital flows; free-standing companies involved private capital flows.
2. I have argued this for many years and it is now accepted in the best of the work on multinational enterprise. See, for example, E. M. Graham, *Global Corporations and National Governments* (Washington, 1996), 24ff., and the *World Investment Report 1996*. There is now a large body of work on the history of FDI. See G. Jones, *The Evolution of International Business* (London, 1996). The long history is also coming to be accepted (albeit gradually) in the more general work of economic historians; see notes to Chapter 1 herein.
3. The quotation is from R. E. Caves, who at the same time insists on the importance of multinationals in the service sector: *Multinational Enterprise and Economic Analysis* (2nd edn., Cambridge, 1996), 5n. Interestingly, Caves himself seems caught in that mind-set when he defines multinationals in terms of 'plants' abroad, yet, as his text points out, he knows better. As one of the wisest writers on multinational enterprises has written, the 'distinction [between "plants" and "services"] is imbedded in the data and in the discussion [of multinationals]. It is hard to escape from the concentration on manufacturing as the only form of "production"' (R. E. Lipsey to Wilkins, 26 Aug. 1996). Yet, escape we must.
4. I have always paid attention to service-sector multinationals. For a reflection of the current interest, see J. J. Boddewyn, M. B. Halbrich, and A. C. Perry, 'Service Multinationals', *Journal of International Business Studies*, 17 (Fall 1986), 41–57. The concentration on manufacturing creates numerous problems. Thus, recently one scholar talked about infrastructure, assisting production, failing to recognize that infrastructure investments *produce services* directly.
5. See, for example, B. Gomes-Casseres, 'Group versus Group: How Alliance Networks Compete', *Harvard Business Review* (July–Aug. 1994) (repr. no. 94402) and B. Gomes-Casseres, *The Alliance Revolution* (Cambridge, Mass., 1996).
6. See O. E. Williamson, 'The Modern Corporation: Origins, Evolution, Attributes', *Journal of Economic Literature*, 19 (Dec. 1981), 1537–68, and O. E. Williamson, 'Transaction Cost Economics: The Governance of Contractual Relations', *Journal of Law and Economics*, 20 (Oct. 1979), 233–61. D. F. Spulber, in 'Market Microstructure and Intermediation', *Journal of Economic Perspectives*, 10 (Summer 1996), 135–52, has three actors in private transactions: firms, households, and intermediaries (the economic agents that facilitate transactions). This addition is not necessary in my view, if we perceive firms as producers of goods *and services*. In the context of our studies, promoters, accountants, engineers, and so forth were firms that produced services and thus facilitated the transactions of other, free-standing, firms.
7. Caves, *Multinational Enterprise*, 26.
8. D. L. Swenson, 'Foreign Mergers and Acquisitions in the USA', in K. A. Froot (ed.), *Foreign Direct Investment* (Chicago, 1993), 255.
9. Jean-François Hennart, Chapter 2 herein, disagrees.
10. Caves, *Multinational Enterprise*, is a literature survey.
11. The criticism was originally made by T. A. B. Corley in discussions with the

author. For the key role of Stephen Hymer in the evolution of the theory of multinational enterprise, see M. Casson (ed.), *Multinational Corporations* (Aldershot, 1990). Hymer, by looking at the international operations of domestic firms, placed the study of multinationals squarely in the field of industrial organization. The newer international trade literature adopts the findings of industrial organization theorists on scale economies and imperfect competition in an attempt to understand the multinational enterprise. Contributors to the new international trade theories (who seek to analyse multinationals) include James Markusen, Elhanan Helpman, Wilfrid Ethier, and Ronald Jones. For an excellent sample of such work, see G. M. Grossman (ed.), *Imperfect Competition and International Trade* (Cambridge, Mass., 1992). For the student of the history of multinational enterprise, the world of imperfect markets and the functioning of enterprise under conditions of imperfect information are a given.

12. On the background, see Mira Wilkins, Chapter 1 herein.
13. Chapters 2 (Hennart), 3 (Casson), 8 (Miller).
14. M. Casson, *The Firm and the Market* (Cambridge, Mass., 1987), 1.
15. There is a long literature on ownership and control. Start with A. A. Berle and G. C. Means, *The Modern Corporation and Private Property* (New York, 1968) and see also M. Wilkins, 'Defining a Firm: History and Theory', in P. Hertner and Geoffrey Jones (eds.), *Multinationals: Theory and History* (Aldershot, 1986), 81–4. Clearly, however, as is evident in discussions in this book, the issues are far from resolved.
16. In my introduction, I dealt with the matter of free-standing companies that came to be joined in wider enterprise groups. It should be noted that some companies were from their origins set up in the UK by the wider enterprise groups. I wondered in Chapter 1 and still wonder whether these should be designated free-standing. The merchant group was the multinational enterprise and some of these entities were from their origin part of it.
17. Chapters 14 (Hausman and Neufeld), 15 (Marchildon), and 2 (Hennart). The conclusions are my own, and still tentative. Marchildon's discussion, based on new archival data, on Montreal Engineering and the extent to which Royal Securities internalized its services offers strong support for the view that success is based on internalizing or virtually internalizing the required core competencies.
18. For an extremely interesting and highly relevant discussion of corporate finance in the USA and Germany (and Japan), see S. D. Prowse, 'Corporate Finance in an International Perspective', *Economic Review* (Federal Reserve of Dallas) (3rd Quarter 1996), 2–15. The data presented in Harm Schröter's Chapter 12 herein on different national expectations in finance is congruent with this discussion.
19. These comments on information asymmetries were stimulated by a talk by Assaf Razin at the University of Miami, 20 September 1996. My comments are not, however, those of Razin. See A. Razin, E. Sadka, and Chi-Wa Yuen, 'A Pecking Order Theory of Capital Inflows and International Tax Principles', (Discussion Paper 1381, Centre for Economic Policy Research, London, 1996). Their 'pecking order' on information asymmetries in private sector international transactions was: direct investment, portfolio debt, portfolio equity (with the first—in their stylized model—circumventing information asymmetries, through the dispatch of managers abroad). Jean-François Hennart, Chapter 2 herein, has certain suggestions in this regard.
20. This is not by any means unique to the study of free-standing companies, albeit the study of free-standing companies is in keeping with historical studies of enterprise, including my own and that of Alfred Chandler. See also R. R. Nelson and S. G. Winter, *An Evolutionary Theory of Economic Change* (Cambridge, Mass.,

1982); B. Kogut, 'Foreign Direct Investment as a Sequential Process', in C. P. Kindleberger and D. B. Audretsch (eds.), *The Multinational Corporation in the 1980s* (Cambridge, Mass., 1983), 38–56; and especially the excellent work by G. Jones, *The Evolution of International Business.*

21. Harm Schröter, Chapter 12 herein, makes this very valid point. If we could identify head offices without using registration at all, this would clearly be the way to proceed.
22. I have found especially useful R. E. Lipsey and M. Y. Weiss, 'Foreign Production and Exports in Manufacturing Industries', *Review of Economics and Statistics*, 63 (Nov. 1981), 488–94; I. B. Kravis and R. E. Lipsey, 'The Location of Overseas Production and Production for Exports by US Multinational Firms', *Journal of International Economics*, 12 (May 1982), 201–23; M. Blomström and R. E. Lipsey, 'The Export Performance of US and Swedish Multinationals', *Review of Income and Wealth*, 35 (Sept. 1989), 245–64. I also find of great interest the work on trade in intermediate components as well as outputs being done by some of the new international trade theorists.
23. When the literature discusses 'trade' and 'trade creation', it often does so in a context of international trade. On the other hand, I believe it is important to look at foreign-owned firms in the context of generation of economic activity that includes both domestic and international (import and export) trade.
24. L. E. Davis and R. A. Huttenback, *Mammon and the Pursuit of Empire: The Economics of British Imperialism* (abridged edn., Cambridge, 1988), 64–83.
25. There are major difficulties in pursuing this research and I am not sure whether it is possible to answer this question. One may be forced to hold too many things constant so the results might not be meaningful.
26. There exists a huge literature on the costs and benefits of British capital exports on the British economy, but this has just begun to be broken down by *type* of capital export.
27. J. M. Keynes, 'Foreign Investment and National Advantage', *Nation* (London), 9 Aug. 1924.
28. These individuals (including T. A. B. Corley) look to G. D. N. Worswick and D. G. Tipping, *Profits in the British Economy 1909–1938* (Oxford, 1967), 87. In 1909, for example, the *number* of British firms operating abroad assessed represented only 3% of the British total but 14.6% of the gross income.
29. R. C. Michie, *The City of London: Continuity and Change, 1850–1990* (London, 1992), 112.
30. K. H. Kennedy, 'Biography of Leslie Urquhart', *Australian Corporate History Bulletin*, 2/1 (May 1986), 8.
31. See M. Wilkins, 'Multinational Corporations: An Historical Account', in R. Rowthorn and R. Kozul-Wright (eds.), *Transnational Corporations and the Global Economy* (London, forthcoming).
32. In this connection, the application to free-standing companies of the concepts in A. Rodriquez-Clare, 'Multinationals, Linkages, and Economic Development', *American Economic Review*, 86 (Sept. 1996), 852–73, would be exciting.
33. Ben P. A. Gales and Keetie E. Sluyterman, Chapter 11 herein, found that in the case of Dutch free-standing companies the entrepreneurial initiative typically came from abroad. My findings have been that the entrepreneurial initiative could come from any one of the three locales. It has often been assumed that the foreigner exploited; if only development had been national, it would have been better. Yet we have the case of Bolivia, one of the world's poorest countries, where the entrepreneurship was Bolivian. The reliance on London and New York was only financial. The free-standing company served the purpose of a significant Bolivian entrepreneur. Much of the development

literature discusses the alignment between foreign capital and local élites; perhaps the free-standing-company concept adds fuel to that literature, albeit with a different twist.

34. Whether they were an inferior form *vis-à-vis* profits to the shareholders, home-country economic development and host-country economic growth may be very different.
35. There has been a sizeable literature that assumes that these investments were by definition 'exploitative'. Research on the free-standing company as a type of multinational enterprise suggests that such an approach may well be deeply flawed.
36. In the development of commodity trade, we have *no* data pre-1914 (actually pre-1977) on how much trade was intra-company trade. The preliminary evidence on free-standing companies is that they developed resources, while often the associated merchant house arranged what was in effect *intra*-company trade. We eagerly await Geoffrey Jones's new work on trading companies that will cast light on this research lacuna. The phrase 'home bias' has been used by contemporary students of foreign investments to indicate that investors prefer home to foreign investments—even when returns abroad are higher than at home. I am using the phrase to indicate that investors preferred to invest securities in their own currency rather than in a foreign currency. Free-standing companies, which were designed to capture the higher returns abroad, typically had their equity (and usually their debt as well) denominated in the currency of the home country—the source of capital.
37. On this see Gales and Sluyterman, Chapter 11, and Harm Schröter, Chapter 12 herein. I am defining empire in traditional terms, not in the sweeping terms of Casson, Chapter 3 herein.
38. G. D. Snooks, *The Dynamic Society* (London, 1996), 433–4.

SELECT BIBLIOGRAPHY

This bibliography is a guide to some of the relevant secondary sources on the history of free-standing companies. It does not include all of the references cited in the text.

Directories, Manuals, and Reference Works

Dictionary of Business Biography (4 vols.).

Directory of Directors (London).

El Colegio de México, *Estadísticas económicas del Porfiriato: Fuerza de trabajo y actividad económica por sectores* (Mexico City, 1960).

Farr and Co., *Manual of Sugar Companies* (New York, 1925).

Handbuch des belgischen Wirtschaftslebens, pt. I (Göttingen/Berlin, 1916).

Instituto Nacional de Estadística, Geografía e Informática (INEGI), *Estadísticas históricas de Mexico* (2 vols.; 2nd edn., Aguascalientes, 1990).

Le Maistre, G. H., *Investor's India Year Book* (Calcutta, 1912).

Mexico, Ministerio de Hacienda, *The Mexican Yearbook: A Statistical, Financial, and Economic Annual, Compiled from Official and Other Returns. Issued under the Auspices of the Department of Finance, 1909–10* (London, 1909).

Ministero di Agricoltura, Industria e Commercio (ed.), *Bollettino ufficiale delle societá per azioni, anno 1891.*

Moody's Banking and Finance Manual.

Moody's Manual of Industrial Securities.

Moody's Manual of Public Utility Securities.

Mrs Van Nierop & Baak's Naamlooze Vennootschappen (1912).

Public Utility Compendium.

Recueil Financier.

Russian Year-Book for 1912 (London, 1912).

Salings Börsen-Jahrbuch.

Schweizerisches Börsen-Handbuch.

Seyd's London Commercial List.

Stock Exchange Yearbook (London).

Stopford, J. M., *Directory of Multinationals* (1992).

Thacker's Directory of the Chief Industries of India (Calcutta).

United States Bureau of the Census, *Historical Statistics of the United States from Colonial Times to 1970* (2 vols.; Washington, 1975).

Van Oss' Effectenboek (1915/16, 1939).

World Investment Report.

Books and Articles

À Campo, J. N. F. M., *Koninklijke Paketvaart Maatschappij: Stoomvaart en staatsvorming in de Indonesische archipel, 1888–1914* (Hilversum, 1992).

—— 'Strength, Survival and Success: A Statistical Profile of Corporate Enterprise in Colonial Indonesia 1883–1913', in *Jahrbuch für Wirtschaftsgeschichte* (1995).

ABO, T., 'ITT's International Business Activities, 1920–1940', *Annals of the Institute of Social Science*, 24 (1982–3), 104–28.

AHMED, N. Z., 'Some Aspects of the History of British Investments in the Private Sector of the Indian Economy 1875–1914', M.Sc. Econ. thesis (London School of Economics, 1955).

ALBERT, B., *An Essay on the Peruvian Sugar Industry, 1880–1920* (Norwich, 1976).

ALLEN, G. C., and DONNITHORNE, A. G., *Western Enterprise in Indonesia and Malaya* (London, 1957).

ALVESSON, M., and LINDKVIST, L., 'Transactions Costs, Clans and Corporate Culture', *Journal of Management Studies*, 30 (1993), 427–52.

AMERICAN & FOREIGN POWER COMPANY Inc., *The Foreign Power System* (New York, 1953).

Andrew Yule & Co. Ltd. 1863–1963 (London, 1963).

ANTROBUS, H. A., *History of the Assam Company* (Edinburgh, 1957).

ARMSTRONG, C., and NELLES, H. V., 'A Curious Capital Flow: Canadian Investment in Mexico, 1902–1910', *Business History Review*, 58 (1984), 178–203.

—— —— *Monopoly's Moment: The Organization and Regulation of Canadian Utilities, 1830–1930* (Philadelphia, 1986).

—— —— *Southern Exposure: Canadian Promoters in Latin America and the Caribbean, 1896–1930* (Toronto, 1988).

—— —— 'Corporate Enterprise in the Public Service Sector: The Performance of Canadian Firms in Mexico and Brazil, 1896–1930', in C. Marichal (ed.), *Foreign Investment in Latin America: Impact on Economic Development, 1850–1930* (Milan, 1994), 69–82.

BAIROCH, P., 'La Suisse dans le contexte international aux XIXe et XXe siècles', in P. Bairoch and M. Körner (eds.), *Die Schweiz in der Weltwirtschaft (15.–20. Jh.)/La Suisse dans l'économie mondiale (15e–20e s.)* (Zurich, 1990), 103–40.

BAKER, M., PITT, R. D., and PITT, J. M., *The Illustrated History of Newfoundland Light & Power* (St John's, 1990).

BAMBERG, J. H., *The History of the British Petroleum Company*, ii (Cambridge, 1994).

BASKIN, J., 'The Development of Corporate Financial Markets in Britain and in the United States, 1600–1914: Overcoming Asymmetric Information', *Business History Review*, 62 (Summer 1988), 199–237.

BEAUD, C. P., 'Investments and Profits of the Multinational Schneider Group: 1894–1943', in A. Teichova, M. Lévy-Leboyer, and H. Nussbaum (eds.), *Multinational Enterprise in Historical Perspective* (Cambridge, 1986).

BECKER, D. G., *The New Bourgeoisie and the Limits of Dependency: Mining, Class, and Power in 'Revolutionary' Peru* (Princeton, 1983).

BELLAVANCE, C., *Shawinigan Water and Power 1898–1963: Formation et déclin d'un groupe industriel au Québec* (Quebec, 1994).

BENITO, G., 'Disvestment of Foreign Production Operations', paper presented at the 2nd Workshop in International Business (University of Vaasa, Finland, 1995).

BEREND, I., and RANKI, G., *The European Periphery and Industrialization 1780–1914* (Cambridge, 1982).

BERLE, A. A., and MEANS, G. C., *The Modern Corporation and Private Property* (New York, 1968).

BERMÚDEZ MIRAL, O., *Historia del salitre desde sus orígenes hasta la Guerra del Pacífico* (Santiago, 1963).

BERNSTEIN, M., *The Mexican Mining Industry, 1890–1950: A Study of the Interaction of Politics, Economics, and Technology* (New York, 1964).

BLAKEMORE, H., *British Nitrates and Chilean Politics, 1886–1896: Balmaceda and North* (London, 1973).

—— *From the Pacific to La Paz: The Antofagasta (Chili) and Bolivia Railway Company, 1888–1988* (London, 1989).

BLOMSTRÖM, M., and LIPSEY, R. E., 'The Export Performance of US and Swedish Multinationals', *Review of Income and Wealth*, 35 (Sept. 1989), 245–64.

BODDEWYN, J. J., HALBRICH, M. B., and PERRY, A. C., 'Service Multinationals', *Journal of International Business Studies*, 17 (Fall 1986), 41–57.

BORNER, S., and WEHRLE, F., *Die Sechste Schweiz* (Zurich, 1984).

BOSCH, K. D., *Nederlandse beleggingen in de Verenigde Staten* (Amsterdam, 1948).

[BRAND, W.], *1879 HVA 1979: Honderd jaar geschiedenis der Verenigde HVA Maatschappijen NV* (Amsterdam, 1979).

BRODER, A., 'Banking and the Electrotechnical Industry in Western Europe', in R. Cameron and V. I. Bovykin (eds.), *International Banking, 1870–1914* (New York, 1991), 468–84.

BROWN, J. C., *Oil and Revolution in Mexico* (Berkeley, Calif., 1993).

BUCHANAN, N. S., 'Service Contracts in the Electric Bond and Share Company: A Further Note', *Journal of Land and Public Utility Economics*, 7 (May 1935), 209–10.

—— 'The Origin and Development of the Public Utility Holding Company', *Journal of Political Economy*, 44 (Feb. 1936), 31–53.

BUCKLEY, P. J., and CASSON, M. C., *The Future of the Multinational Enterprise* (London, 1976).

BURNS, E., *Modern Finance* (London, 1920).

BUSSIÈRE, E., *PARIBAS: 1872–1992, Europe and the World* (Antwerp, 1992).

BUTLIN, S. J., *Australia and New Zealand Bank* (London, 1961).

CAIRNCROSS, Sir ALEC, *Home and Foreign Investment, 1870–1913* (Cambridge, 1953).

CAMERON, R., *France and the Economic Development of Europe 1800–1914* (Princeton, 1961).

—— and BOVYKIN, V. I. (eds.), *International Banking 1870–1914* (New York, 1991).

CARLSON, W. B., *Innovation as a Social Process: Elihu Thomson and the Rise of General Electric, 1870–1900* (Cambridge, 1991).

CAROSSO, V., *Investment Banking in America* (Cambridge, Mass., 1970).

CARSON, J. S., 'The Power Industry', in L. J. Hughlett (ed.), *Industrialization of Latin America* (Westport, Conn., 1970; repr. of 1946 edn.).

CARSTENSEN, F., 'Numbers and Reality: A Critique of Foreign Investment Estimates in Tsarist Russia', in M. Lévy-Leboyer (ed.), *La Position internationale de la France* (Paris, 1977), 275–83.

CASSEL, G., *et al.*, *Foreign Investments* (Chicago, 1928).

CASSIS, Y., *La City de Londres 1870–1914* (Paris, 1987).

—— (ed.), *Finance and Financiers in European History 1880–1960* (Cambridge, 1992).

CASSON, M., *The Entrepreneur* (Oxford, 1982).

—— 'The Theory of Foreign Direct Investment', in P. J. Buckley and M. Casson (eds.), *The Economic Theory of the Multinational Enterprise* (London, 1985).

—— 'General Theories of the Multinational Enterprise: Their Relevance to Business History', in P. Hertner and G. Jones (eds.), *Multinationals: Theory and History* (Aldershot, 1986), 42–63.

—— *The Firm and the Market* (Cambridge, Mass., 1987).

—— 'Internalisation Theory and Beyond', in P. J. Buckley (ed.), *New Horizons in International Business: Research Priorities for the 1990s* (Aldershot, 1991), 4–27.

—— 'Institutional Diversity in Overseas Enterprise: Explaining the Free-Standing Company', *Business History*, 36 (Oct. 1994), 95–108.

—— *The Organization of International Business* (Aldershot, 1995).

—— *Information and Organization* (Oxford, 1997).

—— and PANICCIA, I., 'Business Networks and Industrial Districts: A Comparison of Northern Italy and South Wales', University of Reading Discussion Paper in Economics, No. 301 (1995).

CAVES, R. E., *Multinational Enterprise and Economic Analysis* (Cambridge, 1982; 2nd edn., 1996).

CAVIERES, E., *Comercio chileno y comerciantes ingleses, 1820–1880* (Valparaiso, 1988).

CHALLIES, J. B., 'Water Powers of Canada: Their Nature, Extent and Administration', *The Transactions of the First World Power Conference*, i (London, 1924), 165–225.

CHANDLER, A. D., Jr., *The Visible Hand* (Cambridge, Mass., 1977).

—— 'The Growth of the Transnational Industrial Firm in the United States and the United Kingdom: A Comparative Analysis', *Economic History Review*, 2nd ser., 33 (1980), 396–410.

—— *Scale and Scope: The Dynamics of Industrial Capitalism* (Cambridge, Mass., 1990).

—— 'Organizational Capabilities and the Economic History of the Industrial Enterprise', *Journal of Economic Perspectives*, 6 (Summer 1992), 79–100.

CHAPMAN, S. D., *The Rise of Merchant Banking* (London, 1984).

—— 'British-Based Investment Groups before 1914', *Economic History Review*, 2nd ser., 38 (May 1985), 230–51.

—— *Merchant Enterprise in Britain* (Cambridge, 1992).

CHAUDHURI, K. N., 'The East India Co. in the 17th and 18th Centuries', in L. Blussé and F. Gaastra (eds.), *Companies and Trade* (Leiden, 1981).

CHLEPNER, B.-S., *Le Marché financier belge depuis cent ans* (Brussels, 1930).

CLAUDE, H., *Histoire, réalité et destin d'un monopole: La Banque des Pays Bas et son groupe, 1872–1968* (Paris, 1969).

CLAYTON, L. A., *Grace: W. R. Grace & Co., the Formative Years, 1850–1930* (Ottawa, Ill., 1985).

CLEMENTS, R. V., 'British Controlled Enterprise in the West between 1870 and 1900 and Some Agrarian Reactions', *Agricultural History*, 27 (1953), 137–41.

COASE, R. H., 'The Nature of the Firm', *Economica*, NS 4 (Nov. 1937), 386–405.

COATSWORTH, J. H., 'Obstacles to Economic Growth in Nineteenth-Century Mexico', *American Historical Review*, 83 (1978), 80–100.

—— *Growth against Development: The Economic Impact of Railroads in Porfirian Mexico* (DeKalb, Ill., 1981).

COERVER, D. M., 'The Perils of Progress: The Mexican Department of Fomento during the Boom Years 1880–1884', *Inter-American Economic Affairs*, 31 (1977), 41–62.

COLINET, C., *L'Organisation professionelle des bourses de valeurs mobilières en Belgique* (Brussels, 1913).

CORAM, T. C., 'The Role of British Capital in the Development of the United States, 1600–1914', M.Sc. thesis (University of Southampton, 1967).

CORLEY, T. A. B., *A History of the Burmah Oil Company 1886–1924* (London, 1983).

—— 'Britain's Overseas Investments in 1914 Revisited', *Business History*, 36 (Jan. 1994), 71–88.

—— 'Foreign Direct Investment and British Economic Deceleration 1870–1914', in H. Pohl (ed.), *Transnational Investment from the 19th Century to the Present, Zeitschrift für Unternehmensgeschichte* (Occasional Papers, 81; Stuttgart, 1994) 153–72.

—— 'Free-Standing Companies, their Financing, and Internalisation Theory', *Business History*, 36 (Oct. 1994), 109–17.

—— 'The Ultimate Synthesis? Towards an Integration of Business History, Social Science and Managerial Theory', Conference on Business History, Erasmus University, Rotterdam (Oct. 1994).

COTTRELL, P. L., *British Overseas Investment in the Nineteenth Century* (London, 1975).

—— *Industrial Finance 1830–1914* (London, 1980).

—— 'The Coalescence of a Cluster of Corporate International Banks, 1855–1875', *Business History*, 33 (July 1991), 31–52.

COUYOUMDJIAN, J. R., 'El mercado del salitre durante la primera guerra y la posguerra, 1914–1921', *Historia* (Santiago), 12 (1974–5), 13–55.

COWEN, M., 'Capital, Nation and Commodities: The Case of Forestal Land, Timber and Railway Company in Argentina and Africa, 1900–1945', in J. J. van Helten and Y. Cassis (eds.), *Capitalism in a Mature Economy: Financial Institutions, Capital Exports and British Industry, 1870–1939* (London, 1990), 186–216.

CRAMMOND, E., 'British Investments Abroad', *Quarterly Review*, 207 (1907), 249–53.

CRESPO, A., *Los Aramayo de Chichas: Tres generaciones de mineros bolivianos* (Barcelona, 1981).

CRONE, G. C. E., *H. G. Th. Crone, 1790–1940: Gedenkboek uitgegeven ter gelegenheid van het 150-jarige bestaan der firma op 2 juni 1940* (Haarlem, 1940).

CUSHMAN, J. W., 'The Khaw Group: Chinese Business in Early Twentieth Century Penang', *Journal of Southeast Asian Studies*, 17 (1986), 58–79.

DAEMS, H., *The Holding Company and Corporate Control* (Leiden, 1978).

DAUNTON, M. J., 'Inheritance and Succession in the City of London in the Nineteenth Century', *Business History*, 30 (July 1988), 269–86.

DAVENPORT HINES, R. P. T., and JONES, G. (eds.), *British Business in Asia since 1860* (Cambridge, 1989).

DAVIES, H. H., 'Short History of Duncan Fox', unpublished manuscript (1966).

DAVIS, L. E., and CULL, R. J., *International Capital Markets and American Economic Growth, 1820–1914* (Cambridge, 1994).

—— and GALLMAN, R. E., 'Savings, Investment, and Economic Growth: The United States in the Nineteenth Century', in J. A. James and M. Thomas (eds.), *Capitalism in Context: Essays on Economic Development and Cultural Change in Honor of R. M. Hartwell* (Chicago, 1994), 216–26.

—— and HUTTENBACK, R. A., *Mammon and the Pursuit of Empire: The Political Economy of British Imperialism, 1860–1912* (Cambridge, 1986).

DAWSON, F. G., *The First Latin American Debt Crisis: The City of London and the 1822–1825 Loan Bubble* (New Haven, Conn., 1990).

DE JONGE, J. A., *De industrialisatie in Nederland tussen 1850 en 1914* (Nijmegen, 1968).

DEUSTUA, J., 'The Socavón of Quiulacocha and the Steam Engine Company: Technology and Capital Investment in Cerro de Pasco, 1820–1840', in R. Miller (ed.), *Region and Class in Modern Peruvian History* (Liverpool, 1987), 35–75.

—— 'Mining Markets, Peasants and Power in 19th-Century Peru', *Latin American Research Review*, 29 (1994), 29–54.

Drabble, J. H., *Rubber in Malaya 1876–1922* (Kuala Lumpur, 1973).

—— and DRAKE, P. J., 'More on the Financing of Malayan Rubber, 1905–23', *Economic History Review*, 2nd ser., 27 (1974), 108–20.

—— —— 'The British Agency Houses in Malaysia: Survival in a Changing World', *Journal of Southeast Asian Studies*, 12 (1981), 297–328.

DUMOULIN, M., *Les Relations économique italo-belges 1861–1914* (Academie Royale de Belgique, Mémoires de la Classe des Lettres, Collections in 8°, 2nd ser., vol. 65, pl. 2; Brussels, 1990).

DUNNING, J. H., *American Investment in British Manufacturing Industry* (London, 1958).

—— *International Production and the Multinational Enterprise* (London, 1981).

—— 'Changes in the Level and Structure of International Production: The

Last One Hundred Years', in M. Casson (ed.), *The Growth of International Business* (London, 1983), 84–139.

DUNNING, J. H., *Explaining International Production* (London, 1988).

—— *Multinational Enterprise and the Global Economy* (Wokingham, Berks., 1993).

—— and MORGAN, E. V., *An Economic Study of the City of London* (London, 1971).

EDELSTEIN, M., *Overseas Investment in the Age of High Imperialism: The United Kingdom, 1850–1914* (New York, 1982).

—— 'Foreign Investment and Accumulation', in R. Floud and D. McCloskey (eds.), *The Economic History of Britain since 1700*, ii. *1860–1939* (2nd edn., Cambridge, 1994), 173–96.

EISFELD, C., *Das Niederländische Bankwesen* (The Hague, 1916).

Electric Utility Regulation Board, National Construction Commission, Nanking, 'Electric Power Development in China', *Transactions of the Third World Power Conference*, ii (Washington, 1938).

—— 'Organization of Private Electric Utilities in China', *Transactions of the Third World Power Conference*, v (Washington, 1938).

ERICKSON, C., *British Industrialists 1850–1950* (Cambridge, 1959).

EVANS, G. H., *Business Incorporations in the United States 1800–1943* (New York, 1948).

FEDERICO, G., and TONIOLO, G., 'Italy', in R. Sylla and G. Toniolo (eds.), *Patterns of European Industrialization: The Nineteenth Century* (New York, 1991), 197–217.

FEINSTEIN, C. H., 'Capital Formation in Great Britain', *Cambridge Economic History of Europe* vii, pt. I (Cambridge, 1978).

—— 'Britain's Overseas Investments in 1913', *Economic History Review*, 2nd ser., 43 (May 1990), 288–95.

FEIS, H., *Europe: The World's Banker, 1870–1914* (New York, 1965; repr. of 1930 edn.).

FERRIER, R. W., *The History of the British Petroleum Company*, i. *1901–1932* (Cambridge, 1982).

FIELDHOUSE, D. K., 'The Multinational: A Critique of a Concept', in A. Teichova, M. Lévy-Leboyer, and H. Nussbaum (eds.), *Multinational Enterprise in Historical Perspective* (Cambridge, 1986), 9–29.

—— *Merchant Capital and Decolonization: The United Africa Company 1929–1987* (Oxford, 1994).

FISHLOW, A., 'Lessons from the Past: Capital Markets during the 19th Century and the Interwar Period', *International Organization*, 39 (Summer 1985), 383–439.

FOREMAN-PECK, J., 'Foreign Trade and Economic Growth', in D. H. Aldcroft and S. P. Ville (eds.), *The European Economy 1750–1914: A Thematic Approach* (Manchester, 1994).

FRANKO, L. G., *The European Multinationals* (Stamford, Conn., 1976).

FRY, R., *Bankers in West Africa* (London, 1976).

GALES, B. P. A., and SLUYTERMAN, K. E., 'Outward Bound: The Rise of Dutch Multinationals', in G. Jones and H. G. Schröter (eds.), *The Rise of Multinationals in Continental Europe* (Aldershot, 1993), 65–98.

GARCÍA HERAS, R., 'Las companías ferroviarias británicas y el control de cambios en la Argentina durante la Gran Depresión', *Desarrollo Económico*, 29 (1990), 477–505.

GERRETSON, F. C., *History of the Royal Dutch* (4 vols.; Leiden, 1953–7).

GERRIETS, M., 'The Rise and Fall of a Free-Standing Company in Nova Scotia: The General Mining Association', *Business History*, 34 (July 1992), 16–48.

GHISALBERTI, C., *La codificazione del diritto in Italia, 1865–1942* (Rome, 1985).

GIBB, G. S., and KNOWLTON, E. H., *The Resurgent Years, 1911–1927: The History of the Standard Oil Company (New Jersey)* (New York, 1956).

GIBBS, R. (ed.), *Dos siglos de cooperación México–Gran Bretaña* (Mexico City, 1983).

GLADSTONE, J. S., *History of Gillanders, Arbuthnot & Co. and Ogilvy Gillanders & Co.* (London, 1910).

GOMES-CASSERES, B., 'Group versus Group: How Alliance Networks Compete', *Harvard Business Review* (July–Aug. 1994) (reprint no. 94402).

—— *The Alliance Revolution* (Cambridge, Mass., 1996).

GOSLINGA, C. Ch., *The Dutch in the Caribbean and in Surinam 1791–1942* (Assen, 1990).

GRAHAM, E. M., *Global Corporations and National Governments* (Washington, 1996).

GREEN, E., 'Export Bankers: The Migration of British Bank Personnel to the Pacific Region, 1850–1914', in O. Checkland, S. Nishimura, and N. Tamaki (eds.), *Pacific Banking 1859–1959* (London, 1994).

GREENHILL, R. G., 'The Nitrate and Iodine Trades, 1880–1914', in D. C. M. Platt (ed.), *Business Imperialism, 1840–1930* (Oxford, 1977), 231–83.

—— 'Investment Group, Free-Standing Company or Multinational? Brazilian Warrant, 1909–1952', *Business History*, 37 (Jan. 1995), 86–111.

—— and MILLER, R. M., 'The Peruvian Government and the Nitrate Trade, 1873–1879', *Journal of Latin American Studies*, 5 (1973), 107–31.

GRIFFITHS, P., *History of the Indian Tea Industry* (London, 1967).

GROSSMAN, G. M. (ed.), *Imperfect Competition and International Trade* (Cambridge, Mass., 1992).

GUY, D. J., 'Dependency, the Credit Market, and Argentine Industrialization, 1873–1906', *Business History Review*, 58 (1984), 532–61.

HABAKKUK, H. J., 'Free Trade and Commercial Expansion 1853–1870', in J. Holland Rose, A. P. Newton and E. A. Benians (eds.), *The Cambridge History of the British Empire*, ii (Cambridge, 1940).

HABER, S. H., *Industry and Underdevelopment: The Industrialization of Mexico, 1890–1940* (Stanford, Calif., 1989).

HACCOÛ, J. F., *De Indische exportproducten: Hun beteekenis voor Indië en Nederland* (Leiden, 1947).

—— *Management of Direct Investments in Less Developed Countries* (Leiden, 1957).

—— 'Nederlands-Indië economisch: Een beeld van groei en strijd', in H. Baudet and I. J. Brugmans (eds.), *Balans van Beleid: Terugblik op de laatste halve eeuw van Nederlands-Indië* (Assen, 1961).

HALL, A. R., *The London Capital Market and Australia 1870–1914* (Canberra, 1963).

—— (ed.), *The Export of Capital from Britain 1870–1914* (London, 1968).

HALSEY, F. M., *Investments in Latin America and the British West Indies* (Washington, 1918).

HANNAH, L., 'Delusions of Durable Dominance OR The Invisible Hand Strikes Back: A Critique of the New Orthodoxy in Internationally Comparative Business History', manuscript (1994).

HANSON, S. G., *Economic Development in Latin America* (Washington, 1951).

HARMS, B., *Volkswirtschaft und Weltwirtschaft: Versuch der Begründung einer Weltwirtschaftslehre* (Jena, 1912).

HARRISON, G., *Bird & Co. of Calcutta . . . 1864–1964* (Calcutta, 1964).

HARVEY, C. E., *The Rio Tinto Company: An Economic History of a Leading International Mining Concern, 1873–1954* (Penzance, Cornwall, 1981).

—— and PRESS, J., 'Overseas Investment and the Professional Advance of British Metal Mining Engineers, 1851–1914', *Economic History Review*, 2nd ser., 42 (1989), 64–86.

—— —— 'The City and International Mining, 1870–1914', *Business History*, 32 (July 1990), 98–119.

HAUSMAN, W. J., and NEUFELD, J. L., 'The Rise and Fall of Public Utility Holding Companies', unpublished working paper (Feb. 1992).

—— —— 'The Rise and Fall of The American & Foreign Power Company: A Lesson from the Past?', *Electricity Journal*, 10 (1997), 46–53.

HEATH, H. J., 'Los primeros escarceos del imperialismo en México: Las casas comerciales británicas, 1821–1867', *Historias* (Mexico City), 22 (1989), 77–89.

—— 'British Merchant Houses in Mexico, 1821–1860: Conforming Business Practices and Ethics', *Hispanic American Historical Review*, 73 (1993), 261–90.

HENNART, J. F., *A Theory of Multinational Enterprise* (Ann Arbor, Mich., 1982).

—— 'What is Internalization?', *Weltwirtschaftliches Archiv-Review of World Economics*, 122/4 (1986), 791–804.

—— 'A Transaction Costs Theory of Equity Joint Ventures', *Strategic Management Journal*, 9/4 (1988), 361–74.

—— 'The Transaction Cost Theory of the Multinational Enterprise', in C. Pitelis and R. Sugden (eds.), *The Nature of the Transnational Firm* (London, 1991).

—— 'The Transaction Costs Theory of Joint Ventures: An Empirical Study of Japanese Subsidiaries in the United States', *Management Science*, 37 (Apr. 1991), 483–97.

—— 'Explaining the "Swollen Middle": Why Most Transactions are a Mix of Market and Hierarchy', *Organization Science*, 4 (Nov. 1993), 529–47.

—— 'International Financial Capital Transfers: A Transaction Cost Framework', *Business History*, 36 (Jan. 1994), 51–70.

—— 'Free-Standing Firms and the Internalisation of Markets for Financial Capital: A Response to Casson', *Business History*, 36 (Oct. 1994), 118–31.

HERTNER, P., 'Das Auslandskapital in der italienischen Wirtschaft,

1883–1914: Probleme seiner Quantifizierung und Auswertung', in K. Borchardt, E. Schremmer, and W. Zorn (eds.), *Weltwirtschaftliche und währungspolitische Probleme seit dem Ausgang des Mittelalters* (Stuttgart, 1981), 93–121.

—— 'Financial Strategies and Adaptation to Foreign Markets: The German Electro-Technical Industry and its Multinational Activities, 1890s to 1939', in A. Teichova, M. Lévy-Leboyer, and H. Nussbaum (eds.), *Multinational Enterprise in Historical Perspective* (Cambridge, 1986), 145–59.

—— 'The German Electrotechnical Industry in the Italian Market before the Second World War', in G. Jones and H. Schröter (eds.), *The Rise of Multinationals in Continental Europe* (Aldershot, 1993), 155–72.

HILLMAN, J., 'The Emergence of the Tin Industry in Bolivia', *Journal of Latin American Studies*, 16 (1984), 404–37.

HOBSON, C. K., *The Export of Capital* (London, 1914).

HOOD, N., and YOUNG, S., *The Economics of Multinational Enterprise* (London, 1979).

HOUSTON, T., and DUNNING, J. H., *UK Industry Abroad* (London, 1976).

HOW, D., *Canada's Mystery Man of High Finance: The Story of Izaak Walton Killam and his Glittering Wife Dorothy* (Huntsport, NS, 1986).

HOYNCK VAN PAPENDRECHT, A., *Gedenkboek A. van Hoboken & Co, 1774–1924* (Rotterdam, 1924).

—— *Tabak Maatschappij Arendsburg, 1877–1927* (Rotterdam, 1927).

HUENEMANN, R. W., *The Dragon and the Iron Horse: The Economics of Railroads in China, 1876–1937* (Cambridge, Mass., 1984).

HUGHES, T. P., *Networks of Power: Electrification in Western Society, 1880–1930* (Baltimore, 1983).

HUNT, W., *Heirs of Great Adventure: The History of Balfour, Williamson and Company Limited* (2 vols.; London, 1951, 1960).

IGARTUA, J. E. '"Corporate" Strategy and Locational Decision-Making: The Duke-Price Alcoa Merger, 1925', *Journal of Canadian Studies*, 20 (1985), 82–101.

IMLAH, A. H., *Economic Elements in the Pax Britannica* (Cambridge, Mass., 1958).

JAMES, M., *Merchant Adventurer: The Story of W. R. Grace* (Wilmington, Del., 1993).

JONES, C., 'Commercial Banks and Mortgage Companies', in D. C. M. Platt (ed.), *Business Imperialism, 1840–1930: An Enquiry Based on British Experience in Latin America* (Oxford, 1977), 17–52.

—— *International Business in the Nineteenth Century* (Brighton, 1987).

—— 'The Origins of Modern Multinational Corporations: British Firms in Latin America, 1850–1930', in C. Marichal (ed.), *Foreign Investment in Latin America* (Milan, 1994), 27–39.

—— 'Los antecedentes de la moderna corporación transnacional: Los grupos de inversión británicos en América Latina', in C. Marichal (ed.), *Las inversiones extranjeras en América Latina, 1850–1930* (Mexico City, 1995), 70–95.

JONES, C., 'Institutional Forms of British Foreign Direct Investment in South America', *Business History*, 39 (Apr. 1997), 21–41.

JONES, G., 'Lombard Street on the Riviera: The British Clearing Banks and Europe 1900–1960', *Business History*, 24 (Apr. 1982), 186–210.

—— 'The Expansion of British Multinational Manufacturing, 1890–1939', in A. Okochi and T. Inoue (eds.), *Overseas Business Activities* (Tokyo, 1984), 125–53.

—— (ed.), *British Multinationals: Origins, Management and Performance* (Aldershot, 1986).

—— 'The Performance of British Multinational Enterprise, 1890–1945', in P. Hertner and G. Jones (eds.), *Multinationals: Theory and History* (Aldershot, 1986), 96–112.

—— *Banking and Empire in Iran*, i. *The History of the British Bank of the Middle East* (Cambridge, 1986).

—— 'Competition and Competitiveness in British Banking, 1918–71', in G. Jones and M. Kirby (eds.), *Competitiveness and the State* (Manchester, 1991), 120–40.

—— *British Multinational Banking, 1830–1990* (Oxford, 1993).

—— 'The Making of Global Enterprise', *Business History*, 36 (Jan. 1994), 1–17.

—— 'Organization and Strategy in British-Based International Business before and after 1914', manuscript (University of Reading, 1995).

—— *The Evolution of International Business* (London, 1996).

—— 'Big Business, Management and Competitiveness in Twentieth Century Britain', in A. D. Chandler, Jr., F. Amatori, and T. Hikino (eds.), *Big Business and the Wealth of Nations* (Cambridge, 1997).

—— and SCHRÖTER, H. (eds.), *The Rise of Multinationals in Continental Europe* (Aldershot, 1993).

JONES, L., JONES, C., and GREENHILL, R., 'Public Utility Companies', in D. C. M. Platt (ed.), *Business Imperialism, 1840–1930* (Oxford, 1977), 77–118.

JOSLIN, D. M., *A Century of Banking in Latin America: To Commemorate the Centenary in 1962 of the Bank of London and South America Ltd.* (London, 1963).

KATZ, F., *The Secret War in Mexico: Europe, the United States and the Mexican Revolution* (Chicago, 1981).

—— 'Mexico: Restored Republic and Porfiriato, 1867–1910', in L. Bethell (ed.), *The Cambridge History of Latin America*, v (Cambridge, 1986), 3–78.

KELLER, D. N., *Stone & Webster, 1889–1989: A Century of Integrity and Service* (New York, 1989).

KEMPEES, J. C. J., 'De Nederlandsche Hypotheekbanken in de Verenigde Staten van Noord-Amerika en in Canada', *De Economist* (1919), 655–95, 759–93, 866–909.

KENNEDY, K. H.,'Biography of Leslie Urquhart', *Australian Corporate History Bulletin*, 2/1 (May 1986), 8.

KERR, W. G., *Scottish Capital on the American Credit Frontier* (Austin, Tex., 1976).

KEYNES, J. M., 'Foreign Investment and National Advantage', *Nation* (London), 9 Aug. 1924.

KINDERSLEY, R., 'British Foreign Investments in 1929', *Economic Journal*, 41 (Sept. 1931), 370–843, repr. in M. Wilkins (ed.), *British Overseas Investments* (New York, 1977).

—— 'British Overseas Investments, 1938', *Economic Journal*, 49 (Dec. 1939), 678–795; repr. in M. Wilkins (ed.), *British Overseas Investments* (New York, 1977).

KING, F. H. H., *The History of the Hongkong and Shanghai Banking Corporation* (Cambridge, 1987).

KING, T., *Consolidated of Baltimore, 1816–1950* (Baltimore, 1950).

KINROSS, J., *Fifty Years in the City* (London, 1982).

KIRSCH, H. W., *Industrial Development in a Traditional Society: The Conflict of Entrepreneurship and Modernization in Chile* (Gainesville, Fla., 1977).

KLING, B. B., and PEARSON, M. N. (eds.), *The Age of Partnership: Europeans in Asia before Dominion* (Honolulu, 1979).

KNIGHT, F. H., *Risk, Uncertainty, and Profit* (Boston, 1921).

KOGUT, B., 'Foreign Direct Investment as a Sequential Process', in C. P. Kindleberger and D. B. Audretsch (eds.), *The Multinational Corporation in the 1980s* (Cambridge, Mass., 1983).

KOJIMA, K., and OZAWA, T., *Japan's General Trading Companies: Merchants of Economic Development* (Paris, 1984).

KÖNIG, H., 'Belgische Kapitalanlagen in Italien', unpublished dissertation (University of Kiel, 1920).

KORSTEN, J., '"Little More than a Brass Nameplate Someplace in the City": De free-standing company in Nederland 1910–1928', MA thesis (Nijmegen, 1992).

KRAVIS, I. B., and LIPSEY, R. E., 'The Location of Overseas Production and Production for Exports by US Multinational Firms', *Journal of International Economics*, 12 (May 1982), 201–23.

KUBICEK, R. V., *Economic Imperialism in Theory and Practice: The Case of South African Gold Mining Finance 1886–1914* (Durham, NC, 1979).

KURGAN VAN HENTENRIJK, G., 'Un aspect de l'exportation des capiteaux en Chine: Les Entreprises Franco-Belges, 1896–1914', in M. Lévy-Leboyer (ed.), *La Position internationale de la France* (Paris, 1977), 203–13.

—— *Rail, finance et politique: Les Entreprises Philippart (1865–1890)* (Brussels, 1982).

—— 'The Groupe Philippart: An Experience of Multinational Enterprise in Railway and Banking in Western Europe, 1865–1880', in A. Teichova, M. Lévy-Leboyer, and H. Nussbaum (eds.), *Multinational Enterprise in Historical Perspective* (Cambridge, 1986), 65–73.

LAZONICK, W., 'Learning and the Dynamics of International Competitive Advantage', in R. Thomson (ed.), *Learning and Technological Change* (New York, 1993).

LENZ, F., 'Wesen und Struktur des deutschen Kapitalexports vor 1914', *Weltwirtschaftliches Archiv*, 18 (1922), 42–54.

LEWIS, C., *America's Stake in International Investments* (Washington, 1938).

LEWIS, C. M., *British Railways in Argentina, 1857–1914: A Case Study of Foreign Investment* (London, 1983).

LINDBLAD, J. Th., 'De handel tussen Nederland en Nederlands-Indië, 1874–1939', *Economisch-en sociaal-historisch jaarboek*, 41 (1988), 253–61.

—— 'Foreign Investment in Late-Colonial and Post-Colonial Indonesia', *Economic and Social History in the Netherlands*, 3 (1991), 183–208.

—— 'Ondernemen in Nederlands-Indië, 1900–1940', *Bijdragen en Mededelingen betreffende de geschiedenis der Nederlanden*, 108 (1993), 710.

LIPSEY, R. E., and WEISS, M. Y., 'Foreign Production and Exports in Manufacturing Industries', *Review of Economics and Statistics*, 63 (Nov. 1981), 488–94.

LOKANATHAN, P. S., *Industrial Organisation in India* (London, 1935).

LUDLOW, L., and MARICHAL, C. (eds.), *Banca y poder en México (1800–1925)* (Mexico City, 1986).

MCCALEB, W. F., *Present and Past Banking in Mexico* (New York, 1920).

MCDOWALL, D., *The Light: Brazilian Traction, Light and Power Company Limited, 1899–1945* (Toronto, 1988).

MACGREGOR, D. H., *Enterprise, Purpose and Profit* (Oxford, 1934).

MCKAY, J., *Pioneers for Profit* (Chicago, 1970).

—— *Tramways and Trolleys* (Princeton, 1976).

MAMALAKIS, M. J., *The Growth and Structure of the Chilean Economy from Independence to Allende* (New Haven, Conn., 1976).

MARCHILDON, G. P., 'British Investment Banking and Industrial Decline before the Great War: A Case Study of Capital Outflow to Canadian Industry', *Business History*, 33 (July 1991), 72–92.

—— '"Hands across the Water": Canadian Industrial Financiers in the City of London, 1905–20', *Business History*, 34 (July 1992), 65–95.

—— *Profits and Politics: Beaverbrook and the Gilded Age of Canadian Finance* (Toronto, 1996).

MARIANNO, M., *SUDAMERIS Brasil: 80 anos de trabalho* (São Paulo, 1991).

MARICHAL, C., *A Century of Debt Crises in Latin America: From Independence to the Great Depression, 1820–1930* (Princeton, 1989).

—— 'Foreign Loans, Banks and Capital Markets in Mexico, 1880–1910', in R. Liehr (ed.), *La deuda pública en América Latina en perspectiva histórica* (Frankfurt, 1995).

MARKUSEN, J. R., 'The Boundaries of Multinational Enterprises and Theory of International Trade', *Journal of Economic Perspectives*, 9 (Spring 1995), 169–89.

MARSHALL, H., SOUTHARD, F. A., Jr., and TAYLOR, K. W., *Canadian–American Industry* (New Haven, Conn., 1936).

MAYO, J., 'Before the Nitrate Era: British Commission Houses and the Chilean Economy, 1851–1880', *Journal of Latin American Studies*, 11 (1979), 283–302.

—— 'La Compañía de Salitres de Antofagasta y la Guerra del Pacífico', *Historia* (Santiago), 14 (1979), 71–102.

MEES, A. C., *NV Internationale Crediet- en Handels-Vereeniging 'Rotterdam': Gedenkboek uitgegeven bij het vijf- en zeventig jarig bestaan op 28 augustus 1938* (Rotterdam, 1938).

MEYER, L., *Su Majestad británica contra la Revolución Mexicana, 1900–1950: El fin de un imperio informal* (Mexico City, 1991).

MICHIE, R. C., *The London and New York Stock Exchanges, 1850–1914* (London, 1987).

—— *The City of London: Continuity and Change, 1850–1990* (London, 1992).

MIKESELL, R., and WHITNEY, J., *The World Mining Industry* (Boston, 1987).

MILLER, R., 'The Making of the Grace Contract: British Bondholders and the Peruvian Government, 1885–1890', *Journal of Latin American Studies*, 8 (1976), 73–100.

—— 'Small Business in the Peruvian Oil Industry: Lobitos Oilfields Limited before 1934', *Business History Review*, 56 (1982), 400–23.

—— 'The Grace Contract, the Peruvian Corporation, and Peruvian History', *Ibero-Amerikanisches Archiv*, 9 (1983), 319–48.

—— 'Transferencia de técnicas: La construcción y administración de ferrocarriles en la costa occidental de Sudamérica', *Siglo XIX: Cuadernos de historia*, 7 (1993), 65–102.

—— *Britain and Latin America in the Nineteenth and Twentieth Centuries* (London, 1993).

—— 'The London Capital Market and Latin American Public Debt, 1860–1930', in Reinhard Liehr (ed.), *La deuda pública en América Latina en perspectiva histórica* (Frankfurt, 1995), 91–116.

—— 'Multinational Manufacturing Firms', in C. M. Lewis and R. Miller (eds.), *British Business in Latin America, 1850–1950* (forthcoming).

MILWARD, A., and SAUL, S. B., *The Development of the Economies of Continental Europe 1850–1914* (London, 1977).

MITCHELL, S. A., *S. Z. Mitchell and the Electrical Industry* (New York, 1960).

MITRE, A., *Los patriarcas de la plata: Estructura socioeconómica de la minería boliviana en el siglo XIX* (Lima, 1977).

MOGGRIDGE, D. E., 'British Controls on Long-Term Capital Movements, 1924–1931', in D. N. McCloskey (ed.), *Essays on a Mature Economy: Britain after 1840* (London, 1971), 133–58.

MORRIS, M. D., 'South Asia Entrepreneurship and the Rashomon Effect, 1840–1947', *Explorations in Economic History*, 16 (1979), 341–61.

MUIRHEAD, S., *Crisis Banking in the East: The History of the Chartered Mercantile Bank of India, London and China 1853–1893* (Aldershot, 1996).

MUNCH, F. J., 'The Anglo-Dutch–American Petroleum Industry in Mexico: The Formative Years during the Porfiriato 1900–1910', *Revista de Historia de América*, 84 (1977), 135–87.

MUNRO, J. F., 'Shipping Subsidies and Railway Guarantees: William Mackinnon, Eastern Africa and the Indian Ocean, 1860–93', *Journal of African History*, 28 (1987), 209–23.

—— 'Scottish Overseas Enterprise and the Lure of London: The Mackinnon Shipping Group, 1847–1893', *Scottish Economic and Social History*, 8 (1988), 73–87.

NAVA OTEO, G., 'La Minería', in D. C. Villegas (ed.), *Historia moderna de México*, vol. vii. *El Porfiriato: La vida económica*, pt. 1 (Mexico City, 1965), 179–310.

NAVIN, T., and SEARS, M., 'The Rise of a Market for Industrial Securities', *Business History Review*, 29 (1955), 105–38.

NELSON, R. R., and WINTER, S. G., *An Evolutionary Theory of Economic Change* (Cambridge, Mass., 1982).

NICHOLAS, S. J., 'British Multinational Investment before 1939', *Journal of European Economic History*, 11 (Winter 1982), 605–30.

NICKALLS, G. (ed.), *Great Enterprise: A History of Harrisons & Crosfield* (London, 1990).

NICOLAU D'OLWER, L., 'Las inversiones extranjeras', in D. Cosío Villegas (ed.), *Historia Moderna de México*, vii. *El Porfiriato: La vida económica*, pt. 2 (Mexico City, 1965), 973–1177.

NORTH, D., *Institutions, Institutional Change and Economic Performance* (Cambridge, 1990).

—— 'Economic Performance through Time', *American Economic Review*, 84 (June 1994), 359–68.

O'BRIEN, T. F., 'The Antofagasta Company: A Case Study of Peripheral Capitalism', *Hispanic American Historical Review*, 60 (1980), 1–31.

—— *The Nitrate Industry and Chile's Crucial Transition, 1870–1891* (New York, 1982).

—— '"Rich beyond the Dreams of Avarice": The Guggenheims in Chile', *Business History Review*, 63 (1989), 122–59.

—— *The Revolutionary Mission: American Enterprise in Latin America, 1900–1945* (Cambridge, 1996).

O'HAGAN, H. O., *Leaves from my Life* (2 vols; London, 1929).

OPPENHEIMER, R. N., 'National Capital and National Development: Financing Chile's Central Valley Railroads', *Business History Review*, 56 (1982), 54–75.

OUCHI, W. G., 'Markets, Bureaucracies and Clans', *Administrative Science Quarterly*, 25 (1980), 129–41.

PAISH, G., 'Great Britain's Capital Investments in Other Lands', *Journal of the Royal Statistical Society*, 72 (1909), 471–5; rep. in M. Wilkins (ed.), *British Overseas Investments* (New York, 1977).

PALACIOS MOREYRA, C., *La deuda anglo-peruana, 1822–1890* (Lima, 1983).

PASSER, H., *The Electrical Manufacturers, 1875–1900* (Cambridge, Mass., 1953).

PATERSON, D. G., 'The Failure of British Business in Canada, 1890–1914', in H. Krooss (ed.), *Proceedings of the Business History Conference* (Bloomington, Ind., 1975), 14–31.

—— *British Direct Investment in Canada 1890–1914: Estimates and Determinants* (Toronto, 1976).

PAYNE, P., *The Early Scottish Limited Companies, 1856–1896* (Edinburgh, 1980).

PEETERS, W., 'Belgische Investeringen in het Buitenland 1873–1914. Deel I. Directe Private Investeringen. Het nominaal kapitaal van Naamloze Vennootschappen werkzaam in het buitenland', Paper for the Workshop on Quantitative Economic History (K. U. Leuven, Feb. 1994).

PENROSE, E. T., 'Limits to the Growth and Size of Firms', *American Economic Review*, 45 (May 1955), 531–43; repr. in E. T. Penrose, *The Growth of Firms, Middle East Oil and Other Essays* (London, 1971), 30–42.

—— *The Theory of the Growth of the Firm* (Oxford, 1959; 3rd edn., 1995).

PERCIVAL, J., *The Archives of the Peruvian Corporation* (London, 1980).

PIRET, R., *L'Évolution de la législation belge sur les sociétés anonymes* (Tournai/ Paris, 1946).

PLATT, D. C. M. (ed.), *Business Imperialism 1840–1930: An Enquiry Based on British Experience in Latin America* (Oxford, 1977).

—— 'British Portfolio Investment before 1870: Some Doubts', *Economic History Review*, 2nd ser., 33 (1980), 1–16.

—— *Britain's Investment Overseas on the Eve of the First World War: The Use and Abuse of Numbers* (London, 1986).

PLETCHER, D. M., 'The Fall of Silver in Mexico, 1870–1910, and its Effect on American Investments', *Journal of Economic History*, 18 (1958), 33–55.

PORTER, M., *The Competitive Advantage of Nations* (London, 1990).

PROWSE, S. D., 'Corporate Finance in an International Perspective', *Economic Review* (Federal Reserve of Dallas) (3rd Quarter 1996), 2–15.

PURSER, W. F. C., *Metal-Mining in Peru: Past and Present* (New York, 1971).

QUIROZ, A. W., 'Financial Leadership and the Formation of Peruvian Élite Groups, 1884–1930', *Journal of Latin American Studies*, 20 (1988), 49–81.

—— *Banqueros en conflicto: Estructura financiera y economía peruana, 1884–1930* (Lima, 1989).

—— *Domestic and Foreign Finance in Modern Peru, 1850–1950: Financing Visions of Development* (London, 1993).

RAMACHANDRAN, N., *Foreign Plantation Investment in Ceylon, 1899–1958* (Colombo, 1963).

RAMOS, P., 'Um Estudo da Evolução e da Estrutura da Agroindústria Canavieira do Estado de São Paulo (1930–1982)', unpublished MA dissertation (School of Business Administration of the Fundação Getulio Vargas in São Paulo, 1983).

RANDALL, R. W., *Real del Monte: A British Mining Venture in Mexico* (Austin, Tex., 1972).

RANDALL, S. J., 'The Development of Canadian Business in Puerto Rico', *Revista/Review Interamericana*, 7 (1977), 16–20.

RAY, R. J. (ed.), *Entrepreneurship and Industry in India 1800–1947* (Bombay, 1992).

RAZIN, A., SADKA, E., and CHI-WA YUEN, 'A Pecking Order Theory of Capital Inflows and International Tax Principles' (Discussion Paper 1381, Centre for Economic Policy Research, London, 1996).

REMER, C. F., *Foreign Investment in China* (New York, 1933).

RICHARDSON, G. B., 'The Organisation of Industry', *Economic Journal*, 82 (Sept. 1972), 883–96.

RICHARDSON, P., and VAN HELTEN, J.-J., 'The Development of the South African Gold-Mining Industry, 1895–1918', *Economic History Review*, 2nd ser., 38/3 (1984), 319–40.

RIPPY, J. F., 'Latin America and the British Investment "Boom" of the 1820's', *Journal of Modern History*, 19 (1947), 122–9.

—— 'The Peak of British Investment in Latin American Mines', *Inter-American Economic Affairs*, 2 (1948), 41–8.

—— *British Investments in Latin America, 1822–1949* (Minneapolis, 1959).

ROBERTS, R., *Schroders: Merchants and Bankers* (London, 1992).

ROBERTS, R., 'What's in a Name? Merchants, Merchant Bankers, Accepting Houses, Issuing Houses, Industrial Bankers, and Investment Bankers', *Business History*, 35 (July 1993), 22–38.

RODRIQUEZ-CLARE, A., 'Multinationals, Linkages, and Economic Development', *American Economic Review*, 86 (Sept. 1996), 852–73.

ROEHL, T., 'A Transaction Cost Approach to International Trading Structures: The Case of the Japanese General Trading Company', *Hitotsubashi Journal of Economics*, 24 (1983), 119–35.

ROSENZWEIG, F., 'El desarrollo económico de México de 1877 a 1911', *El trimestre económico* (Mexico City), 32 (1965), 405–54.

Royal Institute of International Affairs, *The Problem of International Investment* (Oxford, 1937).

RUNGTA, R. S., *Rise of Business Corporations in India* (Calcutta, 1970).

RUTNAGUR, S. M., *Bombay Industries: The Cotton Mills* (Bombay, 1927).

SÁNCHEZ, L. A., *Historia de una industria peruana: Cervecería Backus y Johnston S.A.* (Lima, 1978).

SAUL, S. B., *Studies in British Overseas Trade, 1870–1914* (Liverpool, 1960).

SAYERS, R. S., *The Bank of England, 1891–1944* (Cambridge, 1976).

SCARBOROUGH, C., . . . *about Oxo* (London, 1965).

SCHATZL, L., *The Nigerian Tin Industry* (Ibadan, 1971).

SCHIJF, H., *Netwerken van een financieel-economische elite: Personele verbindingen in het Nederlandse bedrijfsleven aan het eind van de negentiende eeuw* (Amsterdam, 1993).

SCHMITZ, C. J., 'Patterns of Scottish Portfolio Foreign Investment 1860–1914', unpublished report to ESRC (1994).

SCHNEIDER, J., SCHWARZER, O., and ZELLFELDER, F. (eds.), *Währungen der Welt I: Europäische und nordamerikanische Devisenkurse 1777–1914*, i (Stuttgart, 1991).

SCHRÖTER, H. G., 'Die Auslandsinvestitionen der deutschen chemischen Industrie 1870 bis 1930', in *Zeitschrift für Unternehmensgeschichte*, 35 (1990), 1–22.

—— 'Etablierungs- und Verteilungsmuster der schweizerischen Auslandsproduktion von 1870 bis 1914', in P. Bairoch and M. Körner (eds.), *Die Schweiz in der Weltwirtschaft (15.–20. Jh.)/La Suisse dans l'économie mondiale (15e–20e s.)* (Zurich, 1990), 391–407.

—— *Aufstieg der Kleinen: Multinationale Unternehmen aus fünf kleinen Staaten vor 1914* (Berlin, 1993).

—— 'On the Specific Freedom of Manœuvre of Small States and their Businessmen: Economic Mediation between Great Britain and Soviet Russia in 1921', in C. Due-Nielsen, H. Kirchhoff, K. C. Lammers, and T. Nybom (eds.), *Konflikt od samarbejde: Festskrift til Carl-Axel Gemzell* (Copenhagen, 1993), 53–66.

—— 'Small European States and Cooperative Capitalism 1900–1980', in A. Chandler, Jr., F. Amatori, and T. Hikino (eds.), *Big Business and the Wealth of Nations* (Cambridge, 1997).

SCHRÖTER, V., *Die deutsche Industrie auf dem Weltmarkt 1929 bis 1932* (Frankfurt, 1984).

SCHURZ, W. L., *Rubber Production in the Amazon Valley* (Washington, 1925).

SCOTT, W. R., *The Constitution and Finance of English, Scottish and Irish Joint-Stock Companies to 1720*, i. *The General Development of the Joint-Stock System to 1720* (Cambridge, 1912).

SEGAL, H., and SIMON, M., 'British Foreign Capital Issues, 1865–94', *Journal of Economic History*, 21 (Dec. 1961), 567–81.

SEGRETO, L., 'Du "Made in Germany" au "Made in Switzerland": Les Sociétés financières suisses pour l'industrie électrique dans l'entre-deux-guerres', in M. Trédé (ed.), *Électricité et électrification dans le monde* (Paris, 1992), 347–67.

—— 'Imprenditori e finanzieri', in G. Mori (ed.), *Storia dell'industria electrica in Italia*, i (Rome, 1992).

SEN, S. K., *The House of Tata 1839–1939* (Calcutta, 1975).

—— 'The Pattern of British Enterprise in India 1854–1914', in R. J. Ray (ed.), *Entrepreneurship and Industry in India* (Bombay, 1992).

SEXTON, J., *Monenco: The First 75 Years* (n.p., 1982).

SIMON, M., 'The Enterprise and Industrial Composition of New British Portfolio Foreign Investment, 1865–1914', *Journal of Development Studies*, 3 (1967), 280–92.

—— 'The Pattern of New British Portfolio Foreign Investment, 1865–1914', in J. H. Adler (ed.), *Capital Movements and Economic Development* (London, 1967).

SIMPSON, R., 'Organization of Private Gas and Electric Utilities', *Transactions of the Third World Power Conference*, v (Washington, 1938), 47–68.

SLUYTERMAN, K. E., *Ondernemen in sigaren: Analyse van bedrijfsbeleid in vijf Nederlandse sigarenfabrieken in de perioden 1856–1865 en 1925–1934* (Tilburg, 1983).

—— *Driekwart eeuw CSM: Cash flow, Strategie en Mensen* (Diemen, 1995).

SMITH, G. D., *From Monopoly to Competition: The Transformation of Alcoa, 1888–1986* (Cambridge, 1988).

SNOOKS, G. D., *The Dynamic Society* (London, 1996).

SNOWDEN, K. A., 'Mortgage Rates and American Capital Market Development in the Late Nineteenth Century', *Journal of Economic History*, 47 (1987).

SPENCE, C. C., *British Investment and the American Mining Frontier* (Ithaca, NY, 1958).

SPULBER, D. F., 'Market Microstructure and Intermediation', *Journal of Economic Perspectives*, 10 (Summer 1996), 135–52.

STAHL, K., *The Metropolitan Organisation of British Colonial Trade* (London, 1951).

STALLINGS, B., *Banker to the Third World: US Portfolio Investment in Latin America, 1900–1986* (Berkeley, Calif., 1987).

STANG, G., 'Entrepreneurs and Managers: The Establishment and Organisation of British Firms in Latin America in the Nineteenth and Twentieth Centuries', *Historisk Tidskriff*, 1 (1982), 40–60.

STEWART, R. E., 'Scottish Company Accounting 1870–1920', unpublished Ph.D. diss. (University of Glasgow, 1986).

STILLSON, R. T., 'The Financing of Malayan Rubber, 1905–1923', *Economic History Review*, 2nd ser., 24 (1971), 589–98.

'STONE & WEBSTER', *Fortune*, 2 (Nov. 1930), 92–4.
STONE, I., 'British Direct and Portfolio Investment in Latin America before 1914', *Journal of Economic History*, 37 (1977), 690–722.
—— *The Composition and Distribution of British Investment in Latin America, 1865 to 1913* (Ph.D. diss., Columbia University, 1962, New York, 1987).
STOPFORD, J. M., 'The Origins of British-Based Multinational Manufacturing Enterprise', *Business History Review*, 48 (Autumn 1974), 303–35.
SUBRAHMANYAM, S. (ed.), *Merchants, Markets and the State in Early Modern India* (Bombay, 1990).
SVEDBERG, P., 'The Portfolio Direct Composition of Private Foreign Investment in 1914 Revisited', *Economic Journal*, 88 (1978), 763–77.
SWENSON, D. L., 'Foreign Mergers and Acquisitions in the United States', in K. A. Froot (ed.), *Foreign Direct Investment* (Chicago, 1993).
SZMRECSÁNYI, T., 'Growth and Crisis of the Brazilian Sugar Industry, 1914–1939', *Rivista di storia economica*, 5 (June 1988), 193–219, 268–70.
TERVOOREN, W., *Die Finanzierung von Kautchukplantagen* (The Hague, 1930).
Thomas Sivewright Catto 1879–1959: A Personal Memoir (Edinburgh, 1962).
THOMSON, R. (ed.), *Learning and Technological Change* (New York, 1993).
THORP, R., and BERTRAM, G., *Peru, 1890–1977: Growth and Policy in an Open Economy* (New York, 1978).
TIPTON, F. B., and ALDRICH, R., *An Economic and Social History of Europe, 1890–1939* (Baltimore, 1987).
TISCHENDORF, A., 'British Investments in Latin American and African Mines', *Inter-American Economic Affairs*, 6 (1953), 29–37.
—— *Great Britain and Mexico in the Era of Porfirio Díaz* (Durham, NC, 1961).
TSURUMI, Y., *Multinational Management* (Boston, 1977).
TUMA, E. H., 'Suez Canal: Another Dimension in the European Network', *Journal of European Economic History*, 24 (Winter 1995), 619–33.
TURRELL, R., and VAN HELTEN, J.-J., 'The Rothschilds, the Exploration Company, and Mining Finance', *Business History*, 28 (Apr. 1986), 181–205.
UNITED NATIONS, *International Capital Movements during the Inter-War Period* (Lake Success, NY, 1949).
UNITED STATES DEPARTMENT OF COMMERCE, *American Direct Investments in Foreign Countries—1936* (Washington, 1938).
UNITED STATES FEDERAL TRADE COMMISSION, *Report on Cooperation in American Export Trade* (2 vols.; Washington, 1916).
—— *Control of Power Companies* (Washington, 1927).
—— *Utility Corporations* (Washington, 1929–35).
VAN DEN BOSCH, W. J. P., *Cultuur-Maatschappij Pondok-Gedeh, 1887–1912* (The Hague, 1912).
VAN DER ENG, P. J., 'The Real Domestic Product of Indonesia, 1880–1989', *Explorations in Economic History*, 29 (1992), 343–73.
—— *Agricultural Growth in Indonesia since 1880: Productivity Change and the Impact of Government Policy* (Groningen, 1993).
VAN DER WEE, HERMAN, 'Investment Strategy of Belgian Industrial Enterprise

between 1830 and 1980 and its Influence on the Economic Development of Europe', in G. Verbeke (ed.), *Belgium and Europe* (Brussels, 1981).

—— 'La Politique d'investissement de la Société Générale de Belgique 1822–1913', *Histoire Économie et Société* (1982), 603–20.

—— 'Large Firms in Belgium, 1892–1974: An Analysis of their Structure and Growth', in D. C. Coleman and P. Mathias (eds.), *Enterprise and History* (Cambridge, 1984), 199–211.

—— and GOOSENS, M., 'Belgium', in R. Cameron and V. I. Bovykin (eds.), *International Banking 1870–1914* (New York, 1991), 122–7.

VAN DER ZWAAG, J., *Verloren tropische zaken: De opkomst en ondergang van de Nederlandse handel- & cultuurmaatschappijen in het voormalige Nederlands-Indië* (Meppel, 1991).

VAN HELTEN, J.-J., 'Mining, Share Manias and Speculation: British Investment in Overseas Mining, 1880–1913', in J.-J. van Helten and Y. Cassis (eds.), *Capitalism in a Mature Economy: Financial Institutions, Capital Exports and British Industry, 1870–1939* (Aldershot, 1990), 159–85.

—— and JONES, G., 'British Business in Malaysia and Singapore since the 1870s', in R. P. T. Davenport-Hines and G. Jones (eds.), *British Business in Asia since 1860* (Cambridge, 1989), 157–88.

VAN HINTE, J., *Nederlanders in Amerika: Een studie over landverhuizers en volkplanters in de 19e en 20ste eeuw in de Vereenigde Staten van Amerika* (Groningen, 1928).

VAN SOEST, J., *Olie als water: De Curaçaose economie in de eerste helft van de twintigste eeuw* (Zutphen, 1977).

VEENENDAAL, A. J., Jr., 'The Dutch Connection: Salomon Frederik van Oss and Dutch Investment in Oklahoma', *The Chronicles of Oklahoma*, 65 (1987), 252–67.

—— 'An Example of "Other People's Money": Dutch Capital in American Railroads', *Business and Economic History*, 2nd ser., 21 (1992), 147–57.

—— *Slow Train to Paradise: How Dutch Investment Helped Build American Railroads* (Stanford, Calif., 1996).

VELIZ, C., 'Egaña, Lambert, and the Chilean Mining Associations of 1825', *Hispanic American Historical Review*, 55 (1975), 637–63.

VERNON, R., 'International Investment and International Trade in the Product Cycle', *Quarterly Journal of Economics*, 80 (1966), 190–207.

—— *Sovereignty at Bay* (New York, 1971).

VEULEMANS, H., 'Gemengde Banken en Holdings in Belgie Tijdens de 19e en Begin 20e Eeuw', unpublished manuscript (Leuwen, 1974).

WALLACE, D. R., *The Romance of Jute* (London, 1928).

WELLS, L. T., Jr., 'Mobile Exporters: New Foreign Investors in East Asia', in K. A. Froot (ed.), *Foreign Direct Investment* (Chicago, 1993).

WHITE, E., 'The Stock Market Boom and Crash of 1929 Revisited', *Journal of Economic Perspectives*, 4 (Spring 1990), 67–83.

WILKINS, M., *The Emergence of Multinational Enterprise: American Business Abroad from the Colonial Era to 1914* (Cambridge, Mass., 1970).

—— *The Maturing of Multinational Enterprise: American Business Abroad from 1914 to 1970* (Cambridge, Mass., 1974).

WILKINS, M., 'The Role of Private Business in the International Diffusion of Technology', *Journal of Economic History*, 34 (Mar. 1974), 168–88.

—— 'Multinational Enterprises', in H. Daems and H. van der Wee (eds.), *The Rise of Managerial Capitalism* (Louvain, 1974), 213–35.

—— 'Modern European Economic History and the Multinationals', *Journal of European Economic History*, 6 (Winter 1977), 575–95.

—— (ed.), *British Overseas Investments, 1907–1948* (New York, 1977).

—— 'Defining a Firm: History and Theory', in P. Hertner and G. Jones (eds.), *Multinationals: Theory and History* (Aldershot, 1986), 80–95.

—— 'European Multinationals in the United States 1875–1914', in A. Teichova, M. Lévy-Leboyer, and H. Nussbaum (eds.), *Multinational Enterprise in Historical Perspective* (Cambridge, 1986), 55–64.

—— 'The History of European Multinationals: A New Look', *Journal of European Economic History*, 15 (Winter 1986), 483–510.

—— 'Efficiency and Management: A Comment on Gregory Clark's "Why isn't the Whole World Developed?"', *Journal of Economic History*, 47 (Dec. 1987), 981–3.

—— 'European and North American Multinationals, 1870–1914: Comparisons and Contrasts', *Business History*, 30 (Jan. 1988), 8–45.

—— 'The Free-Standing Company, 1870–1914: An Important Type of British Foreign Direct Investment', *Economic History Review*, 2nd ser., 41 (May 1988), 259–82.

—— *The History of Foreign Investment in the United States to 1914* (Cambridge, Mass., 1989).

—— 'The Impact of Multinational Corporations', *South African Journal of Economic History*, 4 (Mar. 1989), 4–20.

—— 'Japanese Multinationals in the United States: Continuity and Change, 1879–1990', *Business History Review*, 64 (Winter 1990), 585–629.

—— (ed.), *The Growth of Multinationals* (Aldershot, 1991).

—— 'The Neglected Intangible Asset: The Influence of the Trade Mark on the Rise of the Modern Corporation', *Business History*, 34 (Jan. 1992), 66–95.

—— 'Multinational Corporations: An Historical Account', in R. Rowthorn and R. Kozul-Wright (eds.), *Transnational Corporations and the Global Economy* (London, forthcoming).

—— and HILL, F. E., *American Business Abroad: Ford on Six Continents* (Detroit, 1964).

WILLIAMSON, O. E., 'Transaction Cost Economics: The Governance of Contractual Relations', *Journal of Law and Economics*, 20 (Oct. 1979), 233–61.

—— 'The Modern Corporation: Origins, Evolution, Attributes', *Journal of Economic Literature*, 19 (Dec. 1981), 1537–68.

—— 'Corporate Finance and Corporate Governance', *Journal of Finance*, 63/3 (1988), 569–98.

WILSON, C., *The History of Unilever* (3 vols.; New York, 1968).

WINKLER, M., *Investments of United States Capital in Latin America* (Boston, 1929).

WORSWICK, G. D. N., and TIPPING, D. G., *Profits in the British Economy 1909–1938* (Oxford, 1967).
WRIGHT, A., and CARTWRIGHT, H. A., *Twentieth Century Impressions of British Malaya* (London, 1908).
WRIGHT, H. K., *Foreign Enterprise in Mexico: Laws and Politics* (Chapel Hill, NC, 1971).
YERGIN, D., *The Prize: The Epic Quest for Oil, Money and Power* (New York, 1993).
YIP YAT HOONG, *The Development of the Tin Mining Industry of Malaya* (Kuala Lumpur, 1969).
YOUNG, D., *Member for Mexico: A Biography of Weetman Pearson, First Viscount Cowdray* (London, 1966).
YOUNG, G. F. W., 'German Banks and German Direct Investment in Latin America, 1880–1940', in Carlos Marichal (ed.), *Foreign Investment in Latin America* (Milan, 1994), 57–67.
ZAMAGNI, V., *Dalla periferia al centro: La seconda rinascita economica dell'Italia, 1861–1981* (Bologna, 1990).

INDEX

Page numbers in *italics* indicate a table.

The manufacturer's authorised representative in the EU for product safety is Oxford University Press España S.A. of el Parque Empresarial San Fernando de Henares, Avenida de Castilla, 2 – 28830 Madrid (www.oup.es/en or product.safety@oup.com). OUP España S.A. also acts as importer into Spain of products made by the manufacturer.

www.ingramcontent.com/pod-product-compliance
Lightning Source LLC
LaVergne TN
LVHW021054220926
848484LV00020B/481
* 9 7 8 0 1 9 8 2 9 0 3 2 2 *